YAMAHA | OUTBOARDS
1992-98 REPAIR MANUAL

SELOC™

President	Dean F. Morgantini, S.A.E.
Vice President–Finance	Barry L. Beck
Vice President–Sales	Glenn D. Potere
Executive Editor	Kevin M. G. Maher, A.S.E.
Manager–Marine/Recreation	James R. Marotta, A.S.E., S.T.S.
Manager–Professional	George B. Heinrich III, A.S.E., S.A.E.
Manager–Consumer	Richard Schwartz, A.S.E.
Manager–Production	Ben Greisler, S.A.E.
Production Assistant	Melinda Possinger
Project Managers	Will Kessler, A.S.E., S.A.E., Todd W. Stidham, A.S.E., Ron Webb
Schematics Editor	Christopher G. Ritchie, A.S.E.
Editor	James R. Marotta, A.S.E., S.T.S.

Brought to you by

CHILTON™
MARINE

Manufactured in USA
© 1999 W. G. Nichols
1020 Andrew Drive
West Chester, PA 19380
ISBN 0-89330-047-0
1234567890 8765432109

www.Chiltonsonline.com

Contents

1 GENERAL INFORMATION

1-2 GENERAL INFORMATION   **1-8** SAFETY

2 TUNING

2-2 TUNING

3 MAINTENANCE

3-2 MAINTENANCE   **3-13** EMERGENCY SERVICE
3-6 PRE-SEASON CHECKLIST   **3-15** WINTER STORAGE
3-7 LUBRICATION

4 FUEL SYSTEM

4-2 FUEL AND COMBUSTION   **4-52** FUEL PUMP SERVICE
4-3 FUEL SYSTEM   **4-59** ELECTRONIC FUEL
4-6 TROUBLESHOOTING   INJECTION
4-9 CARBURETOR SERVICE

5 OIL INJECTION

5-2 OIL INJECTION SYSTEM   **5-10** SERVICING
5-7 TROUBLESHOOTING   **5-38** WIRING DIAGRAMS

6 IGNITION SYSTEM

6-2 IGNITION SYSTEM   **6-37** YAMAHA
6-7 TROUBLESHOOTING   MICROCOMPUTER
6-24 SERVICING   IGNITION SYSTEM (YMIS)

7 TIMING AND SYNCHRONIZATION

7-2 TIMING AND
SYNCHRONIZATION

Contents

8-2 POWERHEAD MECHANICAL   **8-58** POWERHEAD REFINISHING

POWERHEAD 8

9-2 ELECTRICAL   **9-20** TACHOMETERS
9-6 CHARGING CIRCUIT   **9-20** WIRING DIAGRAMS
9-11 CRANKING CIRCUIT

ELECTRICAL 9

10-2 LOWER UNIT   **10-5** LOWER UNIT SERVICE
10-4 TROUBLESHOOTING   **10-11** LOWER UNIT OVERHAUL

LOWER UNIT 10

11-2 TRIM & TILT   **11-3** POWER TILT SYSTEM
11-2 HYDRO TILT LOCK SYSTEM   **11-7** POWER TRIM/TILT SYSTEM

TRIM AND TILT 11

12-2 REMOTE CONTROLS

REMOTE CONTROLS 12

13-2 HAND REWIND STARTER

HAND REWIND STARTER 13

13-10 GLOSSARY   **13-15** INDEX

GLOSSARY/ MASTER INDEX

Other titles
Brought to you by

CHILTON™
MARINE

Title	Part #
Chrysler Outboards, All Engines, 1962-84	018-7
Force Outboards, All Engines, 1984-96	024-1
Honda Outboards, All Engines 1988-98	1200
Johnson/Evinrude Outboards, 1-2 Cyl, 1956-70	007-1
Johnson/Evinrude Outboards, 1-2 Cyl, 1971-89	008-X
Johnson/Evinrude Outboards, 1-2 Cyl, 1990-95	026-8
Johnson/Evinrude Outboards, 3, 4 & 6 Cyl, 1973-91	010-1
Johnson/Evinrude Outboards, 3-4 Cyl, 1958-72	009-8
Johnson/Evinrude Outboards, 4, 6 & 8 Cyl, 1992-96	040-3
Kawasaki Personal Watercraft, 1973-91	032-2
Kawasaki Personal Watercraft, 1992-97	042-X
Marine Jet Drive, 1961-96	029-2
Mariner Outboards, 1-2 Cyl, 1977-89	015-2
Mariner Outboards, 3, 4 & 6 Cyl, 1977-89	016-0
Mercruiser Stern Drive, Type I, Alpha/MR, Bravo I & II, 1964-92	005-5
Mercruiser Stern Drive, Alpha I (Generation II), 1992-96	039-X
Mercruiser Stern Drive, Bravo I, II & III, 1992-96	046-2
Mercury Outboards, 1-2 Cyl, 1965-91	012-8
Mercury Outboards, 3-4 Cyl, 1965-92	013-6
Mercury Outboards, 6 Cyl, 1965-91	014-4
Mercury/Mariner Outboards, 1-2 Cyl, 1990-94	035-7
Mercury/Mariner Outboards, 3-4 Cyl, 1990-94	036-5
Mercury/Mariner Outboards, 6 Cyl, 1990-94	037-3
Mercury/Mariner Outboards, All Engines, 1995-99	1416
OMC Cobra Stern Drive, Cobra, King Cobra, Cobra SX, 1985-95	025-X
OMC Stern Drive, 1964-86	004-7
Polaris Personal Watercraft, 1992-97	045-4
Sea Doo/Bombardier Personal Watercraft, 1988-91	033-0
Sea Doo/Bombardier Personal Watercraft, 1992-97	043-8
Suzuki Outboards, All Engines, 1985-99	1600
Volvo/Penta Stern Drives 1968-91	011-X
Volvo/Penta Stern Drives, Volvo Engines, 1992-93	038-1
Volvo/Penta Stern Drives, GM and Ford Engines, 1992-95	041-1
Yamaha Outboards, 1-2 Cyl, 1984-91	021-7
Yamaha Outboards, 3 Cyl, 1984-91	022-5
Yamaha Outboards, 4 & 6 Cyl, 1984-91	023-3
Yamaha Outboards, All Engines, 1992-98	1706
Yamaha Personal Watercraft, 1987-91	034-9
Yamaha Personal Watercraft, 1992-97	044-6
Yanmar Inboard Diesels, 1975-98	7400

SAFETY NOTICE

Proper service and repair procedures are vital to the safe, reliable operation of all marine engines, as well as the personal safety of those performing repairs. This manual outlines procedures for servicing and repairing outboards using safe, effective methods. The procedures contain many NOTES, CAUTIONS and WARNINGS which should be followed, along with standard procedures, to eliminate the possibility of personal injury or improper service which could damage the vessel or compromise its safety.

It is important to note that repair procedures and techniques, tools and parts for servicing marine engines, as well as the skill and experience of the individual performing the work, vary widely. It is not possible to anticipate all of the conceivable ways or conditions under which these engines may be serviced, or to provide cautions as to all possible hazards that may result. Standard and accepted safety precautions and equipment should be used during cutting, grinding, chiseling, prying, or any other process that can cause material removal or projectiles.

Some procedures require the use of tools specially designed for a specific purpose. Before substituting another tool or procedure, you must be completely satisfied that neither your personal safety, nor the performance of the marine engine, will be compromised.

Although information in this manual is based on industry sources and is complete as possible at the time of publication, the possibility exists that some vehicle manufacturers made later changes which could not be included here. While striving for total accuracy, Chilton Marine cannot assume responsibility for any errors, changes or omissions that may occur in the compilation of this data.

PART NUMBERS

Part numbers listed in this reference are not recommendations by Chilton Marine for any product brand name. They are references that can be used with interchange manuals and aftermarket supplier catalogs to locate each brand supplier's discrete part number.

SPECIAL TOOLS

Special tools are recommended by the marine manufacturer to perform a specific task. Use has been kept to a minimum, but, where absolutely necessary, they are referred to in the text by the part number of the tool manufacturer. These tools can be purchased, under the appropriate part number, from your local dealer or regional distributor, or an equivalent tool can be purchased locally from a tool supplier or parts outlet. Before substituting any tool for the one recommended, read the SAFETY NOTICE at the top of this page.

ACKNOWLEDGMENTS

Chilton Marine expresses sincere appreciation to the following companies who supported the production of this manual by providing information, products and general assistance:

- Yamaha Motor Corporation—Cypress, CA
- Clews and Strawbridge—Malvern, PA
- Marine Mechanics Institute—Orlando, FL

Special thanks to Dan Ostrosky and Dan Caviness for providing the literature to get this book started; to Bret Glaser, for teaching us everything we know about Yamaha outboards; to Mike Benfer and Robert Strickler, for the technical info and to Ed Reed for your overall guidance in the finer points of marine engine repair.

ALL RIGHTS RESERVED

FOREWORD

This is a comprehensive tune-up and repair manual for Yamaha outboards manufactured between 1992 and 1998. Competition, high-performance, and commercial units (including aftermarket equipment), are not covered. The book has been designed and written for the professional mechanic, the do-it-yourselfer, and the student developing his mechanical skills.

Professional Mechanics will find it to be an additional tool for use in their daily work because of the many special techniques described.

Boating enthusiasts interested in performing their own work and in keeping their unit operating in the most efficient manner will find the step-by-step illustrated procedures used throughout the manual extremely valuable. In fact, many have said this book almost equals an experienced mechanic looking over their shoulder giving them advice.

Students and Instructors have found the chapters divided into practical areas of interest and work. Technical trade schools, from Florida to Michigan and west to California, as well as the U.S. Navy and Coast Guard, have adopted these manuals as a standard classroom text.

Troubleshooting sections have been included in many chapters to assist the individual performing the work in quickly and accurately isolating problems to a specific area without unnecessary expense and time-consuming work. As an added aid and one of the unique features of this book, many worn parts are illustrated to identify and clarify when an item should be replaced.

Illustrations and procedural steps are so closely related and identified with matching numbers that, in some cases, captions are not used. Exploded drawings show internal parts and their interrelationship with the major component.

GENERAL INFORMATION 1-2
INTRODUCTION 1-2
CLEANING, WAXING AND POLISHING 1-2
CONTROLLING CORROSION 1-2
    USING ZINC ANODES 1-2
SERIAL NUMBERS 1-3
PROPELLERS 1-3
    DIAMETER & PITCH 1-3
    PROPELLER SELECTION 1-4
    CAVITATION 1-4
    VIBRATION 1-4
    SHOCK ABSORBERS 1-4
    PROPELLER RAKE 1-4
    PROGRESSIVE PITCH 1-5
    CUPPING 1-5
    ROTATION 1-5
    HIGH PERFORMANCE
        PROPELLERS 1-5
JET DRIVE 1-6
    DESCRIPTION & OPERATION 1-6
    IDENTIFICATION 1-6
    OPERATIONAL HINTS 1-6
    POWERHEAD STALL 1-6
    GRILLE BLOCKAGE 1-7
FUEL SYSTEM 1-7
    FUEL TANK 1-7
    TAKING ON FUEL 1-7
    STATIC ELECTRICITY 1-7
    FUEL TANK GROUNDING 1-7
SAFETY 1-8
LOADING 1-8
HORSEPOWER 1-8
FLOTATION 1-8
    LIFE PRESERVERS—PERSONAL
        FLOTATION DEVICES (PFDS) 1-8
EMERGENCY EQUIPMENT 1-10
    VISUAL DISTRESS SIGNALS 1-10
    TYPES & QUANTITIES 1-10
    FIRST AID KITS 1-11
    FIRE EXTINGUISHERS 1-11
COMPASS 1-12
    SELECTION 1-12
    INSTALLATION 1-12
    COMPASS PRECAUTIONS 1-13
ANCHORS 1-13
MISCELLANEOUS EQUIPMENT 1-14
    BILGE PUMPS 1-14
BOATING ACCIDENT REPORTS 1-14
NAVIGATION 1-15
    BUOYS 1-15
    WATERWAY RULES 1-15

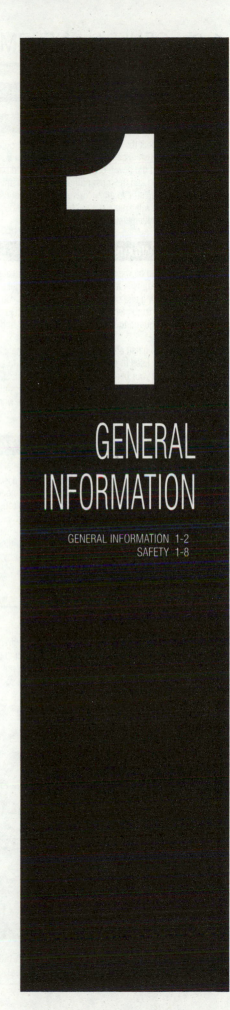

1

GENERAL INFORMATION

GENERAL INFORMATION 1-2
SAFETY 1-8

GENERAL INFORMATION

Introduction

In order to protect the investment of the boat and outboard, they must be cared for properly while being used, as well as when out of the water. Always store the boat with the bow higher than the stern, and be sure to remove the transom drain plug and the inner hull drain plugs. If any type of cover is used to protect the boat, be sure to allow for some movement of air through the hull. Proper ventilation will assure evaporation of any condensation that may form due to changes in temperature and humidity.

Cleaning, Waxing and Polishing

Any boat should be washed with clear water after each use to remove surface dirt and any salt deposits from use in salt water. Regular rinsing will extend the time between waxing and polishing. It will also give you pride of ownership, by having a sharp looking piece of equipment. Elbow grease, a mild detergent and a brush will be required to remove stubborn dirt, oil and other unsightly deposits.

Stay away from harsh abrasives or strong chemical cleaners. A white buffing compound can be used to restore the original gloss to a scratched, dull or faded area. The finish of your boat should be thoroughly cleaned, buffed and polished at least once each season. Take care when buffing or polishing with a marine cleaner not to overheat the surface on which you are working, because you will burn it.

Controlling Corrosion

Since man first started out on the water, corrosion on his craft has been his enemy. The first form was merely rot in the wood and then it was rust, followed by other forms of destructive corrosion in the more modern materials. One defense against corrosion is to use similar metals throughout the boat. Even though this is difficult to do in designing a new boat, particularly the undersides, similar metals should be used whenever and wherever possible.

A second defense against corrosion is to insulate dissimilar metals. This can be done by using an exterior coating of Sea Skin® or by insulating them with plastic or rubber gaskets.

USING ZINC ANODES

◗ See Figures 1, 2 and 3

The proper amount of zinc attached to a boat is extremely important. The use of too much zinc can cause wood burning—by placing the metals close together, they become hot. On the other hand, using not enough zinc will cause

more rapid deterioration of the metal you are trying to protect. If in doubt, consider the fact that it is far better to replace the zinc than to replace planking or other expensive metal parts from having an excess of zinc.

When installing zinc anodes, there are two routes available. One is to install many different zinc anodes on all metal parts and, thus, run the risk of wood burning. Another route, is to use one large zinc anode on the transom of the boat and then connect this to every underwater metallic part through internal bonding. Of the two choices, zinc on the transom is the better way to go.

Most outboards have a zinc anode attached somewhere to the exterior of the lower unit. Zinc anodes, accessible from outside the powerhead, protect the powerhead. Other units have anodes in the powerhead which are not accessible from the exterior.

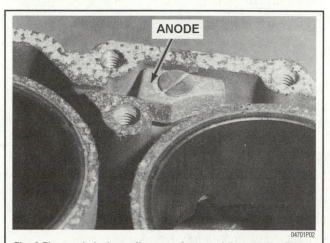

Fig. 2 Zinc anode in the cooling passage around the cylinder. This one is only accessible by disassembling the powerhead

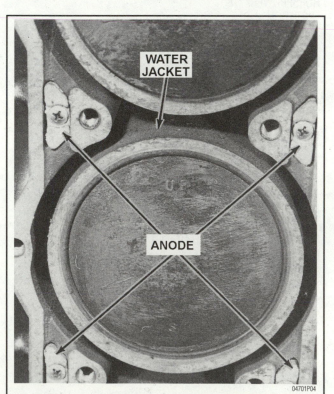

Fig. 1 This zinc is being used as a trim tab. A tab assists in maintaining a true course without fighting the wheel

Fig. 3 This powerhead uses many small zinc anodes spread around the block

Serial Numbers

The outboard serial number and the engine serial number are the manufacturer's key to engine changes. These numbers identify the year of manufacture, the qualified horsepower rating, and the parts book identification. If any correspondence or parts are required, the engine serial number must be used or proper identification is not possible. The accompanying illustrations will be very helpful in locating the engine identification tag for the various models.

The outboard number is usually stamped on the plate attached to the port side of the clamp bracket.

The powerhead serial number is usually stamped on the port side of the cylinder block.

➡ **As a theft prevention measure, a special label with the outboard serial number is usually bonded to the starboard side of the clamp bracket. Any attempt to remove this label will result in cracks across the serial number.**

Propellers

▶ See Figures 4, 5 and 6

As you know, the propeller is actually what moves the boat through the water. This is how it is done: The propeller operates in water in much the same manner as a wood screw or auger passing through wood. The propeller "bites" into the water as it rotates. Water passes between the blades and out to the rear in the shape of a cone. This "biting" through the water is what propels the boat.

All units covered in this manual are equipped, from the factory, with a through-the-propeller exhaust. With these units, exhaust gas is forced out through the propeller.

DIAMETER & PITCH

▶ See Figures 7 and 8

Only two dimensions of the propeller are of real interest to the boat owner: diameter and pitch. These two dimensions are stamped on the propeller hub and always appear in the same order, the diameter first and then the pitch. Propellers furnished with the outboard by the manufacturer for units covered in this manual have a letter designation following the pitch size. This letter indicates the propeller type. For instance, the numbers and letter 9⅞ x 10½ —F stamped on the back of one blade indicates the propeller diameter to be 9⅞ in., with a pitch of 10½ in., and it is a Type F.

The diameter is the measured distance from the tip of one blade to the tip of the other.

The pitch of a propeller is the angle at which the blades are attached to the hub. This figure is expressed in inches of water travel for each revolution of the propeller. In our example of a 9⅞ in. x 10½ in., the propeller should travel 10½ inches through the water each time it revolves. If the propeller action was perfect and there was no slippage, then the pitch multiplied by the propeller rpm would be the boat speed.

Most outboard manufacturers equip their units with a standard propeller, having a diameter and pitch they consider to be best suited to the engine and boat. Such a propeller allows the engine to run as near to the rated rpm and horsepower (at full throttle) as possible for the boat design.

The blade area of the propeller determines its load-carrying capacity. A two-blade propeller is used for high-speed running under very light loads.

A four-blade propeller is installed in boats intended to operate at low speeds under very heavy loads such as tugs, barges or large houseboats. The three-blade propeller is the happy medium covering the wide range between high performance units and load carrying workhorses.

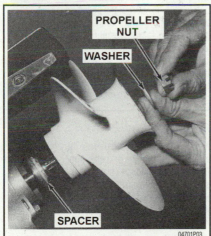

Fig. 4 Typical propeller attaching hardware includes a washer, castle nut and cotter pin to hold the nut in place

Fig. 5 Here is the propeller attaching hardware from an end view. Now you can see how everything fits together

Fig. 6 This propeller should have been replaced long before the damage progressed to this extent

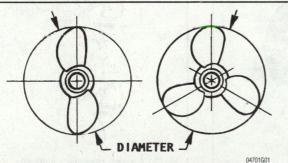

Fig. 7 Diameter and pitch are the two basic dimensions of a propeller. Diameter is measured across the circumference of a circle scribed by the propeller blades.

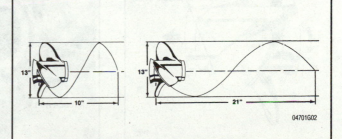

Fig. 8 This diagram illustrates the pitch dimension of a propeller. The pitch is the theoretical distance a propeller would travel through water if there were no friction

PROPELLER SELECTION

There is no one propeller that will do the proper job in all cases. The list of sizes and weights of boats is almost endless. This fact, coupled with the many boat-engine combinations, makes the propeller selection for a specific purpose a difficult task. Actually, in many cases the propeller may be changed after a few test runs. Proper selection is aided through the use of charts set up for various engines and boats. These charts should be studied and understood when buying a propeller. However, bear in mind that the charts are based on average boats with average loads; therefore, it may be necessary to make a change in size or pitch, in order to obtain the desired results for the hull design or load condition.

Propellers are available with a wide range of pitch. Remember, a low pitch design takes a smaller bite of water than a high pitch propeller. This means the low pitch propeller will travel less distance through the water per revolution. However, the low pitch will require less horsepower and will allow the engine to run faster.

All engine manufacturers design their units to operate with full throttle at, or slightly above, the rated rpm. If the powerhead is operated at the rated rpm, several positive advantages will be gained.

- Spark plug life will be increased.
- Better fuel economy will be realized.
- Steering will be easier.
- The boat and power unit will provide best performance.

Therefore, take time to make the proper propeller selection for the rated rpm of the engine at full throttle with what might be considered an average load. The boat will then be correctly balanced between engine and propeller throughout the entire speed range.

A reliable tachometer must be used to measure powerhead speed at full throttle, to ensure that the engine achieves full horsepower and operates efficiently and safely. To test for the correct propeller, make a test run in a body of smooth water with the lower unit in forward gear at full throttle. If the reading is above the manufacturer's recommended operating range, try propellers of greater pitch, until one is found allowing the powerhead to operate continually within the recommended full throttle range.

If the engine is unable to deliver top performance and the powerhead is properly tuned, then the propeller may not be to blame. Operating conditions have a marked effect on performance. For instance, an engine will lose rpm when run in very cold water. It will also lose rpm when run in salt water, as compared with fresh water. A hot, low-barometer day will also cause the engine to lose power.

CAVITATION

♦ **See Figure 9**

Cavitation is the forming of voids in the water just ahead of the propeller blades. Marine propulsion designers are constantly fighting the battle against the formation of these voids, due to excessive blade tip speed and engine wear. The voids may be filled with air or water vapor, or they may actually be a partial vacuum. Cavitation may be caused by installing a piece of equipment too close to the lower unit, such as the knot indicator pickup, depth sounder or bait tank pickup.

VIBRATION

The propeller should be checked regularly to ensure that all blades are in good condition. If any of the blades becomes bent or nicked, this condition will set up vibrations in the drive unit and motor. If the vibration becomes very serious, it will cause a loss of power, efficiency, and boat performance. If the vibration is allowed to continue over a period of time, it can have a damaging effect on many of the operating parts.

Vibration in boats can never be completely eliminated, but it can be reduced by keeping all parts in good working condition and through proper maintenance and lubrication. Vibration can also be reduced in some cases by increasing the number of blades. For this reason, many racers use two-blade propellers, while luxury cruisers have four- and five-blade propellers installed.

SHOCK ABSORBERS

♦ **See Figure 10**

The shock absorber in the propeller plays a very important role in protecting the shafting, gears and engine against the shock of a blow, should the propeller strike an underwater object. The shock absorber allows the propeller to stop rotating at the instant of impact, while the power train continues turning.

How much impact the propeller is able to withstand, before causing the shock absorber to slip, is calculated to be more than the force needed to propel the boat, but less than the amount that could damage any part of the power train. Under normal propulsion loads of moving the boat through the water, the hub will not slip. However, it will slip if the propeller strikes an object with a force that would be great enough to stop any part of the power train.

If the power train was to absorb an impact great enough to stop rotation, even for an instant, something would have to give, resulting in severe damage. If a propeller is subjected to repeated striking of underwater objects, it will eventually slip on its clutch hub under normal loads. If the propeller should start to slip, a new shock absorber/cushion hub will have to be installed.

PROPELLER RAKE

♦ **See Figure 11**

If a propeller blade is examined on a cut extending directly through the center of the hub, and if the blade is set vertical to the propeller hub, the propeller is said to have a zero degree (0°.) rake. As the blade slants back, the rake increases. Standard propellers have a rake angle from 0° to 15°.

A higher rake angle generally improves propeller performance in a cavitating or ventilating situation. On lighter, faster boats, a higher rake often will increase performance by holding the bow of the boat higher.

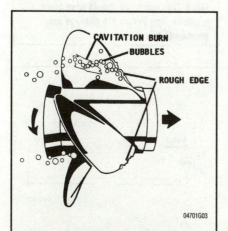

Fig. 9 Cavitation (air bubbles formed at the propeller) is a problem constantly being fought by the manufacturers

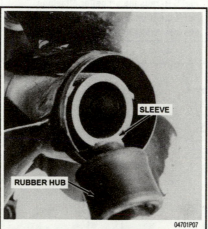

Fig. 10 If your propeller should start to slip after striking underwater objects, inspect and/or replace the rubber hub

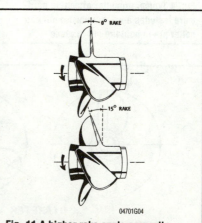

Fig. 11 A higher rake angle generally improves propeller performance and, in lighter boats, tends to hold the bow of the boat higher

PROGRESSIVE PITCH

▶ See Figure 12

Progressive pitch is a blade design innovation that improves performance when forward and rotational speed is high and/or the propeller breaks the surface of the water.

Progressive pitch starts low at the leading edge and progressively increases to the trailing edge. The average pitch over the entire blade is the number assigned to that propeller. In the illustration of the progressive pitch, the average pitch assigned to the propeller would be 21.

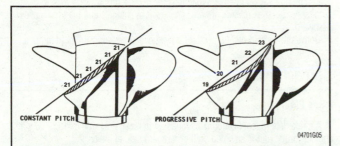

CONSTANT PITCH   PROGRESSIVE PITCH

04701G05

Fig. 12 Comparison of a constant and progressive pitch propeller. Notice how the pitch of the progressive propeller (right) changes to give the blade more thrust

CUPPING

▶ See Figure 13

If the propeller is cast with an edge curl inward on the trailing edge, the blade is said to have a cup. In most cases, cupped blades improve performance. The cup helps the blades to HOLD and not break loose, when operating in a cavitating or ventilating situation.

A cup has the effect of adding to the propeller pitch. Cupping usually will reduce full-throttle engine speed about 150 to 300 rpm below that of the engine equipped with the same pitch propeller without a cup to the blade. A propeller repair shop is able to increase or decrease the cup on the blades. This change, as explained, will alter powerhead rpm to meet specific operating demands. Cups are rapidly becoming standard on propellers.

In order for a cup to be the most effective, the cup should be completely concave (hollowed) and finished with a sharp corner. If the cup has any convex rounding, the effectiveness of the cup will be reduced.

ROTATION

▶ See Figure 14

Propellers are manufactured as right-hand (RH) rotation or left-hand (LH) rotation. The standard propeller for outboard units is RH rotation.

A right-hand propeller can easily be identified by observing it. Observe how the blade of the right-hand propeller slants from the lower left to upper right. The left-hand propeller slants in the opposite direction, from lower right to upper left.

When the RH propeller is observed rotating from astern the boat, it will be rotating clockwise when the outboard unit is in forward gear. The left-hand propeller will rotate counterclockwise.

HIGH PERFORMANCE PROPELLERS

▶ See Figures 15 and 16

The term high performance is usually associated with, or has the connotation of, something used only for racing. The Yamaha high performance propeller does not fit this category and is not considered an aftermarket item.

The Yamaha high performance propeller is made of stainless steel with sophisticated designed blades, and carries an embossed P for positive identification.

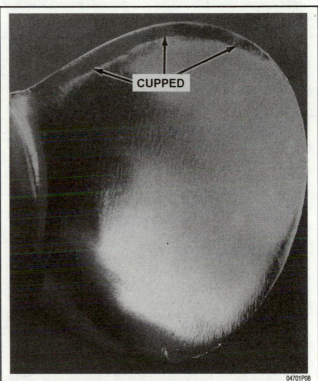

CUPPED

04701P08

Fig. 13 Propeller with a cupped leading edge. Cupping gives the propeller a better hold in the water

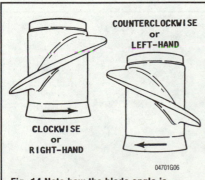

COUNTERCLOCKWISE or LEFT-HAND

CLOCKWISE or RIGHT-HAND

04701G06

Fig. 14 Note how the blade angle is reversed on these right and left-hand propellers. Right-hand propellers are by far the most popular for outboard units

HIGH PERFORMANCE PROPELLER

SPACER

04701G08

Fig. 15 Exploded view of a high performance propeller mounting arrangement. Note the special three-prong spacer

04701P09

Fig. 16 Notice how the blades on this high performance propeller are more narrow and have more pitch than a standard propeller

The accompanying illustration of a high performance propeller clearly shows the unique design of the long blades and other features. This propeller is the weedless type, having extra sharp blades.

Installation of a high performance propeller requires raising the transom height, trim out after planing, and installation of a special design trim tab. Installation of a water pressure gauge is highly recommended, because raising the transom height will affect the amount of water entering the lower unit through the intake holes. An inadequate amount of water taken in will certainly cause powerhead cooling problems.

The high performance propeller has standard attaching hardware with the exception of the inner spacer, which is a special three-pronged design.

Jet Drive

DESCRIPTION & OPERATION

▶ See Figure 17

The jet drive unit is designed to permit boating in areas prohibited for a boat equipped with a conventional propeller drive system. The housing of the jet drive barely extends below the hull of the boat, allowing passage in ankle-deep water, white water rapids, and over sand bars or in shoal water which would foul a propeller drive.

The jet drive provides reliable propulsion with a minimum of moving parts. Simply stated, water is drawn into the unit through an intake grille by an impeller which is driven by a driveshaft off the crankshaft of the powerhead, and then expelled under pressure through an outlet nozzle directed away from the stern of the boat.

As the speed of the boat increases and reaches planing speed, the jet drive discharges water freely into the air, and only the intake grille touches the water.

The jet drive is provided with a gate arrangement and linkage permitting the boat to be operated in reverse. When the gate is moved downward over the exhaust nozzle, the pressure stream is reversed by the gate and the boat moves sternward.

Conventional controls are used for powerhead speed, movement of the boat, and shifting.

IDENTIFICATION

▶ See Figure 18

A model letter identification is stamped on the rear, port side casing. A serial number for the unit is stamped on the starboard side of the casing.

OPERATIONAL HINTS

Wear on the jet impeller and water intake grille will be greatly reduced if the intake of sand, gravel and rocks can be avoided.

When approaching a beach, develop the habit of shutting down the powerhead in water less than six inches below the hull. If the water under the hull becomes less than three inches deep, loose particles on the floor will be sucked into the intake grille. The manufacturer recommends keeping the powerhead speed within the idle range when moving through water less than twelve inches under the hull. Once the water depth increases, with more than a foot of water under the hull, the boat speed may be increased. As boat speed increases, the danger of sucking up rocks is greatly reduced. The faster the boat moves, the ability to suck up rocks becomes negligible, because of the short span of time which the grille is over the rocks.

POWERHEAD STALL

▶ See Figures 19 and 20

If a rock should be sucked up, pass through the grille and jam between the jet impeller and intake wall, the engine will stall, or attempt to stall. If the powerhead sounds as if it is attempting to stall, shut the powerhead down IMMEDIATELY.

The shear pin will most likely prevent any damage to the powerhead. An indication the shear pin has actually done its job and has interrupted the drive train, is a sudden increase in powerhead rpm. Again, the unit should be shut down AT ONCE. If the shear pin has sheared, little or no cooling water will be available to the powerhead. Remove and replace the shear pin.

04701P10

Fig. 17 Notice how the housing of the jet drive barely extends below the hull of the boat

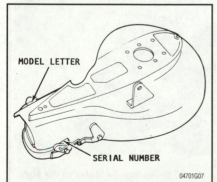

04701G07

Fig. 18 The model letter is embossed on the port side and the serial number on the starboard side of the jet drive

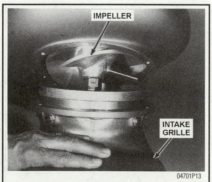

04701P13

Fig. 19 The intake grille must be removed to clear an obstruction lodged between the impeller and the housing

04701P11

Fig. 20 The shear pin is attached to the impeller shaft and prevents powerhead damage if the unit should become jammed

GRILLE BLOCKAGE

If a sudden loss of power to move the boat is experienced, the cause is probably an object blocking the intake grille. A paper or plastic bag, large section of kelp or seaweed, or even a large flat rock may be preventing the intake and exhaust of sufficient water to propel the boat.

If the boat if left unattended in shallow water with the jet drive in the water, and there is considerable wave action, the cavity around the impeller could fill with sand in about three hours or less. Therefore, if the boat is to be left for any period of time under the conditions just described, raise the outboard unit to the full UP and locked position.

If a large quantity of sand should be deposited in the jet drive cavity, any attempt to start the powerhead would fail. The outboard unit must be raised, and the sand flushed out with buckets of water before returning the unit to operational status.

Fuel System

FUEL TANK

▶ **See Figures 21, 22 and 23**

All parts of the fuel system should be selected and installed to provide maximum service and protection against leakage. Reinforced flexible sections should be installed in fuel lines where there is a lot of motion, such as at the engine connection. The flaring of copper tubing should be annealed (heated and cooled slowly) after it is formed as a protection against hardening.

Fig. 21 This tank was taken from the hot sun to a cool location without loosening the vent cap. As the fuel cooled, a vacuum was created inside the tank, causing it to buckle inward

Compression fittings should NOT be used because they are so easily overtightened, which places them under a strain and subjects them to fatigue. Such conditions will cause the fitting to leak after it is connected a second time.

The capacity of the fuel filter must be large enough to handle the demands of the engine as specified by the engine manufacturer.

A manually-operated valve should be installed if anti-siphon protection is not provided. This valve should be installed in the fuel line as close to the gas tank as possible. Such a valve will maintain anti-siphon protection between the tank and the engine.

The supporting surfaces and hold-downs must fasten the tank firmly and they should be insulated from the tank surfaces. This insulation material should be non-abrasive and non-absorbent. Fuel tanks installed in the forward portion of the boat should be especially well secured and protected because shock loads in this area can be as high as 20 to 25 g's (1 g equals the force of gravity).

TAKING ON FUEL

The fuel tank of the boat should be kept full to prevent water from entering the system through condensation caused by temperature changes. Water droplets forming is one of the greatest enemies of the fuel system. By keeping the tank full, the air space in the tank is kept to an absolute minimum and there is no room for moisture to form. It is a good practice not to store fuel in the tank over an extended period, say for six months. Today, fuels contain ingredients that change into gums when stored for any length of time. These gums and varnish products will cause carburetor problems and poor spark plug performance.

An additive, such as Yamaha Fuel Conditioner and Stabilizer, can be used to prevent gums and varnish from forming.

STATIC ELECTRICITY

In very simple terms, static electricity is called frictional electricity. It is generated by two dissimilar materials moving over each other. One form is gasoline flowing through a pipe or into the air. Another form is when you brush your hair or walk across a synthetic carpet and then touch a metal object. All of these actions cause an electrical charge. In most cases, static electricity is generated during very dry weather conditions, but when you are filling the fuel tank on a boat, it can happen at any time.

FUEL TANK GROUNDING

▶ **See Figure 24**

One area of protection against the buildup of static electricity is to have the fuel tank properly grounded (also known as bonding). Bonding must accomplish a direct metal-to-metal contact from the fuel hose nozzle to the water in

Fig. 22 A three-position valve permits fuel to be drawn from multiple tanks or to be shut off completely. Shutting off the fuel prevents accidental siphoning

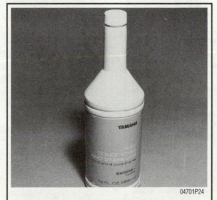

Fig. 23 The use of an approved fuel additive, such as this Yamaha Fuel Conditioner and Stabilizer, will prevent fuel from souring for up to twelve months

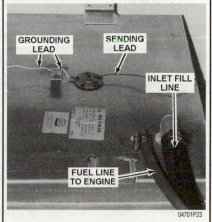

Fig. 24 A properly connected and grounded inboard fuel tank

which the boat is floating. If the fill pipe is made of metal, and the fuel nozzle makes a good contact with the deck plate, then a good ground is made.

As an economy measure, some boats use rubber or plastic filler pipes because of compound bends in the pipe. Such a fill line does not give any kind of ground; if your boat has this type of installation and you do not want to replace the filler pipe with a metal one, it is possible to connect the deck fitting to the tank with a copper wire. The wire should be 8 gauge or larger.

The fuel line from the tank to the engine should provide continuous metal-to-metal contact for proper grounding. If any part of this line is plastic or another non-metallic material, then a copper wire must be connected to bridge the non-metallic material. The power train provides a ground through the engine and drive shaft, to the propeller in the water.

Fiberglass fuel tanks pose problems of their own. Fortunately, this material has almost totally disappeared as a suitable substance for fuel tanks. If, however, the boat you are servicing does have a fiberglass tank, or one is being installed or repaired, it is almost mandatory that you check with the Coast Guard Recreational Boating Standards Office in your district before proceeding with any work. The new standards are very specific and the Coast Guard is extremely rigid about enforcing the regulations.

Anything you can feel as a shock is enough to set off an explosion. Did you know that under certain atmospheric conditions you can cause a static explosion yourself, particularly if you are wearing synthetic clothing. It is almost a certainty you could cause a static spark if you are not wearing insulated rubber-soled shoes.

As soon as the deck fitting is opened, fumes are released to the air. Therefore, to be safe, you should ground yourself before opening the fill pipe deck fitting. One way to ground yourself is to dip your hand in the water to discharge electricity in your body before opening the filler cap. Another method is to touch the engine block or any metal fitting on the dock which goes down into the water.

SAFETY

Loading

▶ **See Figure 25**

In order to receive maximum enjoyment, safety and performance from your boat, take care not to exceed the load capacity given by the manufacturer. A plate attached to the hull indicates the U.S. Coast Guard capacity information in pounds for persons and gear. If the plate states the maximum person capacity to be 750 pounds and you assume each person to weigh an average of 150 lbs., then the boat could carry five persons safely. If you add another 250 lbs. for motor and gear, and the maximum weight capacity for persons and gear is 1,000 lbs. or more, then the five persons and gear would be within the limit.

Try to load the boat evenly on both sides (port and starboard). If you place more weight on one side than on the other, the boat will list to the heavy side and make steering difficult. You will also get better performance by placing heavy supplies aft of the center, to keep the bow light for more efficient planing.

Much confusion arises from the terms, certification, requirements, approval, regulations, etc. Perhaps the following may clarify a couple of these points.

• The Coast Guard does not approve boats in the same manner as they approve life jackets. The Coast Guard applies a formula to inform the public of what is safe for a particular craft.

• If a boat has to meet a particular regulation, it must have a Coast Guard certification plate. The public has been led to believe this indicates approval of the Coast Guard. Not so.

• The certification plate means a willingness of the manufacturer to meet the Coast Guard regulations for that particular craft. The manufacturer may recall a boat if it fails to meet the Coast Guard requirements.

• The Coast Guard certification plate may or may not be metal. The plate is a regulation for the manufacturer. It is only a warning plate and the public does not have to adhere to the restrictions set forth on it. Again, the plate sets forth information as to the Coast Guard's opinion for safety on that particular boat.

• Coast Guard approved equipment is equipment which has been approved by the Commandant of the U. S. Coast Guard and has been determined to be in compliance with Coast Guard specifications and regulations relating to the materials, construction and performance of such equipment.

Horsepower

The maximum horsepower engine for each individual boat should not be increased by any significant amount without checking requirements from the Coast Guard in the local area. The Coast Guard determines horsepower requirements based on the length, beam and depth of the hull. TAKE CARE NOT to exceed the maximum horsepower listed on the plate, otherwise the warranty on the boat, and possibly the insurance, may become void.

Flotation

If the boat is less than 20 ft. overall, a Coast Guard and Boating Industry of America (BIA), now changed to National Marine Manufacturers Association (NMMA), requirement is that the boat must have buoyant material built into the hull (usually foam) to keep it from sinking if it should become swamped. Coast Guard requirements are mandatory, but those of the NMMA are voluntary.

Protection against sinking is defined as the ability of the flotation material to keep the boat from sinking when filled with water and with passengers clinging to the hull. One restriction is that the total weight of the motor, passengers and equipment aboard does not exceed the maximum load capacity listed on the plate.

LIFE PRESERVERS—PERSONAL FLOTATION DEVICES (PFDs)

The Coast Guard requires at least one Coast Guard approved life-saving device be carried on board all motorboats for each person on board. Such devices are identified by a tag indicating Coast Guard approval; they include life preservers, buoyant vests, ring buoys and buoyant cushions. Cushions used for seating are serviceable if air cannot be squeezed out of it. Once air is released when the cushion is squeezed, it is no longer fit as a flotation device. New foam cushions dipped in a rubberized material trap air and are almost indestructible.

Life preservers have been classified by the Coast Guard into five types of categories. All PFDs presently acceptable on recreational boats fall into one of these five designations. All PFDs MUST be U.S. Coast Guard approved, in good and serviceable condition, and of an appropriate size for the persons who intend to wear them. Wearable PFDs MUST be readily accessible and throwable devices, and MUST be immediately available for use.

Type I Personal Flotation Device

▶ **See Figure 26**

A Type I PFD has the greatest required buoyancy and is designed to turn most UNCONSCIOUS persons in the water from a face down position to a vertical or slightly backward position. The adult size device provides a minimum buoyancy of 22 pounds and the child size provides a minimum buoyancy of 11 pounds. The Type I PFD provides the greatest protection to its wearer and is most effective for all waters and conditions.

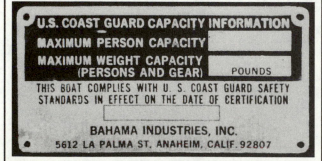

U.S. COAST GUARD CAPACITY INFORMATION
MAXIMUM PERSON CAPACITY
MAXIMUM WEIGHT CAPACITY
(PERSONS AND GEAR) POUNDS

THIS BOAT COMPLIES WITH U. S. COAST GUARD SAFETY STANDARDS IN EFFECT ON THE DATE OF CERTIFICATION

BAHAMA INDUSTRIES, INC.
5612 LA PALMA ST. ANAHEIM, CALIF. 92807

04701P20

Fig. 25 A U.S. Coast Guard certification plate is affixed to all new boats. This plate indicates the amount of occupants, gear and horsepower appropriate for safe operation of the craft

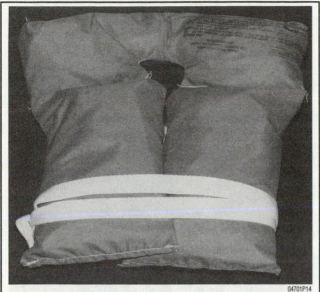

04701P14

Fig. 26 Type I PFD approved life jacket. This type of flotation device provides the greatest amount of buoyancy

04701P15

Fig. 27 Type IV PFD cushion intended to be thrown to a person in the water. If air can be squeezed out of the cushion, it is faulty and should be replaced

Type II Personal Flotation Device

A Type II PFD is designed to turn its wearer in a vertical or slightly backward position in the water. The turning action is not as pronounced as with a Type I. The device will not turn as many different types of persons under the same conditions as the Type I. An adult size device provides a minimum buoyancy of 15 ½ pounds, the medium child size provides a minimum of 11 pounds, and the infant and small child sizes provide a minimum buoyancy of 7 pounds.

Type III Personal Flotation Device

A Type III PFD is designed to permit the wearer to place himself (herself) in a vertical or slightly backward position. The Type III device has the same buoyancy as the Type II PFD, but it has little or no turning ability. Many of the Type III PFDs are designed to be particularly useful when water skiing, sailing, hunting, fishing, or engaging in other water sports. Several of this type will also provide increased hypothermia protection.

Type IV Personal Flotation Device

♦ **See Figures 27 and 28**

A Type IV PFD is designed to be thrown to a person in the water, and grasped and held by the user until rescued. It is NOT designed to be worn. The most common Type IV PFD is a ring buoy or a buoyant cushion.

Type V Personal Flotation Device

A Type V PFD is any PFD approved for restricted use.

Coast Guard regulations state, in general terms: For all boats, one Type I, II, III or IV device shall be carried on board for each person in the boat. On boats over 16 ft., one Type I, II or III device shall be carried on board for each person in the boat, plus one Type IV device.

It is an accepted fact that most boating people own life preservers, but too few actually wear them. There is little or no excuse for not wearing one because the modern, comfortable designs available today do not subtract from an individual's boating pleasure. Make a life jacket available to the crew and advise each member to wear it. If you are a crew member, ask the skipper to issue one,

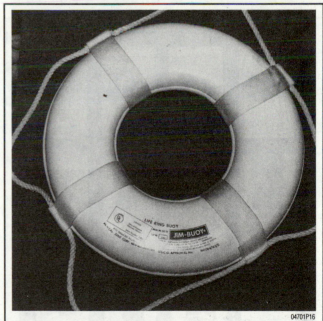

04701P16

Fig. 28 Type IV PFD ring buoy intended to be thrown to a person in the water. On ocean cruisers, this type of device usually has a weighted pole with a flag and light attached to the buoy

especially when boating in rough weather, cold water, or when running at high speed. Naturally, a life jacket should be a must for non-swimmers anytime they are out on the water in a boat.

Emergency Equipment

VISUAL DISTRESS SIGNALS

♦ **See Figures 29 and 30**

Since January 1, 1981, Coast Guard Regulations require all recreational boats which fall into one of the following two categories to be equipped with visual distress signals:

• Boats used on coastal waters, including the Great Lakes, territorial seas and those waters directly connected to the Great Lakes and territorial seas, up to a point where the waters are less than two miles wide.

• Boats owned in the United States, when operating on the high seas.

The only exceptions are during daytime (sunrise to sunset) for:

• Recreational boats less than 16 ft. (5 meters) in length.

• Boats participating in organized events such as races, regattas or marine parades.

• Open sailboats not equipped with propulsion machinery and less than 26 ft. (8 meters) in length.

• Manually propelled boats.

➡ **The above listed boats need to carry visual distress signals when used on these waters at night.**

Pyrotechnic visual distress signaling devices MUST be United States Coast Guard (USCG) approved, in serviceable condition and stowed to be readily accessible. If they are marked with a date showing the serviceable life, this date must not have passed. Launchers produced before January 1, 1981, and intended for use with approved signals, are not required to be USCG approved.

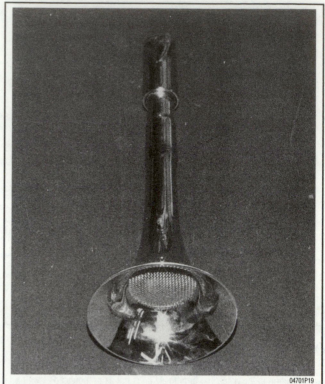

04701P19

Fig. 30 A sounding device should be mounted close to the helmsman for use in sounding emergency alarms

USCG approved pyrotechnic visual distress signals and associated devices include:

• Pyrotechnic red flares, hand-held or aerial.

• Pyrotechnic orange smoke, hand-held or floating.

• Launchers for aerial red meteors or parachute flares.

Non-pyrotechnic visual distress signaling devices must carry the manufacturer's certification that they meet USCG requirements. They must be in serviceable condition and stowed so as to be readily accessible.

• Orange distress flag at least 3 x 3 feet with a black square and ball on an orange background.

• Electric distress light—not a flashlight, but an approved electric distress light which MUST automatically flash the international SOS distress signal (...---...) four to six times each minute.

TYPES & QUANTITIES

♦ **See Figure 31**

The following variety and combination of devices may be carried in order to meet the requirements.

• Three hand-held red flares (day and night).

• One electric distress light (night only).

• One hand-held red flare and two parachute flares (day and night).

• One hand-held orange smoke signal, two floating orange smoke signals (day) and one electric distress light (day and night).

If young children are frequently aboard your boat, careful selection and proper stowage of visual distress signals becomes especially important. If you elect to carry pyrotechnic devices, you should select types in tough packaging which are not easy to ignite, should the devices fall into the hands of children.

Coast Guard approved pyrotechnic devices carry an expiration date. This date CANNOT exceed 42 months from the date of manufacture, and at such time the device can no longer be counted toward the minimum requirements.

➡ **In some states, the launchers for meteors and parachute flares may be considered a firearm. Therefore, check with your state authorities before acquiring such a launcher.**

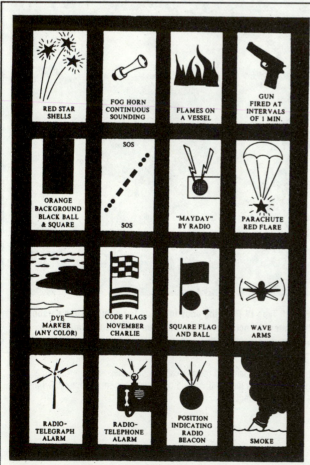

04701G09

Fig. 29 Internationally accepted distress signals

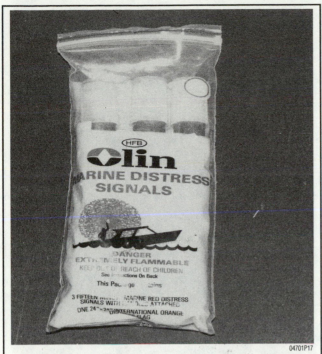

Fig. 31 Moisture protected flares should be carried on board any craft for use as a distress signal

FIRST AID KITS

▶ **See Figure 32**

The first aid kit is similar to an insurance policy or life jacket. You hope you don't have to use it, but if needed, you want it there. It is only natural to overlook this essential item because, let's face it, who likes to think of unpleasantness when planning to have only a good time. However, the prudent skipper is prepared ahead of time, and is thus able to handle the emergency without a lot of fuss.

Good commercial first aid kits are available, such as the Johnson and Johnson Marine First-Aid Kit. With a very modest expenditure, a well-stocked and adequate kit can be prepared at home.

Any kit should include instruments, supplies and a set of instructions for their use. Instruments should be protected in a watertight case and should include: scissors, tweezers, tourniquet, thermometer, safety pins, eye-washing cup and a hot water bottle. Supplies in the kit should include: assorted bandages in addition to various sizes of Band-Aids® (or other adhesive strips), adhesive tape, absorbent cotton, applicators, petroleum jelly, antiseptic (liquid and ointment), local ointment, aspirin, eye ointment, antihistamine, ammonia inhalant, sea-sickness pills, antacid pills and a laxative. You may want to consult your family physician about including antibiotics. Be sure your kit contains

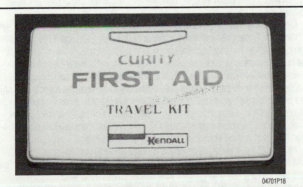

Fig. 32 Always carry an adequately stocked first aid kit on board for the safety of the crew and guests

a first aid manual, because even though you have taken the Red Cross course, you may be the patient and have to rely on an untrained crew member for care.

FIRE EXTINGUISHERS

▶ **See Figure 33**

All fire extinguishers must bear Underwriters Laboratory (UL) Marine Type approved labels. With the UL certification, the extinguisher does not have to have a Coast Guard approval number. The Coast Guard classifies fire extinguishers according to their size and type.

Types B-I and B-II are designed for extinguishing flammable liquids, and are required on all motorboats.

The Coast Guard considers a boat having one or more of the following conditions as a boat of closed construction, subject to fire extinguisher regulations.

- Inboard engine or engines.
- Closed compartments under thwarts and seats, wherein portable fuel tanks may be stored.
- Double bottoms not sealed to the hull or which are not completely filled with flotation materials.
- Closed living spaces.
- Closed stowage compartments in which combustible or flammable material is stored.
- Permanently installed fuel tanks.

Detailed classification of fire extinguishers is by agent and size:

- B-I contains 1¼ gallons foam, 4 pounds carbon dioxide, 2 pounds dry chemical, and 2½ pounds Freon®.
- B-II contains 2½ gallons foam, 15 pounds carbon dioxide, and 10 pounds dry chemical.

The class of motorboat dictates how many fire extinguishers are required on board. One B-II unit can be substituted for two B-I extinguishers.

Dry chemical fire extinguishers without gauges or indicating devices must be weighed and tagged every 6 months. If the gross weight of a carbon dioxide (CO_2) fire extinguisher is reduced by more than 10 percent of the net weight, the extinguisher is not acceptable and must be recharged.

Fig. 33 An approved fire extinguisher should be mounted close to the helmsman for emergency use

➡Read labels on fire extinguishers. If the extinguisher is UL listed, it is approved for marine use. Seloc suggests that you double the number of on board fire extinguishers, as recommended by the Coast Guard. Coast guard requirements are a bare minimum for safe operation. Your boat, family and crew must certainly be worth much more than bare minimum.

Compass

SELECTION

♦ **See Figure 34**

The safety of the boat and her crew may depend on her compass. In many areas, weather conditions can change so rapidly that, within minutes, a skipper may find himself socked in by a fog bank, rain squall or just poor visibility. Under these conditions, he may have no other means of keeping to his desired course except with the compass. When crossing an open body of water, his compass may be the only means of making an accurate landfall.

Fig. 34 Don't hesitate to spend a few extra dollars for a good, reliable compass. If in doubt, seek advice from a knowledgeable boater or marine shop

During thick weather when you can neither see nor hear the expected aids to navigation, attempting to run out the time on a given course can disrupt the pleasure of the cruise. The skipper gains little comfort in a chain of soundings that does not match those given on the chart for the expected area. Any stranding, even for a short time, can be an unnerving experience.

A pilot will not knowingly accept a cheap parachute. By the same token, a good boater should not accept a bargain in lifejackets, fire extinguishers, or compass. Take the time and spend the few extra dollars to purchase a compass to fit your expected needs. Regardless of what the salesman may tell you, postpone buying until you have had the chance to check more than one make and model.

Lift each compass, tilt and turn it, simulating expected motions of the boat. The compass card should have a smooth and stable reaction.

The card of a good quality compass will come to rest without oscillations about the lubber's line. Reasonable movement in your hand, comparable to the rolling and pitching of the boat, should not materially affect the reading.

INSTALLATION

♦ **See Figure 35**

Proper installation of the compass does not happen by accident. Make a critical check of the proposed location to be sure compass placement will permit the helmsman to use it with comfort and accuracy. First, the compass should be

Fig. 35 The compass is a delicate instrument and deserves respect. It should be mounted securely and in a position where it can be easily observed by the helmsman

placed directly in front of the helmsman, and in such a position that it can be viewed without body stress as he sits or stands in a posture of relaxed alertness. The compass should be in the helmsman's zone of comfort. If the compass is too far away, he may have to bend forward to watch it; too close and he must rear backward for relief.

Second, give some thought to comfort in heavy weather and poor visibility conditions during the day and night. In some cases, the compass position may be partially determined by the location of the wheel, shift lever and throttle handle.

Third, inspect the compass site to be sure the instrument will be at least two feet from any engine indicators, bilge vapor detectors, magnetic instruments, or any steel or iron objects. If the compass cannot be placed at least two feet (six feet would be better) from one of these influences, then either the compass or the other object must be moved, if first order accuracy is to be expected.

Once the compass location appears to be satisfactory, give the compass a test before installation. Hidden influences may be concealed under the cabin top, forward of the cabin aft bulkhead, within the cockpit ceiling, or in a wood-covered stanchion.

Move the compass around in the area of the proposed location. Keep an eye on the card. A magnetic influence is the only thing that will make the card turn. You can quickly find any such influence with the compass. If the influence cannot be moved away or replaced by one of non-magnetic material, test to determine whether it is merely magnetic, a small piece of iron or steel, or some magnetized steel. Bring the north pole of the compass near the object, then shift and bring the south pole near it. Both the north and south poles will be attracted if the compass is demagnetized. If the object attracts one pole and repels the other, then the compass is magnetized. If your compass needs to be demagnetized, take it to a shop equipped to do the job PROPERLY.

After you have moved the compass around in the proposed mounting area, hold it down or tape it in position. Test everything you feel might affect the compass and cause a deviation from a true reading. Rotate the wheel from hard over-to-hard over. Switch on and off all the lights, radios, radio direction finder, radio telephone, depth finder and, if installed, the shipboard intercom. Sound the electric whistle, turn on the windshield wipers, start the engine (with water circulating through the engine), work the throttle, and move the gear shift lever. If the boat has an auxiliary generator, start it.

If the card moves during any one of these tests, the compass should be relocated. Naturally, if something like the windshield wipers causes a slight deviation, it may be necessary for you to make a different deviation table to use only when certain pieces of equipment are operating. Bear in mind, following a course that is off only a degree or two for several hours can make considerable difference at the end, putting you on a reef, rock or shoal.

Check to be sure the intended compass site is solid. Vibration will increase pivot wear.

Now, you are ready to mount the compass. To prevent an error on all courses, the line through the lubber line and the compass card pivot must be exactly parallel to the keel of the boat. You can establish the fore-and-aft line of the boat with a stout cord or string. Use care to transfer this line to the compass site. If necessary, shim the base of the compass until the stile-type lubber line (the one affixed to the case and not gimbaled) is vertical when the boat is on an even keel. Drill the holes and mount the compass.

COMPASS PRECAUTIONS

♦ **See Figure 36**

Many times an owner will install an expensive stereo system in the cabin of his boat. It is not uncommon for the speakers to be mounted on the aft bulkhead up against the overhead (ceiling). In almost every case, this position places one of the speakers in very close proximity to the compass, mounted above the ceiling.

As we all know, a magnet is used in the operation of the speaker. Therefore, it is very likely that the speaker, mounted almost under the compass in the cabin will have a very pronounced effect on the compass accuracy.

Consider the following test and the accompanying photographs as proof:

First, the compass was read as 190 degrees while the boat was secure in her slip.

Next, a full can of soda pop in an aluminum can was placed on one side and the compass read as 204 degrees, a good 14 degrees off.

Next, the full can was moved to the opposite side of the compass and again a reading was observed, this time as 189 degrees, 11 degrees off from the original reading.

Finally, the contents of the can were consumed, the can placed on both sides of the compass with NO effect on the compass reading.

Two very important conclusions can be drawn from these tests.
• Something must have been in the contents of the can to affect the compass so drastically.
• Keep even innocent things clear of the compass to avoid any possible error in the boat's heading.

➡ **Remember, a boat moving through the water at 10 knots on a compass error of just 5 degrees will be almost 1.5 miles off course in only ONE hour. At night, or in thick weather, this could very possibly put the boat on a reef, rock or shoal with disastrous results.**

Anchors

♦ **See Figure 37**

One of the most important pieces of equipment in the boat, next to the power plant, is the ground tackle carried. The engine makes the boat go, and the anchor and its line are what hold it in place when the boat is not secured to a dock or on the beach.

The anchor must be of suitable size, type and weight to give the skipper peace of mind when the boat is at anchor. Under certain conditions, a second, smaller, lighter anchor may help to keep the boat in a favorable position during a non-emergency daytime situation.

In order for the anchor to hold properly, a piece of chain must be attached to

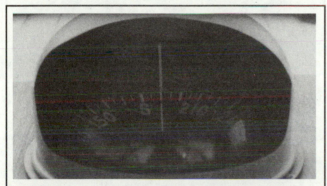

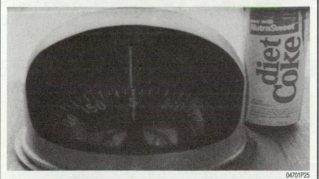

04701P25

Fig. 36 Innocent objects close to the compass may cause serious problems and lead to disaster

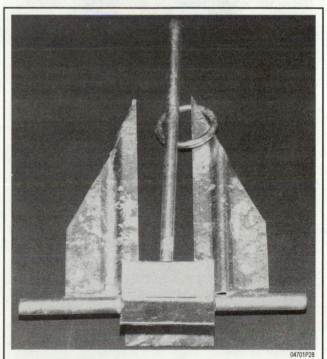

04701P28

Fig. 37 The weight of the anchor must be sufficient to secure the boat without dragging

the anchor, and then the nylon anchor line attached to the chain. The amount of chain should equal or exceed the length of the boat. Such a piece of chain will ensure that the anchor stock will lay in an approximate horizontal position and permit the flutes to dig into the bottom and hold.

Miscellaneous Equipment

▶ **See Figures 38, 39 and 40**

In addition to the equipment you are legally required to carry in the boat and the items previously mentioned, some extra items will add to your boating pleasure and safety. Practical suggestions include: a bailing device (bucket, pump, etc.), boat hook, spare propeller, spare engine parts, tools, an auxiliary means of

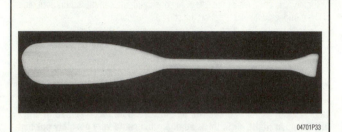

04701P33

Fig. 38 A typical wooden oar should be kept on board as an auxiliary means of propulsion. It can also function as a grab hook for someone fallen overboard

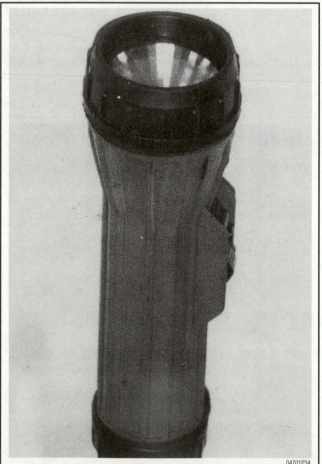

04701P34

Fig. 39 Make sure the flashlight has a fresh set of batteries at the beginning of every boating season

04701P35

Fig. 40 A spare can of gasoline can keep you from becoming stranded on the water. Make sure the container is approved for marine use

propulsion (oars), spare can of gasoline, flashlight, and extra warm clothing. The area of your boating activity, weather conditions, length of stay aboard your boat, and the specific purpose will all contribute to the kind and amount of stores you put aboard. When it comes to personal gear, heed the advice of veteran boaters who say to decide on how little you think you can get by with, then cut it in half.

BILGE PUMPS

▶ **See Figure 41**

Automatic bilge pumps should be equipped with an overriding manual switch. They should also have an indicator in the operator's position to advise the helmsman when the pump is operating. Select a pump that will stabilize its temperature within the manufacturer's specified limits when it is operated continuously. The pump motor should be a sealed or arcless type, suitable for a marine atmosphere. Place the bilge pump inlets so that excess bilge water can be removed at all normal boat trims. The intakes should be properly screened to prevent the pump from sucking up debris from the bilge. Intake tubing should be of a high quality and stiff enough to resist kinking and/or collapsing under maximum pump suction condition if the intake becomes blocked.

Boating Accident Reports

In the United States, new federal and state regulations require an accident report to be filed with the nearest state boating authority within 48 hours, if a person is lost, disappears, or is injured. Injured is defined as requiring medical attention beyond first aid.

Accidents involving only property or equipment damage MUST be reported within 10 days if the damage is in excess of $200. Some states are more stringent and require reporting of accidents with property damage less than $200.

A $500 penalty may be assessed for failure to submit the report.

Take time to make a copy of the report to keep for your records or for the

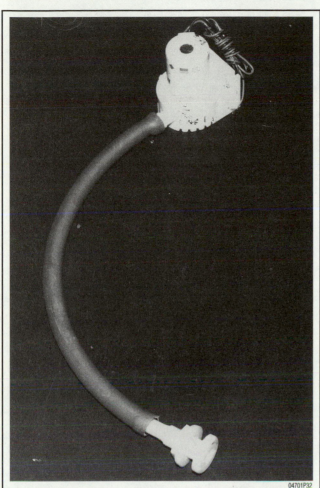

Fig. 41 The bilge pump line must be cleaned frequently to ensure the pump will be effective in an emergency

insurance company. Once the report is filed, the Coast Guard will not give out a copy, even to the person who filed the report.

The report must give details of the accident and include:

- The date, time and exact location of the occurrence.
- The name of each person who died, was lost, or injured.
- The number and name of the vessel.
- The names and addresses of the owner and operator.

If the operator cannot file the report for any reason, each person on board MUST notify the authorities, or determine that the report has been filed.

Navigation

BUOYS

♦ **See Figures 42 and 43**

In the United States, a buoyage system is used as an assist to all boaters of all size craft to navigate our coastal waters and our navigable rivers in safety. When properly read and understood, these buoys and markers will permit the boater to cruise with comparative confidence that he will be able to avoid reefs, rocks, shoals and other hazards.

In the spring of 1983, the Coast Guard began making modifications to U.S. aids to navigation in support of an agreement sponsored by the International Association of Lighthouse Authorities (IALA) and signed by representatives from most of the maritime nations of the world. The primary purpose of the modifications is to improve safety by making buoyage systems around the world more alike and less confusing.

In nautical terms, the front of the boat is the bow, and the rear is the stern. The terms port and starboard are used to refer to the left and right side of the boat, when looking forward. One easy way to remember this basic fundamental is to consider that the words port and left both have four letters and go together.

WATERWAY RULES

On the water, certain basic safe-operating practices must be followed. You should learn and practice them, for to know is to be able to handle your boat with confidence and safety. Knowledge of what to do, and not do, will add a great deal to the enjoyment you will receive from your boating investment.

The best advice possible, as well as a Coast Guard requirement since 1981 for boats over 39 ft., 4 in. (12 meters) in length, is to obtain an official copy of

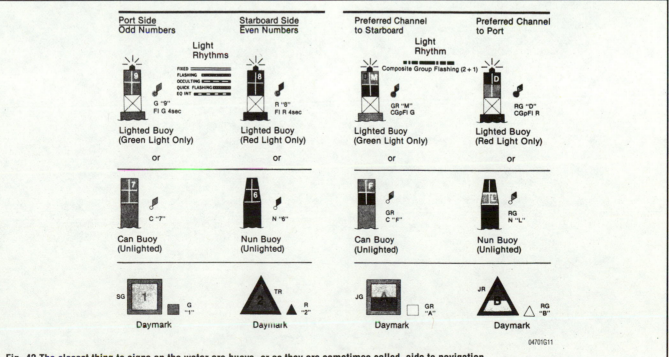

Fig. 42 The closest thing to signs on the water are buoys, or as they are sometimes called, aids to navigation

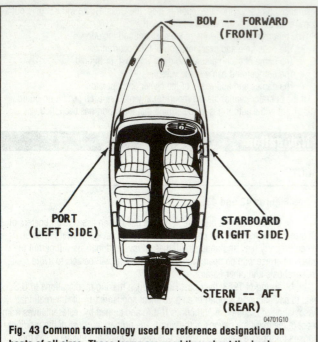

Fig. 43 Common terminology used for reference designation on boats of all sizes. These terms are used throughout the book

the "Rules of the Road," which includes Inland Waterways, Western Rivers, and the Great Lakes for study and ready reference.

The following two paragraphs give a very brief, condensed, and abbreviated synopsis of the rules. They should not be considered in any way as covering the entire subject.

Powered boats must yield the right-of-way to all boats without motors, except when being overtaken. When meeting another boat head-on, keep to starboard, unless you are too far to port to make this practical. When overtaking another boat, the right-of-way belongs to the boat being overtaken. If your boat is being passed, you must maintain course and speed.

When two boats approach at an angle and there is danger of collision, the boat to port must give way to the boat to starboard. Always keep to starboard in a narrow channel or canal. Boats underway must stay clear of vessels fishing with nets, lines or trawls. (Fishing boats are not allowed to fish in channels or to obstruct navigation.

TUNING 2-2
ROUTINE TUNE-UP 2-2
TUNE-UP SEQUENCE 2-2
COMPRESSION CHECK 2-2
    CHECKING COMPRESSION 2-2
    LOW COMPRESSION 2-3
SPARK PLUGS 2-3
    SPARK PLUG HEAT RANGE 2-3
    SPARK PLUG SERVICE 2-4
    REMOVAL 2-4
    INSPECTION 2-4
    READING SPARK PLUGS 2-4
    GAPPING SPARK PLUGS 2-4
    INSTALLATION 2-4
SPARK PLUG WIRES 2-5
    CHECKING & REPLACING 2-5
BROKEN REED 2-6
BREAKER POINTS (MAGNETO) IGNITION
  SYSTEM 2-6
    TESTING 2-7
    REPLACEMENT 2-7
    ADJUSTMENT 2-8
CDI IGNITION SYSTEMS 2-9
BATTERY 2-9
STARTER MOTOR 2-9
INTERNAL WIRING HARNESS 2-9
CARBURETORS 2-9
    TACHOMETER CONNECTIONS 2-9
    IDLE SPEED ADJUSTMENT 2-10
FUEL SYSTEM 2-11
    FUEL INSPECTION 2-11
    FUEL PUMP INSPECTION 2-11
    FUEL FILTER SERVICE 2-12
WATER PUMP CHECK 2-12
PROPELLER 2-13
LOWER UNIT 2-13
JET DRIVE UNITS 2-14
    GATE POSITION & SHIFT LEVER 2-14
    IMPELLER 2-14
PERFORMANCE TESTING 2-15
SPECIFICATIONS CHART
  GENERAL ENGINE SPECIFICATIONS 2-16

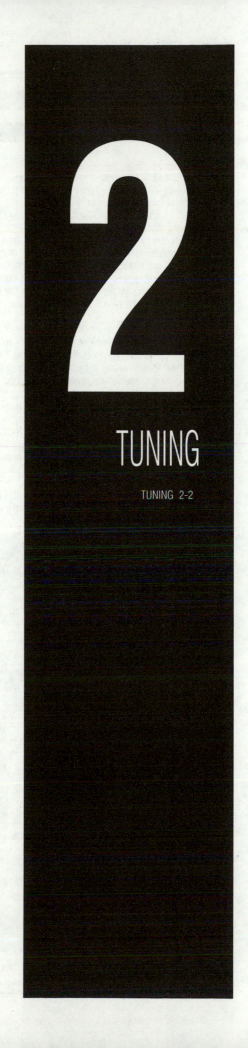

2

TUNING

TUNING 2-2

TUNING

Routine Tune-Up

♦ See Figure 1

A proper tune-up is the key to long and trouble-free engine life, and the work can yield its own rewards. Studies have shown that a properly tuned and maintained engine can achieve better fuel mileage than an out-of-tune engine. As a conscientious boater, set aside a Saturday morning, say once a month, to check or replace items which could cause major problems later. Keep your own personal log to jot down which services you performed, how much the parts cost you, the date, and the number of hours on the engine at the time. Keep all receipts for such items as engine oil and filters, so that they may be referred to in case of related problems or to determine operating expenses. As a do-it-yourselfer, these receipts are the only proof you have that the required maintenance was performed. In the event of a warranty problem, these receipts will be invaluable.

The efficiency, reliability, fuel economy and enjoyment available from engine performance are all directly dependent on having your outboard tuned properly. The importance of performing service work in the proper sequence cannot be over emphasized. Before making any adjustments, check the specifications. Never rely on memory when making critical adjustments.

Before beginning to tune any engine, ensure the engine has satisfactory compression. An engine with worn or broken piston rings, burned pistons, or scored cylinder walls, will not perform properly no matter how much time and expense is spent on the tune-up. Poor compression must be corrected or the tune-up will not give the desired results.

A practical maintenance program that is followed throughout the year, is one of the best methods of ensuring the engine will give satisfactory performance. As they say, you can spend a little time now or a lot of time later.

The extent of the engine tune-up is usually dependent on the time lapse since the last service. A complete tune-up of the entire engine would entail almost all of the work outlined in this manual. However, this is usually not necessary in most cases.

In this section, a logical sequence of tune-up steps will be presented in general terms. If additional information or detailed service work is required, refer to the section containing the appropriate instructions.

Each year higher compression ratios are built into modern outboard engines and the electrical systems become more complex. Therefore, the need for reliable, authoritative, and detailed instructions becomes more critical. The information in this section fulfill that requirement.

Tune-Up Sequence

During a major tune-up, a definite sequence of service work should be followed to return the engine its maximum performance level. This type of work should not be confused with troubleshooting (attempting to locate a problem when the engine is not performing satisfactorily). In many cases, these two areas will overlap, because many times a minor or major tune-up will correct the malfunction and return the system to normal operation.

The following list is a suggested sequence of tasks to perform during a tune-up.

• Perform a compression check of each cylinder.
• Inspect the spark plugs to determine their condition. Test for adequate spark at the plug.
• Start the engine in a body of water and check the water flow through the engine.
• Check the gear oil in the lower unit.
• Check the carburetor adjustments and the need for an overhaul.
• Check the fuel pump for adequate performance and delivery.
• Make a general inspection of the ignition system.
• Test the starter motor and the solenoid, if so equipped.
• Check the internal wiring.
• Check the timing and synchronization.

Compression Check

Cylinder compression test results are extremely valuable indicators of internal engine condition. The best marine mechanics automatically check an engine's compression as the first step in a comprehensive tune-up. Obviously, it is useless to try to tune an engine with extremely low or erratic compression readings, since a simple tune-up will not cure the problem.

The pressure created in the combustion chamber may be measured with a gauge that remains at the highest reading it measures during the action of a one-way valve. This gauge is inserted into the spark plug hole. A compression test will uncover many mechanical problems that can cause rough running or poor performance.

If the powerhead shows any indication of overheating, such as discolored or scorched paint, inspect the cylinders visually through the transfer ports for possible scoring. It is possible for a cylinder with satisfactory compression to be scored slightly. Also, check the water pump. The overheating condition may be caused by a faulty water pump.

CHECKING COMPRESSION

♦ See Figures 2 and 3

Prepare the engine for a compression test as follows:

1. Run the engine until it reaches operating temperature. The engine is at operating temperature a few minutes after the upper radiator hose gets hot. If the test is performed on a cold engine, the readings will be considerably lower than normal, even if the engine is in perfect mechanical condition.

2. Label and disconnect the spark plug wires. Always grasp the molded cap and pull it loose with a twisting motion to prevent damage to the connection.

3. Clean all dirt and foreign material from around the spark plugs, and then remove all the plugs. Keep them in order by cylinder for later evaluation.

4. Ground the spark plug leads to the engine to render the ignition system inoperative while performing the compression check.

5. Insert a compression gauge into the No. 1, top, spark plug opening.

6. Crank the engine with the starter through at least 4 complete strokes with

Fig. 1 A Yamaha outboard mounted on a boat. The cowling is removed in preparation to make tuning adjustments

04702P01

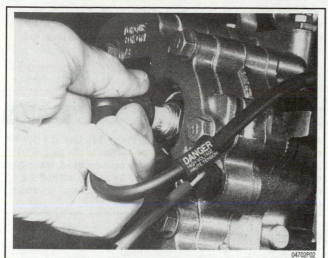

Fig. 2 Removing the high tension lead. Always use a twist and pull motion on the boot to prevent damage to the wire

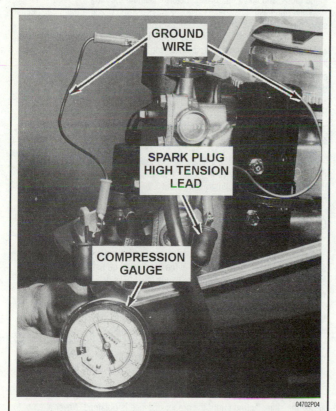

Fig. 3 All spark plugs should be grounded while making compression tests. This action will prevent placing an extra load on the ignition coil

the throttle at the wide-open position, to obtain the highest possible reading. Record the reading.

7. Repeat the test and record the compression for each cylinder.

8. A variation between cylinders is far more important than the actual readings. A variation of more than 15 psi (103 kPa), between cylinders indicates the lower compression cylinder is defective. Not all engines will exhibit the same compression readings. In fact, two identical engines may not have the same compression. Generally, the rule of thumb is that the lowest cylinder should be within 25% of the highest (difference between the two readings).

9. If compression is low in one or more cylinders, the problem may be worn, broken, or sticking piston rings, scored pistons or worn cylinders.

V6 Models

In recent years, Yamaha has modified the cylinder head design on some V6 models in an attempt to keep the temperature of each head the same. This action has changed the shape of the combustion chamber, and therefore the volume and compression pressure of each cylinder.

As a general rule, the pressure between pairs of cylinders which share the same crankshaft throw, should be approximately the same. Cylinder No. 1 should be the same as cylinder No. 2; cylinder No. 3 should be the same as cylinder No. 4; and so on.

Normally, on a V6 powerhead, cylinder No. 1 and No. 2 will have the highest compression pressure. Cylinder No. 5 and No. 6 will have the lowest compression pressure. The design modification has brought about one exception to this rule, and this is for the 175HP and 200HP in 1986 only. Cylinder No. 3 and No. 4 will have an even higher compression pressure than cylinder No. 1 and No. 2. Cylinder No. 5 and No. 6 will still have the lowest compression pressure.

➡ **Use of an engine cleaner, available at any automotive parts house, will help to free stuck rings and to dissolve accumulated carbon. Follow the directions on the container.**

LOW COMPRESSION

Compression readings that are generally low indicate worn, broken, or sticking piston rings, scored pistons or worn cylinders, and usually indicate an engine that has a lot of hours on it. Low compression in two adjacent cylinders (with normal compression in the other cylinders) indicates a blown head gasket between the low-reading cylinders. Other problems are possible (broken ring, hole burned in a piston), but a blown head gasket is most likely.

Spark Plugs

◆ **See Figure 4**

Spark plug life and efficiency depend upon the condition of the engine and the combustion chamber temperatures to which the plug is exposed. These temperatures are affected by many factors, such as compression ratio of the engine, air/fuel mixtures and the type of normally placed on your engine.

Factory installed plugs are, in a way, compromise plugs, since the factory has no way of knowing what typical loads your engine will see. However, most people never have reason to change their plugs from the factory recommended heat range.

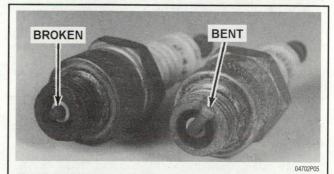

Fig. 4 Damaged spark plugs. Notice the broken electrode on the left plug. The electrode must be found and retrieved prior to returning the powerhead to service

SPARK PLUG HEAT RANGE

◆ **See Figure 5**

Spark plug heat range is the ability of the plug to dissipate heat. The longer the insulator (or the farther it extends into the engine), the hotter the plug will operate; the shorter the insulator (the closer the electrode is to the block's cooling passages) the cooler it will operate. A plug that absorbs little heat and remains too cool will quickly accumulate deposits of oil and carbon since it is

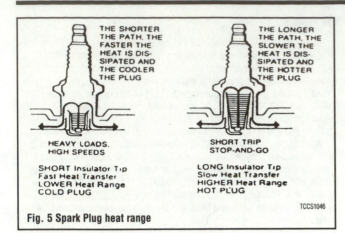

THE SHORTER THE PATH, THE FASTER THE HEAT IS DISSIPATED AND THE COOLER THE PLUG

THE LONGER THE PATH, THE SLOWER THE HEAT IS DISSIPATED AND THE HOTTER THE PLUG

HEAVY LOADS, HIGH SPEEDS

SHORT Insulator Tip
Fast Heat Transfer
LOWER Heat Range
COLD PLUG

SHORT TRIP STOP-AND-GO

LONG Insulator Tip
Slow Heat Transfer
HIGHER Heat Range
HOT PLUG

TCCS1046

Fig. 5 Spark Plug heat range

not hot enough to burn them off. This leads to plug fouling and consequently to misfiring. A plug that absorbs too much heat will have no deposits but, due to the excessive heat, the electrodes will burn away quickly and might possibly lead to pre-ignition or other ignition problems. Pre-ignition takes place when plug tips get so hot that they glow sufficiently to ignite the air/fuel mixture before the actual spark occurs. This early ignition will usually cause a pinging during heavy loads.

SPARK PLUG SERVICE

➡ **New technologies in spark plug and ignition system design have pushed the recommended replacement interval to every 100 hours of operation (6 months). However, this depends on usage and conditions. This holds true unless internal engine wear or damage cause plug fouling. If you suspect this, you may wish to remove and inspect the plugs before the recommended time.**

Spark plugs should only require replacement once a season. The electrode on a new spark plug has a sharp edge, but with use, this edge becomes rounded by wear, causing the plug gap to increase. As the gap increases, the plug's voltage requirement also increases. It requires a greater voltage to jump the wider gap and about two to three times as much voltage to fire a plug at high speeds than at idle.

Tools needed for spark plug replacement include a ratchet, short extension, spark plug socket (there are two types; either $\frac{13}{16}$ inch or $\frac{5}{8}$ inch, depending upon the type of plug), a combination spark plug gauge and gapping tool, and a can of penetrating oil or anti-seize type grease for engines with aluminum heads.

When removing spark plugs, work on one at a time. Don't start by removing the plug wires all at once, because unless you number them, they may become mixed up. Take a minute before you begin and number the wires with tape.

REMOVAL

1. Disconnect the negative battery cable, and if the engine has been run recently, allow the engine to thoroughly cool. Attempting to remove plugs from a hot cylinder head could cause the plugs to seize and damage the threads in the cylinder head. Especially on aluminum heads!
2. Carefully twist the spark plug wire boot to loosen it, then pull the boot using a twisting motion and remove it from the plug. Be sure to pull on the boot and not on the wire, otherwise the connector located inside the boot may become separated.

➡ **A spark plug wire removal tool is recommended as it will make removal easier and help prevent damage to the boot and wire assembly.**

3. Using compressed air (and safety glasses), blow debris from the spark plug well to assure that no harmful contaminants are allowed to enter the combustion chamber when the spark plug is removed. If compressed air is not available, use a rag or a brush to clean the area. Compressed air is available from both an air compressor or from compressed air in cans available at photography stores.

➡ Remove the spark plugs when the engine is cold, if possible, to prevent damage to the threads. If plug removal is difficult, apply a few drops of penetrating oil to the area around the base of the plug, and allow it a few minutes to work.

4. Using a spark plug socket that is equipped with a rubber insert to properly hold the plug, turn the spark plug counterclockwise to loosen and remove the spark plug from the bore.

✳✳ WARNING

Avoid the use of a flexible extension on the socket. Use of a flexible extension may allow a shear force to be applied to the plug. A shear force could break the plug off in the cylinder head, leading to costly and frustrating repairs. In addition, be sure to support the ratchet with your other hand—this will also help prevent the socket from damaging the plug.

INSPECTION

Evaluate each cylinder's performance by comparing the spark condition. Check each spark plug to be sure they are all of the same manufacturer and have the same heat range rating. Inspect the threads in the spark plug opening of the block, and clean the threads before installing the plug.

When purchasing new spark plugs, always ask the dealer if there has been a spark plug change for the engine being serviced.

Crank the engine through several revolutions to blow out any material which might have become dislodged during cleaning. Always use a new gasket (if applicable). The gasket must be fully compressed on clean seats to complete the heat transfer process and to provide a gas tight seal in the cylinder.

READING SPARK PLUGS

▶ **See Figures 6 thru 12**

Your spark plugs are the single most valuable indicator of your engine's internal condition. Study your spark plugs carefully every time you remove them. Compare them to illustrations shown to identify the most common plug conditions.

GAPPING SPARK PLUGS

Check spark plug gap before installation. The ground electrode (the L-shaped one connected to the body of the plug) must be parallel to the center electrode and the specified size wire gauge must pass between the electrodes with a slight drag.

Always check the gap on new plugs as they are not always set correctly at the factory. Do not use a flat feeler gauge when measuring the gap on a used plug, because the reading may be inaccurate. A round-wire type gapping tool is the best way to check the gap. The correct gauge should pass through the electrode gap with a slight drag. If you're in doubt, try a wire that is one size smaller and one larger. The smaller gauge should go through easily, while the larger one shouldn't go through at all.

Wire gapping tools usually have a bending tool attached. Use this tool to adjust the side electrode until the proper distance is obtained. Never attempt to bend the center electrode. Also, be careful not to bend the side electrode too far or too often as it may weaken and break off within the engine, requiring removal of the cylinder head to retrieve it.

INSTALLATION

1. Inspect the spark plug boot for tears or damage. If a damaged boot is found, the spark plug boot and possible the entire wire will need replacement.
2. Apply a thin coating of antiseize on the thread of the plug. This is extremely important on aluminum head engines.
3. Carefully thread the plug into the bore by hand. If resistance is felt before the plug completely bottomed, back the plug out and begin threading again.

Fig. 6 A normally worn spark plug should have light tan or gray deposits on the firing tip (electrode)

Fig. 7 A carbon-fouled plug, identified by soft, sooty black deposits, may indicate an improperly tuned vehicle. Check the air cleaner, ignition components and the engine control system.

Fig. 8 A physically damaged spark plug may be evidence of severe detonation in that cylinder. Watch that cylinder carefully between services, as a continued detonation will not only damage the plug, but could also damage the engine

Fig. 9 An oil-fouled spark plug indicates an engine with worn piston rings and/or bad valve seals allowing excessive oil to enter the combustion chamber

Fig. 10 This spark plug has been left in the engine too long, as evidenced by the extreme gap—Plugs with such an extreme gap can cause misfiring and stumbling accompanied by a noticeable lack of power

Fig. 11 A bridged or almost bridged spark plug, identified by the build-up between the electrodes caused by excessive carbon or oil build-upon the plug

✳✳ WARNING

Do not use the spark plug socket to thread the plugs. Always carefully thread the plug by hand or using an old plug wire to prevent the possibility of crossthreading and damaging the cylinder head bore.

4. Carefully tighten the spark plug. If the plug you are installing is equipped with a crush washer, seat the plug, then tighten to 10–15 ft. lbs. (14–20 Nm) or about ¼ turn to crush the washer. Whenever possible, spark plugs should be tightened to the factory torque specification.

5. Apply a small amount of silicone dielectric compound to the end of the spark plug lead or inside the spark plug boot to prevent sticking, then install the boot to the spark plug and push until it clicks into place. The click may be felt or heard. Gently pull back on the boot to assure proper contact.

Spark Plug Wires

CHECKING & REPLACING

At every tune-up/inspection, visually check the spark plug wires for burns, cuts, or breaks in the insulation. Check the boots on the coil and at the spark plug. Replace any wire that is damaged.

Once a year, usually when you change your spark plugs, check the resistance of the spark plug wires with an ohmmeter. Wires with excessive resistance will cause misfiring and may make the engine difficult to start. In addition worn wires will allow arcing and misfiring in humid conditions.

Remove the spark plug wire from the engine. Test the wires by connecting one lead of the ohmmeter to the coil end of the wire and the other lead to the spark plug end of the wire. Resistance should measure approximately 7000 ohms per foot of wire.

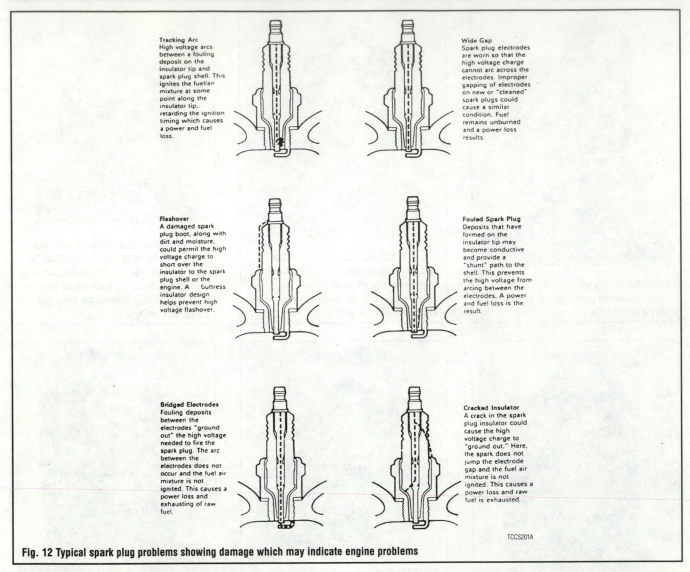

Fig. 12 Typical spark plug problems showing damage which may indicate engine problems

Tracking Arc
High voltage arcs between a fouling deposit on the insulator tip and spark plug shell. This ignites the fuel/air mixture at some point along the insulator tip, retarding the ignition timing which causes a power and fuel loss.

Wide Gap
Spark plug electrodes are worn so that the high voltage charge cannot arc across the electrodes. Improper gapping of electrodes on new or "cleaned" spark plugs could cause a similar condition. Fuel remains unburned and a power loss results.

Flashover
A damaged spark plug boot, along with dirt and moisture, could permit the high voltage charge to short over the insulator to the spark plug shell or the engine. A buttress insulator design helps prevent high voltage flashover.

Fouled Spark Plug
Deposits that have formed on the insulator tip may become conductive and provide a "shunt" path to the shell. This prevents the high voltage from arcing between the electrodes. A power and fuel loss is the result.

Bridged Electrodes
Fouling deposits between the electrodes "ground out" the high voltage needed to fire the spark plug. The arc between the electrodes does not occur and the fuel air mixture is not ignited. This causes a power loss and exhausting of raw fuel.

Cracked Insulator
A crack in the spark plug insulator could cause the high voltage charge to "ground out." Here, the spark does not jump the electrode gap and the fuel air mixture is not ignited. This causes a power loss and raw fuel is exhausted.

TCCS201A

When installing a new set of spark plug wires, replace the wires one at a time so there will be no confusion. Coat the inside of the boots with dielectric grease to prevent sticking. Install the boot firmly over the spark plug until it clicks into place. The click may be felt or heard. Gently pull back on the boot to assure proper contact. Route the wire the same as the original and install it in a similar manner on the engine. Repeat the process for each wire.

Broken Reed

♦ **See Figure 13**

A broken reed is usually caused by metal fatigue over a long period of time. The failure may also be due to the reed flexing too far because the reed stop has not been adjusted properly or the stop has become distorted.

If the reed is broken, the loose piece must be located and removed, before the powerhead is returned to service. The piece of reed may have found its way into the crankcase, behind the bypass cover. If the broken piece cannot be located, the powerhead must be completely disassembled until it is located and removed.

An excellent check for a broken reed on an operating powerhead is to hold an ordinary business card in front of the carburetor. Under normal operating conditions, a very small amount of fine mist will be noticeable, but if fuel begins to appear rapidly on the card from the carburetor, one of the reeds is broken and causing the backflow through the carburetor onto the card. A broken reed will cause the powerhead to operate roughly and pop back through the carburetor.

➠**The reeds must never be turned over in an attempt to correct a problem. Such action would cause the reed to flex in the opposite direction and break in a very short time.**

Breaker Points (Magneto) Ignition System

♦ **See Figures 14 and 15**

All 2HP outboards up to 1994 use a breaker points (magneto) ignition system. The 1995 and later 2HP outboards are equipped with CDI ignition. The following paragraphs give a brief description of breaker point function. For more information on the breaker point ignition system, refer to the "Ignition" section in this manual

Magnetos installed on outboard engines will usually operate over extremely long periods of time without requiring adjustment or repair. However, if ignition system problems are encountered, and the usual corrective actions such as replacement of spark plugs does not correct the problem, the magneto output should be checked to determine if the unit is functioning properly.

Unfortunately, the breaker point set is located under the flywheel. This location requires the hand rewind starter to be removed and the flywheel to be pulled in order to replace the point set.

When checking point gap, the manufacturer made provisions for the point gap to be checked with a feeler gauge through one of two slots cut into the top of the flywheel for this purpose. Only the hand rewind starter needs to be removed to perform the task of point adjustment.

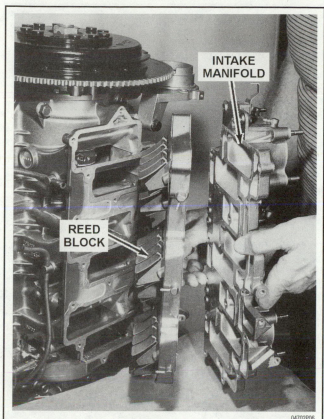

Fig. 13 The reed block on V4 and V6 powerheads may be serviced without disassembling the powerhead

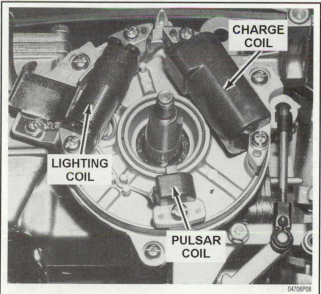

Fig. 14 After the flywheel is removed, components on the stator plate may be easily serviced

The condition and gap of the breaker points will greatly affect engine performance. Burned or badly oxidized points decrease the amount of current passage and point gaps that are too narrow or too wide will not allow the coil to function properly. This all results in a weak spark.

Slightly pitted contacts can be dressed with a points file. Oxidized, dirty or oil points can be cleaned with alcohol. In the end, new points are always preferable to used points. Given their low cost, it is a wise investment to start the year out with a fresh set.

Fig. 15 Breaker points ignition system point set as seen through the access window in the flywheel—2 HP engine shown

➡High primary voltage will darken and roughen the breaker points within a short period. This is not cause for alarm.

The condenser absorbs the surge of high voltage from the coil and prevents current from arcing across the points as they open. Condensers can be tested with a special tester. However, condensers are also inexpensive and should be replaced whenever the points are serviced.

The breaker point set is installed on the stator base under the flywheel. Point gap is usually set to 0.014 in. (0.35mm). This is an important setting because an error of just 0.0015 in (0.038mm) will alter engine timing.

TESTING

Check the resistance across the contacts. If the test indicates zero resistance, the points are serviceable. A slight resistance across the points will affect idle operation. A high resistance may cause the ignition system to malfunction and loss of spark. Therefore, if any resistance across the points is indicated, the point set should be replaced.

REPLACEMENT

✳✳ CAUTION

Always rotate the crankshaft in the standard direction of rotation (clockwise). If rotated counterclockwise, the water pump impeller may be damaged.

1. Disconnect the negative battery cable.
2. Remove the flywheel.
3. There is a single screw attaching the point set to the stator base. Remove this screw . Take special care not to drop it.
4. Label and disconnect the coil and condenser leads from the points. Remove the points set from the stator plate.
5. There is a single screw attaching the condenser to the stator base. Remove this screw . Take special care not to drop it.
6. Install the new breaker point set on the stator base. Ensure the pivot point on the bottom of the point set engages the hole in the stator base. Install but do not tighten the hold-down screw.
7. Install the new condenser on the stator base. Install and securely tighten the hold-down screw.
8. Attach the coil and condenser leads to the points set.
9. Squeeze the felt lubrication wick on the stator plate to see if it is dry. If dry, lubricate it with a few (1or 2) drops of 30W motor oil.

➡Do not over lubricate the wick. Excessive lubrication will cause premature point set failure.

10. Install the flywheel.
11. Connect the negative battery cable.

ADJUSTMENT

▶ **See Figures 16, 17, 18 and 19**

Dial Indicator and Ohmmeter Method

The point gap may be checked using an ohmmeter and a dial gauge without removing the hand rewind starter or the flywheel. This procedure is not necessary if the point gap has already been checked using a feeler gauge.

1. Remove the spark plug and install a dial gauge into the spark plug opening. Rotate the flywheel until the piston reaches TDC (top dead center). Set the dial gauge at Zero.

❊❊ CAUTION

Always rotate the crankshaft in the standard direction of rotation (clockwise). If rotated counterclockwise, the water pump impeller may be damaged.

2. Disconnect the white lead at the quick disconnect fitting and remove the black ground lead from the horseshoe bracket. Set the ohmmeter on the 1000 scale. Make contact with the black ohmmeter lead to the black ground lead and the red ohmmeter lead to the white lead from the stator plate.

3. When the points are closed, the meter will indicate continuity by registering a reading. The actual value of the reading is not important.

4. When the points are open, creating an open in the circuit, the meter will register an infinite resistance—an air gap. Therefore, the meter needle will swing either to the far right or to the far left, depending on the scale of the ohmmeter.

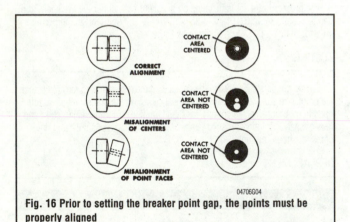

Fig. 16 Prior to setting the breaker point gap, the points must be properly aligned

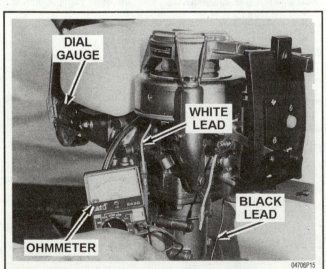

Fig. 17 The point gap may be checked without removing any major parts by using an ohmmeter and a dial indicator gauge

Fig. 18 The flywheel on some powerheads has a window to permit point gap adjustment using a screwdriver and feeler gauge

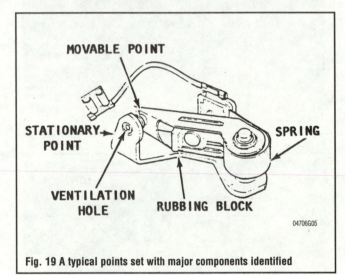

Fig. 19 A typical points set with major components identified

5. Slowly rotate the flywheel counterclockwise and observe the two positions of the meter needle. If the point gap is correct, the meter needle will swing from open to close between 0.04–0.05 in. (1.0–1.2mm) BTDC (before top dead center).

6. If the point gap is incorrect, the gap must be adjusted or the point set replaced.

Feeler Gauge Method

1. Install the flywheel nut on the crankshaft and rotate the stator base to the wide open throttle position.

2. Place a wrench on the flywheel nut and rotate the crankshaft clockwise until the breaker point rubbing block rests on a high point on the cam. In this position the points will be fully open.

3. Loosen the point set hold-down screw. Insert a screwdriver in the adjusting notch and move the point set base to obtain a point gap of 0.014 in. (0.35mm) when measured with a flat feeler gauge. The gap is correct when the feeler gauge offers a slight drag as it is slipped between the points contacts.

➡ **The point gap is an important setting because an error of just 0.0015 in (0.038mm) will alter engine timing.**

4. When the gap is correct, tighten the hold-down screw securely and recheck the point gap.

CDI Ignition Systems

♦ **See Figure 20**

All outboards, except the 1994 and prior 2HP model, are equipped with a Capacitor Discharge Ignition (CDI) System. There are no adjustable components in this system. If it is determined that the ignition system is not functioning properly, refer to the "Ignition" section of this manual for complete troubleshooting procedures.

Various engines are equipped with the Yamaha Microcomputer Ignition System (YMIS). YMIS is essentially a standard CDI type ignition with computer controls. There are no adjustable components in this system.

Battery

Difficulty in starting accounts for almost half of the service required on boats each year. A survey by Champion Spark Plug Company indicated that roughly one third of all boat owners experienced a "won't start" condition in a given year. When an engine won't start, most people blame the battery when, in fact, it may be that the battery has run down in a futile attempt to start an engine with other problems.

Maintaining your battery in peak condition may be though of as either tune-up or maintenance material. Most wise boaters will consider it to be both. A complete check up of the electrical system in your boat at the beginning of the boating season is a wise move. Continued regular maintenance of the battery will ensure trouble free starting on the water.

A complete battery service procedure is included in the "Maintenance" section of this manual. The following are a list of basic electrical system service procedures that should be performed as part of any tune-up.
- Check the battery for solid cable connections
- Check the battery and cables for signs of corrosion damage
- Check the battery case for damage or electrolyte leakage
- Check the electrolyte level in each cell
- Check to be sure the battery is fastened securely in position
- Check the battery's state of charge and charge as necessary
- Check battery voltage while cranking the starter. Voltage should remain above 9.5 volts
- Clean the battery, terminals and cables
- Coat the battery terminals with dielectric grease or terminal protector

Starter Motor

♦ **See Figure 21**

The starter motor system includes the battery, starter motor, solenoid, ignition switch and in some cases a relay.

The frequency of starts governs how often the motor should be removed and reconditioned. The manufacturer recommends removal and overhaul every 1000 hours.

When checking the starter motor circuit during a tune-up, ensure the battery has the proper rating and is fully charged. Many starter motors are needlessly overhauled, when the battery is actually the culprit.

Connect one lead of a voltmeter to the positive terminal of the starter motor. Connect the other meter lead to a good ground on the engine. Check the battery voltage under load by turning the ignition switch to the START position and observing the voltmeter reading. If the reading is 9 ½ volts or greater, and the starter motor fails to operate, repair or replace the starter motor.

Internal Wiring Harness

♦ **See Figure 22**

Corrosion is probably a boater's worst enemy. It is especially harmful to wiring harnesses and connectors. Small amounts of corrosion can cause havoc in an electrical system and make it appear as if major problems are present.

The following are a list of checks that should be performed as part of any tune-up.
- Perform a through visual check of all wiring harnesses and connectors on the vessel
- Check for frayed or chafed insulation, loose or corroded connections between wires and terminals
- Unplug all connectors and check terminal pins to be sure they are not bent or broken
- Lubricate and protect all terminal pins with dielectric grease to provide a water tight seal
- Check any suspect harness for continuity between the harness connection and terminal end. Repair any wire that shows no continuity (infinite resistance)

Carburetors

It may be necessary to adjust the carburetor while the outboard unit is running in a test tank or with the boat in a body of water. For maximum performance, the idle rpm and other carburetor adjustments should be made under actual operating (load) conditions.

TACHOMETER CONNECTIONS

♦ **See Figures 23 and 24**

A tachometer is installed as standard equipment on many models covered in this manual. If adjustments need to be made with the outboard running it might be necessary to attach a tachometer closer to the powerhead than the one installed on the control panel.

Some outboards covered in this manual use a CDI system firing a twin lead ignition coil twice for each crankshaft revolution. If an induction tachometer is installed to measure powerhead speed, the tachometer will probably indicate double the actual crankshaft rotation.

1. On manual start models except the 2HP model, connect the two tachometer leads to the two green leads from the stator. Either tachometer lead may be connected to either green lead.

2. On electric start models, open the remote control box. Locate the Black and Green leads or on models equipped with a tachometer, disconnect the Black and Green leads from the tachometer. Connect the Black lead to the ground terminal of the auxiliary tachometer and the Green lead to the input or hot terminal of the auxiliary tachometer.

Fig. 20 The control unit for outboards equipped with YMIS is located on the rear of the power head

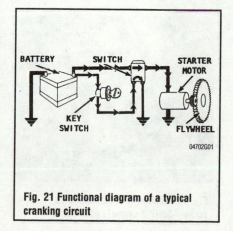

Fig. 21 Functional diagram of a typical cranking circuit

Fig. 22 Any time electrical gremlins are present, always check the harness connectors for pins which are bent, broken or corroded

Fig. 23 Two green lighting coil leads are located inside a sheath on the powerhead. Use these leads to connect a tachometer to the powerhead

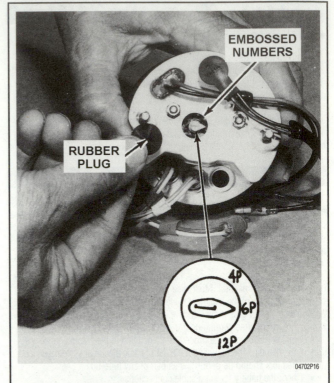

Fig. 24 Checking a tachometer for the correct calibration

3. On the 2HP model, connect the positive tachometer lead to the primary negative terminal of the coil (usually a small black lead), and the negative tachometer lead to a suitable ground.

4. If a tachometer is purchased from Yamaha or another manufacturer, it should be calibrated for the model matching the particular model powerhead. Remove the rubber plug from the back of the meter. Observe the ring with 4P, 6P, and 12P embossed around the ring. These numbers indicate the number of possible poles used on the flywheel magnetos. Determine the number of poles on the flywheel and using a slotted screwdriver, move the arrow until it points toward the desired pole setting.

IDLE SPEED ADJUSTMENT

◆ **See Figures 25, 26, 27 and 28**

➡Remember, the powerhead will not start without the emergency tether in place behind the kill switch knob.

❊❊ CAUTION

Water must circulate through the lower unit to the engine any time the engine is run to prevent damage to the water pump in the

lower unit. Just five seconds without water will damage the water pump. Never operate the engine at high speed with a flush device attached. The engine, operating at high speed with such a device attached, would runaway from lack of a load on the propeller, causing extensive damage.

➡The 2HP model has only one carburetor adjustment screw—the idle speed screw on the starboard side of the carburetor. This screw controls the amount of air entering the powerhead instead of fuel.

1. Remove the cowling and attach a tachometer as required.
2. Start the engine and allow it to warm to operating temperature.
3. The idle speed is regulated by the throttle stop screw. The screw sets the position of the throttle plate inside the carburetor throat.
4. Note the idle speed on the tachometer. If the idle speed is not within specification, rotate the idle speed screw until the idle speed falls within specification. The idle speed specification is noted in the Tune-Up Specifications chart.
5. Rotating the idle speed screw clockwise increases powerhead speed, and rotating the screw counterclockwise decreases powerhead speed.

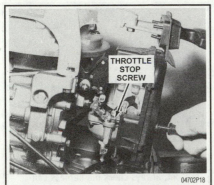

Fig. 25 Location of the throttle stop screw —2-cylinder powerhead

Fig. 26 Location of the throttle stop screw—30HP 3-cylinder powerhead

Fig. 27 Location of the throttle stop screw—all other 3-cylinder powerheads except the 30HP

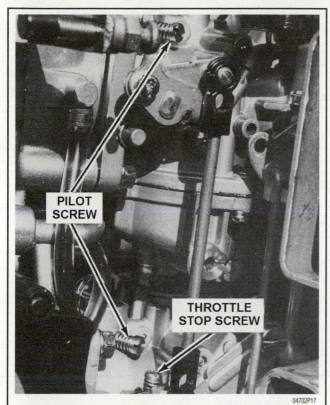

Fig. 28 The idle speed is regulated by the throttle stop screw which sets the position of the throttle plate inside the carburetor throat—V4 and V6 powerhead

Fuel System

FUEL INSPECTION

Most often, tune-ups are performed at the beginning of the boating season. If the fuel system in your boat was properly winterized, there should be no problem with starting the outboard for the first time in the spring. If problems exist, perform the following checks.

1. If the condition of the fuel is in doubt, drain, clean, and fill the tank with fresh fuel.

2. Visually check all fuel lines for kinks, leaks, deterioration or other damage.

3. Disconnect the fuel lines and blow them out with compressed air to dislodge any contamination or other foreign material.

4. Check the line between the fuel pump and the carburetor while the powerhead is operating and the line between the fuel tank and the pump when the powerhead is not operating. A leak between the tank and the pump many times will not appear when the powerhead is operating, because the suction created by the pump drawing fuel will not allow the fuel to leak. Once the powerhead is shut down and the suction no longer exists, fuel may begin to leak.

FUEL PUMP INSPECTION

▶ See Figure 29

If the powerhead operates as if the load on the boat is being constantly increased and decreased, even though an attempt is being made to hold a constant powerhead speed, the problem can most likely be attributed to the fuel pump.

Many times, a defective fuel pump diaphragm is mistakenly diagnosed as a problem in the ignition system. The most common problem is a tiny pin-hole in the diaphragm or a bent check valve inside the fuel pump. Such a small hole will permit gas to enter the crankcase and wet foul the spark plug at idle-speed.

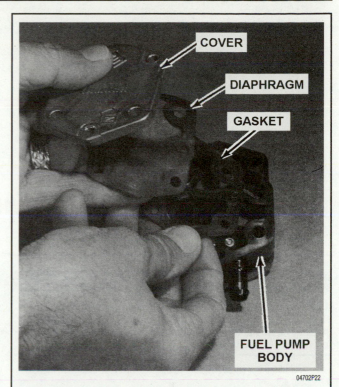

Fig. 29 Arrangement of the vacuum operated fuel pump parts. A tiny hole in the diaphragm can affect fuel pump performance

During high-speed operation, gas quantity is limited, the plug is not foul and will therefore fire in a satisfactory manner.

If the fuel pump fails to perform properly, an insufficient fuel supply will be delivered to the carburetor. This lack of fuel will cause the engine to run lean, lose rpm or cause piston scoring.

Pressure Check

▶ See Figures 30 and 31

➡If an integral fuel pump carburetor is installed, the fuel pressure cannot be checked.

1. Mount the outboard unit in a test tank, or on the boat in a body of water.

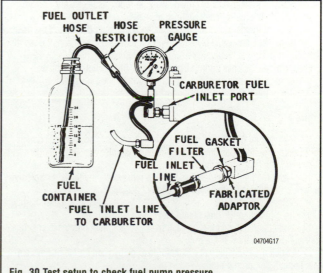

Fig. 30 Test setup to check fuel pump pressure

Fig. 31 Lack of adequate fuel, possibly caused by a defective fuel pump, caused the hole burned into the top of this piston

✳✳ CAUTION

Never operate the engine at high speed with a flush device attached. The engine, operating at high speed with such a device attached, would runaway from lack of a load on the propeller, causing extensive damage.

2. Install the fuel pressure gauge in the fuel line between the fuel pump and the carburetor.
3. Start the engine and check the fuel pressure.
4. Remember, the powerhead will not start without the emergency tether in place behind the kill switch knob.

✳✳ CAUTION

Water must circulate through the lower unit to the engine any time the engine is run to prevent damage to the water pump in the lower unit. Just five seconds without water will damage the water pump.

5. Operate the powerhead at full throttle and check the pressure reading. The gauge should indicate at least 2 psi.

FUEL FILTER SERVICE

Integral Fuel Tank Filter

1. Drain the fuel in the tank into a suitable container.
2. Remove the fuel tank to provide working room, as necessary.
3. Loosen the fuel petcock clamp screw or nut.
4. Remove the petcock from the clamp and tank, then disconnect the hose.
5. Clean the filter assembly in solvent and blow it dry with compressed air. If excessively dirty or contaminated with water, replace the filter.
6. Install the petcock on the clamp and tank, then connect the hose.
7. Tighten the fuel petcock clamp screw or nut.
8. Check the fuel filter installation for leakage.

Inline Filter

1. Place a pan or clean cloth under the inline filter to absorb spilled fuel.
2. Slide the hose retaining clips off the filter nipple with a pair of pliers and disconnect the hoses from the filter.
3. Clean the filter assembly in solvent to remove any particles. If excessively dirty or contaminated with water, replace the filter.
4. Reinstall the hoses on the filter nipples. Make sure the embossed arrow on the filter points in the direction of fuel flow.
5. Slide the retaining clips on each hose over the filter nipples to ensure a leak-free connection.
6. Check the fuel filter installation for leakage by priming the fuel system with the fuel line primer bulb.

Canister Type Filter

EXCEPT 76° V6 ENGINE

➥On some models, it may be possible to service the filter element without removing the canister.

1. On models with metal clips, slide each hose retaining clip off the filter assembly cover nipples with a pair of pliers. Disconnect the hoses from the cover and plug the hoses to prevent fuel leakage.
2. On models with plastic clips, unsnap the plastic clips holding the hoses to the filter assembly cover. Disconnect the hoses from the cover and plug the hoses with golf tees to prevent fuel leakage.
3. Remove the nut securing the filter cover to its mounting bracket. Remove the cover and canister assembly.
4. Unscrew the canister from the filter assembly cover. Remove the filter element from the canister.
5. Drain the canister and wipe the inside dry with a clean lint-free cloth or paper towel.
6. Remove and discard the cover O-ring and gasket, as required.
7. Clean the filter screen with solvent to remove any particles. If the filter screen is severely clogged or damaged, replace it.
8. Install a new O-ring seal and gasket in the filter canister, as required.
9. Install the filter and the filter canister. Tighten the canister securely.
10. If removed, connect the inlet and outlet hoses to the canister cover.
11. Install the nut securing the filter cover to its mounting bracket and tighten securely.
12. On models with metal clips, slide each hose retaining clip onto the filter assembly cover nipples with a pair of pliers.
13. On models with plastic clips, snap the plastic clips holding the hoses to the filter assembly cover.
14. Check the fuel filter installation for leakage by priming the fuel system with the fuel line primer bulb.

76° V6 ENGINE

1. Unscrew the ring nut securing the canister to the filter assembly cover.
2. Remove the canister and filter element from the cover.
3. Remove the filter element and spring from the canister.
4. Drain the canister and wipe the inside dry with a clean lint-free cloth or paper towel.
5. Remove and discard the cover O-ring and old gasket.
6. Clean the filter screen with solvent to remove any particles. If the filter screen is severely clogged or damaged, replace it.
7. Install a new O-ring seal and gasket in the filter canister.
8. Install the spring and filter into the filter canister.
9. Install the canister assembly onto the filter assembly cover and screw on the ring nut. Tighten the ring nut securely.
10. Check the fuel filter installation for leakage by priming the fuel system with the fuel line primer bulb.

Water Pump Check

◆ See Figures 32 and 33

➥The water pump must be in very good condition for the engine to deliver satisfactory service. The pump performs an extremely important function by supplying enough water to properly cool the engine. In most cases, it is advisable to overhaul the complete water pump assembly at least once a year, or anytime the lower unit is disassembled for service.

✳✳ CAUTION

Sometimes during adjustment procedures, it is necessary to run the engine with a flush device attached to the lower unit. Never operate the engine over 1000 rpm with a flush device attached, because the engine may runaway due to the no-load condition on the propeller. A runaway engine could be severely damaged.

As the name implies, the flush device is primarily used to flush the engine after use in salt water or contaminated fresh water. Regular use of the flush device will prevent salt or silt deposits from accumulating in the water passage-

Fig. 32 This water pump impeller has seen better days. If left in service, serious engine overheating problems would be encountered

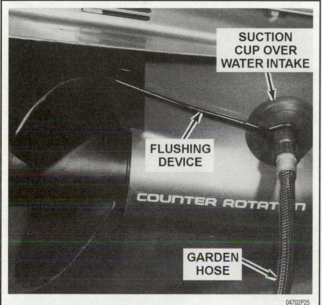

Fig. 33 This popular and inexpensive flushing device may be purchased at almost any marine store. This item should be included in every boat owner's tool kit

Fig. 34 Always use anti-seize compound when installing the propeller to the shaft

way. During and immediately after flushing, keep the outboard unit in an upright position until all of the water has drained from the intermediate housing. This will prevent water from entering the power head by way of the intermediate housing and the exhaust ports, during the flush. It will also prevent residual water from being trapped in the intermediate housing and other passageways.

All powerheads covered in this manual have water exhaust ports which deliver a tattle-tale stream of water, if the water pump is functioning properly during engine operation. Water pressure at the cylinder block should be checked if an overheating condition is detected or suspected.

To test the water pump, the lower unit or jet drive must be placed in a test tank or the boat moved into a body of water. The pump must now work to supply a volume of water to the powerhead. A tattle-tale stream of water should be visible from the pilot hole beneath the cover cowling.

Lack of adequate water supply from the water pump through the engine will cause any number of powerhead failures, such as stuck rings, scored cylinder walls and burned pistons.

Propeller

▶ See Figure 34

The performance of your outboard will be critically affected by your choice of propeller. The engine speed depends on the propeller size and the boat load. If the engine speed is too high or too low for good engine performance, the performance and longevity of the powerhead may be compromised.

Outboards are fitted with propellers chosen to perform well over a range of applications. However there are many uses where a propeller with a different pitch would be better suited for the application. For a greater operating load, a smaller pitch propeller is more suitable as it enables the correct engine speed to be maintained. Conversely, a larger pitch propeller is more suitable for a smaller operating load.

Check the propeller blades for nicks, cracks, or bent condition. If the propeller is damaged, the local marine dealer can make repairs or send it out to a shop specializing in such work.

Any time the propeller is visible, check the shaft seal to be sure it is not leaking. Check the area just forward of the seal to be sure a fish line is not wrapped around the shaft.

Lower Unit

▶ See Figure 35

Lower unit lubricant should be replaced after the first 10 hours of use and then again every 100 hours of use.

The first few times gearcase lubricant is drained, from a counterrotating lower unit, a discoloration may be noticed. This condition is quite normal and is no cause for alarm unless accompanied by the presence of metal chips. The discoloration is due to the use of molybdenum-disulfide assembly grease at the factory.

Check the lubricant level only after the unit has been allowed to cool. Add Yamaha Gear Case Lubricant, or equivalent to bring the lubricant level to specification.

➡ If the lubricant appears milky brown, or if large amounts of lubricant must be added to bring the lubricant up to the full mark, a thorough check should be made to determine the cause of the loss.

✳✳ WARNING

Never use regular automotive-type grease in the lower unit, because it expands and foams too much. Outboard lower units do not have provisions to accommodate such expansion.

Fig. 35 Lower unit and propeller cleaned, serviced and ready for work

➥It is important to note that some outboards should be placed in the upright position and some in the fully tilted position for lower unit lubricant service. Consult your owner's manual for the proper position for lubricant service for your outboard.

For information on replacing the lower unit lubricant, refer to the "Maintenance" section of this manual.

Jet Drive Units

The gate of a jet drive unit MUST be properly adjusted to obtain maximum performance from the outboard unit. When properly adjusted, the gate will permit the pump to deliver its full potential of thrust with no drag.

GATE POSITION & SHIFT LEVER

♦ **See Figures 36, 37, 38 and 39**

The shift lever adjustment should be checked from time to time to ensure the gate is firmly against the rubber pad beneath the pump housing, when the unit is in the FORWARD position (wide open).

With the gate against the rubber pad, any rattle noises will be avoided as the boat moves through the water. Proper positioning of the gate in forward gear will prevent wave action from accidentally shifting the gate into reverse as the boat is operated through violent maneuvers.

When the shift lever is in the FORWARD position, a leaf spring prevents the lever from returning to the NEUTRAL position and allowing the gate to rise. Shifting may be accomplished with one hand by moving the leaf spring to one side with a thumb, and then moving the lever.

During the tune-up, make a thorough check of the linkage and gate movement to ensure maximum thrust and use of the horsepower developed by the powerhead.

IMPELLER

Excessively rounded jet impeller edges will reduce the efficiency of the jet drive.

A proper scoop angle for the water intake grille will enhance the drive's performance. The vertical axis of the outboard drive shaft must be completely vertical or slightly inclined under and toward the boat to provide the best scoop angle.

Trimming the outboard unit to position the jet drive away from the boat reduces the scoop angle and may cause jet impeller slippage and even cavitation burns on the impeller blades.

The term cavitation burn is a common expression used throughout the world among people working with pumps, impeller blades, and forceful water movement.

Burns on the impeller blades are caused by cavitation air bubbles exploding with considerable force against the impeller blades. The edges of the blades may develop small dime size areas resembling a porous sponge, as the aluminum is actually eaten by the condition just described.

Fig. 36 The gate on this jet drive is in the neutral position

Fig. 37 A leaf spring prevents the lever from returning to the neutral position and allowing the gate to rise

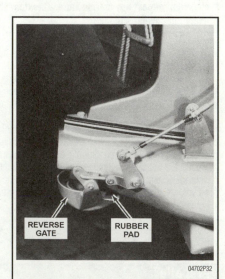

Fig. 38 The reverse gate should make firm contact with the rubber pad on the under side of the housing when placed in the forward position

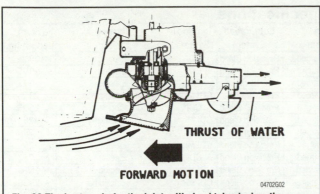

Fig. 39 The best angle for the inlet grille is obtained when the surface of the grille is at a slight incline under and toward the boat

Performance Testing

▶ See Figure 40

Operation of the outboard unit, mounted on a boat with some type of load, is the ultimate test. Failure of the power unit or the boat under actual movement through the water may be detected much more quickly than operating the power unit in a test tank.

Before testing the boat, check the boat bottom carefully for marine growth or evidence of a hook or a rocker in the bottom. Either one of these conditions will greatly reduce performance.

Mount the motor on the boat. Install the remote control cables, as required, and check for proper adjustment.

Make an effort to test the boat with what might be considered an average gross load. The boat should ride on an even keel, without a list to port or starboard. Adjust the motor tilt angle, if necessary, to permit the boat to ride slightly higher than the stern. If heavy supplies are stowed aft of the center, the bow will be light and the boat will plane more efficiently. For this test the boat must be operated in a body of water. If the motor is equipped with an adjustable trim tab, the tab should be adjusted to permit boat steerage in either direction with equal ease.

Check the engine rpm at full throttle. If the rpm is not within specified range, a propeller change may be in order. A higher pitch propeller will decrease rpm, and a lower pitch propeller will increase rpm.

If the outboard unit is equipped with a jet drive, check to be sure the vertical axis of the outboard drive shaft is vertical or slightly inclined under and toward the boat to provide the best scoop angle. For maximum low speed engine performance, the idle mixture and the idle rpm should be readjusted under actual operating conditions.

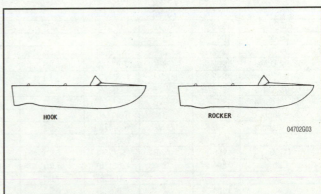

Fig. 40 Boat performance will be drastically imparted if the bottom is damaged by a dent (hook) or a bulge (rocker)

General Engine Specifications

Model	Years	Cylinders	Displace Cu.In. (cc)	Compression Ratio	Fuel System	Lubrication System	Ignition System	Starting System	Shaft Length (in.)
2	1995-98	1	2.6(43)	7.4:1	Loop Charged	100:1 Premix	CDI	Manual	15
2	1992-94	1	2.6(43)	7.4:1	Loop Charged	100:1 Premix	Magneto	Manual	15
3	1992-98	1	4.3(70)	6.9:1	Loop Charged	100:1 Premix	CDI	Manual	15/20
4	1992-98	1	5.0(83)	7.0:1	Cross Flow	100:1 Premix	CDI	Manual	15/20
5	1995-98	1	6.3(103)	6.5:1	Cross Flow	100:1 Premix	CDI	Manual	15/20
6	1992-98	2	10(165)	7.0:1	Cross Flow	100:1 Premix	CDI	Manual	15/20
8	1992-98	2	10(165)	7.0:1	Cross Flow	100:1 Premix	CDI	Manual/Electric	15/20
9.9	1992-98	2	15(246)	6.8:1	Loop Charged	100:1 Premix	CDI	Manual or Electric w/Manual	15/20
15	1992-98	2	15(246)	6.8:1	Loop Charged	100:1 Premix	CDI	Manual or Electric w/Manual	15/20
20	1996-98	2	24(395)	7.2:1	Loop Charged	100:1 Premix	CDI	Manual	15/20
25	1996-98	2	24(395)	7.2:1	Loop Charged	Precision Blend	CDI	Manual or Electric w/Manual	15/20
25	1992-95	2	24(395)	7.2:1	Loop Charged	100:1 Premix	CDI	Manual or Electric w/Manual	15/20
25	1996-98	3	30(496)	6.8:1	Loop Charged	100:1 Premix	CDI	Manual	15/20
30	1992-93	2	30(496)	7.0:1	Loop Charged	100:1 Premix	CDI	Manual/Electric	20
30	1992-98	3	30(496)	6.8:1	Loop Charged	Precision Blend	CDI	Manual/Electric	15/20
40	1992-93	2	36(592)	6.5:1	Loop Charged	100:1 Premix	CDI	Manual/Electric	15/20
40	1998	3	43(689)	6.0:1	Loop Charged	Precision Blend	CDI Micro	Manual/Electric	15/20
40	1992-97	3	43(689)	6.0:1	Loop Charged	Precision Blend	CDI	Manual/Electric	15/20
50	1992-97	3	43(689)	6.0:1	Loop Charged	Precision Blend	CDI	Electric	20
70	1998	3	52(849)	6.2:1	Loop Charged	Precision Blend	CDI Micro	ElectricPrime	20
70	1992-97	3	52(849)	6.2:1	Loop Charged	Precision Blend	CDI Micro	Electric	20
85	1992-93	3	70(1140)	5.2:1	Loop Charged	50:1 Premix	CDI	Electric	20
90	1998	3	70(1140)	5.9:1	Loop Charged	Precision Blend	CDI Micro	ElectricPrime	20
90	1992-97	3	70(1140)	5.9:1	Loop Charged	Precision Blend	CDI Micro	Electric	20
115	1993-98	90' V4	106(1730)	6.5:1	Loop Charged	Precision Blend	CDI	Electric	20
115	1992	90' V4	106(1730)	6.5:1	Loop Charged	50:1 Premix	CDI	Electric	20/25
130	1992-98	90' V4	106(1730)	6.8:1	Loop Charged	Precision Blend	CDI	Electric	20/25
150	1996-98	90' V6	158(2596)	5.8:1	Loop Charged	Precision Blend	CDI Micro	Electric	20
150	1992-95	90' V6	158(2596)	5.8:1	Loop Charged	Precision Blend	CDI	Electric	20
175	1992-94	90' V6	158(2596)	5.9:1	Loop Charged	Precision Blend	CDI	Electric	20
200	1996-98	90' V6	158(2596)	6.0:1	Loop Charged	Precision Blend	CDI Micro	Electric	20
200	1992-95	90' V6	158(2596)	6.0:1	Loop Charged	Precision Blend	CDI	Electric	20
225	1992-97	90' V6	191(3130)	6.4:1	Loop Charged	Precision Blend	CDI Micro	Electric	20

04702C01

General Engine Specifications

Model	Years	Cylinders	Displace Cu.In. (cc)	Compression Ratio	Fuel System	Lubrication System	Ignition System	Starting System	Shaft Length (in.)
115SW	1995-98	90° V4	106(1730)	6.5:1	Loop Charged	Precision Blend	CDI	Electric	20/25
130SW	1995-98	90° V4	106(1730)	6.8:1	Loop Charged	Precision Blend	CDI	Electric	20/25
150C	1998	90° V6	158(2596)	6.2:1	Loop Charged	50:1 Premix	CDI	Electric	20/25
150SW	1996-98	90° V6	158(2596)	5.8:1	Loop Charged	Precision Blend	CDI Micro	Electric	20/25
150SW	1992-95	90° V6	158(2596)	5.8:1	Loop Charged	Precision Blend	CDI	Electric	20/25
175SW	1996-98	90° V6	158(2596)	5.9:1	Loop Charged	Precision Blend	CDI Micro	Electric	25
175SW	1994-95	90° V6	158(2596)	5.9:1	Loop Charged	Precision Blend	CDI	Electric	25
200SW	1996-98	90° V6	158(2596)	6.0:1	Loop Charged	Precision Blend	CDI Micro	Electric	25
200SW	1994-95	90° V6	158(2596)	6.0:1	Loop Charged	Precision Blend	CDI	Electric	25
225 V76X SW	1994-95	76° V6	191(3130)	5.6:1	Loop Charged	Precision Blend	CDI Micro	Electric	25/30
225SW	1996-98	76° V6	191(3130)	5.8:1	EFI Loop Charged	Precision Blend	CDI Micro	ElectricPrime	25/30
250 V76X SW	1992-95	76° V6	191(3130)	5.5:1	Loop Charged	Precision Blend	CDI Micro	Electric	25/30
250SW	1998	76° V6	191(3130)	5.7:1	EFI Loop Charged	Precision Blend	CDI Micro	ElectricPrime	25/30
250SW	1996-97	76° V6	191(3130)	5.7:1	EFI Loop Charged	Precision Blend	CDI Micro	Electric	25/30
28 Jet Drive	1992-98	3	43(689)	6.0:1	Loop Charged	Precision Blend	CDI	Manual/Electric	(1)
35 Jet Drive	1992-98	3	43(689)	6.0:1	Loop Charged	Precision Blend	CDI	Electric	(1)
65 Jet Drive	1992-98	3	70(1140)	5.9:1	Loop Charged	Precision Blend	CDI Micro	Electric	(1)
80 Jet Drive	1992-98	90° V4	106(1730)	6.7:1	Loop Charged	Precision Blend	CDI	Electric	(1)
105 Jet Drive	1996-98	90° V6	158(2596)	6.2:1	Loop Charged	Precision Blend	CDI Micro	Electric	(1)
145 Jet Drive	1992-95	90° V6	158(2596)	5.9:1	Loop Charged	Precision Blend	CDI	Electric	20
90 Inshore	1997-98	3	70(1140)	5.9:1	Loop Charged	Precision Blend	CDI Micro	ElectricPrime	17.5
B115 Inshore	1998	90° V4	106(1730)	6.5:1	Loop Charged	Precision Blend	CDI	Electric	17.5
C115	1994-98	90° V4	106(1730)	6.5:1	Loop Charged	50:1 Premix	CDI	Electric	20/25
C150	1996-97	90° V6	158(2596)	6.2:1	Loop Charged	50:1 Premix	CDI	Electric	20/25
C25	1994-97	2	26(430)	7.0:1	Loop Charged	100:1 Premix	CDI	Manual or Electric w/Manual	15/20
C30	1994-97	2	30(496)	7.0:1	Loop Charged	100:1 Premix	CDI	Manual or Electric w/Manual	20
C40	1994-97	2	36(592)	6.5:1	Loop Charged	100:1 Premix	CDI	Manual/Electric	15/20
C40	1998	3	43(689)	6.0:1	Loop Charged	50:1 Premix	CDI Micro	ElectricPrime	20
C50	1998	3	43(689)	6.0:1	Loop Charged	50:1 Premix	CDI Micro	ElectricPrime	20
C55	1992-95	2	46(760)	6.5:1	Loop Charged	50:1 Premix	CDI	Electric	20
C60	1996-98	3	52(849)	6.1:1	Loop Charged	50:1 Premix	CDI Micro	ElectricPrime	20
C75	1998	3	70(1140)	5.9:1	Loop Charged	50:1 Premix	CDI Micro	ElectricPrime	20
C75	1995-96	3	70(1140)	4.5:1	Loop Charged	50:1 Premix	CDI	Electric	20
C75	1994	3	70(1140)	4.5:1	Loop Charged	50:1 Premix	CDI	Electric	20
C80	1997	3	70(1140)	5.9:1	Loop Charged	Precision Blend	CDI Micro	Electric	20
C85	1994-96	3	70(1140)	5.2:1	Loop Charged	50:1 Premix	CDI	Electric	20
C90	1998	3	70(1140)	5.9:1	Loop Charged	50:1 Premix	CDI Micro	ElectricPrime	20
E48	1996-98	2	46(760)	6.5:1	Loop Charged	50:1 Premix	CDI	Manual	20
E60	1996-98	3	52(849)	6.1:1	Loop Charged	50:1 Premix	CDI	Manual	20
E75	1996-98	3	70(1140)	4.5:1	Loop Charged	50:1 Premix	CDI	Manual	20
P40	1998	3	43(689)	6.0:1	Loop Charged	Precision Blend	CDI Micro	ElectricPrime	20
P60	1998	3	52(849)	6.2:1	Loop Charged	Precision Blend	CDI Micro	ElectricPrime	20
P75	1998	3	70(1140)	5.9:1	Loop Charged	Precision Blend	CDI Micro	ElectricPrime	20
Pro 50	1992-96	3	43(689)	6.0:1	Loop Charged	Precision Blend	CDI	Electric	20
Pro 60	1992-97	3	52(849)	6.2:1	Loop Charged	Precision Blend	CDI Micro	Electric	20
Pro 75	1996-97	3	70(1140)	5.9:1	Loop Charged	Precision Blend	CDI Micro	Electric	20
Pro V 115	1993-96	90° V4	106(1730)	6.5:1	Loop Charged	Precision Blend	CDI	Electric	20
Pro V 175	1996-97	90° V6	158(2596)	5.6:1	Loop Charged	Precision Blend	CDI Micro	Electric	20
Pro V 175	1994-95	90° V6	158(2596)	5.6:1	Loop Charged	Precision Blend	CDI	Electric	20
Pro V 150	1996-97	90° V6	158(2596)	5.8:1	Loop Charged	Precision Blend	CDI Micro	Electric	20
Pro V 150	1992-95	90° V6	158(2596)	5.6:1	Loop Charged	Precision Blend	CDI	Electric	20
Pro V 200	1996-97	90° V6	158(2596)	6.0:1	Loop Charged	Precision Blend	CDI Micro	Electric	20
Pro V 200	1992-95	90° V6	158(2596)	6.0:1	Loop Charged	Precision Blend	CDI	Electric	20
Pro V Max 150	1997	90° V6	158(2596)	6.6:1	Loop Charged	Precision Blend	CDI Micro	Electric	17.5
V Max 150	1998	90° V6	158(2596)	5.8:1	Loop Charged	Precision Blend	CDI Micro	Electric	20
V Max 150SW TRP	1998	90° V6	158(2596)	6.6:1	Loop Charged	Precision Blend	CDI Micro	Electric	17.5
V Max 175SW	1998	90° V6	158(2596)	5.6:1	Loop Charged	Precision Blend	CDI Micro	Electric	20
V Max 200	1998	90° V6	158(2596)	6.0:1	Loop Charged	Precision Blend	CDI Micro	Electric	20
V Max 200 3.1	1998	76° V6	191(3130)	5.9:1	EFI Loop Charged	Precision Blend	CDI Micro	ElectricPrime	20
V Max 225 3.1	1998	76° V6	191(3130)	5.9:1	EFI Loop Charged	Precision Blend	CDI Micro	ElectricPrime	20

(1) Fits 25 in. Transom

04702C02

MAINTENANCE 3-2
INTRODUCTION 3-2
FIBERGLASS HULLS 3-2
  BELOW WATERLINE 3-2
PROPELLER SERVICE 3-3
TRIM TABS AND LEAD WIRES 3-3
BATTERY 3-3
  CLEANING 3-4
  CHECKING SPECIFIC GRAVITY 3-4
  BATTERY TERMINALS 3-5
  BATTERY & CHARGING SAFETY
    PRECAUTIONS 3-5
  BATTERY CHARGERS 3-5
  REPLACING BATTERY CABLES 3-5
FUEL AND FUEL TANKS 3-5
PRE-SEASON CHECKLIST 3-6
LUBRICATION 3-7
GENERAL INFORMATION 3-7
LUBRICANTS 3-9
INSIDE THE BOAT 3-9
PROPELLER DRIVE 3-9
  DRAINING 3-9
  WATER IN THE LOWER UNIT 3-9
  FILLING 3-10
JET DRIVE 3-10
  LUBRICATION 3-10
  FLUSHING 3-12
EMERGENCY SERVICE 3-13
EMERGENCY TETHER 3-13
SUBMERGED ENGINE 3-13
  SUBMERGED ENGINE—SALT
    WATER 3-13
  SUBMERGED ENGINE—WHILE
    RUNNING 3-13
  SUBMERGED ENGINE—FRESH
    WATER 3-13
JUMP STARTING 3-14
  JUMPER CABLES 3-14
  JUMP STARTING
    PRECAUTIONS 3-14
  JUMP STARTING PROCEDURE 3-14
WINTER STORAGE 3-15
FUEL STABILIZER 3-15
BATTERY STORAGE 3-16
SPECIFICATIONS CHARTS
  PERIODIC MAINTENANCE 3-2
  PERIODIC LUBRICATION 3-9
  GEAR OIL CAPACITY 3-11

3

MAINTENANCE

MAINTENANCE 3-2
PRE-SEASON CHECKLIST 3-6
LUBRICATION 3-7
EMERGENCY SERVICE 3-13
WINTER STORAGE 3-15

MAINTENANCE

Introduction

♦ See Figure 1

Most engine repair work can be directly or indirectly attributed to lack of proper care for the engine. This is especially true of care during the off-season period. There is no way on this green earth for a mechanical engine, particularly an outboard motor, to be left sitting idle for an extended period of time, say for six months, and then be ready for instant satisfactory service.

Imagine if you will, leaving your boat for six months, and then expecting to turn the key, have it roar to life, and be able to drive off in the same manner as a daily occurrence.

It is critical for an outboard engine to be run at least once a month, preferably, in the water, but if this is not possible, then a flush attachment must be connected to the lower unit.

Water must circulate through the lower unit to the powerhead anytime the powerhead is operating to prevent damage to the water pump in the lower unit. Just five seconds without water will damage the water pump impeller.

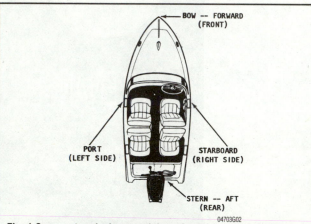

Fig. 1 Common terminology used throughout the world for reference designation on boats of all sizes

☀☀ CAUTION

Never operate the engine at high speed with a flush device attached. The engine, operating at high speed with such a device attached, would runaway from lack of load on the propeller, causing extensive damage.

At the same time, the shift mechanism should be operated through the full range several times and the steering operated from hard-over to hard-over.

Only through a regular maintenance program can the owner expect to receive long life and satisfactory performance at minimum cost.

Fiberglass Hulls

Fiberglass reinforced plastic hulls are tough, durable, and highly resistant to impact. However, like any other material they can be damaged. One of the advantages of this type of construction is the relative ease with which it may be repaired. Because of its break characteristics, and the simple techniques used in restoration, these hulls have gained popularity throughout the world. From the most congested urban marina, to isolated lakes in wilderness areas, to the severe cold of far off northern seas, and in sunny tropic remote rivers of primitive islands or continents, fiberglass boats can be found performing their daily task with a minimum of maintenance.

A fiberglass hull has almost no internal stresses. Therefore, when the hull is broken or stove-in, it retains its true form. It will not dent to take an out-of-shape set. When the hull sustains a severe blow, the impact will be either absorbed by deflection of the laminated panel or the blow will result in a definite, localized break. In addition to hull damage, bulkheads, stringers, and other stiffening structures attached to the hull may also be affected and therefore, should be checked. Repairs are usually confined to the general area of the rupture.

BELOW WATERLINE

A foul bottom can seriously affect boat performance. This is one reason why racers, large and small, both powerboat and sail, are constantly giving attention to the condition of the hull below the waterline.

In areas where marine growth is prevalent, a coating of vinyl, anti-fouling bottom paint should be applied. If growth has developed on the bottom, it can be removed with a solution of Muriatic acid applied with a brush or swab and then rinsed with clear water. Always use rubber gloves when working with Muriatic acid and take extra care to keep it away from your face and hands. The fumes are toxic. Therefore, work in a well-ventilated area, or if outside, keep your face on the windward side of the work.

Barnacles have a nasty habit of making their home on the bottom of boats which have not been treated with anti-fouling paint. Actually they will not harm the fiberglass hull, but can develop into a major nuisance.

If barnacles or other crustaceans have attached themselves to the hull, extra work will be required to bring the bottom back to a satisfactory condition. First,

Periodic Maintenance

Component	Service	Initial			Thereafter Every	
		10 Hours	50 Hours	100 Hours	100 Hours	200 Hours
Spark Plug	C,A	*	*	*	*	
Greasing Points	G			*	*	
Lower Unit Oil	R	*		*	*	
Fuel System	I			*	*	
Fuel Filter	C,A	*	*	*	*	
Fuel Tank	C,A					*
Idling Speed	A			*	*	
Anode	I/R			*	*	
Outboard Motor Case	I		*	*	*	
Cooling Water Passages	C,A		*	*	*	
Propeller	I		*	*	*	
Cotter Pin	I/R		*	*	*	
Battery	I	*				
Carburetor	I/A	*		*	*	
Ignition Timing	I/A	*		*	*	
Bolts and Nuts	T	*		*	*	

C - Clean
A- Adjust
G- Grease
I- Inspect
R- Replace
T- Retighten

04703C02

if practical, put the boat into a body of fresh water and allow it to remain for a few days. A large percentage of the growth can be removed in this manner. If this remedy is not possible, wash the bottom thoroughly with a high-pressure fresh water source and use a scraper. Small particles of hard shell may still hold fast. These can be removed with sandpaper.

Propeller Service

▶ See Figures 2 and 3

The propeller should be checked regularly to be sure all the blades are in good condition. If any of the blades become bent or nicked, this condition will set up vibrations in the motor. Remove and inspect the propeller. Use a file to trim nicks and burrs. Take care not to remove any more material than is absolutely necessary. For a complete check, take the propeller to your marine dealer where the proper equipment and knowledgeable mechanics are available to perform a proper job at modest cost.

Inspect the propeller shaft to be sure it is still true and not bent. If the shaft is not perfectly true, it should be replaced.

Install the thrust hub. Coat the propeller shaft splines with Perfect Seal No. 4, and the rest of the shaft with a good grade of anti-corrosion lubricant. Install the front spacer, the propeller, the washer and the propeller nut.

Position a block of wood between the propeller and the anti-cavitation tab to keep the propeller from turning. Tighten the propeller nut to proper torque specification. Adjust the nut to enable the cotter pin to be threaded through the propeller nut and shaft. Bend the two ends of the cotter pin in opposite directions around the nut. This action will prevent the nut from backing off the shaft.

Fig. 3 A block of wood inserted between the propeller and the anti-cavitation plate will prevent the propeller from turning while the nut is being removed or installed

sive parts. It is normal for the tab to show signs of erosion. The tabs are inexpensive and should be replaced frequently.

Clean the exterior surface of the unit thoroughly. Inspect the finish for damage or corrosion. Clean any damaged or corroded areas, and then apply primer and matching paint.

Check the entire unit for loose, damaged, or missing parts.

An anode is attached across both clamp brackets. It also serves as protection for the coil of hydraulic hoses beneath the trim/tilt unit between the brackets.

Lead wires provide good electrical continuity between various brackets which might be isolated from the trim tab by a coating of lubricant between moving parts.

Battery

Batteries which are not maintained on a regular basis can fall victim to parasitic loads (small current drains which are constantly drawing current from the battery).

Fig. 2 An application of antiseize on the propeller shaft splines will prevent the propeller from freezing to the shaft and facilitate easier removal for the next service

Trim Tabs and Lead Wires

▶ See Figures 4, 5, 6 and 7

Check the trim tab and the anode (zinc) heads. Replace them, if necessary. The trim tab must make a good ground inside the lower unit. Therefore, the trim tab and the cavity must not be painted. In addition to trimming the boat, the trim tab acts as a zinc electrode to prevent electrolysis from acting on more expen-

Fig. 4 Such extensive erosion of a trim tab compared with a new tab suggests an electrolysis problem or complete disregard for periodic maintenance

04703P09

Fig. 5 Although many outboards use the trim tab as an anode, other types of anodes are also used throughout the powerhead

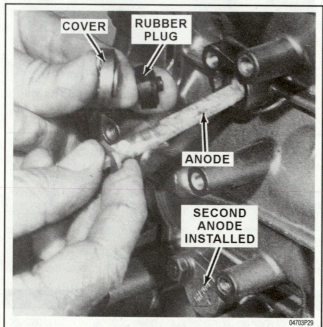

COVER RUBBER PLUG

ANODE

SECOND ANODE INSTALLED

04703P29

Fig. 6 Anodes installed in the water jacket of a powerhead provide added protection against corrosion

Normal parasitic loads may drain a battery on boat that is in storage and not used frequently. Boats that have additional accessories with increased parasitic load may discharge a battery sooner. Storing a boat with the negative battery cable disconnected or battery switch turned off will minimize discharge due to parasitic loads.

CLEANING

Keep the battery clean, as a film of dirt can help discharge a battery that is not used for long periods. A solution of baking soda and water mixed into a paste may be used for cleaning, but be careful to flush this off with clear water.

➡**Do not let any of the solution into the filler holes on non-sealed batteries. Baking soda neutralizes battery acid and will de-activate a battery cell.**

CHECKING SPECIFIC GRAVITY

The electrolyte fluid (sulfuric acid solution) contained in the battery cells will tell you many things about the condition of the battery. Because the cell plates must be kept submerged below the fluid level in order to operate, maintaining

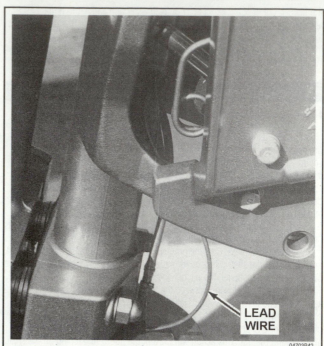

LEAD WIRE

04703P42

Fig. 7 One of the many lead wires used to connect bracketed parts. Lead wires are used as an assist in reducing corrosion

the fluid level is extremely important. In addition, because the specific gravity of the acid is an indication of electrical charge, testing the fluid can be an aid in determining if the battery must be replaced. A battery in a boat with a properly operating charging system should require little maintenance, but careful, periodic inspection should reveal problems before they leave you stranded.

❋❋ CAUTION

Battery electrolyte contains sulfuric acid. If you should splash any on your skin or in your eyes, flush the affected area with plenty of clear water. If it lands in your eyes, get medical help immediately.

As stated earlier, the specific gravity of a battery's electrolyte level can be used as an indication of battery charge. At least once a year, check the specific gravity of the battery. It should be between 1.20 and 1.26 on the gravity scale. Most parts stores carry a variety of inexpensive battery testing hydrometers. These can be used on any non-sealed battery to test the specific gravity in each cell.

Conventional Battery

A hydrometer is required to check the specific gravity on all batteries that are not maintenance-free. The hydrometer has a squeeze bulb at one end and a nozzle at the other. Battery electrolyte is sucked into the hydrometer until the float or pointer is lifted from its seat. The specific gravity is then read by noting the position of the float/pointer. If gravity is low in one or more cells, the battery should be slowly charged and checked again to see if the gravity has come up. Generally, if after charging, the specific gravity of any two cells varies more than 50 points (0.50), the battery should be replaced, as it can no longer produce sufficient voltage to guarantee proper operation.

Check the battery electrolyte level at least once a month, or more often in hot weather or during periods of extended operation. Electrolyte level can be checked either through the case on translucent batteries or by removing the cell caps on opaque-case types. The electrolyte level in each cell should be kept filled to the split ring inside each cell, or the line marked on the outside of the case.

If the level is low, add only distilled water through the opening until the level is correct. Each cell is separate from the others, so each must be checked and filled individually. Distilled water should be used, because the chemicals and minerals found in most drinking water are harmful to the battery and could significantly shorten its life.

If water is added in freezing weather, the battery should be warmed to allow the water to mix with the electrolyte. Otherwise, the battery could freeze.

Maintenance-Free Batteries

Although some maintenance-free batteries have removable cell caps for access to the electrolyte, the electrolyte condition and level is usually checked using the built-in hydrometer "eye." The exact type of eye varies between battery manufacturers, but most apply a sticker to the battery itself explaining the possible readings. When in doubt, refer to the battery manufacturer's instructions to interpret battery condition using the built-in hydrometer.

The readings from built-in hydrometers may vary, however a green eye usually indicates a properly charged battery with sufficient fluid level. A dark eye is normally an indicator of a battery with sufficient fluid, but one that may be low in charge. In addition, a light or yellow eye is usually an indication that electrolyte supply has dropped below the necessary level for battery (and hydrometer) operation. In this last case, sealed batteries with an insufficient electrolyte level must usually be discarded.

BATTERY TERMINALS

At least once a season, the battery terminals and cable clamps should be cleaned. Loosen the clamps and remove the cables, negative cable first. On batteries with top mounted posts, the use of a puller specially made for this purpose is recommended. These are inexpensive and available in most parts stores.

Clean the cable clamps and the battery terminal with a wire brush, until all corrosion, grease, etc., is removed and the metal is shiny. It is especially important to clean the inside of the clamp thoroughly (a wire brush is useful here), since a small deposit of foreign material or oxidation there will prevent a sound electrical connection and inhibit either starting or charging. It is also a good idea to apply some dielectric grease to the terminal, as this will aid in the prevention of corrosion.

After the clamps and terminals are clean, reinstall the cables, negative cable last; Do not hammer the clamps onto battery posts. Tighten the clamps securely, but do not distort them. Give the clamps and terminals a thin external coating of grease after installation, to retard corrosion.

Check the cables at the same time that the terminals are cleaned. If the insulation is cracked or broken, or if its end is frayed, that cable should be replaced with a new one of the same length and gauge.

BATTERY & CHARGING SAFETY PRECAUTIONS

Always follow these safety precautions when charging or handling a battery.

1. Wear eye protection when working around batteries. Batteries contain corrosive acid and produce explosive gas a byproduct of their operation. Acid on the skin should be neutralized with a solution of baking soda and water made into a paste. In case acid contacts the eyes, flush with clear water and seek medical attention immediately.

2. Avoid flame or sparks that could ignite the hydrogen gas produced by the battery and cause an explosion. Connection and disconnection of cables to battery terminals is one of the most common causes of sparks.

3. Always turn a battery charger OFF, before connecting or disconnecting the leads. When connecting the leads, connect the positive lead first, then the negative lead, to avoid sparks.

4. When lifting a battery, use a battery carrier or lift at opposite corners of the base.

5. Ensure there is good ventilation in a room where the battery is being charged.

6. Do not attempt to charge or load-test a maintenance-free battery when the charge indicator dot is indicating insufficient electrolyte.

7. Disconnect the negative battery cable if the battery is to remain in the boat during the charging process.

8. Be sure the ignition switch is OFF before connecting or turning the charger ON. Sudden power surges can destroy electronic components.

9. Use proper adapters to connect charger leads to batteries with non-conventional terminals.

BATTERY CHARGERS

Before using any battery charger, consult the manufacturer's instructions for its use. Battery chargers are electrical devices that change Alternating Current (AC) to a lower voltage of Direct Current (DC) that can be used to charge a marine battery. There are two types of battery chargers—manual and automatic.

A manual battery charger must be physically disconnected when the battery has come to a full charge. If not, the battery can be overcharged, and possibly fail. Excess charging current at the end of the charging cycle will heat the electrolyte, resulting in loss of water and active material, substantially reducing battery life.

➡ As a rule, on manual chargers, when the ammeter on the charger registers half the rated amperage of the charger, the battery is fully charged. This can vary, and it is recommended to use a hydrometer to accurately measure state of charge.

Automatic battery chargers have an important advantage—they can be left connected (for instance, overnight) without the possibility of overcharging the battery. Automatic chargers are equipped with a sensing device to allow the battery charge to taper off to near zero as the battery becomes fully charged. When charging a low or completely discharged battery, the meter will read close to full rated output. If only partially discharged, the initial reading may be less than full rated output, as the charger responds to the condition of the battery. As the battery continues to charge, the sensing device monitors the state of charge and reduces the charging rate. As the rate of charge tapers to zero amps, the charger will continue to supply a few milliamps of current—just enough to maintain a charged condition.

REPLACING BATTERY CABLES

Battery cables don't go bad very often, but like anything else, they can wear out. If the cables on your boat are cracked, frayed or broken, they should be replaced.

When working on any electrical component, it is always a good idea to disconnect the negative (-) battery cable. This will prevent potential damage to many sensitive electrical components

Always replace the battery cables with one of the same length, or you will increase resistance and possibly cause hard starting. Smear the battery posts with a light film of dielectric grease, or a battery terminal protectant spray once you've installed the new cables. If you replace the cables one at a time, you won't mix them up.

➡ Any time you disconnect the battery cables, it is recommended that you disconnect the negative (-) battery cable first. This will prevent you from accidentally grounding the positive (+) terminal when disconnecting it, thereby preventing damage to the electrical system.

Before you disconnect the cable(s), first turn the ignition to the OFF position. This will prevent a draw on the battery which could cause arcing. When the battery cable(s) are reconnected (negative cable last), be sure to check all electrical accessories are all working correctly.

Fuel and Fuel Tanks

◆ See Figure 8

Take time to check the fuel tank and all of the fuel lines, fittings, couplings, valves, flexible tank fill and vent. Turn on the fuel supply valve at the tank. If the gas was not drained at the end of the previous season, make a careful inspec-

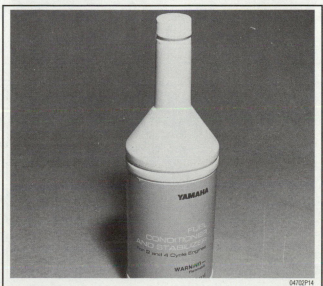

04702P14

Fig. 8 Yamaha fuel conditioner and stabilizer will prevent fuel from souring for up to twelve months

tion for gum formation. When gasoline is allowed to stand for long periods of time, particularly in the presence of copper, gummy deposits form.

This gum can clog the filters, lines, and passageway in the carburetor. Check the fuel tank for the following:

- Adequate air vent in the fuel cap.
- Fuel line of sufficient size, should be $\frac{5}{16}$–$\frac{3}{8}$ (8mm to 9.5mm).
- Filter on the end of the pickup is too small or is clogged.
- Fuel pickup tube is too small.

PRE-SEASON CHECKLIST

▶ **See Figures 9 thru 15**

Satisfactory performance and maximum enjoyment can be realized if a little time is spent in preparing the outboard unit for service at the beginning of the season. Assuming the unit has been properly stored, a minimum amount of work is required to prepare the unit for use. The following steps outline an adequate and logical sequence of tasks to be performed before using the outboard the first time in a new season.

1. Lubricate the outboard according to the manufacturer's recommendations.

2. Perform a tune-up on the engine. This should include replacing the spark plugs and making a thorough check of the ignition system. The ignition system check should include the ignition coils, stator assembly, condition of the wiring and the battery.

3. If a built-in fuel tank is installed, take time to check the gasoline tank and all fuel lines, fittings, couplings, valves, including the flexible tank fill and vent. Turn on the fuel supply valve at the tank. If the fuel was not drained at the end of the previous season, make a careful inspection for gum formation. If a six-gallon fuel tank is used, take the same action. When gasoline is allowed to stand for long periods of time, particularly in the presence of copper, gummy deposits form. This gum can clog the filters, lines, and passageways in the carburetor.

4. Replace the oil in the lower unit.

5. Replace the fuel filter.

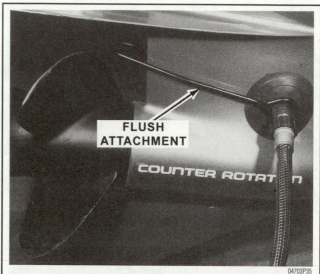

Fig. 11 This popular and inexpensive flushing device should be included in every boat owner's maintenance kit

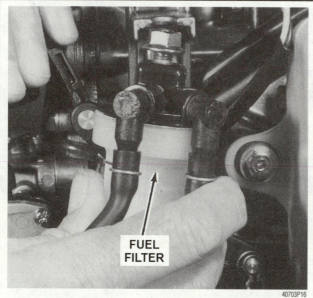

Fig. 9 Removing the fuel filter for inspection and possible replacement

Fig. 10 Make a pre-season check of the fuel line coupling at the fuel joint to ensure a proper and clean connection

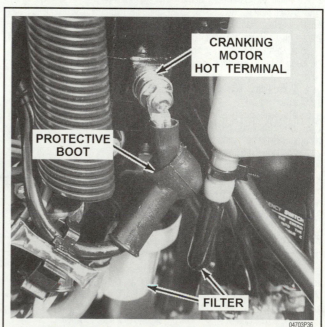

Fig. 12 Electrical and fuel system components should be checked on a regular basis

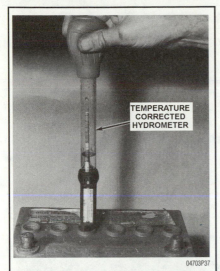

Fig. 13 Checking the condition of the battery electrolyte using a hydrometer

Fig. 14 A water separating fuel filter installed inside the boat on the transom

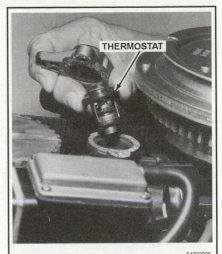

Fig. 15 The thermostat is usually located in an accessible place for easy maintenance or replacement

6. If servicing an engine without precision lube, add oil to the fuel tank at the ratio of 25:1 for the first ten hours of operation after the unit is brought out of storage. This ratio will ensure adequate lubrication of moving parts which have been drained of oil during the storage period. After the first ten hours of operation, the normal 50:1 or 100:1 oil/fuel mixture may be used.

➡ **Use only outboard marine oil in the mixture, never automotive oils. Automotive engine oils are not designed to burn completely, only to lubricate. Therefore, automotive oil, if used in a two stroke powerhead, will leave an undesirable residue.**

7. Close all water drains. Check and replace any defective water hoses. Check to be sure the connections do not leak. Replace any spring-type hose clamps with band-type clamps, if they have lost their tension or if they have distorted the water hose.

8. The engine can be run with the lower unit in water to flush it. If this is not practical, a flush attachment may be used. This unit is attached to the water pick-up in the lower unit. Attach a garden hose, turn on the water, allow the water to flow into the engine for awhile, and then run the engine.

✳✳ CAUTION

Water must circulate through the lower unit to the powerhead anytime the powerhead is operating to prevent damage to the water pump in the lower unit. Just five seconds without water will damage the water pump impeller.

9. Check the exhaust outlet for water discharge. Check for leaks. Check operation of the thermostat.

10. Check the electrolyte level in the battery and the voltage for a full charge. Clean and inspect the battery terminals and cable connections. Take time to check the polarity, if a new battery is being installed. Cover the cable connections with grease or special protective compound as a prevention to corrosion formation. Check all electrical wiring and grounding circuits.

11. Check all electrical parts on the engine and lower portions of the hull. Rubber boots help keep electrical connections clean and reduce the possibility of arcing.

➡ **Electric cranking motors and high tension wiring harnesses should be of a marine type that cannot cause an explosive mixture to ignite.**

12. If a water separating filter is installed between the fuel tank and the powerhead fuel filter, replace the element at least once each season. This filter removes water and fuel system contaminants such as dirt, rust, and other solids, thus reducing potential problems.

✳✳ CAUTION

Before putting the boat in the water, take time to verify the drain plugs are installed. Countless number of boating excursions have had a very sad beginning because the boat was eased into the water only to have the boat begin to fill with the water.

LUBRICATION

General Information

▶ See Figures 16 thru 21

Lubrication plays a prominent role in operation, enjoyment, and longevity of every outboard unit. If an outboard unit is operated in salt water the frequency of applying lubricant to fittings is usually cut in half from the time interval for the same fitting if the unit is used in fresh water. The few minutes involved in moving around the outboard applying lubricant and at the same time making a visual inspection of its general condition will pay in rich rewards with years of trouble free service.

It is not uncommon to see outboard units well over 20 years of age moving a boat through the water as if the unit had recently been purchased from the current line of models. An inquiry with the proud owner will undoubtedly reveal his main credit for its performance to be regular periodic maintenance.

The Maintenance chart can be used as a guide to periodic maintenance while the outboard is being used during the season.

In addition to the normal lubrication listed in the Lubrication chart, the prudent owner will inspect and make checks on a regular basis.

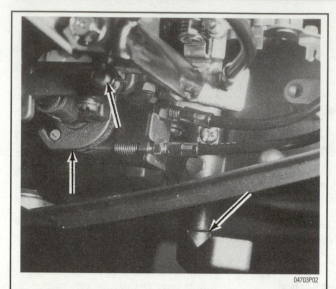

Fig. 16 Various lubrication points on the powerhead which should be maintained regularly to ensure a long service life with minimal downtime

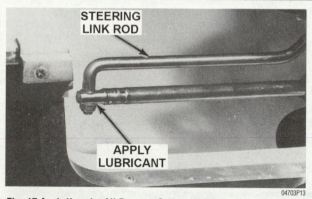

Fig. 17 Apply Yamaha All Purpose Grease to the steering link rod joint

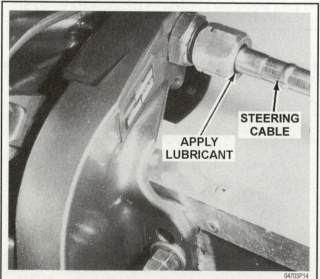

Fig. 18 The steering cable should be lubricated with Yamaha All Purpose Grease also

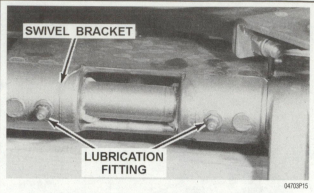

Fig. 19 Location of the two lubrication fittings on the swivel bracket

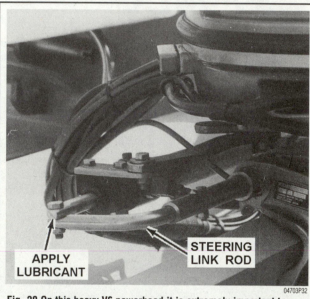

Fig. 20 On this heavy V6 powerhead it is extremely important to keep the steering cable well lubricated

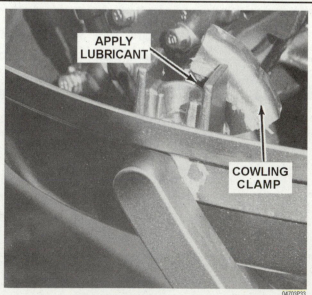

Fig. 21 The cowling clamp should also be lubricated with Yamaha All Purpose Grease

Periodic Lubrication

Component	Lubricant	Frequency	
		Fresh Water	**Salt Water**
Throttle Linkage	1	100 Hours	50 Hours
Throttle Control Lever	1	100 Hours	50 Hours
Throttle Grip housing	1	100 Hours	50 Hours
Throttle Lonk Journal	1	100 Hours	50 Hours
Shift Lever Journal	1	100 Hours	50 Hours
Shift Mechanism	1	100 Hours	50 Hours
Steering Pivot Shaft	1	100 Hours	50 Hours
Clowling Clamp Lever Journal	1	100 Hours	50 Hours
Choke Lever	1	100 Hours	50 Hours
Swivel Bracket	1	100 Hours	50 Hours
Clamp Bolt	1	100 Hours	50 Hours
Tilt Mechanism	1	100 Hours	50 Hours
Propeller Shaft	1	100 Hours	50 Hours
Lower Unit	2	100 Hours	50 Hours
Jet Drive	1	10 Hours	5 Hours

1- Yamaha All Purpose Lubricant
2- Yamaha Gear Case Lubricant

04703C01

Lubricants

♦ See Figures 22 and 23

❄❄ WARNING

Lubricants recommended in the lubrication procedures in this manual are NOT interchangeable as each is designed to perform under different conditions.

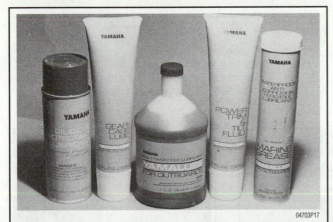

Fig. 22 Yamaha recommended lubricants and additives will not only keep the unit within the limits of the warranty but will also contribute to dependable performance and reduced maintenance costs

Yamaha or Yamalube All Purpose Marine Grease

All-purpose marine grease is a general outboard lubricant, chemically formulated to resist salt water. This lubricant is recommended for application to bearings, bushings, and oil seals.

Yamalube Lubricant

Yamalube lubricant is a two-stroke engine oil. It is a petroleum based, clean burning lubricant. Yamalube reduces carbon deposits and ensures maximum pro-

Fig. 23 Yamaha products, available from your local dealer, will do much to keep the outboard unit looking sharp and running right

tection against engine wear. No oil additives are recommended by the manufacturer. Yamalube contains ashless detergent to minimize piston rings from sticking.

Yamaha or Yamalube Gearcase Lubricant

Yamaha or Yamalube Gearcase Lubricant contains high viscosity additives to protect the lower unit gears at high speed operation. The lubricant will extend gear life, reduce gear noise, minimize friction, and has a cooling affect on the lower unit moving parts.

Yamaha or Yamalube Power Trim and Tilt Fluid

Yamaha or Yamalube power trim and tilt fluid is a highly refined hydraulic fluid. This product has a high detergent content and additives to keep seals pliable. A high grade automatic transmission fluid, Dexron® or Type F, may be substituted if the Yamalube fluid is not available.

➡ **If a substitute fluid is used to top off the reservoir, the system should be drained and filled with a single product at the first opportunity. Brand names should never be mixed, if its possible to avoid.**

Inside the Boat

The following points may be lubricated with Yamalube All Purpose lubricant:
• Remote control cable ends next to the hand nut. DO NOT over-lubricate the cable.

Fig. 24 A suitable container positioned under a fully tilted lower unit, ready to receive lubricant as it drains

Fig. 25 On this single cylinder outboard the oil level and fill holes are close together, suggesting a small quantity of oil is used

Fig. 26 When draining the lower unit, ensure it is fully tilted and a drain pan of adequate capacity is place to catch the lubricant

- Steering arm pivot socket.
- Exposed shaft of the cable passing through the cable guide tube.
- Steering link rod to steering cable.

Propeller Drive

DRAINING

▶ See Figures 24, 25, and 26

➡ **Never remove the vent or filler plugs when the lower unit is hot. Expanded lubricant will be released through the plug hole.**

1. Place a suitable container under the lower unit.
2. Loosen the oil level plug on the lower unit. This step is important! If the oil level plug cannot be loosened or removed, the complete lower unit lubricant service cannot be performed.
3. Remove the fill plug from the lower end of the gear housing and then the oil level plug.
4. Allow the lubricant to completely drain from the lower unit.
5. Inspect the lubricant for the presence of a milky white substance, water or metallic particles. If any of these conditions are present, the lower unit should be serviced immediately.

WATER IN THE LOWER UNIT

▶ See Figures 27 and 28

Water in the lower unit is usually caused by fishing line, or other foreign material, becoming entangled around the propeller shaft and damaging the seal. If the line is not removed, it will cut the propeller shaft seal and allow water to enter the lower unit. Fish line has also been known to cut a groove in the propeller shaft.

The propeller should be removed each time the boat is hauled from the water at the end of an outing and any material entangled behind the propeller removed before it can cause expensive damage. The small amount of time and effort involved in pulling the propeller is repaid many times by reduced maintenance and service work, including the replacement of expensive parts.

FILLING

▶ See Figure 29

1. Place the outboard in the proper position for filling the lower unit. The lower unit should not list to either port or starboard.
2. Insert the lubricant tube into the oil fill hole at the bottom lower unit, and inject lubricant until the excess begins to come out the oil level hole.

Fig. 27 This lower unit was destroyed because the bearing carrier was frozen due to lack of lubrication

Fig. 28 Excellent view of rope and fishing line entangled behind the propeller. Entangles fishing line can actually cut through the seal allowing water to enter the lower unit and lubricant to escape. Check this area constantly

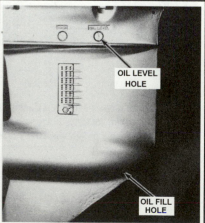

Fig. 29 Inject lubricant through the oil fill hole until the excess begins to come out the oil level hole

Gear Oil Capacity

Model	Years	Right Hand Rotation Oz.(cc)	Left Hand Rotation Oz.(cc)
2	1990-98	1.5(45)	-
3	1990-98	2.5(75)	-
4	1990-98	3.6(105)	-
5	1994-98	3.6(105)	-
6	1990-98	5.4(160)	-
8	1990-98	5.4(160)	-
9.9	1990-98	6.0(185)	-
9.9	1996-98	6.0(185)	-
15	1990-95	6.0(185)	-
15	1996-98	6.0(185)	-
20	1996-97	12.7(375)	-
25	1990-98	12.7(375)	-
25 (3CYL)	1996-98	6.8(200)	-
C25	1990-97	6.1(180)	-
30 (3CYL)	1990-98	6.8(200)	-
C30	1990-92	6.1(180)	-
C30	1993-97	10.8(320)	-
40	1990-94	14(415)	-
40 (3CYL)	1995-98	14.5(430)	-
C40 (3CYL)	1998-98	14.5(430)	-
C40	1990-97	10.6(315)	-
E48	1995-98	16.9(500)	-
50/P50	1990-94	14(415)	-
50/P50	1995-98	14.5(430)	-
C55	1990-95	16.9(500)	-
C60	1996-98	20.6(610)	-
E60	1995-98	20.6(610)	-
P60	1991	20.6(610)	-
P60	1992-98	20.6(610)	-
70	1990-91	20.6(610)	-
70	1992-98	20.6(610)	-
C75	1994-96	20.6(610)	-
C75	1998-98	20.6(610)	-
E75	1995-96	20.6(610)	-
E75	1997-98	20.6(610)	-
P75	1996-98	20.6(610)	-
C80	1997	20.6(610)	-
C85	1990-96	20.6(610)	-
90	1990-91	20.6(610)	-
90/B90/C90	1992-98	20.6(610)	-
115/B115/C115/P115	1990-98	25.7(760)	-
130/L130/S130	1990-98	25.7(760)	24.2 oz. (715 cc)
150	1990-95	33.1(980)	29.4 oz. (870 cc)
150/D150/P150/S150/L150	1996-98	(2)	(2)
C150	1996-98	(2)	(2)
DX150/LX150/PX150/SX150	1999	(3)	(3)
P150	1990-95	33.1(980)	-
175	1990-95	33.1(980)	-
P175	1994-95	33.1(980)	-
P175/S175	1996-98	33.1(980)	
200	1990-95	33.1(980)	30.4 oz. (900 cc)
P200	1991-95	33.1(980)	
P200/S200/L200	1996-98	33.1(980)	30.4 oz (870cc)
LX200/SX200	1999	30.5(870)	30.5(870) (1)
V200	1998	38.9(1150)	33.8 oz. (1000 cc)
V200	1999	40.5 (1150)	-
225	1990-93	33.1(980)	-
225 (2.6L)	1994-95	33.1(980)	-
225 (2.6L)	1996-97	31.1(980)	-
225L	1994-95	33.1(980)	-
225U (3.1L)	1995	38.9(1150)	33.8 oz. (1000 cc)
225X	1994-95	38.9(1150)	33.8 oz. (1000 cc)
L225/S225/V225	1998-98	38.9(1150)	33.8 oz. (1000 cc)
S225X/S225U (3.1L)	1996	38.9(1150)	33.8 oz. (1000 cc)
S225X/S225U (3.1L)	1997	38.9(1150)	33.8 oz. (1000 cc)
250	1990-95	38.9(1150)	33.8 oz. (1000 cc)
L250/S250	1998-98	38.9(1150)	33.8 oz. (1000 cc)
S250HP	1996	38.9(1150)	33.8 oz. (1000 cc)
S250HP	1997	38.9(1150)	33.8 oz. (1000 cc)

(1) LX, SX 34.5 oz (980cc)

(2) Except D150 and L150 33.1 oz (980cc), D150 30.4 oz (900cc) and L150 29.4 oz (870cc)

(3) DX150 31.5 oz (900cc), LX150 30.5 oz (870cc), PX150 and SX150 34.5 oz (980cc)

04703C03

3. Using new gaskets, install the oil level plug first, then install the oil fill plug.

➡**Ensure the gaskets are properly positioned to prevent water from entering the housing.**

4. Place the used lubricant in a suitable container for transportation to an authorized recycling station.

Jet Drive

LUBRICATION

▶ **See Figures 30 and 31**

Jet drive care falls between a tune-up procedure and a maintenance procedure. Jet drives should be lubricated after each operating period, after 10 hours of operation.

In addition, after every 50 hours of operation, grease should be pumped into the bearings to purge any moisture.

1. Removing the cap on the end of the excess grease hose from the grease fitting on the side of the jet drive.

2. Use a grease gun to inject Yamalube All Purpose Grease, or equivalent, into the fitting until grease exits from the capped end of the excess grease hose.

3. Note the color of the grease being expelled from the excess grease hose. During the break-in period, some discoloration of the grease is normal. If the grease should turn dark gray after the break-in period, the jet drive assembly should be serviced immediately. Seals ad bearings should be inspected and replaced as necessary.

4. If moisture is being expelled from the excess grease hose, the jet drive should be disassembled and the seals replaced.

The bearing and seal housing installed on the jet unit drive shaft is lubricated through an externally mounted Zerk fitting. This fitting is located at the top of the jet drive casing on the port side.

To lubricate through the fitting, first push the coupling aside to release the coupling and the hose from the fitting. DO NOT attempt to pull on the coupling or the hose. Pushing the coupling aside is the answer.

Pump Yamalube All Purpose Marine Grease into the fitting until the old grease emerges from the hose coupler. Internal passageways are provided through the outer jet drive housing and the bearing and the seal housing to route the lubricant. When the old grease emerges from the hose coupling, there is no doubt the system has been properly lubricated. Wipe off the excess grease, and then snap the coupler back into place over the fitting.

The fitting should be lubricated every ten hours of jet drive operation.

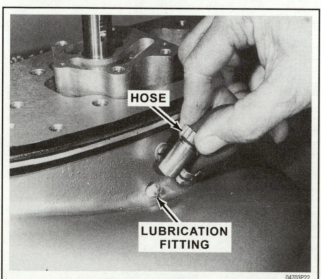

Fig. 30 Removing the hose is accomplished by deflecting the hose to one side to snap it free of the fitting. Do not attempt to pull the hose off the fitting

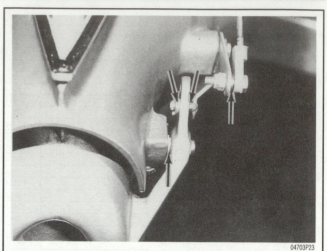

Fig. 31 The arrows indicate pivot points to be lubricated with Yamaha All Purpose Grease

Every 50 hours of jet drive operation, pump enough new grease into the fitting to replace the old grease. A distinct change in color between the old grease and the new grease will be noted, indicating the unit is filled with the new lubricant.

When the unit is new, a slight discoloration may be expected, as the new seals are broken in.

If the old grease contains tiny beads of water, the seals are beginning to break down. If the old grease emerging from the hose coupling is a dark dirty gray color, the seals have already broken down and water is attacking the bearings.

Lubricate the gate control linkage pivot points at regular intervals. These points are indicated in the accompanying illustration.

FLUSHING

Regular flushing of the jet drive will prolong the life of the powerhead, by clearing the cooling system of possible obstructions.

Models With a Flushing Plug

▶ **See Figure 32**

Most jet drives are equipped with a plug on the port side just above the lubrication hose.

1. Remove the plug and gasket, install the flush adapter, connect the garden hose and turn on the water supply.

2. Start and operate the powerhead at a fast idle for about 15 minutes. Disconnect the flushing adapter and replace the plug.

➡**The procedure just described will only flush the powerhead cooling system, not the jet drive. To flush the jet drive unit, direct a stream of high pressure water through the intake grille.**

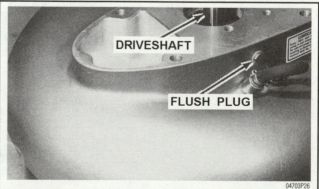

Fig. 32 Most jet drives are equipped with a flushing plug on the side of the unit

Models Without a Flushing Plug

◆ **See Figure 33**

Units not equipped with a flushing plug can be suitably modified by drilling and tapping a small hole in the port side of the jet drive unit to accept a flush adapter. Proceed as follows:

1. The jet drive must be dropped from the intermediate housing and disassembled.

2. Deflect the lubrication hose coupler sideways to remove it from the grease fitting and secure the hose out of the way.

3. Drill a ¹⁵⁄₆₄ in. hole above the grease fitting, as illustrated. Using a 8mm x 1.25 tap thread the hole. Blow away all metal chips from the interior and exterior of the housing, using compressed air.

4. Install the plug and gasket (available at the local Yamaha dealer). Assemble and install the jet drive to the intermediate housing.

5. The powerhead may now be flushed as described in the previous section for units with the flush plug.

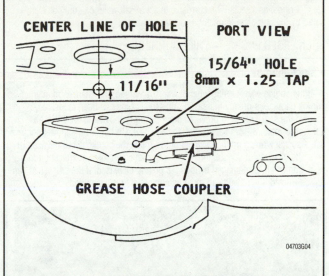

Fig. 33 On models not equipped with a flushing plug, a hole should be drilled and tapped to receive a plug as illustrated

EMERGENCY SERVICE

Emergency Tether

◆ **See Figure 34**

Most outboards are equipped with an emergency tether by the manufacturer. This tether must be in place behind the kill switch or the powerhead will not start. If the powerhead is operating and the tether is removed, the unit will immediately shut down.

The purpose of this tether is two fold.

• **As a Safety Feature**—when this tether is used as intended by the manufacturer, the boat operator attaches the belt hook onto their clothing at any convenient location. Should the operator be thrown overboard or knocked forward away from the outboard unit, the tether will be pulled free of the kill button and the powerhead will be shut down.

• **As a Security Feature**—If the boat is moored and will be left unattended, the owner can take the entire emergency tether with them. Without the tether in place behind the kill button, the powerhead cannot be started. Any attempt to start the powerhead and steal the boat will be unsuccessful—unless the thief is familiar with this particular security device.

The plastic tether Yamaha uses acts as a spacer, moving the kill button out slightly and allowing an internal contact to be closed, permitting the ignition circuit to be completed and the powerhead to be started.

The kill button may now be depressed to shut the powerhead down with the tether in place. If the tether is pulled free from behind the kill button, the button

pops inward and the ignition circuit is opened. With the kill switch in this position, no amount of cranking will result in powerhead startup.

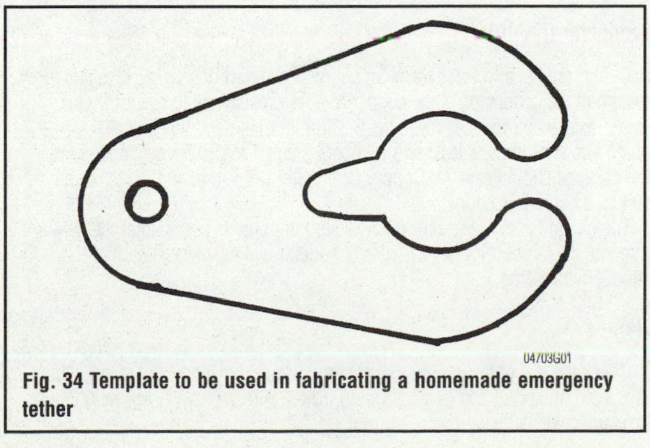

If the boat owner loses their tether and is unable to obtain one immediately from the local Yamaha dealer, an emergency substitute tether may be made using only a common knife and a couple pieces of plastic.

1. Obtain a piece of plastic from the cover of a container of margarine, whipped topping, or similar product.

2. Using the illustrated pattern, cut out about four shapes. Stack the four cutouts together, secure them and then insert them behind the kill switch.

➡ **If the material described is not available, obtain some other pliable material and cut the shape indicated. The thickness of the substitute tether device should be approximately ⅛ in. (3mm).**

3. Use this device only in an emergency situation and purchase the proper tether from the local Yamaha dealer at the first opportunity. By substituting this home made tether, both the safety and the security features intended by the manufacturer have been lost.

Submerged Engine

A submerged engine is always the result of an unforeseen accident. Once the engine is recovered, special care and service procedures must be closely followed in order to return the unit to satisfactory performance.

Never, again we say never allow an engine that has been submerged to stand more than a couple hours before following the procedures outlined in this section and making every effort to get it running. Such delay will result in serious internal damage. If all efforts fail and the engine cannot be started after the following procedures have been performed, the engine should be disassembled, cleaned, assembled, using new gaskets, seals, and O-rings, and then started as soon as possible.

Submerged engine treatment is divided into three unique problem areas: Submersion in salt water; submerged while powerhead was running; and a submerged unit in fresh water.

The most critical of these three circumstances is the engine submerged in salt water, with submersion while running, a close second.

SUBMERGED ENGINE—SALT WATER

Never attempt to start the engine after it has been recovered. This action will only result in additional parts being damaged and the cost of restoring the engine increased considerably. If the engine was submerged in salt water the

Fig. 34 Template to be used in fabricating a homemade emergency tether

complete unit MUST be disassembled, cleaned, and assembled with new gaskets, O-rings, and seals. The corrosive effect of salt water can only be eliminated by the complete job being properly performed.

SUBMERGED ENGINE—WHILE RUNNING

♦ **See Figure 35**

If the engine was running when it was submerged, the chances of internal engine damage is greatly increased. After the engine has been recovered, remove the spark plugs to prevent compression in the cylinders. Make an attempt to rotate the crankshaft with the flywheel. On larger horsepower engines, use a socket wrench on the flywheel nut to rotate the crankshaft. If the attempt fails, the chances of serious internal damage, such as: bent connecting rod, bent crankshaft, or damaged cylinder, is greatly increased. If the crankshaft cannot be rotated, the powerhead must be completely disassembled.

PISTON ASSEMBLY

04703P20

Fig. 35 Easy removal of the exhaust cover will provide access to inspect the condition of the cylinder bores, pistons and the rings. Such inspection may reveal the cause of strange noises in the powerhead

❊❊ CAUTION

Never attempt to start a powerhead that has been submerged. If there is water in the cylinder, the piston will not be able to compress the liquid. The result will most likely be a bent connecting rod.

SUBMERGED ENGINE—FRESH WATER

As an aid to performing the restoration work, the following steps are numbered and should be followed in sequence.
1. Recover the engine as quickly as possible.
2. Remove the cowling and the spark plugs.
3. Remove the carburetor float bowl cover, or the bowl.
4. Flush the outside of the engine with fresh water to remove silt, mud, sand, weeds, and other debris. DO NOT attempt to start the engine if sand has entered the powerhead. Such action will only result in serious damage to powerhead components. Sand in the powerhead means the unit must be disassembled.

❊❊ CAUTION

Never attempt to start a powerhead that has been submerged. If there is water in the cylinder, the piston will not be able to compress the liquid. The result will most likely be a bent connecting rod.

5. Remove as much water as possible from the powerhead. Most of the water can be eliminated by first holding the engine in a horizontal position with the spark plug holes down, and then cranking the powerhead with a socket wrench on the flywheel nut. Rotate the crankshaft through at least 10 complete revolutions. If you are satisfied there is no water in the cylinders, remove the moisture.
6. Alcohol will absorb moisture. Therefore, pour alcohol into the carburetor throat and again crank the powerhead.
7. Rotate the outboard in the horizontal position until the spark plug openings are facing upward. Pour alcohol into the spark plug openings and again rotate the crankshaft.
8. Rotate the outboard in the horizontal position until the spark plug openings are again facing down. Pour engine oil into the carburetor throat and, at the same time, rotate the crankshaft to distribute oil throughout the crankcase.
9. Rotate the outboard in the horizontal position until the spark plug holes are again facing upward. Pour approximately one teaspoon of engine oil into each spark plug opening. Rotate the crankshaft to distribute the oil in the cylinders.
10. Install and connect the spark plugs.
11. Install the carburetor float bowl cover, or the bowl.
12. Obtain fresh fuel and attempt to start the engine. If the powerhead will start, allow it to run for approximately an hour to eliminate any unwanted moisture remaining in the powerhead.

❊❊ CAUTION

Water must circulate through the lower unit to the powerhead anytime the powerhead is operating to prevent damage to the water pump in the lower unit. Just five seconds without water will damage the water pump impeller.

13. If the powerhead fails to start, determine the cause, electrical or fuel, correct the problem, and again attempt to get it running. Never allow a powerhead to remain sitting for more than a couple hours without following the procedures in this section and attempting to start it. If attempts to start the powerhead fail, the unit should be disassembled, cleaned, assembled, using new gaskets, seals, and O-rings, as soon as possible.

Jump Starting

Whenever a unit is jump started, precautions must be followed in order to prevent the possibility of personal injury or damage. Remember that batteries contain a small amount of explosive hydrogen gas which is a by-product of battery charging. Sparks should always be avoided when working around batteries, especially when attaching jumper cables. To minimize the possibility of accidental sparks, follow the procedure carefully.

❊❊ CAUTION

Never hook the batteries up in a series circuit or the entire electrical system will go up in smoke, including the starter!

JUMPER CABLES

There are four things to consider when buying jumper cables:

Conductor (Cable)

Cables are usually made from copper, which minimizes power loss due to heating of the conductor, since copper has less resistance to electrical current (more resistance produces more heat). Aluminum is sometimes used, but the gauge size should be at least two numbers smaller to deliver the same power. The package should say "All Copper Conductor"; if not, push the insulation back to be sure it is copper.

The gauge (size) of the conductor is also important. The smaller the gauge numbers the larger the wire. A larger conductor will carry more current longer, without overheating.

Clamps

Check the feel of the clamps. They should resist twisting from side to side, have a strong spring and good gripping power. A higher amperage rating means the clamps will withstand more current.

Insulation

The conductor is insulated with vinyl or rubber to protect the user. Quality cables will retain their flexibility in cold temperatures without cracking or breaking.

Length

Buy the shortest cables possible to safely do the job. Longer cables mean increased resistance and power loss, but they should be at least 8–10 feet for most situations.

JUMP STARTING PRECAUTIONS

- Be sure that both batteries are of the same voltage. Most batteries used by units covered in this manual utilize a 12 volt charging system.
- Be sure that both batteries are of the same polarity (have the same terminal, in most cases NEGATIVE grounded).
- Be sure that the boats are not touching or a short could occur.
- On serviceable batteries, be sure the vent cap holes are not obstructed.
- Do not smoke or allow sparks anywhere near the batteries.
- In cold weather, make sure the battery electrolyte is not frozen. This can occur more readily in a battery that has been in a state of discharge.
- Do not allow electrolyte to contact your skin or clothing.

JUMP STARTING PROCEDURE

1. Make sure that the voltages of the 2 batteries are the same. Most batteries and charging systems are of the 12 volt variety.
2. Place the fully charged booster battery into a position so the jumper cables can reach the dead battery.
3. Turn all lights and accessories OFF. Make sure the ignition is turned to the OFF position.
4. Cover the battery cell caps with a rag, but do not cover the terminals.

5. Make sure the terminals on both batteries are clean and free of corrosion or proper electrical connection will be impeded. If necessary, clean the battery terminals before proceeding.
6. Identify the positive (+) and negative (-) terminals on both batteries.
7. Connect the first jumper cable to the positive (+) terminal of the dead battery, then connect the other end of that cable to the positive (+) terminal of the booster (good) battery.
8. Connect one end of the other jumper cable to the negative (-) terminal on the booster battery and the final cable clamp to an bolt on the powerhead. Try to pick a ground on the powerhead that is positioned away from the battery in order to minimize the possibility of the clamps touching should one loosen during the procedure. Do not connect this clamp to the negative (-) terminal of the bad battery.

✳✳ CAUTION

Be very careful to keep the jumper cables away from moving parts.

9. Attempt to start the outboard with the dead battery. Crank the starter for no more than 10 seconds at a time and let it cool for at least 20 seconds between tries. If the powerhead does not start in three tries, it is likely that something else is also wrong or that the battery needs additional time to charge.
10. Once the powerhead is started, allow it to run at idle for a few seconds to make sure that it is operating properly.
11. Turn ON lights and other accessories, if equipped, in order to reduce the severity of voltage spikes and subsequent risk of damage to the powerhead's electrical systems when the cables are disconnected. This step is especially important to any powerhead equipped with computer controls.
12. Carefully disconnect the cables in the reverse order of connection. Start with the negative cable that is attached to the powerhead ground, then the negative cable on the donor battery. Disconnect the positive cable from the donor battery and finally, disconnect the positive cable from the formerly dead battery. Be careful when disconnecting the cables from the positive terminals not to allow the alligator clips to touch any metal or a short and sparks will occur.

WINTER STORAGE

Taking extra time to store the boat properly at the end of each season will increase the chances of satisfactory service at the next season. Remember, storage is the greatest enemy of an outboard motor. The unit should be run on a monthly basis. The boat steering and shifting mechanism should also be worked through complete cycles several times each month. If a small amount of time is spent in such maintenance, the reward will be satisfactory performance, increased longevity and greatly reduced maintenance expenses.

For many years there has been the widespread belief simply shutting off the fuel at the tank and then running the powerhead until it stops is the proper procedure before storing the engine for any length of time. Right? WRONG!

First, it is not possible to remove all fuel in the carburetor by operating the powerhead until it stops. Considerable fuel is trapped in the float chamber and other passages and in the line leading to the carburetor. The only guaranteed method of removing all fuel is to take the time to remove the carburetor, and drain the fuel.

Secondly, if the powerhead is operated with the fuel supply shut off until it stops, the fuel and oil mixture inside the powerhead is removed, leaving bearings, pistons, rings, and other parts without any protective lubricant.

Proper storage involves adequate protection of the unit from physical damage, rust, corrosion, and dirt. The following steps provide an adequate maintenance program for storing the unit at the end of a season.

1. Empty all fuel from the carburetor.
2. Drain the fuel tank and the fuel lines. Pour approximately one quart (0.96 liters) of Benzol (Benzine) into the fuel tank, and then rinse the tank and pickup filter with the Benzol. Drain the tank. Store the fuel tank in a cool dry area with the vent OPEN to allow air to circulate through the tank. Do not store the fuel tank on bare concrete. Place the tank to allow air to circulate around it.

3. Clean the carburetor fuel filter with Benzol.
4. Drain, and then fill the lower unit with Yamaha Gear Case Lubricant.
5. Lubricate the throttle and shift linkage. Lubricate the steering pivot shaft with Yamalube or equivalent.
6. Clean the outboard unit thoroughly. Coat the powerhead with a commercial corrosion and rust preventative spray. Install the cowling, and then apply a thin film of fresh engine oil to all painted surfaces.
7. Remove the propeller. Apply Perfect Seal or a waterproof sealer to the propeller shaft splines, and then install the propeller back in position.
8. Be sure all drain holes in the gear housing are open and free of obstruction. Check to be sure the flush plug has been removed to allow all water to drain. Trapped water could freeze, expand, and cause expensive castings to crack.
9. Always store the outboard unit off the boat with the lower unit below the powerhead to prevent any water from being trapped inside.

Fuel Stabilizer

◆ **See Figure 36**

Yamaha Fuel Conditioner and Stabilizer is recommended for use at all times, during operation of the powerhead and during the storage period. The material absorbs water in the fuel system and protects against corrosion.

If used during operation, this fuel additive will prevent the formation of gum and varnish deposits and greatly extend the period between required carburetor overhaul.

When added to the fuel during storage, the additive will prevent the fuel from souring for up to twelve full months.

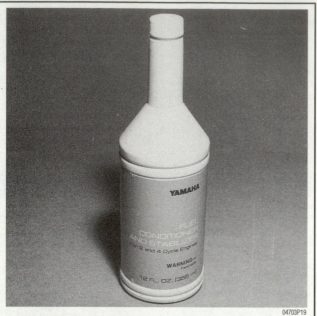

Fig. 36 Yamaha gasoline stabilizer and conditioner can be used to prevent the fuel from souring for up to a year

Battery Storage

Remove the batteries from the boat and keep them charged during the storage period. Clean the batteries thoroughly of any dirt or corrosion, and then charge them to full specific gravity reading. After they are fully charged, store them in a clean cool dry place where they will not be damaged or knocked over.

Never store the battery with anything on top of it or cover the battery in such a manner as to prevent air from circulating around the filler caps. All batteries, both new and old, will discharge during periods of storage, more so if they are hot than if they remain cool. Therefore, the electrolyte level and the specific gravity should be checked at regular intervals. A drop in the specific gravity reading is cause to charge them back to a full reading.

In cold climates, exercise care in selecting the battery storage area. A fully-charged battery will freeze at about 60 degrees below zero. A discharged battery, almost dead, will have ice forming at about 19 degrees above zero.

Always remove the drain plug and position the boat with the bow higher than the stern. This will allow any rain water and melted snow to drain from the boat and prevent trailer sinking. This term is used to describe a boat that has filled with rain water and ruined the interior, because the plug was not removed or the bow was not high enough to allow the water to drain properly.

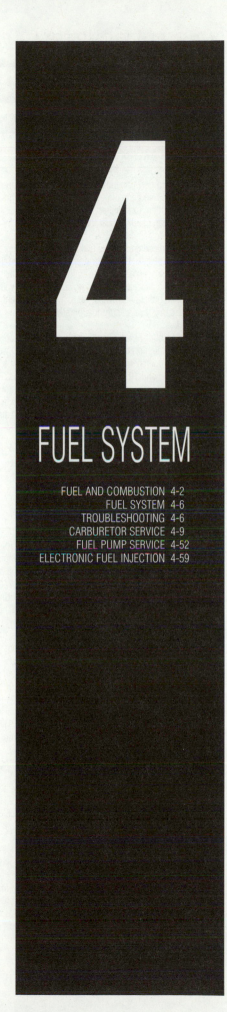

FUEL AND COMBUSTION 4-2
FUEL 4-2
  RECOMMENDATIONS 4-2
  OCTANE RATING 4-2
  VAPOR PRESSURE AND
    ADDITIVES 4-2
  THE BOTTOM LINE WITH FUELS 4-2
  HIGH ALTITUDE OPERATION 4-2
  ALCOHOL-BLENDED FUELS 4-2
COMBUSTION 4-3
  ABNORMAL COMBUSTION 4-3
  FACTORS AFFECTING
    COMBUSTION 4-3
FUEL SYSTEM 4-3
CARBURETION 4-3
  GENERAL INFORMATION 4-3
  CARBURETOR CIRCUITS 4-4
  BASIC FUNCTIONS 4-4
  DUAL-THROAT CARBURETORS 4-5
  REMOVING FUEL FROM THE
    SYSTEM 4-5
FUEL PUMP 4-6
TROUBLESHOOTING 4-6
FUEL SYSTEM 4-6
  LOGICAL TROUBLESHOOTING 4-7
  COMMON PROBLEMS 4-7
FUEL PUMP 4-8
FUEL LINE 4-8
  COMMON PROBLEMS 4-9
COMBUSTION RELATED PISTON
  FAILURES 4-9
CARBURETOR SERVICE 4-9
CARBURETOR IDENTIFICATION 4-9
1–2-CYLINDER POWERHEADS 4-10
2 HP AND 3 HP MODEL 4-10
  REMOVAL & DISASSEMBLY 4-10
  CLEANING & INSPECTION 4-13
  ASSEMBLLY & INSTALLATION 4-13
4 HP AND 5 HP MODELS 4-15
  REMOVAL 4-16
  DISASSEMBLY 4-17
  CLEANING & INSPECTION 4-17
  ASSEMBLY & INSTALLATION 4-18
6 HP, 8 HP, 9.9 HP AND 15 HP
  MODELS 4-21
  REMOVAL 4-21
  DISASSEMBLY 4-23
  CLEANING & INSPECTION 4-24
  ASSEMBLY 4-25
  FLOAT ADJUSTMENT 4-25
  INSTALLATION 4-27
25 HP AND 30 HP MODELS 4-28
  REMOVAL 4-28
  DISASSEMBLY 4-29
  CLEANING & INSPECTION 4-31
  ASSEMBLY 4-31
  INSTALLATION 4-33
3-CYLINDER POWERHEADS 4-33
  REMOVAL 4-34

  DISASSEMBLY 4-37
  CLEANING & INSPECTION 4-38
  ASSEMBLY 4-39
  INSTALLATION 4-41
  TACHOMETER CONNECTIONS 4-44
V4 & V6 POWERHEADS 4-44
  REMOVAL 4-44
  DISASSEMBLY 4-45
  CLEANING & INSPECTION 4-47
  ASSEMBLY 4-48
  INSTALLATION 4-50
  CHOKE SOLENOID
    ADJUSTMENT 4-51
FUEL PUMP SERVICE 4-52
1–2-CYLINDER FUEL PUMPS 4-52
  DESCRIPTION & OPERATION 4-52
  FUEL PRESSURE CHECK 4-53
TYPE II FUEL PUMP 4-54
  REMOVAL & DISASSEMBLY 4-54
  CLEANING & INSPECTION 4-54
  ASSEMBLY & INSTALLATION 4-54
EXCEPT 1–2-CYLINDER FUEL
  PUMPS 4-54
  DESCRIPTION & OPERATION 4-54
  FUEL PUMP PRESSURE CHECK 4-55
  REMOVAL & DISASSEMBLY 4-57
  CLEANING & INSPECTION 4-57
  ASSEMBLY & INSTALLATION 4-58
ELECTRONIC FUEL INJECTION 4-59
FUEL INJECTION BASICS 4-59
YAMAHA TUNED PORT INJECTION 4-59
FUEL INJECTION COMPONENTS 4-59
  ELECTRONIC CONTROL
    SYSTEM 4-59
  FUEL DELIVERY SYSTEM 4-61
  AIR INDUCTION GROUP 4-61
CONTROLLED COMBUSTION
  SYSTEM 4-61
NORMAL VS. FAIL SAFE CONTROL 4-62
  NORMAL MODE 4-62
  FAIL SAFE CONTROL (RETURN TO
    PORT) MODE 4-62
SPECIFICATIONS CHARTS
  CARBURETOR IDENTIFICATION 4-9
  FLOAT HEIGHT 4-40
TROUBLESHOOTING CHARTS
  NORMAL VS. FAIL SAFE CONTROL
    MODES 4-62
  EFI DIAGNOSTIC CODES 4-62

4

FUEL SYSTEM

FUEL AND COMBUSTION 4-2
FUEL SYSTEM 4-6
TROUBLESHOOTING 4-6
CARBURETOR SERVICE 4-9
FUEL PUMP SERVICE 4-52
ELECTRONIC FUEL INJECTION 4-59

FUEL AND COMBUSTION

Fuel

RECOMMENDATIONS

Reformulated gasoline fuels are now found in many market areas. Current testing indicates no particular problems with using this fuel. Shelf life is shorter and, because of the oxygenates, a slight leaning out at idle may be experienced. This slightly lean condition can be compensated for by adjusting idle mixture screws.

Fuel recommendations have become more complex as the chemistry of modern gasoline changes. The major driving force behind the changes in gasoline chemistry is the search for additives to replace lead as an octane booster and lubricant. These new additives are governed by the types of emissions they produce in the combustion process. Also, the replacement additives do not always provide the same level of combustion stability, making a fuel's octane rating less meaningful.

In the search for new fuel additives, automobiles are used as the test medium. Not one high performance two cycle engine was tested in the process of determining the chemistry of today's gasoline.

In the 1960's and 1970's, leaded fuel was common. The lead served two functions. The lead served as an octane booster (combustion stabilizer) and, in four cycle engines, served as a valve seat lubricant. For two cycle engines, the primary benefit of lead was to serve as a combustion stabilizer. Lead served very well for this purpose, even in high heat applications.

Today, all lead has been removed from the gasoline process. This means that the benefit of lead as an octane booster has been eliminated. Several substitute octane boosters have been introduced in the place of lead. While many are adequate in an automobile, most do not perform nearly as well as lead did, even though the octane rating of the fuel is the same.

OCTANE RATING

A fuel's octane rating is a measurement of how stable the fuel is when heat is introduced. Octane rating is a major consideration when deciding whether a fuel is suitable for a particular application. For example, in an engine, we want the fuel to ignite when the spark plug fires and not before, even under high pressure and temperatures. Once the fuel is ignited, it must burn slowly and smoothly, even though heat and pressure are building up while the burn occurs. The unburned fuel should be ignited by the traveling flame front, not by some other source of ignition, such as carbon deposits or the heat from the expanding gasses. A fuel's octane rating is known as a measurement of the fuel's anti-knock properties (ability to burn without exploding).

Usually a fuel with a higher octane rating can be subjected to a more severe combustion environment before spontaneous or abnormal combustion occurs. To understand how two gasoline samples can be different, even though they have the same octane rating, we need to know how octane rating is determined.

The American Society of Testing and Materials (ASTM) has developed a universal method of determining the octane rating of a fuel sample. The octane rating you see on the pump at a gasoline station is known as the pump octane number. Look at the small print on the pump. The rating has a formula. The rating is determined by the R+M/2 method.

Therefore, the number you see on the pump is the average of two other octane ratings.

The Research Octane Reading is a measure of a fuel's anti-knock properties under a light load, or part throttle conditions. During this test, combustion heat is easily dissipated.

The Motor Octane Rating is a measure of a fuel's anti-knock properties under a heavy load, or full throttle conditions, when heat buildup is at maximum.

Because a two cycle engine has a power stroke every revolution, with heat buildup every revolution, it tends to respond more to the motor octane rating of the fuel than the research octane rating. Therefore, in an outboard motor, the motor octane rating of the fuel is the best indication of how it will perform, not the research octane. Unfortunately, the user has no way of knowing for sure the exact motor octane rating of the fuel.

VAPOR PRESSURE AND ADDITIVES

Two other factors besides octane rating affect how suitable the fuel is for a particular application.

Fuel vapor pressure is a measure of how easily a fuel sample evaporates. Many additives used in gasoline contain aromatics. Aromatics are light hydrocarbons distilled off the top of a crude oil sample. They are effective at increasing the research octane of a fuel sample, but can cause vapor lock on a very hot day. If you have an inconsistent running engine and you suspect vapor lock, use a piece of clear fuel line to look for bubbles, indicating that the fuel is vaporizing.

One negative side effect of aromatics is that they create additional combustion products such as carbon and varnish. If your engine requires high octane fuel to prevent detonation, de-carbon the engine more frequently with an internal engine cleaner to prevent ring sticking due to excessive varnish buildup.

Besides aromatics, two types of alcohol are used in fuel today as octane boosters, ethanol and methanol. Again, alcohol tends to raise the research octane of the fuel. This usually means they will have limited benefit in an outboard motor. Also, alcohol contains oxygen, which means that since it is replacing gasoline without oxygen content, alcohol fuel blends cause the fuel-air mixture to be leaner.

THE BOTTOM LINE WITH FUELS

If we could buy fuel of the correct octane rating, free of alcohol and aromatics, this would be our first choice.

Yamaha continues to recommend unleaded fuel. This is almost a redundant recommendation due to the near universal unavailability of any other type fuel.

According to the fuel recommendations that come with your outboard, there is no engine in the product line that requires more than 89 octane. Most Yamaha engines need only 86 octane or less. An 89 octane rating generally means middle grade unleaded. Premium unleaded is more stable under severe conditions, but also produces more combustion products. Therefore, when using premium unleaded, more frequent de-carboning is necessary.

Regardless of the fuel octane rating you choose, try to stay with a name brand fuel. You never know for sure what kinds of additives or how much is in off brand fuel.

HIGH ALTITUDE OPERATION

At elevated altitudes there is less oxygen in the atmosphere than at sea level. Less oxygen means lower combustion efficiency and less power output. Power output is reduced three percent for every thousand feet above sea level. At ten thousand feet, power is reduced 30 percent from that available at sea level.

Re-jetting for high altitude does not restore this lost power. Re-jetting simply corrects the air-fuel ratio for the reduced air density, and makes the most of the remaining available power. If you re-jet an engine, you are locked into the higher elevation. You cannot operate at sea level until you re-jet for sea level. Understand that going below the elevation jetted for your motor will damage the engine. As a general rule, jet for the lowest elevation anticipated. Spark plug insulator tip color is the best guide for high altitude jetting.

If you are in an area of known poor fuel quality, you may want to use fuel additives. Today's additives are mostly alcohol and aromatics, and their effectiveness may be limited. It is difficult to find additives without ethanol, methanol, or aromatics. If you use octane boosters frequent de-carboning may be necessary. If possible, the best policy is to use name brand pump fuel with no additional additives except Yamaha fuel conditioner and Ring-Free™.

ALCOHOL-BLENDED FUELS

The Environmental Protection Agency mandated a phase-out of the leaded fuels. Lead was used to boost the octane of fuel. By January of 1986, the maximum allowable amount of lead was 0.1 gm/gal, down from 1.1 gm/gal.

Gasoline suppliers, in general, feel that the 0.1 gm/gal limit is too low to make lead of any real use to improve octane. Therefore, alternate octane improvers are being used. There are multiple methods currently employed to improve octane but the most inexpensive additive seems to be alcohol.

There are, however, some special considerations due to the effects of alcohol in fuel. You should know about them and what steps to take when using alcohol-blended fuels commonly called gasohol.

Alcohol in fuel is either methanol (wood alcohol) or ethanol (grain alcohol). Either type can have serious effects when applied to outboard motor applications.

The leaching affect of alcohol will, in time, cause fuel lines and plastic components to become brittle to the point of cracking. Unless replaced, these cracked lines could leak fuel, increasing the potential for hazardous situations.

➡**Yamaha fuel lines and plastic fuel system components have been specially formulated to resist alcohol leaching effects.**

When gasohol becomes contaminated with water, the water combines with the alcohol then settles to the bottom. This leaves the gasoline and the oil for models using premix, on a top layer. With alcohol-blended fuels, the amount of water necessary for this phase separation to occur is 0.5% by volume.

All fuels have chemical compounds added to reduce the tendency towards phase separation. If phase separation occurs, however, there is a possibility of a lean oil/fuel mixture with the potential for engine damage. With oil-injected outboards (Precision Blend models), phase separation will be less of a problem because the oil is injected separately rather than being premixed.

Combustion

A two cycle engine has a power stroke every revolution of the crankshaft. A four cycle engine has a power stroke every other revolution of the crankshaft. Therefore, the two cycle engine has twice as many power strokes for any given RPM. If the displacement of the two types of engines is identical, then the two cycle engine has to dissipate twice as much heat as the four cycle engine. In such a high heat environment, the fuel must be very stable to avoid detonation. If any parameters affecting combustion change suddenly (the engine runs lean for example), uncontrolled heat buildup occurs very rapidly in a two cycle engine.

ABNORMAL COMBUSTION

There are two types of abnormal combustion:
- Pre-ignition—Occurs when the air-fuel mixture is ignited by some other incandescent source other than the correctly timed spark from the spark plug.
- Detonation—Occurs when excessive heat and or pressure ignites the air/fuel mixture rather than the spark plug. The burn becomes explosive.

FUEL SYSTEM

Carburetion

GENERAL INFORMATION

The carburetor is merely a metering device for mixing fuel and air in the proper proportions for efficient engine operation. At idle speed, an outboard engine requires a mixture of about 8 parts air to 1 part fuel. At high speed or under heavy duty service, the mixture may change to as much as 12 parts air to 1 part fuel.

Float Systems

▶ **See Figure 1**

A small chamber in the carburetor serves as a fuel reservoir. A float valve admits fuel into the reservoir to replace the fuel consumed by the engine. If the carburetor has more than one reservoir, the fuel level in each reservoir (chamber) is controlled by identical float systems.

Fuel level in each chamber is extremely critical and must be maintained accurately. Accuracy is obtained through proper adjustment of the floats. This adjustment will provide a balanced metering of fuel to each cylinder at all speeds.

Following the fuel through its course, from the fuel tank to the combustion chamber of the cylinder, will provide an appreciation of exactly what is taking place. In order to start the engine, the fuel must be moved from the tank to the carburetor by a squeeze bulb installed in the fuel line. This action is necessary

FACTORS AFFECTING COMBUSTION

The combustion process is affected by several interrelated factors. This means that when one factor is changed, the other factors also must be changed to maintain the same controlled burn and level of combustion stability.

Compression

Determines the level of heat buildup in the cylinder when the air-fuel mixture is compressed. As compression increases, so does the potential for heat buildup.

Ignition Timing

Determines when the gasses will start to expand in relation to the motion of the piston. If the gasses begin to expand too soon, such as they would during pre-ignition or in an overly advanced ignition timing, the motion of the piston opposes the expansion of the gasses, resulting in extremely high combustion chamber pressures and heat.

As ignition timing is retarded, the burn occurs later in relation to piston position. This means that the piston has less distance to travel under power to the bottom of the cylinder, resulting in less usable power.

Fuel Mixture

Determines how efficient the burn will be. A rich mixture burns slower than a lean one. If the mixture is too lean, it can't become explosive. The slower the burn, the cooler the combustion chamber, because pressure buildup is gradual.

Fuel Quality (Octane Rating)

Determines how much heat is necessary to ignite the mixture. Once the burn is in progress, heat is on the rise. The unburned poor quality fuel is ignited all at once by the rising heat instead of burning gradually as a flame front of the burn passing by. This action results in detonation (pinging).

Other Factors

In general, anything that can cause abnormal heat buildup can be enough to push an engine over the edge to abnormal combustion, if any of the four basic factors previously discussed are already near the danger point, for example, excessive carbon buildup raises the compression and retains heat as glowing embers.

because the fuel pump does not have sufficient pressure to draw fuel from the tank during cranking before the engine starts.

The fuel for some small horsepower units is gravity fed from a tank mounted at the rear of the powerhead. Even with the gravity feed method, a small fuel pump may be an integral part of the carburetor.

After the engine starts, the fuel passes through the pump to the carburetor. All systems have some type of filter installed somewhere in the line between the tank and the carburetor. Many units have a filter as an integral part of the carburetor.

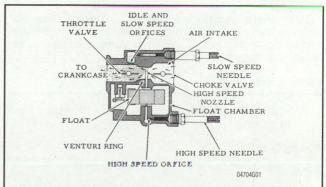

Fig. 1 Fuel flow through a venturi, showing principle and related parts controlling intake and outflow

At the carburetor, the fuel passes through the inlet passage to the needle and seat, and then into the float chamber (reservoir). A float in the chamber rides up and down on the surface of the fuel. After fuel enters the chamber and the level rises to a predetermined point, a tang on the float closes the inlet needle and the flow entering the chamber is cut off. When fuel leaves the chamber as the engine operates, the fuel level drops and the float tang allows the inlet needle to move off its seat and fuel once again enters the chamber. In this manner, a constant reservoir of fuel is maintained in the chamber to satisfy the demands of the engine at all speeds.

A fuel chamber vent hole is located near the top of the carburetor body to permit atmospheric pressure to act against the fuel in each chamber. This pressure assures an adequate fuel supply to the various operating systems of the powerhead.

Air/Fuel Mixture

♦ See Figure 2

A suction effect is created each time the piston moves upward in the cylinder. This suction draws air through the throat of the carburetor. A restriction in the throat, called a venturi, controls air velocity and has the effect of reducing air pressure at this point.

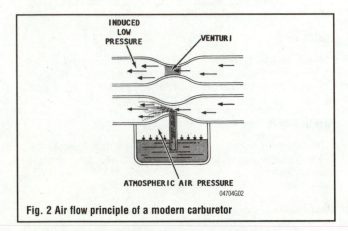

Fig. 2 Air flow principle of a modern carburetor

The difference in air pressures at the throat and in the fuel chamber, causes the fuel to be pushed out of metering jets extending down into the fuel chamber. When the fuel leaves the jets, it mixes with the air passing through the venturi. This fuel/air mixture should then be in the proper proportion for burning in the cylinders for maximum engine performance.

In order to obtain the proper air/fuel mixture for all engine speeds, some models have high and low speed jets. These jets have adjustable needle valves which are used to compensate for changing atmospheric conditions. In almost all cases, the high-speed circuit has fixed high-speed jets and are not adjustable.

A throttle valve controls the flow of air/fuel mixture drawn into the combustion chambers. A cold powerhead requires a richer fuel mixture to start and during the brief period it is warming to normal operating temperature. A choke valve is placed ahead of the metering jets and venturi. As this valve begins to close, the volume of air intake is reduced, thus enriching the mixture entering the cylinders.

When this choke valve is fully closed, a very rich fuel mixture is drawn into the cylinders.

The throat of the carburetor is usually referred to as the barrel. Carburetors with single, double, or four barrels have individual metering jets, needle valves, throttle and choke plates for each barrel. Single and two barrel carburetors are fed by a single float and chamber.

CARBURETOR CIRCUITS

The following section illustrates the circuit functions and locations of a typical marine carburetor.

Starting Circuit

♦ See Figure 3

The choke plate is closed, creating a partial vacuum in the venturi. As the piston rises, negative pressure in the crankcase draws the rich air-fuel mixture from the float bowl into the venturi and on into the engine.

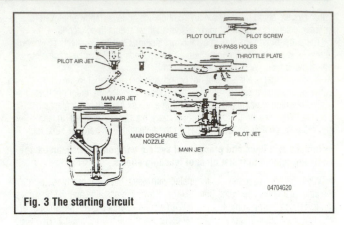

Fig. 3 The starting circuit

Low Speed Circuit

♦ See Figure 4

Zero–one-eighth throttle, when the pressure in the crankcase is lowered, the air-fuel mixture is discharged into the venturi through the pilot outlet because the throttle plate is closed. No other outlets are exposed to low venturi pressure. The fuel is metered by the pilot jet. The air is metered by the pilot air jet. The combined air-fuel mixture is regulated by the pilot air screw.

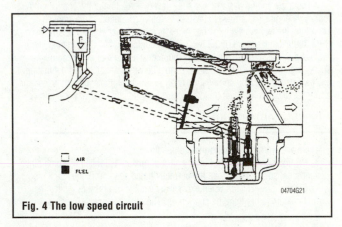

Fig. 4 The low speed circuit

Mid-Range Circuit

♦ See Figure 5

One-eighth–three-eighths throttle, as the throttle plate continues to open, the air-fuel mixture is discharged into the venturi through the bypass holes. As the throttle plate uncovers more bypass holes, increased fuel flow results because of the low pressure in the venturi. Depending on the model, there could be two, three or four bypass holes.

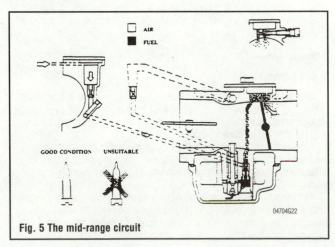

Fig. 5 The mid-range circuit

High Speed Circuit

♦ See Figure 6

Three-eighths–wide-open throttle, as the throttle plate moves toward wide open, we have maximum air flow and very low pressure. The fuel is metered through the main jet, and is drawn into the main discharge nozzle. Air is metered by the main air jet and enters the discharge nozzle, where it combines with fuel. The mixture atomizes, enters the venturi, and is drawn into the engine.

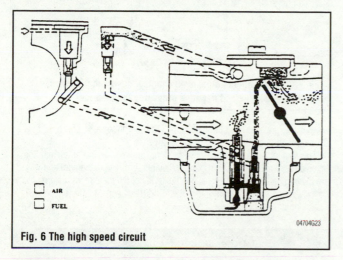

Fig. 6 The high speed circuit

BASIC FUNCTIONS

♦ See Figure 7

The carburetor systems on in line engines require careful cleaning and adjustment if problems occur. These carburetors are complicated but not too complex to understand. All carburetors operate on the same principles.

Traditional carburetor theory often involves a number of laws and principles. To troubleshoot carburetors learn the basic principles, watch how the carburetor comes apart, trace the circuits, see what they do and make sure they are clean. These are the basic steps for troubleshooting and successful repair.

The diagram illustrates several carburetor basics. If you blow through the straw an atomized mixture (air and fuel droplets) comes out. When you blow through the straw a pressure drop is created in the straw column inserted in the liquid. In a carburetor this is mostly air and a little fuel. The actual ratio of air to fuel differs with engine conditions but is usually from 15 parts air to one part fuel at optimum cruise to as little as 7 parts air to one part fuel at full choke.

If the top of the container is covered and sealed around the straw what will happen? No flow. This is typical of a clogged carburetor bowl vent. If the base of the straw is clogged or restricted what will happen? No flow or low flow. This represents a clogged main jet. If the liquid in the glass is lowered and you blow through the straw with the same force what will happen? Not as much fuel will

flow. A lean condition occurs. If the fuel level is raised and you blow again at the same velocity what happens? The result is a richer mixture.

Yamaha carburetors control air flow semi-independently of RPM. This is done with a throttle plate. The throttle plate works in conjunction with other systems or circuits to deliver correct mixtures within certain RPM bands. The idle circuit pilot outlet controls from 0–⅛ throttle. The series of small holes in the carburetor throat called transition holes control the ⅛–⅜ throttle range. At wide open throttle the main jet handles most of the fuel metering chores, but the low and mid-range circuits continue to supply part of the fuel.

Enrichment is necessary to start a cold engine. Fuel and air mix does not want to vaporize in a cold engine. In order to get a little fuel to vaporize, a lot of fuel is dumped into the engine. On many older inline engines a choke plate is used for cold starts. This plate restricts air entering the engine and increases the fuel to air ratio.

The Prime Start enrichment system on the latest engines is controlled by a heated wax pellet. This pellet is heated by current from the stator. Temperature is monitored and enrichment is automatic. Earlier inline engines used choke plates, or electric solenoid enrichment systems.

DUAL-THROAT CARBURETORS

The carburetor systems on V4 and V6 engines require careful cleaning and adjustment if problems occur. These carburetors are not difficult to understand. All carburetors operate on the same principles. For best results, trace and analyze one circuit at a time.

Beginning in 1996, all Saltwater series 90 degree V engines have an additional jet in the carburetor. This pull over or enrichment jet improves mid-range response while maintaining fuel economy. Additional enrichment is necessary to start a cold engine. Fuel/air mixes to not want to vaporize in a cold engine. In order to get a little fuel to vaporize, a lot of fuel is dumped into the engine. On most V4 and V6 engines, a choke plate is used for cold starts. This plate restricts air entering the engine and increases the fuel/air ratio.

The enrichment system on the 90-degree 225 hp engines is controlled by a microprocessor. Temperature and throttle position are monitored and enrichment is automatic. A pair of injectors with different diameters are used to provide enrichment.

REMOVING FUEL FROM THE SYSTEM

♦ See Figures 8 and 9

For many years there has been the widespread belief that simply shutting off the fuel at the tank and then running the engine until it stops is the proper procedure before storing the engine for any length of time. Right? Wrong!

It is not possible to remove all of the fuel in the carburetor by operating the engine until it stops. Some fuel is trapped in the float chamber and other passages and in the line leading to the carburetor. The only guaranteed method of removing ALL of the fuel is to take the time to remove the carburetor, and drain the fuel.

If the engine is operated with the fuel supply shut off until it stops, the fuel and oil mixture inside the engine is removed, leaving bearings, pistons, rings, and other parts with little protective lubricant, during long periods of storage.

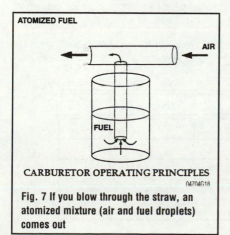

Fig. 7 If you blow through the straw, an atomized mixture (air and fuel droplets) comes out

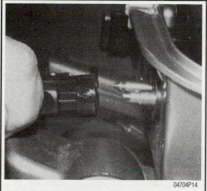

Fig. 8 Typical fuel line quick disconnect fitting

Fig. 9 Fuel shutoff knob on a 4 hp outboard

Proper procedure involves:
1. Shutting off the fuel supply at the tank.
2. Disconnecting the fuel line at the tank.
3. Operating the engine until it begins to run rough, then stopping the engine, which will leave some fuel/oil mixture inside.
4. Removing and draining the carburetor.

By disconnecting the fuel supply, all small passages are cleared of fuel even though some fuel is left in the carburetor. A light oil should be put in the combustion chamber as instructed in the owner's manual. On some model carburetors the high-speed jet plug can be removed to drain the fuel from the carburetor.

For short periods of storage, simply running the carburetor dry may help prevent severe gum and varnish from forming in the carburetor. This is especially true during hot weather.

Fuel Pump

▸ **See Figure 10**

A fuel pump is a basic mechanical device that utilizes crankcase positive and negative pressures to pump fuel from the fuel tank to the carburetors.

This device contains a flexible diaphragm and two check valves (flappers or fingers) that control flow. As the piston goes up, crankcase pressure drops (negative pressure) and the inlet valve opens, pulling fuel from the tank. As the piston nears TDC, pressure in the pump area is neutral (atmospheric pressure). At this point both valves are closed. As the piston comes down, pressure goes

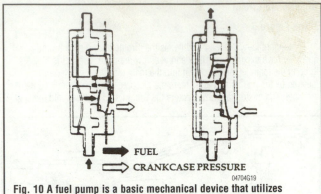

Fig. 10 A fuel pump is a basic mechanical device that utilizes crankcase positive and negative pressures to pump fuel

up (positive pressure) and the fuel is pushed toward the carburetor bowl by the diaphragm through the now open outlet valve.

This is a reliable method to move fuel but can have several problems. Sometimes an engine backfire can rupture the diaphragm. The diaphragm and valves are moving parts subject to wear. The flexibility of the diaphragm material can go away, reducing or stopping flow. Rust or dirt can hang a valve open and reduce or stop fuel flow.

TROUBLESHOOTING

Fuel System

Troubleshooting fuel systems requires the same techniques used in other areas. A thorough, systematic approach to troubleshooting will pay big rewards. Build your troubleshooting checklist, with the most likely offenders at the top. Use your experience to adjust your list for local conditions. Everyone has been tempted to jump into the carburetor on a vague hunch. Pause a moment and review the facts when this urge occurs.

In order to accurately troubleshoot a carburetor or fuel system problem, you must first verify that the problem is fuel related. Many symptoms can have several different possible causes. Be sure to eliminate mechanical and electrical systems as the potential fault. Carburetion is the number one cause of most engine problems, but there are other possibilities.

One of the toughest tasks with a fuel system is the actual troubleshooting. Several tools are at your disposal for making this process very simple. A timing light works well for observing carburetor spray patterns. Look for the proper amount of fuel and for proper atomization in the two fuel outlet areas (main nozzle and bypass holes). The strobe effect of the lights helps you see in detail the fuel being drawn through the throat of the carburetor. On multiple carburetor engines, always attach the timing light to the cylinder you are observing so the strobe doesn't change the appearance of the patterns. If you need to compare two cylinders, change the timing light hookup each time you observe a different cylinder.

Pressure testing fuel pump output can determine whether the fuel spray is adequate and if the fuel pump diaphragms are functioning correctly. A pressure gauge placed between the fuel pumps and the carburetors will test the entire fuel delivery system. Normally a fuel system problem will show up at high speed where the fuel demand is the greatest. A common symptom of a fuel pump output problem is surging at wide open throttle, but normal operation at slower speeds. To check the fuel pump output, install the pressure gauge and

accelerate the engine to wide open throttle. Observe the pressure gauge needle. It should always swing up to some value between 5–6 psi and remain steady. This reading would indicate a system that is functioning properly.

If the needle gradually swings down toward zero, fuel demand is greater than the fuel system can supply. This reading isolates the problem to the fuel delivery system (fuel tank or line). To confirm this, an auxiliary tank should be installed and the engine retested. Be aware that a bad anti-siphon valve on a built-in tank can create enough restriction to cause a lean condition and serious engine damage.

If the needle movement becomes erratic, suspect a ruptured diaphragm in the fuel pump.

A quick way to check for a ruptured fuel pump diaphragm is while the engine is at idle speed, to squeeze the primer bulb and hold steady firm pressure on it. If the diaphragm is ruptured, this will cause a rough running condition because of the extra fuel passing through the diaphragm into the crankcase. After performing this test you should check the spark plugs for cylinders that the fuel pump supplies. If the spark plugs are OK, but the fuel pumps are still suspected, you should remove the fuel pumps and completely disassemble them. Rebuild or replace the pumps as needed.

To check the boat's fuel system for a restriction, install a vacuum gauge in the line before the fuel pump. Run the engine under load at wide open throttle to get a reading. Vacuum should read no more than 4.5 in. Hg (15.2 kPa) for engines up to and including 200 hp, and should not exceed 6.0 in. Hg (20.2 kPa) for engines greater than 200 hp.

To check for air entering the fuel system, install a clear fuel hose between the fuel screen and fuel pump. If air is in the line, check all fittings back to the boat's fuel tank.

Spark plug tip appearance is a good indication of combustion efficiency. The tip should be a light tan. A white insulator or small beads on the insulator indi-

CIRCUIT/POSITION	0	1/8	1/4	3/8	1/2	5/8	3/4	WOT
IDLE								
BYPASS								
MID-RANGE								
MAIN JET								
CHOKE/ENRICHENER								

cate too much heat. A dark or oil fouled insulator indicates incomplete combustion. To properly read spark plug tip appearance, run the engine at the rpm you are testing for about 15 second and then immediately turn the engine OFF without changing the throttle position.

Reading spark plug tip appearance is also the proper way to test jet verifications in high altitude.

The following chart explains the relationship between throttle position and carburetion circuits.

LOGICAL TROUBLESHOOTING

The following paragraphs provide an orderly sequence of tests to pinpoint problems in the fuel system.
1. Gather as much information as you can.
2. Duplicate the condition. Take the boat out and verify the complaint.
3. If the problem cannot be duplicated, you cannot fix it. This could be a product operation problem.
4. Once the problem has been duplicated, you can begin troubleshooting. Give the entire unit a careful visual inspection. You can tell a lot about the engine from the care and condition of the entire rig. What's the condition of the propeller and the lower unit? Remove the hood and look for any visible signs of failure. Are there any signs of head gasket leakage. Is the engine paint discolored from high temperature or are there any holes or cracks in the engine block? Perform a compression and leak down test. While cranking the engine during the compression test, listen for any abnormal sounds. If the engine passes these simple tests we can assume that the mechanical condition of the engine is good. All other engine mechanical inspection would be too time consuming at this point.
5. Your next step is to isolate the fuel system into two sub-systems. Separate the fuel delivery components from the carburetors. To do this, substitute the boat's fuel supply with a known good supply. Use a 6 gallon portable tank and fuel line. Connect the portable fuel supply directly to the engine fuel pump, bypassing the boat fuel delivery system. Now test the engine. If the problem is no longer present, you know where to look. If the problem is still present, further troubleshooting is required.
6. When testing the engine, observe the throttle position when the problem occurs. This will help you pinpoint the circuit that is malfunctioning. Carburetor troubleshooting and repair is very demanding. You must pay close attention to the location, position and sometimes the numbering on each part removed. The ability to identify a circuit by the operating RPM it affects is important. Often your best troubleshooting tool is a can of cleaner. This can be used to trace those mystery circuits and find that last speck of dirt. Be careful and wear safety glasses when using this method.

COMMON PROBLEMS

Fuel Delivery

▶ See Figure 11

Many times fuel system troubles are caused by a plugged fuel filter, a defective fuel pump, or by a leak in the line from the fuel tank to the fuel pump. A defective choke may also cause problems. would you believe, a majority of

Fig. 11 An excellent way of protecting fuel hoses against contamination is an end cap filter

starting troubles which are traced to the fuel system are the result of an empty fuel tank or aged sour fuel.

Sour Fuel

▶ See Figure 12

Under average conditions (temperate climates), fuel will begin to break down in about four months. A gummy substance forms in the bottom of the fuel tank and in other areas. The filter screen between the tank and the carburetor and small passages in the carburetor will become clogged. The gasoline will begin to give off an odor similar to rotten eggs. Such a condition can cause the owner much frustration, time in cleaning components, and the expense of replacement or overhaul parts for the carburetor.

Even with the high price of fuel, removing gasoline that has been standing unused over a long period of time is still the easiest and least expensive preventative maintenance possible. In most cases, this old gas can be used without harmful effects in an automobile using regular gasoline.

The gasoline preservative additive Yamaha Fuel Conditioner and Stabilizer for 2 cycle engines, will keep the fuel fresh for up to twelve months. If this particular product is not available in your area, other similar additives are produced under various trade names.

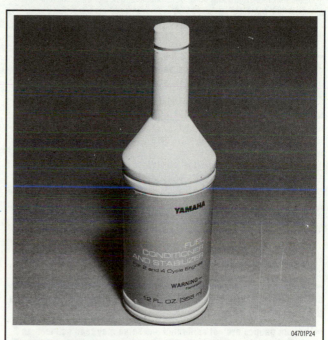

Fig. 12 The use of an approved fuel additive, such as this Yamaha Fuel Conditioner and Stabilizer, will prevent fuel from souring for up to twelve months

Choke Problems

When the engine is hot, the fuel system can cause starting problems. After a hot engine is shut down, the temperature inside the fuel bowl may rise to 200 degrees F and cause the fuel to actually boil. All carburetors are vented to allow this pressure to escape to the atmosphere. However, some of the fuel may percolate over the high-speed nozzle.

If the choke should stick in the open position, the engine will be hard to start. If the choke should stick in the closed position, the engine will flood, making it very difficult to start.

In order for this raw fuel to vaporize enough to burn, considerable air must be added to lean out the mixture. Therefore, the only remedy is to remove the spark plugs, ground the leads, crank the powerhead through about ten revolutions, clean the plugs, reinstall the plugs, and start the engine.

If the needle valve and seat assembly is leaking, an excessive amount of fuel may enter the reed housing in the following manner. After the powerhead is shut down, the pressure left in the fuel line will force fuel past the leaking needle valve. This extra fuel will raise the level in the fuel bowl and cause fuel to overflow into the reed housing.

A continuous overflow of fuel into the reed housing may be due to a sticking inlet needle or to a defective float, which would cause an extra high level of fuel in the bowl and overflow into the reed housing.

Fuel Pump

▶ See Figure 13

Fuel pump testing is an excellent way to pinpoint air leaks, restricted fuel lines and fittings or other fuel supply related performance problems.

When a fuel starvation problem is suspected such as engine hesitation or engine stopping, perform the following fuel system test:

1. Connect the piece of clear fuel hose to a side barb of the "T" fitting O.
2. Connect one end of the long piece of fuel hose to the vacuum gauge and the other end to the center barb of the "T" fitting.

➡**Use a long enough piece of fuel hose so the vacuum gauge may be read at the helm.**

3. Remove the existing fuel hose from the fuel tank side of the fuel pump, and connect the remaining barb of the "T" fitting to the fuel hose.
4. Connect the short piece of clear fuel hose to the fuel check valve leading from the fuel filter. If a check valve does not exist, connect the clear fuel hose directly to the fuel filter.
5. Check the vacuum gauge reading after running the engine long enough to stabilize at full power.

➡**The vacuum is to not exceed 4.5 in. Hg (15.2 kPa) for up to 200 hp engines. The vacuum is to not exceed 6.0 in. Hg (20.3 kPa) for engines greater than 200 hp.**

6. An anti-siphon valve (required if the fuel system drops below the top of the fuel tank) will cause a 1.5 to 2.5 in. Hg (8.4 kPa) increase in vacuum.
7. If high vacuum is noted, move the T-fitting to the fuel filter outlet O and retest.
8. Continue to the fuel filter inlet and along the remaining fuel system until a large drop in vacuum locates the problem.
9. A good clean water separator fuel filter will increase vacuum about 0.5 in. Hg (1.7 kPa).
10. Small internal passages inside a fuel selector valve, fuel tank pickup, or fuel line fittings may cause excessive fuel restriction and high vacuum.
11. Unstable and slowly rising vacuum readings, especially with a full tank of fuel, usually indicates a restricted vent line.

➡**Bubbles in the clear fuel line section indicate an air leak, making for an inaccurate vacuum test. Check all fittings for tightened clamps and a tight fuel filter.**

➡**Vacuum gauges are not calibrated and some may read as much as 2 in. Hg (6.8 kPa) lower than the actual vacuum. It is recommended to perform a fuel system test while no problems exist to determine vacuum gauge accuracy.**

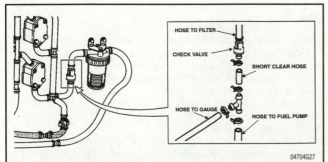

04704G27

Fig. 13 Connecting a fuel pressure gauge inline in preparation for a fuel pump test

Fuel Line

▶ See Figures 14, 15 and 16

On most installations, the fuel line is provided with quick-disconnect fittings at the tank and at the engine. If there is reason to believe the problem is at the quick-disconnects, the hose ends should be replaced as an assembly. For a small additional expense, the entire fuel line can be replaced and thus eliminate this entire area as a problem source for many future seasons.

04704P18

Fig. 14 To test the fuel pickup in the fuel tank, operate the squeeze bulb and observe fuel flowing from the disconnected line at the fuel pump. Discharge fuel into an approved container.

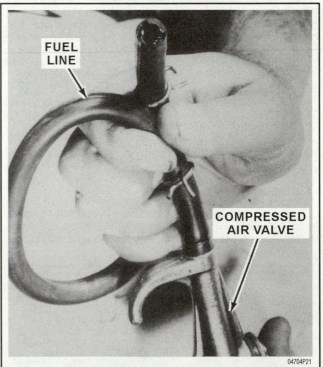

04704P21

Fig. 15 Many times restrictions suck as foreign material may be cleared from the fuel lines using compressed air. Ensure the open end of the hose is pointing in a clear direction to avoid personal injury

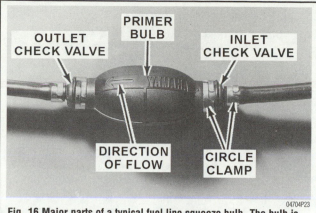

Fig. 16 Major parts of a typical fuel line squeeze bulb. The bulb is used to prime the fuel system until the powerhead is operating and the pump can deliver the required amount of fuel to run the engine

The primer squeeze bulb can be replaced in a short time. First, cut the hose line as close to the old bulb as possible. Slide a small clamp over the end of the fuel line from the tank. Next, install the small end of the check valve assembly into this side of the fuel line. The check valve always goes towards the fuel tank. Place a large clamp over the end of the check valve assembly. Use Primer Bulb Adhesive when the connections are made. Tighten the clamps. Repeat the procedure with the other side of the bulb assembly and the line leading to the engine.

COMMON PROBLEMS

Rough Engine Idle

If an engine does not idle smoothly, the most reasonable approach to the problem is to perform a tune-up to eliminate such areas as:
- Defective points
- Faulty spark plugs
- Timing out of adjustment

Other problems that can prevent an engine from running smoothly include:
- An air leak in the intake manifold
- Uneven compression between the cylinders
- Sticky or broken reeds

Of course any problem in the carburetor affecting the air/fuel mixture will also prevent the engine from operating smoothly at idle speed. These problems usually include:
- Too high a fuel level in the bowl
- A heavy float
- Leaking needle valve and seat
- Defective automatic choke
- Improper adjustments for idle mixture or idle speed

Excessive Fuel Consumption

Excessive fuel consumption can be the result of any one of four conditions, or a combination of all.
- Inefficient engine operation.
- Faulty condition of the hull, including excessive marine growth.
- Poor boating habits of the operator.
- Leaking or out of tune carburetor.

If the fuel consumption suddenly increases over what could be considered normal, then the cause can probably be attributed to the engine or boat and not the operator.

Marine growth on the hull can have a very marked effect on boat performance. This is why sail boats always try to have a haul-out as close to race time as possible.

While you are checking the bottom, take note of the propeller condition. A bent blade or other damage will definitely cause poor boat performance.

If the hull and propeller are in good shape, then check the fuel system for possible leaks. Check the line between the fuel pump and the carburetor while the engine is running and the line between the fuel tank and the pump when the engine is not running. A leak between the tank and the pump many times will not appear when the engine is operating, because the suction created by the pump drawing fuel will not allow the fuel to leak. Once the engine is turned off and the suction no longer exists, fuel may begin to leak.

If a minor tune-up has been performed and the spark plugs, points, and timing are properly adjusted, then the problem most likely is in the carburetor and an overhaul is in order.

Check the needle valve and seat for leaking. Use extra care when making any adjustments affecting the fuel consumption, such as the float level or automatic choke.

Engine Surge

If the engine operates as if the load on the boat is being constantly increased and decreased, even though an attempt is being made to hold a constant engine speed, the problem can most likely be attributed to the fuel pump, or a restriction in the fuel line between the tank and the carburetor.

Combustion Related Piston Failures

When an engine has a piston failure due to abnormal combustion, fixing the mechanical portion of the engine is the easiest part. The hard part is determining what caused the problem, in order to prevent a repeat failure. Think back to the four basic areas that affect combustion to find the cause of the failure.

Since you probably removed the cylinder head. Inspect the failed piston, look for excessive deposit buildup that could raise compression, or retain heat in the combustion chamber. Statically check the wide open throttle timing. Be sure that the timing is not over advanced. It is a good idea to seal these adjustments with paint to detect tampering.

Look for a fuel restriction that could cause the engine to run lean. Don't forget to check the fuel pump, fuel tank and lines, especially if a built in tank is used. Be sure to check the anti-siphon valve on built in tanks.

If everything else looks good, the final possibility is poor quality fuel.

CARBURETOR SERVICE

Carburetor Identification

▶ **See Figure 17**

Several years ago Yamaha changed carburetor vendors from Teikei to Nikki. The service procedures for both manufactured carburetors remain identical, except for the float arrangement. The Teikei carburetor installed on all V4 and V6 models, have a figure 8 shaped float in an elongated float bowl. This carburetor also has a single needle and seat assembly.

After the vendor change, all V4 and V6 models are equipped with Nikki carburetors. This carburetor has two individual float bowls, two floats—one for each bowl—with a separate needle and seat assembly for each float.

The carburetors are easily identified. The shape of the bowl is a dead giveaway. The single float bowl identifies the Teikei and the double float bowl identifies the Nikki.

The float level and pilot screw settings are different for each vendor carburetor.

Carburetor Identification

Identification Stamp	Model	Fuel Pump Type
K	2, 3 hp	Gravity
600	4, 5 hp	Integral Fuel Pump
6G100	6, 8 hp	Integral Fuel Pump
6E772	9.9 hp	Integral Fuel Pump
6E802	15 hp	Integral Fuel Pump
6H770, 6H771	25 hp	Vac. Operated Fuel Pump
68973	30 hp	Vac. Operated Fuel Pump

04704C01

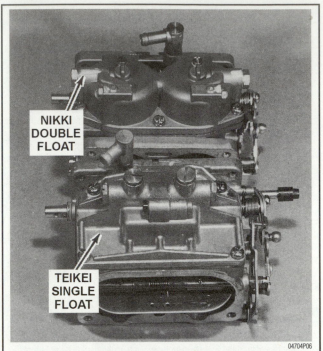

Fig. 17 Identifying characteristics of Nikki or Teikei carburetors. Both carburetors are essentially the same, except for float arrangement

1–2-Cylinder Powerheads

◆ See Figures 18 and 19

2 hp and 3 hp Model

◆ See Figure 20

This carburetor is a single-barrel, float feed type with a manual choke. Fuel to the carburetor is gravity fed from a fuel tank mounted at the rear of the power-head.

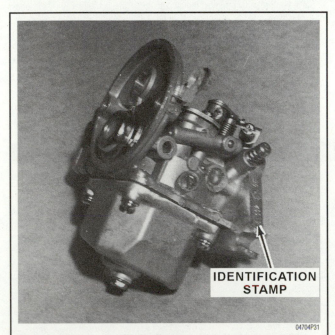

Fig. 18 Carburetor number identification embossed on the carburetor flange—1- and 2-cylinder powerheads

Fig. 19 Carburetor repair kits, available at your local service dealer, contain the necessary components to perform a carburetor overhaul. In most cases, an illustration showing the parts contained in the package is included in the cleaning and inspection portion for each carburetor.

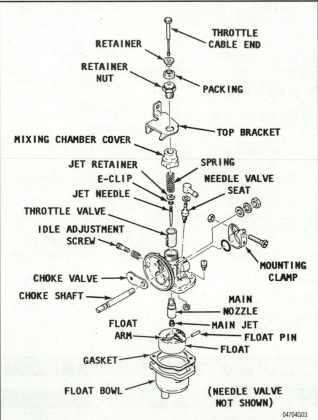

Fig. 20 Exploded view of carburetor with major parts identified—2 hp and 3 hp model

REMOVAL & DISASSEMBLY

◆ See accompanying illustrations

Good shop practice dictates a carburetor repair kit be purchased and new parts be installed any time the carburetor is disassembled.

Make an attempt to keep the work area organized and to cover parts after they have been cleaned. This practice will prevent foreign matter from entering passageways or adhering to critical parts.

1. Remove the screws on one half of the spark plug cover. Remove four more screws securing one-half of the cowling. Separate the cowling half from which the screws were removed. Remove the four screws securing the other half of the cowling and remove it from the engine. The spark plug cover will remain attached to one of the cowling halves.

➡**Observe the different length screws used to secure the cowling halves to the powerhead. Remember their location as an aid during assembling.**

2. Remove the two Philips screws securing the intake silencer and the screw securing the throttle control knob to the throttle lever. Remove the knob.

3. Hold the choke knob with one hand and remove the nut on the back side of the intake silencer with a wrench and the other hand. Slide the lockwasher free of the choke shaft.

4. Pull the choke knob with the choke shaft attached out through the hole in the intake silencer. The choke valve and slotted washer will come out with the shaft. Place these small items in order on the workbench as an aid during installation.

5. Carefully separate the White lead (engine stop button lead), from the quick disconnect fitting anchored to the powerhead. Disconnect the black lead, ground, at the horseshoe bracket. Thread the small screw back into the bracket as a precaution against the screw being lost. Lift the intake silencer free of the engine with the wire leads attached to the stop button.

6. Loosen the bolt on the clamp securing the carburetor to the powerhead.

7. Close the fuel valve. Be prepared to catch a small amount of fuel with a cloth when the fuel line is disconnected. Disconnect the fuel line at the carburetor. Remove the carburetor from the reed valve housing. The clamp will come off with the carburetor.

8. Pry off the circlip, and then remove the pivot pin attaching the throttle control lever to the carburetor. Remove the screw, spring, washer, and nut from the carburetor top bracket.

9. Loosen, but do not remove the top retainer brass nut on the carburetor. Hold the carburetor securely with one hand and unscrew the mixing chamber cover with the other, using a pair of pliers.

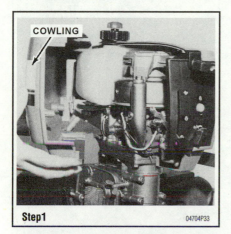

Step 1 04704P33

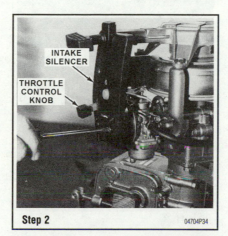

Step 2 04704P34

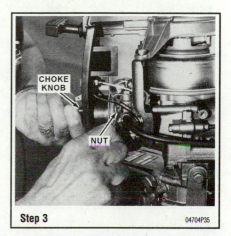

Step 3 04704P35

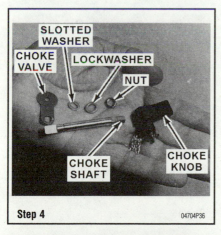

Step 4 04704P36

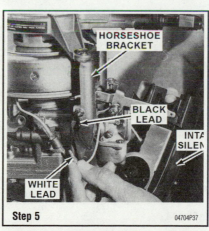

Step 5 04704P37

Step 6 04704P38

Step 7 04704P39

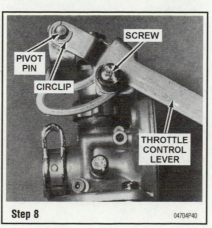

Step 8 04704P40

Step 9 04704P41

10. Lift out the throttle valve assembly.

11. Compress the spring in the throttle valve assembly to allow the throttle cable end to clear the recess in the base of the throttle valve and to slide down the slot.

12. Disassemble the throttle valve consisting of the throttle valve, spring, jet needle (with an E-clip on the second groove), jet retainer, and throttle cable end.

13. Remove and discard the two screws securing the float bowl to the carburetor body. Remove the float bowl. Lift out the float. A new pair of float bowl screws are provided in the carburetor rebuild kit.

14. Push the float pin free using a fine pointed awl.

15. Lift out the float arm and needle valve. Slide the needle valve free of the arm.

16. Unscrew the main jet from the main nozzle. Remove and discard the float bowl gasket.

17. Count and record the number of turns required to lightly seat the idle adjustment screw. The number of turns will give a rough adjustment during installation. Back out the idle speed screw and discard the screw, but save the spring. a new screw is provided in the carburetor rebuild kit to ensure a damaged screw is not used again. this screw is most important for maximum performance.

18. Pry out and discard the carburetor sealing ring.

➡ It is not necessary to remove the E-clip from the jet needle, unless replacement is required or if the powerhead is to be operated at a significantly different elevation.

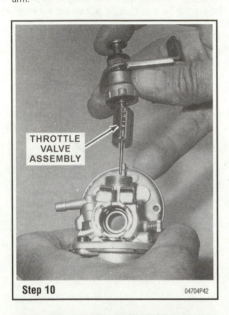

Step 10 04704P42

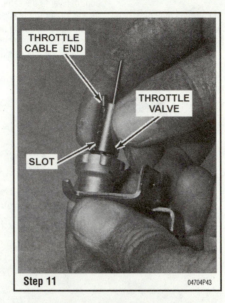

Step 11 04704P43

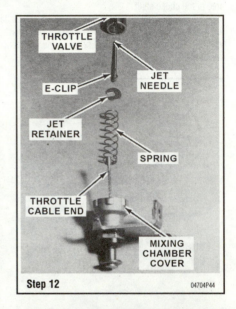

Step 12 04704P44

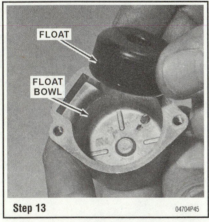

Step 13 04704P45

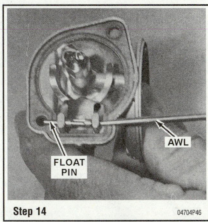

Step 14 04704P46

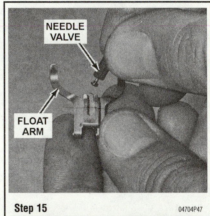

Step 15 04704P47

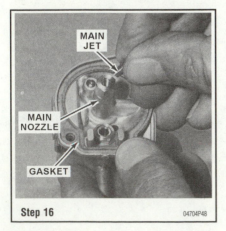

Step 16 04704P48

Step 17 04704P49

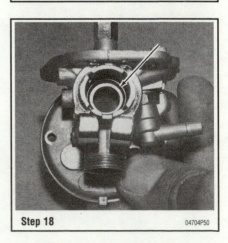

Step 18 04704P50

CLEANING & INSPECTION

♦ **See Figures 21 and 22**

※※ CAUTION

Never dip rubber parts, plastic parts, diaphragms, or pump plungers in carburetor cleaner. These parts should be cleaned only in solvent, and then blown dry with compressed air.

Place all metal parts in a screen-type tray and dip them in carburetor cleaner until they appear completely clean, then blow them dry with compressed air.

Blow out all passages in the castings with compressed air. Check all parts and passages to be sure they are not clogged or contain any deposits. Never use a piece of wire or any type of pointed instrument to clean drilled passages or calibrated holes in a carburetor.

Move the throttle shaft back and forth to check for wear. If the shaft appears to be too loose, replace the complete throttle body because individual replacement parts are not available.

Inspect the main body, airhorn, and venturi cluster gasket surfaces for cracks and burrs which might cause a leak. Check the float for deterioration. Check to be sure the float spring has not been stretched. If any part of the float is damaged, the unit must be replaced. Check the float arm needle contacting surface and replace the float if this surface has a groove worn in it.

Inspect the tapered section of the idle adjusting needles and replace any that have developed a groove.

As previously mentioned, most of the parts which should be replaced during a carburetor overhaul are included in overhaul kits available from your local marine dealer. One of these kits will contain a matched fuel inlet needle and seat. This combination should be replaced each time the carburetor is disassembled as a precaution against leakage.

ASSEMBLY & INSTALLATION

♦ **See accompanying illustrations**

1. Install a new carburetor O-ring into the carburetor body.
2. Apply an all-purpose lubricant to a new idle speed screw. Install the idle speed screw and spring.
3. Install the main jet into the main nozzle and tighten it just snug with a screwdriver.

Fig. 21 Metal parts from our disassembled 2 hp carburetor in a basket ready to be immersed in carburetor cleaner

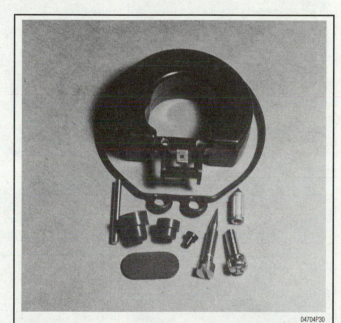

Fig. 22 A carburetor repair kit, like this one for our disassembled carburetor, are available at your local service dealer. They contain the necessary components to perform a carburetor overhaul

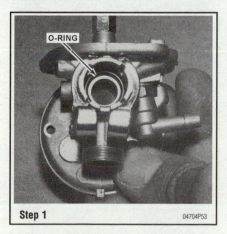

Step 1

Step 2

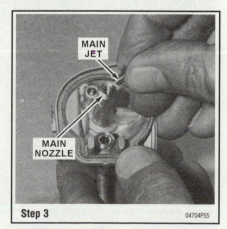

Step 3

4. Slide a new needle valve into the groove of the float arm.

5. Lower the float arm into position with the needle valve sliding into the needle valve seat. Now, push the float pin through the holes in the carburetor body and hinge using a small awl or similar tool.

6. Hold the carburetor body in a perfect upright position. Check the float hinge adjustment. The vertical distance between the top of the hinge and the top of the gasket should be 0.16 in. (4mm). Carefully, bend the hinge, if necessary, to achieve the required measurement.

7. Position a new float bowl gasket in place on the carburetor body. Install the float into the float bowl. Place the float bowl in position on the carburetor body, and then secure it with the two Phillips head screws.

8. If the E-clip on the jet needle is lowered, the carburetor will cause the powerhead to operate rich. Raising the E-clip will cause the powerhead to operate lean. Higher altitude raise E-clip to compensate for rarefied air. Begin to assemble the throttle valve components by inserting the E-clip end of the jet needle into the throttle valve (the end with the recess for the throttle cable end). Next, place the needle retainer into the throttle valve over the E-clip and align the retainer slot with the slot in the throttle valve.

9. Thread the spring over the end of the throttle cable and insert the cable into the retainer end of the throttle valve. Compress the spring and at the same time, guide the cable end through the slot until the end locks into place in the recess.

10. Position the assembled throttle valve in such a manner to permit the slot to slide over the alignment pin while the throttle valve is lowered into the carburetor. This alignment pin permits the throttle valve to only be installed one way in the correct position. Carefully tighten the mixing chamber cover with a pair of pliers.

11. Slide the pivot pin through the top carburetor bracket and then through the upper hole in the throttle control lever. Secure the pin with the circlip. Slide the spring, then the washer over the screw and align the slot in the control lever with the threaded hole in the top carburetor bracket. Install the screw until the lever moves freely with just enough friction to provide the operator with a feel of the throttle opening.

12. Position the carburetor clamp over the carburetor mounting collar, with the locking bolt and nut in place in the clamp. Slide the carburetor into place on the reed valve housing.

Step 4   04704P56

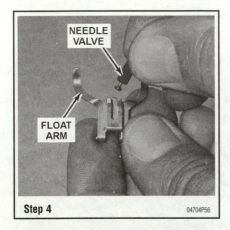

Step 5   04704P57

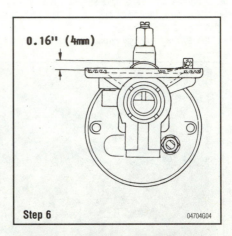

0.16" (4mm)

Step 6   04704G04

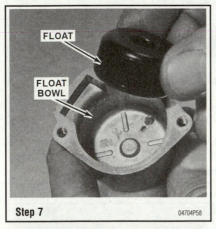

Step 7   04704P58

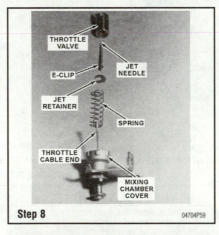

Step 8   04704P59

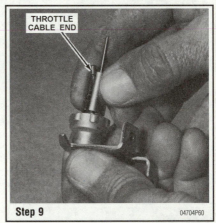

Step 9   04704P60

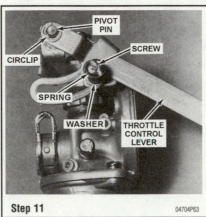

Step 10   04704P61

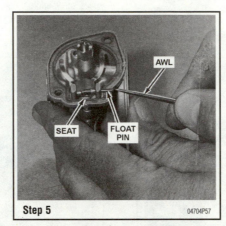

Step 11   04704P63

Step 12   04704P64

13. Secure the carburetor in place by tightening the bolt and nut securely.

14. Hold the intake silencer up to the carburetor. Connect the white lead (engine stop button lead) to the quick disconnect fitting anchored at the top of the powerhead. Attach the black ground lead to the screw on the horseshoe powerhead bracket.

15. Push the choke knob onto the slotted end of the choke shaft. Place the threaded end through the intake silencer and slide the choke valve, followed by the slotted washer, onto the protruding threaded end past the threads onto the slotted part of the shaft. Position the intake silencer up against the carburetor.

16. Hold the choke knob. Slide the lock washer onto the end of the choke shaft, and then thread on the nut.

➡**Starting this nut is not an easy task. Holding the nut with an alligator clip may prove helpful. Tighten the nut just snugly. Connect the fuel hose to the carburetor.**

Install the throttle control knob onto the throttle lever and secure it with the Phillips head screw. Secure the intake silencer to the carburetor with the two Phillips head screws.

Slowly tighten the idle speed screw until it barely seats, then back it out the same number of turns recorded during disassembly. If the number of turns was not recorded, back the screw out 1-¾ turns as a rough adjustment.

17. Install the two halves of the cowling around the powerhead.

18. Secure the cowling with the attaching screws. Eight screws hold the cowling halves in place plus one more for the spark plug cover.

➡**As noted during disassembly, the screws are different lengths. Ensure the proper size are used to the correct location.**

Mount the outboard unit in a test tank, or the boat in a body of water, or connect a flush attachment and hose to the lower unit. Start the engine and check the completed work. Allow the powerhead to warm to normal operating temperature. Adjust the idle speed to specification.

4 hp and 5 hp Models

◆ See Figure 23

This carburetor contains an integral fuel pump.

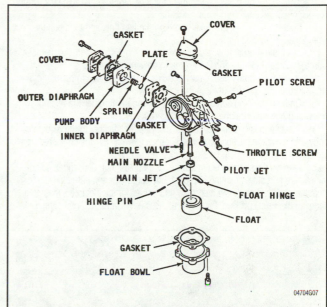

Fig. 23 Exploded view of carburetor with major parts identified—4 hp and 5 hp model

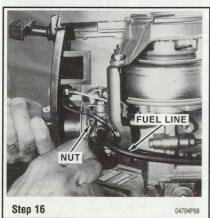

Step 13   04704P65

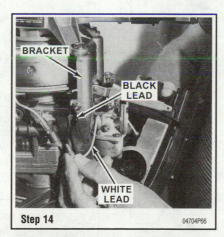

Step 14   04704P66

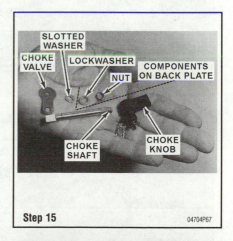

Step 15   04704P67

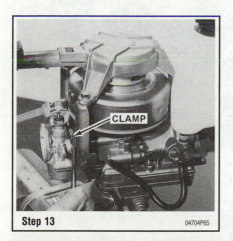

Step 16   04704P68

Step 17   04704P71

Step 18   04704P72

REMOVAL

♦ **See accompanying illustrations**

1. If servicing a 4 hp model, turn off the fuel supply at the base of the fuel tank by turning the fuel knob to the **OFF** position.

If servicing a 5 hp model, disconnect the fuel joint from the fuel tank. Protect the disconnected ends from contamination.

2. Squeeze the wire type hose clamp on the fuel line, and then pull the hose free of the fuel inlet fitting.

If servicing a 4 hp model, plug the fuel line with a screw and slip the hose clamp in place. Tape the line to the tank to prevent loss of fuel.

If servicing a 5 hp model, allow the excess fuel in the line to drain into a cloth, to prevent spilling fuel into the lower cowling.

3. On both the 4 hp and 5 hp models, loosen the throttle wire retaining screw and pull the wire free of the brass barrel.

4. Remove the two Phillips screws securing the silencer to the carburetor body and move the silencer to one side out of the way. Pry the choke rod from the carburetor linkage using a small blade screwdriver.

5. Remove the starboard side carburetor mounting nut. Loosen but do not remove the port side mounting nut. Grasp the carburetor and pull it forward to clear the starboard stud, and then slide it to the left for the slot in the mounting flange to clear the port stud. Remove and discard the carburetor mounting gasket.

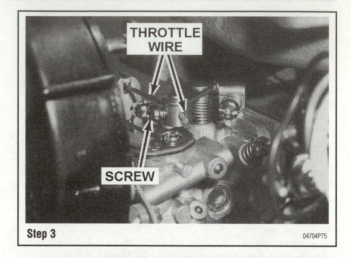

Step 3   04704P75

Step 1   04704P73

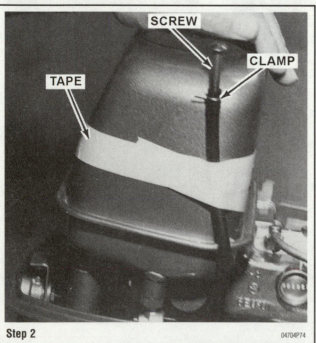

Step 2   04704P74

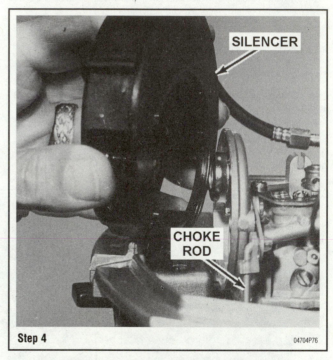

Step 4   04704P76

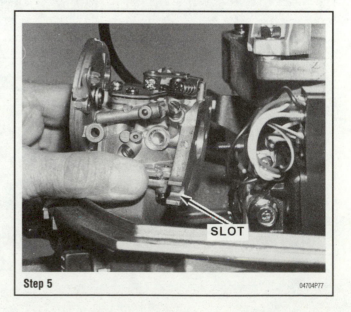

Step 5   04704P77

DISASSEMBLY

♦ **See accompanying illustrations**

1. Remove the four Phillips screws securing the float bowl to the carburetor. Remove the float bowl. Lift off and discard the float bowl gasket.

2. Push out the hinge pin using an awl. Lift out the float. The needle valve will come out with the float.

3. Slide the needle valve free of the slot in the float.

4. Remove the main jet from the turret of the float bowl.

5. Unscrew and remove the main nozzle from deep inside the turret.

6. Remove the three Phillips screws securing the top cover. Remove the top cover and the gasket.

7. Back out the pilot screw and pilot jet. The number of turns need not be recorded because during installation a definite number of turns from the lightly seated position will be listed. Slide the pilot screw spring free.

8. Remove the four Phillips screws securing the fuel pump to the carburetor body.

If the fuel pump gaskets and diaphragms are to be used again, carefully disassemble the fuel pump. Use care during disassembly and note the order of the gaskets and diaphragms. The membranes are fragile and may be easily punctured or stretched. Disassembly involves removing first, the cover, then the outer diaphragm, and finally the cover gasket.

9. Remove the fuel pump body. Take care not to lose the spring and plate as they are held under tension by the pump body. Remove the inner diaphragm, and then the pump body gasket.

CLEANING & INSPECTION

♦ **See Figures 24, 25, 26 and 27**

❋❋ CAUTION

Never dip rubber parts, plastic parts, diaphragms, or pump plungers in carburetor cleaner. These parts should be cleaned only in solvent, and then blown dry with compressed air.

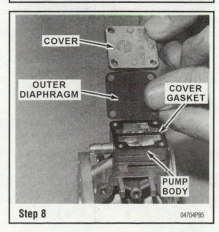

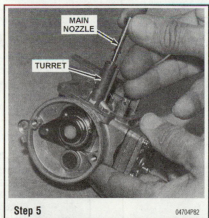

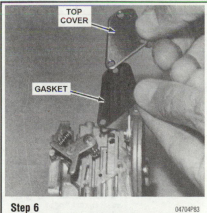

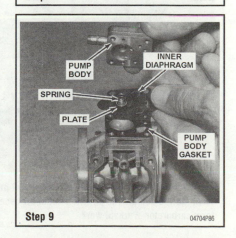

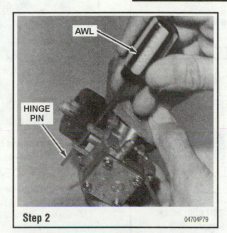

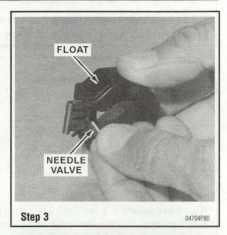

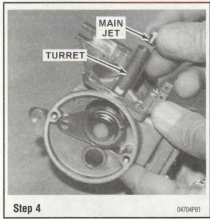

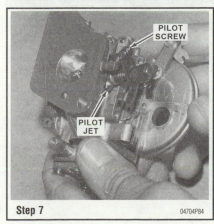

Place all the metal parts in a screen-type tray and dip them in carburetor cleaner until they appear completely clean, free of gum and varnish which accumulates from stale fuel. Blow the parts dry with compressed air.

Blow out all passageways in the castings with compressed air. Check all of the parts and passages to be sure they are not clogged or contain any deposits.

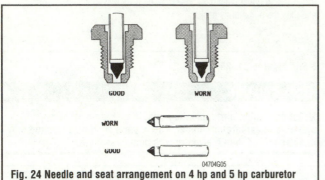

Fig. 24 Needle and seat arrangement on 4 hp and 5 hp carburetor showing worn and new needle for comparison

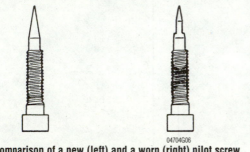

Fig. 25 Comparison of a new (left) and a worn (right) pilot screw. Note the ridge which has developed on the worn screw

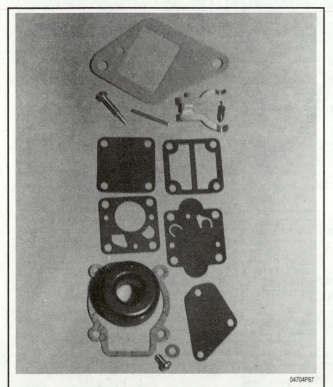

Fig. 26 A carburetor service kit is available at modest cost from the local marine dealer. The kit will contain all necessary parts to perform carburetor overhaul work

Fig. 27 Metal parts from our disassembled 4 hp and 5 hp carburetor in a basket ready to be immersed in carburetor cleaner

Never use a piece of wire or any type of pointed instrument to clean drilled passages or calibrated holes in a carburetor.

Make a thorough inspection of the fuel pump diaphragms for the tiniest pin hole. If one is discovered, the hole will only get bigger. Therefore, the diaphragms must be replaced in order to obtain full performance from the powerhead.

Carefully inspect the casting for cracks, stripped threads, or plugs for any sign of leakage. Inspect the float hinge in the hinge pin area for wear and the float for any sign of leakage.

Examine the inlet needle for wear and if there is any evidence of wear, the inlet needle must be replaced.

Always replace any and all worn parts.

ASSEMBLY & INSTALLATION

▶ **See accompanying illustrations**

1. Position first, the pump body gasket, then the inner diaphragm, next the plate, then the spring onto the carburetor body in the order given. The plate and

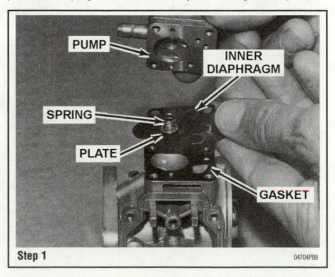

Step 1

spring must index with the round hole on the underside of the pump body. When the pump body is placed over the spring, ensure all the parts are aligned and the spring seats in an upright position between the plate and the pump body. Hold it all together for the next step.

2. Place the cover gasket, the outer diaphragm and the cover over the pump body. Visually check to be sure the holes are aligned before threading the screws through the many layers of fuel pump parts. If the screws are forced through, one of the fragile parts may be damaged. Secure the parts together with the four attaching screws.

3. Install the pilot jet snugly. Install the pilot screw and spring. Slowly

rotate the pilot screw into the carburetor body until it barely seats. From this position, back it out the appropriate number of turns. Fine idle adjustment will be made later using the throttle stop screw.

4. Install the gasket and top carburetor cover.
5. Thread the main nozzle into the float bowl turret and tighten it just snug.
6. Install the main jet over the main nozzle and tighten it snugly.
7. Slide the needle valve into the slot of the float.
8. Lower the float and needle valve assembly over the turret, engaging the needle valve into the needle seat. Position the float hinge between the mounting posts and install the hinge pin securing the float in place.

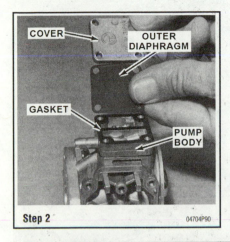

Step 2   04704P90

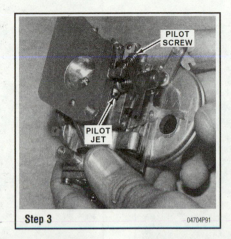

Step 3   04704P91

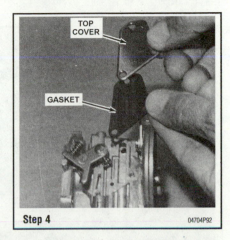

Step 4   04704P92

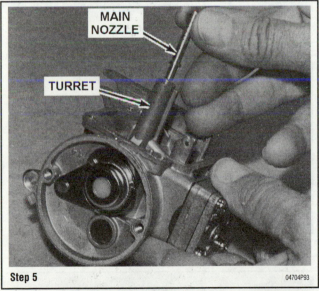

Step 5   04704P93

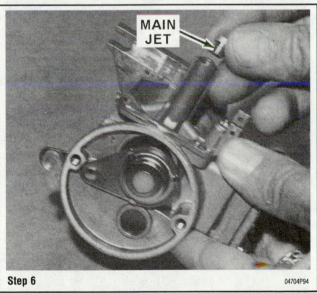

Step 6   04704P94

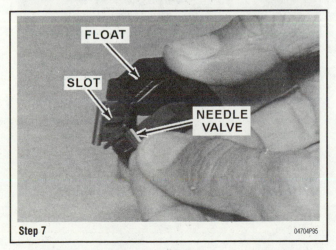

Step 7   04704P95

Step 8   04704P96

9. Hold the carburetor inverted, as shown. Measure the distance between the carburetor body to the top of the float. This distance should be 0.85–0.89 in. (21.5–22.5mm). This dimension, with the carburetor inverted, places the lower surface of the float parallel to the carburetor body. If necessary, carefully bend the tab on the float to obtain the correct measurement. Install the float bowl to the carburetor body and secure it with the four Phillips screws.

10. Install the carburetor mounting gasket. Slide the port side slotted end of the carburetor mounting flange onto the stud first. The nut and washer should not have been removed during disassembly. Move the starboard side of the carburetor mounting flange onto the left stud. Install the left nut and washer, and then tighten both nuts to 5.8 ft. lbs. (8Nm).

11. Snap the choke link into place. Connect the fuel line to the fuel pump inlet fitting. Install the silencer to the carburetor body and secure it in place with the two Phillips screws.

12. Thread the throttle wire through the holder first, and then through the brass barrel. Tighten the screw to retain the wire. The wire should project out from the barrel approximately 0.12–0.16 in. (3–4mm).

13. If servicing a 4 hp model, open the fuel valve at the base of the tank by turning the fuel knob to the **ON** position.

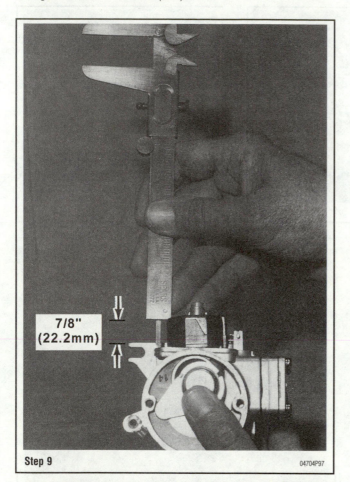

7/8" (22.2mm)

Step 9 04704P97

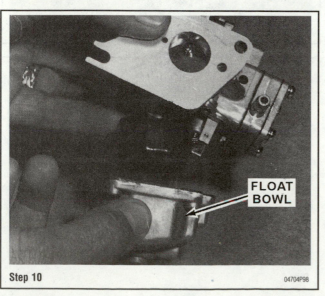

FLOAT BOWL

Step 10 04704P98

SILENCER

CHOKE LINK

Step 11 04704P00

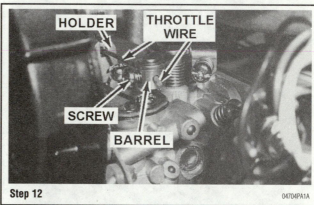

HOLDER

THROTTLE WIRE

SCREW

BARREL

Step 12 04704PA1A

FUEL KNOB

Step 13 04704PA1B

Step 14   04704PA2

If servicing a 5 hp model, connect the fuel line from the tank to the carburetor at the fuel joint.

14. Mount the outboard unit in a test tank, on the boat in a body of water, or connect a flush attachment and hose to the lower unit. Connect a tachometer to the powerhead. Start the engine and check the completed work. Allow the powerhead to warm to normal operating temperature. Adjust the throttle stop screw until the powerhead idles at specification.

6 hp, 8 hp, 9.9 hp and 15 hp Models

▶ See Figure 28

This carburetor contains an integral fuel pump.

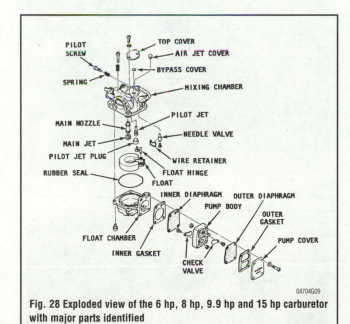

Fig. 28 Exploded view of the 6 hp, 8 hp, 9.9 hp and 15 hp carburetor with major parts identified

REMOVAL

▶ See accompanying illustrations

1. Disconnect the fuel hose at the fuel joint. Protect the ends from contamination. Disconnect the fuel line at the fuel pump inlet fitting.
2. On 6 hp and 8 hp model only, pry the small choke link from the plastic fitting on the carburetor using a small slotted screwdriver.
3. Remove the three Phillips screws retaining the front panel to the lower cowling. The panel must be removed to gain access to the carburetor.

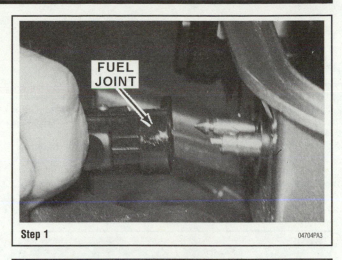

Step 1   04704PA3

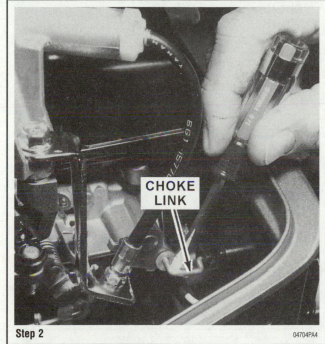

Step 2   04704PA4

Step 3   04704PA5

4. Pull the panel forward and set it to one side out of the way. It is not necessary to disconnect the kill switch harness or the fuel connection.

5. On 6 hp and 8 hp model only, pry the throttle link from the starboard side of the carburetor with a small slotted screwdriver. On the 9.9 and 15 hp units a throttle roller moving on the throttle cam is used instead of the throttle link. The roller arrangement cannot be disconnected from the carburetor.

6. It should be noted that the 9.9 hp and 15 hp carburetor has a different silencer and choke setup than the other units.

7. It should also be noted that the 9.9 hp and 15 hp carburetor has a unique linkage arrangement.

8. Reach through the opening of the front panel and remove the two long bolts which secure both the silencer and the carburetor to the powerhead. Remove the silencer. On the 9.9 and the 15 hp model the choke rod will slide out of the choke lever and the choke roller will slide out of the choke shaft cradle. Remove the carburetor. Remove and discard the carburetor mounting gasket.

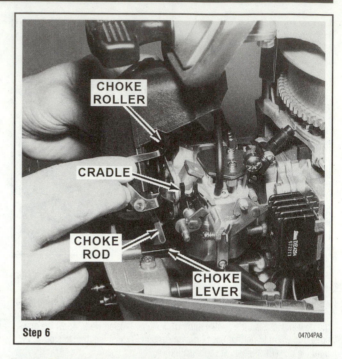

Step 6   04704PA8

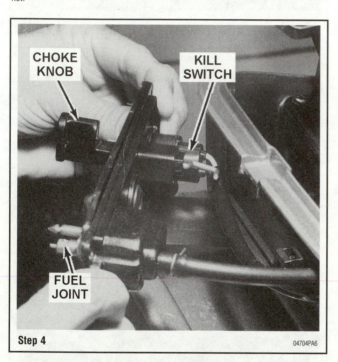

Step 4   04704PA6

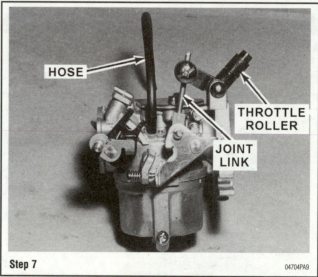

Step 7   04704PA9

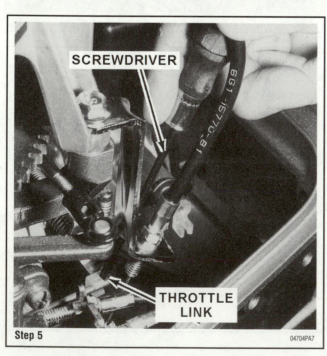

Step 5   04704PA7

Step 8   04704PA0

DISASSEMBLY

♦ See accompanying illustrations

1. Remove the pilot screw and spring. The number of turns out from a lightly seated position will be given during assembling.

Remove the two screws securing the top cover and lift off the cover. Gently pry the two rubber plugs out with an awl. Remove the oval air jet cover and the round bypass cover.

2. Remove the four screws securing the fuel pump to the carburetor body. Disassemble the pump cover, the outer gasket, the outer diaphragm, the pump body, the inner diaphragm, and finally the inner gasket in that specific order.

3. Remove the screws from both sides of the fuel pump body. Remove the check valves.

4. Remove the four screws securing the float bowl cover in place. Lift off the float bowl. Remove and discard the rubber sealing ring.

5. Remove the small Phillips screw securing the float hinge to the mounting posts. Lift out the float, the hinge pin and the needle valve. Slide the hinge pin free of the float.

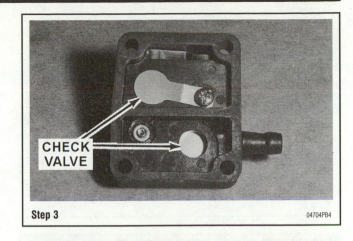

Step 3

Step 1

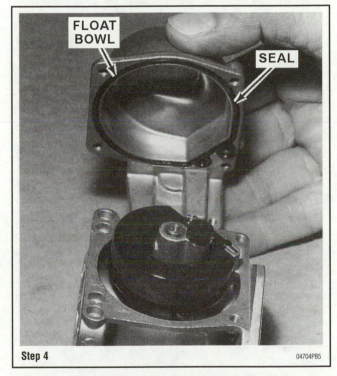

Step 4

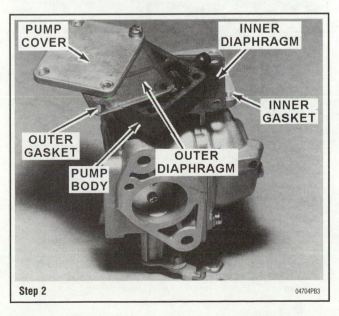

Step 2

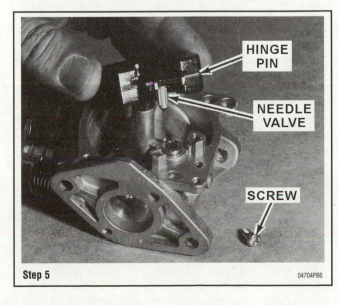

Step 5

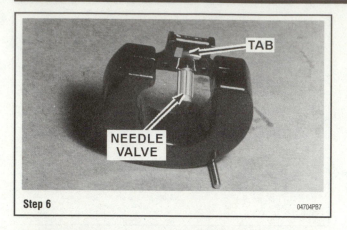

Step 6   04704PB7

use a piece of wire or any type of pointed instrument to clean drilled passages or calibrated holes in a carburetor.

Move the throttle shaft back and forth to check for wear. If the shaft appears to be too loose, replace the complete throttle body because individual replacement parts are not available.

Inspect the main body, airhorn, and venturi cluster gasket surfaces for cracks and burrs which might cause a leak. Check the float for deterioration. Check to be sure the float spring has not been stretched. If any part of the float is damaged, the unit must be replaced. Check the float arm needle contacting surface and replace the float if this surface has a groove worn in it.

Inspect the tapered section of the idle adjusting needles and replace any that have developed a groove.

As previously mentioned, most of the parts which should be replaced during a carburetor overhaul are included in overhaul kits available from your local marine dealer. One of these kits will contain a matched fuel inlet needle and seat. This combination should be replaced each time the carburetor is disassembled as a precaution against leakage.

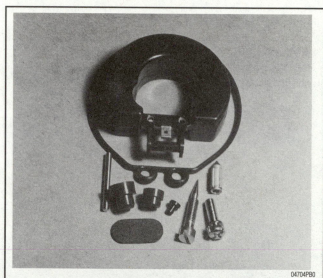

Fig. 29 Good shop practice dictates a carburetor rebuild kit be purchased and new parts, especially gaskets and O-rings be installed any time the carburetor is disassembled. This photo includes parts in a repair kit for the 6 hp, 8 hp, 9.9 hp and 15 hp carburetor

Step 7   04704PB8

6. Slide the wire attaching the needle valve to the float free of the tab.

7. Use the proper size slotted screwdriver and remove the main jet, then unscrew the main nozzle from beneath the main jet. Remove the plug, and then unscrew the pilot jet located beneath the plug.

CLEANING & INSPECTION

▸ **See Figures 24, 25, 29 and 30**

Inspect the check valves in the fuel pump for varnish build up as well as any deformity.

Never dip rubber parts, plastic parts, diaphragms, or pump plungers in carburetor cleaner. These parts should be cleaned only in solvent, and then blown dry with compressed air.

Place all metal parts in a screen-type tray and dip them in carburetor cleaner until they appear completely clean, then blow them dry with compressed air.

Blow out all passages in the castings with compressed air. Check all parts and passages to be sure they are not clogged or contain any deposits. Never

Fig. 30 Remove all rubber and plastic parts before immersing metal parts of the 6 hp, 8 hp, 9.9 hp and 15 hp carburetor in cleaning solution

ASSEMBLY

▶ **See accompanying illustrations**

1. Install the main nozzle into the center hole and tighten it snugly. Install the main jet on top of the nozzle and tighten it snugly also. Install the pilot jet into the center hole and then the plug. Tighten the jet and the plug securely.

2. For the 6 hp and 8 hp units, slide the wire attached to the needle valve onto the float tab. For the 9.9 hp and 15 hp units, insert the needle valve into the needle seat.

3. For the 6 hp and 8 hp units, slide the hinge pin through the float hinge. Lower the float and needle assembly down into the float chamber and guide the needle valve into the needle seat. Check to be sure the hinge pin indexes into the mounting posts. Secure the pin in place with the small Phillips screw.

For the 9.9 hp and 15 hp units, place the float hinge arm between the mounting posts and secure the arm in place with the hinge pin.

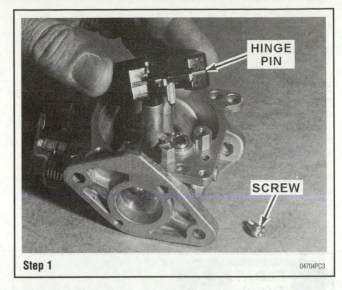

Step 1   04704PC3

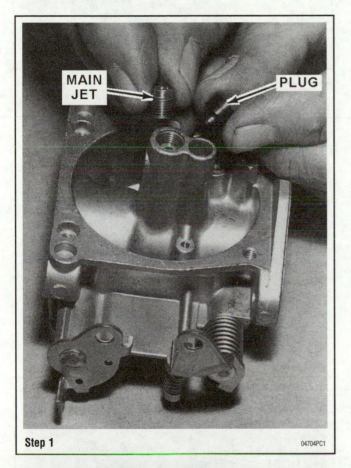

Step 1   04704PC1

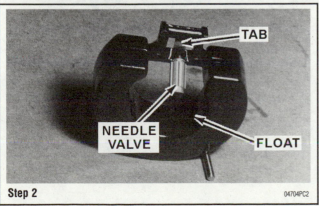

Step 2   04704PC2

FLOAT ADJUSTMENT

▶ **See accompanying illustrations**

1. For the 6 hp and 8 hp units, invert the carburetor and allow the float to rest on the needle valve. Measure the distance between the top of the float and the mixing chamber housing. This distance should be 0.47–0.63 in. (12–16mm). This dimension, with the carburetor inverted, places the lower surface of the float parallel to the carburetor body. If the dimension is not within the limits listed, the needle valve must be replaced.

For the 9.9 hp and 15 hp units, invert the carburetor and install the float bowl gasket. Measure the distance from top surface of the gasket to the top of the hinge, as shown in the accompanying illustration. The measurement should be 0.06–0.10 in. (1.5–2.5mm). carefully bend the float arm, as required, to obtain a satisfactory measurement. Install the float.

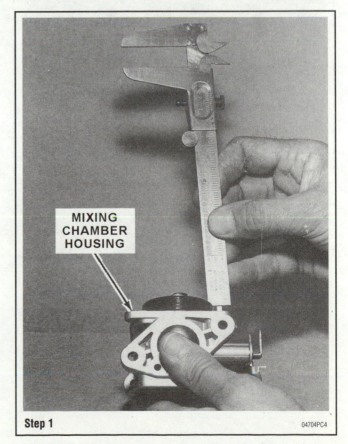

Step 1   04704PC4

2. Insert the rubber sealing ring into the groove in the float bowl. Install the float bowl and secure it in place with the four Phillips screws.

3. Place the check valves, one at a time, in position on both sides of the fuel pump body. Secure each valve with the attaching screw.

4. Assemble the fuel pump components onto the carburetor body in the following order, the inner gasket, the inner diaphragm, the pump body, the outer diaphragm, the outer gasket, and finally the pump cover. Check to be sure all the parts are properly aligned with the mounting holes. Secure it all in place with the four attaching screws.

Install the oval air jet cover and the round bypass cover in their proper recesses. Place the top cover over them, no gasket is used. Install and tighten the two attaching screws.

5. Slide the spring over the pilot screw, and then install the screw. Tighten the screw until it barely seats. For the 6 hp and 8 hp powerheads, back the pilot screw out 1-⅛. For the 9.9 hp and 15 hp powerheads, back the screw out 1-⅜ turns.

6. Prior to installation the hose and joint link are connected on the 9.9 hp and 15 hp carburetors.

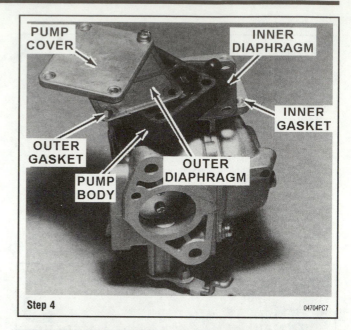

Step 4   04704PC7

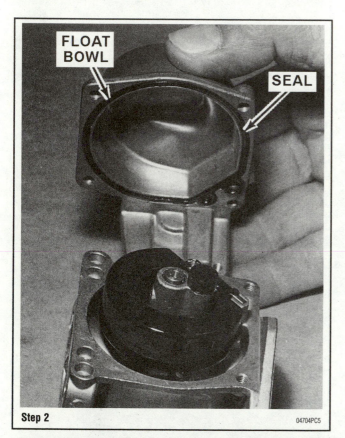

Step 2   04704PC5

Step 5   04704PC9

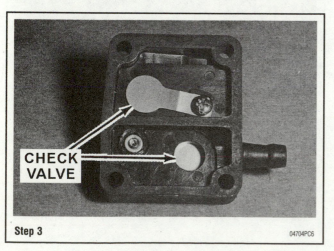

Step 3   04704PC6

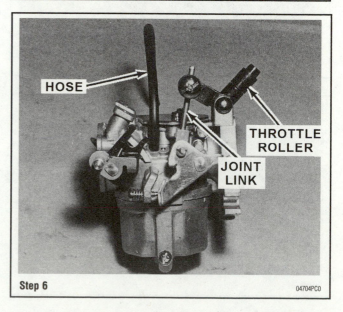

Step 6   04704PC0

INSTALLATION

▶ **See accompanying illustrations**

1. Place a new carburetor mounting gasket onto the two pins on the intake manifold.

For the 6 hp and 8 hp units, align the carburetor and the silencer with the two mounting holes. Start the bolts, and then tighten them, through the opening in the front panel, to a torque value of 5.8 ft. lbs. (8Nm).

For the 9.9 hp and 15 hp units, move the carburetor into place. Guide the choke rod through the slot in the choke lever and at the same time guide the throttle roller into the throttle shaft cradle. Start the mounting nuts, and then tighten them, through the opening in the front panel, to a torque value of 5.8 ft. lbs. (8Nm).

2. For the 6 hp and 8 hp units, snap the throttle link into the plastic fitting on the starboard side of the carburetor.

3. Install the front panel and secure it in place with the three Phillips screws.

4. Snap the small choke link into the plastic fitting on the starboard side of the carburetor. Check the action of the choke knob to be sure there is no evidence of binding.

5. Connect the fuel line to the fuel pump. Connect the fuel line from the tank with the fuel joint.

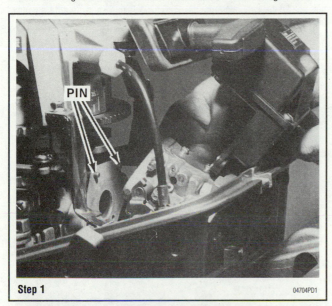

Step 1   04704PD1

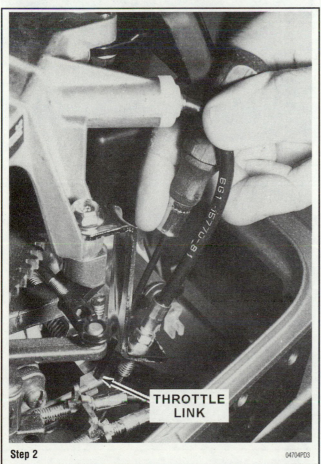

Step 2   04704PD3

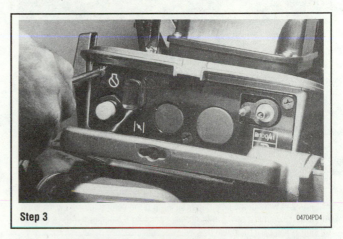

Step 3   04704PD4

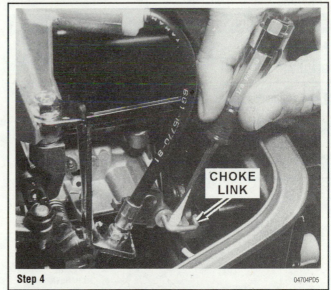

Step 4   04704PD5

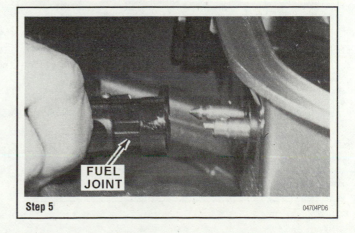

Step 5   04704PD6

Step 6   04704PD7

6. Mount the outboard unit in a test tank, on the boat in a body of water, or connect a flush attachment and hose to the lower unit. Connect a tachometer to the powerhead.

Start the engine and check the completed work. Remember, the powerhead will not start without the emergency tether in place behind the kill switch knob. Allow the powerhead to warm to normal operating temperature. Adjust the throttle stop screw until the powerhead idles at specification.

25 hp and 30 hp Models

▶ See Figure 31

REMOVAL

▶ See accompanying illustrations

1. Remove the powerhead cowling. Remove the three Phillips head screws securing the silencer cover to the carburetor.

On models equipped with a manual choke, snap the choke link from the plastic fitting at the carburetor.

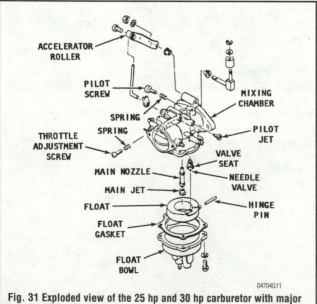

04704G11

Fig. 31 Exploded view of the 25 hp and 30 hp carburetor with major parts identified

On models equipped with an electric choke solenoid, disconnect the solenoid lead at the quick disconnect fitting directly beneath the carburetor. Disconnect the ground lead at the screw on the crankcase. Remove the tiny metal ring from the choke solenoid link. This ring passes through a hole in the link and acts as a retaining ring. Therefore, take care not to lose the ring.

Remove the link. Remove the two screws securing the solenoid to the mounting bracket and remove the choke solenoid. Loosen the screw at the barrel retaining the joint rod connecting the throttle arm to the accelerator arm. Pull the rod free of the barrel.

2. Squeeze the wire type fuel hose clamp and move it back on the fuel line. Work the fuel line free of the inlet fitting. Remove the two carburetor mounting nuts and lift the carburetor from the powerhead. Remove and discard the mounting gasket.

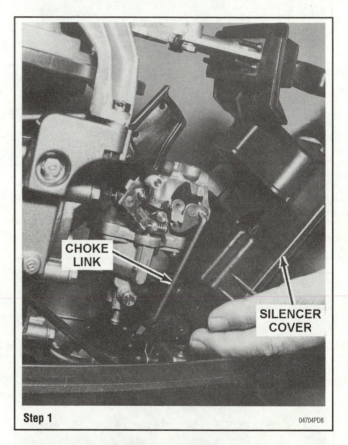

Step 1   04704PD8

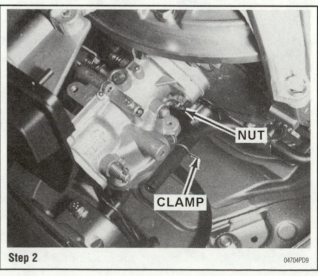

Step 2   04704PD9

DISASSEMBLY

♦ **See accompanying illustrations**

1. Remove the nut and washer from the long bolt. Slide the bolt and throttle cam free of the carburetor.

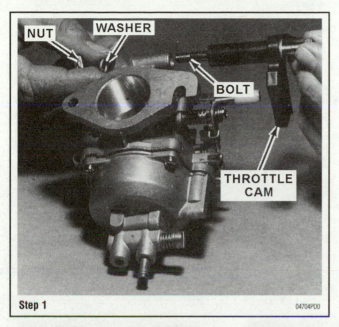

Step 1   04704PD0

2. Remove the pilot screw and spring. Inspect the tapered end. Usually this part is supplied in the rebuild kit for this carburetor. The screw must be replaced if any ridges appear on the tapered end.

3. Remove the pilot jet on the opposite side of the carburetor.

➡**Perform the next two steps only if the throttle shaft or throttle plate is worn, bent, or damaged. Installing the two screws onto the throttle plate is not an easy task. If the accelerator roller is the only defective part, perform only the first part of the next step.**

4. To remove the accelerator roller, first remove the screw next to the roller and the bracket will come free of the carburetor. Next, remove the circlip from the end of the arm and roller will slide free.

To remove the throttle plate, using a very small Phillips screwdriver, remove the two small screws securing the throttle plate to the throttle shaft. Take care not to strip the heads and do not lose the screws. Jar the plate free of the carburetor throat. Pry the E-clip from the end of the throttle shaft.

5. Pull out the throttle shaft. Notice how one end of the return spring hooks around the bracket and the other end hooks around a post. Count the number of turns the spring unwinds when it is unhooked.

➡**Perform the next step only if the choke shaft or the choke plate is worn or bent or if the flapper valve or its return spring is defective. To assemble these parts is not an easy task.**

6. Using a very small Phillips screwdriver, remove the two screws securing the choke plate to the choke shaft. Count the number of turns the return spring is wound. Drive out the rolled pin from the choke shaft. Slide the spring free of the rolled pin. Pull out the choke shaft and unhook the other end of the return spring from the post on the carburetor.

7. Remove the drain valve and spring from the base of the float bowl.

Step 2   04704PE1

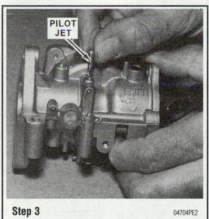

Step 3   04704PE2

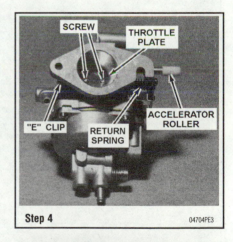

Step 4   04704PE3

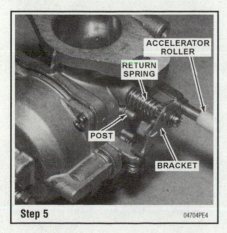

Step 5   04704PE4

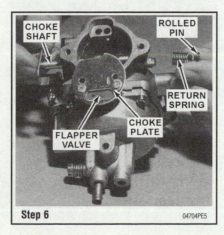

Step 6   04704PE5

Step 7   04704PE6

8. Remove the four Phillips head screws securing the fuel bowl to the mixing chamber.

9. Lift the fuel bowl from the mixing chamber. Remove and discard the gasket.

10. Push the pin free of the mounting posts using a long pointed awl. The pin must be pushed out in the direction of the arrow embossed on one of the mounting posts. Once the end of the pin clears the float hinge, the float may be lifted free, leaving the pin still in the other mounting post.

11. Lift out the needle valve from the needle seat. Take care not to damage the pointed end of the valve.

12. Using the proper size socket, remove the needle seat. Remove and discard the gasket.

13. Remove the main jet, and then the main nozzle from the center of the mixing chamber.

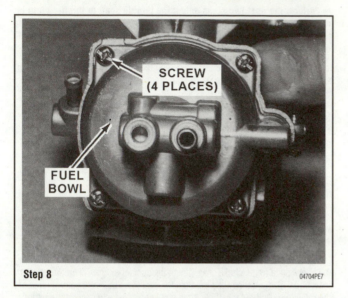

Step 8
04704PE7

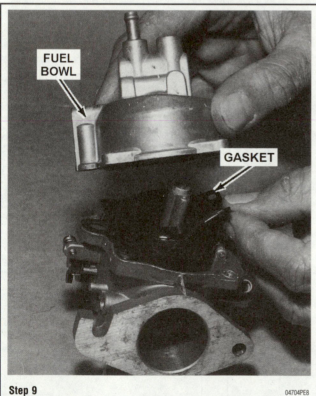

Step 9
04704PE8

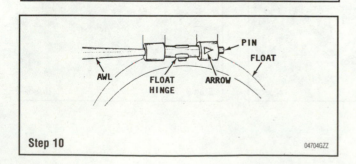

Step 10
04704GZZ

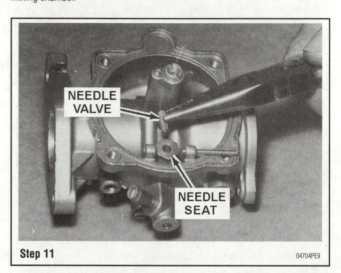

Step 11
04704PE9

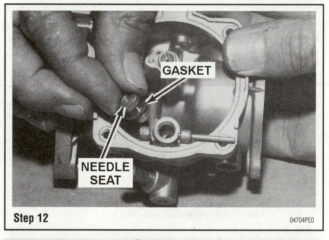

Step 12
04704PE0

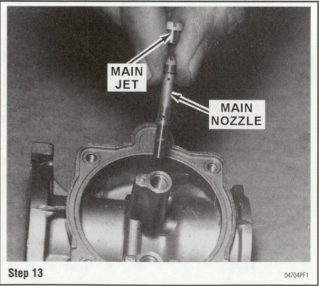

Step 13
04704PF1

CLEANING & INSPECTION

♦ See Figures 32, 33 and 34

✳✳ CAUTION

Never dip rubber parts, plastic parts, diaphragms, or pump plungers in carburetor cleaner. These parts should be cleaned only in solvent, and then blown dry with compressed air.

Place all metal parts in a screen-type tray and dip them in carburetor cleaner until they appear completely clean, then blow them dry with compressed air.

Blow out all passages in the castings with compressed air. Check all parts and passages to be sure they are not clogged or contain any deposits. Never use a piece of wire or any type of pointed instrument to clean drilled passages or calibrated holes in a carburetor.

Move the throttle shaft back and forth to check for wear. If the shaft appears to be too loose, replace the complete throttle body because individual replacement parts are not available.

Inspect the main body, airhorn, and venturi cluster gasket surfaces for cracks and burrs which might cause a leak. Check the float for deterioration. Check to be sure the float spring has not been stretched. If any part of the float is damaged, the unit must be replaced. Check the float arm needle contacting surface and replace the float if this surface has a groove worn in it.

Inspect the tapered section of the idle adjusting needles and replace any that have developed a groove.

Fig. 32 The mixing chamber of the 25 hp and 30 hp carburetor must not be immersed in cleaning solution. The chamber contains plastic bushings around the throttle shaft. These bushings are pressed into place and are not normally removed

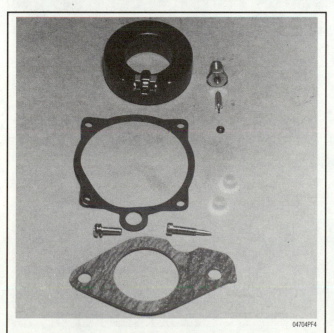

Fig. 33 Typical carburetor overhaul kit

Fig. 34 Good shop practice dictates a carburetor rebuild kit be purchased and new parts, especially gaskets and O-rings be installed any time the carburetor is disassembled. This photo includes parts in a repair kit for the 25 hp and 30 hp carburetor

As previously mentioned, most of the parts which should be replaced during a carburetor overhaul are included in overhaul kits available from your local marine dealer. One of these kits will contain a matched fuel inlet needle and seat. This combination should be replaced each time the carburetor is disassembled as a precaution against leakage.

ASSEMBLY

♦ See accompanying illustrations

1. Insert the main nozzle into the center of the mixing chamber and tighten the nozzle snugly using a slotted screwdriver. Install the main jet over the nozzle and tighten the jet snugly.

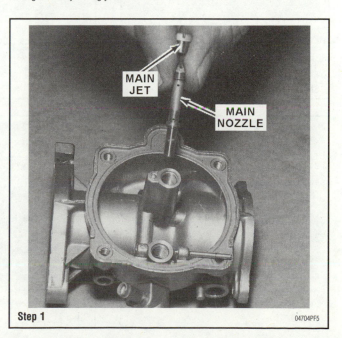

Step 1

2. Slide a new gasket onto the shaft of the needle seat. Install and tighten the needle seat just snug, using the proper size socket.

3. Insert the needle valve into the needle seat. Position the float between the two mounting posts. Push the hinge pin through the posts and hinge until the end of the pin is flush with the outer edge of the mounting post.

4. Invert (turn upside down) the carburetor. Now, rotate the carburetor until the axis of the float is about a 60,dg angle with vertical, as indicated in the accompanying illustration. With the carburetor in this position, measure the distance from the top edge of the mixing chamber to the top of the float. This distance should be 0.69–0.73 in. (17.5–18.5mm).

5. If the measurement is not within these limits, carefully bend the tang to obtain a satisfactory measurement.

6. Position a new float bowl gasket in place on the mating surface of the carburetor. Install the float bowl and secure it with the four Phillips head screws.

7. Install the pilot jet. Tighten the jet until it seats snugly.

8. Slide the spring onto the drain valve shaft. Install the valve and spring into the base of the fuel bowl.

9. Insert the choke shaft through the carburetor. Rotate the shaft to permit the flattened surface of the shaft to face upward in the carburetor throat. Lower the choke plate into the throat, aligning the notch with the air jet housing. Secure the plate to the shaft with the two small Phillips head screws. This is not an easy task. A magnetic screwdriver may prove very helpful in starting the screws in their holes.

Slide the return spring onto the choke shaft and hook the end onto the post on the carburetor. Wind the spring the same number of turns as recorded during disassembly. Hold tension on the spring and at the same time insert the roll pin. Test the return action of the plate when the choke shaft is rotated and then released. Adjust the tension on the spring if necessary to obtain a smooth and complete return of the plate when the shaft is released.

10. Slide the return spring onto the throttle shaft and hook one end onto the bracket. Wind the spring the same number of turns recorded during disassembly. Insert the shaft through the carburetor and hook the tensioned end of the spring onto the post on the carburetor body. Test the return action of the plate when the throttle shaft is rotated and then released. Adjust the tension on the

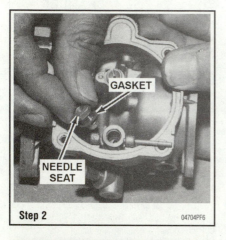

Step 2   04704PF6

GASKET

NEEDLE SEAT

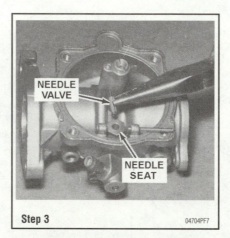

Step 3   04704PF7

NEEDLE VALVE

NEEDLE SEAT

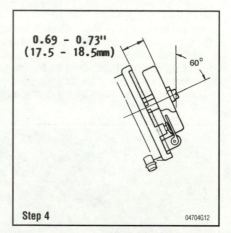

Step 4   04704G12

0.69 – 0.73"
(17.5 – 18.5mm)

60°

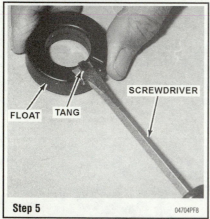

Step 5   04704PF8

SCREWDRIVER

FLOAT   TANG

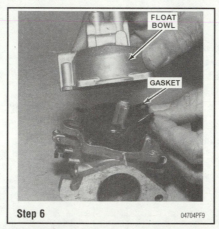

Step 6   04704PF9

FLOAT BOWL

GASKET

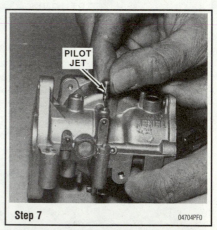

Step 7   04704PF0

PILOT JET

Step 8   04704PG1

FUEL BOWL

DRAIN VALVE

SPRING

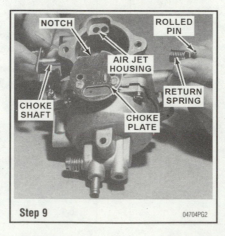

Step 9   04704PG2

NOTCH

ROLLED PIN

AIR JET HOUSING

RETURN SPRING

CHOKE SHAFT

CHOKE PLATE

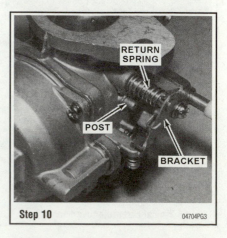

Step 10   04704PG3

RETURN SPRING

POST

BRACKET

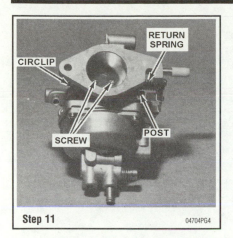

Step 11   04704PG4

Step 12   04704PG5

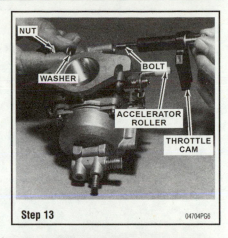

Step 13   04704PG6

spring, by increasing the number of spring turns, if necessary, to obtain a smooth and complete return of the plate when the shaft is released.

11. Rotate the shaft slightly in either direction to allow the flattened surface of the shaft to face upward in the carburetor throat. Lower the throttle plate into the carburetor throat and onto the shaft with the holes in the plate aligned with the holes in the shaft. Secure the plate with the two small Phillips head screws. A magnetic screwdriver may prove most helpful to guide the screws into their holes.

Install the circlip onto the end of the throttle shaft. If the accelerator roller was removed, slide a new roller onto the arm and secure it in place with a circlip.

12. Slide the spring onto the pilot screw shaft, and then install the screw. Tighten the pilot screw until it just barely seats. From this position, back the screw out 1-½ turns.

13. Slide the long bolt through the throttle cam and the carburetor. Install the washer, and then tighten the nut securely. Check the throttle cam action against the accelerator roller. The accelerator should roll smoothly on the throttle cam.

INSTALLATION

▶ **See accompanying illustrations**

1. Place a new carburetor mounting gasket on the powerhead studs. Install the carburetor and secure it in place with the washers and nuts. Tighten the nuts alternately and evenly to a torque value of 5.6 ft. lbs. (8Nm). Connect the fuel line onto the carburetor inlet fitting.

2. Units with electric solenoid, Slide the joint rod up into the barrel on the accelerator arm and tighten the screw to secure it in place. The length of this rod

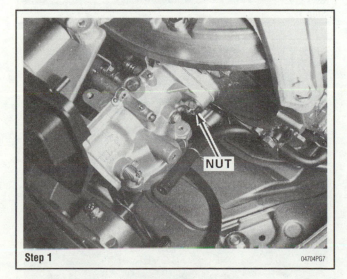

Step 1   04704PG7

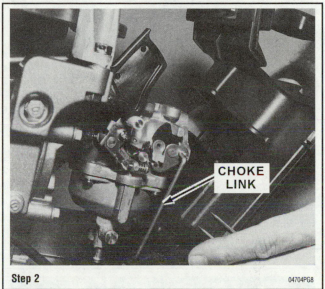

Step 2   04704PG8

must be adjusted by first pushing down on the rod until the throttle arm makes contact with the wide open throttle stop. Hold this position and make sure the accelerator roller contacts the throttle cam. Tighten the screw at the barrel.

Install the solenoid to the mounting bracket on the carburetor. Secure it with the two screws. Connect the ground lead to the crankcase with the screw. Connect the solenoid lead at the quick disconnect fitting beneath the carburetor. Attach the choke solenoid link onto the choke arm. Secure the link with the tiny retaining ring.

Units with manual choke, Snap the choke link into the plastic fitting on the carburetor.

All units, Install the silencer cover. Secure the cover in place with the three Phillips head screws.

Start the engine and check the completed work. Remember, the powerhead will not start without the emergency tether in place behind the kill switch knob. Allow the powerhead to warm to normal operating temperature. Adjust the throttle stop screw by inserting a screwdriver through the opening in the silencer until the powerhead idles within specification.

3-Cylinder Powerheads

▶ **See Figures 35, 36 and 37**

Three carburetors are used on the 3-cylinder outboard powerheads. Complete, detailed and illustrated procedures for these carburetors follow. Removal procedures may vary slightly due to differences in linkage. These differences will be noted whenever they make a substantial change in a procedure.

Fig. 35 The three carburetors installed on the powerhead are identical. The only difference is in the adjustment procedure

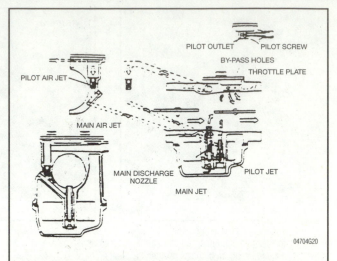

Fig. 37 Exploded view of the carburetor used on 3-cylinder power-heads with all major parts are identified

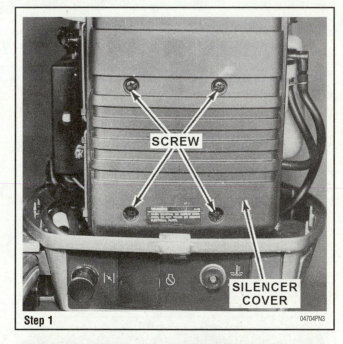

Step 1

Fig. 36 Single carburetor disconnected from the series of carburetors and ready for service

REMOVAL

Model 30 hp

♦ See accompanying illustrations

1. Remove the four Philips head screws securing the air silencer cover to the flame arrestor.
2. Lift the silencer cover free of the flame arrestor.

Step 2

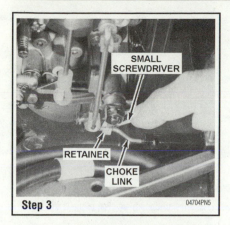

Step 3   04704PN5

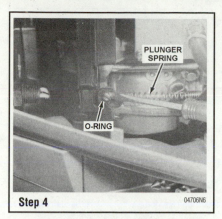

Step 4   04706N6

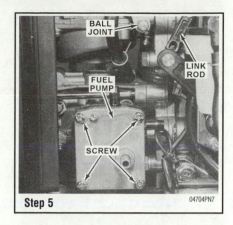

Step 5   04704PN7

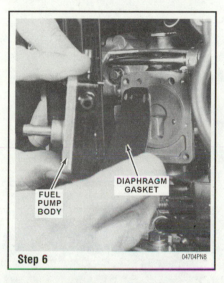

Step 6   04704PN8

Step 7   04704PN9

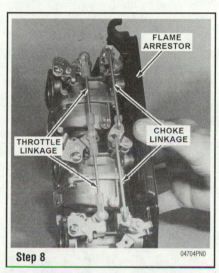

Step 8   04704PN0

3. Use a small screwdriver and pry the choke link free of the plastic retainer at the bottom carburetor.

4. Pry off the TINY O-ring which acts as a retainer for the plunger spring to the carburetor linkage. Take care not to lose this little O-ring. Unhook the plunger spring from the carburetor linkage.

5. Disconnect all three hoses leading to the fuel pump.

6. Remove the two hoses leading to the upper and lower carburetors. The third hose leading to the fuel filter may remain in place. Remove the four outer Philips head screws on the fuel pump cover. Pry off the small link rod from the ball joint on the carburetor linkage. Remove the fuel pump body and the diaphragm/gasket. These two items usually stick together.

7. Loosen all six bolts securing the carburetor to the reed block housing. Remove only the upper four bolts. The lower two bolts can only be removed after the carburetor is lifted clear of the lower cowling.

8. Gently ease the flame arrestor from the three carburetors. Remove and discard the one piece gasket, which stretches from the top carburetor to the bottom carburetor.

Disconnect the throttle and choke linkage. Place each piece of linkage on the work bench in order as it is removed, as an aid during installation. Scribe a mark on the float bowl of each carburetor, 1, 2, 3 to ensure each is installed back in its original location.

Model 40 hp, 50 hp, 70 hp and 90 hp Carburetors

♦ **See accompanying illustrations**

1. Remove the four screws securing the air silencer to the carburetor front plate. Carburetors mounted on 40 and 50 hp units have two short upper screws and two long lower screws. All other models have equal length screws.

2. Use a small screwdriver and pry the choke link free of the plastic retainer at the bottom carburetor.

3. Squeeze the wire clamp with a pair of needlenose pliers and gently pull off the fuel intake hose from the T fitting. If the open end of the hose shows signs of weeping fuel, plug the end of the hose with a suitable screw.

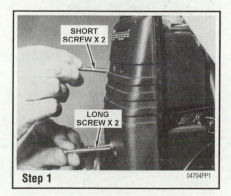

Step 1   04704PP1

Step 2   04704PP2

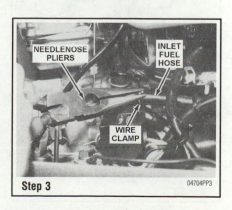

Step 3   04704PP3

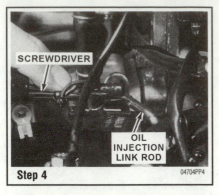

Step 4   04704PP4

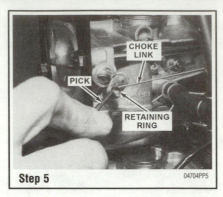

Step 5   04704PP5

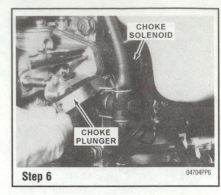

Step 6   04704PP6

4. Use a small screwdriver and pry the oil injection link rod free of the plastic retainer on the bottom carburetor.

5. Pry off the TINY O-ring which acts as a retainer for the choke link to the carburetor linkage. Take care not to lose this tiny O-ring.

6. Unhook the choke link from the carburetor and slide the choke plunger from the choke solenoid.

7. Remove the oil injection tank mounting bolts (if any) to the front plate. The 70 hp unit has a single bolt, and the 90 hp has three bolts. Loosen the six long bolts securing the carburetor front plate, and the carburetors to the reed block housing. Only the four uppermost bolts may be removed at this time. The two lower bolts will not clear the bottom cowling, and can only be removed after the carburetor is lifted clear of the bottom cowling.

8. Gently ease the three carburetors from the reed block housing. The front plate and the two lower bolts will also be removed with the carburetor assembly.

These items can be removed once the carburetors are clear of the bottom cowling.

9. Remove and discard the one piece gasket used for all three carburetors.

10. If the choke solenoid is to be removed, loosen the Phillips head screw on the bottom of the choke bracket and pull the solenoid from the retaining bracket.

11. Squeeze the ends of the wire clamps at the inlet fitting of each of the three carburetors and gently pull the fuel hoses from each fitting.

➡ **The T-fitting in the fuel line is located between the middle and bottom carburetors.**

12. Disconnect the throttle and choke linkage. Place each piece of linkage on the work bench in order as it is removed, as an aid during installation. Scribe a mark on the float bowl of each carburetor, 1, 2, 3 to ensure each is installed in its original location.

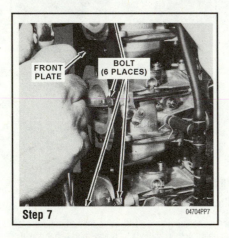

Step 7   04704PP7

Step 8   04704PP9

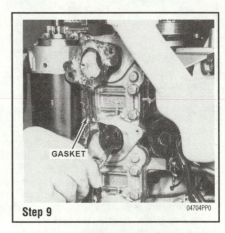

Step 9   04704PP0

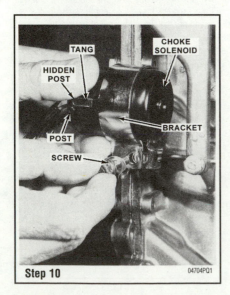

Step 10   04704PQ1

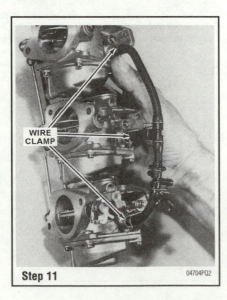

Step 11   04704PQ2

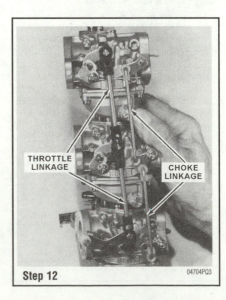

Step 12   04704PQ3

DISASSEMBLY

♦ See accompanying illustrations

The following procedures pick up the work after the carburetors have been removed from the powerhead. The procedures for each of the three carburetors is identical, even for the 30 hp unit which has a carburetor with the fuel pump attached to the middle carburetor. Any differences in float drop measurement, pilot screw turns, jets, or any other adjustments will be clearly identified for the carburetor including location and model.

1. Remove the four Phillips head screws and lockwashers securing the fuel bowl to the mixing chamber.
2. Remove and discard the O-ring around the fuel bowl.
3. Loosen, but do not remove, the Phillips head screw retaining the hinge pin in its groove. Grasp the float and gently lift until the hinge pin can clear the retaining screw. The needle valve, attached to the tang on the float will also slide out of the needle seat.
4. Pull the hinge pin from the float. Unhook the wire clip and needle valve from the tang on the float.
5. Pry the small plastic plug from the center turret of the mixing chamber.
6. Use a suitable size screwdriver and remove the pilot jet located under the plug.
7. Remove the main jet from the center turret of the mixing chamber.
8. Invert the mixing chamber and shake it, keeping a hand over the center turret. The main nozzle should fall free from the turret. If the nozzle refuses to fall out, gently reach in with a pick or similar instrument to raise the nozzle.
9. Obtain the correct size thin walled socket and remove the valve seat. Remove and discard the O-ring.

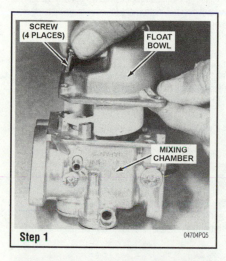

Step 1   04704PQ5

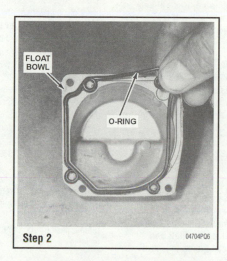

Step 2   04704PQ6

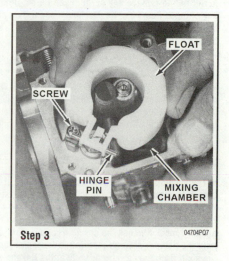

Step 3   04704PQ7

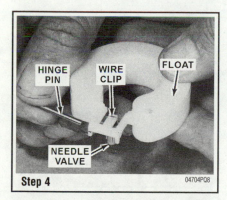

Step 4   04704PQ8

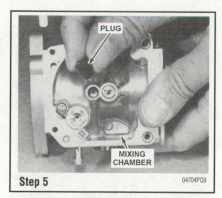

Step 5   04704PQ9

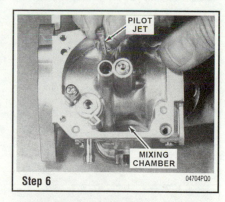

Step 6   04704PQ0

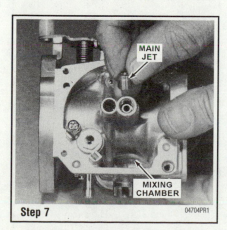

Step 7   04704PR1

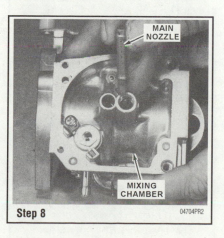

Step 8   04704PR2

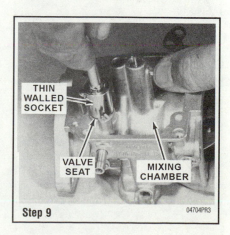

Step 9   04704PR3

10. Remove the two Phillips head screws securing the top cover to the top of the mixing chamber. Lift off the cover.

11. Observe three flat rubber plugs, two large and one small. Lift off the large rubber plug closest to the throttle plate. Lift off the remaining large rubber plug and the metal plate beneath it. The first rubber plug does not and should not have a metal plate under it.

12. Lift off the small rubber plug and plate.

13. Remove the pilot screw and spring from the carburetor. It is not necessary to count the number of turns in to a lightly seated position as a guide for installation, as the number of turns will be specified in the installation procedures.

➡Normal carburetor overhaul work stops at this point. However, if noticeable wear has taken place on either the throttle shaft, the choke shaft, or the throttle or choke plates, the following two steps may be performed to remove any of the listed items. Bear in mind, it is unlikely any of these items can be purchased separately at the dealer. If they have worn beyond use and cannot be repaired, a new carburetor should be purchased.

14. Remove the two Phillips head screws securing the throttle shaft to the throttle plate. Rotate the shaft to provide sufficient clearance to permit the plate to slide from the shaft and out the carburetor bore. Use a punch and remove the roll pin from the end of the throttle shaft, and then remove the small white plastic spacer. Unhook the spring from the other end of the shaft and note the number of turns required to loosen or remove the spring. Pull the shaft from the carburetor body at the linkage end.

15. Remove the two Phillips head screws securing the choke plate to the choke shaft.

➡The accompanying illustration shows a hole in the lower portion of the choke plate. Not all models have this hole, some have a perfectly solid choke plate. Remove the choke plate. Use a punch and remove the roll pin from the end of the choke shaft and then remove the small white plastic spacer. Unhook the spring from the other end of the shaft and note the number of turns required to loosen or remove the spring. Pull the shaft from the carburetor body at the linkage end.

CLEANING & INSPECTION

♦ See Figures 24, 25, 38, 39 and 40

✵✵ CAUTION

Never dip rubber or plastic parts, in carburetor cleaner. These parts should be cleaned only in solvent, and then blown dry with compressed air.

Place all metal parts in a screen type tray and dip them in carburetor cleaner until they appear completely clean, then blow them dry with compressed air.

Blow out all passages in the castings with compressed air. Check all parts and passages to be sure they are not clogged or contain any deposits. Never use a piece of wire or any type of pointed instrument to clean drilled passages or calibrated holes in a carburetor.

Move the throttle and choke shafts back and forth to check for wear. If the shaft appears to be too loose, replace the complete mixing chamber because individual replacement parts are not available.

Inspect the mixing chamber, and fuel bowl gasket surfaces for cracks and burrs which might cause a leak. Check the float for deterioration. Check to be sure the needle valve spring has not been stretched. If any part of the float is damaged, the float must be replaced. Check the needle valve rubber tip contacting surface and replace the needle valve if this surface has a groove worn in it.

Inspect the tapered section of the pilot screw and replace the screw if it has developed a groove.

As previously mentioned, most of the parts which should be replaced during a carburetor overhaul are included in an overhaul kit available from your local marine dealer. One of these kits will contain a matched fuel inlet needle and seat. This combination should be replaced each time the carburetor is disassembled as a precaution against leakage.

TOP COVER

Step 10 04704PR4

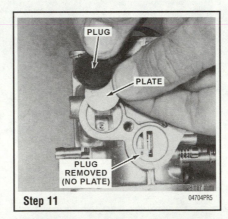

PLUG / PLATE / PLUG REMOVED (NO PLATE)

Step 11 04704PR5

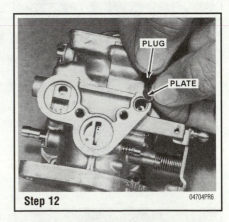

PLUG / PLATE

Step 12 04704PR6

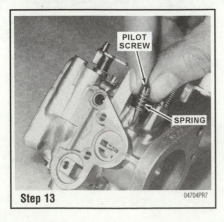

PILOT SCREW / SPRING

Step 13 04704PR7

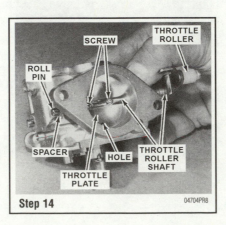

SCREW / THROTTLE ROLLER / ROLL PIN / SPACER / HOLE / THROTTLE PLATE / THROTTLE ROLLER SHAFT

Step 14 04704PR8

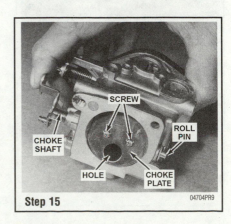

SCREW / CHOKE SHAFT / ROLL PIN / HOLE / CHOKE PLATE

Step 15 04704PR9

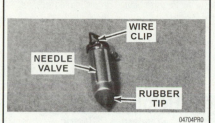

Fig. 38 A wire clip secures the needle valve to the float. If this wire should break or slip free of the float, the fuel supply will be cut off

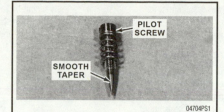

Fig. 39 Inspect the taper on the end of the pilot screw for ridges or signs of roughness. Good shop practice dictates a new pilot screw be installed each time the carburetor is overhauled

Fig. 40 Some of the parts included in the repair kit for the 3-cylinder powerhead carburetors

ASSEMBLY

◆ **See accompanying illustrations**

1. Insert the choke shaft from the port side of the carburetor, and at the same time wind the spring the same number of turns it unwound during disassembly. Hook the spring in place over the tab on the casting. If the spring was broken, missing or whatever, and a new spring is being installed, then estimate the tension and check the return action. Adjust the spring tension as necessary to obtain a smooth and complete return of the plate when the shaft is released.

Hold spring tension on the shaft while the roll pin is installed. Slide the white plastic retainer over the small end of the shaft. Push the roll pin into the hole. Rotate the shaft to permit the flattened surface of the shaft to face upwards in the carburetor bore. Position the choke plate over the two screw holes. If there is a hole on the plate, the hole is positioned at the bottom of the carburetor bore. Thread the two small Phillips head screws firmly through the plate and into the shaft.

✳✳ CAUTION

No torque specification is available from the manufacturer for these two small screws, but imagine what damage would occur if one of these screws vibrated loose and chewed its way through the reeds and into the combustion chamber!

2. Insert the throttle shaft from the port side of the carburetor, and at the same time, wind the spring the same number of turns it unwound during disassembly. Hook the spring in place over the tab on the casting. If the spring was broken, missing or whatever, and a new spring is being installed, then estimate the tension and check the return action. Adjust the spring tension as necessary to obtain a smooth and complete return of the plate when the shaft is released. Hold spring tension on the shaft while the roll pin is installed. Slide the white plastic retainer over the small end of the shaft. Push the roll pin into the hole. Rotate the shaft to provide sufficient clearance for the throttle plate to slide into the bore and behind the shaft. Align the plate with the screw holes. Thread the two small Phillips head screws through the shaft and into the throttle plate. Again, no torque specifications are provided by the manufacturer for tightening these two screws, but they could cause as much damage as loose choke shaft screws!

3. Slide a new spring over the pilot screw.

4. Install the pilot screw into the carburetor. Tighten the pilot screw until it barely seats. From this position, back out the screw the specified number of turns. Take notice, each year of manufacture has a different pilot screw setting. Furthermore, each carburetor has a different screw setting on certain models.

5. Place the small metal plug in position over the smallest hole on top of the carburetor. Place the smallest rubber plug over the plate.

6. Place the large metal plug in position over the large hole on top of the carburetor, nearest the fuel fitting, and then place one of the large rubber plugs

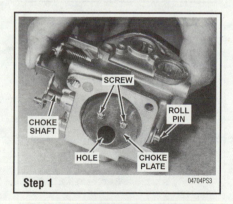

Step 1

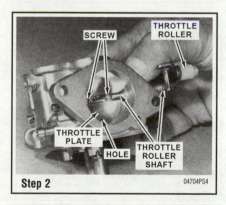

Step 2

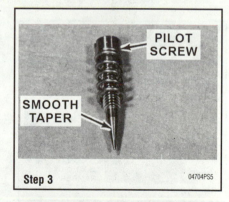

Step 3

Step 4

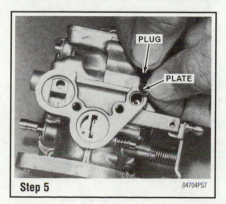

Step 5

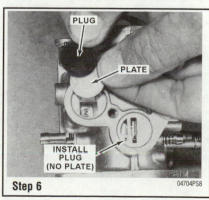

Step 6

over the plate. Place the remaining large rubber plug over the remaining hole. This plug is installed without a metal plate beneath it.

7. Position the top cover over all three plugs. Install and tighten the cover with the two Phillips head screws.

8. Slide a new O-ring over the shaft of the valve seat. Install and tighten the seat snugly, using a thin walled socket.

9. Insert the main nozzle into the aft hole on the center turret. Position the series of holes in the nozzle to face port and starboard when installed.

10. Install the main jet over the main nozzle. Tighten the jet until it seats snugly.

11. Install the pilot jet into the forward hole on the center turret. Tighten the jet until it seats snugly.

12. Install the plug over the pilot jet. Push the plug in securely. A loose plug could wedge itself between the float and the float bowl.

13. Check to be sure the wire clip is securely in position around the needle valve. Slide the clip over the tang on the float, and check to see if the needle valve can be moved freely.

14. Slide the hinge pin through the hole in the float.

15. Lower the float assembly over the center turret, guiding the needle valve into the needle seat and positioning the end of the hinge pin under its retaining screw. Tighten the screw securely.

16. Hold the mixing chamber in the inverted position, (as it has been held during the past few steps). Measure the distance between the top of the float and the gasket surface of the mixing chamber. This distance should be as specified in the chart.

17. Apply a coat of Yamalube All Purpose Marine Grease to both sides of the fuel bowl O-ring. Install the O-ring into the groove of the fuel bowl.

18. Install the fuel bowl onto the mixing chamber, matching the one cutaway corner with the other. Install and tighten the four attaching screws.

Float Height

Model	Standard	Metric
30hp	11/16 in.	17.5mm
40hp	9/16 in.	14.0mm
50hp	9/16 in.	14.0mm
70hp	9/16 in.	14.0mm
90hp	3/4 in.	19.5mm

NOTE: If the measurement is not within these limits, inspect the valve seat, needle valve, and wire clip. Do not attempt to correct the reading by bending the tab on the float. The float is made of plastic and it will break before it bends. The float is made of plastic and it will break before it bends

04704C02

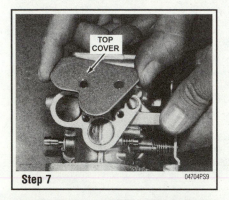

Step 7   04704PS9

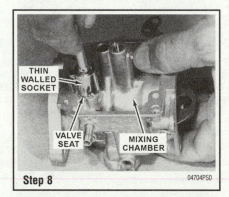

Step 8   04704PS0

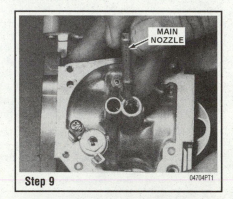

Step 9   04704PT1

Step 10   04704PT2

Step 11   04704PT3

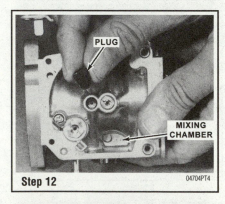

Step 12   04704PT4

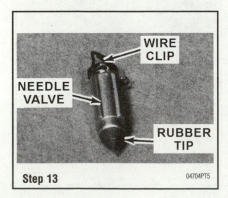

Step 13   04704PT5

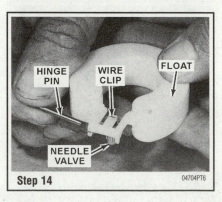

Step 14   04704PT6

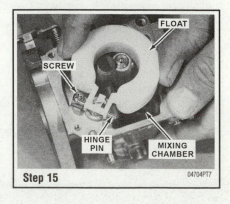

Step 15   04704PT7

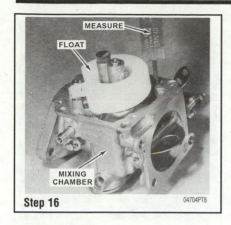

Step 16   04704PT8

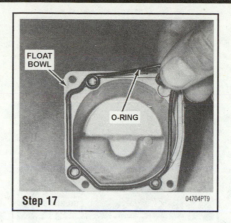

Step 17   04704PT9

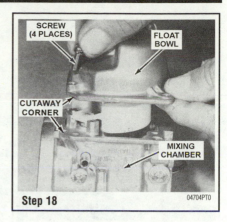

Step 18   04704PT0

INSTALLATION

Model 30 hp

▶ **See accompanying illustrations**

1. Identify each carburetor by the mark scribed on the float bowl during removal. Check to be sure the small pieces of linkage were installed onto the correct carburetor. The throttle roller belongs on the carburetor with the fuel pump attached. Place the three carburetors in line on the work bench. Install the throttle and choke linkage. Place a new one piece gasket on the carburetor throats and align the flame arrestor to the carburetor assemblies.

2. Install the two lower bolts through the flame arrestor before moving the three carburetors into position on the reed block housing. These two bolts will not clear the bottom cowling after the carburetors are installed. Install the

other four bolts. Tighten all six bolts alternately and evenly to 5.8 ft. lbs. (8Nm).

3. Install the diaphragm/gasket and fuel pump body. Align the holes for the screws before attempting to insert the screws. A misaligned diaphragm can be easily torn or punctured.

4. Install and tighten the four Phillips head screws securing the fuel pump body to the carburetor. Hook the plunger spring onto the carburetor linkage and slip the O-ring in over the linkage to secure it in place. Snap the small link rod onto the ball joint on the carburetor linkage.

5. Install the fuel hose from the fuel filter to the fitting at the center of the fuel pump. Install the short fuel hose from the top fuel pump fitting to the upper carburetor. Install the longer fuel hose from the side fuel pump fitting to the lower carburetor with the bend in the hose closest to the pump side fitting. Secure all connections with the wire clamps.

6. Snap the choke link back onto the plastic fitting on the lower carburetor.

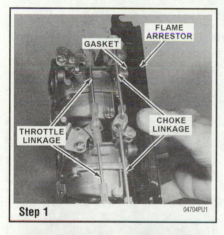

Step 1   04704PU1

Step 2   04704PU2

Step 3   04704PU3

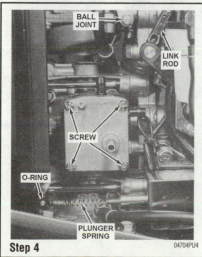

Step 4   04704PU4

Step 5   04704PU5

Step 6   04704PU6

Step 7   04704PU7

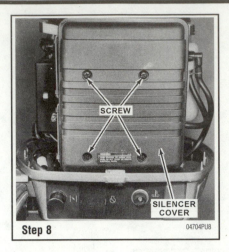

Step 8   04704PU8

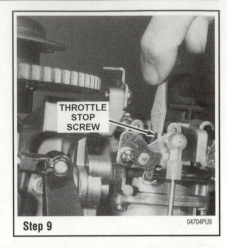

Step 9   04704PU9

Check the action of the choke linkage on the starboard side of the carburetors by pulling the choke lever out and pushing it in.

7. Install the silencer cover over the flame arrestor.

8. Install and tighten the four Phillips head screws securing the silencer cover in place.

9. Mount the outboard unit in a test tank, or put the boat in a body of water, or connect a flush attachment and hose to the lower unit. Connect a tachometer to the powerhead.

✳✳ CAUTION

Never operate the engine at high speed with a flush device attached. The engine, operating at high speed with such a device attached, would runaway from lack of a load on the propeller, causing extensive damage.

Start the engine and check the completed work.

✳✳ CAUTION

Water must circulate through the lower unit to the powerhead any-time the powerhead is operating to prevent damage to the water

pump in the lower unit. Just five seconds without water will damage the water pump impeller.

Allow the powerhead to warm to normal operating temperature. Adjust the throttle stop screw until the powerhead idles at specification. Rotating the throttle stop screw clockwise increases powerhead speed, and rotating the screw counterclockwise decreases powerhead speed.

Models 40, 50, 70, and 90 hp

◆ See accompanying illustrations

1. Identify each carburetor by the mark scribed on the fuel bowl during removal. Check to be sure the small pieces of linkage were installed on the correct carburetor. The throttle roller MUST be installed on the lower carburetor. Place all three carburetors in line on the work bench. Install the choke and throttle linkage on the port side of the carburetors.

2. Turn the carburetors over on the workbench to rest on their port sides. Push each fuel hose onto its respective fuel inlet fitting on the starboard side. The T fitting is located between the middle and bottom carburetor. Secure each hose with the wire clamp.

3. Place the choke solenoid into the bracket, with the tang on the bracket indexing between the two posts on the solenoid. Push in the solenoid until the

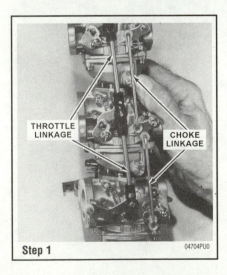

Step 1   04704PU0

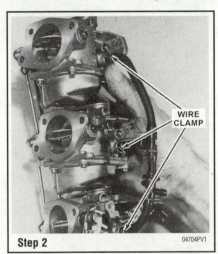

Step 2   04704PV1

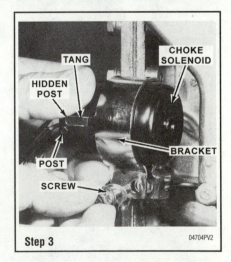

Step 3   04704PV2

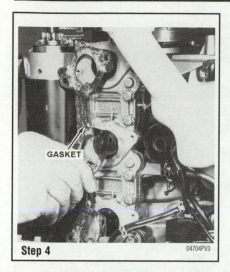

Step 4   04704PV3

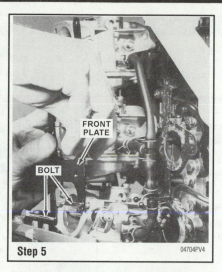

Step 5   04704PV4

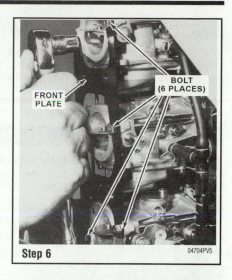

Step 6   04704PV5

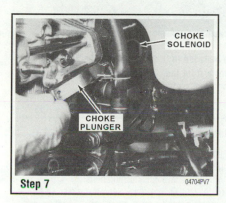

Step 7   04704PV7

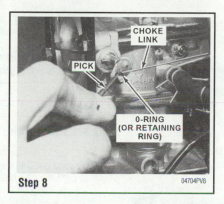

Step 8   04704PV8

Step 9   04704PV9

posts rest against the bracket band. Tighten the screw on the bracket to secure the solenoid.

4. Place a new gasket in position over the reed block housing. The manufacturer recommends no sealant at this location.

5. Install the two lower bolts through the front plate and carburetors before moving the carburetor assembly into position on the reed block housing. These two bolts will not clear the bottom cowling after the carburetors are installed.

6. Install the other four bolts. Tighten all six bolts alternately and evenly to a torque value of 5.8 ft. lbs. (8Nm). Install the oil tank mounting bolts (if any) to the front plate. 70 hp unit has a single lower bolt, 90 hp unit has three retaining bolts.

7. Slide the choke plunger into the solenoid with the flat side facing outward, to align with the solenoid bore.

8. Hook the choke link onto the carburetor linkage and slip the tiny O-ring over the linkage to secure the link in place. If the choke link is properly adjusted, the embossed line on the choke plunger will be aligned with the edge of the solenoid bore. To change the alignment of the choke plunger, loosen the

screw on the bottom of the choke solenoid bracket, and move the solenoid in or out of its bracket until the correct alignment is obtained, and the plunger does not bind in its bore.

9. Snap the oil injection link rod back into the plastic retainer.

10. Connect the fuel line from the fuel filter to the T fitting between the middle and bottom carburetors.

11. Snap the choke link back onto the plastic fitting on the lower carburetor. Check the action of the choke linkage on the starboard side of the carburetors by pulling the choke lever out and pushing it in. At the same time check the action of the choke link and plunger in the solenoid bore.

12. Install the four screws securing the air silencer to the carburetor front plate. 40 and 50 hp units have two short upper screws and two long lower screws. All other models have screws of equal length.

Mount the outboard unit in a test tank, on the boat in a body of water, or connect a flush attachment and hose to the lower unit. Connect a tachometer to the powerhead.

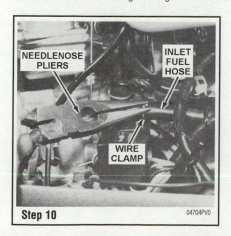

Step 10   04704PV0

Step 11   04704PW1

Step 12   04704PW2

⚜ CAUTION

Never operate the engine at high speed with a flush device attached. The engine, operating at high speed with such a device attached, would runaway from lack of a load on the propeller, causing extensive damage.

Start the engine and check the completed work.

⚜ CAUTION

Water must circulate through the lower unit to the powerhead anytime the powerhead is operating to prevent damage to the water pump in the lower unit. Just five seconds without water will damage the water pump impeller.

Allow the powerhead to warm to normal operating temperature. Adjust the throttle stop screw until the powerhead idles at specification. Rotating the throttle stop screw clockwise increases powerhead speed, and rotating the screw counterclockwise decreases powerhead speed.

TACHOMETER CONNECTIONS

Manual Start Model

Connect the two tachometer leads to the two Green leads from the stator. These two Green leads are encased inside a sheath, but the connecting ends are exposed. The leads are connected to a pair of Green female leads. Either tachometer lead may be connected to either Green lead from the stator.

Electric Start Model

The following instructions apply to a model without a tachometer installed, or for a model with a tachometer installed, but a second meter is needed to assist in making adjustments.

Inside the control box, the Green lead with the female end connector is input or signal lead. The Black lead with either a male or female end connector is the tachometer return or ground lead.

Connect the tachometer to these two leads per the instructions with the meter, input and ground.

Start the engine and check the completed work.

V4 & V6 Powerheads

◆ See Figure 41

Yamaha V4 powerheads use two carburetors and V6 powerheads use three carburetors. Complete, detailed, illustrated, procedures to remove, service, and install the carburetors follow. Removal procedures may vary slightly due to differences in linkage.

As explained in the description of the carburetors, the float arrangement and adjustments differ due to a change in carburetor vendor. These differences are noted whenever they make a substantial change in a procedure.

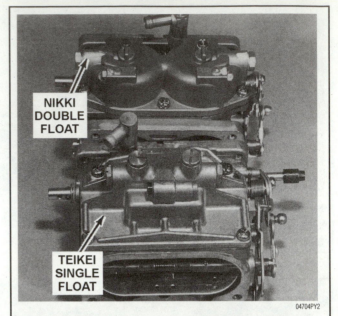

Fig. 41 Procedures are included in the text for both the Teikei single float carburetor (bottom) and for the Nikki dual float carburetor (top)

REMOVAL

◆ See accompanying illustrations

1. Disconnect the fuel line from the tank at the fuel joint. Remove the screws securing the outer silencer cover to the inner silencer cover. V4 models have eight attaching bolts, V6 models have ten attaching bolts.

2. On V4 models, pry off the little O-ring which serves as a retainer for the choke solenoid pull wire. Take care not to lose this small part. Slip off the end of the pull wire from the carburetor linkage. Remove the choke pull wire and plunger from the solenoid. Disconnect the single Blue lead at its quick disconnect fitting. The solenoid may remain mounted to the inner silencer cover. The cover is removed in a later step.

3. Pry the choke link from its retainer on the port side of the bottom carburetor.

4. Snip the three plastic hose retainers and gently pull off the fuel supply hoses from the carburetors.

5. Remove the bolts securing the inner silencer cover to the carburetors. Separate the cover from the carburetors a short distance, and then gently pull off the oil tank breather hose (top) and the fuel recirculation hose (bottom) from the aft side of the inner silencer cover.

On models equipped with YMIS, mark the original location of the throttle position sensor before removal. If this sensor is misaligned during installation, a digital type voltmeter is needed to correctly reset the sensor on its mounting bracket, because voltages in the $\frac{1}{10}$ range must be accurately read. A mis-

Step 1

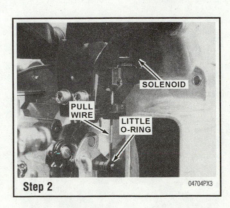

Step 2

Step 3

FUEL SUPPLY HOSE (V4 2 PLCS) (V6 3 PLCS)

Step 4 04704PX5

BREATHER HOSE

RECIRCULATION HOSE

Step 5 04704PX6

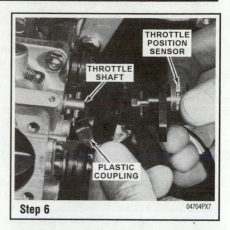

THROTTLE POSITION SENSOR

THROTTLE SHAFT

PLASTIC COUPLING

Step 6 04704PX7

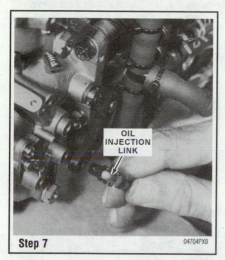

OIL INJECTION LINK

Step 7 04704PX8

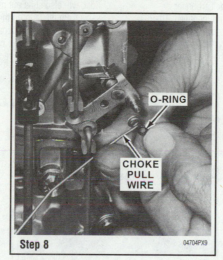

O-RING

CHOKE PULL WIRE

Step 8 04704PX9

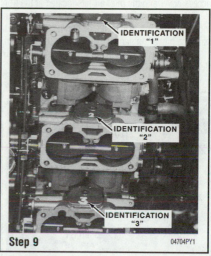

IDENTIFICATION "1"

IDENTIFICATION "2"

IDENTIFICATION "3"

Step 9 04704PY1

GASKET (3 PLCS)

Step 10 04704PY1

aligned sensor could send misleading signals to the microcomputer and consequently effect the ignition timing.

6. After marking the position of the throttle sensor, remove the two securing screws and lift out the sensor from its plastic coupling. Slide the plastic coupling from the throttle shaft.

7. On the starboard side of the bottom carburetor, pry the oil injection link from the linkage.

8. On V6 models, pry off the little O-ring which serves as a retainer for the choke solenoid pull wire. Take care not to lose this small part. Slip off the end of the pull wire from the carburetor linkage. The choke solenoid need not be removed on these models.

9. Identify each carburetor by inscribing or painting a 1, 2 and 3 (if applicable) on the mixing chamber cover to ensure each carburetor will be installed back into the same position from which it was removed.

10. Remove the mounting nuts, four on each carburetor, and then remove the carburetors as an assembly. Each carburetor has a separate gasket which may either come away with the carburetor, or remain on the intake manifold. Remove and discard these gaskets.

Place the carburetor assembly on the workbench and remove each piece of linkage one at a time. Arrange the linkage on the workbench as it was installed on the carburetors, as an assist during assembling.

DISASSEMBLY

▶ **See accompanying illustrations**

The following procedures pick up the work after the carburetors have been removed from the powerhead, as outlined in the previous steps. The procedures for each of the two or three carburetors is identical, except for the powerheads equipped with YMIS. The top carburetor on a powerhead equipped with YMIS has an extension on the throttle shaft for the throttle position sensor.

Where differences occur in the single (Teikei) and dual (Nikki) float designs, both sets of procedures are included. Therefore, perform the following procedures for each of the carburetors.

→ **Any differences in float drop measurement, pilot screw turns, jets, or any other adjustments will be clearly identified for the carburetor including location and model.**

1. On Teikei carburetors, use a small screwdriver and remove the pilot air jets and the main air jets. On some Teikei carburetors, the main air jets are not removable, because the jet does not have a screwdriver slot. The jet is flush with the carburetor body.

Keep the pilot air jets and the main air jets separated and identified. They look identical and may easily be confused, one for the other. The main air jets have the higher numerical value embossed on them.

2. On Nikki carburetors, remove the Phillips screw securing the jet access cover to the carburetor. Remove the access cover and the gasket beneath the cover. Discard the gasket.

3. Use a small screw driver and remove the main air jets located under the access cover and the pilot air jets located at the front of the carburetor.

Keep the pilot air jets and the main air jets separated and identified. They look identical and may easily be confused, one for the other. The main air jets have the higher numerical value embossed on them.

4. Remove the two bypass screws from the mixing chamber. Remove and discard the two O-rings.

5. Remove both pilot screws and springs. It is not necessary to count the number of turns in to a lightly seated position, as a guide for installation. The number of turns will be specified in the installation procedures.

6. Remove the securing screws and lift off the float bowl. Do not attempt to remove the gasket at this time.

7. Remove the two main jets and drain screws from the underneath side of the float bowl. Remove and discard the gaskets and O-rings.

8. On Teikei carburetors, remove the small Phillips head screw retaining the hinge pin.

9. Grasp the float lightly. Use a small pair of needle nose pliers and draw out the hinge pin from its mounting posts.

10. Gently lift up the float. The needle valve, attached to the tang on the float, will also slide out of the needle seat.

11. Unhook the wire loop and needle valve from the tang on the float.

12. On Nikki carburetors, slide the hinge pin outward to release the float.

13. Gently lift up the float. The needle valve, attached to the tang on the float, will also slide out of the needle seat. Unhook the wire loop and needle valve from the tang on the float. Remove the other float in a similar manner.

14. Remove and discard the float bowl gasket from the mixing chamber.

15. Remove the two main nozzles from the mixing chamber.

16. Obtain the correct size thin walled socket and remove the needle seat.

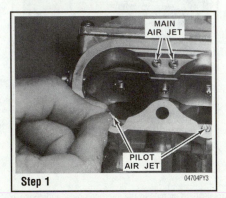

Step 1 — MAIN AIR JET / PILOT AIR JET — 04704PY3

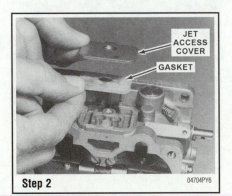

Step 2 — JET ACCESS COVER / GASKET — 04704PY6

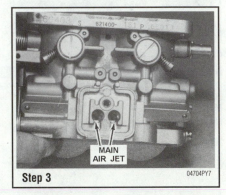

Step 3 — MAIN AIR JET — 04704PY7

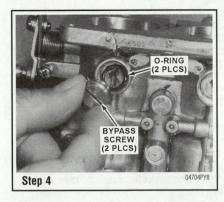

Step 4 — O-RING (2 PLCS) / BYPASS SCREW (2 PLCS) — 04704PY8

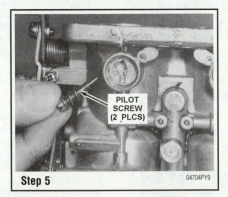

Step 5 — PILOT SCREW (2 PLCS) — 04704PY9

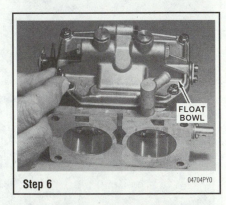

Step 6 — FLOAT BOWL — 04704PY0

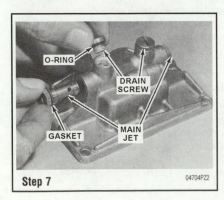

Step 7 — O-RING / DRAIN SCREW / GASKET / MAIN JET — 04704PZ2

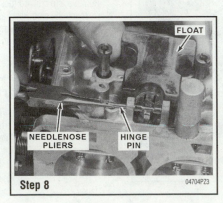

Step 8 — FLOAT / NEEDLENOSE PLIERS / HINGE PIN — 04704PZ3

Step 9 — HINGE PIN / SCREW — 04704PZ4

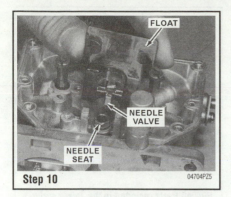

Step 10

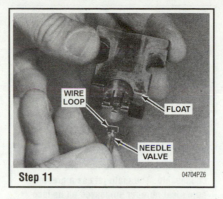

Step 11

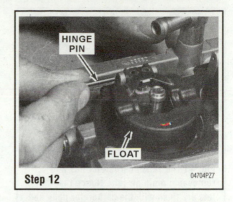

Step 12

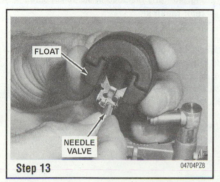

Step 13

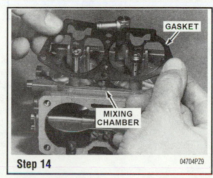

Step 14

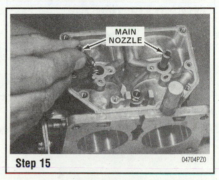

Step 15

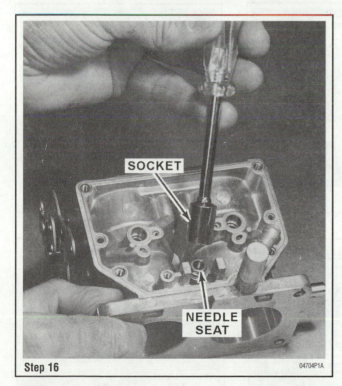

Step 16

Place all metal parts in a screen type tray and dip them in carburetor cleaner until they appear completely clean, then blow them dry with compressed air.

Blow out all passages in the castings with compressed air. Check all parts and passages to be sure they are not clogged or contain any deposits. Never use a piece of wire or any type of pointed instrument to clean drilled passages or calibrated holes in a carburetor.

Move the throttle and choke shafts back and forth to check for wear. If the shaft appears to be too loose, replace the complete mixing chamber because individual replacement parts are not available.

Inspect the mixing chamber, and fuel bowl gasket surfaces for cracks and burrs which might cause a leak. Check the floats for deterioration. Check to be sure the needle valve loop has not been stretched. If any part of the float is damaged, the float must be replaced. Check the needle valve tip contacting surface and replace the needle valve if this surface has a groove worn in it.

Inspect the tapered section of the pilot screw and replace the screw if it has developed a groove.

As previously mentioned, most of the parts which should be replaced during a carburetor overhaul are included in an overhaul kit available from your local marine dealer. One of these kits will contain a matched fuel inlet needle and

CLEANING & INSPECTION

▶ See Figures 24, 25, 38, 39, 42, 43, 44 and 45

❄❄ CAUTION

Never dip rubber or plastic parts in carburetor cleaner. These parts should be cleaned only in solvent, and then blown dry with compressed air.

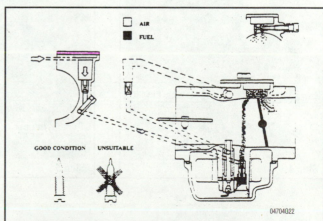

Fig. 42 Exploded view of a Teikei single float carburetor. The Nikki carburetor incorporates a double float arrangement.

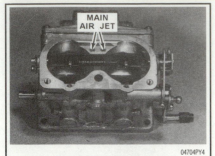

Fig. 43 The Teikei carburetor has non-removable main air jets. Notice that the jets are flush with the carburetor body and do not have a screwdriver slot

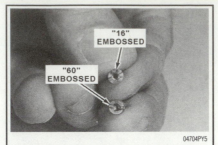

Fig. 44 The pilot jet (above) and the main jet (bottom) look similar, but are not interchangeable. The main jet has a greater numerical number embossed on its face as indicated

Fig. 45 Parts included in the Teikei carburetor repair kit

seat. This combination should be replaced each time the carburetor is disassembled as a precaution against leakage.

ASSEMBLY

◆ **See accompanying illustrations**

1. Install and tighten the needle seat snugly, using a thin walled socket.
2. Install the two main nozzles into the mixing chamber. Tighten them securely.

3. Place a new float bowl gasket in position over the mixing chamber.
4. On Teikei carburetors, check to be sure the wire loop is securely in position around the needle valve. Slide the loop over the tang on the float, and then check to ensure the needle valve can be moved freely.
5. Lower the float assembly into the mixing chamber guiding the needle valve into the needle seat.
6. Use a small pair of needle nose pliers and slide the hinge pin through the mounting post and the float hinge. Position the end of the hinge pin to clear its retaining screw.

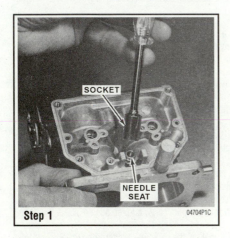

Step 1

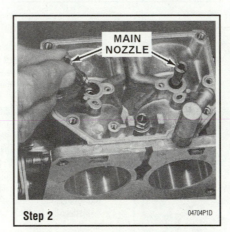

Step 2

Step 3

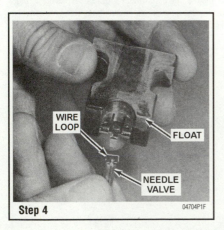

Step 4

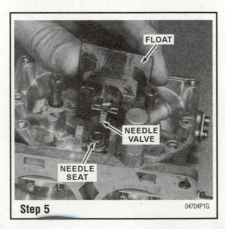

Step 5

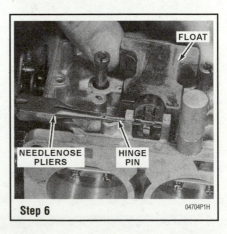

Step 6

Step 7 04704P1J

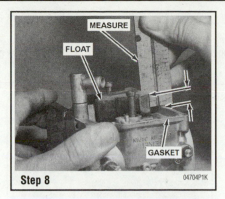

Step 8 04704P1K

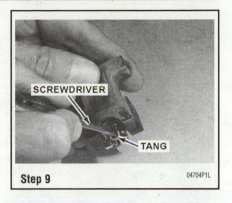

Step 9 04704P1L

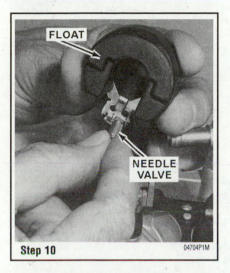

Step 10 04704P1M

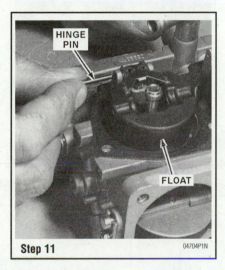

Step 11 04704P1N

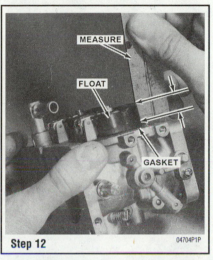

Step 12 04704P1P

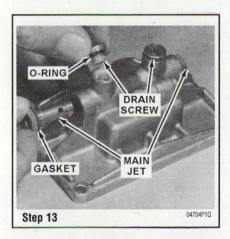

Step 13 04704P1Q

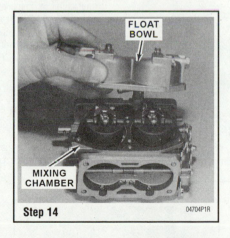

Step 14 04704P1R

Step 15 04704P1S

7. Install and tighten the retaining screw.

8. Hold the mixing chamber in the inverted position, (as it has been held during the past few steps). Measure the distance between the top of the float and the gasket. This distance should be ½ in. (12.5 mm).

If the distance is not as specified, remove the float and needle valve. Gently bend the tab on the float using a small screwdriver to correct the float level measurement.

9. On Nikki carburetors, check to be sure the wire loop is securely in position around the needle valve. Slide the loop over the tang on the float, and then check to ensure the needle valve can be moved freely. Lower the float assembly into the mixing chamber guiding the needle valve into the needle seat. Install the other float in the same manner.

10. Slide the hinge pin through the mounting posts and float hinge, until the pin ends are flush with the mounting posts.

11. Hold the mixing chamber in the inverted position, (as it has been held during the past few steps). Measure the distance between the top of the float and the gasket. This distance should be ⅝ in. (16 mm).

12. If the distance is not as specified, remove the float and needle valve. Gently bend the tab on the float using a small screwdriver to correct the float level measurement. Repeat the float level measurement for the other float.

13. Install new gaskets on the main jets. Install the jets into the float bowl and tighten them securely. Install new O-rings around the two drain screws. Install the screws into the float bowl and tighten them securely.

14. Lower the float bowl over the floats. Take care not to disturb the float level adjustment. Install and tighten the attaching hardware.

15. Slide new springs over the pilot screws. Install the pilot screws into the carburetor. Tighten each screw until it barely seats. From this position, back out the screw the specified number of turns.

➡ **Take notice, each year of manufacture could have a different pilot screw setting. Furthermore, on certain models, the port screw has a different setting from the starboard screw.**

16. Install new O-rings around the two bypass screws, and then install them into the mixing chamber.

17. On Teikei carburetors, identify the pilot air jets and the main air jets. The main air jets have a higher numerical value embossed on them. Install the two sets of jets in the locations indicated in the accompanying illustration. On some Teikei carburetors, the main air jets are not replaceable.

18. On Nikki carburetors, identify the pilot air jets and the main air jets. The main air jets have a larger number embossed on them. Install the main air jets under the access cover and the pilot air jets located at the front of the carburetor.

19. Position a new gasket over the mixing chamber and place the jet access cover over the gasket. Install and tighten the Phillips head screw securing the cover.

O-RING (2 PLCS)
BYPASS SCREW (2 PLCS)
Step 16   04704P1T

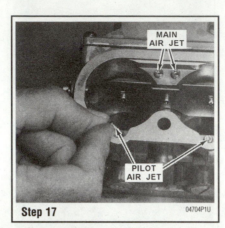

MAIN AIR JET
PILOT AIR JET
Step 17   04704P1U

MAIN AIR JET
Step 18   04704P1V

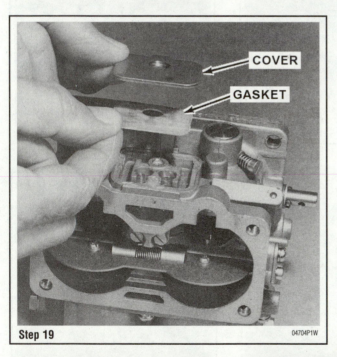

COVER
GASKET
Step 19   04704P1W

INSTALLATION

♦ **See accompanying illustrations**

1. Identify each carburetor by the mark scribed on the mixing chamber during removal. Check to be sure the small pieces of linkage were installed onto the correct carburetor. On V4 models, the throttle roller is used on the lower carburetor. On V6 models, the throttle roller is used on the center carburetor.

The choke and oil injection link retainers are located on the bottom carburetor. Place the carburetors in line on the work bench. Install the throttle and choke linkage. Place a new gasket onto the studs of the intake manifold. The manufacturer recommends NO sealant at this location. Install and tighten the four mounting nuts for each carburetor to a torque value of 5.8 ft. lbs. (8Nm).

2. On V6 models, hook the choke solenoid pull wire loop into the linkage between the two choke rods. Slide the little O-ring over the linkage ball to retain the wire loop. The choke plunger adjustment is performed later.

3. On the starboard side of the bottom carburetor, snap the oil injection link rod into the linkage. If the length of this rod was accidentally changed adjust the length to specifications.

4. On YMIS models, slide one end of the plastic coupling over the throttle shaft extension and the other end of the coupling over the throttle position sensor shaft. Engage the pins of both shafts into the slots of the plastic coupling. Install the sensor onto the bracket on the top carburetor, using the attaching hardware, in exactly the same location, matching the marks made during removal.

GASKET (3 PLCS)
Step 1   04704P1X

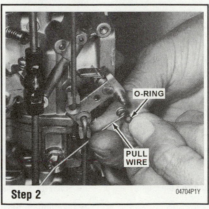

O-RING
PULL WIRE
Step 2   04704P1Y

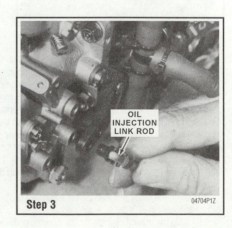

OIL INJECTION LINK ROD
Step 3   04704P1Z

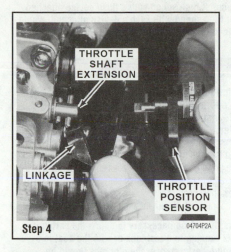

Step 4

Step 5

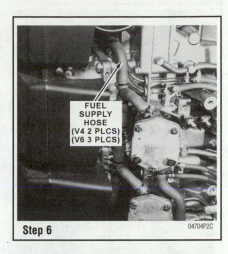

Step 6

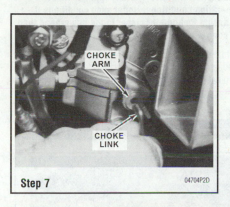

Step 7

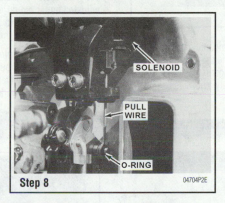

Step 8

Step 9

➡On models equipped with YMIS, If the throttle position sensor is misaligned during installation, a digital type voltmeter is needed to correctly reset the sensor on its mounting bracket because voltages in its setting range must be accurately read. A misaligned sensor will send misleading signals to the microcomputer and consequently affect the ignition timing. If no locating marks were made during removal, carefully examine the bracket for traces of an outline made by the sensor and try to mount the sensor as near to the original location as possible. A difference of 0.04 in. (1mm) corresponds to 2,dg of throttle angle.

5. Bring the inner silencer cover up to the installed carburetors. Install the hose leading from the oil tank to the uppermost fitting on the cover. Install the fuel recirculation hose onto the lower fitting on the cover.

6. Place new hose clamps over the three fuel supply hoses. Slide the hoses over the inlet fittings, and then secure them with the hose clamps.

7. On the port side of the bottom carburetor, snap the choke link onto the carburetor choke arm. Check the action of the choke linkage on the side of the carburetors by moving the choke lever in and out.

8. On V4 models, hook the choke solenoid pull wire loop into the linkage between the two choke rods. Slide the little O-ring over the linkage ball to retain the wire loop. The choke plunger adjustment is performed later. Connect the single Blue lead at the quick disconnect fitting.

9. Install the outer silencer cover to the inner silencer cover. V4 Models have eight attaching screws, V6 models have ten attaching screws. Connect the fuel line at the fuel joint.

CHOKE SOLENOID ADJUSTMENT

▶ **See accompanying illustrations**

Mount the outboard unit in a test tank, on a boat in a body of water, or connect a flush attachment and hose to the lower unit. Connect a tachometer to the powerhead.

1. Pull out the choke knob on the lower cowling, to fully close the choke butterflies.

2. Check to ensure the mark on the plunger is flush with the surface of the solenoid. The V4 model choke solenoid should look as illustrated

3. Check to ensure the mark on the plunger is flush with the surface of the solenoid. The V6 model choke solenoid should look as illustrated.

Step 1

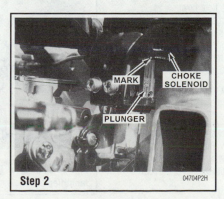

Step 2

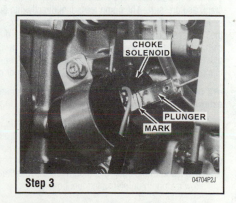

Step 3

SCREWDRIVER

THROTTLE STOP SCREW

Step 4

04704P2K

If the mark is not aligned, adjustment of the solenoid mounting position is required. Loosen the attaching hardware which secures the solenoid in its bracket and move the solenoid until the mark on the plunger is flush with the surface of the solenoid. Tighten the bolts to hold this newly adjusted position.

➡Never operate the engine at high speed with a flush device attached. The engine, operating at high speed with such a device attached, would runaway from lack of a load on the propeller, causing extensive damage.

✳✳ CAUTION

Water must circulate through the lower unit to the powerhead anytime the powerhead is operating to prevent damage to the water pump in the lower unit. Just five seconds without water will damage the water pump impeller.

4. Allow the powerhead to warm to normal operating temperature. Adjust the throttle stop screw until the powerhead idles at the specified speed. Rotating the throttle stop screw clockwise increases powerhead speed. Rotating the screw counterclockwise decreases powerhead speed.

Time and synchronize the fuel system with the ignition system.

➡Due to local conditions, it may be necessary to adjust the carburetor while the outboard unit is running in a test tank or with the boat in a body of water. For maximum performance, the idle rpm should be adjusted under actual operating conditions. Under such conditions it might be necessary to attach a tachometer closer to the powerhead than the one installed on the control panel.

Open the remote control box. Disconnect the Black and Green leads. Connect the Black lead to the ground terminal of the auxiliary tachometer and the Green lead to the input or hot terminal of the auxiliary tachometer. Start the engine and check the completed work.

FUEL PUMP SERVICE

1–2-Cylinder Fuel Pumps

DESCRIPTION & OPERATION

2–5 hp powerheads may not have a fuel pump of any type. Fuel is provided to the carburetor by gravity flow from the fuel tank atop the powerhead.

The fuel pump on some powerheads is an integral part of the carburetor. Therefore, do not search for a separate fuel pump on these powerheads. This integral fuel pump is covered under Carburetor C.

The following section provides detailed instructions to service the fuel pump on powerheads equipped with an external fuel pump.

The next few paragraphs briefly describe operation of the separate fuel pump used on powerheads covered in this manual. This description is followed by detailed procedures for testing the pressure, testing volume, removing, servicing, and installing the fuel pump.

Two different model fuel pumps may be found on 1–2-cylinder Yamaha powerheads. Type I fuel pump is an integral part of the carburetor. Type II diaphragm displacement fuel pump.

Type I

▶ **See Figures 46 and 47**

This pump consists of a series of diaphragms and check valves operated by crankcase pressure. The pump feeds fuel directly into the float bowl.

As the piston moves upward, a suction, or negative pressure, is created in the crankcase. This low pressure acts upon the inner diaphragm through the carburetor. The inner diaphragm is therefore pulled inward. When the diaphragm moves inward, the check valve opens and fuel is drawn from the bottom of the fuel pump exterior chamber into the fuel pump interior chamber.

➡If the primer bulb is activated prior to powerhead start, the fuel pump exterior chamber will be filled with fuel.

As the piston moves downward, a positive pressure is created in the crankcase causing the inner diaphragm to be pushed outward. The delivery check valve opens under pressure and allows fuel to flow into the upper part of the exterior chamber and on into the carburetor float bowl.

The function of the outer diaphragm is to absorb the pulsations of the fuel and allow a smooth uninterrupted fuel flow.

HOSE STAY

THROTTLE STOP SCREW

04704PL9

Fig. 46 This carburetor has an integral Type I fuel pump. The pump operates under crankcase pressure to deliver fuel to the float bowl

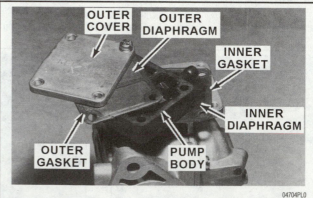

OUTER COVER

OUTER DIAPHRAGM

INNER GASKET

INNER DIAPHRAGM

OUTER GASKET

PUMP BODY

04704PL0

Fig. 47 An integral Type I fuel pump with major parts and areas identified

Type II

♦ **See Figures 48, 49 and 50**

The Type II fuel pump is a separate unit from the carburetor. A short description follows and service procedures are also listed.

This pump is a diaphragm displacement type. The pump is attached to the crankcase and is operated by crankcase impulses. A hand-operated squeeze bulb is installed in the fuel line to fill the fuel pump and carburetor with fuel prior to powerhead start. After the powerhead is operating, the pump is able to supply an adequate fuel supply to the carburetor to meet engine demands under all speeds and condition.

The pump consists of a spring loaded inner diaphragm, a spring loaded outer diaphragm, two valves, one for inlet (suction) and the other for outlet (discharge), and a small opening leading directly into the crankcase. The suction and compression created as the piston travels up and down in the cylinder, causes the diaphragms to flex.

As the piston moves upward, the inner diaphragm will flex inward displacing volume on its opposite side to create suction. This suction will draw fuel in through the inlet valve.

When the piston moves downward, compression is created in the crankcase. This compression causes the inner diaphragm to flex in the opposite direction. This action causes the discharge valve to lift off its seat. Fuel is then forced through the discharge valve into the carburetor.

The function of the outer diaphragm is to absorb the pulsations of the fuel and allow a smooth uninterrupted fuel flow.

The Type II fuel pump has the capacity to lift fuel two feet and deliver approximately five gallons per hour at four pounds pressure psi.

Problems with the fuel pump are limited to possible leaks in the flexible neoprene suction lines, a punctured diaphragm, air leaks between sections of the pump assembly, or possibly from the valves becoming distorted or not seating properly.

FUEL PRESSURE CHECK

♦ **See Figures 51 and 52**

✷✷ CAUTION

Lack of an adequate fuel supply will cause the powerhead to run lean, lose rpm, or cause piston scoring and burning.

➡ **If an integral fuel pump carburetor is installed, the fuel pressure cannot be checked.**

Fuel pressure should be checked if a fuel tank, other than the one supplied by the outboard unit's manufacturer, is being used. When the tank is checked, be sure the fuel cap has an adequate air vent. Verify the size of the fuel line from the tank to be sure it is of adequate size to accommodate powerhead demands.

An adequate size line would be one measuring from $5/16$–$3/8$ in. (7.94 to 9.52mm) ID (inside diameter). Check the fuel strainer on the end of the pickup in the fuel tank to be sure it is not too small and is not clogged. Check the fuel pickup tube. The tube must be large enough to accommodate the powerhead fuel demands under all conditions. Be sure to check the filter at the carburetor. Sufficient quantities of fuel cannot pass through into the carburetor to meet powerhead demands if this screen becomes clogged.

1. Mount the outboard unit in a test tank, or on the boat in a body of water.

✷✷ CAUTION

Never operate the engine at high speed with a flush device attached. The engine, operating at high speed with such a device attached, would runaway from lack of a load on the propeller, causing extensive damage.

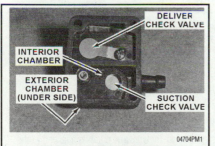

Fig. 48 Major parts of a typical fuel line squeeze bulb used to prime the system and deliver fuel to the carburetor until the powerhead is operating and the pump can deliver the required amount of fuel

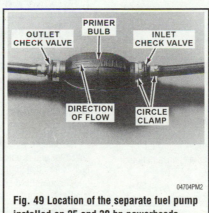

Fig. 49 Location of the separate fuel pump installed on 25 and 30 hp powerheads

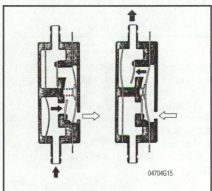

Fig. 50 Cross section drawing of a typical diaphragm displacement type fuel pump

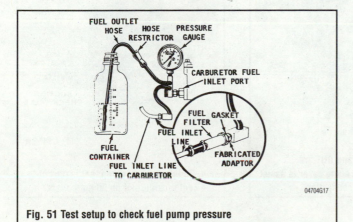

Fig. 51 Test setup to check fuel pump pressure

Fig. 52 Lack of adequate fuel, possibly caused by a defective fuel pump, caused the hole burned into the top of this piston

2. Install the fuel pressure gauge in the fuel line between the fuel pump and the carburetor.

3. Start the engine and check the fuel pressure.

4. Remember, the powerhead will not start without the emergency tether in place behind the kill switch knob.

> ### ❋❋ CAUTION
>
> **Water must circulate through the lower unit to the engine any time the engine is run to prevent damage to the water pump in the lower unit. Just five seconds without water will damage the water pump.**

5. Operate the powerhead at full throttle and check the pressure reading. The gauge should indicate at least 2 psi.

Type II Fuel Pump

➡**Disassembly and assembling should be performed on a clean work surface. Make every effort to prevent foreign material from entering the fuel pump or adhering to the diaphragms.**

REMOVAL & DISASSEMBLY

◆ **See Figure 53**

1. Disconnect the fuel line fuel joint. Disconnect the inlet and outlet hose from the fuel pump. Remove the two bolts securing the pump to the crankcase.

2. Remove the pump and move it to a suitable clean work surface. Remove the three screws securing the pump together. Take care not to let the spring fly out or to lose the cup.

3. Now, carefully separate the parts and keep them in order as an assist in assembling. as a check valve is removed, take time to observe and remember how each valve faces, because it must be installed in exactly the same manner, or the pump will not function.

CLEANING & INSPECTION

Wash all metal parts thoroughly in solvent, and then blow them dry with compressed air. Use care when using compressed air on the check valves. Do not hold the nozzle too close because the check valve can be damaged from an excessive blast of air.

Inspect each part for wear and damage. Verify that the valve seats provide a flat contact area for the valve. Tighten all check valve connections firmly as they are replaced.

Test each check valve by blowing through it with your mouth. In one direction the valve should allow air to pass through. In the other direction, air should not pass through.

Check the diaphragms for pin holes by holding it up to the light. If pin holes are detected or if the diaphragm is not pliable, it MUST be replaced.

ASSEMBLY & INSTALLATION

◆ **See Figure 54**

1. Proper operation of the fuel pump is essential for maximum powerhead performance. Therefore, always use new gaskets.

➡**Never use any type of sealer on fuel pump gaskets.**

2. Place the appropriate check valves on the appropriate sides of the pump body with the fold in the valve facing up. Take care not to damage the very fragile and flat surface of the valve. Secure each check valve in place with a Phillips head screw. Tighten the screw securely.

3. Place the spring, the cup (on top of the spring), the diaphragm, the gasket, and finally the inner cover on the pump body. Hold these parts together and turn the pump over. Install the diaphragm gasket and outer pump cover.

4. Check to be sure the holes for the screws are all aligned through the cover, diaphragms, and gaskets.

5. If the diaphragms are not properly aligned, a tear would surely develop when the screws are installed.

6. Install the three Phillips head screws through the various parts and tighten the screws securely.

7. Position the mounting gasket onto the crankcase and the fuel pump against the gasket.

8. Secure the pump to the powerhead with the two bolts.

9. Connect the fuel line from the filter to the fitting embossed with the word in. Connect the fuel line to the carburetor onto the fitting embossed with the word out.

10. Secure the fuel lines with the wire type clamps.

11. Connect the fuel supply at the fuel joint.

Except 1–2-Cylinder Fuel Pumps

DESCRIPTION & OPERATION

◆ **See Figures 55 and 56**

The next few paragraphs briefly describe operation of the separate fuel pumps used on several Yamaha powerheads. This description is followed by detailed procedures for testing the pressure, testing volume, removing, servicing, and installing the fuel pump.

➡**One fuel pump is used on 3-cylinder and V4 powerheads and two fuel pumps are used on V6 powerheads.**

The pump is a diaphragm displacement type. The pump is attached to the crankcase and is operated by crankcase impulses. A hand-operated squeeze bulb is installed in the fuel line to fill the fuel pump and carburetor with fuel prior to powerhead start. After the powerhead is operating, the pump is able to supply an adequate fuel supply to the carburetor to meet engine demands under all speeds and conditions.

04704PM3

Fig. 53 Disassembly of a Type II fuel pump with major components identified

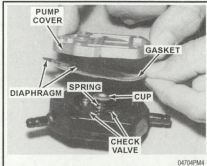

04704PM4

Fig. 54 The words IN and OUT are embossed on the fuel pump cover to assist in making the proper connections

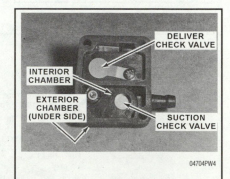

04704PW4

Fig. 55 Integral fuel pump that is part of the center carburetor on 30 hp models

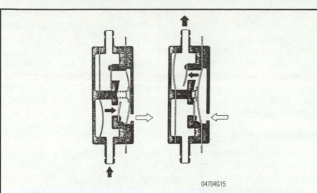

Fig. 56 Cross section drawing of the diaphragm displacement type fuel pump installed on all powerheads except the 30 hp model

The pump consists of a spring loaded inner diaphragm, a spring loaded outer diaphragm, two valves, one for inlet (suction) and the other for outlet (discharge), and a small opening leading directly into the crankcase. The suction and compression created as the piston travels up and down in the cylinder, causes the diaphragms to flex.

The pump is a diaphragm displacement type. The pump is attached to the crankcase and is operated by crankcase impulses. A hand-operated squeeze bulb is installed in the fuel line to fill the fuel pump and carburetor with fuel prior to powerhead start. After the powerhead is operating, the pump is able to supply an adequate fuel supply to the carburetor to meet engine demands under all speeds and condition.

As the piston moves upward, the inner diaphragm will flex inward displacing volume on its opposite side to create suction. This suction will draw fuel in through the inlet valve.

When the piston moves downward, compression is created in the crankcase. This compression causes the inner diaphragm to flex in the opposite direction. This action causes the discharge valve to lift off its seat. Fuel is then forced through the discharge valve into the carburetor.

The function of the outer diaphragm is to absorb the pulsations of the fuel and allow a smooth uninterrupted fuel flow.

This design fuel pump has the capacity to lift fuel two feet and deliver approximately five gallons per hour at four pounds pressure psi.

Problems with the fuel pump are limited to possible leaks in the flexible neoprene suction lines, a punctured diaphragm, air leaks between sections of the pump assembly, or possibly from the valves becoming distorted or not seating properly.

FUEL PUMP PRESSURE CHECK

♦ See Figure 57

Lack of an adequate fuel supply will cause the powerhead to run lean, lose rpm, or cause piston scoring. If an integral fuel pump carburetor is installed, the fuel pressure cannot be checked.

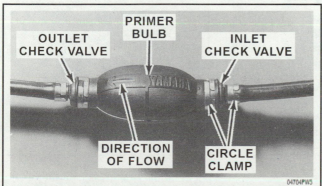

Fig. 57 Major parts of a typical fuel line squeeze bulb. The bulb is used to prime the system and deliver fuel to the carburetor until the powerhead is operating and the pump can deliver the required amount of fuel on its own

Fuel pressure should be checked if a fuel tank, other than the one supplied by the outboard unit's manufacturer, is being used. When the tank is checked, be sure the fuel cap has an adequate air vent. Verify the size of the fuel line from the tank to be sure it is of adequate size to accommodate powerhead demands.

An adequate size line would be one measuring from $\frac{5}{16}$–$\frac{3}{8}$ (7.94 to 9.52mm) ID (inside diameter). Check the fuel strainer on the end of the pickup in the fuel tank to be sure it is not too small and is not clogged. Check the fuel pickup tube. The tube must be large enough to accommodate the powerhead fuel demands under all conditions. Be sure to check the filter at the carburetor. Sufficient quantities of fuel cannot pass through into the carburetor to meet powerhead demands if this screen becomes clogged.

3-Cylinder Powerheads

♦ See Figures 58 and 59

Mount the outboard unit in a test tank, or on the boat in a body of water.

> ※※ CAUTION
>
> **Never operate the engine at high speed with a flush device attached. The engine, operating at high speed with such a device attached, would runaway from lack of a load on the propeller, causing extensive damage.**

Install the fuel pressure gauge in the fuel line between the fuel pump and the carburetor.

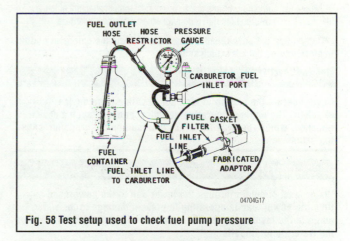

Fig. 58 Test setup used to check fuel pump pressure

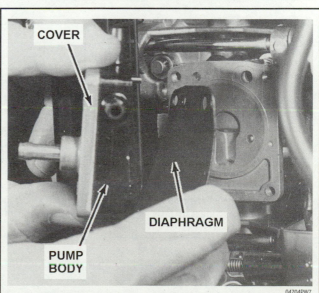

Fig. 59 The integral fuel pump used on the 30 hp model is mounted on the port side of the center carburetor

Start the engine and check the fuel pressure.

➡Remember, the powerhead will not start without the emergency tether in place behind the kill switch knob.

※ CAUTION

Water must circulate through the lower unit to the engine any time the engine is run to prevent damage to the water pump in the lower unit. Just five seconds without water will damage the water pump.

Operate the powerhead at full throttle and check the pressure reading. The gauge should indicate at least 2 psi.

V4 & V6 Powerheads

▶ **See Figures 60, 61 and 62**

Obtain about a foot (30cm) of fuel hose the same size as used on the powerhead being serviced. Obtain a T-fitting compatible with the fuel hose and a pressure gauge.

VACUUM CHECK

If servicing the pump on a V4 powerhead, remove the hose clamps and fuel hose between the fuel filter and the fuel pump. If servicing the pump on a V6 powerhead, remove the fuel filter and existing T fitting.

Replace this hose with the temporary fuel hose cut into workable lengths, with a T fitting installed at the mid-point of the new hose.

Connect the pressure gauge to the open T fitting.

Mount the outboard unit in a test tank, connect a flush attachment to the lower unit, or move the boat into a body of water. Start the powerhead.

➡Remember, the powerhead will not start without the emergency tether in place behind the kill switch knob.

※ CAUTION

Never operate the engine at high speed with a flush device attached. The engine, operating at high speed with such a device attached, would runaway from lack of a load on the propeller, causing extensive damage.

※ CAUTION

Water must circulate through the lower unit to the powerhead anytime the powerhead is operating to prevent damage to the water pump in the lower unit. Just five seconds without water will damage the water pump impeller.

Observe the vacuum reading on the pressure gauge. When the powerhead is operating between 4700 and 5500 rpm, the gauge should register 2.13 in. Hg (7.2 kPa) vacuum.

If the fuel pumps do not pull this amount of vacuum, insufficient fuel is reaching the cylinders. This may cause a surge, or a loss of power. Check the fuel hoses for a restriction before removing and replacing the fuel pumps.

Remove the temporary fuel hoses and install the original hoses. Secure the hoses to the inlet fittings on the carburetors with new hose clamps. If a decision has been reached to replace the fuel pumps.

PRESSURE CHECK

If servicing the pump on a V4 powerhead, remove the hose clamps and fuel hose between the fuel filter and the fuel pump. If servicing the pump on a V6 powerhead, remove the fuel filter and existing T fitting.

Replace this hose with the temporary fuel hose cut into workable lengths, with a T fitting installed at the mid-point of the new hose.

Connect the pressure gauge to the open T fitting.

Mount the outboard unit in a test tank, connect a flush attachment to the lower unit, or move the boat into a body of water. Start the powerhead.

➡Remember, the powerhead will not start without the emergency tether in place behind the kill switch knob.

※ CAUTION

Never operate the engine at high speed with a flush device attached. The engine, operating at high speed with such a device attached, would runaway from lack of a load on the propeller, causing extensive damage.

※ CAUTION

Water must circulate through the lower unit to the powerhead anytime the powerhead is operating to prevent damage to the water pump in the lower unit. Just five seconds without water will damage the water pump impeller.

Observe the pressure reading on the gauge. When the powerhead is operating between 4700 and 5500 rpm, the gauge should register 5.7 psi.

If the fuel pumps do not produce this amount of pressure, insufficient fuel is reaching the cylinders. This may cause a surge, or a loss of power. Check the fuel hoses for a restriction before removing and replacing the fuel pumps.

Remove the temporary fuel hoses and install the original hoses. Secure the hoses to the inlet fittings on the carburetors with new hose clamps. If a decision has been reached to replace the fuel pumps.

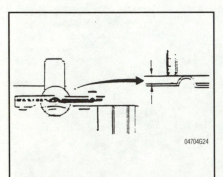

04704G24

Fig. 60 Gauge connections required to perform vacuum and pressure tests on V4 powerhead fuel pump

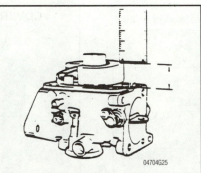

04704G25

Fig. 61 Gauge connections required to perform vacuum and pressure tests on V4 powerhead fuel pump

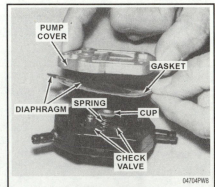

04704PW8

Fig. 62 Exploded view of the fuel pump used on all models except the 30 hp unit

REMOVAL & DISASSEMBLY

▶ **See accompanying illustrations**

➡Disassembly and assembling should be performed on a clean work surface. Make every effort to prevent foreign material from entering the fuel pump or adhering to the diaphragms.

1. Disconnect the fuel line fuel joint.
2. Disconnect the inlet and outlet hose from the fuel pumps. Remove the two bolts securing the pumps to the crankcase.
3. Remove the pumps and move it to a suitable clean work surface. Remove the three screws securing the pump together. Take care not to let the spring fly out or to lose the cup.
4. Separate the back cover from the pump body. If the gasket and diaphragm are to be used again, take great care in peeling them away from the surface of the cover. Remove the spring and cup. Separate the parts and keep them in order as an assist in assembling.

Remove the front cover from the pump body. If the diaphragm and gasket are to be used again, take great care in peeling them away from the surface of the cover. Separate the parts and keep them in order as an assist in assembling.

5. Remove the check valves and take time to observe and remember how each valve faces, because it MUST be installed in exactly the same manner, or the pump will not function.

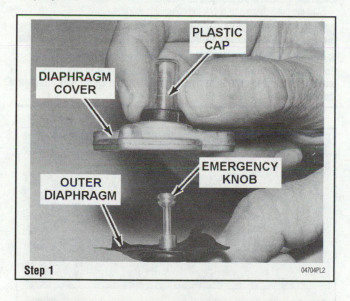

Step 1   04704PL2

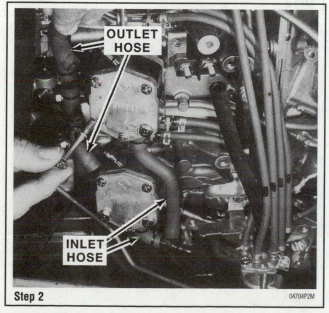

Step 2   04704P2M

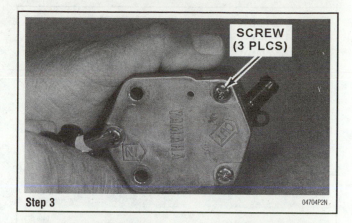

Step 3   04704P2N

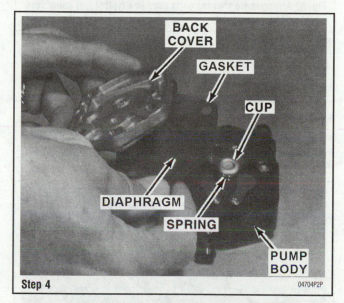

Step 4   04704P2P

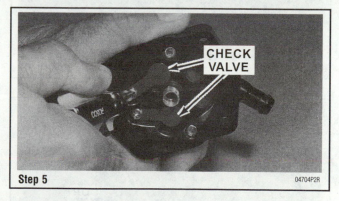

Step 5   04704P2R

CLEANING & INSPECTION

▶ **See Figure 63**

Wash all metal parts thoroughly in solvent, and then blow them dry with compressed air. Use care when using compressed air on the check valves. Do not hold the nozzle too close because the check valve can be damaged from an excessive blast of air.

Inspect each part for wear and damage. Verify that the valve seats provide a flat contact area for the valve. Tighten all check valve connections firmly as they are replaced.

Test each check valve by blowing through it with your mouth. In one direction the valve should allow air to pass through. In the other direction, air should not pass through.

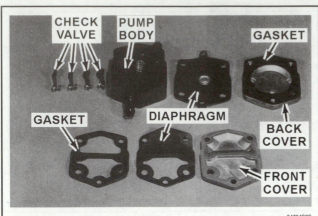

Fig. 63 Arrangement showing parts used in a typical fuel pump used on V4 and V6 powerheads

Check the diaphragms for pin holes by holding it up to the light. If pin holes are detected or if the diaphragm is not pliable, it must be replaced.

ASSEMBLY & INSTALLATION

▶ **See accompanying illustrations**

➡ **Proper operation of the fuel pump is essential for maximum power-head performance. Therefore, always use new gaskets. Never use any type of sealer on fuel pump gaskets.**

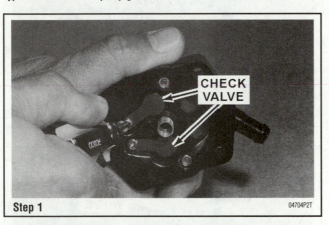

Step 1

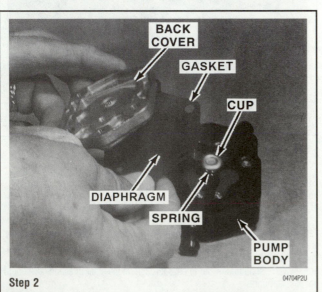

Step 2

1. Place the appropriate check valves on the appropriate sides of the pump body with the fold in the valve facing up. Take care not to damage the very fragile and flat surface of the valve. Secure each check valve in place with a Phillips head screw. Tighten the screw securely.

2. Place the spring, the cup (on top of the spring), the diaphragm, the gasket, and finally the inner cover on the pump body. Hold these parts together and turn the pump over.

Install the gasket and then the diaphragm onto the pump body. Install the front cover.

3. Check to be sure the holes for the screws are all aligned through the cover, diaphragms, and gaskets. If the diaphragms are not properly aligned, a tear would surely develop when the screws are installed.

Install the three Phillips head screws through the various parts and tighten the screws securely.

Position the mounting gasket onto the crankcase and the fuel pump against the gasket.

Secure the pumps to the powerhead with the two bolts.

4. Connect the fuel line from the filter to the fitting embossed with the word **IN**. Connect the fuel line to the carburetor onto the fitting embossed with the word out.

Secure the fuel lines with the wire type clamps.

Connect the fuel supply at the fuel joint.

Mount the outboard unit in a test tank, connect a flush attachment to the lower unit, or move the boat into a body of water.

Start the powerhead and check the completed work.

✴✴ CAUTION

Water must circulate through the lower unit to the powerhead any-time the powerhead is operating to prevent damage to the water pump in the lower unit. Just five seconds without water will damage the water pump impeller.

Step 3

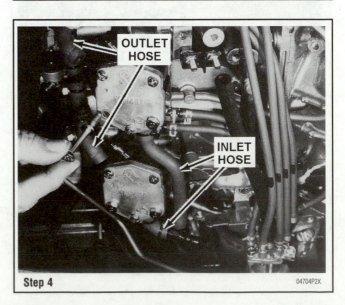

Step 4

ELECTRONIC FUEL INJECTION

Beginning with the 1996 model year, Saltwater Series V76 engines are equipped with electronic fuel injection (EFI). This system improves low speed smoothness, reduces maintenance, improves durability, and increases fuel efficiency. The Electronic Control Unit (computer) is capable of adjusting fuel delivery and ignition timing Over a wide range. Unlike carburetor-equipped engines, these new fuel-injected engines can automatically adjust for changes in altitude, air temperature, and barometric pressure. This precise control over engine operation results in crisp throttle response and maximum efficiency over a broad range of conditions.

Fuel Injection Basics

▶ **See Figure 64**

Fuel injection is not a new invention. Even as early as the 1950s, various automobile manufacturers experimented with mechanical-type injection systems. There was even a vacuum tube equipped control unit offered for one system! This might have been the first "electronic fuel injection system." Early problems with fuel injection revolved around the control components. The electronics were not very smart or reliable. These systems have steadily improved since. Today's fuel injection technology, responding to the need for better economy and emission control, has become amazingly reliable and efficient. Computerized engine management, the brain of fuel injection, continues to get more reliable and more precise.

Components needed for a basic computer-controlled system are as follows:
- A computer-controlled engine manager, which is the Electronic Control Unit (or ECU), with a set of internal maps to follow.
- A set of input devices to inform the ECU of engine performance parameters.
- A set of output devices. Each device is controlled by the ECU. These devices modify fuel delivery and timing. Changes to fuel and timing are based on input information matched to the map programs.

This list gets a little more complicated when you start to look at specific components. Some fuel injection systems may have twenty or more input devices. On many systems, output control can extend beyond fuel and timing. The Yamaha Fuel Injection System provides more than just the basic functions, but is still straight forward in its layout. There are twelve input devices and six output controls. The diagram on the following page shows the input and output devices with their functions.

There are several fuel injection delivery methods. Throttle body injection is relatively inexpensive and was used widely in early automotive systems. This is usually a low pressure system running at 15 PSI or less. Often an engine with a single carburetor was selected for throttle body injection. The carburetor was recast to hold a single injector. and the original manifold was retained. Throttle body injection is not as precise or efficient as port injection.

Multi-port fuel injection is defined as one or more electrically activated solenoid injectors for each cylinder. Multi-port injection generally operates at higher pressures than throttle body systems. The Yamaha system operates at 35.5 PSI.

Port injectors can be triggered two ways. One system uses simultaneous injection. All injectors are triggered at once. The fuel "hangs around" until the pressure drop in the cylinder pulls the fuel into the combustion chamber.

The second type is more precise and follows the firing order of the engine. Each cylinder gets a squirt of fuel precisely when needed.

Yamaha Tuned Port Injection

Yamaha uses the tuned port, sequential method of fuel injection. The injectors are located between the throttle air valves and the reed valves. The ECU controls fuel and ignition timing in two stages. In stage one, the ECU controls ignition timing and fuel injection volume according to information gathered about engine speed from the Crankshaft Position Sensor (CPS) and throttle opening from the Throttle Position Sensor (TPS).

In stage two, the ECU fine tunes the fuel mixture according to information from several other sensors, especially the Oxygen sensor. This second stage is sometimes referred to as closed loop mode. Closed-loop mode means that the oxygen sensor information is used to control enrichment. In an open loop condition, one or more sensors (the oxygen sensor is usually the critical input) is missing or out of range. Open-loop operation controls the engine by a fixed map or pre-programmed information in the ECU. An additional feature of the Yamaha system is return-to-port capability or limp mode. If there is a major sensor failure that prevents the ECU from processing, the engine is run on a minimum performance map. The only input that will shut the engine down completely is battery voltage. If the battery is disconnected or the battery voltage falls below 9 volts, the fuel pump quits pumping so the engine stops.

Fuel Injection Components

▶ **See Figure 65**

The Yamaha fuel injection system is divided into three component groups. These are:
- Electronic control system
- Fuel system
- Air induction group

The air induction and fuel systems are the delivery agents for the fuel/ air mixture. The fuel delivery system is controlled by the electronic control system. The electronic control system can be further subdivided into input sensors (the informants), outputs (the workers that make adjustments to fuel and timing), and the computer (the boss or decision maker).

ELECTRONIC CONTROL SYSTEM

The electronic control system has the largest number of individual components.

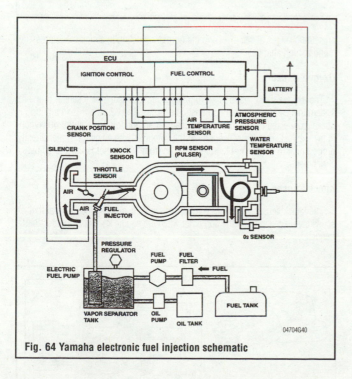

Fig. 64 Yamaha electronic fuel injection schematic

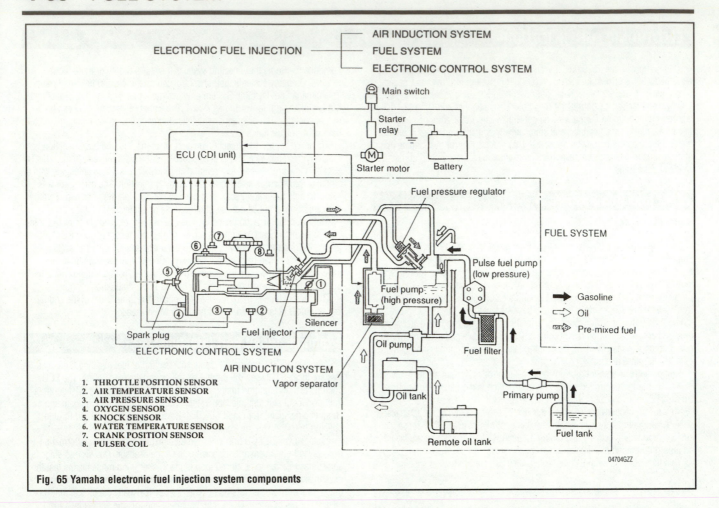

Fig. 65 Yamaha electronic fuel injection system components

Throttle Position Sensor

▶ See Figure 66

The TPS signals the ECU/CDI unit how much throttle opening the operator is requesting.

Air Temperature Sensor

▶ See Figure 67

The air temperature sensor monitors air temperature under the cowl and reports the information to the ECU/CDT in a continuous stream.

Air Temperature Sensor

The atmospheric pressure sensor works like a barometer and reports barometric pressure. This sensor allows the computer to compensate for barometric pressure changes at sea level and the normal reduction in atmospheric pressure found at high altitudes.

Oxygen Sensor

The oxygen sensor is the fine-tuning sensor. This is the only sensor in the system that can monitor the combustion process. The 02 sensor is in a blind pocket connected to the combustion chamber. It monitors the amount of oxygen in the exhaust. This sensor reports to the computer with a voltage signal directly proportional to oxygen content. Information from this sensor is used to adjust enrichment.

Knock Sensor

The knock sensor works like a microphone. It contains a tuned crystal that sends a voltage signal to the computer when the engine knocks at a prescribed frequency.

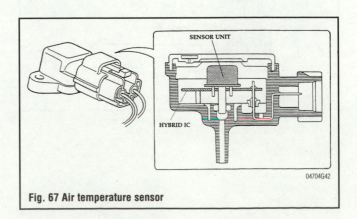

Fig. 66 Throttle position sensor and schematic

Fig. 67 Air temperature sensor

Water Temperature Sensor

The water temperature sensor monitors cooling water temperature. This is essential information during cold starts and warm-up.

Crankshaft Position Sensor

The crank position sensor is a coil and magnet that tracks the crankshaft location. This information is combined with pulser firing information to yield ignition and fuel injection timing. Additionally, this information combined with an internal clock results in a highly accurate RPM counter.

Pulser Coil

The pulser coil is considered an input and an output. It provides the timing signal for fuel injection pulses (input). The pulser signal is also processed by the computer to accomplish timing changes. Once this processing occurs it becomes an output.

Additional Inputs

Additional inputs include:
- The key switch, which tells the computer when to begin the program
- The thermoswitch (overheat) for overheat information
- Oil level sensor information
- The shift cut switch
- The lanyard switch
- The gray over-rev loop lead

Although not strictly inputs, battery power and ground are essential for computer operation. This computer also monitors battery voltage. As battery voltage drops, the injectors would open more slowly, decreasing fuel delivery volume. Therefore, when the computer detects low battery voltage, it makes adjustments to injector "time on" to keep fuel delivery volume correct.

Return To Port

Disconnecting the red emergency lead allows the operator to put the computer into a fixed fuel delivery mode. This fixed mode is rich at idle and lean above 4000 rpm. When the emergency lead is disconnected the operator should not exceed 4000 rpm.

FUEL DELIVERY SYSTEM

Fuel injectors require clean, water-free, pressurized gasoline. The Yamaha fuel delivery system uses four filters, a vapor separator tank assembly, a two-speed electric fuel pump, a set of pulse or mechanical fuel pumps, and the six rail-mounted fuel injectors. Oil mixing is accomplished with a standard oil pump. This pump injects oil into the vapor separator tank.

Fuel Supply and the Vapor Separator Tank

The supply side of this system is similar to Yamaha carbureted engines. Fuel is pulled from the six gallon or boat tank through a primer bulb and hose to the engine-mounted fuel filter (paper filter #1). Next the mechanical pumps push the fuel on to the separator tank.

The vapor separator tank is a multipurpose reservoir. It acts as a "burp" tank for any air in the supply side of the system. This ensures that the high-pressure pump does not pump any air. The separator tank is vented into the air intake to recirculate any vapor that accumulates. Fuel is pumped from the separator by an internally mounted two-stage electric fuel pump. Fuel drawn in through the bottom of this pump passes through a 400-mesh screen (filter #2). High-pressure fuel from this pump (35.5 PSI) keeps the injectors charged. Pressurizing the fuel in the injector fuel rail retards gum formation. Often, EFI engines will crank after a year of storage.

The pump is designed to supply more fuel to the injectors than maximum demand requires. The regulator controls this over supply by diverting excess high pressure fuel through a filter (filter #4) and then back to the separator. This loop (separator tank to the injectors through the regulator and back to the separator tank) is typical of most fuel injection systems.

Oil Injection

The separator also functions as the mixing chamber for oil and fuel. Oil is injected into the separator tank by the engine-driven oil pump. The amount of oil delivered to the separator tank is dependent upon engine RPM and throttle opening. The supply side of the oil injection system is similar to previous PBS models.

The Fuel Injectors

▶ See Figure 68

The center fed fuel injectors in this system consist of a fuel filter (filter #3), a coil, an actuator, a return spring, and a nozzle. The injector coil wire is connected to the ECU. When fuel delivery is needed, the injector is retracted by current fed through the coil. The coil pulls the actuator back electromagnetically. The pull on the actuator overcomes the spring that normally holds it closed. The pressurized fuel sprays out of the nozzle into the reed valves. The amount of time the current is on determines the amount of fuel injected. The ECU can vary injector time on for two reasons. The first reason is that engine demand has changed. The second possibility is that demand is steady but the ECU has detected a drop in system voltage. The computer will leave the injector on slightly longer to compensate for slower injector opening response (and less fuel delivery) because of the lower voltage.

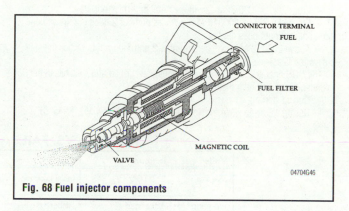

CONNECTOR TERMINAL
FUEL
FUEL FILTER
MAGNETIC COIL
VALVE
04704G46

Fig. 68 Fuel injector components

AIR INDUCTION GROUP

▶ See Figure 69

There are six individual induction tracts in a single bank. There is one tract for each cylinder. Each induction tract has an air throttle valve and an injector. The throttle position sensor is mounted on the port side of the #1 throttle valve. Throttle valve synchronization procedures are similar to inline engines. These engines will require synchronization less frequently than carburetor-equipped engines. Tight synchronization and correct throttle position sensor adjustment, however, are critical as they have been with previous V76X engines.

Controlled Combustion System

The Controlled Combustion System (CCS) improves low speed stability for trolling. The engine is designed to run on 5 cylinders between 500 and 850 RPM. Between 850 and 2000 RPM only 4 cylinders are operating. This reduces noise, increases slow speed stability and improves fuel economy.

It is an inventive solution to the problems associated with running a large displacement engine at trolling speed. A large displacement engine is not working hard enough at low speeds to maintain peak combustion efficiency. It is also difficult to meter small amounts of fuel and air precisely through large diameter carburetors and intakes. These problems can result in excessive fuel consumption and roughness when trolling for extended periods. The CCS effectively shrinks engine size by limiting fuel delivery to 4 or 5 cylinders, depending on RPM. Fuel injection also solves the metering problems encountered with large bore carburetors. The overall effect is a smooth, fuel-efficient engine at low speeds.

This new system does not require a scan tool to access the diagnostic system. The V76X diagnostic lamp works on this system also.

The new ECU now has more maps to cover a wider range of operating situations. This ECU also has more inputs to make decisions and takes a wider range of output actions than its predecessors.

To improve low-speed smoothness at reduced throttle settings, cylinder #5 does not fire between idle and 850 RPM. Cylinders #5 and #2 do not fire between 850 RPM and 2000 RPM, again depending upon throttle opening.

If the shift cut switch is activated during CCS operation, the following cylinders do not fire:

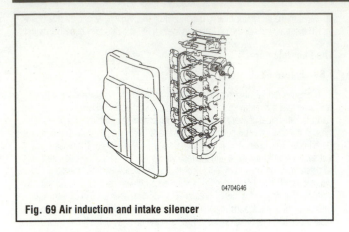

04704G46

Fig. 69 Air induction and intake silencer

- From idle to 2000 RPM—cylinder number 5 does not fire
- From 850 RPM to2000 RPM—cylinder number 2 does not fire and one additional cylinder does not fire
- Above 2000 RPM—cylinders number 2 and 5 do not fire when the shift cut switch is activated.

The CCS operates selectively as previously described and switches to full 6-cylinder operation under the following conditions:
- During starting
- During warm-up when the water temperature is below 113°F (45°C)

- When the oxygen sensor is not functioning
- Under acceleration
- When decelerating
- When the knock sensor is activated
- When the warning system is activated (RPM reduction, horn and red indicator activated due to overheat, low oil, or dual engine problem)
- When there is a sensor failure.

Normal vs. Fail Safe Control

NORMAL MODE

The following chart lists normal occurring modes or MAPS of operation. The adjustments made to fuel and ignition are in the right columns. On Condition describes what puts the computer into that particular mode or turns it on.

If the computer goes to Fail Safe Control, a sensor has malfunctioned. Oxygen feed back operation and Controlled Combustion are suspended. When Controlled Combustion stops, the engine runs on all six cylinders at all times. This may result in rough idling.

FAIL SAFE CONTROL (RETURN TO PORT) MODE

The nine diagnostic code numbers and their effects on engine operation are listed below. Note that a loose battery cable (with a single battery installation) will stop the engine due to no fuel delivery.

NORMAL VS. FAILSAFE CONTROL MODES

Mode	Ignition	Fuel	"ON" Condition	"OFF" Condition
Starting	7° BTDC	Initial Injection	Key switch position "START"	Engine speed exceeds approx. 700 RPM
Warming Up	Advanced	Richer	Engine speed exceeds approximately 700 RPM	Engine temperature 113°F and up
Idling	5 or 4 cylinder firing	Minimized fuel for off ignition cylinders	Engine speed approx. 2,000 RPM or less and throttle valve closed	Engine speed exceeds approx. 2,000 RPM or throttle valve widely open
Gentle Acceleration	Normal	Normal	Slowly opening throttle valve	
Rapid Acceleration	Normal	Richer	Throttle valve widely opened	Engine speed exceeds approx. 5,000 RPM or throttle valve closed
Knocking	Retard the timing step by step	Normal	Knocking signal entered	Close the throttle valve to less than 1/4 opening

04704C99

EFI DIAGNOSTIC CODES

TROUBLE		RESULT		
Code	Part	Ignition	Fuel	Output
13	Pulser Coil	Off ignition according to the sensor(s)	6 cylinder injection with the MAP (Group Injection)	Maximum speed not reached
14	Crank Angle Sensor	7° BTDC	Normal (Sequential Injection)	Maximum speed not reached (higher idling)
15	Engine Temperature Sensor	Advanced timing at idle (7° BTDC)	Fixed fuel enrichment when starting	Higher idling
17	Knocking Sensor	7° BTDC	Richer	Maximum speed not reached and higher idling
18	Throttle Position Sensor	7° BTDC	According to engine speed only	Maximum speed not reached
19	Yellow Emergency Leads (removed)	7° BTDC	Group Injection	Tachometer Signal stops and higher idling. Maximum speed not reached
22	Atmosphere Pressure Sensor	Normal	MAP data on 35.5 PSI fixed	Richer at high altitude
23	Atmosphere Temperature Sensor	Normal	MAP data on 5°C fixed	Maximum speed not reached. Richer above 5°C
24	Battery Cable (Loosened)		Fuel stops	Engine stops

04704C98

OIL INJECTION SYSTEM 5-2
DESCRIPTION AND OPERATION 5-2
  SYSTEM COMPONENTS 5-3
TROUBLESHOOTING 5-7
WIRE COLORS 5-7
GENERAL INFORMATION 5-7
  MAIN (ENGINE) OIL TANK
    OVERFLOWING 5-7
  OIL WILL NOT TRANSFER 5-8
  EXCESSIVE SMOKE AT IDLE 5-9
SERVICING 5-10
3-CYLINDER POWERHEADS 5-10
OIL INJECTION SYSTEM 5-10
  REMOVAL 5-10
  INSTALLATION 5-12
  BLEEDING 5-15
  ADJUSTMENT 5-17
  TESTING 5-19
OIL PUMP 5-21
  DISASSEMBLY 5-21
  CLEANING & INSPECTING 5-21
  ASSEMBLY 5-22
V4 AND V6 POWERHEADS 5-23
MAIN OIL TANK 5-23
  REMOVAL 5-23
  INSTALLATION 5-23
  TESTING 5-24
REMOTE OIL TANK 5-24
  TESTING 5-24
  REMOVAL 5-25
  CLEANING & INSPECTING 5-26
  INSTALLATION 5-26
OIL PUMP 5-27
  REMOVAL 5-27
  DISASSEMBLY 5-27
  CLEANING & INSPECTING 5-28
  ASSEMBLY 5-29
  INSTALLATION 5-31
  BLEEDING 5-32
INJECTION CONTROL LINK ROD 5-33
  ADJUSTMENT 5-33
OIL INJECTION WARNING SYSTEM 5-33
  DESCRIPTION & OPERATION 5-33
  TROUBLESHOOTING 5-35
  OPERATIONAL CHECK 5-36
WIRING DIAGRAMS 5-38
SPECIFICATIONS CHART
  OIL PUMP OUTPUT
  SPECIFICATIONS 5-9
TROUBLESHOOTING CHART
  OIL TRANSFER PUMP
  TROUBLESHOOTING CHART 5-8

5

OIL INJECTION

OIL INJECTION SYSTEM 5-2
TROUBLESHOOTING 5-7
SERVICING 5-10
WIRING DIAGRAMS 5-38

OIL INJECTION SYSTEM

Description and Operation

▶ **See Figures 1, 2, 3 and 4**

In the past, two-stroke outboard motors required the oil and gas to be mixed. This method supplied the engine with the oil necessary for lubrication.

This system, while simple, has several drawbacks:

• The boat owner has to remember to mix oil with the gas. The owner also has to remember the correct mix ratio. This is a messy and sometimes confusing task for many customers.

• If the owner forgets to add oil the engine can be ruined. There is no simple way for the customer to verify or remember if oil has been added.

• Even when the oil is mixed at the correct ratio, this ratio is not perfect for all engine speeds. An engine may need as little as 200:1 (200 parts gas to 1 part oil) at idle and as much as 50:1 (50 parts gas to 1 part oil) at wide open throttle. Mix ratios must be set rich for safety. This means that at idle, the motor may be getting more oil than it needs. This can foul plugs and produces large clouds of smoke.

The Precision Blend System (PBS) system used by Yamaha solves many of the problems associated with premixing. At the heart of the system is a mechan-ical oil pump driven by a brass gear on the crankshaft. As engine rpm changes, so does oil pump output. An arm on the side of the pump is connected to the carburetor linkage. As the carburetors open, the arm moves to increase the pump's stroke. The increased stroke produces an increase in oil output.

By having a pump that is sensitive to engine rpm and carburetor opening, the engine receives the exact amount of oil at all times. This increases engine life and reduces oil consumption and smoke. The oil feed lines from the pump go directly into the intake manifold. By having oil delivered to the intake, any change in oil delivery is almost instantaneous.

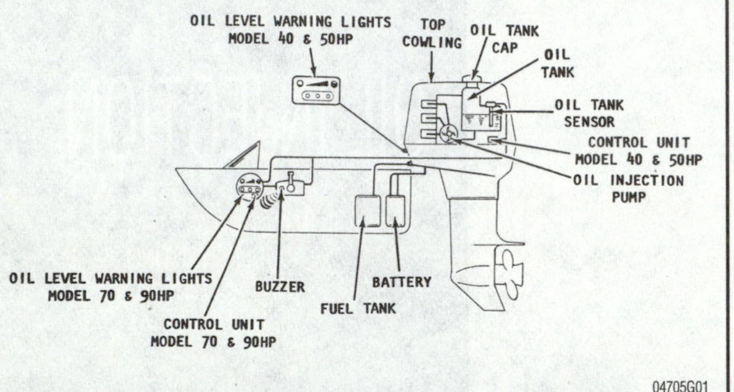

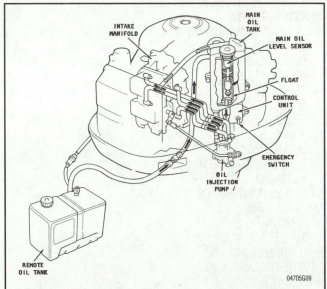

Fig. 3 Typical oil injection system showing relative position and function of major components—V4 and V6 powerheads

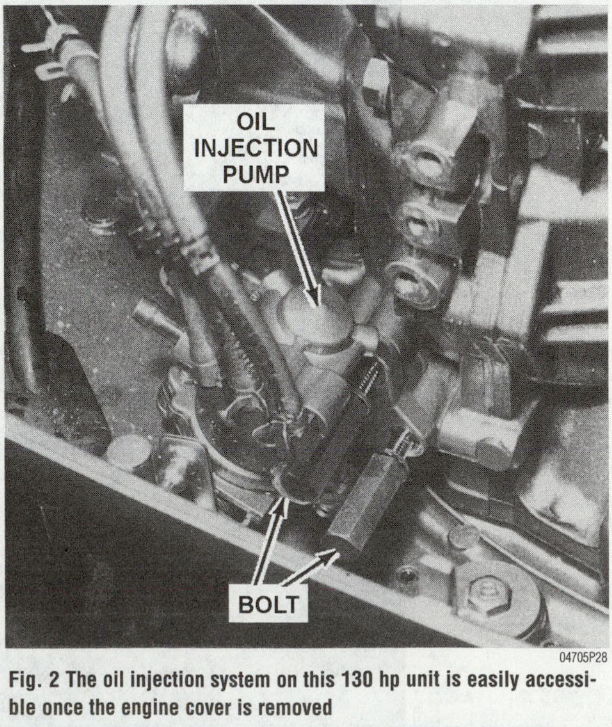

Fig. 1 Simplified functional diagram of an oil injection system. The diagram depicts the relative location of the major components

Fig. 2 The oil injection system on this 130 hp unit is easily accessible once the engine cover is removed

Fig. 4 Major components of a 3-cylinder powerhead oil injection system

Other oil injection systems deliver oil to the carburetor bowl. Oil mixed in the carburetor bowl will take several seconds to enter the engine. If engine rpm or load changes rapidly, the slower response of a bowl-mix system may leave the engine momentarily under-oiled or over-oiled.

The PBS system also reduces the mess associated with premixing the oil and gas. The fuel is in one tank and the oil in another. Another feature of the PBS is a low-oil level warning indicator. The oil level is microprocessor monitored. When the oil level is low, a warning indicator flashes and rpm is reduced to 2,000.

For safety's sake, a hold circuit is built into the PBS system. Once the rpm reduction has been activated, the system must be reset to bring back full rpm operation. rpm will not automatically increase even if the oil tank is refilled. The reset for late models is to return to idle and on older models the ignition key must be cycled from **OFF** to **ON**.

Finally, a holding system protects the owner from an unexpected increase in rpm if he accidentally refills the PBS with the engine running.

SYSTEM COMPONENTS

➡ **The system components discussed in this section are inclusive of all components installed on all Yamaha outboards. Not all components are installed on every outboard.**

On a powerheads equipped with Yamaha Microcomputer Ignition System (YMIS), an extra lead from the oil injection control unit to the microcomputer is used. Other than this one difference, the oil injection systems installed on most powerheads are identical.

Main Oil Tank

▶ **See Figures 5 and 6**

Oil supply to the oil injection pump is gravity feed from the oil tank. A breather for the tank is located next to the filler cap. This breather must remain open at all times.

The main oil tank is mounted on the powerhead. The oil tank filler is easily accessible on top of the cowling. A transparent plastic water/dust trap, located at the bottom of the main oil tank, is used to trap contaminates.

Remote Oil Tank

▶ **See Figure 7**

V4 and V6 powerheads use a remote oil tank installed in a convenient location in the boat. The remote tank feeds the main oil tank with fresh oil when the level of the main tank drops below 0.53 U.S. quarts (0.5 liters).

Oil Tank Sensors

▶ **See Figures 8 and 9**

An oil level sensor is mounted in the main oil tank. The sensor consists of a float sliding up and down in the sensor shaft between stops. The float rises and

Fig. 5 Most systems have a transparent water/dust trap located at the bottom of the main oil tank

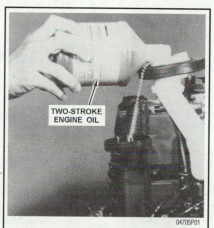

Fig. 6 Filling the oil tank with a quality two-stroke engine oil such as Yamalube

Fig. 7 The remote oil tank may be installed in any convenient location on the boat, but should be close to the outboard unit

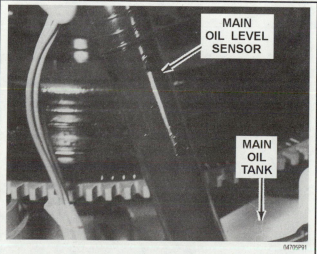

Fig. 8 The design of the main oil sensor on powerheads equipped with YMIS differs from the one used on standard CDI ignition powerheads. However, both use a small oil filter inside the sensor

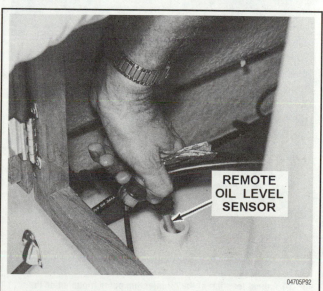

Fig. 9 Removing the oil level sensor from a remote oil tank

falls with the level of the oil. This sensor monitors the remaining oil level in the tank and, if the oil level falls to a dangerously low level or if the oil filter should become clogged, it sends signals to the oil level lights, the warning buzzer and on some powerheads , the control unit. The sensor signal sent to the control unit automatically causes powerhead rpm to be reduced.

On models with main and remote oil tanks, the oil level in the main tank is replenished after it falls to 0.53 U.S. quarts (0.5 liters). The oil tank sensor signals the feed pump in the remote tank to replenish the main tank. Oil will be pumped up from the remote tank to the main tank, until the level in the main tank reaches 0.9 U.S. quarts (0.85 liters). If there is no oil in the remote tank, the Yellow warning light will come on to inform the operator of the condition of the remote tank. Under this condition, the powerhead will operate strictly on the oil remaining in the main tank.

When the oil level in the main tank falls to 0.3 U.S. quarts (0.3 liters), the oil level sensor will activate the Red warning light, cause the buzzer to sound and send a signal to the ignition control unit. The signal received by the ignition control unit will automatically cause powerhead rpm to be reduced.

There is no ignition cutout switch. Theoretically, it is possible to operate the powerhead when the main oil tank is dry, leading to overheating and seizure. However, the manufacturer has incorporated enough visual and audible danger signals to alert the operator well before any internal engine damage occurs.

➡ **If the warning system should operate and the buzzer sound, the powerhead must be shut down and the oil in the tank replenished. Filling the tank will cancel the engine speed restrictions.**

Oil Injection Pump

♦ **See Figures 10, 11, 12 and 13**

The oil injection pump is a positive displacement type unit driven by a worm gear and two short shafts from the lower end of the crankshaft. A gear pressed onto the lower end of the crankshaft drives the worm gear and a short shaft indexed with a second short shaft to the pump. This second short shaft to the pump drives the plunger cam. With each revolution of the plunger cam, the plunger moves up and down three times pumping oil to the cylinders.

A link from the lower carburetor operates the oil injection pump lever. This lever affects the movement of the plunger cam by limiting the plunger stroke. In this manner, the amount of oil leaving the pump is regulated. As throttle movement is advanced and crankshaft rotation is increased, the amount of oil entering the intake manifold will increase. The mixing ratio depends upon the angle of the pump lever shaft. The pump lever shaft is directly connected to the throttle plate

Fig. 11 An oil injection pump removed from the powerhead. Note the oil hose nipples and the ball where the link rod attaches

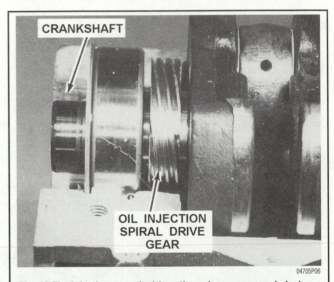

Fig. 12 The injection pump is driven through a worm gear indexing with a spiral gear pressed onto the lower end of the driveshaft—3-cylinder powerheads

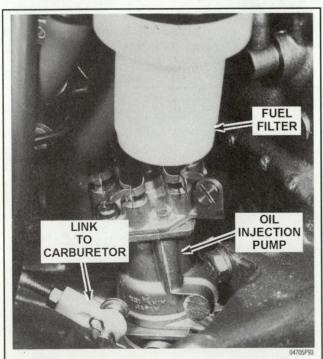

Fig. 10 Typical location of the oil injection pump mounted on the powerhead—3-Cylinder powerhead

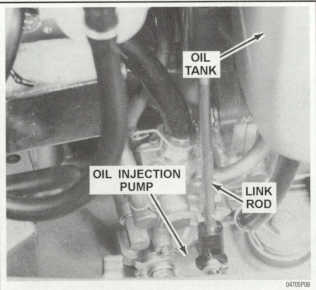

Fig. 13 Typical location of the oil injection pump mounted on the powerhead—V4 and V6 powerhead

via a link rod. If the lever angle is between 0° and 5°, the mixing ratio is 200:1. If the lever angle is between 5° and 50°, the mixing ratio is between 200:1 and 50:1.

The oil leaves the pump and is delivered to the cylinders through a series of four or six transparent hoses.

Oil Feed Pump

▶ **See Figure 14**

The oil feed pump is located at the rear of the remote oil tank. The unit is an electrically-operated gear type pump capable of delivering oil from the remote tank to the main tank.

The pump is activated to start and stop by signals from the oil sensor in the main tank. Under normal operation conditions, when the oil level in the main tank falls to a predetermined low level, the sensor sends a signal and the oil feed pump is activated. The pump will deliver oil to the main tank until the oil level in the main tank reaches a predetermined full quantity. At this time, another signal is sent to the oil feed pump and pumping from the remote tank ceases.

The oil feed pump will pump oil until only 1.6 U.S. quarts (1.5 liters) remain in the tank. However, a manual override of the main oil tank sensor will permit the pump to be activated and the remote tank drained of all oil. This override action is accomplished by activating the emergency switch on the control box. A detailed explanation of the emergency switch is given in later paragraphs.

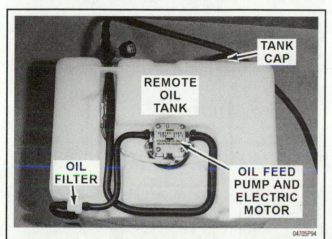

Fig. 14 This remote oil tank has been removed from the boat to clearly show the oil feed pump and electric motor. The oil filter, normally hidden, is also visible

Control Unit

▶ **See Figures 15 and 16**

The control unit may be installed in the bottom cowling, in the warning light display, at the rear of the instrument panel or directly beneath the main oil injection tank on the powerhead.

The control unit receives input signals from the oil level sensors in both oil tanks and determines which light should illuminate on the display. The control unit also sends signals to the buzzer in the remote control box and to the CDI unit to reduce powerhead speed under specified conditions.

Tilt Switch

The tilt switch is a function of the control unit and is incorporated inside the unit. Should the powerhead be tilted during operation, the sensors in both tanks would register a false reading. This condition could cause unnecessary transfer of oil from the remote tank to the main tank, possibly filling and overflowing the tank. The tilt switch senses the angle of the powerhead at all times. If the unit is tilted beyond 35° to the vertical, the tilt switch cuts out the oil feed pump circuit until the powerhead returns to 20° or less.

Emergency Switch

The emergency switch is located on the face of the control unit directly beneath the main oil tank on the powerhead. A decal on the control box describes the purpose of the switch. Because the decal may no longer be legible, the wording is given here:

Holding up the emergency switch pumps reserve oil into the main oil tank so you can continue cruising.

When the switch is held in the up position, the operator is able to manually override the signal from the main oil tank sensor and cause the oil feed pump to completely drain the remote tank.

The emergency switch should only be activated if the operator is unable to replenish the remote tank and is forced to use the tank's reserve capacity. If the emergency switch is released before all the oil is pumped to the main tank, the necessity of bleeding the oil feed pump may be avoided. If the remote tank is pumped completely dry, the feed pump must be purged of air.

Buzzer

▶ **See Figure 17**

The buzzer is installed in the remote control box and warns the operator of a possible problem. The most common cause is low oil level in the remote tank. However, the buzzer can be activated by a signal from three different sensors—the overrev sensor, the overheating sensor, and the low oil sensor. If the buzzer sounds due to a signal from the overrev or overheating sensor, the signal will be

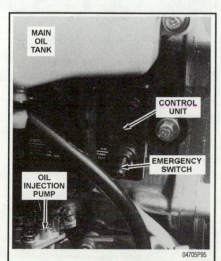

Fig. 15 Location of the control unit in relation to other oil injection components. The tilt switch is incorporated into the control unit

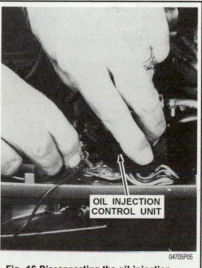

Fig. 16 Disconnecting the oil injection control unit on this 40 hp model in preparation for testing

Fig. 17 On larger engines with forward controls, the buzzer and its harness are neatly tucked inside the crowded remote control box

accompanied by a sudden (noticeable) drop in powerhead rpm and the Red warning light will come on.

If the buzzer sounds and the Red light comes on but powerhead rpm is not reduced, then the signal responsible for activating the buzzer and light is from the sensor in the remote oil tank. Adding oil to the tank will correct the problem.

Warning Light Display

SINGLE LAMP SYSTEM

♦ See Figures 18, 19 and 20

The warning light display is located either on the front of the powerhead or built into the tachometer. The light colors and their significance are explained in the following paragraphs.

➡If the warning system fails (no lights come on) the oil level must be checked immediately. Operate the powerhead at reduced speed and with caution until the unit can be properly serviced.

THREE LED SYSTEM

Three colored warning lights, a Green round light, a Yellow oil can or round light, and a Red round light are used on some powerheads. These lights warn the operator of a low oil or overheating condition Different combinations of lights with or without the buzzer can indicate a variety of conditions.

Green Light Comes On, Buzzer Does Not Sound—During normal operating conditions, if the powerhead has an adequate supply of oil, the Green light is always on. This Green light informs the operator there is more than 0.5 U.S. quarts (0.5 liters) is in the main tank, and at least 1.6 U.S. quarts (1.5 liters) in the remote tank.

Green Or Yellow Light Comes On, Buzzer Sounds—This condition should be accompanied with a sudden drop in engine rpm. The oil level in both tanks is acceptable. The problem lies in one or both banks of cylinders because an overheating condition is developing. The powerhead should be shut down immediately; the problem isolated; and corrective action taken. Continued operation of the powerhead with one of these lights on and the buzzer sounding could lead to serious and expensive internal damage and seizure.

Yellow Light Comes On, Buzzer Does Not Sound—If the Yellow light comes on, the operator is advised only a reserve quantity of oil remains in the remote tank. In order to pump this reserve oil, approximately 1.6 U.S. quarts (1.5 liters) to the main tank, the operator must hold the emergency switch in the up position. The Yellow light will remain on until the remote tank is replenished with oil.

Red Light Comes On, Buzzer Sounds—If this condition is accompanied with a sudden drop in powerhead rpm, the problem is an overheating condition. One or both banks of cylinders has experienced prolonged excessive temperatures and is in immediate danger of seizing. Shut the powerhead down immediately.

If this signal is not accompanied with a drop in powerhead rpm, then a dangerously low oil level condition exists, which requires the operator's immediate attention. There is almost no oil left. The main tank has less than 0.3 U.S. quarts (0.3 liters) and the remote tank has less than 1.6 U.S. quarts (1.5 liters).

➡If the Red light is ON, the buzzer should be sounding. Check the operation of the buzzer as soon as possible if it does not sound.

Green And Red Lights Come On Buzzer Sounds—If the Green and Red lights both come on simultaneously, a problem has arisen in the transfer of oil from the remote tank to the main tank. There is adequate oil in the remote tank but either the oil feed pump has failed or there is a blockage in one of the oil lines. Again, this situation demands immediate action by the operator. Shut down the powerhead at once. In order to return the boat to its point of origin, the oil in the remote tank must be manually transferred to the main tank. Once the main tank has an adequate supply, the powerhead may be restarted.

➡If the Green and Red lights are ON, the buzzer should be sounding. Check the operation of the buzzer as soon as possible if it does not sound.

Hose Network

♦ See Figures 21, 22, 23, 24 and 25

Oil from the main oil tank is gravity fed to the oil injection pump. From the injection pump, oil is routed through a series of transparent hoses and delivered to the intake manifold.

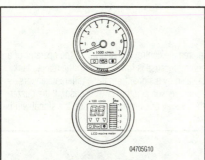

Fig. 18 The warning light display on some models is a part of the tachometer face. The typical older (upper) and newer (lower) style tachometer faces are shown

Fig. 19 A single LED type oil lever indicator is used on this 30 hp model powerhead

Fig. 20 The oil warning light display on this 40 hp model uses three colored warning lights

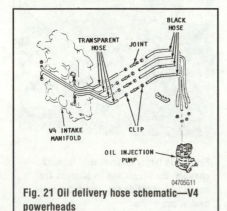

Fig. 21 Oil delivery hose schematic—V4 powerheads

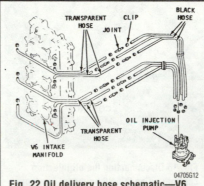

Fig. 22 Oil delivery hose schematic—V6 powerheads

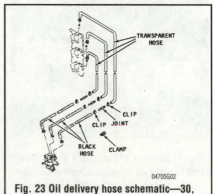

Fig. 23 Oil delivery hose schematic—30, 40 and 50 hp model powerheads

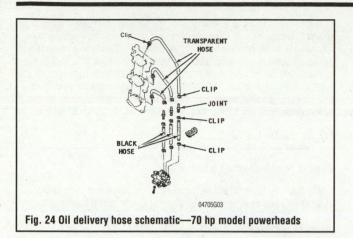

Fig. 24 Oil delivery hose schematic—70 hp model powerheads

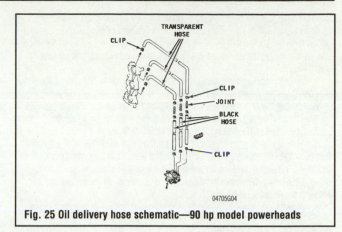

Fig. 25 Oil delivery hose schematic—90 hp model powerheads

TROUBLESHOOTING

Wire Colors

The Yamaha electrical system is designed to use the ground side of any electrical component for control rather than the power side. This means the warning lights, oil transfer pump, and warning buzzer have power when the main switch is in the **ON** position. Also, if the Pink wire is shorted to ground, the buzzer and rpm reduction feature will operate.

The color code of the wires coming from the precision blend control unit are as follows:

- Red—Battery power +12 volts
- Yellow—Main switched power +12 volts
- Black—Ground
- Pink—Warning horn rpm reduction control

The color code of the wires coming from the remote oil tank are as follows:

- Black—Ground lead for oil level sensor
- Black/Red—Oil level sensor signal
- Brown—Switched power +12 volts
- Blue—Control lead for transfer pump ground

General Information

This section is divided into the most common problem areas and complaints concerning the Precision Blend System.

MAIN (ENGINE) OIL TANK OVERFLOWING

General Troubleshooting Information

When the engine oil tank overflows, it could be caused by a mechanical problem, electrical problem, or both. Electrical problems are usually caused by the engine oil sender not turning the oil pump **OFF** when the oil tank is full.

On all V6 engines up to 1989 and all V4 engines to present, the White wire from the engine oil tank sends the signal to the oil control unit to shut off the oil transfer pump. Current V6 engines use a Blue wire with a White tracer. This wire connects to ground to activate the control unit to stop the transfer pump. If it is not grounded, check to see if the Black wire to the sending unit is grounded.

The only components left are the oil control unit and the wire harness. When the engine oil tank overfills, assuming you have not mounted the remote tank higher than the engine. It is caused by the Blue wire to the transfer pump being grounded. Whenever the ignition key is in the **ON** position, the oil transfer pump has a positive 12 volts supplied to it on the brown wire. If the Blue wire running to the pump is grounded, the oil transfer pump will run.

So why would the Blue wire be grounded? Well, the harness may have a screw through it, grounding the Blue wire or the oil control unit may have grounded the Blue wire for some reason.

Why would the oil control unit ground the Blue wire when the engine oil tank is full? Either the sender is telling it to ground the Blue wire or the control unit is grounded internally.

Here are two items to check before replacing the engine oil tank sending unit. Check if the filter is turned (on the sending unit) blocking the vent hole at the top. Also check if the White or Blue/White wire is connected to the Black wire (in the sending unit) when the float is all the way in the up position. If the engine oil tank sending unit connects the White or Blue/White wire to the Black wire (in the sending unit) when the float is all the way up, there is nothing wrong with the sending unit. If all harnesses check good, odds are you have a bad oil control unit.

Overflowing Tanks with No Evidence of Defective Parts

♦ See Figure 26

Check the following items to prevent the needless replacement of parts when attempting to diagnose overflowing tank problems.

A very low battery voltage with main switch **ON** is usually caused when a customer leaves the main (key) switch in the **ON** position while the boat is in storage. After a time, the battery will discharge to the point where the voltage drops and the electronic circuitry on the engine cannot operate properly. When this happens, the transfer pump will start transferring oil to the engine oil tank, overflowing it. Operation returns to normal after the battery is charged.

An improper location of the filter screen on the engine oil level sender may cause an overflow condition. All engines have a tubular plastic screen installed around the oil level sender. This screen has a vent hole near the top of the tube. This hole lines up at the center of the flat area on the sender. It is to let air escape so oil may pass through the screen. The fitting at the bottom of the tube is offset and should line up with the oil tank outlet.

Sometimes when someone is inspecting an engine, they will twist or turn the top of the oil sender. The offset outlet of the screen will keep the filter screen

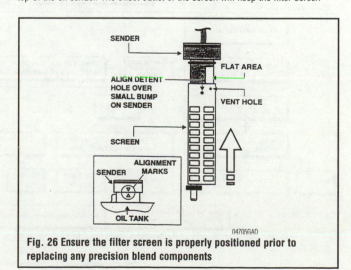

Fig. 26 Ensure the filter screen is properly positioned prior to replacing any precision blend components

from twisting, but the sender itself will twist easily, causing the filter screen tube to distort and bind the up and down action of the sensor float. If this does not occur, then the screen will twist so the vent hole is blocked. Either of these conditions will cause the sensor to malfunction and cause the engine oil tank to overflow.

Twisting the oil sender back to the correct position may not correct the problem because the screen inside the oil talk may be in the wrong position.

Remember the following when installing and aligning the screen:

1. The vent hole goes at the center of the flat area on the oil sender.
2. The offset outlet fitting aligns with the oil tank outlet.
3. There is an alignment detent hole on the screen that fits over a small bump on the sender just to the side of the flat area. This alignment bump is even with the arrow marking on the side of the sender cap.
4. Make sure the above mentioned arrow marking on the sender cap aligns with the arrow marking on the oil tank.
5. Make sure to check the screen for plugging and clean it, if necessary.

Remote Oil Tank Location

When picking the mounting location for the remote oil tank, or the engine oil tank is overflowing when the motor is not in use, note the relative height of the remote oil tank in relation to the engine oil tank. If the remote oil tank is located where the oil level is above the engine oil tank inlet, then (through normal gravity and siphoning), the remote oil will drain into the engine tank, causing it to overfill. This is especially possible with pontoon or house boats. If this occurs, the remote oil tank must be relocated below the level of the engine oil tank. This problem may also occur when a trailered boat is parked on a steep hill. Make sure you ask your customers about their boat storage location if they have this complaint.

Dual Engine Installations

A common problem on dual engine installations is one engine (e.g. port engine) begins to smoke heavily and stalls. This problem may occur on either engine in a dual installation, depending on the way the engines are used. If you come across this problem, make sure the harnesses and oil lines are matched up and connected to the proper engines.

During rigging or routine maintenance, the harness connecting the starboard engine to the sub-oil tank (boat mounted tank) was connected instead to the main oil tank of the port engine. When the oil level in the starboard main tank decreased, the control unit turned on the transfer pump to refill the tank of the starboard engine. Because of the improperly connected harness, the control unit sent the oil to the main tank forcing the oil to pass the in-line check valves and into the intake manifold; making the engine smoke and stall. Because the port tank never received any oil, the shut down of the transfer pump did not occur.

OIL WILL NOT TRANSFER

General Troubleshooting Information

The following items should be checked prior to performing in-depth troubleshooting when oil will not transfer from the remote tank to the main tank.

1. Pre-1990 V6's and all V4's use a Mercury switch in the control unit to prevent oil from transferring when the engine is tilted. When testing a control unit, make sure it is positioned properly.
2. 1990–95 V6's (2.6 liter) use the trim sender to stop the transfer when the engine is tilted. If you have one of these units and it will not transfer oil, then check the trim gauge to see if it is reading solid Black with the engine tilted in the down position. If this occurs, then replace the sender. Also, note that this system is not compatible with aftermarket trim meters.
3. 1996–98 2.6 liter V6 and all V76 3.1 liter outboards require the engine to be running to transfer oil.

Engine Oil Sender Hold Circuit

▶ See Figure 27

All V4 and V6 engines contain an rpm sensing hold circuit. The engine speed must be reduced below approximately 1300 rpm or the throttle must be returned to idle to reset the system, provided the oil tank has been refilled.

Some models control this rpm hold inside the CDI computer unit. Others use a hold circuit built into the engine oil level sensor. Hold circuit sensors can be identified by an "H" molded into the top of the sensor.

OIL TRANSFER PUMP TROUBLESHOOTING CHART

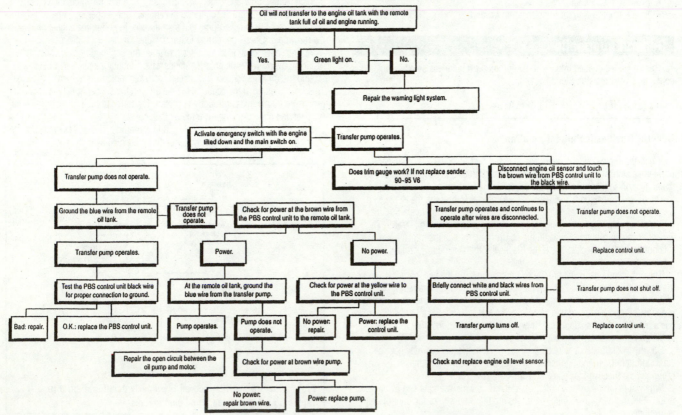

04705C02

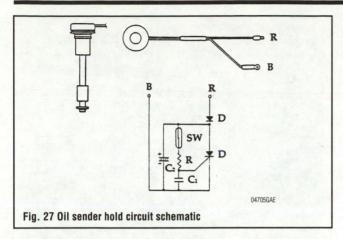

Fig. 27 Oil sender hold circuit schematic

Sensors with the oil level hold circuits may be tested just like a diode. Ohmmeter polarity is important. If the hold circuit appears to be bad, reverse the ohmmeter leads and try again. The circuit should only function when polarity is correct .

➡**If you are using a digital voltmeter, select the diode setting if the meter has one.**

1. Position the float at the top of the sender.
2. Connect the positive lead of the ohmmeter (not necessarily the Red lead depending on your meter) to the warning system lead (Blue/Red or Red).
3. Connect the negative lead of the ohmmeter to the Black ground lead on the sensor.
4. Use the 10 scale on your meter. If you are using a digital voltmeter, select the diode setting if the meter has one.
5. At this time, the meter reading should be infinite or open. Move the float to the bottom of the sensor. You should now have some resistance reading between zero and infinity.
6. Move the float to the top of the sensor. The resistance reading should stay between 0 and infinity.
7. Momentarily disconnect and then reconnect the ohmmeter. The resistance reading should be infinite or open again.

EXCESSIVE SMOKE AT IDLE

When the engine exhaust smoke is too thick at idle, check the following:
- Disconnected oil pump linkage
- Oil pump linkage for free movement
- Oil pump linkage adjustment
- Carburetion synchronization and idle fuel adjustment
- Quality of oil being used
- Oil pump output check valves for proper sealing

- Engine recirculation check valves not sealing
- Leaking fuel pump diaphragms
- Leaking exhaust gaskets
- Excessive oil passing through vent hose to the air box. This may be caused by an oil sender not fully inserted, causing a high oil level in engine oil tank.
- Oil pump driveshaft seal leaking. Remove pump and check for out of position or damaged seal.

Oil Pump Check Valve

If the oil pump check valve is suspected, it may be tested using a combination vacuum pump and gauge.
1. The check valve should seal at some value above zero inches of mercury.
2. If the gauge returns all the way to zero, the check valve is leaking and should be replaced.

Oil Pump Output Test

Prior to testing the oil pump output, premix an appropriate quantity of 2-stroke oil with the fuel being run during the test. Check the I.D. mark on the pump before testing. Bleed any air from the system.

➡**When checking the output with a measuring syringe, make sure the wall surface of the syringe is not coated with oil. If it is, the measurement may be incorrect. When measuring a small amount of oil, measure with a plastic hose connected between the discharge port of the oil pump and the bottom of the measuring syringe (12cc or larger.)**

OIL PUMP OUTPUT SPECIFICATIONS

Model	Oil Pump ID MARK	Oil Pump Output cc/3 min.
25HP	6J200	0.7 ~ 0.9
30HP	6J801	0.6 ~ 0.8
40/50HP, P50	6H404	1.4 ~ 1.8
P60, 70HP	6H302	2.0 ~ 2.4
90HP	6H102	2.8 ~ 3.4
P115, 115HP	6N600	2.9 ~ 3.5
130HP	6N700	4.3 ~ 5.3
P150, 150/175HP	6R300	2.6 ~ 3.2
P175, 200HP	6R400	3.1 ~ 3.7
P200, 225 (L-90° V)	6R501	4.3 ~ 5.3
225 (X/U-V76X), 250HP	61A01	5.9 ~ 7.3
S225V/S250V	62J00	5.9 ~ 7.3
S225W/S250W V200W/V225W	65L00	5.3 ~ 7.9

04705C04

SERVICING

3-Cylinder Powerheads

The oil injection tank on the 3-cylinder powerheads covered in this manual is attached to the powerhead. On some models the tank is installed on the port side, on other models on the starboard side.

The oil tank is easily accessible and may be moved aside to facilitate removal of the flywheel, without draining the tank or disconnecting the oil lines.

However, the oil injection pump is located down in the lower cowling. Some parts of the fuel system must be removed to gain access to the pump.

Removal procedures vary depending on the outboard model being serviced. Therefore, the following instructions are listed under separate headings or grouped together under a multiple heading when the steps are valid for more than one powerhead.

Oil Injection System

REMOVAL

30 Hp Model

◆ **See accompanying illustrations**

The following procedures include removal of all parts of the oil injection system. If the unit being serviced does not require certain items to be removed, simply skip those steps and continue with the necessary work.
1. Disconnect the inlet fuel hose at the fuel joint and the outlet fuel hose at the fuel pump.
2. Using a small screwdriver, pry the tiny retaining O ring, securing the

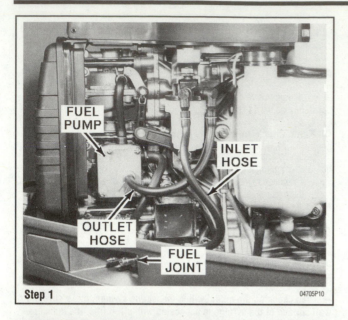

FUEL PUMP

INLET HOSE

OUTLET HOSE

FUEL JOINT

Step 1   04705P10

CHOKE PLUNGER SPRING

O-RING

Step 2   04705P11

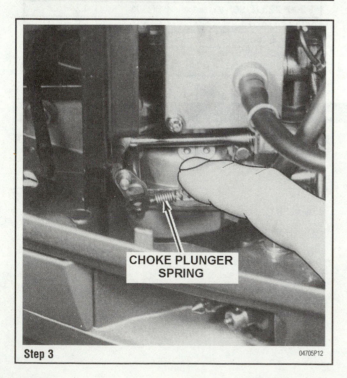

CHOKE PLUNGER SPRING

Step 3   04705P12

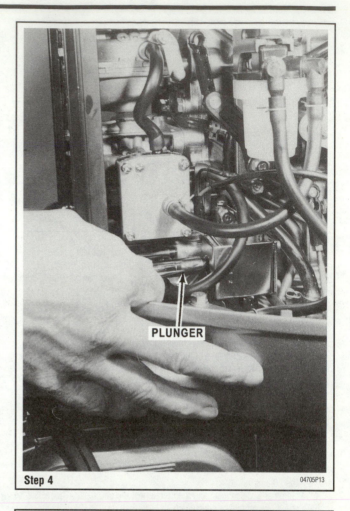

PLUNGER

Step 4   04705P13

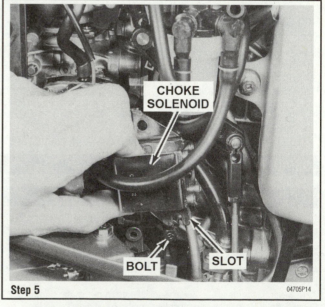

CHOKE SOLENOID

BOLT   SLOT

Step 5   04705P14

end of the choke plunger spring to the carburetor linkage, free. Take care not to lose this O-ring.

3. Unhook the choke plunger spring from the carburetor linkage.

4. Pull the plunger free of the choke solenoid.

5. Loosen and remove the top choke solenoid attaching bolt. The solenoid ground wire is attached to this top bolt. Loosen, but do not remove the bottom attaching bolt. The choke solenoid has a slotted lower bracket which will now clear the bottom bolt.

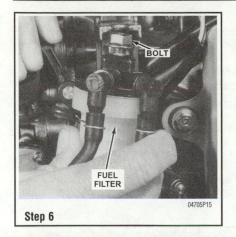

BOLT

FUEL FILTER

Step 6

04705P15

"T" FITTING

Step 7

04705P16

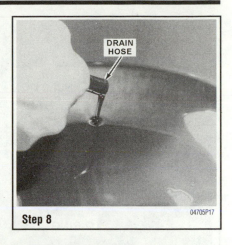

DRAIN HOSE

Step 8

04705P17

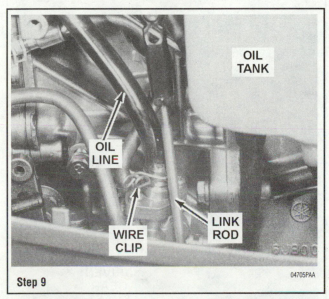

OIL TANK

OIL LINE

WIRE CLIP

LINK ROD

Step 9

04705PAA

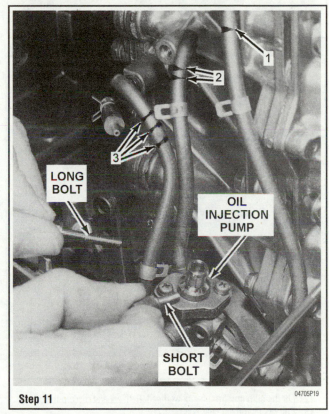

1

2

3

LONG BOLT

OIL INJECTION PUMP

SHORT BOLT

Step 11

04705P19

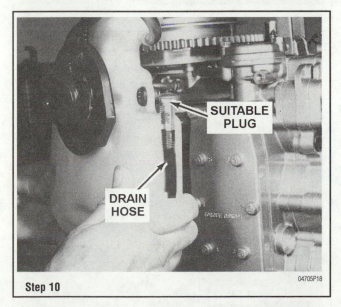

SUITABLE PLUG

DRAIN HOSE

Step 10

04705P18

the Y fitting. Pry off the oil line at the T fitting which leads from the bottom of the oil tank.

8. Drain the oil from the oil tank into the container. Inspect the condition of the oil as it drains. The color should be clear. If the color is murky or milky, the oil is contaminated with water or other impurities.

9. Obtain a suitable size plug (a bolt will do) and plug the end of the drain hose to prevent oil from draining into the lower cowling.

10. Pry the oil pump control link free from the upper ball joint. Squeeze the two loops of the wire clip together and at the same time pull up on the oil line to free the line from the fitting on the oil pump. This line will contain some oil, therefore, be prepared to plug the line with a bolt, or similar device.

Take note of the oil line routing, as an aid during installation. The oil is routed behind the fuel filter bracket, behind the oil level gauge cap and in front of the oil tank, following a groove in the tank.

Loosen and remove the three bolts securing the oil tank. Carefully lift the tank free of the powerhead. Set the tank upright in a safe place.

11. Locate the three oil delivery lines and mark each one to ensure correct connection to the proper cylinder during installation. Disconnect the three oil lines from the intake manifold. Remove the two bolts securing the oil pump. Note the forward bolt is longer than the aft bolt.

6. Loosen, but do not remove the nut on the top of the fuel filter bracket. Slide the fuel filter, together with the two fuel lines away from the bracket. Place the fuel filter in an upright position to prevent spilling the fuel inside.

7. Position a suitable container close by to catch the oil from the tank. Obtain a short piece of cord. Tie the oil line to the oil tank fill neck just below

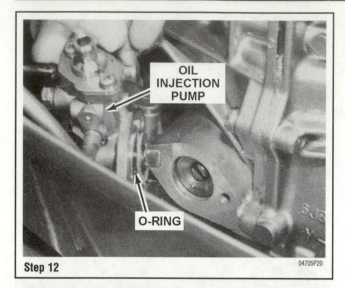

OIL
INJECTION
PUMP

O-RING

Step 12   04705P20

DRIVEN
GEAR
SHAFT

Step 13   04705P21

12. Lift the oil pump from the powerhead. Remove and discard the O-ring.
13. Pull out the driven gear shaft.

Except 30 Hp Models

1. Pull out the tiny cotter pin from the oil injection lever.
2. Pry the oil injection link rod free of the ball joint on the pump lever.
3. Position a suitable container under the lower cowling to receive oil drained from the tank. Compress the wire clamp with a pair of needle nose pliers and push the clamp up along the oil line. Squeeze the oil line to restrict the flow of oil while pulling it free of the fitting. Allow the contents of the tank to drain into the container.
4. Remove the flame arrestor and carburetor assemblies.
5. Locate the three oil delivery lines and mark each one to ensure correct connection to the proper cylinder during installation. Slide the three clips back, one on each of the lines. Gently pull each line free of its fitting at the intake manifold.
6. Loosen and remove the remaining bolts securing the oil tank. Some bolts on 70 hp and 90 hp units were removed. Carefully lift the tank free of the powerhead. Set the tank upright in a safe place.
7. Remove the two bolts securing the oil pump to the powerhead. Lift out the oil pump and then remove and discard the O-ring.
8. Pull the driven gear shaft straight out of the powerhead.

INSTALLATION

30 Hp Model

▶ **See accompanying illustrations**

1. Push in the driven gear shaft.
2. Install a new O-ring on the oil injection pump. Check to be sure the shaft of the oil injection pump will index into the slot at the center of the crankshaft driven gear. If the two are no longer aligned, rotate the slotted shaft on the pump to match the slot in the driven gear. Install the oil pump with the pump shaft indexed with the slot in the crankshaft driven gear.
3. Secure the pump with the two attaching bolts. Remember, the forward bolt is longer than the aft bolt. Tighten the bolts securely. Connect the three oil delivery lines to their original locations (as recorded during disassembling), at the intake manifold.

DRIVEN
GEAR
SHAFT

Step 1   04705P44

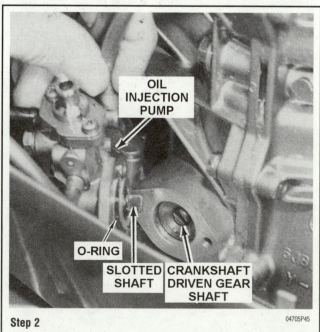

OIL
INJECTION
PUMP

O-RING

SLOTTED
SHAFT

CRANKSHAFT
DRIVEN GEAR
SHAFT

Step 2   04705P45

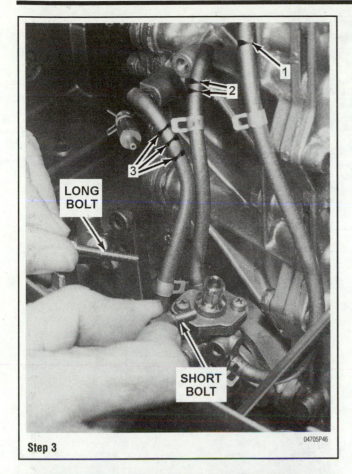

Step 3
04705P46

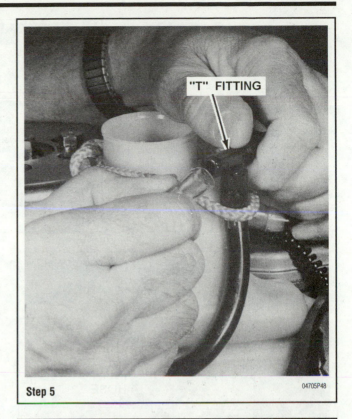

Step 5
04705P48

Step 4
04705P47

Step 6
04705P49

4. Install the oil tank to the powerhead. Secure the tank with the three attaching bolts. Route the oil line from the T fitting, snugly across the front of the tank, tucked into the groove, then behind the oil level gauge cap, behind the fuel filter bracket, and finally down to the oil pump. Check to be sure this oil line will not be crimped or flattened when the tank is installed. A free flow of oil through an unrestricted line is critical for adequate powerhead lubrication.

5. Remove the plug from the end of the drain hose and attach the hose to the T fitting. Remove the rope securing the oil lines to the fill neck.

6. Install the fuel filter into its mounting bracket and tighten the top securing bolt.

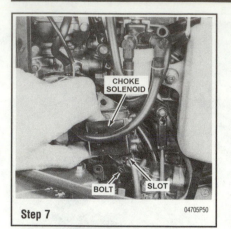

Step 7   04705P50

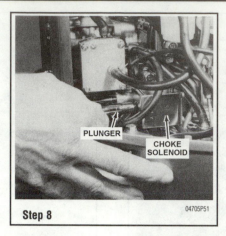

Step 8   04705P51

Step 9   04705P52

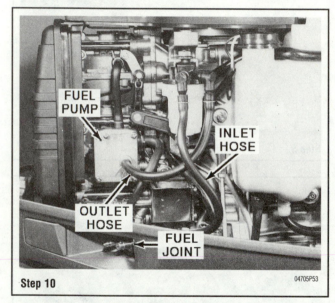

Step 10   04705P53

Step 1   04705P54

7. Position the slot in the lower choke solenoid bracket over the bolt and slide the solenoid down over the bolt. Install the top mounting bolt with the Black ground lead. Tighten both bolts alternately and evenly to a torque value of 5.8 ft. lbs. (8 Nm).

8. Insert the plunger into the choke solenoid with the groove which runs along its length facing inward toward the powerhead.

9. Hook the end of the plunger spring onto the carburetor linkage and secure it in place with the tiny O-ring.

10. Connect the fuel filter inlet hose to the fuel joint and the outlet hose to the fuel pump. Top off or fill the oil tank with Yamalube two cycle outboard oil or an equivalent 2-stroke engine oil with a BIA certified rating TC-W. This oil is suitable for use through a temperature range of 14°F to 140°F (–10°C to 60°C). The tank will hold 0.9 gal US (0.8 L).

☀☀ WARNING

Any time the oil tank hose is disconnected, the oil injection pump must be purged (bled) of any trapped air. Failure to bleed the system could lead to powerhead seizure due to lack of adequate lubrication. Therefore, bleed the system.

Except 30 Hp Models

♦ **See accompanying illustrations**

1. Push the driven gear shaft into the powerhead to index with the bronze drive gear around the crankshaft.

2. Install a new O-ring on the oil injection pump. Check to be sure the shaft of the oil injection pump will index into the slot at the center of the crankshaft

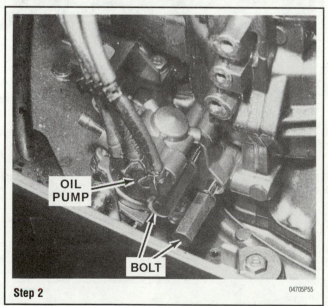

Step 2   04705P55

driven gear. If the two are no longer aligned, rotate the slotted shaft on the pump to match the slot in the driven gear. Install the oil pump with the pump shaft indexed with the slot in the crankshaft driven gear.

Secure the pump with the two attaching bolts. Tighten the bolts securely.

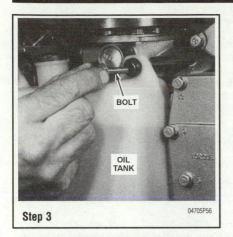

BOLT

OIL TANK

Step 3   04705P56

WIRE CLAMP

Step 4   04705P57

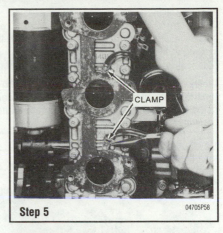

CLAMP

Step 5   04705P58

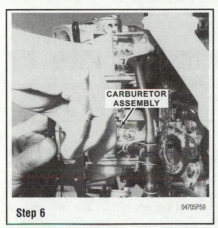

CARBURETOR ASSEMBLY

Step 6   04705P59

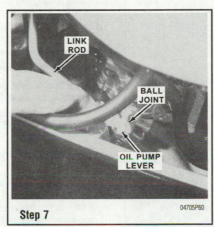

LINK ROD

BALL JOINT

OIL PUMP LEVER

Step 7   04705P60

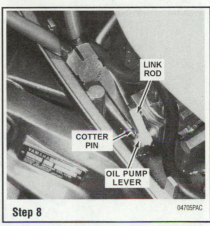

LINK ROD

COTTER PIN

OIL PUMP LEVER

Step 8   04705PAC

TWO-STROKE ENGINE OIL

Step 9   04705P61

3. Install the oil tank to the powerhead. Secure the tank with the attaching bolts. On 70 hp and 90 hp units, the remaining tank attaching bolts will be installed later. Route the oil line behind the tank. Check to be sure this oil line will not be crimped or flattened when the tank is installed. A free flow of oil through an unrestricted line is critical for adequate powerhead lubrication.

4. Install the oil line from the tank to the pump at the inlet fitting. Secure the line with the wire clamp.

5. Connect the three oil delivery lines to their original locations (as recorded during disassembling), at the intake manifold.

6. Install the carburetor assemblies and the flame arrestor.

7. Slide the oil injection link rod onto the ball joint of the oil pump lever. If the length of the rod was accidentally altered, adjust the rod to the specified length.

8. Insert the tiny cotter pin through the oil injection pump lever to secure the link rod.

9. Fill the oil tank with Yamalube two cycle outboard oil (or an equivalent 2-stroke engine oil with a BIA certified rating TC-W). This oil is suitable for use through a temperature range of 14°F to 140°F (−10°C to 60°C).

✳✳ CAUTION

Any time the oil tank hose is disconnected, the oil injection pump must be purged (bled) of any trapped air. Failure to bleed the system could lead to powerhead seizure due to lack of adequate lubrication. Therefore, bleed the system per the instructions.

BLEEDING

Purging air (bleeding) procedures differ significantly for two groups of powerheads. Therefore, separate instructions are presented as follows:

30 Hp and 40 Hp Manual Start

◆ **See accompanying illustrations**

The following procedures are to be performed any time the oil injection system has been opened (other than to add oil to the tank) and air has entered the system.

1. Pry off the oil injection control link rod at the upper ball joint.
Prepare a 50:1 gasoline/oil mixture to operate the powerhead. Jury-rig a setup to provide this mixture to the fuel pump during the bleeding operation.

✳✳ CAUTION

Water must circulate through the lower unit to the powerhead anytime the powerhead is operating to prevent damage to the water pump in the lower unit. Just five seconds without water will damage the water pump impeller.

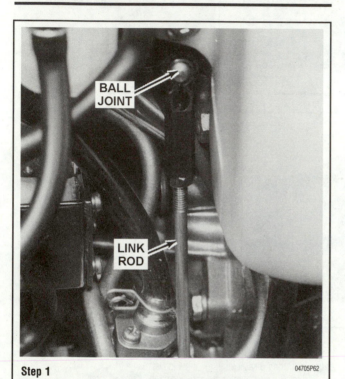

Step 1   04705P62

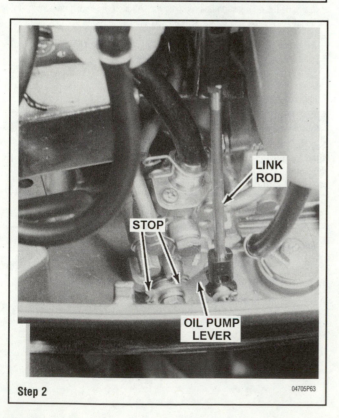

Step 2   04705P63

Start the powerhead. Operate the powerhead only at idle speed throughout the bleeding procedure.

2. Depress the link rod to obtain the richest setting until the oil pump lever hits a stop. Check the transparent oil feed lines. Air bubbles will probably be observed moving through the line and into the cylinders. Watch for a solid oil flow with no air bubbles. When no more air bubbles are visible, connect the link rod to the upper ball joint and shut down the engine. The oil injection system is now operational. The powerhead may be operated on the regular fuel tank in the normal manner.

Except 30 Hp and 40 Hp Manual Start

♦ **See accompanying illustrations**

The following procedures are to be performed any time the oil injection system has been opened (other than to add oil to the tank) and air has entered the system.

1. If servicing a 40 hp or 50 hp electric start, prepare about a ten minute supply of 100:1 premix fuel and oil in a separate container. If servicing a 70 hp or 90 hp, prepare a 50:1 premix using Yamalube, or other quality two-stroke oil. Check the level of oil in the oil tank and replenish as necessary.
Connect a flush device to the lower unit.

✳✳ WARNING

Never operate the powerhead over 1000 rpm with a flush device attached, because the engine may runaway due to no load on the propeller. A runaway engine could be severely damaged.

Start the engine.

✳✳ WARNING

Water must circulate through the lower unit to the powerhead anytime the powerhead is operating to prevent damage to the water pump in the lower unit. Just five seconds without water will damage the water pump impeller.

2. Place a suitable cloth under the air bleed screw. Remove the air bleed screw and allow oil to flow from the opening until a bubble-free flow of oil is obtained.

➡Because the fuel and oil premix is being fed through the carburetor in addition to oil from the oil injection system being fed directly into the cylinders, the powerhead will be operating on a heavy mixture of oil.

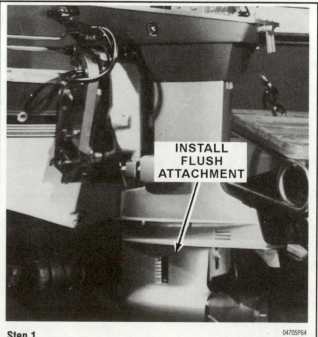

Step 1   04705P64

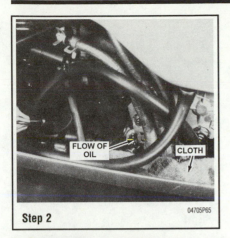

Step 2   04705P65

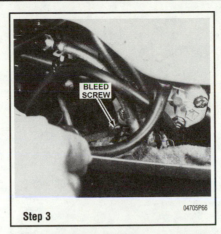

Step 3   04705P66

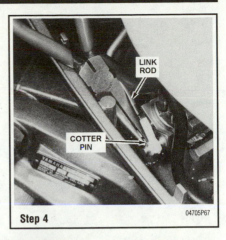

Step 4   04705P67

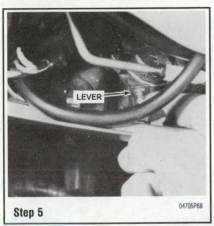

Step 5   04705P68

Step 6   04705P69

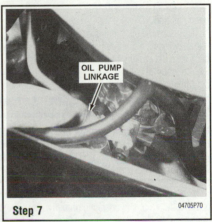

Step 7   04705P70

3. Install and tighten the bleed screw. Should the oil flow very slowly into the delivery hoses, check the vent on the oil tank to be sure it is clear.

4. Remove the cotter pin and then the link rod from the oil injection pump lever.

5. Turn the lever to the fully open position counterclockwise as far as possible. Allow the powerhead to idle at 800 rpm for about ten minutes.

6. Hold a suitable cloth under the oil line fitting at cylinder No. 1. Remove the oil delivery line and allow the oil to flow into the cloth. Observe the oil flow for a few minutes to be sure no air bubbles are present. Reconnect the line. Shut down the powerhead and remove the flushing device.

7. Connect the oil pump linkage and check its adjustment. With the throttle shut, the oil injection pump lever should be at the minimum stroke position.

ADJUSTMENT

Correct adjustment of the link rod from the carburetor to the oil injection pump lever is critical. If this rod is out of adjustment, an oil starvation condition could develop leading to premature wear and over-heating. Incorrect adjustment of the link rod could also lead to excessive oil delivery resulting in a smoking powerhead, fouled spark plugs, or erratic performance.

If the oil injection system has been removed to facilitate powerhead removal or for any other reason, it is quite possible the link rod may require adjustment.

➡**Since the procedures differ substantially for three groups of power-heads, separate instructions are given in the following short sections. The necessary instructions are detailed to adjust the control link rod for proper oil flow to the cylinders.**

30 Hp and 40 Hp Manual Start

▸ **See accompanying illustrations**

1. Pry off the oil injection control link rod at the upper ball joint and loosen the link rod locknut.

Step 1   04705P71

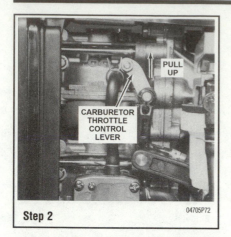

CARBURETOR THROTTLE CONTROL LEVER

PULL UP

Step 2   04705P72

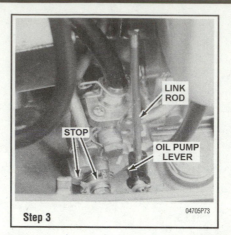

LINK ROD

STOP

OIL PUMP LEVER

Step 3   04705P73

OIL LIGHT (OFF)

Step 4   04705P74

2. Pull up on the carburetor throttle control lever to set the lever at the full open position.

3. Rotate the oil pump lever clockwise to the richest position until the oil pump lever hits a stop. Adjust the length of the link rod until it can be snapped back onto the ball joint on the carburetor control lever without any movement at the other end of the rod. Snap the link rod in place and tighten the locknut to hold the new adjusted length.

✳✳ WARNING

Water must circulate through the lower unit to the powerhead anytime the powerhead is operating to prevent damage to the water pump in the lower unit. Just five seconds without water will damage the water pump impeller.

4. Start the powerhead and check the oil warning light on the front cowling panel. If the system is operating properly; the light should remain off.

Except 30 Hp and 40 Hp Manual Start

▶ See accompanying illustrations

1. Loosen the center carburetor idle adjustment screw.

2. Remove the cotter pin and pry the oil injection link rod from the ball joint on the oil injection pump. Loosen the locknut on the link rod.

3. Pull the throttle roller forward on 40 hp and 50 hp units to open the throttle plates. On 70 hp and 90 hp units, push the throttle roller down against the throttle cam to fully close the throttle plates.

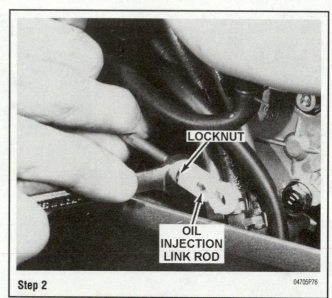

LOCKNUT

OIL INJECTION LINK ROD

Step 2   04705P76

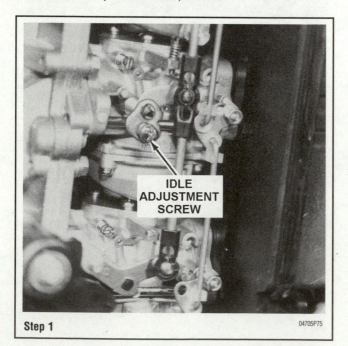

IDLE ADJUSTMENT SCREW

Step 1   04705P75

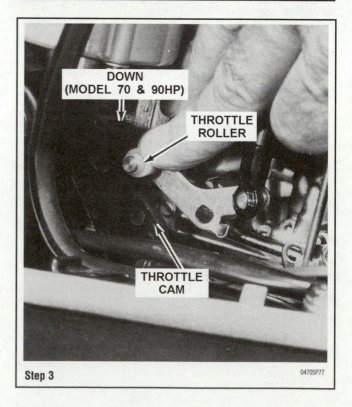

DOWN (MODEL 70 & 90HP)

THROTTLE ROLLER

THROTTLE CAM

Step 3   04705P77

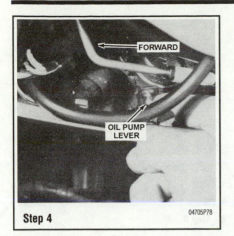

Step 4   04705P78

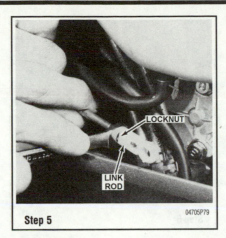

Step 5   04705P79

Step 6   04705P80

4. Push the oil pump lever forward until the lever contacts the stop and align the embossed mark on the pump lever with the mark on the oil injection pump body.

5. Adjust the length of the link rod until the rod can be snapped back onto the ball joint on the oil pump without any movement at the other end of the rod. Snap the link rod in place and tighten the locknut to hold the adjustment. Install the cotter pin.

6. Tighten the center carburetor idle adjustment screw snugly.

TESTING

30 Hp Model

▶ **See accompanying illustrations**

1. Disconnect the spark plug leads from the spark plugs. Lift out the oil level gauge cap with the sensor attached. Wrap a shop towel around the sensor to prevent dripping oil on the deck. Set the sensor aside.

2. Adjust a vernier caliper to read 4 ¼ in. (107mm). Make a mark on the oil tank 4 ¼ in. (107mm) from the top of the sensor neck. Install the sensor assembly. Turn the main switch to the **ON** position but do not start the power-head.

3. Position a suitable container close by to receive the oil from the tank. Obtain a short piece of cord. Tie the oil line to the oil tank fill neck just below the T fitting, as shown. Pry off the oil line at the T fitting which leads from the bottom of the oil tank.

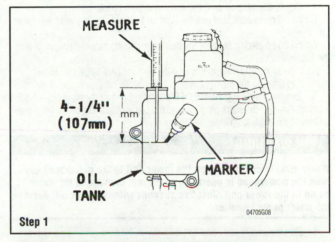

Step 1   04705G08

Step 2   04705P81

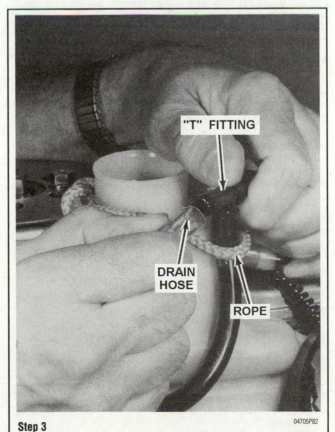

Step 3   04705P82

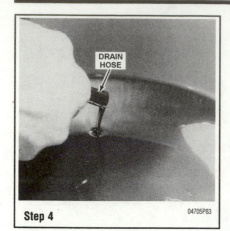

Step 4   04705P83

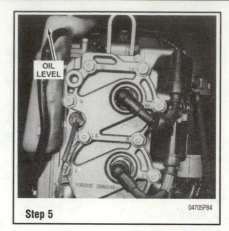

Step 5   04705P84

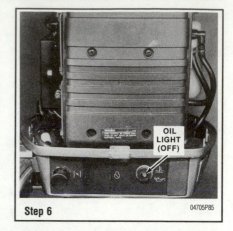

Step 6   04705P85

4. Slowly drain the oil until the warning system operates:
On the 30 hp manual start unit the light on the front cowling panel will come on.
On the 30 hp electric start the light on front cowling panel will come on and the buzzer will sound.
As soon as the system operates or if the oil level falls below the scribed mark, stop draining the oil.

5. Turn the main switch to the **OFF** position. Connect the drain hose to the T fitting. Connect the spark plug leads to the spark plugs. Top off the oil in the oil tank to the mark just below the top hose.

✳✳ WARNING

Water must circulate through the lower unit to the powerhead anytime the powerhead is operating to prevent damage to the water pump in the lower unit. Just five seconds without water will damage the water pump impeller.

6. Start the engine and check the oil light on the front cowling panel The light should remain off for both the manual and electric start 30 hp unit. The warning buzzer should not sound on the electric start 30 hp units.

Except 30 Hp Model

♦ **See accompanying illustrations**

The following procedures check the operation of the buzzer and the Green, Yellow, and Red lights to ensure they come on at the proper time. Correct operation of the buzzer and lights is essential to warn the operator of a low oil level in the tank. This simple procedure should be performed at the start of each season to verify the warning system is functioning correctly as a protection against expensive powerhead service work. Inadequate lubrication can almost destroy a powerhead.

After these tests are completed, the injection system should be bled.

1. Place a suitable container under the oil tank and remove the bottom hose. Temporarily block the hose to prevent moisture, dirt, etc., from entering the system. Turn the ignition switch the **ON** position.

2. The Red light should come on and the buzzer should sound. Obtain Yamalube or equivalent two-stroke oil. The Red light should go off, the buzzer should stop sounding and the Yellow light should come on after the following pre-measured quantities of oil have been added for the models listed:

- 40/50 Hp —0.35 qts. (0.33 liter)
- 70 Hp —0.14 qts.(0.13 liter)
- 90 Hp —0.39 qts. (0.37 liter)

The Yellow light should go out and the Green light should come on after the following pre-measured quantities of oil have been added for the models listed:

- 40/50 Hp —0.18 qts. (0.17 liter)
- 70 Hp —0.37 qts. (0.35 liter)
- 90 Hp —0.61 qts. (0.58 liter)

The CDI unit received a message to limit engine rpm, due to the low oil condition. Therefore, turn the switch to off to cancel the message.

If the lights change color when the correct amount of oil is added to the tank, fill the tank to capacity and then bleed the oil injection pump and the system.

If there is a problem with the lights, perform the testing procedures outlined in this section.

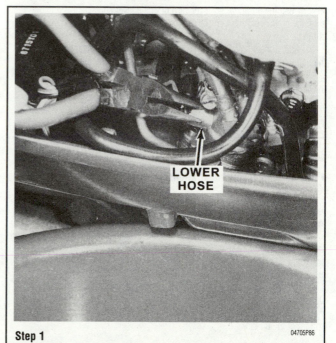

Step 1   04705P86

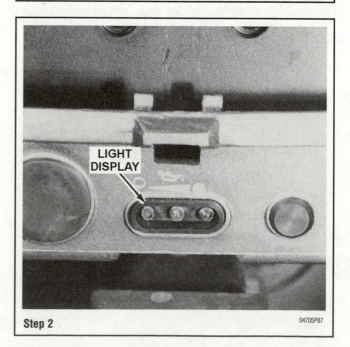

Step 2   04705P87

Oil Pump

DISASSEMBLY

♦ **See Figure 28 and accompanying illustrations**

1. Remove the two Phillips head screws and remove the pump cover.
2. Remove and discard the O-ring around the pump cover.

Fig. 28 Oil injection pump removed from the powerhead and ready for disassembly. Note the hose nipples and link rod ball

3. Normally the cover would remain intact, because individual replacement parts are not available. The only reason the cover would be disassembled would be to replace a broken or missing return spring. To replace the spring, first loosen and remove the nut at the end of the lever shaft. Next, unhook the return spring from the lever and count the number of turns needed to unwind the spring. If the spring is missing or broken, remove what is left. Pull out the lever shaft.
4. Pull out the plunger cam and spring from the pump body.
5. Remove and discard the O-ring around the worm shaft. Pull out the worm shaft.
6. Inspect the condition of the oil seal around the worm shaft. Remove this seal only if another is available to take its place. If the seal is still in a serviceable condition, leave it in place, because the seal will be destroyed during removal.

CLEANING & INSPECTING

♦ **See Figures 29, 30 and 31**

Rinse the pump body and pump cover in solvent and then blow dry with compressed air. Check all parts and passages to be sure they are not clogged or contain any deposits. Do not aim the compressed air directly into the oil distributor of the pump body, because such action may damage the small check valves at the three outlet fittings. These check valves are not serviceable, as it is impossible to separate the outlet fittings from the pump body. If it is determined a check valve is stuck in the open position, a new oil pump must be purchased and installed.

Inspect the condition of the worm shaft threads/teeth and the plunger cam gear teeth for excessive wear and missing or chipped teeth.

If the pump had a tendency to leak oil, only two possible areas may be at fault. The first would be the gasket under the bleed screw. If this gasket is missing, then the pump would definitely leak at this point. The second area to check is the O-ring around the worm shaft. If the O-ring is distorted in any way, the pump will leak profusely at this point.

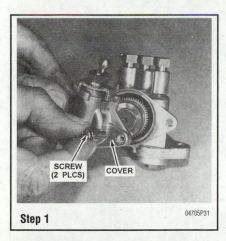

Step 1

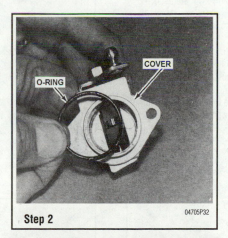

Step 2

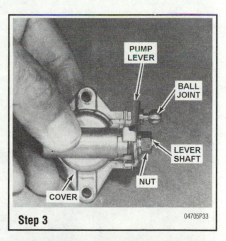

Step 3

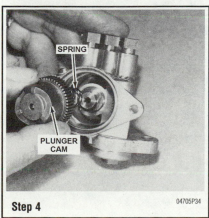

Step 4

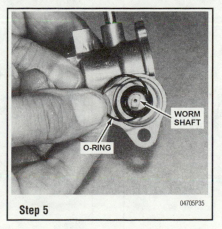

Step 5

Step 6

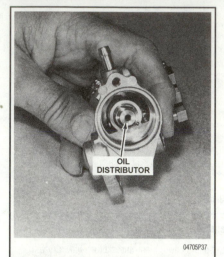

Fig. 29 A small passage in the oil distributor leads to a series of check valves. The check valves must not be subjected to compressed air

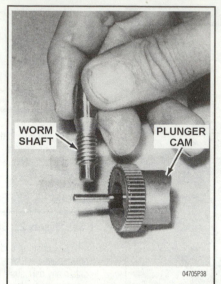

Fig. 30 Inspecting the threads and teeth of the worm shaft and plunger cam

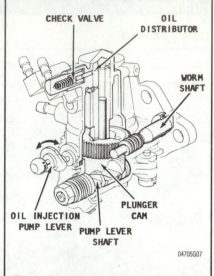

Fig. 31 Cut away view of an oil pump with major parts identified

ASSEMBLY

▸ **See accompanying illustrations**

1. If the oil seal was removed from around the worm shaft, install a new one with the lip of the seal facing outward to the exterior of the pump.

2. Push the worm shaft through the oil seal until it seats inside the pump body. Install a new O-ring around the worm shaft and push it firmly into the groove in the mating surface. An incorrectly installed O-ring will almost certainly cause the pump to leak oil at this location.

3. Place the spring over the post of the plunger cam. Install the plunger cam with the post sliding into the oil distributor.

4. If the pump cover was disassembled to replace the return spring, begin to assemble the pump cover by sliding the lever shaft into the cover. Next, hook the L-shaped end of the spring onto the groove of the cover, and then wind the spring clockwise seven full turns. Hold on to the tensioned spring, and at the same time install the pump lever over the shaft. Seat the lever onto the shaft with the ball joint facing upward (as installed on the powerhead). Hook the

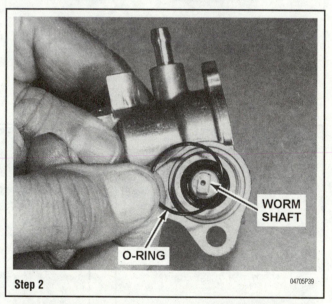

Step 2

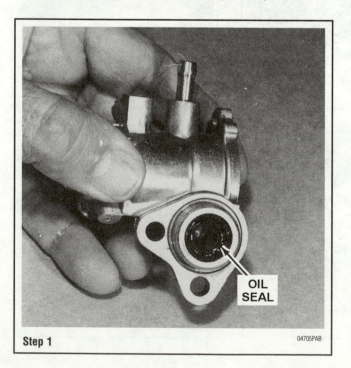

Step 1

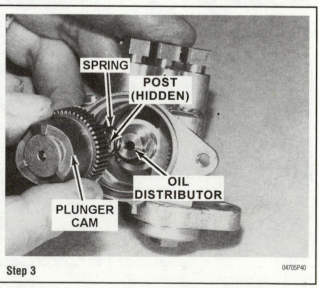

Step 3

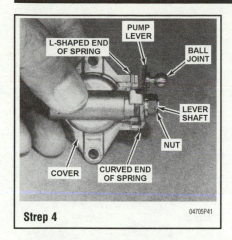

Strep 4   04705P41

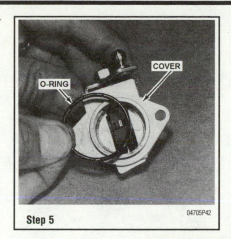

Step 5   04705P42

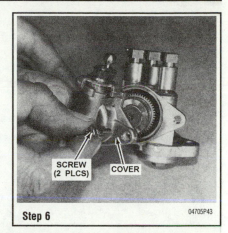

Step 6   04705P43

curved end of the tensioned spring over the wider of the two stops. Install and tighten the lockwasher and nut.

5. Install a new O-ring around the pump cover.

6. Install the cover over the pump body and secure it in place with the two attaching Phillips head screws. Tighten the screws securely. The pump is now ready for installation onto the powerhead.

V4 and V6 Powerheads

The oil injection system used on V4 and V6 powerheads appears similar to the system used on 3-cylinder powerheads. However, it varies enough to treat it as a separate system. Procedures covered in this section are for V4 and V6 powerheads only.

Main Oil Tank

REMOVAL

◗ See accompanying illustrations

1. Place some shop cloths in the bottom of the lower cowling to catch any oil which may drain during disconnection of oil supply lines. Disconnect the oil

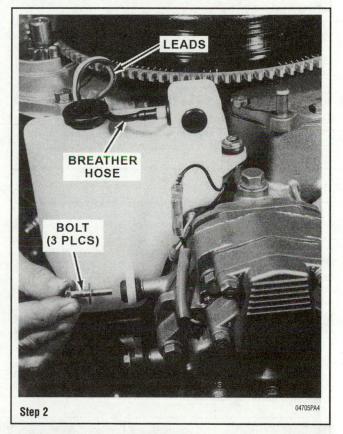

Step 2   04705PA4

supply line leading from the main oil tank to the oil pump beneath the tank by compressing the wire clamp with a pair of needle nose pliers and pushing the clamp up along the oil line. Squeeze the oil line to restrict the flow of oil while pulling it free of the fitting. Plug the line quickly with a suitable screw to prevent loss of oil.

2. Remove the main oil tank breather hose from the air box cover. Disconnect the leads from the oil level sensor cap at their quick disconnect fittings. Loosen and remove the three bolts securing the oil tank. Carefully lift the tank free of the powerhead. Set the tank upright in a safe place.

INSTALLATION

◗ See accompanying illustrations

1. Install the oil tank to the powerhead. Secure the tank with the attaching bolts. Install the main oil tank breather hose to the air box cover. Check around the tank to be sure no oil line will be crimped or flattened when the tank is installed. Secure the line with the wire clamp. A free flow of oil through an unrestricted line is critical for adequate powerhead lubrication.

Step 1   04705PA3

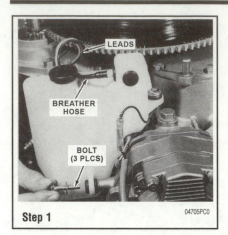

Step 1   04705PC0

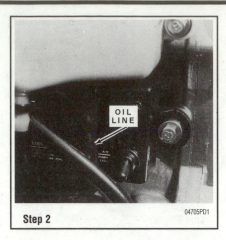

Step 2   04705PD1

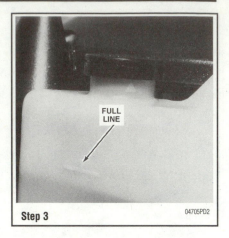

Step 3   04705PD2

2. Install the oil line from the tank to the pump at the inlet fitting. Connect the leads from the oil level sensor cap at their quick connect fittings.

3. Fill the oil tank to the top line embossed on the tank. Use only Yamalube two cycle outboard oil (or an equivalent 2-stroke engine oil with a BIA certified rating TC-W). This oil is suitable for use through a temperature range of 14°F to 140°F (-10°C to 60°C).

✳✳ WARNING

Any time the oil tank hose is disconnected, the oil injection pump must be purged (bled) of any trapped air. Failure to bleed the system could lead to powerhead seizure due to lack of adequate lubrication.

TESTING

▶ **See accompanying illustrations**

1. Pull out the tiny cotter pin from the oil pump shaft. Slide the plastic spacer from the shaft. Pry the oil pump link rod from the ball joint on the pump shaft. Turn the pump lever all the way clockwise to set the pump stroke to maximum.

2. Prepare a 50:1 gasoline/oil mixture to operate the powerhead. Jury rig a setup to provide this mixture to the fuel pump during this step.

✳✳ CAUTION

Water must circulate through the lower unit to the powerhead any-time the powerhead is operating to prevent damage to the water pump in the lower unit. Just five seconds without water will damage the water pump impeller.

Start the powerhead. Operate the powerhead only at idle speed throughout this procedure.

Allow the powerhead to idle for about ten minutes.

Obtain a small container and have a shop towel handy to catch any oil drips. Using a pair of needlenose pliers, squeeze the clamp on the No. 1 cylinder delivery hose. Push the clamp up the hose. Gently pull the hose from the fitting on the intake manifold and immediately hold it over the container. Observe the flow of oil for five full minutes to verify the pump is functioning correctly.

➡ **The prepared oil/fuel mixture will provide adequate lubrication during this test.**

A steady slow pulsing flow with no air bubbles may be expected. The manufacturer gives no specified amount per minute in this case. Reconnect the line. Shut down the powerhead and remove the flushing device.

3. Snap the oil injection link rod back onto the ball joint on the pump shaft. Slide the plastic spacer onto the shaft and install the tiny cotter pin. If the length of the rod was accidentally altered, adjust the rod to the specified length.

Remote Oil Tank

TESTING

▶ **See accompanying illustrations**

1. Check to see if the remote tank contains at least ¾ U.S. quart (0.7 liter). Obtain 12 volt battery and two leads. Position a suitable container under the oil supply line. Make contact with the lead from the negative battery terminal to the Brown female terminal in the harness connector. Make contact with the lead from the positive battery terminal to the Blue female terminal in the harness connector. The oil line should emit a strong, solid flow of oil.

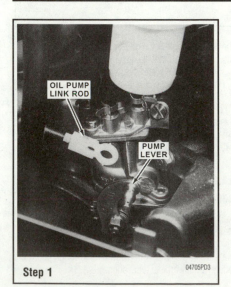

Step 1   04705PD3

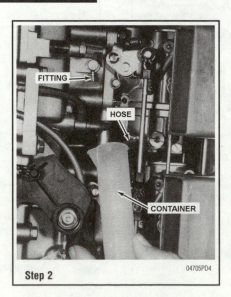

Step 2   04705PD4

Step 3   04705PD5

Step 1   04705PD6

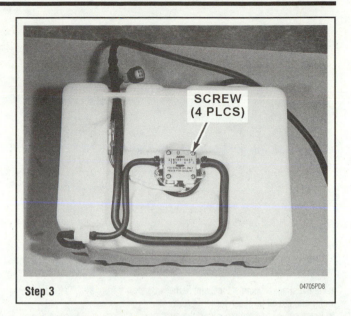

Step 3   04705PD8

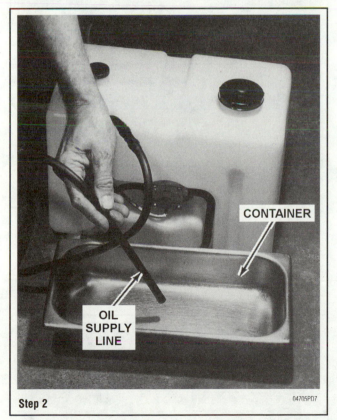

Step 2   04705PD7

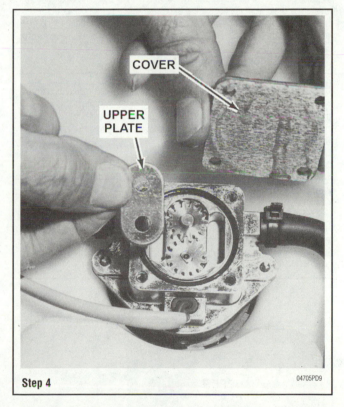

Step 4   04705PD9

3. Remove the four Phillips head screws securing the pump cover.
4. Lift off the cover and upper plate.

REMOVAL

▶ **See accompanying illustration**

Each boat will probably have the remote oil tank mounted in a different location using different securing hardware. All tanks are mounted in a holder with a securing strap across the top of the tank. Therefore the following removal procedures begin with this strap.

1. Remove the nut and long bolt securing the top strap to the holder. Set

2. Obtain a measuring cup or cylinder and measure the rate at which oil is delivered. The flow of oil should be 0.2 U.S. quarts (0.2 liters) per minute. Perform the test over a three minute period and average the reading.

If the pump is allowed to empty the tank of oil and pump air, the feed pump must be purged of air.

If the flow of oil is less than specified, proceed with these steps to service the pump and check all oil lines for leaks, kinks, or restrictions.

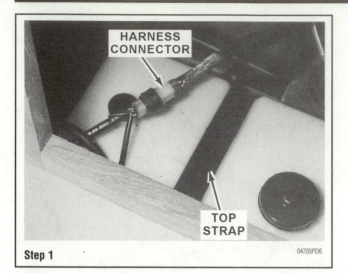

Step 1   04705PD6

aside the strap. Disconnect the wire harness connector from the oil feed pump motor and the oil level sensor.

Place some shop cloths around the oil supply line hose joint to catch any oil which may drain from the hose. Snip the clamp with a pair of dykes. Squeeze the oil line to restrict the flow of oil while pulling it free of the fitting. Plug the line quickly with a suitable screw to prevent loss of oil. Lift out the remote tank.

CLEANING & INSPECTING

Inspect the two cavities of the pump body for any foreign material which might wedge between the teeth of the pump. Momentarily connect the Brown and Blue leads to the 12 volt battery. Check to ensure the teeth rotate smoothly. Inspect the condition of the O-ring in the groove of the pump body, replace if necessary.

INSTALLATION

▶ **See accompanying illustrations**

1.   Fill the cavities and coat the gear teeth with oil to prime the pump. Install the upper plate over the two small shafts. Check to be sure the O-ring is correctly seated in the groove of the pump body. Place the pump cover in position over the pump, with the screw holes aligned.

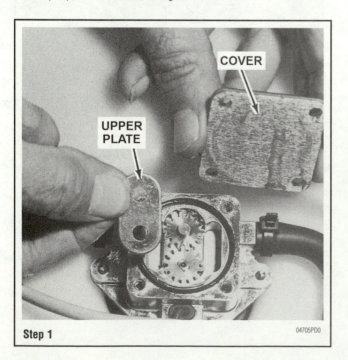

Step 1   04705PD0

2.   Secure the cover to the pump with the four Phillips head screws. Tighten the screws securely. If questionable test result were obtained and the pump was subsequently overhauled, go back and repeat the test outlined. If the flow of oil is still not within specifications and the lines have been checked for leaks, obstructions, and kinks, then the feed pump must be removed and replaced.

3.   Install the tank into the boat. Slide a new hose clamp onto the remote tank hose, and then connect the hose to the hose from the main tank. Tighten

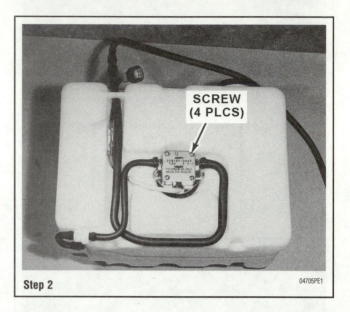

Step 2   04705PE1

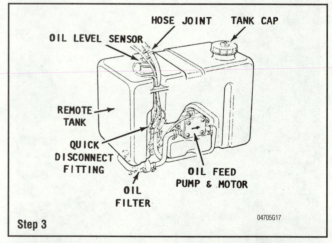

Step 3   04705G17

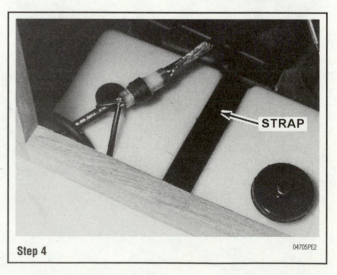

Step 4   04705PE2

the hose clamp at the joint. Connect the two halves of the wire harness connector together. They will only fit one way.

4. Bring the strap across the tank and secure the strap to the holder with the long bolt and nut.

Purge the air from the remote oil tank feed pump.

Oil Pump

REMOVAL

♦ **See accompanying illustrations**

1. Pull out the tiny cotter pin from the oil pump shaft. Slide the plastic spacer from the shaft. Pry the oil pump link rod from the ball joint on the pump shaft.

2. Wrap a small piece of masking tape around each of the oil supply lines and write the cylinder number on each piece of tape. Taking time to identify the lines will ensure each will be connected back in its original location.

➥**An illustration showing the numbered discharge fittings will be given later in the assembly procedures as a guide to installing the correct hose onto the correct fitting.**

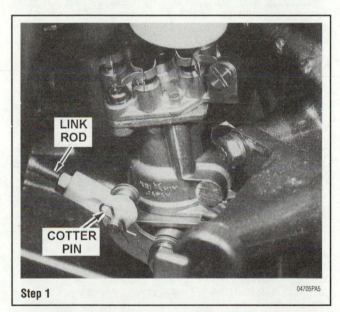

Step 1 04705PA5

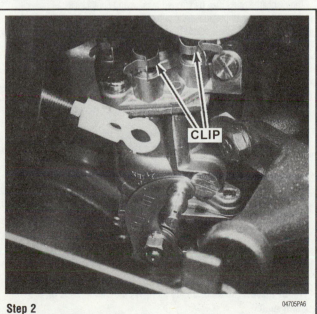

Step 2 04705PA6

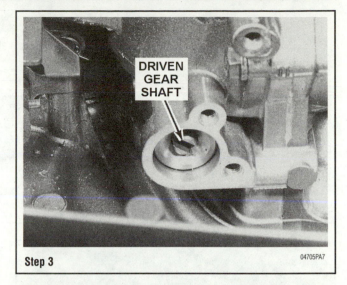

Step 3 04705PA7

Slide the clips back, one on each oil line. Gently pull each line free of its fitting at the pump cover. Remove the two bolts securing the oil pump. Lift the oil pump from the powerhead. Remove and discard the O-ring.

3. Pull out the driven gear shaft.

DISASSEMBLY

♦ **See accompanying illustrations**

1. Remove and discard the O-ring around the worm shaft. Pull out the worm shaft.

2. Remove the two Phillips head screws, and then remove the shaft housing. Remove and discard the O-ring.

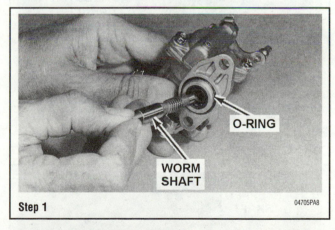

Step 1 04705PA8

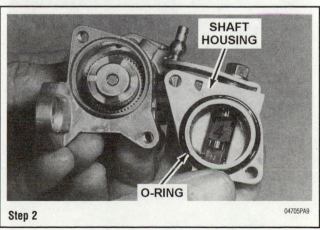

Step 2 04705PA9

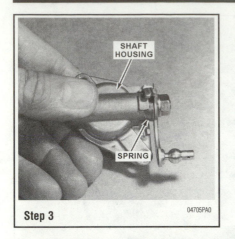

Step 3   04705PA0

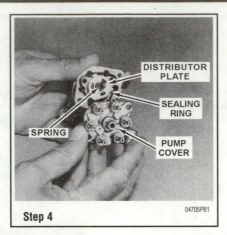

Step 4   04705PB1

Step 5   04705PB2

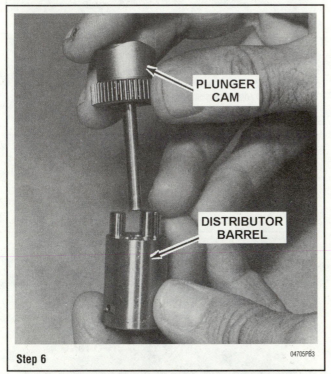

Step 6   04705PB3

3. Normally the shaft housing would remain intact, because individual replacement parts are not available. The only reason the housing would be disassembled is to replace a broken or missing return spring.

To replace the spring, first loosen and remove the nut at the end of the lever shaft. Next, unhook the return spring from the lever and count the number of turns needed to unwind the spring. If the spring is missing or broken, remove what is left. Pull out the lever shaft.

4. Remove the two Phillips head screws, and then lift off the pump cover. Remove the spring and distributor plate. Remove and discard the sealing ring.

5. Push out the plunger cam and distributor barrel as an assembly. Do not allow the assembly to fly apart.

6. Remove the plunger cam from the distributor barrel.

7. Lift out the two stepped shafts and springs from the distributor barrel. Notice the smaller end of the shaft and the spring are located inside the barrel.

CLEANING & INSPECTING

▶ **See Figures 32, 33 and 34**

Rinse the pump body and pump cover in solvent or soak them in contact cleaner for several hours and then lightly blow dry with compressed air.

Check all parts and passages to be sure they are not clogged or contain any deposits. Do not aim the compressed air directly into the pump cover because such action may damage the small check balls at the discharge fittings by causing them to spin. These check balls are not serviceable, as it is impossible to separate the discharge fittings from the pump cover. If it is determined a check ball is stuck in the open position, a new oil pump must be purchased and installed.

The discharge ports may be cleaned by spraying contact cleaner past each check ball from the underside of the pump cover. This may cause the check balls to be lifted from their seats. To reseat the balls, place the pump cover on a clean shop cloth with the discharge fittings facing upward. Obtain a 1/16 in. drill bit and a small hammer. Insert the blunt end of the bit into a discharge fitting and lightly tap on the pointed end with the hammer to seat the ball. Repeat this procedure for all the fittings.

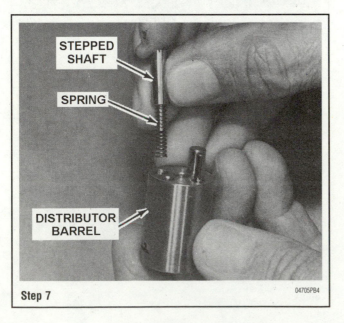

Step 7   04705PB4

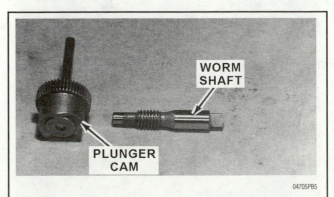

04705PB5

Fig. 32 Inspect the teeth on the plunger cam and threads on the worm shaft

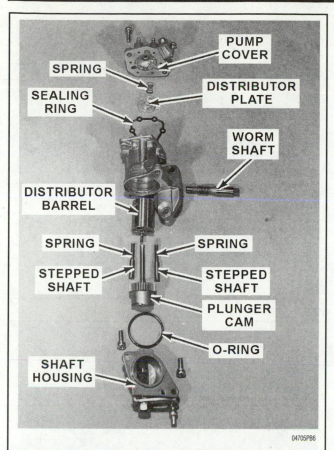

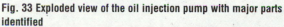

Fig. 33 Exploded view of the oil injection pump with major parts identified

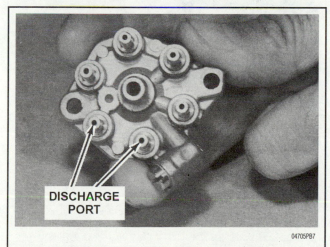

Fig. 34 The discharge ports may be cleaned using contact cleaner and a 1/16 inch drill bit

Inspect the condition of the worm shaft threads/teeth and the plunger cam gear teeth for excessive wear and missing or chipped teeth.

If the pump had a tendency to leak oil, only two possible areas may be at fault. The first would be the gasket under the bleed screw. If this gasket is missing, then the pump would definitely leak at this point. The second area to check is the O-ring around the worm shaft. If the O-ring is distorted in any way, the pump will leak profusely at this point.

Inspect the condition of the oil seal around the worm shaft. Remove this seal only if another is available to take its place. If the seal is still in a serviceable condition, leave it in place, because the seal will be destroyed during removal.

ASSEMBLY

◆ **See accompanying illustrations**

1. Slide the spring over the smaller end of the stepped shaft and insert this end first into the distributor barrel. Install the other shaft in a similar manner.

2. Slide the shaft of the plunger cam into the distributor barrel. Notice the small stubby shaft on the distributor barrel is the only shaft which will index into one of the three notches on the gear of the cam. The other two stepped shafts rest against the shoulder of the gear. This installation IS correct as it provides the pumping action when the plunger cam oscillates.

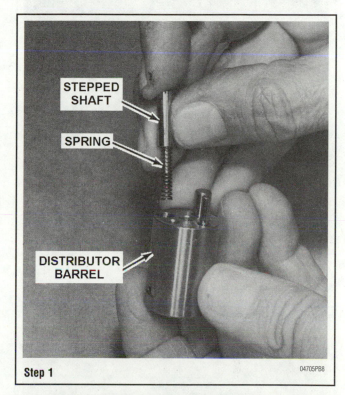

Step 1

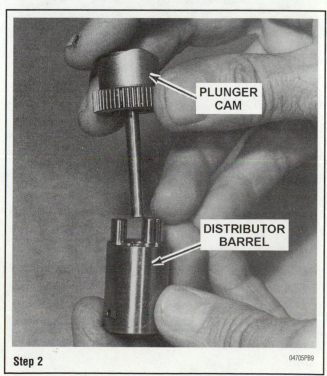

Step 2

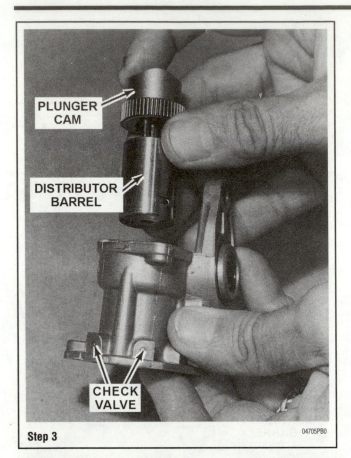

PLUNGER CAM

DISTRIBUTOR BARREL

CHECK VALVE

Step 3   04705PB0

SHAFT HOUSING

O-RING

Step 4   04705PC1

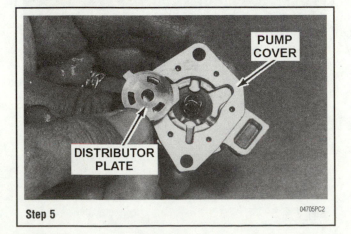

PUMP COVER

DISTRIBUTOR PLATE

Step 5   04705PC2

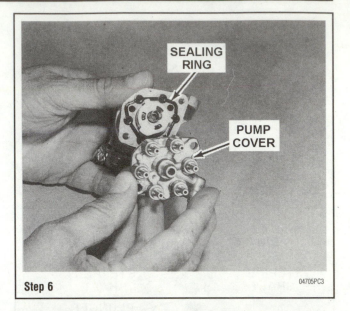

SEALING RING

PUMP COVER

Step 6   04705PC3

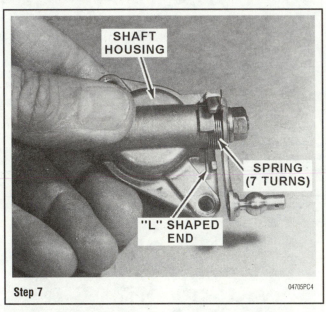

SHAFT HOUSING

SPRING (7 TURNS)

"L" SHAPED END

Step 7   04705PC4

3. Hold the assembly together and insert it through the body of the pump with the barrel end closest to the check valves on the pump body after installation.

4. Install a new O-ring around the shaft housing. Install the housing over the pump body and secure it in place with the two attaching Phillips head screws. Tighten the screws securely.

5. Match the pump cover to the pump body. Separate them and notice how the distributor plate aligns with the cover following installation.

6. Install a new sealing ring around the pump body. Place the distributor plate over the distributor barrel to match the notches in the cover when it is installed. Center the spring onto the distributor plate.

Bring the pump cover down over the pump body, the spring must center itself inside the cover and the plate must index into the notches of the cover. Hold the cover down against the spring tension while the two Phillips head screws are installed and tightened securely.

7. If the shaft housing was disassembled, replace the return spring, begin to assemble the housing by sliding the lever shaft into the cover. Next, hook the L-shaped end of the spring behind the projection on the housing, and then wind the spring counterclockwise seven full turns. Hold onto the tensioned spring, and at the same time install the pump lever over the shaft. Seat the lever onto the shaft with the ball joint facing upward (as installed on the powerhead). Hook the curved end of the tensioned spring over the stop. Install and tighten the lockwasher and nut.

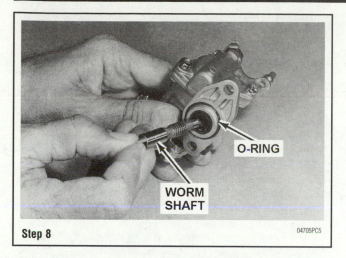

Step 8   04705PC5

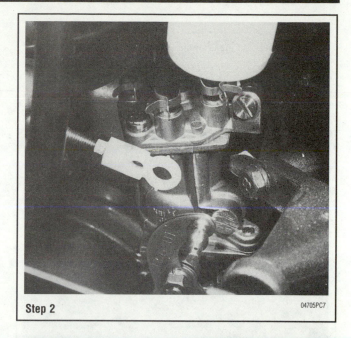

Step 2   04705PC7

8. If the oil seal was removed from around the worm shaft, install a new one with the lip of the seal facing outward to the exterior of the pump.

Push the worm shaft through the oil seal until it seats inside the pump body. Install a new O-ring around the worm shaft and push it firmly into the groove in the mating surface. An incorrectly installed O-ring will almost certainly cause the pump to leak oil at this location. The pump is now ready for installation onto the powerhead.

INSTALLATION

‣ **See accompanying illustrations**

1. Push the driven gear shaft into the powerhead to index with the bronze drive gear around the crankshaft.

2. Install a new O-ring on the oil injection pump. Check to be sure the shaft of the oil injection pump will index into the slot at the center of the crankshaft driven gear. If the two are no longer aligned, rotate the slotted shaft on the pump to match the slot in the driven gear. Install the oil pump with the pump shaft indexed with the slot in the crankshaft driven gear.

Secure the pump with the two attaching bolts. Tighten the bolts securely.

3. Install each of the oil supply lines onto their respective discharge fittings. If the lines were not identified as to which cylinder they originated from, the lines will have to be traced back. On V4 powerheads, there are two long lines leading from cylinders 1 and 3, and two short lines leading from cylinders 2 and 4. On V6 powerheads there is one long line leading from cylinder No. 1; four medium length lines leading from cylinders No. 2, 3, 4, and 5, and one short line leading from cylinder No. 6.

4. Snap the oil injection link rod back onto the ball joint on the pump shaft. Slide the plastic spacer onto the shaft and install the tiny cotter pin. If the length of the rod was accidentally altered, adjust the rod to the specified length.

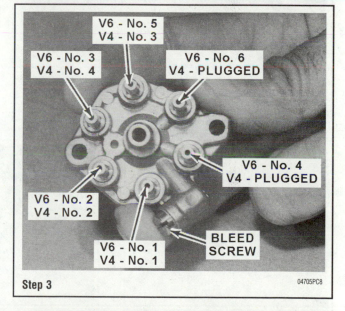

Step 3   04705PC8

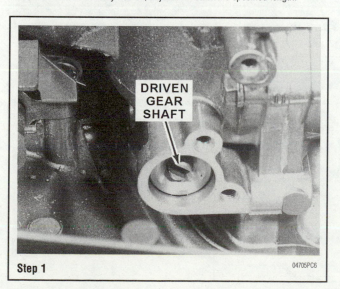

Step 1   04705PC6

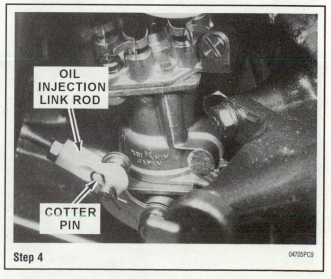

Step 4   04705PC9

BLEEDING

♦ **See accompanying illustrations**

1. Prepare about a ten minute supply of 50:1 premix using Yamalube, or other quality two-stroke oil. Jury-rig a setup to provide this mixture to the fuel pump during this purging procedure. Check the level of oil in the oil tank and replenish as necessary. Connect a flush device to the lower unit. Start the engine.

✳✳ WARNING

Never operate the powerhead over 1000 rpm with a flush device attached, because the engine may runaway due to no load on the propeller. A runaway engine could be severely damaged.

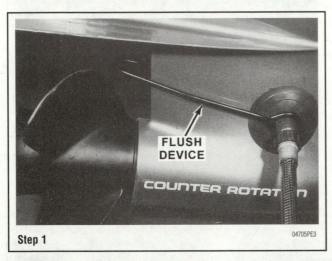

FLUSH DEVICE

COUNTER ROTATION

Step 1   04705PE3

✳✳✳ WARNING

Water must circulate through the lower unit to the powerhead anytime the powerhead is operating to prevent damage to the water pump in the lower unit. Just five seconds without water will damage the water pump impeller.

2. Place a suitable cloth under the air bleed screw. Remove the air bleed screw and allow oil to flow from the opening until a bubble free flow of oil is obtained. On models equipped with a check valve ball on the main tank breather, a long thin object such as a nail or a tooth pick can be used to depress the check valve ball to quicken the flow of oil through the bleed screw.

➡ Because the fuel and oil premix is being fed through the carburetor in addition to oil from the oil injection system being fed directly into the cylinders, the powerhead will be operating on a heavy mixture of oil.

3. Install and tighten the bleed screw.
4. Pull out the tiny cotter pin from the oil pump shaft. Slide the plastic spacer from the shaft. Pry the oil pump link rod from the ball joint on the pump shaft. Turn the pump lever all the way clockwise to set the pump stroke to maximum.
5. Obtain a small container and have a shop towel handy to catch any oil drips. Using a pair of needlenose pliers, squeeze the clamp on cylinder No. 1 delivery hose. Push the clamp up the hose. Gently pull the hose from the fitting on the intake manifold and immediately hold it over the container.

➡ The prepared oil/fuel mixture will provide adequate lubrication while the system is being purged.

6. Observe the flow of oil for five full minutes to verify the pump is functioning correctly. A steady slow pulsing flow with no air bubbles may be expected. The manufacturer gives no specified amount per minute in this case. Reconnect the line. Shut down the powerhead and remove the flushing device.
7. Snap the oil injection link rod back onto the ball joint on the pump shaft. Slide the plastic spacer onto the shaft and install the tiny cotter pin. Check the adjustment, with the throttle shut. The oil injection pump lever should be at the

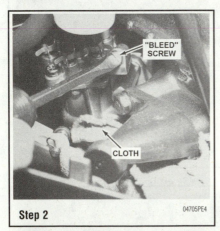

"BLEED" SCREW

CLOTH

Step 2   04705PE4

CHECK VALVE BALL

Step 3   04705PE5

"BLEED" SCREW

Step 4   04705PE6

OIL PUMP LINK ROD

PUMP LEVER

Step 5   04705PE7

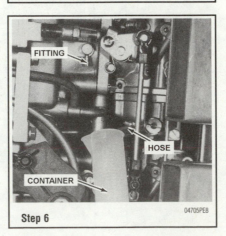

FITTING

HOSE

CONTAINER

Step 6   04705PE8

OIL PUMP LINK ROD

COTTER PIN

Step 7   04705PE9

minimum stroke position. If the length of the rod was accidentally altered, adjust the rod to the specified length.

Injection Control Link Rod

ADJUSTMENT

▶ **See accompanying illustrations**

Correct adjustment of the link rod from the carburetor to the oil injection pump lever is critical. If this rod is out of adjustment, an oil starvation condition could develop leading to premature wear and overheating. Incorrect adjustment of the link rod could also lead to excessive oil delivery resulting in a smoking powerhead, fouled spark plugs, or erratic performance.

If the oil injection system has been removed to facilitate powerhead removal or for any other reason, it is quite possible the link rod may require adjustment.

1. Close the throttle valves by pushing up on the throttle lever on the starboard side of the lower carburetor.

2. Pull out the tiny cotter pin from the oil pump shaft. Slide the plastic spacer from the shaft. Pry the oil pump link rod from the ball joint on the pump shaft. Turn the pump lever all the way counterclockwise to set the pump stroke to minimum.

3. Loosen the locknut on the link rod. Adjust the length of the link rod until

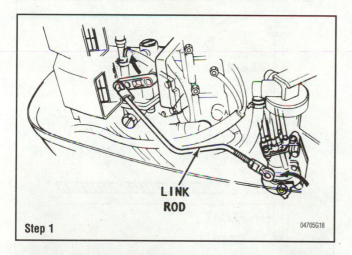

LINK ROD

Step 1   04705G18

LINK ROD

PUMP LEVER

Step 2   04705PF2

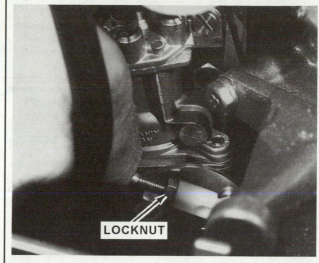

LOCKNUT

Step 3   04705PF3

the rod can be snapped back onto the ball joint on the oil pump without any movement at the other end of the rod. Snap the link rod in place and tighten the locknut to hold the adjustment. Install the plastic spacer and the cotter pin.

Oil Injection Warning System

DESCRIPTION & OPERATION

Single Lamp System

▶ **See Figure 35**

The single lamp warning system is the simplest system used by Yamaha. The oil tank is located under the engine cowling. Inside the oil tank is a sensor. This sensor has a single switch located near the bottom of the sensor shaft. The switch is closed when the sensor float is down near the bottom of the shaft.

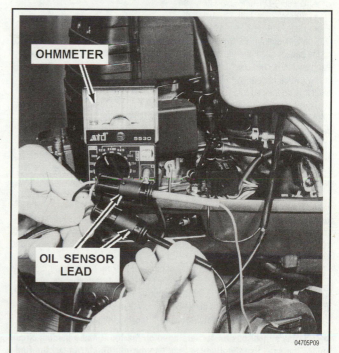

OHMMETER

OIL SENSOR LEAD

04705P09

Fig. 35 Testing the oil level sensor with a multimeter set to the 1000 ohm scale

When the switch is closed, the circuit is complete between ground (Black) and the warning system (Pink).

The system is powered by the magneto's charge coil. No battery is needed. This also means that the system can only operate when the engine is running.

A Red warning light is wired in between the Capacitor Discharge Ignition (CDI) box and the oil tank sensor.

When the oil tank runs low, the float on the sensor rests down at the bottom. This closes the switch inside of it. Current from the CDI box now has a path to ground, and the warning light now glows to indicate a problem. The sensor switch closing also tells the CDI box to lower the rpm to 2,000.

Please note that the overheat sensor is also connected to the warning light. When the engine gets too hot, the overheat sensor closes its switch, completing the Pink lead circuit to ground. This completes the same circuit that the low oil circuit is on. The light comes on, the rpm is reduced The same warning occurs for overheat or low oil. What would happen if the boat operator was at wide open throttle, the warning kicked in, and reduced the rpm to 2,000? If the operator stayed at the helm with the throttle open and sent someone to fill the oil tank what might happen? As the tank filled and the sensor switch went open, the engine rpm would return to wide open. This sudden acceleration could possibly injure someone.

To prevent a sudden return to a previous throttle setting, a holding circuit is built into the PBS. This circuit won't allow the engine to return to full throttle operation with the warning on until the ignition is cycled off and then back on. This resets the system.

Three LED System

This system uses three LEDs (light emitting diodes) to indicate the amount of oil left in the injector tank. This system is used on many of the three cylinder models. The oil tank is located underneath the cowling on the side of the powerhead.

The three colors are Green, Yellow and Red. Green indicates a full to near full tank Yellow indicates that about a third of the tank is left. Refilling should be done soon. Red indicates that the system is very low on oil and something must be done immediately. When the Red lamp comes on, the rpm reduction is switched on and the warning buzzer sounds.

The primary components of this system are the tank sensor, LED lamp assembly and the control unit. The 1994 and earlier three LED systems required battery voltage to operate. Beginning in 1995 the Yellow/Red wire from the CDI powers the system and no battery is required.

The three indicator system uses the following lights to signal the operator of the level in the oil tank:

- Green—Oil Tank Over 30% Full
- Yellow—Oil Tank 10-30% Full
- Red—Oil Tank Less Than 10%

The tank sensor has two switches built in. One switch is located near the top of the sensor shaft and the other switch is located near the bottom. One side of each switch is connected to ground through the Black wire. The other end of the upper switch is connected to a Green wire while the other end of the lower switch is connected to a Green/Red wire. When the oil tank level is near the full mark, the sensor's magnetic float closes the circuit on the upper switch. This completes the circuit between ground and the Green wire. The control unit receives this signal and turns on the Green LED lamp (full tank).

As oil is consumed, the oil level drops in the tank. The sensor float follows the oil level. When the float reaches a point between the two switches in the sensor neither switch is closed. This "no switch closed" signal triggers the control unit to shut off the Green and turn on the Yellow.

If the oil level continues to drop, the sensor float will drop down and close the lower switch. This completes the circuit between the Green/Red wire and ground. When the control unit gets this signal, the Yellow light is turned off, and the Red light is turned on. This also activates the warning system including rpm reduction. The Green/Red wire from the oil tank sensor is also connected to the Pink warning wire.

The whole system is operated by making and breaking the path to ground. As a switch is grounded or non-grounded, the control unit reads this and reacts. The control unit and lamps are located either on the engine pan or in the gauge. Either way, the electronics are the same. This system also uses the holding circuit discussed under single lamp systems to prevent unintended acceleration.

➥ If a tank sensor has an "H" stamped on the top it has a holding circuit under the cap. Use the diode setting on your multimeter to test the Red lamp circuit. The 90 hp may or may-not have a "H" stamped on the top of the oil level sensor. However, these units all have a holding circuit

built into them. The holding circuit is either in the oil level sensor or in the oil control unit itself.

V4 & V6 Precision Blend

◗ See Figures 36 and 37

Yamaha's most advanced PBS system is used on the V4 and V6 engines. Larger motors consume more oil. An engine-mounted oil tank for V motors that would have sufficient capacity to satisfy customer demands would take up excessive space and add additional weight to the engine.

A large remote tank is included in this system to supply oil to the smaller tank (main tank) under the cowling. Oil is pumped from the remote tank (sub-tank or reservoir) to the main tank using an electric transfer pump.

Each tank has a sensor to monitor the oil level. A control unit takes the information from the sensors and decides when oil needs to be pumped from the remote tank to the main tank. The control unit also uses this sensor information to decide which light in the gauge to illuminate (Green, Yellow, or Red). The control unit also kicks in the warning systems (rpm reduction, buzzer, etc.) when the Red light is lit.

While very early Yamaha outboards used incandescent bulbs in the PBS gauge, the current PBS gauges use LCD indicators. An LCD arrow points at a colored block to indicate oil status.

Now look at the two oil tank sensors and the control unit in more detail. The

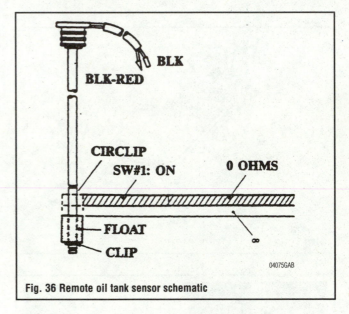

Fig. 36 Remote oil tank sensor schematic

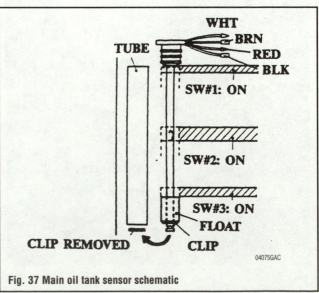

Fig. 37 Main oil tank sensor schematic

main tank sensor has three magnetic switches inside its shaft. If one of these switches closes, it completes the path to ground for that circuit.

The remote tank sensor has only one switch at the bottom of the sensor shaft. When the switch is closed, the circuit is complete to ground. This switch's color code is Black/Red.

Now, put everything together to see how it works. Start with both the main and remote tanks filled.

As the engine consumes oil, the float in the main tank drops. About halfway down the shaft, the magnetic float closes the switch on the Blue/Green wire. The control unit senses this connection and turns on the transfer pump. The transfer Pump already has 12 volts on one leg when the key is **ON**. The ground path is through the control unit. When the control unit turns the pump, it completes the path to ground.

The pump fills up the main tank. As the main tank sensor float moves up toward the top of the shaft, the Blue/Green switch opens and the Blue/White switch closes. The control unit senses this and turns the pump off. This cycle of turning the pump off and on continues as long as the oil supply in the remote tank is high enough to keep the remote tank switch closed.

During this time, the control unit turns on the Green light at the gauge.

The remote tank level falls as oil is transferred to the main engine tank When the remote tank level is down to less than a quarter tank, the sensor float drops to the bottom of the shaft. This opens the switch on the remote tank sensor.

When the remote tank switch opens, two things happen. First, the control unit turns on the Yellow low light at the gauge. Next, the control unit blocks any call for automatic oil transfer from the remote to the main tank The remaining oil in the remote tank can now only be transferred manually using the emergency override switch.

If the operator continues to run the engine without refilling the remote tank, the main engine tank will run out of oil. With no more oil coming from the remote tank, the main tank oil level drops to a point where the float closes the switch on the Blue/Red wire at the bottom of the sensor. This immediately turns on the Red light at the gauge and activates the other warning systems.

Another feature of this system is the circuit to turn off the oil pump when the engine is tilted over 30 degrees. Without this, the angle of the tilted engine could let the pump stay on even after the main tank is filled.

On older models, a mercury switch was used to decide when the motor had over 30 degrees tilt. V6 models through 1995 use the trim sender on the motor to decide tilt angle. The V4 series continue to use a mercury switch to reference 30 degrees.

Beginning in 1990 the oil control unit was placed inside the CDI box. On older models, the control unit is a separate component. The emergency switch is built on to the oil control unit. On many current production models, the emergency switch is separate part mounted next to the CDI box.

Another point of interest is the hold circuit on the YMIS equipped models. This circuit is in the CDI or YMIS module. On non-YMIS engines, the hold circuit is in the sensor.

The introduction of the SMART system technology in 1996 affected the oil injection on these models. The SMART system allows oil transfer only when the engine is running (except for initial service). This eliminates the need for trim sender information in the oil control unit. Problems such as oil transfer due to extended key-on/engine-off were also eliminated.

When rigging is completed, fill the remote tank at least one-quarter full. Turn on the ignition switch and, within 5 seconds, the oil pump will run for 180 seconds. If you do not get the full 180 seconds of transfer, check to see if first switch has closed. If enough oil transferred to close the first switch, then pump shut off was normal.

During normal operation with the engine running, the second switch turns the transfer pump on. When the oil level reaches the top of the tank (first switch closed) or after 90 seconds of transfer, the pump shuts off. The transfer pump will not run if the remote tank is low (third switch closed) while the engine is running. The transfer pump will not run if the engine is **OFF**.

The oil transfer will not take place with the main tank sender disconnected. If the main tank sensor is disconnected with the key **ON** the buzzer will sound.

Models	Years	Warning System
OIL WARNING SYSTEM OPERATION CHART		
25 30, 40M	88 ~ 97 87 ~	Single warning light in lower pan. Warning horn only used with remote control. Light and 2000rpm reduction activates with less than 20% oil remaining in oil tank.
40E 50 (see Below)	84 ~ 84 ~	Three warning lights in lower pan. Warning horn located in remote control. Green light: all OK. Yellow light with 1/3 oil remaining. Red light , horn, and 2000rpm reduction with 10% oil remaining. System reset by turning main switch off.
PRO 50	88 ~	Three warning lights in tachometer. Warning horn located in remote control. Green light: all OK. Yellow light with 1/3 oil remaining. Red light , horn, and 2000rpm reduction with 10% oil remaining. System reset by turning main switch off.
40TLH 50ETMLD 50TLHP PRO 60 PRO 75	96 ~ 90 91 ~ 91 ~ 96 ~	Three warning indicators in tachometer and warning horn. Multifunction tachometer full-indicator activated: all OK. Center indicator activated with 1/3 oil remaining. Red indicator activated and 2000rpm reduction with 10% oil remaining. System reset by turning main switch off.
70 90	84 to 85 84 to 85	Three warning indicators in small gauge. Green indicator activated: all OK. Yellow indicator activated with 1/3 oil remaining. Red indicator and horn activated 2000rpm reduction with 10% oil remaining. System reset by turning main switch off.
70 90	86 to 87 86 to 87	Same as above 70 & 90 except oil lights located in tachometer. A control unit was required.
70 90	88 ~	Same as above 70 & 90 except multifunction tachometer used with warning indicators.
115 All V-6	84 to 85 84 to 85	Three warning lights in a large gauge. Green light activated: all OK. Yellow light activated with 1/2 gallon of oil remaining in remote oil tank. Emergency switch on oil control unit will transfer remaining oil if needed. Red light and horn activated and 2000rpm reduction with engine oil tank only 10% oil remaining. System reset by turning main switch off. A mercury switch (located inside the control unit) will not allow oil to transfer if the engine is tilted.
115 All V-6 PRO V 150	86 to 87 86 to 87 86 to 88	Same as above except oil lights located in tachometer.
115 & 130 All V-6 PRO V 150	88 ~ 88 to 89 89	Same as above except oil lights located in multifunction tachometer. Indicators flash when gauge turned on. "90" ~ Loose battery warning, RPM reduction and lights and horn activated.
115 ~ 200	90 to 95	The loose battery warning activates when the CDI does not sense the presence of a battery in the circuit. This may be caused by a loose battery terminal on the battery or engine or a loose fuse causing a momentary break in the power supply. If this happens, the warning buzzer will sound and engine speed will reduce to about 2000rpm. All three oil lights will flash.
All V-6	90 to 95	Oil control unit and emergency switch are combined with CDI. Oil will not transfer when engine is tilted up. This is detected by the trim sender. All other operations are the same except system is reset by returning the throttle to idle and engine RPM dropping below 1300rpm.
V6-3.1L V6-2.6L	90 ~ 94 ~	Operation is the same as above except oil will not transfer when the engine is not running. For initial filling, the oil pump will operate for 180 seconds when the remote oil tank is full and the engine oil tank is empty.

04705C01

TROUBLESHOOTING

Single Lamp System

This a very simple system to check. The following components are involved: Charge coil, Ignitor (CDI) box and Warning lamp.

Oil tank sensor Troubleshooting strategy is problem dependent. What is wrong will determine you troubleshooting direction. Is the system staying on all the time? Not coming on at all? Gather information.

The oil tank sensor operation can be checked by running the motor and grounding, then ungrounding the Pink harness lead going to the sensor. When grounded, the warning system should engage. When ungrounded, the system should operate normally.

If the system works correctly when doing this check, investigate the sensor itself. Do not forget that the overheat sensor is also connected in this circuit. If there is an overheat, the operator will get the same warning. To isolate the low oil warning from the overheat, disconnect the overheat sensor Pink lead from the circuit. Now only the oil warning system is operating.

If the engine is running, it is probable that the charge coil is good. It is necessary for ignition.

The only component that can't be directly checked is the CDI box. Remember that all other components can be directly checked. If they are all good, then the CDI box is the only remaining source of the problem.

Three LED System

There are basically two parts to this system. The oil tank sensor and the lamp/control unit. The lamp assembly and the control unit come only as an assembly.

Begin troubleshooting by identifying the problem. Is the system totally dead? Is one light out? Are the lights dim?

This system requires a battery in good condition. Play the percentages and check out the battery before jumping into the electronics. Also don't forget to check the grounds on the system. Total failure or dim lights (high resistance) can be a symptom of bad grounds.

Make sure the Yellow wire to the control unit has 12 volts and the Black wire is grounded.

A quick way to troubleshoot this system is to disconnect the sensor. With the power on and the tank sensor disconnected, the control unit is getting a "no switch closed." You should have a Yellow lamp. If this works ground the Green wire. The control unit is being told the upper sensor switch is closed. The Green lamp should come on. The last check is to ground the Green/Red wire. The control unit should read this as a closed lower sensor switch. The Red lamp should come on.

If these tests give the correct readings, the control unit and lamps are OK. A failure of one or all the lamps will require replacement of the brain/lamp assembly.

If the lamps are OK, the oil tank sensor needs to be resistance checked.

This system can be checked out quickly once you understand how it works. Other PBS Related Problems

Excessive smoke at idle is a common problem. The following items should be inspected. They are listed in the order of their probability.

- The oil pump linkage is disconnected
- The oil pump linkage is binding
- The oil pump linkage is out of adjustment
- The unit needs carburetor synchronization and idle fuel adjustment
- The oil is not Yamalube. Some oil brands smoke excessively when all adjustments are correct.
- The oil line check valves are leaking.

Some special notes regarding electrical problems bear mentioning. This is a "ground control" system. If you have a short to ground on a control (sensor) lead the, control unit will think a switch is closed. Watch for pinched wires. Check color codes and watch out for incorrect connections.

V4 & V6 Precision Blend

As with any electrical problem, the best troubleshooting strategy begins with good preparation, knowledge of the system to be checked, and a Seloc manual. Don't forget to get details about the problem. Good information can vastly reduce troubleshooting time.

Note when the problem occurs and how long it occurs. Is only part of the system not working? Is the whole system dead? These questions can make a difference.

Remember that this system has only one component that is difficult to check and that is the control module. All other pieces have direct tests. Your goal is to check the components that can be checked. If they are good, the control module is the prime suspect.

Start off with the basics. Are all fuses in good shape? Is the battery fully charged? Is current getting to the precision blend system? Is there oil in both tanks?

A quick check for the tank sensors is to bypass them. Remember that as each sensor lead from the control unit is grounded, the unit activates or turns off a circuit.

Start with the main tank sensor. Disconnect the sensor leads from the main harness. We know that when the Blue/Green lead is grounded through its switch, the transfer pump turns on. The same thing can happen if we jump the harness side Blue/Green to the harness side Black. This is doing the same thing as closing the switch.

If the system is good, the transfer pump will now turn **ON** and stay on. If it doesn't, the wiring, pump, or the control module could be bad.

To turn the pump off, jump between the Blue/White and Black on the harness side. The pump should stop. Again, if it doesn't, check the wiring and the control module.

Next, activate the Red lamp and the warning system by jumping between the Blue/Red and Black wires. The Red lamp and other warning systems should activate. If not, check the wiring and the control module.

Remember that if the system wouldn't work before, and these bypass checks give proper operation, the main tank sensor is the problem. The beauty of these checks is that they were quick and didn't require taking the sensor out of the tank.

The remote tank sensor is the next item to check. It has only one switch on the Black/Red wire. Disconnect the sensor from the wiring harness. Jump between the Black/Red and Black wires on the harness side. The Green light should come on in automatic mode.

Disconnect the jumper. With the circuit open, the Yellow light should come on and the transfer pump should not work.

Like before, if the jumps allow the system to work when they wouldn't before, the sensor is at fault. If the jumps don't solve the problem, the failure is elsewhere in the system.

To check the transfer pump operation, try the emergency bypass switch first with the key on. If the pump runs, the problem is elsewhere. If the pump doesn't run, go directly to the pump. Connect the brown lead to the pump to the positive side of a battery and the negative lead to the Blue pump lead. If the pump works, the problem is elsewhere. If the pump still won't operate, the pump is bad.

If the pump, sensors, and wiring all check out, the only item left is the control module.

Don't forget that some systems use a mercury switch (V4s), or the trim sender (1990–1995 V6s) to detect a 30 degree tilt angle on the motor. V76 motors and SMART systems do not allow the pump to run with the engine **OFF**. A problem in this area could also cause failures.

OPERATIONAL CHECK

⬦ **See Figure 38 and accompanying illustrations**

The following procedures check the operation of the buzzer and the Green, Yellow, and Red lights to ensure they come on at the proper time. Correct operation of the buzzer and lights is essential to warn the operator of a low oil level in the tank. This simple procedure should be performed at the start of each season to verify the warning system is functioning correctly as a protection against expensive powerhead service work. Inadequate lubrication can almost destroy a powerhead.

After these tests are completed, the injection system should be purged of air (bled).

➥**The following tests are performed with the powerhead not running, as both oil tanks are to be drained. Running the powerhead with inadequate lubrication will cause damage to internal moving parts and may cause seizure. The battery must be connected for the tests, but the spark plugs should be removed and the high tension leads grounded.**

1. Obtain a suitable container with a large enough capacity to hold all the oil in the main tank. Place some shop cloths in the bottom of the lower cowling to catch any oil which may drain during the removal of the oil supply line.

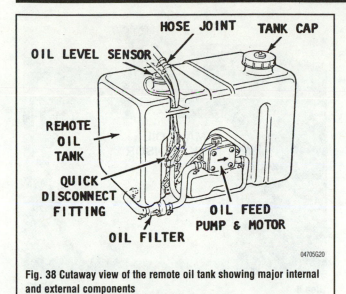

Fig. 38 Cutaway view of the remote oil tank showing major internal and external components

Remove the oil supply line leading from the main oil tank to the oil pump beneath the tank by compressing the wire clamp with a pair of needlenose pliers and pushing the clamp up along the oil line. Squeeze the oil line to restrict the flow of oil while pulling it free of the fitting. Allow the tank to completely drain into the container. Install the line back onto the center fitting on the oil pump.

2. Remove the remote tank from the boat. Once the tank is removed from the boat, completely drain the oil from the tank. Install the empty tank into the boat.

Turn the main switch to the **ON** position. The Red light should illuminate and the buzzer should sound. The oil feed pump should not operate.

3. Begin to add oil to the remote tank. Fill the tank to a little over 1.6 U.S. quarts (1.5 liters).

Turn the main switch to the **ON** position. The Green and the Red light should come on. The buzzer should sound and the oil feed pump should operate.

Continue to add oil to the remote tank until a total of just over 5.3 U.S. quarts (5.0 liters) have been added. Repeat Test B and check to see if the oil is being transferred from the remote tank to the main tank.

4. Check the oil level in the main tank. Continue to hold the main switch in the **ON** position until the oil level reaches the lower mark embossed on the exterior of the tank. Release the main switch.

With the main switch in the **ON** position, the Red light should go out. The Green light should be the only light lit. The buzzer should be silent and the feed pump should not operate. Release the main switch.

5. Remove the remote tank oil level sensor.

Turn the main switch to the **ON** position. Only the Yellow light should come on. The buzzer should not sound and the feed pump should not operate.

Hold the emergency switch in the up position. The oil feed pump should operate. Release the emergency switch and the main switch.

Install the remote oil tank sensor.

6. Turn the main switch to the **ON** position. Tilt the outboard to 35° from the vertical position.

With the main switch in the **ON** position, hold the emergency switch up. The oil feed pump should not operate, if the tilt switch in the control box is functioning correctly. No lights should come on and the buzzer should not sound.

Bring the outboard down to less than 20° from the vertical position.

Step 1

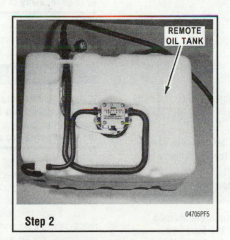

Step 2

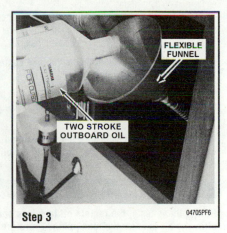

Step 3

Step 4

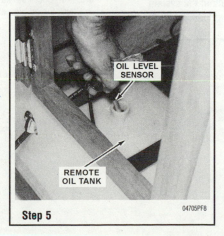

Step 5

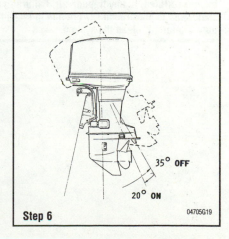

Step 6

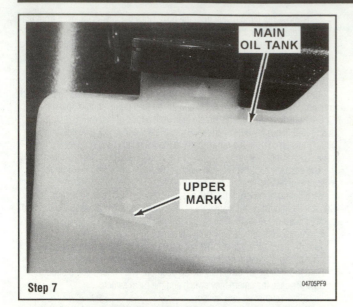

MAIN OIL TANK

UPPER MARK

Step 7   04705PF9

MAIN OIL TANK SENSOR

Step 8   04705PF0

With the main switch in the **ON** position, hold the emergency switch up. The oil feed pump should now operate, if the tilt switch in the control box is functioning correctly. No lights should come on and the buzzer should not sound.

7. Return the outboard to the vertical position, and continue to keep the main switch in the **ON** position while the feed pump transfers oil to the main tank. Continue holding the switch until the oil level reaches the upper mark embossed on the exterior of the tank.

When the oil level in the main tank reaches the upper mark, the feed pump should stop. No lights should come on and the buzzer should not sound.

8. Lift out the main tank oil level sensor half way.

➡**Perform the next test quickly, as the feed pump will be pumping oil into a full tank and may overflow.**

With the main switch in the **ON** position, the feed pump should pump oil up to the main tank. No lights should come on and the buzzer should not sound.

Install the main tank oil level sensor

➡**After the foregoing tests have been completed, the operation of the warning lights, both oil level sensors, and the oil feed pump have been checked.**

✳✳ CAUTION

During these tests, the remote oil tank was completely drained allowing air to enter the feed pump. Therefore, the feed pump must be purged (bled) of any trapped air. Failure to bleed the system could lead to powerhead seizure due to lack of adequate lubrication. Therefore, bleed the system.

✳✳ CAUTION

Never operate the powerhead above a fast idle with a flush attachment connected to the lower unit. Operating the powerhead at a high rpm with no load on the propeller shaft could cause the powerhead to runaway causing extensive damage to the unit.

Remember, the powerhead will not start without the emergency tether in place behind the kill switch knob.

Start the powerhead and allow it to warm to operating temperature.

✳✳ CAUTION

Water must circulate through the lower unit to the powerhead anytime the powerhead is operating to prevent damage to the water pump in the lower unit. Just five seconds without water will damage the water pump impeller.

Check the completed work. If the system is functioning properly, only the Green light should be on and the buzzer should not sound.

Check for oil leaks around all hose connections which were disturbed. Replenish both tanks with Yamalube two stroke outboard oil.

Fill the main tank to the upper line embossed on the tank exterior. Fill the remote tank to a point where the motion of the boat will not cause the tank to over flow. Check the water/dust trap on the bottom of the main tank.

Check the oil filter at the remote tank periodically and replace, as necessary.

WIRING DIAGRAMS

OIL INJECTION SYSTEM SCHEMATIC — 1990–98 3.1 L AND 1996–98 2.6 L

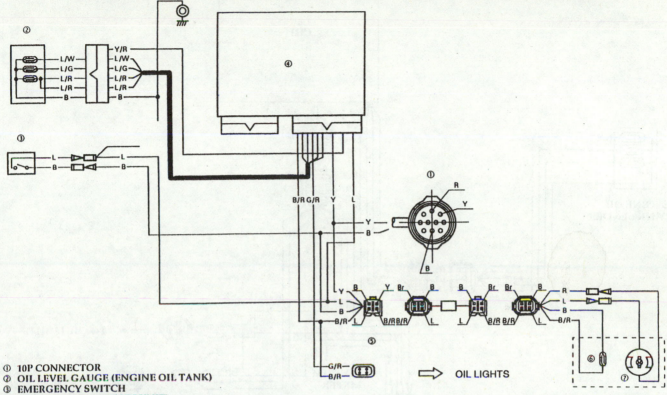

① **10P CONNECTOR**
② **OIL LEVEL GAUGE (ENGINE OIL TANK)**
③ **EMERGENCY SWITCH**
④ **MICROCOMPUTER (CDI UNIT)**
⑤ **4P COUPLER**
⑥ **OIL LEVEL GAUGE (REMOTE OIL TANK)**
⑦ **OIL FEED PUMP**

NOTE: Shown is V76 system. V6 System has different connector plugs.

04705W01

OIL INJECTION SYSTEM SCHEMATIC — 1990–95 2.6 L

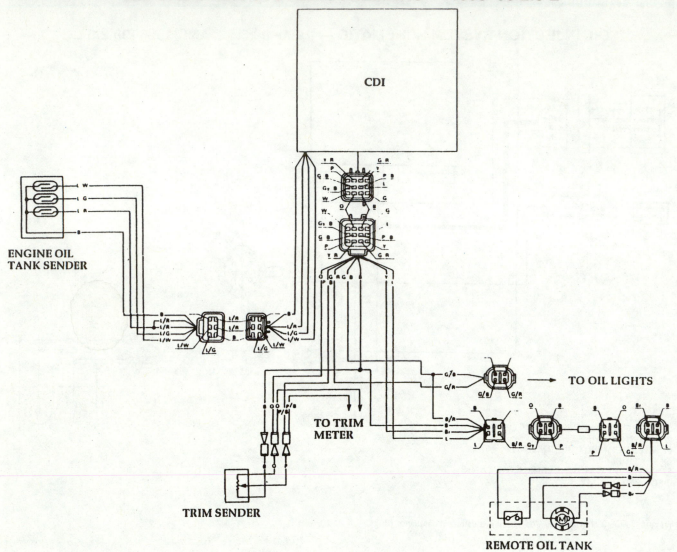

04705W02

IGNITION SYSTEM 6-2
CONTACT BREAKER POINTS IGNITION
 (MAGNETO IGNITION) 6-2
  SERVICING 6-2
CAPACITOR DISCHARGE IGNITION (CDI)
 SYSTEM 6-3
TROUBLESHOOTING 6-7
SPARK PLUGS 6-7
COMPRESSION 6-8
CONDENSER 6-8
BREAKER POINTS 6-8
POLARITY CHECK 6-9
RESISTANCE TESTING PRECAUTIONS 6-9
PULSAR COILS 6-9
CHARGE COILS 6-10
LIGHTING COIL 6-11
IGNITION COILS 6-11
CDI UNIT 6-12
RECTIFIER 6-21
CONTROL UNIT 6-21
SERVICING 6-24
FLYWHEEL AND STATOR PLATE 6-24
  REMOVAL 6-24
  CLEANING AND INSPECTION 6-28
  ASSEMBLY AND INSTALLATION 6-28
CDI UNIT AND IGNITION COILS 6-33
  REMOVAL 6-33
  INSTALLATION 6-35
**YAMAHA MICROCOMPUTER
 IGNITION SYSTEM (YMIS) 6-37**
DESCRIPTION AND OPERATION 6-37
  SYSTEM TYPES 6-37
  CONTROL UNIT 6-37
  THROTTLE POSITION SENSOR 6-38
  CRANKSHAFT POSITION
   SENSOR 6-38
  KNOCK SENSOR 6-39
  THERMO SENSOR 6-39
CONTROL UNIT FUNCTIONS 6-39
  ENGINE START CONTROL 6-39
  ENGINE WARM UP CONTROL 6-39
  IDLE STABILIZING CONTROL 6-40
  IGNITION TIMING CONTROL 6-40
  OVERHEATING CONTROL 6-40
  OVERREV CONTROL 6-40
  KNOCK CONTROL 6-40
  REVERSE DIRECTION CONTROL 6-40
  OPERATING VOLTAGE CONTROL 6-40
SELF DIAGNOSIS 6-40
TROUBLESHOOTING 6-42
  1992–98 60, C60, C80 AND 90
   POWERHEADS 6-42
  1990–95 225 (2.6L) POWERHEAD 6-42
  1996–98 150–225L
   POWERHEADS 6-43
  1990–95 250, 225X, 225U AND
   1996–98 3.1L POWERHEADS 6-43
TESTING 6-43
  CONTROL UNIT 6-43

YMIS POWER SUPPLY 6-44
CRANK POSITION SENSOR 6-44
KNOCK SENSOR 6-45
THERMOSWITCH TEST 6-45
THERMOSENSOR 6-45
THROTTLE POSITION SENSOR 6-46
SPECIFICATIONS CHARTS
CDI UNIT TEST CHARTS 6-14
RECTIFIER TEST CHART 6-22
IGNITION TESTING
 SPECIFICATIONS 6-23
YMIS SYSTEM APPLICATIONS 6-38
DIAGNOSIS CODE TABLES 6-41
YMIS SENSOR CHARACTERISTICS 6-43

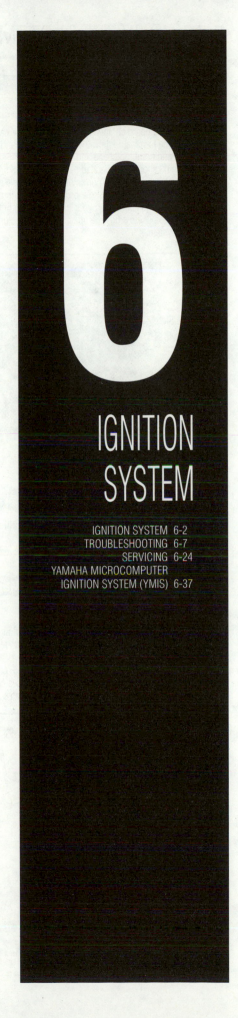

6

IGNITION
SYSTEM

IGNITION SYSTEM 6-2
TROUBLESHOOTING 6-7
SERVICING 6-24
YAMAHA MICROCOMPUTER
IGNITION SYSTEM (YMIS) 6-37

IGNITION SYSTEM

▶ See Figure 1

The less an outboard engine is operated, the more care it needs. Allowing an outboard engine to remain idle will do more harm than if it is used regularly. To maintain the engine in top shape and always ready for efficient operation at any time, the engine should be operated every 3 to 4 weeks throughout the year.

The carburetion and ignition principles of two-cycle engine operation must be understood in order to perform a proper tune-up on an outboard motor. If you have any doubts concerning your understanding of two-cycle engine operation, it would be best to study the operation theory before tackling any work on the ignition system.

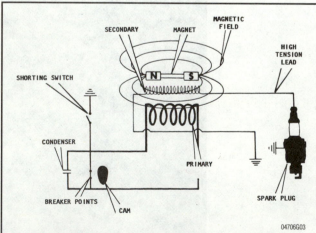

Fig. 1 The ignition system must be properly adjusted and synchronized for optimum powerhead performance

Contact Breaker Points Ignition (Magneto Ignition)

▶ See Figures 2 and 3

As of 1995 all Yamaha outboard engines use a pointless electronic ignition system. Prior to 1995 the 2hp engine was the only model with a point type magneto.

This ignition system uses a mechanically switched, collapsing field to induce spark at the plug. A magnet moving by a coil produces current in the primary coil winding. The current in the primary winding creates a magnetic field. When

Fig. 2 Schematic of a typical magneto ignition system installed on an outboard

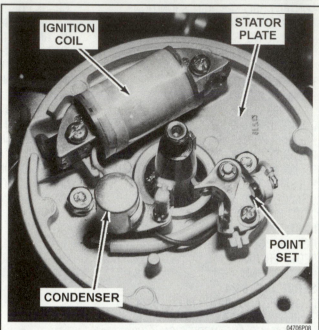

Fig. 3 After the flywheel is removed, components on the stator plate may be easily serviced

the points are closed the current goes to ground. As the breaker points open the primary magnetic field collapses across the secondary field. This induces (transforms) a high voltage potential in the secondary coil winding. This high voltage current travels to the spark plug and jumps the gap.

The point type ignition system contains a condenser that works like a sponge in the circuit. Current that is flowing through the primary circuit tries to keep going. When the breaker point switch opens the current will arc over the widening gap. The condenser is wired in parallel with the points. The condenser absorbs some of the current flow as the points open. This reduces arc over and extends the life of the points.

The flywheel-type magneto unit consists of a stator plate, and permanent magnets built into the flywheel. The ignition coil, condenser and breaker points are mounted on the stator plate.

As the pole pieces of the magnet pass over the heels of the coil, a magnetic field is built up about the coil, causing a current to flow through the primary winding.

At the proper time, the breaker points are separated by action of a cam designed into the collar of the flywheel and the primary circuit is broken. When the circuit is broken, the flow of primary current stops and causes the magnetic field about the coil to break down instantly. At this precise moment, an electrical current of extremely high voltage is induced in the fine secondary windings of the coil. This high voltage is conducted to the spark plug where it jumps the gap between the points of the plug to ignite the compressed charge of air-fuel mixture in the cylinder.

SERVICING

Magnetos installed on outboard engines will usually operate over extremely long periods of time without requiring adjustment or repair. However, if ignition system problems are encountered, and the usual corrective actions such as replacement of spark plugs does not correct the problem, the magneto output should be checked to determine if the unit is functioning properly.

Unfortunately, the breaker point set of the Contact Breaker Points ignition system is located under the flywheel. This location requires the hand rewind starter to be removed, and the flywheel to be pulled in order to replace the point set.

However, the manufacturer made provisions for the point gap to be checked with a feeler gauge through one of two slots cut into the top of the flywheel for this purpose. Therefore, only the hand rewind starter needs to be removed to perform the task of point adjustment.

Point Gap Check

♦ See Figures 4, 5, 6 and 7

The point gap may be checked using an ohmmeter and a dial gauge without removing the hand rewind starter or the flywheel. This procedure is not necessary if the point gap has already been checked using a feeler gauge.

First, remove the spark plug and install a dial gauge into the spark plug opening. Rotate the flywheel until the piston reaches TDC (top dead center). Set the dial gauge at Zero.

Next, disconnect the White lead at the quick disconnect fitting and remove the Black ground lead from the horseshoe bracket. Set the ohmmeter on the 1000 scale. Make contact with the Black ohmmeter lead to the Black ground lead and the Red ohmmeter lead to the White lead from the stator plate.

When the points are closed, the meter will indicate continuity by registering a reading. The actual value of the reading is not important.

When the points are open, creating an open in the circuit, the meter will register an infinite resistance—an air gap. Therefore, the meter needle will swing either to the far right or to the far left, depending on the scale of the ohmmeter.

Now, slowly rotate the flywheel counterclockwise and observe the two positions of the meter needle. If the point gap is correct, the meter needle will swing from open to close between 0.04–0.05 in. (1.0–1.2mm) BTDC (before top dead center).

If the point gap is incorrect, the gap must be adjusted or the point set replaced.

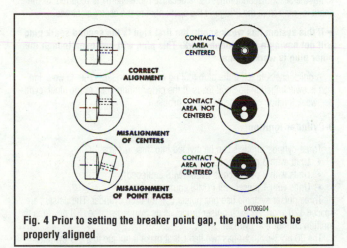

Fig. 4 Prior to setting the breaker point gap, the points must be properly aligned

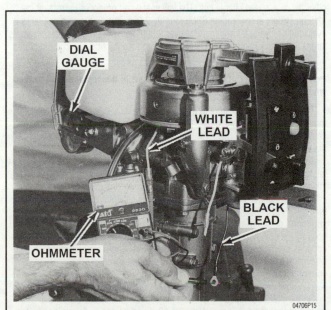

Fig. 5 The point gap may be checked without removing any major parts by using an ohmmeter and a dial indicator gauge

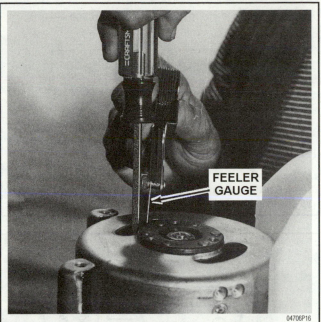

Fig. 6 The flywheel on some powerheads has a window to permit point gap adjustment using a screwdriver and feeler gauge

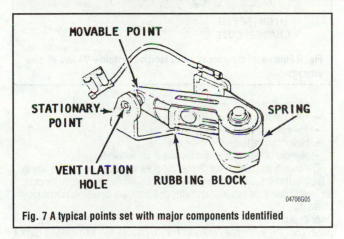

Fig. 7 A typical points set with major components identified

The procedures outlined in the following service section for the Contact Breaker Points ignition system provide detailed instructions to adjust or replace the breaker point set on 1-cylinder units covered in this manual.

Capacitor Discharge Ignition (CDI) System

♦ See Figures 8 and 9

1-Cylinder Ignition

In its simplest form, a CDI ignition is composed of the following elements:

- Magneto
- Pulser coil
- Charge, or source coil
- Igniter (CDI) box
- Ignition coil
- Spark plug

Other components such as main switches, stop switches, or computer systems may be included, though, these items are not necessary for basic CDI operation.

To understand basic CDI operation, it is important to understand the basic theory of induction. Induction theory states that if we move a magnet (magnetic field) past a coil of wire (or the coil by the magnet), AC current will be generated in the coil.

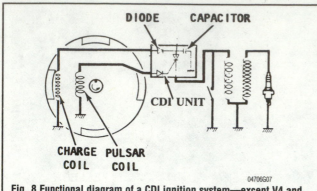

04706G07

Fig. 8 Functional diagram of a CDI ignition system—except V4 and V6 powerheads

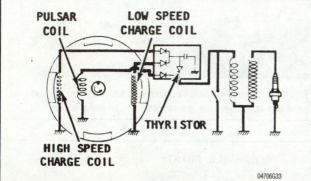

04706G33

Fig. 9 Functional diagram of a CDI ignition system—V4 and V6 powerheads

The amount of current produced depends on several factors:
- How fast the magnet moves past the coil
- The size of the magnet(strength)
- How close the magnet is to the coil
- Number of turns of wire and the size of the windings

The current produced in the charge coil goes to the CDI box. On the way in, it is converted to DC current by a diode. This DC current is stored in the capacitor located inside the box. As the charge coil produces current, the capacitor stores it.

At a specific time in the magneto's revolution, the magnets go past the pulser coil. The pulser coil is smaller than the charge coil so it has less current output. The current from the pulser also goes into the CDI box. This current signals the CDI box when to fire the capacitor (the pulser may be called a trigger coil for obvious reasons). The current from the capacitor flows out to the ignition coil and spark plug. The pulser acts much like the points in older ignitions systems.

When the pulser signal reaches the CDI box, all the electricity stored in the capacitor is released at once. This current flows through the ignition coil's primary windings.

The ignition coil is a step-up transformer. It turns the relatively low voltage entering the primary windings into high voltage at the secondary windings. This occurs due to a phenomena known as induction.

The high voltage generated in the secondary windings leaves the ignition coil and goes to the spark plug. The spark in turn ignites the air-fuel charge in the combustion chamber.

Once the complete cycle has occurred, the spinning magneto immediately starts the process over again.

Main switches, engine stop switches, and the like are usually connected on the wire in between the CDI box and the ignition coil. When the main switch or stop switch is turned to the OFF position, the switch is closed. This closed switch short-circuits the charge coil current to ground rather than sending it through the CDI box. With no charge coil current through the CDI box, there is no spark and the engine stops or, if the engine is not running, no spark is produced.

2-Cylinder Ignition

Most smaller Yamaha outboards up through the 25 hp model are 2-cylinders with one, dual lead ignition coil.

The system has one pulser coil, one charge coil, a CDI box and a dual lead coil. In this system, both spark plugs spark at the same time. Although both cylinders spark at the same time, only one cylinder is actually producing power. The crankshaft is a 180 degree type which means that as piston number one is at top dead center, piston number two is at bottom dead center. The piston at TDC is compressing a fuel charge that the spark then ignites. At the same moment, the piston at BDC isn't compressing a fuel charge. Actually, there are still exhaust gases going out. The spark in this cylinder has no effect on power production. This combination of engine and ignition design is called waste spark system.

After the crankshaft has rotated another 180 degrees, the two pistons have reversed position. The spark fires again to ignite the fuel charge compressed in cylinder number two and sparks to no effect in cylinder one.

Twin coil CDI operation up to the ignition coil is exactly Like the basic CDI. The difference is in the dual lead ignition coil

On a traditional ignition coil, the current leaves the coil, goes to the spark plug through the cylinder head to ground.

On a dual lead coil, the current leaves the coil, goes through one of the spark plugs, travels through the cylinder head to the second spark plug, and returns to the coil itself. This way one coil can fire two cylinders.

This type of system requires about 30% more voltage than a standard system to fire the second spark plug. This is because more energy is required for the spark to jump from the bridge of the spark plug to the center electrode.

➡ **If this system has weak spark, the first sign is the second spark plug will not having a hot enough spark. This plug will foul even though the other plug is working fine.**

A quick check to tell if the plug fouling on one cylinder is due to weak ignition is switch the ignition coil leads. If the plug fouling goes to the other. cylinder, weak ignition components are the problem.

3-Cylinder Ignition

Three-cylinder models can be divided into three groups:
- Units with 3 pulser coils
- Units with 2 pulser coils (Non-YMIS equipped)
- Units with 1 pulser coil (YMIS equipped)

Three pulser systems use one pulser coil for each cylinder. The pulsers are spaced 120 apart. As each pulser produces its own signal, the CDI box fires the ignition coil for that cylinder.

The 90 hp 3-cylinder has two items that make it unique to the 3-cylinder family. One, it has two charge coils, one called a low speed charge coil and the other the high speed charge coil. The low speed coil produces current for the ignition system at low engine RPM, roughly 2,000. The high speed coil takes over ignition needs for engine RPM over 2,000. Rather than having two separate large coils, the 90 hp has both charge coils and the lighting coil combined into a single unit called a stator.

➡ **The failure of any of these coils will result in the replacement of the whole stator rather than a single coil.**

The second unique feature to the 90 hp is that it uses two pulsers rather than three. Usually there is one pulser per cylinder. In this case, one pulser actually controls two cylinders. These two cylinders are not firing at the same time like the earlier twin models.

To allow two cylinders to fire off one pulser at different times, the pulser must tell the CDI box when to ignite the appropriate cylinder. This is accomplished by taking advantage of a characteristic of the induction process.

As a magnet goes by the pulser, electricity is generated. This current flows to the igniter (CDI) box. The direction the current flows is determined by which end (north or south) of the magnet travels past the coil first. When the north end goes by the coil, current flows in one direction. When the south end of the magnet goes by, the current flows in the opposite direction. This is sometimes referred to as phase or polarity. The CDI box can differentiate the direction of current flow and direct the signal to the appropriate capacitor. The CDI box, in effect, knows which cylinder to fire by the signature of the signal.

On the YMIS equipped 70 & 90 hp units, there is only one pulser coil in the system. It fires the 1 & 3 cylinders. The #2 cylinder firing is determined by the YMIS computer. A failure of the YMIS will extinguish the # 2 spark.

V4 & V6 Ignition

The V4 ignition system works like a basic CDI system with two major differences. First, one pulser fires two cylinders independently of each other. Second, there are two charge coils, one for low speed and one for high speed.

In a basic CDI, one pulser coil sends The signal to fire one ignition coil. In the V4 system two pulser coils fire for separate ignition coils. This means that one two-wire pulser coil fires two separate cylinders at different times in the firing order.

To fire two cylinders off one pulser at different times, the pulser must tell the CDI box when to fire a particular cylinder. This is accomplished by inducing distinctly different electrical signals for each pulser.

When a magnet passes a pulser, electricity is generated. This current flows to the CDI box. The direction of current flow (sometimes referred to as phase) is determined by which end of the magnet, north or south, travels past the coil first. When the north end goes by the pulser coil first, current flows in one direction. When the south end of the magnet goes by first, the current flows in the opposite direction.

The CDI box senses which direction the pulser current is flowing. The direction of flow determines which of the two cylinders controlled by that pulser will fire.

By operating this way, two pulsers can control the operation of four cylinders.

In a basic CDI system, a single charge coil is used to supply the electrical power needed for the ignition.

On larger Yamaha outboards, two charge coils are used to supply the electrical needs of the ignition system. One coil, the low-speed coil, supplies the electrical power from idle up to about 2,000 rpm. The other coil, the high-speed coil supplies electrical power from about 2,000 rpm on up.

On Yamaha CDI systems, the low speed, high speed, and lighting coil are all combined into one unit called a stator. If any of the stator components are bad, the whole assembly is replaced.

The V6 ignition is very similar to the V4 system. The V6 systems has the same low and high-speed charge coils for better electrical output at all speeds.

The V6 uses three pulser coils to fire 6 cylinders. These pulsers operate on the same principle as the V4 pulsers. The SMART ignition use two pulsers and the computer to fire six cylinders. Cylinders two and five are fired by the computer and can run a different timing map from the rest of the engine.

Charge Circuit

EXCEPT V4 AND V6 POWERHEADS

▶ See Figures 10 and 11

Two basic circuits are used with the CDI system, the first of these is the charge circuit. The charge circuit consists of the flywheel magnet, a charge coil, a diode, and a capacitor. As the flywheel magnet passes by the charge coil, a voltage is induced in the coil. As the flywheel continues to rotate and the coil is no longer influenced by the magnet, the magnetic field collapses. Therefore, an alternating current is produced at the charge coil. This AC current is changed to DC by a diode inside the CDI unit.

➡ **A diode is a solid state unit which permits current to flow in one direction but prevents flow in the opposite direction. A diode may also be know as a rectifier.**

The current then passes to a capacitor, also located inside the CDI unit, where it is stored.

Both the V4 and V6 models have two charge coils, one for high speed operation and one for low speed operation. A voltage is induced in the windings of each coil. The magnitude of the voltage depends upon the number of windings (turns) in each coil and the engine rpm.

The voltages generated by these two charge coils are limited by a voltage regulator and stored separately in two condensers. The condensers are charged in stages, each time a magnet passes a charge coil.

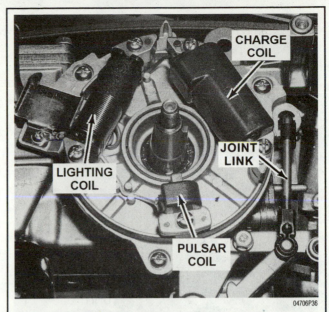

Fig. 10 Stator plate of a 1-cylinder powerhead with major parts identified. The stator plate is rotated through the joint link to advance the timing

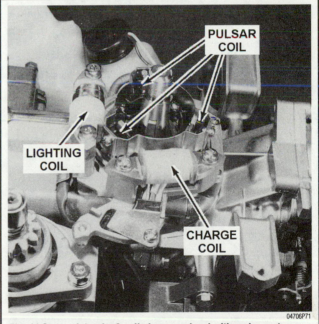

Fig. 11 Stator plate of a 3-cylinder powerhead with major parts identified

V4 AND V6 POWERHEADS

▶ See Figures 12 and 13

The charging system consists of the flywheel magnets, a lighting coil (alternator), a rectifier, voltage regulator, and the battery.

The lighting coil, so named because it may be used to power the lights on the boat when used together with a voltage regulator, allows the powerhead to generate additional electrical current to charge the battery.

Fig. 12 The CDI unit is located on the side of the powerhead and is usually removed for testing

CDI UNIT

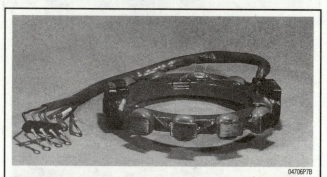

Fig. 13 The charge and lighting coil removed from a V6 powerhead for bench testing

As the flywheel magnets rotate, voltage is induced in the lighting coil located next to the pulsar coils. This alternating current passes through a series of diodes and emerges as DC current. Therefore, it may be stored in the battery. A lighting coil may be identified by its clean laminated copper windings. All other coils are wrapped in tape and their windings are not visible.

The rectifier converts the alternating current into DC, which may then be stored in the battery. The rectifier is a sealed unit and contains four diodes. If one of the diodes is defective, the entire unit must be replaced.

The voltage regulator stabilizes the power output of the coils and extends the life of the light bulbs by preventing power surges.

Pulsar Circuit

♦ See Figure 14

The second circuit used in CDI systems is the pulsar circuit. The pulsar circuit has its own flywheel magnet, a pulsar coil, a diode, and a thyristor. A

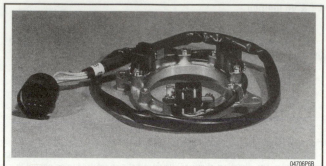

Fig. 14 The pulsar coil removed from a V6 powerhead for bench testing

thyristor is a solid state electronic switching device which permits voltage to flow only after it is triggered by another voltage source.

At the point in time when the ignition timing marks align, an alternating current is induced in the pulsar coil, in the same manner as previously described for the charge coil. This current is then passed to a second diode located in the CDI unit where it becomes DC current and flows on to the thyristor. This voltage triggers the thyristor to permit the voltage stored in the capacitor to be discharged. The capacitor voltage passes through the thyristor and on to the primary windings of the ignition coil.

In this manner, a spark at the plug may be accurately timed by the timing marks on the flywheel relative to the magnets in the flywheel and to provide as many as 100 sparks per second for a powerhead operating at 6000 rpm.

On the V4 models, the two pulsar coils are mounted to produce a pulse every 90° revolution of the crankshaft. Therefore four pulses are produced each crankshaft revolution.

On the V6 models the three pulsar coils are evenly spaced at 120° around the stator plate. The combination of these three pulsars will produce a pulse every 60° revolution of the crankshaft. Therefore six pulses are produced each crankshaft revolution.

Ignition Coils

♦ See Figure 15

Ignition coils, one per cylinder, boost the DC voltage instantly to approximately 20,000 volts to the spark. This completes the primary side of the ignition circuit.

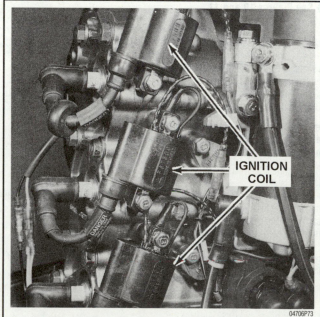

Fig. 15 Most powerheads covered in this manual are equipped with one ignition coil for each cylinder

IGNITION COIL

Once the voltage is discharged from the ignition coil the secondary circuit begins and only stretches from the ignition coil to the spark plugs via extremely large high tension leads. At the spark plug end, the voltage arcs in the form of a spark, across from the center electrode to the outer electrode, and then to ground via the spark plug threads. This completes the ignition circuit.

Ignition Timing

At the point in time when the ignition timing marks align, an alternating current is induced in the pulsar coil, in the same manner as previously described for the charge coil. This current is then passed to a second diode located in the CDI unit where it becomes DC current and flows on to the thyristor. This voltage triggers the thyristor to permit the voltage stored in the capacitor to be dis-

charged. The capacitor voltage passes through the thyristor and on to the primary windings of the ignition coil.

In this manner, a spark at the plug may be accurately timed by the timing marks on the flywheel relative to the magnets in the flywheel and to provide as many as 100 sparks per second for a powerhead operating at 6000 rpm.

Units equipped with an automatic advance type CDI system have no moving or sliding parts. Ignition advance is accomplished electronically—by the electric waves emitted by the pulsar coils. These coils increase their wave output proportionately to engine speed increase, thus advancing the timing.

Units equipped with a mechanical advance type CDI system use a link rod between the carburetor and the ignition base plate assembly. At the time the throttle is opened, the ignition base plate assembly is rotated by means of the link rod, thus advancing the timing.

TROUBLESHOOTING

Accurate troubleshooting of an ignition system is viewed by many as mission impossible. This does not have to be the case. Having a systematic approach to troubleshooting is the key. Your first priority is understanding how the system works.

Get yourself mentally prepared for ignition troubleshooting before you touch the motor. Make notes about how the motor behaves. Is it totally dead? Misfiring? If it is dead, what were the circumstances that led to its demise? Did it run poorly before it died? If it is running, but not well, is this a permanent condition? Only when cold? Only when warm? Under load? Ask yourself a lot of questions. The more information you can gather the faster the repair can be made.

It is easy to forget to ask yourself if the root cause of the failure is truly ignition? Could it be something else? Look at the plug and check the spark. Once you have done the basics, the hands-on troubleshooting begins.

The key to successful troubleshooting is a systematic approach. Do not skip around. On new or unfamiliar equipment try writing up a check list on a 3x5 note card. This makes a handy reference for future troubleshooting.

Use the spark tester to observe spark quality. Does it jump the gap? Is it Blue? Orange spark usually means trouble in the ignition system.

Do not forget to check the ignition controlling components such as the main or stop switches. These can be disconnected from the system. These switches can cause failures that checks of the individual ignition components may not reveal.

Always attempt to proceed with the troubleshooting in an orderly manner. The shot in the dark approach will only result in wasted time, incorrect diagnosis, replacement of unnecessary parts, and frustration.

Spark Plugs

▶ **See accompanying illustrations**

1. Check the plug wires to be sure they are properly connected. Check the entire length of the wires from the plugs to the magneto under the stator plate. If the wires are to be removed from the spark plug, always use a pulling and twisting motion as a precaution against damaging the connection.

2. Attempt to remove the spark plug by hand. This is a rough test to determine if the plug is tightened properly. The attempt to loosen the plug by hand should fail. The plug should be tight and require the proper socket size tool. Remove the spark plug and evaluate its condition.

3. Use a spark tester and check for spark. If a spark tester is not available, hold the plug wire about ¼ in. (6.4mm) from the engine. Rotate the flywheel with the hand pull starter and check for spark. A strong spark over a wide gap must be observed when testing in this manner, because under compression a strong spark is necessary in order to ignite the air-fuel mixture in the cylinder. This means it is possible to think a strong spark is present, when in reality the spark will be too weak when the plug is installed. If there is no spark, or if the spark is weak, the trouble is most likely under the flywheel in the magneto.

4. Reinstall the spark plug and tighten with a torque wrench to the proper specification.

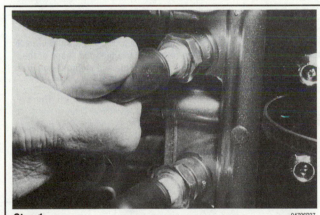

Step 1   04706P37

Step 2   04706P8B

Step 3   04706P38

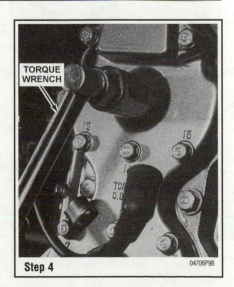

Step 4   04706P9B

Compression

▶ See Figure 16

1. Before spending too much time and money attempting to trace a problem to the ignition system, a compression check of the cylinder should be made. If the cylinder does not have adequate compression, troubleshooting and attempted service of the ignition or fuel system will fail to give the desired results of satisfactory engine performance.

2. Run the engine until it reaches operating temperature. The engine is at operating temperature a few minutes after the upper radiator hose gets hot. If the test is performed on a cold engine, the readings will be considerably lower than normal, even if the engine is in perfect mechanical condition.

3. Label and disconnect the spark plug wires. Always grasp the molded cap and pull it loose with a twisting motion to prevent damage to the connection.

4. Clean all dirt and foreign material from around the spark plugs, and then remove all the plugs. Keep them in order by cylinder for later evaluation.

5. Ground the spark plug leads to the engine to render the ignition system inoperative while performing the compression check.

6. Insert a compression gauge into the No. 1, top, spark plug opening.

7. Crank the engine with the starter through at least 4 complete strokes with the throttle at the wide-open position, to obtain the highest possible reading. Record the reading.

8. Repeat the test and record the compression for each cylinder.

9. A variation between cylinders is far more important than the actual readings. A variation of more than 15 psi (103 kPa), between cylinders indicates the lower compression cylinder is defective. Not all engines will exhibit the same compression readings. In fact, two identical engines may not have the same compression. Generally, the rule of thumb is that the lowest cylinder should be within 25% of the highest (difference between the two readings).

10. If compression is low in one or more cylinders, the problem may be worn, broken, or sticking piston rings, scored pistons or worn cylinders.

➡In recent years the manufacturer has modified the cylinder head design on some models in an attempt to keep the temperature of each head as equal as possible. This action has changed the shape of the combustion chamber, and therefore the volume and compression pressure of each cylinder.

As a general rule, the pressure between pairs of cylinders which share the same crankshaft throw, should be approximately the same. Cylinder No. 1 should be the same as cylinder No. 2; cylinder No. 3 should be the same as cylinder No. 4 and so on.

Normally, on a V6 powerhead, cylinder No. 1 and No. 2 will have the highest compression pressure and cylinders No. 5 and No. 6 will have the lowest compression pressure. The design modification has brought about one exception to

this rule as follows for the 175 hp and 200 hp in 1986 only: cylinders No. 3 and No. 4 will have an even higher compression pressure than cylinders No. 1 and No. 2; cylinders No. 5 and No. 6 will still have the lowest compression pressure.

Condenser

▶ See Figure 17

In simple terms, a condenser is composed of two sheets of tin or aluminum foil laid one on top of the other, but separated by a sheet of insulating material such as waxed paper, etc. The sheets are rolled into a cylinder to conserve space and then inserted into a metal case for protection and to permit easy assembling.

The purpose of the condenser is to prevent excessive arcing across the points and to extend their useful life. When the flow of primary current is brought to a sudden stop by the opening of the points, the magnetic field in the primary windings collapses instantly, and is not allowed to fade away, which would happen if the points were allowed to arc.

The condenser stores the electricity that would have arced across the points and discharges that electricity when the points close again. This discharge is in the opposite direction to the original flow, and tends to smooth out the current. The more quickly the primary field collapses, the higher the voltage produced in the secondary windings and delivered to the spark plugs. In this way, the condenser (in the primary circuit), affects the voltage (in the secondary circuit) at the spark plugs.

Modern condensers seldom cause problems, therefore, it is not necessary to install a new one each time the points are replaced. However, if the points show evidence of arcing, the condenser may be at fault and should be replaced. A faulty condenser may not be detected without the use of special test equipment. Testing will reveal any defects in the condenser, but will not predict the useful life left in the unit.

The modest cost of a new condenser justifies its purchase and installation to eliminate this item as a source of trouble.

Breaker Points

▶ See Figure 18

The breaker points in an outboard motor are an extremely important part of the ignition system. A set of points may appear to be in good condition, but they may be the source of hard starting, misfiring, or poor engine performance. The rules and knowledge gained from association with 4-cycle engines does not necessarily apply to a 2-cycle engine. The points should be replaced every 100 hours of operation or at least once a year. Remember, the less an outboard engine is operated, the more care it needs. Allowing an outboard engine to remain idle will do more harm than if it is used regularly.

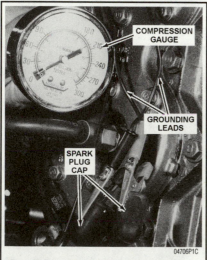

04706P1C

Fig. 16 Preparing to check powerhead cranking compression. Note the jumper leads used to ground the cylinders

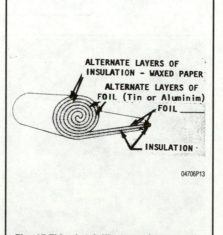

04706P13

Fig. 17 This sketch illustrates how waxed paper, aluminum foil and insulation are rolled in the manufacture of a typical condenser

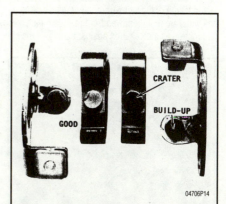

04706P14

Fig. 18 A normal set of breaker points used in a magneto will shoe evidence of a shallow crater and build up after a few hours of operation. The condition of the left set is normal. The right set has been in service for a while and should be replaced

A breaker point set consists of two points. One is attached to a stationary bracket and does not move. The other point is attached to a movable mount. A spring is used to keep the points in contact with each other, except when they are separated by the action of a cam built into the flywheel collar which fits over the crankshaft. Both points are constructed with a steel base and a tungsten cap fused to the base.

To properly diagnose magneto (spark) problems, the theory of electricity flow must be understood. The flow of electricity through a wire may be compared with the flow of water through a pipe. Consider the voltage in the wire as the water pressure in the pipe and the amperes as the volume of water. Now, if the water pipe is broken, the water does not reach the end of the pipe. In a similar manner if the wire is broken the flow of electricity is broken. If the pipe springs a leak, the amount of water reaching the end of the pipe is reduced. Same with the wire. If the installation is defective or the wire becomes grounded, the amount of electricity (amperes) reaching the end of the wire is reduced.

Polarity Check

▶ **See accompanying illustration**

Coil polarity is extremely important for proper battery ignition system operation. If a coil is connected with reverse polarity, the spark plugs may demand from 30 to 40 percent more voltage to fire, or on most CDI systems, there will be no spark. Under such demand conditions, in a very short time the coil would be unable to supply enough voltage to fire the plugs. Any one of the following three methods may be used to quickly determine coil polarity.

1. The polarity of the coil can be checked using an ordinary D.C. voltmeter set on the maximum scale. Connect the positive lead to a good ground. With the engine running, momentarily touch the negative lead to a spark plug terminal. The needle should swing upscale. If the needle swings downscale, the polarity is reversed.

If a voltmeter is not available, a pencil may be used in the following manner: Disconnect a spark plug wire and hold the metal connector at the end of the cable about ¼ in. (6.35mm) from the spark plug terminal. Now, insert an ordinary pencil tip between the terminal and the connector. Crank the engine with the ignition switch on. If the spark feathers on the plug side and has a slight

orange tinge, the polarity is correct. If the spark feathers on the cable connector side, the polarity is reversed.

The firing end of a used spark plug can give a clue to coil polarity. If the ground electrode is dished, it may mean polarity is reversed.

Resistance Testing Precautions

When performing an electrical resistance test on a CDI unit, rectifier unit, or any device where the resistance varies with electrical polarity or applied voltage the following points should be noted:

• There are no standard specifications for the design of either analog or digital test meters.

• When performing resistance testing, some test meter manufacturers will apply positive battery power to the Red test lead, while others apply the positive voltage to the Black lead.

• Some meters (especially digital meters) will apply a very low voltage to the test leads that may not properly activate some devices (e.g., CDI units).

• Be aware there are ohmmeters that have reverse polarity. If your test results all differ from the chart, swap + and - leads and retest.

➡ **Digital meter resistance values are not reliable when testing CDI units, rectifier units, or any device containing semiconductors, transistors, and diodes.**

Pulsar Coils

▶ **See Figures 19 thru 25**

The basic test for a pulser coil is continuity. This measures the actual resistance from one end of the pulser coil to the other. The correct specification for each coil can be found in the Ignition Testing Specifications chart.

1. Adjust the meter to ohms.
2. Connect the tester across the pulser leads and note the reading.

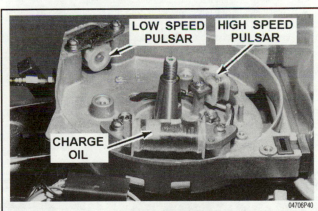

Fig. 19 Location of the low and high speed pulsar coils a 1-cylinder powerhead

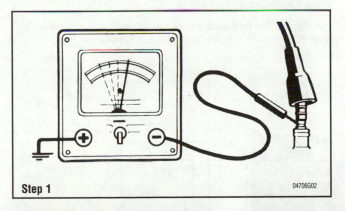

Step 1

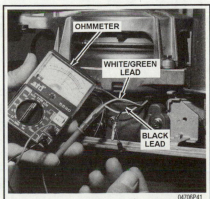

Fig. 20 The proper set up for testing a low speed pulsar coil—1-cylinder powerhead

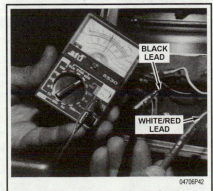

Fig. 21 The proper set up for testing a high speed pulsar coil—1-cylinder powerhead

Fig. 22 The proper set up for testing a pulsar coil—2-cylinder powerhead

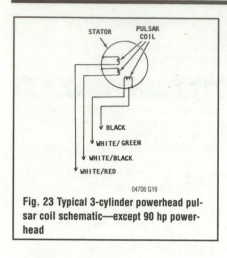

Fig. 23 Typical 3-cylinder powerhead pulsar coil schematic—except 90 hp powerhead

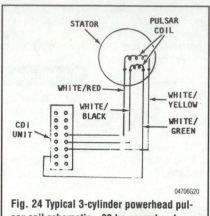

Fig. 24 Typical 3-cylinder powerhead pulsar coil schematic—90 hp powerhead

Fig. 25 The proper set up for testing a pulsar coil—V4 and V6 powerhead

3. Compare the coil reading to the specifications.

4. If the reading is above or below the correct value and beyond the allowable deviation then it must be replaced.

→**Remember that temperature has an affect on resistance. Most resistance specifications are given assuming a temperature of 70° F.**

There are two types of pulser coils. One type has one coil lead connected directly to ground through a Black wire or a grounded bolt hole. The other end of the coil has a color-coded wire. These type coils have one lead listed as Black and the other typically a White wire with a colored tracer.

The other type of pulser coil is not grounded. Instead, both leads go to the CDI box. Both coil leads are typically White with a colored tracer.

When checking either type pulser coil for continuity, connect the ohmmeter to the color wires listed in the Ignition Testing Specifications chart.

A second check must be made on pulser coils that are not grounded on one end. This second check is called a short-to-ground check. Make sure that this type of coil not only has correct resistance (continuity) but also is not shorted to ground (and leaking current to ground).

5. Connect one tester lead to a coil lead.

6. Touch the other tester lead to the engine ground or the mounting point of the pulser.

7. If the pulser is good, the reading on the ohmmeter should be infinity.

8. Any ohm reading other than infinity (O.L on some digital meters) indicates a bad coil. Repair or replace the coil.

→**This second check is just as critical as the standard continuity check.**

Charge Coils

♦ **See Figures 26 thru 31**

The charge coil checks are the same as those for the pulser coil. There are two types of charge coils. One type has a charge coil lead connected to ground. The other type charge coil has both leads go directly to the CDI box. Both charge coil types require the continuity test. This checks the coil's internal resistance. On charge coils that do not have a grounded lead, the short-to-ground test must also be done

The basic test for a charge coil is continuity. This measures the actual resistance from one end of the charge coil to the other. The correct specification for each coil can be found in the Ignition Testing Specifications chart.

1. Adjust the meter to ohms.

2. Connect the tester across the pulser leads and note the reading.

3. Compare the coil reading to the specifications.

4. If the reading is above or below the correct value and beyond the allowable deviation then it must be replaced.

→**Remember that temperature has an affect on resistance. Most resistance specifications are given assuming a temperature of 70° F.**

There are two types of charge coils. One type has one coil lead connected directly to ground through a Black wire or a grounded bolt hole. The other end of the coil has a color-coded wire. These type coils have one lead listed as Black and the other typically a White wire with a colored tracer.

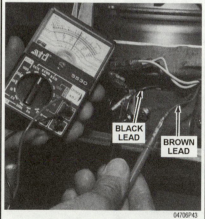

Fig. 26 The proper set up for testing a charging coil—1-cylinder powerhead

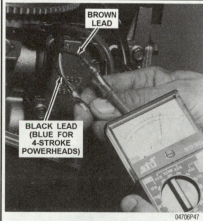

Fig. 27 The proper set up for testing a charge coil—2-cylinder powerhead

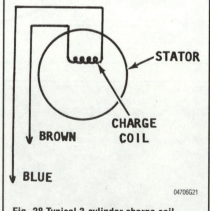

Fig. 28 Typical 3-cylinder charge coil schematic—except 70 hp and 90 hp powerheads

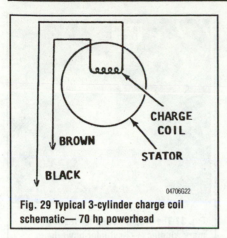

Fig. 29 Typical 3-cylinder charge coil schematic— 70 hp powerhead

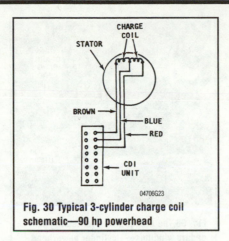

Fig. 30 Typical 3-cylinder charge coil schematic—90 hp powerhead

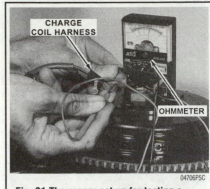

Fig. 31 The proper set up for testing a charge coil—V4 and V6 powerhead

The other type of charge coil is not grounded. Instead, both leads go to the CDI box. Both coil leads are typically White with a colored tracer.

When checking either type charge coil for continuity, connect the ohmmeter to the color wires listed in the specifications.

A second check must be made on charge coils that are not grounded on one end. This second check is called a short-to-ground check. Make sure that this type of coil not only has correct resistance (continuity) but also is not shorted to ground (and leaking current to ground).

5. Connect one tester lead to a coil lead.

6. Touch the other tester lead to the engine ground or the mounting point of the coil.

7. If the coil is good, the reading on the ohmmeter should be infinity. Any ohm reading other than infinity (O.L on some digital meters) indicates a bad coil.

8. Repair or replace the coil.

➡This second check is just as critical as the standard continuity check.

Lighting Coil

◆ See Figures 32, 33 and 34

The basic test for a charge coil is continuity. This measures the actual resistance from one end of the charge coil to the other. The correct specification for each coil can be found in the Ignition Testing Specifications chart.

1. Disconnect the two wires (usually Green) between the stator and the rectifier at the rectifier. Connect the ohmmeter leads to the wires and measure the resistance. Resistance for all powerheads except V4 and V6 should be approximately 0.23–0.84 ohms at 70° F. Resistance for V4 and V6 powerheads should be approximately 0.23 and 0.43 ohms at 70° F.

➡Remember that temperature has an affect on resistance. Most resistance specifications are given assuming a temperature of 70° F.

2. If the resistance is not within specification, the battery will not hold a charge and the boat accessories which depend on this coil for power may not function properly.

➡Never attempt to verify the charging circuit by operating the powerhead with the battery disconnected. Such action would force current (normally directed to charge the battery), back through the rectifier and damage the diodes in the rectifier.

Ignition Coils

◆ See Figures 35 thru 41

Although the best test for an ignition coil is on a dynamic ignition coil tester, resistance checks can also be done.

There are two circuits in an ignition coil, the primary winding circuit and the secondary winding circuit. Both need to be checked.

The tester connection procedure for a continuity check will depend on how the coil is constructed. Generally, the primary circuit is the small gauge wire or wires, while the secondary circuit contains the high tension or plug lead.

Some ignition coils have the primary and/or secondary circuits grounded on one end. On these type coils, only the continuity check is done. On ignition coils that are not grounded on one end, the short-to-ground test must also be done. Regardless of the coil type, compare the resistance with the Electrical Testing Specification chart.

Fig. 32 The proper set up for testing a lighting coil—2-cylinder powerhead

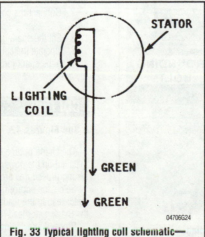

Fig. 33 Typical lighting coil schematic— 3-cylinder powerhead

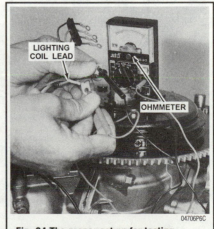

Fig. 34 The proper set up for testing charge coil—V4 and V6 powerhead

Fig. 35 The proper set up for testing primary windings—1-cylinder powerhead

Fig. 36 The proper set up for testing secondary windings—1-cylinder powerhead

Fig. 37 The proper set up for testing primary windings—2-cylinder powerhead

Fig. 38 The proper set up for testing secondary windings—2-cylinder powerhead

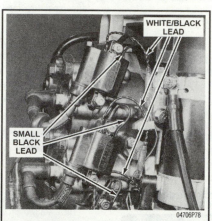

Fig. 39 Setup for testing the primary windings—3-cylinder powerhead

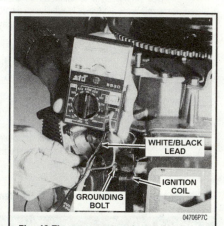

Fig. 40 The proper set up for testing primary windings—V4 and V6 powerhead

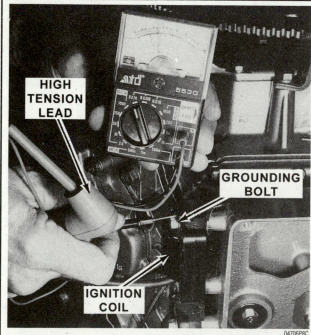

Fig. 41 The proper set up for testing secondary windings—V4 and V6 powerhead

➡When checking the secondary side, remove the spark plug caps to make the measurement. In some cases the cap is bad, not the coil. Bad resistor caps can be the cause of high-speed misfire. Unscrew the cap and check the resistance (5 kilohms). Leaving the cap on during measurement could condemn a good ignition coil.

The other method used to test ignition coils is with a Dynamic Ignition Coil Tester. Since the output side of the ignition coil has very high voltage, a regular voltmeter can not be used. While resistance reading can be valuable, the best tool for checking dynamic coil performance is a dynamic ignition coil tester.

1. Connect the coil to the tester according to the manufacturer's instructions.
2. Set the spark gap according to the specifications.
3. Operate the coil for about 5 minutes.
4. If the spark jumps the gap with the correct spark color, the coil is probably good.

CDI Unit

◆ See Figures 42, 43 and 44

The charts outline testing procedures for the CDI unit. The unit may remain installed on the powerhead, or it may be removed for testing. In either case, the testing procedures are identical.

Select the appropriate scale on the ohmmeter. Make contact with the Red meter lead to the leads called out in the horizontal heading. Make contact with the Black meter lead to the leads called out in the vertical list of leads.

Proceed slowly and carefully in the order given. The asterisk (*) denotes the meter needle should swing toward continuity (zero ohms), and then return to stay at the specified value.

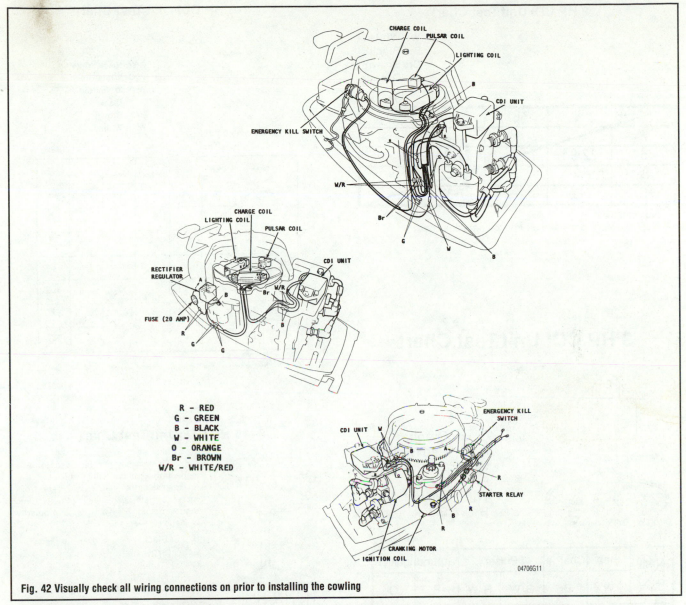

R – RED
G – GREEN
B – BLACK
W – WHITE
O – ORANGE
Br – BROWN
W/R – WHITE/RED

Fig. 42 Visually check all wiring connections on prior to installing the cowling

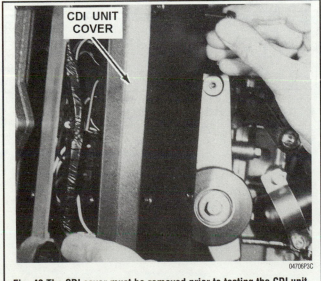

Fig. 43 The CDI cover must be removed prior to testing the CDI unit

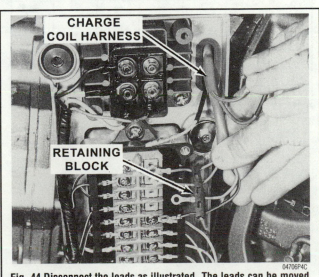

Fig. 44 Disconnect the leads as illustrated. The leads can be moved away from the unit but are still retained by a small block

2 HP CDI Unit Test Chart

W: White
B: Black
Br: Brown
O: Orange

Unit: kΩ

⊖＼⊕	W	B	Br	O
W			∞	•
B	2.2~9.5		2.2~9.5	•
Br	∞		•	•
O	7~30	2~9	7~30	

∞ No continuity
• Needle swings once and returns to home position

04706C01

3 HP CDI Unit Test Chart

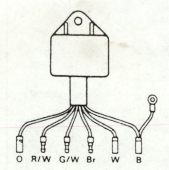

O   : Orange
R/W : Red/White
G/W : Green/White
Br : Brown
W   : White
B   : Black

Unit: kΩ

⊕＼⊖	Stop	Charge	Pulser		Ground	Ignition
	W	Br	G/W	R/W	B	O
W		0	∞	∞	∞	∞ ✻
Br	0		∞	∞	∞	∞ ✻
G/W	23	23		25	9	∞
R/W	20	20	∞		12	∞
B	4	4	∞	12		∞ ✻
O	∞	∞	∞	∞	∞	

∞ : No continuity

✻ : Needle swings once and returns to home position

04706C02

4–5 HP CDI Unit Test Chart

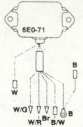

6E0-71

B/W: Black/White
W/G: White/Green
W/R: White/Red
B : Black
Br : Brown
W : White

Unit kΩ

＼Tester (+) (−) Tester		Stop W	Charge Br	Pulser 2 (Low speed) W/G	Pulser 1 (High speed) W/R	Earth B	Ignition B/W
Stop	W		0	∞	∞	∞	✻
Charge	Br	0		∞	∞	∞	✻
Pulser 2 (Low speed)	W/G	18.4 ~ 27.6	18.4 ~ 27.6		20 ~ 30	7.2 ~ 10.8	∞
Pulser 1 (High speed)	W/R	16 ~ 24	16 ~ 24	∞		9.6 ~ 14.4	∞
Earth	B	3.2 ~ 4.8	3.2 ~ 4.8	∞	9.6 ~ 14.4		✻
Ignition	B/W	∞	∞	∞	∞	∞	

∞ : No continuity

✻ : Needle swings once and returns to home position

04706C03

6–15 HP CDI Unit Test Chart

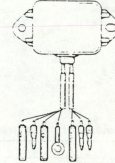

● Digital tester can not be used for this inspection. Use analogue tester.
● C.D.I. resistance values will vary from meter to meter, especially with electronic digital meters. For some testers, polarity of leads is reversed.

B   : Black
Br : Brown
G   : Green
O   : Orange
W   : White
W/R : White/Red

Unit: KΩ

⊖＼⊕	W	B	Br	W/R	O
W		∞	∞	∞	∞
B	∞		7.5 ~ 11.3	∞	•
Br	∞	63.2 ~ 94.8		∞	•
W/R	8.8 ~ 13.2	14.4 ~ 21.6	30.4 ~ 45.6		•
O	∞	∞	∞	∞	

• : Needle swings once and returns to home position.
∞ : Discontinuity

04706C04

25 HP CDI Unit Test Chart

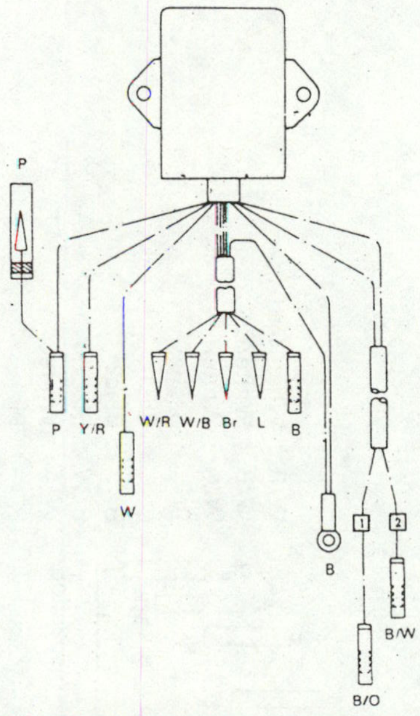

NOTE:
Digital tester can not be used for this inspection. Use analogue tester.

P   : Pink
Y/R : Yellow/Red
W   : White
W/R : White/Red
W/B : White/Black
Br : Brown
L   : Blue
B   : Black
B/O : Black/Orange
B/W : Black/White

Unit: kΩ

+ / −	Thermo switch P	Overheat Y/R	Stop W	Pulser W/R	Pulser W/B	Charge (+) Br	Charge (−) L	Ground B	Ignition B/O	Ignition B/W
P		∞	∞	∞	∞	∞	∞	∞	∞	∞
Y/R	∞		∞	∞	∞	∞	∞	∞	∞	∞
W	∞	∞		∞	∞	∞	∞	∞	∞	∞
W/R	∞	∞	∞		∞	∞	∞	∞	∞	∞
W/B	∞	∞	∞	∞		∞	∞	∞	∞	∞
Br	100K~1M	100K~1M	80K~1M	100K~1M	∞		80K~300K	80K~300K	80K~1M	80K~1M
L	9K~30K	3K~10K	40K~∞	10K~30K	∞	3K~10K		0	2K~8K	2K~8K
B	9K~30K	3K~10K	40K~∞	10K~30K	∞	3K~10K	0		2K~8K	2K~8K
B/O										
B/W										

∞ : Discontinuity

0470625B

C25–C30 HP CDI Unit Test Chart

W   : White   W/R : White/Red
B   : Black   W/B : White/Black
B/O : Black/Orange Br : Brown
B/W : Black/White L   : Blue

Unit: kΩ

Tester (−) / Tester (+)	Stop W	Ground B	Ignition B/O	Ignition B/W	Pulser W/R	Pulser W/B	Charge Br	Charge L
Stop W		∞	∞	∞	∞	∞	∞	∞
Ground B	40~∞		2.0~8.0	2.0~8.0	10~30	∞	3.0~100	0
Ignition B/O	∞	∞		∞	∞	∞	∞	∞
Ignition B/W	∞	∞	∞		∞	∞	∞	∞
Pulser W/R	∞	∞	∞	∞		∞	∞	∞
Pulser W/B	∞	∞	∞	∞	∞		∞	∞
Charge Br	80~1,000	80~300	80~1,000	80~1,000	100~1,000	∞		3.0~10.0
Charge L	40~∞	0	2.0~8.0	2.0~8.0	10~30	∞	3.0~10.0	

∞ : No continuity

0470625A

30 HP (3 Cyl.) CDI Unit Test Chart

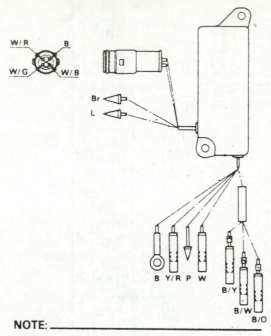

W/R : White/Red
W/B : White/Black
W/G : White/Green
Br : Brown
L : Blue
B : Black
B/W : Black/White
W : White
P : Pink
Y/R : Yellow/Red
B/O : Black/Orange
B/Y : Black/Yellow

NOTE:

- Digital tester can not be used for this inspection. Use analogue tester.
- C.D.I. resistance values will vary from meter to meter, especially with electronic digital meters. For some testers, polarity of leads is reversed.

Unit: kΩ

(+) / (−)	Charge		Pulser			Ground	Overheat	Thermo switch	Ignition			
	Br	L	W/R	W/B	W/G	B	Y/R	P	W	B/O [1]	B/W [2]	B/Y [3]
Br		400^{+400}_{-200}	$1000^{+\infty}_{-500}$	✳	✳	400^{+400}_{-200}	$1000^{+\infty}_{-500}$	✳	140^{+100}_{-40}	$1000^{+\infty}_{-500}$	✳	✳
L	4±2		16±6	✳	✳	0	4.3±2	13±6	62^{+60}_{-30}	4±2	✳	✳
W/R	∞	∞		∞	∞	∞	∞	∞	∞	34^{+30}_{-15}	∞	∞
W/B	✳	✳	∞		✳	✳	✳	✳	✳	∞	34^{+30}_{-15}	∞
W/G	✳	✳	✳	∞		✳	✳	✳	✳	✳	∞	34^{+30}_{-15}
B	4±2	0	16±6	✳	✳		4.3±2	13±6	62^{+60}_{-30}	4±2	✳	✳
Y/R	∞	∞	∞	∞	∞	∞		∞	∞	∞	∞	∞
P	✳	✳	✳	✳	✳	✳	∞		✳	✳	✳	✳
W	✳	✳	✳	✳	✳	✳	✳	∞		✳	✳	✳
B/O [1]	✳	✳	✳	✳	✳	✳	✳	✳	∞		✳	✳
B/W [2]	✳	✳	✳	✳	✳	✳	✳	✳	✳	∞		✳
B/Y [3]	✳	✳	✳	✳	✳	✳	✳	✳	✳	✳	✳	

∞ : Discontinuity

✳ : Needle of tester should swing towards "0" and then slowly swing back to indicate the specified value

04706C06

C40 HP CDI Unit Test Chart

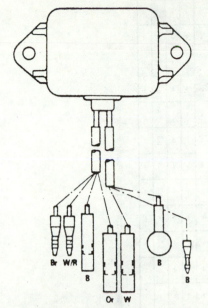

W   : White
W/R : White/Red
Br   : Brown
B   : Black
Or   : Orange

Unit : kΩ

Tester ⊕		Stop	Earth	Charge	Pulser	Ignition
Tester ⊖		White	Black	Brown	White/red	Orange
Stop	White		∞	∞	∞	∞
Earth	Black	9 ~ 19		2 ~ 6	∞	∞
Charge	Brown	80 ~ 160	70 ~ 150		∞	✴
Pulser	White/red	33 ~ 63	7 ~ 17	15 ~ 35		✴
Ignition	Orange	∞	∞	∞	∞	

✴ ..... Needle swings once and returns to home position.
∞ ..... No continuity.

The test indicated by "•" should be made with the condenser completely discharged, and therefore, the needle will not deflect again. If any charge remains in the condenser, the needle will not swing at all.

04706C07

E48 and C55 HP CDI Unit Test Chart

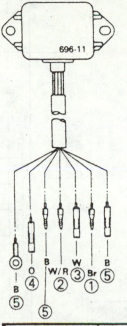

696-11

B   : Black
Br : Brown
O   : Orange
W   : White
W/R : White/Red

Unit: kΩ

Tester ⊕		① Charge coil	② Pulser coil	③ Stop	④ Ignition coil	⑤ Ground
Tester ⊖		Br	W/R	W	O	B
① Charge coil	Br		∞	∞	∞*	79k
② Pulser coil	W/R	38k		11k	∞*	18k
③ Stop	W	∞	∞		∞	∞
④ Ignition coil	O	∞	∞	∞		∞
⑤ Ground	B	9.4k	∞	∞	∞*	

∞* .....Needle swings once and returns to home position.
∞ ....No continuity.

04706C08

40, 50, and Pro 50 HP CDI Unit Test Chart

Y/R : Yellow/Red
P   : Pink
O   : Orange
O/G : Orange/Green
B   : Black

Unit: kΩ

⊖ \ ⊕	Y/R	P	O	O/G	B
Y/R		∞	∞	∞	∞
P	∞		∞	∞	∞
O	20 ~ 80	7 ~ 30		20 ~ 80	6 ~ 24 *
O/G	40 ~ 160	15 ~ 60	9 ~ 36		10 ~ 40 *
B	7 ~ 30	7 ~ 30	5 ~ 20 *	20 ~ 80 *	

The resistance values will vary from meter to meter, especially with electronic digital meters. For some testers, polarity of leads is reversed.
* : Pointer deflects once and returns to specification
∞: Discontinuity

04706C09

Pro 60, C60, 70, 75 and 90 HP CDI Unit Test Chart

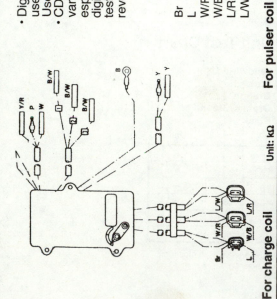

- Digital tester cannot be used for this inspection. Use analogue tester.
- CDI resistance values will vary from meter to meter, especially with electronic digital meters. For some testers, polarity of leads is reversed.

Br : Brown
L : Blue
W/R : White/Red
W/B : White/Black
L/R : Blue/Red
L/W : Blue/White

For charge coil Unit: kΩ

⊕ / ⊖	Br	L	B
Br		12 ~ 29	8 ~ 18
L	15 ~ 40		9.5 ~ 22
B	2.5 ~ 6.7	2.7 ~ 7.0	

For pulser coil Unit: kΩ

⊕ / ⊖	W/R	W/B	B
W/R		35 ~ 500	37.5 ~ 1,000
W/B	37.5 ~ 1,000		28 ~ 175
B	2.7 ~ 7.0	2.7 ~ 7.0	

04706C10

C75 and C85 HP CDI Unit Test Chart

Terminal block (top row): Br, L, R, W/R, W/B, W/Y, (Y)
Terminal block (bottom row): B/W, B/W, B/W, W, P, B, W/G

ON/OFF (Over rev protection)

W : White
B : Black
Br : Brown
L : Blue
R : Red
W/R : White/Red
W/B : White/Black
W/Y : White/Yellow
W/G : White/Green
B/W : Black/White
P : Pink
Y : Yellow

Unit: kΩ ± 20%

⊖ \ ⊕	Stop W	Ground B	Charge Br	Charge L	Charge R	Pulser W/R	Pulser W/B	Pulser W/Y	Pulser W/G	Ign. Coil 1 B/W	Ign. Coil 2 B/W	Ign. Coil 3 B/W	Overheat P	Overheat Y	Over rev "ON"	Over rev "OFF"
W		52	75	∞	120	75	∞	75	52	75	75	75	180	130	55	150
B	12		4.2	∞	13	4.2	∞	4.2	0	4.2	4.2	4.2	75	28	1.7	25
Br	350	250		∞	500	400	∞	400	250	350	350	350	500	14.5	260	500
L	450	350	4.2		1000	500	∞	500	350	500	500	500	1000	28	350	1000
R	160	45	120	∞		120	∞	120	45	110	110	110	500	500	50	60
W/R	4.2	75	120	∞	120		∞	120	75	28	120	120	300	220	80	280
W/B	4.2	75	120	∞	120	120		120	75	120	28	120	300	220	80	280
W/Y	4.2	75	120	∞	120	120	∞		75	120	120	28	300	220	80	280
W/G	12	0	4.2	∞	13	4.2	∞	4.2		4.2	4.2	4.2	75	28	1.7	25
Coil 1 B/W	∞	∞	∞	∞	∞	∞	∞	∞	∞		∞	∞	∞	∞	∞	∞
Coil 2 B/W	∞	∞	∞	∞	∞	∞	∞	∞	∞	∞		∞	∞	∞	∞	∞
Coil 3 B/W	∞	∞	∞	∞	∞	∞	∞	∞	∞	∞	∞		∞	∞	∞	∞
P	∞	∞	∞	∞	∞	∞	∞	∞	∞	∞	∞	∞		∞	∞	∞
Y	∞	∞	∞	∞	∞	∞	∞	∞	∞	∞	∞	∞	∞		∞	∞
"ON"	14.5	1.7	6.5	16.5	6.5	6.5	6.5	6.5	1.7	6.5	6.5	6.5	80	31		29
"OFF"	∞	∞	∞	∞	∞	∞	∞	∞	∞	∞	∞	∞	∞	∞	∞	

∞ : No continuity

NOTE: When working this resistance test, disconnect the lead from the over rev terminal.

04706C11

115, Pro115, and 130 HP CDI Unit Test Chart

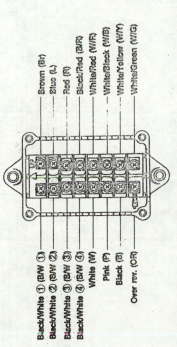

Color code:

B	Black
Br	Brown
G	Green
Gy	Grey
L	Blue
P	Pink
R	Red
W	White
Y	Yellow
B/R	Black/Red
B/W	Black/White
Gy/B	Grey/Black
L/R	Blue/Red
W/B	White/Black
W/G	White/Green
W/R	White/Red
W/Y	White/Yellow

NOTE: CDI resistance values will vary from meter to meter, especially with electronic digital meters. For some testers, polarity of leads is reversed.

For pulser coil — Unit: kΩ

	W/R	W/B	W/Y	W/G	B
W/R	■	22 – 80	22 – 80	22 – 80	13 – 35
W/B	22 – 80	■	22 – 80	22 – 80	13 – 35
W/Y	22 – 80	22 – 80	■	22 – 80	13 – 35
W/G	22 – 80	22 – 80	22 – 80	■	13 – 35
B	2.6 – 7.0	2.6 – 7.0	2.6 – 7.0	2.6 – 7.0	■

For charge coil — Unit: kΩ

	Br	L	R	B/R	B
Br	■	30 – 300	40 – ∞	30 – 300	19 – 60
L	50 – ∞	■	50 – ∞	50 – ∞	35 – 1,000
R	40 – ∞	50 – ∞	■	35 – 1,000	19 – 60
B/R	35 – 1,000	35 – 1,000	2.6 – 7.0	■	35 – 1,000
B	9.0 – 20	2.6 – 7.0	8.5 – 19	2.4 – 6.5	■

04706C21A

C115 HP CDI Unit Test Chart

Lead identification:
- Black/White ① (B/W) ①
- Black/White ② (B/W) ②
- Black/White ③ (B/W) ③
- Black/White ④ (B/W) ④
- White (W)
- Pink (P)
- Black (B)
- Over rev. (OR)
- Brown (Br)
- Blue (L)
- Red (R)
- Black/Red (B/R)
- White/Red (W/R)
- White/Black (W/B)
- White/Yellow (W/Y)
- White/Green (W/G)

	Charge				Pulser				Ignition				Stop	Ground		Over-rev
	Br	L	R	B/R	W/R	W/B	W/Y	W/G	B/W① (Coil 1)	B/W② (Coil 2)	B/W③ (Coil 3)	B/W④ (Coil 4)	W	P	B	OR
Br	■	3.6 – 5.4	105 – 195	105 – 195	98 – 182	98 – 182	98 – 182	98 – 182	91 – 169	91 – 169	91 – 169	91 – 169				105 – 195
L	3.6 – 5.4	■	'06 – 182	'06 – 182	60 – 90	60 – 90	60 – 90	60 – 90	64 – 96	64 – 96	64 – 96	64 – 96				48 – 72
R	105 – 195	'06 – 182	■	3.6 – 5.4	77 – 143	77 – 143	77 – 143	77 – 143	77 – 143	77 – 143	77 – 143	77 – 143				140 – 260
B/R	91 – 169	98 – 182	3.6 – 5.4	■	77 – 143	77 – 143	77 – 143	77 – 143	'64 – 96	'64 – 96	'64 – 96	'64 – 96				112 – 208
W/R	98 – 182	60 – 90	77 – 143	77 – 143	■	64 – 96	64 – 96	64 – 96	29 – 43	56 – 84	29 – 44	60 – 90	112 – 208	140 – 260	68 – 102	119 – 221
W/B	98 – 182	60 – 90	77 – 143	77 – 143	64 – 96	■	64 – 96	64 – 96	60 – 90	56 – 84	29 – 44	60 – 90	105 – 195	60 – 90	'37 – 57	119 – 221
W/Y	98 – 182	60 – 90	77 – 143	77 – 143	60 – 90	60 – 90	■	60 – 90	60 – 90	56 – 84	29 – 44	60 – 90	112 – 208	140 – 260	68 – 102	119 – 221
W/G	98 – 182	64 – 96	77 – 143	64 – 96	60 – 90	64 – 96	60 – 90	■	64 – 96	56 – 84	29 – 44	60 – 90	112 – 208	140 – 260	68 – 102	119 – 221
B/W① (Coil 1)	'64 – 96	'64 – 96	'64 – 96	'64 – 96	29 – 43	60 – 90	60 – 90	60 – 90	■				96 – 182	60 – 90	37 – 57	
B/W② (Coil 2)	98 – 182	64 – 96	'64 – 96	64 – 96	56 – 84	56 – 84	56 – 84	56 – 84		■			12 – 18	122 – 227	36 – 54	
B/W③ (Coil 3)	98 – 182	64 – 96	'64 – 96	64 – 96	29 – 44	29 – 44	29 – 44	29 – 44			■		12 – 18	140 – 260	37 – 57	
B/W④ (Coil 4)	98 – 182	64 – 96	'64 – 96	64 – 96	60 – 90	60 – 90	60 – 90	60 – 90				■	12 – 18	140 – 260	37 – 57	
W					3.0 – 4.6	3.0 – 4.6	3.0 – 4.6	3.0 – 4.6					■			
P					3.2 – 4.6	3.2 – 4.6	3.2 – 4.6	3.2 – 4.6						■		
B	11.8 – 17.8	3.7 – 5.5	11.8 – 17.8	3.6 – 5.5	3.7 – 5.5	3.7 – 5.5	3.2 – 4.6	3.7 – 5.5	3.0 – 4.6	3.2 – 4.6	3.0 – 4.6	3.1 – 4.7	24 – 36	28 – 42	■	17 – 26
OR	105 – 195	48 – 72	140 – 260	112 – 208	119 – 221	119 – 221	119 – 221	119 – 221								■

Note:
1. When making this resistance test, disconnect the lead from the over-rev terminal.
2. The asterisk (*) indicates that the tester needle should swing toward "O" and slowly swing back to stay at the specified value.

04706C12

225 V6 90° CDI Unit Test Chart

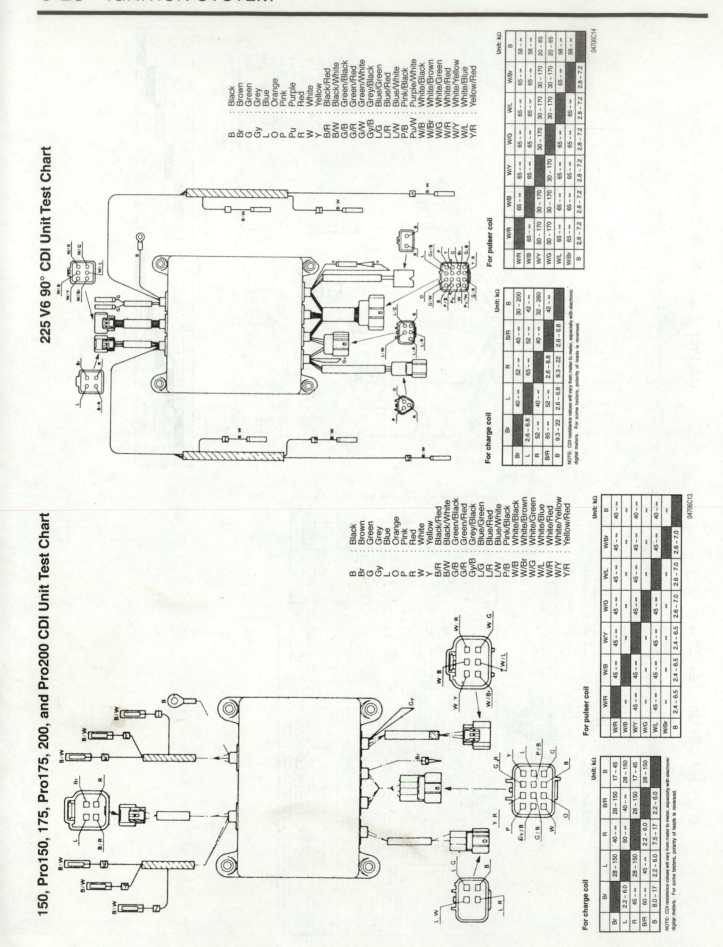

Color code:
- B : Black
- Br : Brown
- G : Green
- Gy : Grey
- L : Blue
- O : Orange
- P : Pink
- Pu : Purple
- R : Red
- W : White
- Y : Yellow
- B/R : Black/Red
- B/W : Black/White
- G/B : Green/Black
- G/R : Green/Red
- G/W : Green/White
- Gy/B : Grey/Black
- L/G : Blue/Green
- L/R : Blue/Red
- L/W : Blue/White
- P/B : Pink/Black
- Pu/W : Purple/White
- W/B : White/Black
- W/Br : White/Brown
- W/G : White/Green
- W/R : White/Red
- W/Y : White/Yellow
- W/L : White/Blue
- Y/R : Yellow/Red

For pulser coil Unit: kΩ

	W/R	W/B	W/Y	W/G	W/L	W/Br	B
W/R		65-∞	65-∞	30-170	65-∞	30-170	58-∞
W/B	65-∞		65-∞	30-170	65-∞	65-∞	58-∞
W/Y	30-170	30-170		30-170	65-∞	65-∞	20-65
W/G	30-170	30-170	30-170		65-∞	65-∞	20-65
W/L	65-∞	65-∞	30-170	65-∞		65-∞	58-∞
W/Br	30-170	65-∞	65-∞	65-∞	65-∞		58-∞
B	2.8-7.2	2.8-7.2	2.8-7.2	2.8-7.2	2.8-7.2	2.8-7.2	

For charge coil Unit: kΩ

	Br	L	R	B/R	B
Br		2.6-6.8	52-∞	65-∞	9.3-22
L	40-∞		52-∞	52-∞	9.3-22
R	52-∞	40-∞		2.6-6.8	2.6-6.8
B/R	40-∞	40-∞	2.6-6.8		2.6-6.8
B	30-200	42-∞	32-260	42-∞	

NOTE: CDI resistance values will vary from meter to meter, especially with electronic digital meters. For some testers, polarity of leads is reversed.

04706C14

150, Pro150, 175, Pro175, 200, and Pro200 CDI Unit Test Chart

Color code:
- B : Black
- Br : Brown
- G : Green
- Gy : Grey
- L : Blue
- O : Orange
- P : Pink
- R : Red
- W : White
- Y : Yellow
- B/R : Black/Red
- B/W : Black/White
- G/B : Green/Black
- G/R : Green/Red
- Gy/B : Grey/Black
- L/G : Blue/Green
- L/R : Blue/Red
- L/W : Blue/White
- P/B : Pink/Black
- W/B : White/Black
- W/Br : White/Brown
- W/G : White/Green
- W/L : White/Blue
- W/R : White/Red
- W/Y : White/Yellow
- Y/R : Yellow/Red

For pulser coil Unit: kΩ

	W/R	W/B	W/Y	W/G	W/L	W/Br	B
W/R		45-∞	45-∞	45-∞	45-∞	45-∞	40-∞
W/B	45-∞		45-∞	45-∞	45-∞	45-∞	40-∞
W/Y	45-∞	45-∞		45-∞	45-∞	45-∞	40-∞
W/G	45-∞	45-∞	45-∞		45-∞	45-∞	40-∞
W/L	45-∞	45-∞	45-∞	45-∞		45-∞	40-∞
W/Br	45-∞	45-∞	45-∞	45-∞	45-∞		
B	2.4-6.5	2.4-6.5	2.4-6.5	2.6-7.0	2.6-7.0	2.6-7.0	

For charge coil Unit: kΩ

	Br	L	R	B/R	B
Br		2.2-6.0	45-∞	60-∞	8.0-17
L	28-150		45-∞	45-∞	2.2-6.0
R	40-∞	50-∞		2.2-6.0	7.5-17
B/R	28-150	28-150	2.2-6.0		2.2-6.0
B	17-45	17-45	28-150	28-150	

NOTE: CDI resistance values will vary from meter to meter, especially with electronic digital meters. For some testers, polarity of leads is reversed.

04706C13

225 and 250 HP V6 76° CDI Unit Test Chart

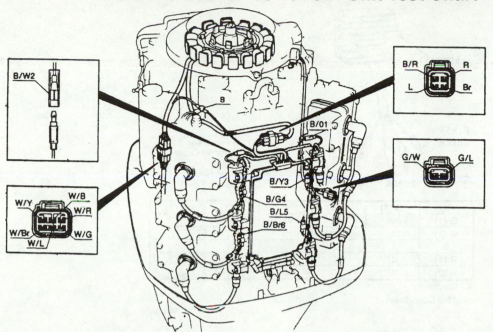

B	: Black
Br	: Brown
L	: Blue
R	: Red
B/R	: Black/Red
B/W	: Black/White
G/L	: Green/Blue
G/W	: Green/White
W/B	: White/Black
W/Br	: White/Brown
W/G	: White/Green
W/L	: White/Blue
W/R	: White/Red
W/Y	: White/Yellow
B/O	: Black/Orange
B/Y	: Black/Yellow
B/G	: Black/Green
B/L	: Black/Blue
B/Br	: Black/Brown

For charge coil

Unit: kΩ

$\ominus$ \ $\oplus$	Br	L	R	B/R	B
Br		200^{+200}_{-200}	200^{+200}_{-200}	200^{+200}_{-200}	50^{+50}_{-25}
L	200^{+200}_{-200}		1000^{+1000}_{-500}	1000^{+1000}_{-500}	20^{+20}_{-10}
R	150^{+150}_{-75}	150^{+150}_{-75}		150^{+150}_{-75}	100^{+100}_{-50}
B/R	200^{+200}_{-100}	200^{+200}_{-100}	200^{+200}_{-100}		150^{+150}_{-75}
B	4 ± 2	4 ± 2	4 ± 2	4 ± 2	

NOTE: CDI resistance values will vary depending on the ohm meter, especially with electronic digital meters. Also, the polarity (+ and −) will be reversed for some tester leads.

For pulser coil

Unit: kΩ

$\ominus$ \ $\oplus$	W/R	W/B	W/Y	W/G	W/L	W/Br	B
W/R		18^{+18}_{-9}	18^{+18}_{-0}	18^{+18}_{-0}	18^{+18}_{-0}	18^{+18}_{-9}	9^{+9}_{-5}
W/B	18^{+18}_{-9}		18^{+18}_{-9}	18^{+18}_{-9}	18^{+18}_{-9}	18^{+18}_{-9}	9^{+9}_{-5}
W/Y	18^{+18}_{-9}	18^{+18}_{-9}		18^{+18}_{-9}	18^{+18}_{-9}	18^{+18}_{-9}	9^{+9}_{-5}
W/G	18^{+18}_{-9}	18^{+18}_{-9}	18^{+18}_{-9}		18^{+18}_{-9}	18^{+18}_{-9}	9^{+9}_{-5}
W/L	18^{+18}_{-9}	18^{+18}_{-9}	18^{+18}_{-9}	18^{+18}_{-9}		18^{+18}_{-9}	9^{+9}_{-5}
W/Br	18^{+18}_{-9}	18^{+18}_{-9}	18^{+18}_{-9}	18^{+18}_{-9}	18^{+18}_{-9}		9^{+9}_{-5}
B	10^{+10}_{-5}	10^{+10}_{-5}	10^{+10}_{-5}	10^{+10}_{-5}	10^{+10}_{-5}	10^{+10}_{-5}	

04706C15

Rectifier

1. The charts outline testing procedures for the rectifier. The unit may remain installed on the powerhead, or it may be removed for testing. In either case, the testing procedures are identical.

2. Select the appropriate scale on the ohmmeter. Make contact with the Red meter lead to the leads called out as (+) and the Black meter lead to the leads called out as (-). Proceed slowly and carefully in the order given.

3. If resistance is not as specified, the rectifier is faulty and should be replaced.

Control Unit

▶ See Figure 45

1. The unit may remain installed on the powerhead, provided the leads are disconnected from the screw terminals of the CDI unit. The unit may also be removed for testing. In either case, the testing procedures are identical.

2. Using an ohmmeter, make contact with the Red meter lead to the leads called out in the horizontal heading. Make contact with the Black meter lead to the leads called out in the vertical list of leads. Proceed slowly and carefully in the order given.

3. If the control unit should fail any of the above resistance tests, it must be removed and replaced with a new unit. Service or adjustment is not possible.

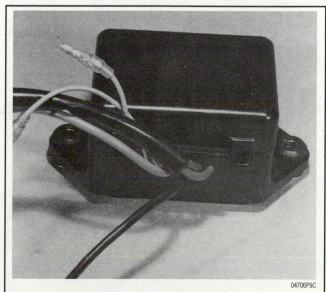

04706P9C

Fig. 45 A control unit removed for bench testing

Rectifier Test Chart — Except V4 and V6 Powerheads

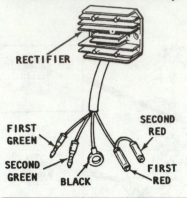

RECTIFIER

FIRST GREEN

SECOND GREEN

BLACK

SECOND RED

FIRST RED

G (1) : First Green
G (2) : Second Green
B : Black
R (1) : First Red
R (2) : Second Red

	G (1)	G (2)	B	R (1)	R (2)
G (1)		NC	NC	C	C
G (2)	NC		NC	C	C
B	C	C		C	C
R (1)	NC	NC	NC		
R (2)	NC	NC	NC		

C: Continuity
NC: No Continuity

04706C16

VOLTAGE REGULATOR RECTIFIER

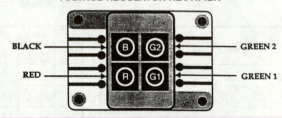

BLACK — B   G2 — GREEN 2

RED — R   G1 — GREEN 1

Negative Test Lead Position		Positive Test Lead Position			
		(1) G1	(2) G2	(3) R	(4) B
	(1) G1		NO	YES	NO
	(2) G2	YES		YES	YES
	(3) R	NO	NO		
	(4) B	YES	YES	YES	

YES = Continuity (Needle moves)   NO = No continuity (Needle does not move)

04706C17

CONTROL UNIT TEST CHART

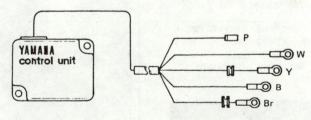

YAMAHA control unit

P
W
Y
B
Br

Unit: kΩ

(+) \ (−)	Brown	Black	White	Yellow	Pink
Brown		∞	∞	∞	∞
Black	20		15	22	∞
White	50	15		60	∞
Yellow	∞	∞	∞		∞
Pink	50	28	75	50	

04706C18

Ignition Testing Specifications

Model	Years	Pulser Coils Low Speed Wire leads (+)	(-)	Resist. Ohms (1)	High Speed Wire leads (+)	(-)	Resistance Ohms (1)	Charge Coil Wire leads (+)	(-)	Resist. Ohms	Ignition Coil Wire leads (+)	(-)	Resist. Kilohms (1)
2	1995-98	-	-	-	-	-	-	Br	B	352	O	B	3.2
3	1992-98	R/W	B	33	G/W	B	310	Br	B	352	O	B	2.6
4	1984-98	W/R	B	33	W/G	B	310	Br	B	275	O	B	2.6 (2)
5	1994-98	W/R	B	33	W/G	B	310	Br	B	275	O	B	2.6

Note: All electrical specifications are plus or minus 20% unless otherwise indicated

(1) Plus or minus 10%

04706C99

Ignition Testing Specifications

Model	Years	Pulser Coils Wire leads (+)	(-)	Resist. Ohms (1)	Peak Voltage Loaded	Unloaded	1000 rpm	Charge Coil Wire leads (+)	(-)	Resistance Ohms	Peak Voltage Loaded	Unloaded	1000 rpm	CDI Output Wire leads (+)	(-)	Peak Voltage Loaded	Unloaded	1000 rpm	Ignition Coil Wire leads (+)	(-)	Resist. Kilohms (1)	Peak Voltage Kilovolts Loaded	Unloaded
6	1992-98	W/R	B	102	-	-	-	Br	B	90	-	-	-	-	-	-	-	-	O	B	5.4	-	-
8	1992-98	W/R	B	102	-	-	-	Br	B	90	-	-	-	-	-	-	-	-	O	B	5.4	-	-
9.9	1992-98	W/R	B	102	-	-	-	Br	B	90	-	-	-	-	-	-	-	-	O	B	3.5 (2)	-	-
15	1992-98	W/R	B	102	-	-	-	Br	B	90	-	-	-	-	-	-	-	-	O	B	3.5 (2)	-	-
20	1996-97	W/R	B	102	5.5	5.5	15	Br	B	380	125	130	125	B/W	GND	105	-	110	B/W	GND	3.2	-	-
25	1992-93	W/R	B	325	4	4	15	Br	B	200	100	100	310	B/W	GND	100	50	260	B/W	GND	2.1	5	4
25	1994-98	W/R	B	346	4	4	15	Br	B	380	100	100	310	B/W	GND	100	50	260	B/W	GND	3.5	5	4
C25	1992-97	W/R	B	105	5	-	-	Br	B	235	190	-	-	O	GND	210	-	-	O	GND	3.5 (3)	6	22
30	1992-98	W/R	B	346	5	5.5	14	Br	B	205	210	220	300	B/W	GND	200	0	290	B/W	GND	6.3	10	30
C30	1992-92	W/R	B	14	5	-	-	Br	B	134	190	-	-	O	GND	210	-	-	O	GND	3.5 (3)	6	22
C30	1993-97	W/R	B	345	-	-	-	Br	B	445	-	-	-	B/W	GND	-	-	-	B/W	GND	3.2	-	-
40	1992-98	(4)	B	196	4	5	10	Br	L	297	200	190	230	B/W	GND	175	0	215	B/W	GND	3.2	6	30
C40	1992-98	W/R	B	14	5	-	-	Br	B	134	190	-	-	O	GND	210	-	-	O	GND	3.5	6	22
E48	1995-98	W/R	B	102	-	-	-	Br	G	90	-	-	-	O	GND	-	-	-	O	GND	5.4	8	20
50/P50	1992-94	W/R	B	196	4	5	10	Br	L	297	200	190	230	B/W	GND	175	0	215	B/W	GND	3.2	6	30
50/P50	1995-97	W/R	B	210	5.5-6.4	6.8-8.3	11-13	Br	L	460	224	263	227	B/W	GND	193	0	200	B/W	GND	3.2	6	30
C55	1992-97	(5)	B	(6)	4	-	-	Br	L	235	175	-	-	O	GND	-150	-	-	O (8)	GND	(9)	8	20
E60	1995-98	W/R	W/B	300	-	-	-	Br	L	170	-	-	-	B/W	GND	-	-	-	B/W	GND	4.1	-	-
P60	1991	(4)	B	130	2.5	2.7	8	Br	B	165	140	170	230	B/W	GND	100	0	200	B/W	GND	4.8	12	20
P60/C60	1992-98	W/R	W/B	300	-	-	-	Br	L	170	-	-	-	B/W	GND	-	-	-	B/W	GND	4.1	-	-
70	1992-98	W/R	W/B	300	-	-	-	Br	L	170	-	-	-	B/W	GND	-	-	-	B/W	GND	4.1	-	-

Note: All electrical specifications are plus or minus 20% unless otherwise indicated

(1) Plus or minus 10%

(2) 1984-92, 1993-95 5.4 Kilohms

(3) 1990-92, 1993-97 5.4 Kilohms

(4) Cylinder 1, W/R; cylinder 2, W/B; cylinder 3, W/G

(5) Cylinder 1, W/R; cylinder 2, W/B

(6) 1989-94, 1995-97 325 Ohms

04706C98

Ignition Testing Specifications

Model	Years	Pulser Coils Wire leads (+)	(-)	Resist. Ohms	Peak Voltage Loaded	Unloaded	1000 rpm	Low Speed Wire leads (+)	(-)	Resist. Ohms	Peak Voltage Loaded	Unloaded	1000 rpm	High Speed Wire leads (+)	(-)	Resist. Ohms	Peak Voltage Loaded	Unloaded	1000 rpm	CDI Output Wire leads (+)	(-)	Peak Voltage Loaded	Unloaded	1000 rpm	Ignition Coil Wire leads (+)	(-)	Resist. Kilohms (1)	Peak Voltage (kV) Loaded	Unloaded
E75	1995-98	W/R (2)	W/Y (2)	380	-	-	-	Br	L	-	-	-	-	R	L	120	-	-	-	B/W	GND	-	-	-	B/W	GND	4.8	-	-
C75	1994-98	W/R (2)	W/Y (2)	380	-	-	-	Br	L	-	-	-	-	R	L	120	-	-	-	B/W	GND	-	-	-	B/W	GND	4.8	-	-
P75	1994-98	W/R (2)	W/Y (2)	330	2.5	0	7	Br	L	120	120	79	75	R	L	120	45	45	155	B/W	GND	95	-	130	B/W	GND	4.8	-	-
C80	1997	W/R (2)	W/Y (2)	300	5	7	14	Br	L	240	100	90	135	R	L	80	60	55	170	B/W	GND	130	-	155	B/W	GND	4.1	-	-
C85	1996-97	W/R (2)	W/Y (2)	380	-	-	-	Br	L	1050	-	-	-	R	L	120	-	-	-	B/W	GND	-	-	-	R/W	GND	4.8	-	-
90/C90	1992-98	W/R	W/B	300	-	-	-	Br	L	240	-	-	-	R	L	80	-	-	-	B/W	GND	-	-	-	B/W	GND	4.1	-	-
115	1992-98	W/R (3)	W/Y (3)	320	3	3	10	Br	R	740	175	175	240	L	B/R	69	50	50	210	B/W	GND	90	0	200	B/W	GND	3.8	5	11
C115	1992-98	W/R (3)	W/Y (3)	320	3	3	10	Br	R	740	175	175	240	L	B/R	69	50	50	210	B/W	GND	90	0	200	B/W	GND	3.8	5	11
P115	1992-96	W/R (3)	W/Y (3)	320	3	3	10	Br	R	740	175	175	240	L	B/R	69	50	50	210	B/W	GND	90	0	200	B/W	GND	3.8	5	11
130	1992-98	W/R (3)	W/Y (3)	320	3	3	10	Br	R	740	175	175	240	L	B/R	69	50	50	210	B/W	GND	90	0	200	B/W	GND	3.8	5	11
150	1992-98	W/R (4)	W/G (4)	320	2.5	3	8	Br	R	-	200	230	270	L	B/R	69	60	60	260	B/W	GND	150	0	250	B/W	GND	3.8	6	22
P150/C150	1992-98	W/R (4)	W/G (4)	320	2.5	3	8	Br	R	-	200	230	270	L	B/R	69	60	60	260	B/W	GND	150	0	250	B/W	GND	3.8	6	22
175	1992-98	W/R (4)	W/G (4)	320	2.5	3	8	Br	R	-	200	230	270	L	B/R	69	60	60	260	B/W	GND	150	0	250	B/W	GND	3.8	6	22
P175	1994-97	W/R (4)	W/G (4)	320	2.5	3	8	Br	R	-	200	230	270	L	B/R	69	60	60	260	B/W	GND	150	0	250	B/W	GND	3.8	6	22
200	1992-98	W/R (4)	W/G (4)	320	2.5	3	8	Br	R	-	200	230	270	L	B/R	69	60	60	260	B/W	GND	150	0	250	B/W	GND	3.8	6	22
P200	1992-97	W/R (4)	W/G (4)	320	2.5	3	8	Br	R	-	200	230	270	L	B/R	69	60	60	260	B/W	GND	150	0	250	B/W	GND	3.8	6	22
225	1982-93	W/R (4)	W/G (4)	320	2.5	3	8	Br	R	-	200	230	270	L	B/R	69	60	60	260	B/W	GND	150	0	250	B/W	GND	3.8	6	22
225L	1994-98	W/R (4)	W/G (4)	320	2.5	3	8	Br	R	-	200	230	270	L	B/R	69	60	60	260	B/W	GND	150	0	250	B/W	GND	3.8	6	22
225X	1994-98	W/R (5)	B	346	-	5.3	18-19 (6)	Br	R	280	-	139-140	222 (7)	L	B/R	280	-	152	221 (8)	B/W	GND	159-160	6.1-6.2	196-197	B/W	GND	2.7	-	-
225U	1995-98	W/R	B	346	-	5.3	18-19 (6)	Br	R	280	-	139-140	222 (7)	L	B/R	280	-	152	221 (8)	B/W	GND	159-160	6.1-6.2	196-197	B/W	GND	2.7	-	-
250	1992-98	W/R (5)	B	346	-	5.3	18-19 (6)	Br	R	280	-	139 140	222 (7)	L	B/R	280	-	152	221 (8)	R/W	GND	159-160	6.1-6.2	196-197	B/W	GND	2.7	-	-

Note: All electrical specifications are plus or minus 20% unless otherwise indicated

(1) Plus or minus 10%

(2) Cylinder 2, W/B (+), W/G (-)

(3) Cylinder 1 and 3; Cylinder 2 and 4, W/B (+), W/G (-)

(4) Cylinder 1 and 4; Cylinder 2 and 5, W/B (+), W/L (-); Cylinder 3 and 6, W/Y (+), W/Br (-)

(5) Cylinder 1; Cylinder 2 and 4, W/B; Cylinder 3, W/Y; Cylinder 5, W/L; Cylinder 6, W/Br

(6) 59-62 volts @ 5500 rpm

(7) 155-160 volts @ 5500 rpm

(8) 165-172 volts @ 5500 rpm

04706C97

SERVICING

Flywheel and Stator Plate

The following short section lists the procedures required to pull the flywheel and remove the stator plate in order to service the ignition system. Removal and installation of the stator plate is necessary in order to gain access to the wiring harness retainer underneath the stator plate. Cleaning and Inspecting procedures in addition to proper assembling and installation steps are also included.

REMOVAL

1 & 2-Cylinder Powerheads

♦ See accompanying illustrations

1. Remove the cowling from the powerhead. Remove the spark plugs using a spark plug socket and ratchet.

2. Remove the mounting hardware securing the hand rewind starter to the powerhead. Move the rewind starter to one side out of the way.

→Do not remove the handle from the starter rope because the rope would immediately rewind inside the starter. Such action would require considerable time and effort to correct.

3. Obtain a flywheel holder. Insert the two indexing pins on the ends of the arms through the holes in the flywheel cover. Hold the cover steady and remove the three cover attaching bolts.

4. Before lifting the cover from the flywheel, scribe a mark on the cover and a matching mark on the flywheel to ensure the cover is installed in the same position from which it is removed.

5. Position the same tool into the flywheel holes. Hold the flywheel from rotating and at the same time remove the flywheel nut.

6. Obtain a flywheel puller. Ensure the puller will pull from the bolt holes in the flywheel and not from around the perimeter of the flywheel.

Never attempt to use a puller which pulls on the outside edge of the flywheel.

Install the puller onto the flywheel, take a strain on the puller with the proper size wrench. Now, continue to tighten on the tool and at the same time, shock the crankshaft with a gentle to moderate tap with a hammer on the end of the tool. This shock will assist in breaking the flywheel loose from the crankshaft.

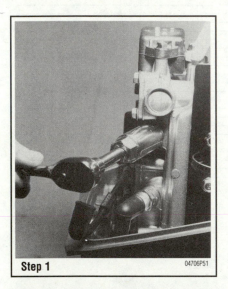

Step 1 04706P51

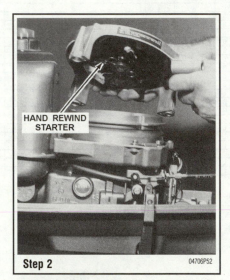

Step 2 04706P52

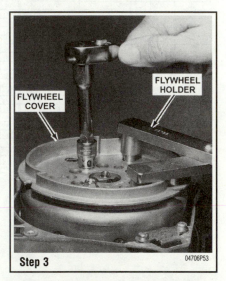

Step 3 04706P53

Step 4 04706P54

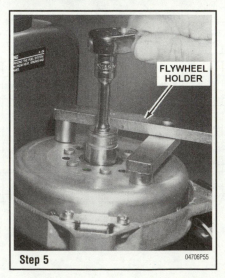

Step 5 04706P55

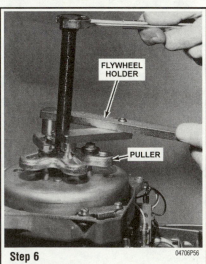

Step 6 04706P56

Step 7

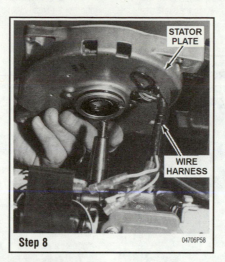

Step 8

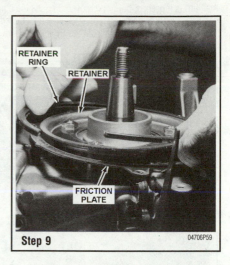

Step 9

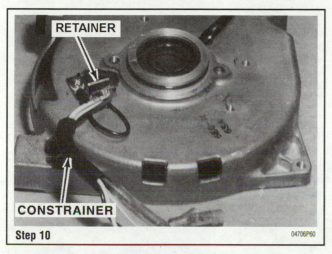

Step 10

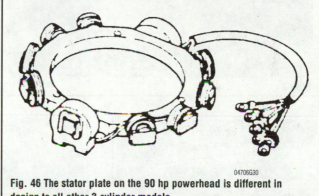

Fig. 46 The stator plate on the 90 hp powerhead is different in design to all other 3 cylinder models

7. Lift the flywheel free of the crankshaft. Remove and save the Woodruff key from the recess in the crankshaft.

8. Unplug the stator harness at the quick disconnect fittings. Remove the bolts securing the stator plate to the powerhead and lift the stator plate free of the crankshaft and powerhead.

9. On the 6 hp, 8 hp, 9.9 hp, 15 hp, 25 hp and 30 hp models, the stator is bolted to a friction plate beneath a retainer. Once the stator plate is removed, this friction plate is free to rotate. Do not disturb the position of this friction plate in relation to the stator plate. Movement of the friction plate will affect powerhead timing.

If it is necessary to remove and replace the friction plate, take time to scribe a mark on the powerhead opposite the small timing hump, as shown in the accompanying illustration.

10. Place the stator plate on a suitable work surface. Remove the screw securing the harness retainer to the plate and unwind the Black plastic harness constrainer. Now, any component mounted on top of the stator plate and tested defective may be removed.

3-Cylinder Powerheads

▶ **See Figure 46 and accompanying illustrations**

The sequence of photographs illustrate the work being performed on a 30 hp powerhead. Where procedural tasks differ for other model units, these differences will be clearly identified and accompanied with captioned illustrations.

➡ **On 30 hp models, the oil injection tank must be moved out of the way to provide clearance for the flywheel to be removed. It is not necessary to drain the oil from the tank, only to release the tank from the powerhead to permit moving it aside for flywheel clearance.**

Remove the plastic cover from the top of the flywheel. Twist the spark plug leads free from the spark plugs to prevent an accident should the powerhead start inadvertently. If servicing a Model 30 hp unit, remove one of the three mounting bolts securing the oil tank.

1. On 30 hp powerheads, remove the other two oil tank mounting bolts and carefully set the tank upright inside the lower cowling.

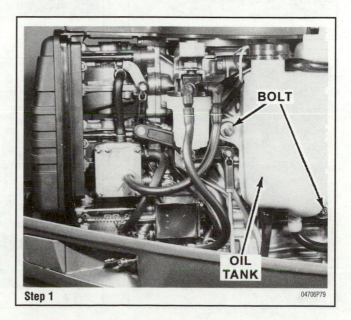

Step 1

2. Wedge a large screwdriver against two of the flywheel cover bolts while the third is loosened, but not removed. Loosen the other two in the same manner. After the three bolts are loosened, they may be removed.

3. Lift the flywheel cover from the flywheel.

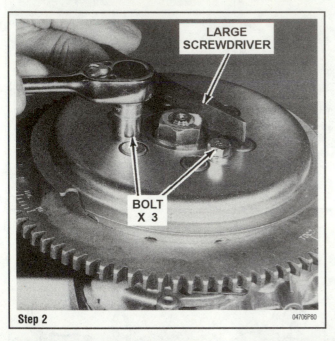

Step 2   04706P80

4. Insert a flywheel holding tool into the two holes provided in the flywheel and hold it steady while the flywheel nut is loosened with a 22mm socket. Remove the flywheel nut and washer.

5. Obtain a flywheel puller. Ensure the puller will pull from the bolt holes in the flywheel and not from around the perimeter of the flywheel.

Never attempt to use a puller which pulls on the outside edge of the flywheel.

Install the puller onto the flywheel, and take a strain on the puller with the proper size wrench. Now, continue to tighten on the tool and at the same time, shock the crankshaft with a gentle to moderate tap with a hammer on the end of the tool. This shock will assist in breaking the flywheel loose from the crankshaft.

✳✳ CAUTION

A violent strike to the center bolt may cause damage to the crankshaft oil seals. Therefore, use only a gentle to moderate tap with the hammer.

6. Lift the flywheel up and free of the crankshaft. The flywheel may seem heavier than it actually is due to the magnetic attraction between the flywheel magnets and the laminated cores of the coils.

7. Pry the link rod from the ball joint under the stator plate. Take care not to alter the length of the link rod.

8. On 30 hp powerheads, unplug the wires at the quick disconnect fittings and at the large harness connector. Loosen and remove the two screws at the forward end of the stator plate. Loosen the two bolts on either side of the lighting coil at the aft end of the stator plate. Carefully lift off the lighting coil and set it aside. Lift off the two spacers and the two bolts. The charge coil is secured to the stator plate, therefore it is not necessary to remove this coil. Remove the Woodruff key from the crankshaft.

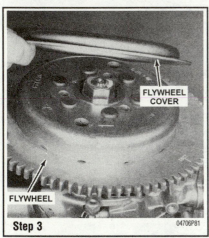

Step 3   04706P81

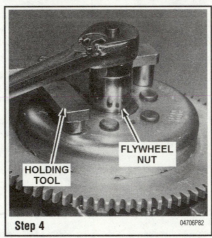

Step 4   04706P82

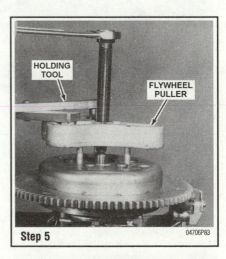

Step 5   04706P83

Step 6   04706P84

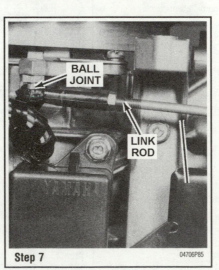

Step 7   04706P85

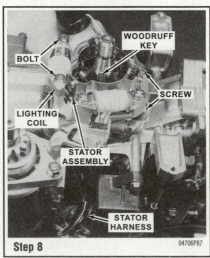

Step 8   04706P87

9. Remove the attaching hardware, and then lift the stator plate free of the powerhead.

On 30 hp powerheads, remove the three screws, the three small angled retainers, and then remove the pulsar assembly. (On all other models the pulsar assembly is an integral part of the stator plate.)

Remove the nylon spacer from the pulsar assembly or the stator plate depending on the model being serviced. Remove and save the Woodruff key from the crankshaft.

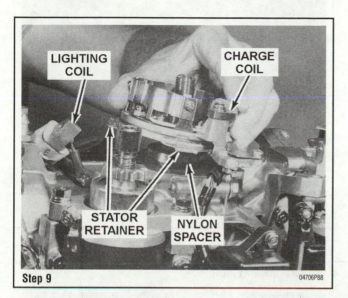

Step 9   04706P88

V4 and V6 Powerheads

♦ **See accompanying illustrations**

1. Disconnect both leads at the battery terminals. Remove the plastic cover over the flywheel. Twist the spark plug leads free from the spark plugs to prevent an accident should the powerhead start inadvertently.

2. Insert a flywheel holding tool into the two holes provided in the flywheel and hold it steady while the flywheel nut is loosened with the correct size socket. Remove the flywheel nut and washer.

3. Obtain a flywheel puller. Ensure the puller will pull from the bolt holes in the flywheel and not from around the perimeter of the flywheel.

Never attempt to use a puller which pulls on the outside edge of the flywheel.

Install the puller onto the flywheel, and take a strain on the puller with the proper size wrench. Now, continue to tighten on the tool and at the same time, shock the crankshaft with a gentle to moderate tap with a hammer on the end of the tool. This shock will assist in breaking the flywheel loose from the crankshaft.

✳✳ CAUTION

A violent strike to the center bolt may cause damage to the crankshaft oil seals. Therefore, use only a gentle to moderate tap with the hammer.

Lift the flywheel up and free of the crankshaft. The flywheel may seem heavier than it actually is due to the magnetic attraction between the flywheel magnets and the laminated cores of the coils. Remove the Woodruff key from the crankshaft.

4. On models not equipped with YMIS, pry the link rod from the ball joint under the stator plate. Take care not to alter the length of the link rod.

5. Remove the bolts and then the cover over the CDI unit and rectifier/regulator.

6. Disconnect the following leads from their terminals on the CDI unit:

Step 1   4706P1D

Step 2   04706P2D

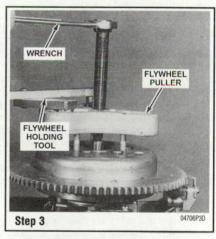

Step 3   04706P3D

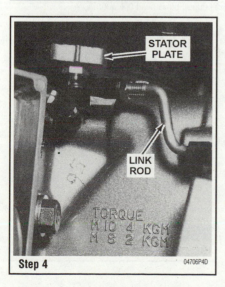

Step 4   04706P4D

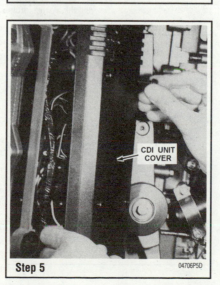

Step 5   04706P5D

Step 6   04706P6D

Brown, Red, Blue and Black/Red. These leads can be lifted away from the edge of the unit and still be secured in a small retainer.

Disconnect the leads between the stator and the rectifier at the rectifier.

Identify the wire harness lead from the stator to the CDI unit or on models equipped with YMIS identify the wire harness lead from the stator to the microcomputer. Disconnect the two halves of the connector.

7. Mark the relative positions of the stator and pulsar assemblies to the powerhead before removal. Marking their positions will enable each to be installed in same location around the crankshaft from which they were removed. Remove the three bolts securing the stator assembly, and then lift it off the powerhead. The charge and lighting coils are considered the stator assembly and are replaced as a set. Next remove the four magneto base retainers and the pulsar assembly attaching hardware. Lift off the pulsar assembly, and remove the retaining collar from the pulsar assembly.

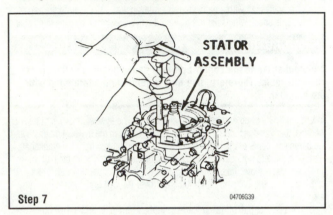

Step 7   04706G39

CLEANING AND INSPECTION

▶ **See Figure 47**

Inspect the flywheel for cracks or other damage, especially around the inside of the center hub. Check to be sure metal parts have not become attached to the magnets. Verify each magnet has good magnetism by using a screwdriver or other suitable tool.

Thoroughly clean the inside taper of the flywheel and the taper on the crankshaft to prevent the flywheel from walking on the crankshaft during operation.

Check the top seal around the crankshaft to be sure no oil has been leaking onto the stator plate. If there is any evidence the seal has been leaking, it must be replaced.

Test the stator assembly to verify it is not loose. Attempt to lift each side of the plate. There should be little or no evidence of movement.

Inspect the stator plate oil seal and the O-ring on the underside of the plate.

Some models have a retainer, a retainer ring, and a friction plate located under the stator. The retainer ring is a guard around the retainer, subject to cracking and wear. Inspect the condition of this guard and replace if it is damaged.

Fig. 47 Always check the flywheel carefully to be sure particles of metal have not stuck to the magnets

ASSEMBLY AND INSTALLATION

1 & 2-Cylinder Powerheads

▶ **See accompanying illustrations**

1. On the 6 hp, 8 hp, 9.9 hp, 15 hp, 25 hp and 30 hp models, place the friction plate down over the crankshaft. Rotate the plate until the hump on the outer edge is aligned with the mark scribed on the powerhead prior to removal. Install the retainer on top of the friction plate and secure it in place with the attaching bolts. Stretch the retainer ring around the retainer with the outer edge of the retainer indexed into the ring groove.

➡ **On the 6 hp, 8 hp, 9.9 hp, 15 hp, 25 hp and 30 hp models, when the stator plate is installed, the mounting bolts thread into the friction plate instead of into the powerhead, as on the other models.**

Make a final check to be sure the hump on the friction plate is still aligned with the scribed mark on the powerhead.

2. Position the stator plate in place over the crankshaft. Secure the plate with the attaching bolts. Tighten the bolts alternately and evenly to a torque value of 5.9 ft. lbs. (8Nm). Connect the stator wire harness wire by wire, color to color.

3. Place a tiny dab of thick lubricant on the curved surface of the Woodruff key to hold it in place while the flywheel is being installed. Press the Woodruff key into place in the crankshaft recess. Wipe away any excess lubricant to prevent the flywheel from walking during powerhead operation.

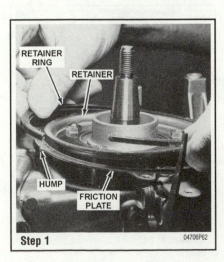

Step 1   04706P62

Step 2   04706P63

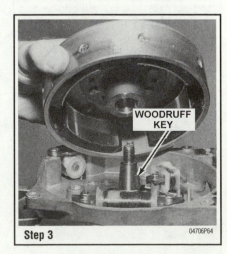

Step 3   04706P64

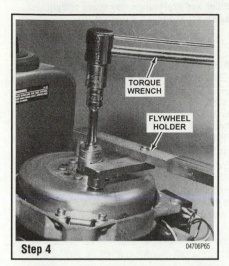

Step 4   04706P65

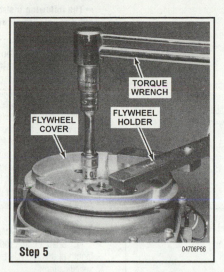

Step 5   04706P66

Step 6   04706P67

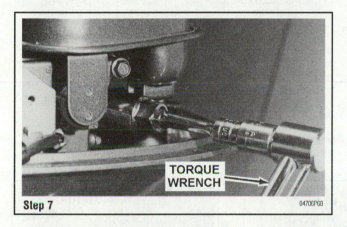

Step 7   04706P68

Check the flywheel magnets to ensure they are free of any metal particles. Double check the taper in the flywheel hub and the taper on the crankshaft to verify they are clean and contain no oil.

Now, slide the flywheel down over the crankshaft with the keyway in the flywheel aligned with the Woodruff key in place on the crankshaft. Rotate the flywheel counterclockwise to be sure it does not contact any part of the stator plate or wiring.

4. Slide the washer onto the crankshaft, and then thread the flywheel nut onto the crankshaft. Obtain a flywheel holding tool. With the pins on the ends of the holder arms indexed into the flywheel holes, tighten the flywheel nut to the following torque value for the models listed.

- Model 4, 5, 6, & 8 hp—32 ft. lbs. (44Nm)
- Model 9.9 & 15 hp—70 ft. lbs. (96Nm)
- Model 25 & 30 hp—100 ft. lbs. (136Nm)

5. Position the flywheel cover in place over the flywheel with the three holes in the cover aligned with the three holes in the flywheel. Install and tighten the three bolts to a torque value of 5.8 ft. lbs. (8Nm).

6. Install the hand rewind starter to the powerhead. Tighten the three attaching bolts to a torque value of 5.8 ft. lbs. (8Nm).

7. Install and tighten the spark plugs to a torque value of 14 ft. lbs. (20Nm). Secure the spark plug leads to the spark plugs.

Install the cowling to the powerhead.

3-Cylinder Powerheads

▶ See Figure 48 and accompanying illustrations

The following procedures pickup the work after the flywheel and stator assembly have been cleaned, inspected, serviced, and assembled.

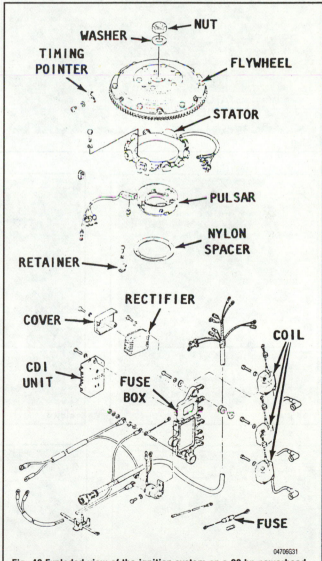

Fig. 48 Exploded view of the ignition system on a 90 hp powerhead with all major parts identified

04706G31

1. Place the nylon spacer around the pulsar assembly or the stator plate, depending on the model being serviced.

On 90 hp models, place the pulsar assembly over the crankshaft. Secure the assembly with the three small angled retainers and the three attaching screws.

Place the stator plate down over the crankshaft.

As required, install the three small angled retainers around the nylon spacer. Secure the retainers with the attaching screws. Install and tighten the stator plate attaching hardware.

2. On 30 hp models, secure the forward end of the stator plate with the two Phillips head screws. Install the lighting coil over the two tall spacers at the aft end of the stator plate.

Install the Woodruff key into the crankshaft. A tiny dab of grease will help hold the key in place while the flywheel is installed.

Connect the stator harness wires, color to color. The large connector plug may only be connected one way.

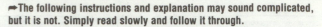

➤The following instructions and explanation may sound complicated, but it is not. Simply read slowly and follow it through.

If the Green lighting wires were disconnected, care must be exercised when the wires are connected.

First, there are two Green wires (may be encased in a plastic tube), one of which ends in a single female connector. The other ends in a double female connector. Be sure to connect the Green wire from the lighting coil with the single female connector to one of the Green wires with a male connector leading from the rectifier.

Next, connect the Green wire from the lighting coil with one of the two female ends with the other Green wire with a male end leading from the rectifier.

Now, the only wire left is the other Green wire from the lighting coil with one of the double female connectors. This wire is to be connected to a Green wire with a male end coming from a wire harness in the bottom of the lower cowling.

In summary, do not connect both Green rectifier leads with male ends to the single Green wire with the double female connector from the lighting coil. Such a connection would render the lighting coil circuit inoperative.

3. Lower the flywheel over the crankshaft with the Woodruff key indexing into the slot in the flywheel.

4. Snap the link rod back onto the ball joint under the stator plate. If the length of this rod has been accidentally changed to adjust the length back to the specifications.

Check the action of the stator plate. The plate should move freely within the limits of travel of the magneto control lever. If any binding is felt, remove the flywheel and check the installation of the stator plate.

5. Install the washer and flywheel nut. Hold the flywheel from rotating using the flywheel holder tool. If servicing a 30 hp unit, tighten the flywheel nut to a torque value of 72 ft. lbs. (100Nm). For all other models, tighten the flywheel nut to a torque value of 115 ft. lbs. (160Nm).

Once again, check the action of the stator plate.

6. Place the flywheel cover over the flywheel and align the three holes with the three threaded holes in the flywheel.

7. Thread all three bolts through the holes of the cover and into the flywheel. Use a large screwdriver wedged between any two of the bolts while tightening the third bolt. Tighten the three bolts securely.

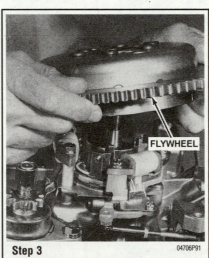

LIGHTING COIL • CHARGE COIL • STATOR RETAINER • NYLON SPACER

Step 1   04706P89

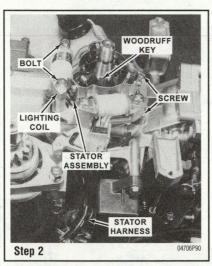

BOLT • WOODRUFF KEY • SCREW • LIGHTING COIL • STATOR ASSEMBLY • STATOR HARNESS

Step 2   04706P90

FLYWHEEL

Step 3   04706P91

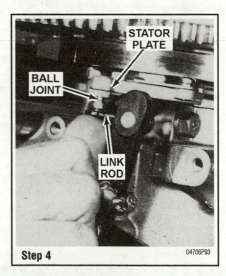

STATOR PLATE • BALL JOINT • LINK ROD

Step 4   04706P93

TORQUE WRENCH • FLYWHEEL HOLDER

Step 5   04706P94

FLYWHEEL COVER

Step 6   04706P95

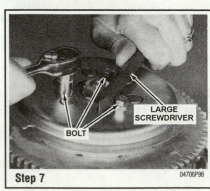

BOLT • LARGE SCREWDRIVER

Step 7   04706P96

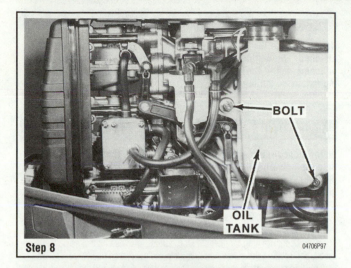

Step 8   04706P97

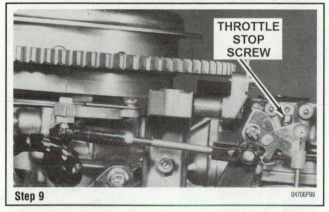

THROTTLE
STOP
SCREW

Step 9   04706P99

8. On 30 hp models, move the oil tank into position. Install and tighten the three retaining bolts.

Connect the spark plug leads to the spark plugs. Install the plastic cover over the flywheel. Install the cowling to the powerhead.

Mount the outboard unit in a test tank, on the boat in a body of water, or connect a flush attachment and hose to the lower unit. Connect a tachometer to the powerhead.

On manual start models, connect the two tachometer leads to the two Green leads from the stator. These two Green leads are encased inside a sheath, but the connecting ends are exposed. The leads are connected to a pair of Green female leads. Either tachometer lead may be connected to either Green lead from the stator.

On electric start models without a tachometer installed, or for a model with a tachometer installed, but a second meter is needed to assist in making adjustments.

Inside the control box, the Green lead with the female end connector is input or signal lead. The Black lead with either a male or female end connector is the tachometer return or ground lead.

Connect the tachometer to these two leads per the instructions with the meter, input and ground.

❊❊ CAUTION

Never operate the engine at high speed with a flush device attached. The engine, operating at high speed with such a device attached, would runaway from lack of a load on the propeller, causing extensive damage.

Start the engine and check the completed work.

❊❊ CAUTION

Water must circulate through the lower unit to the powerhead anytime the powerhead is operating to prevent damage to the water

pump in the lower unit. Just five seconds without water will damage the water pump impeller.

9. Allow the powerhead to warm to normal operating temperature. Adjust the throttle stop screw until the powerhead idles between 700 and 800 rpm for the Model 30 hp unit, and between 750 and 850 rpm for all other models. Rotating the throttle stop screw clockwise increases powerhead speed, and rotating the screw counterclockwise decreases powerhead speed.

Time and synchronize the ignition system with the fuel system.

V4 and V6 Powerheads

▶ See Accompanying Illustrations

The following procedures pickup the work after the flywheel and stator assembly have been cleaned, inspected, serviced, and assembled.

1. Install the retaining collar over the pulsar assembly. Place the pulsar assembly over the crankshaft, with the arm on the retaining collar on the starboard side of the powerhead. Secure the assembly to the upper bearing housing with four retainers.

Place the stator plate down over the crankshaft. The three bolt holes are unevenly spaced, therefore rotate the plate until all three holes align. Install and tighten the three securing bolts.

2. Thread the stator harness wire through the grommet next to the rectifier/regulator. Attach the two Green lighting coil leads to the two forward terminals on the rectifier/regulator. It makes no difference which lead is attached to which terminal. Connect the other four leads to the four forward terminals on the CDI terminal block, starting from the top, Brown, Blue, Red, Black/red in order.

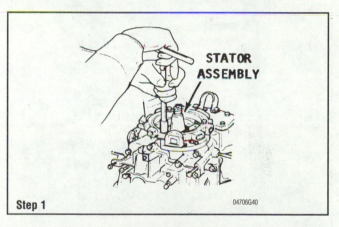

STATOR
ASSEMBLY

Step 1   04706G40

GREEN

BROWN
BLUE
RED
BLACK/RED

Step 2   04706P8D

3. Install the CDI unit cover with the attaching hardware. Tighten the screws securely.

4. On models without YMIS, snap the link rod from the magneto control lever back onto the ball joint on the magneto plate. If the length of this rod was accidentally altered, adjust the rod back to the specified length.

Install the Woodruff key into the crankshaft. A tiny dab of grease will help hold the key in place while the flywheel is installed.

Lower the flywheel over the crankshaft with the Woodruff key indexing into the slot in the flywheel.

Check the action of the magneto plate. For those models equipped with a rod connecting the magneto plate with the magneto control lever, the plate should move freely within the limits of travel of the magneto control lever. If any binding is felt, remove the flywheel and check installation of the stator plate.

5. Install the washer and flywheel nut. Hold the flywheel from rotating using a flywheel holder tool. Tighten the flywheel nut to a torque value of 115 ft. lbs. (160Nm).

Once again, check the action of the stator plate.

6. Connect the spark plug leads to the spark plugs.

Install the plastic cover over the flywheel. Install the cowling to the powerhead.

Install both leads at the battery terminals, the Red lead to the positive terminal and the Black lead to the negative terminal.

Mount the outboard unit in a test tank, on the boat in a body of water, or connect a flush attachment and hose to the lower unit. Connect a tachometer to the powerhead.

※※ CAUTION

Never, operate the engine at high speed with a flush device attached. The engine, operating at high speed with such a device attached, would runaway from lack of a load on the propeller, causing extensive damage.

Start the engine and check the completed work.

※※ CAUTION

Water must circulate through the lower unit to the powerhead anytime the powerhead is operating to prevent damage to the water pump in the lower unit. Just five seconds without water will damage the water pump impeller.

7. Allow the powerhead to warm to normal operating temperature. Adjust the throttle stop screw until the powerhead idles at the correct speed for the model being serviced. Rotating the throttle stop screw clockwise increases powerhead speed, and rotating the screw counterclockwise decreases powerhead speed.

Time and synchronize the ignition system with the fuel system.

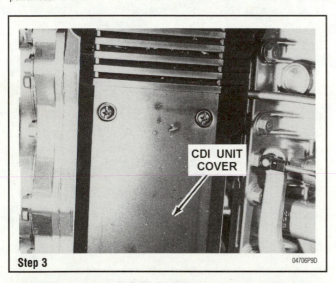

CDI UNIT COVER

Step 3   04706P9D

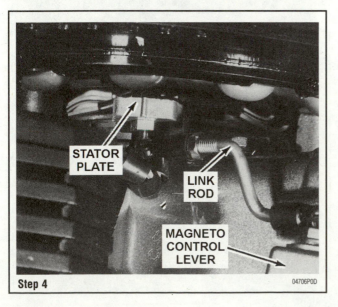

STATOR PLATE

LINK ROD

MAGNETO CONTROL LEVER

Step 4   04706P0D

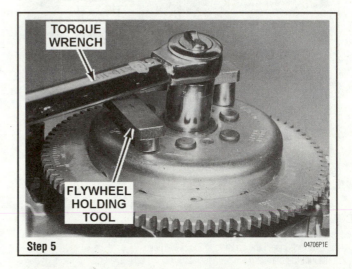

TORQUE WRENCH

FLYWHEEL HOLDING TOOL

Step 5   04706P1E

PLASTIC COVER

Step 6   04706P2E

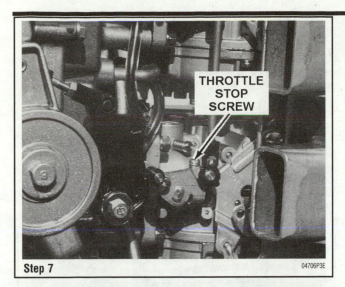

THROTTLE STOP SCREW

Step 7   04706P3E

CDI Unit and Ignition Coils

REMOVAL

Except V4 and V6 Powerheads

♦ **See accompanying illustrations**

1. Disconnect both electrical leads at the battery terminals. Release the quick disconnect fitting and the 10amp fuse holder, directly under the fitting, from the front of the wire cover.

2. Loosen, then remove the single screw securing the cover to the powerhead. Lift the cover free.

3. Disconnect the main harness connector. Disconnect all the wires at their

quick disconnect fittings. Loosen and remove the grounding bolts. This bolt secures four Black ground leads with eye connectors to the powerhead. Such grounding bolts are usually painted Blue at the factory and do not serve any other purpose other than as grounding terminals.

4. Note the White plastic sleeves on the wires leading from the CDI unit to each ignition coil. These sleeves are numbered 1, 2, and 3. Disconnect each wire at the quick disconnect fitting. If these sleeves are missing, then mark each wire to identify to which coil the lead must be reconnected. If these wires are not connected properly, the powerhead cylinders will not fire in the correct sequence. The powerhead may operate, but very poorly.

☛**There is no other way to determine which lead is for which cylinder other than the sleeves or tracing the leads. If the leads are disconnected with no sleeves, and if the leads are not identified by markings or pieces of tape, then a trial and error method must be used to find the correct firing order for the powerhead.**

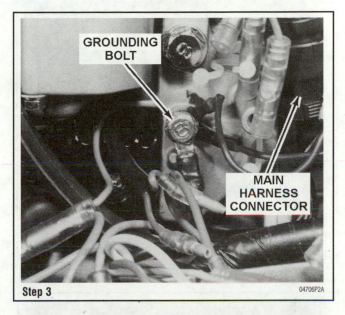

GROUNDING BOLT

MAIN HARNESS CONNECTOR

Step 3   04706P2A

WIRE COVER

10 AMP. FUSE HOLDER

Step 1   04706P00

WIRE COVER

SCREW

Step 2   04706P1A

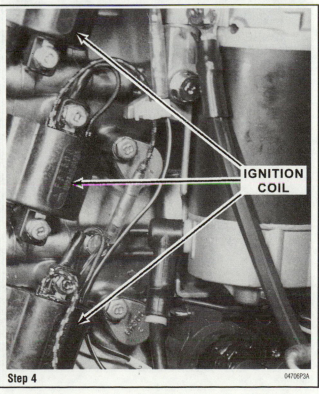

IGNITION COIL

Step 4   04706P3A

5. Remove the two attaching bolts securing the CDI unit to the powerhead. Remove the CDI unit.

6. Twist off each spark plug lead from the spark. Remove the two bolts securing each ignition coil to the powerhead. Remove each coil in turn. The lower mounting bolts of the No. 3 coil will also secure a Black grounding lead with an eye connector to the powerhead. This Black lead comes from a connector plug in the lower cowling.

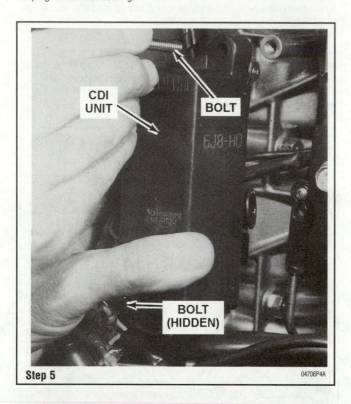

Step 5   04706P4A

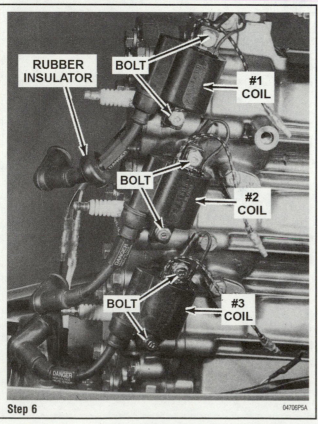

Step 6   04706P5A

V4 and V6 Powerheads

▶ **See accompanying illustrations**

➡ **This procedure also details the removal of the rectifier/regulator assembly.**

1. Disconnect both leads at the battery terminals and remove the CDI unit cover securing bolts. Remove the cover.

Disconnect all the leads on the CDI unit screw terminals, each set of three or four leads are grouped together in a small retaining block for ease of installation. Pull the retaining block, with leads attached from the edge of the mounting bracket. Remove the two screws, one at the top and one at the bottom of the CDI unit and lift the unit out of its mounting bracket.

2. Disconnect all the leads from the rectifier/regulator and remove the two attaching screws. Lift the unit out of its mounting bracket.

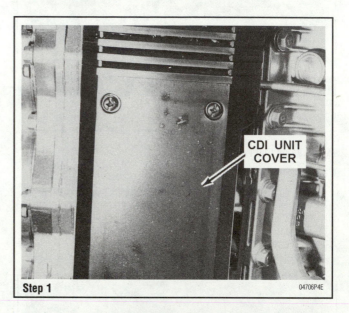

Step 1   04706P4E

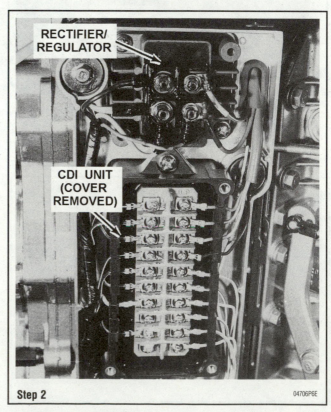

Step 2   04706P6E

3.   Disconnect all the leads from the CDI unit screw terminals. Each set of three or four leads are grouped together in a small retaining block for ease of installation. Pull the retaining block, with leads attached from the edge of the mounting bracket. Disconnect all the leads from the rectifier/regulator. It is not necessary to remove the two components from their mounting bracket. Remove the large attaching bolts and washers from the CDI unit mounting bracket and remove the bracket with the CDI unit and rectifier/regulator still attached.

4.   Remove the spark plug leads with a twisting motion, for models equipped with YMIS rotate the caps counterclockwise, without pulling on them. Note the White plastic sleeves on the wires leading from the CDI unit to each ignition coil. These sleeves are numbered 1,2,3 and so on. Disconnect each wire at the quick disconnect fitting. If these sleeves are missing, then mark each wire to identify which coil the lead must be reconnected . If these wires are not connected properly, the powerhead cylinders will not fire in the correct sequence. The powerhead may operate, but very **poorly.**

→The only way to determine which lead is for which cylinder other than the sleeves is by tracing the leads back to the CDI unit and comparing them to the wiring diagram. These leads are encased in a network of plastic casings which will have to be destroyed in order to trace the leads. If the leads are disconnected with no sleeves, and if the leads are not identified by markings or a piece of tape, then a trial and error method must be used to find the correct firing order for the powerhead.

Remove the two securing bolts from each coil, there will be a small Black grounding lead at each coil attached to one of the securing bolts. All ignition coils on the models covered in this manual are created equal. They may be installed to energize any spark plug.

INSTALLATION

Except V4 and V6 Powerheads

▶ **See accompanying illustrations**

1.   Install each ignition coil to the powerhead with the two attaching bolts. Attach the Black ground lead from the small harness of wires lying in the lower cowling to the bottom mounting bolt of the No. 3 coil. This lead has an eye connector. Tighten the bolts to a torque value of 5.8 ft. lbs. (8Nm). The coil with the rubber insulator is the top coil. The other two may be installed in either the No. 2 or No. 3 location. Install each spark plug lead.

2.   Check to be sure the over rev limiter bridge is connected across the **ON** position on the back side of the CDI unit.

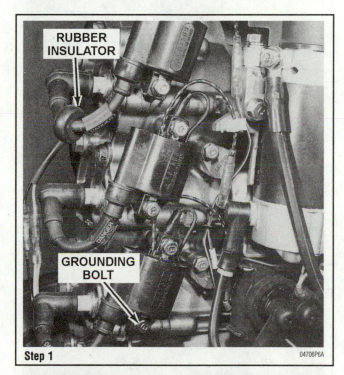

Step 1   04706P6A

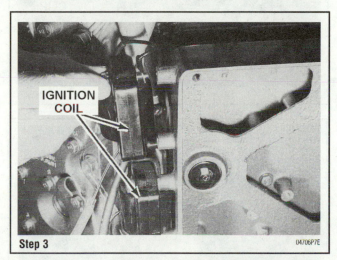

Step 3   04706P7E

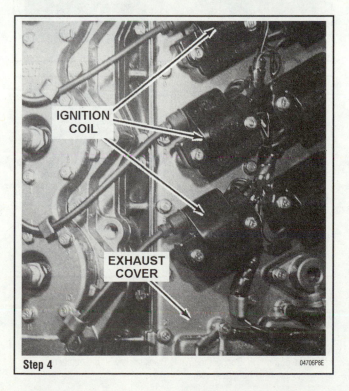

Step 4   04706P8E

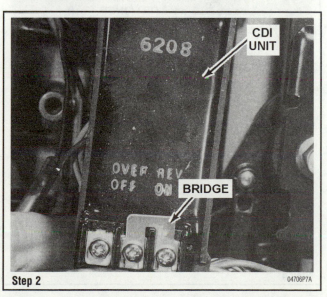

Step 2   04706P7A

3. Install the CDI unit to the powerhead and secure it in place with the two attaching bolts. Tighten the bolts to a torque value of 5.8 ft. lbs. (8Nm). Route the three White/Black leads with numbered sleeves behind the cranking motor relay.

4. Connect the three White/Black leads with the numbered sleeves to the fabric covered coil leads matching sleeve No. 1 to coil No. 1, etc.

→ If the sleeves were lost and the leads not numbered as instructed during disconnecting, the correct firing order may be lost. The only solution is to operate the powerhead, then change leads until the powerhead operates satisfactorily. Hook the No. 1 lead and the fabric covered lead from the No. 2 coil into the small plastic lead retainer next to the cranking motor.

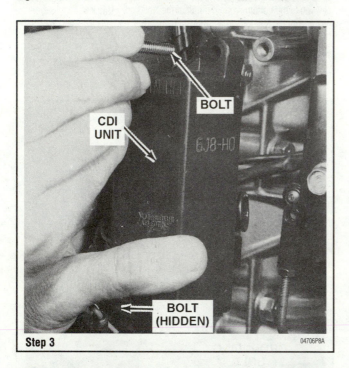

Step 3

Step 4

5. Identify and connect the leads matching color to color using the wiring diagram for the model being serviced, as an assist in making the connections.

Once all connections have been properly made, there will be some Black grounding leads with eye connectors left over.

Gather the eye connectors onto appropriate bolts, usually marked with Blue dye, and ground the leads to the cranking motor bracket (electric start model), or directly to the powerhead (manual start model).

Tuck the leads and connectors into the clips provided at different locations for this purpose.

6. Install the wire cover and neatly tuck in any stray leads. Secure the cover to the powerhead with a single Phillips head screw.

7. Snap the 10-amp fuse and the wire connector from the fuse to the outside of the wire cover. Connect both electrical leads to the proper battery terminal.

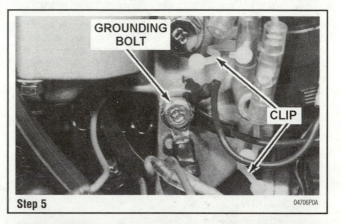

Step 5

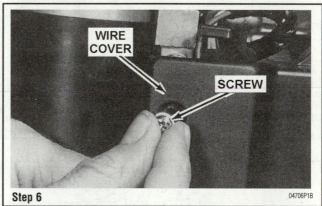

Step 6

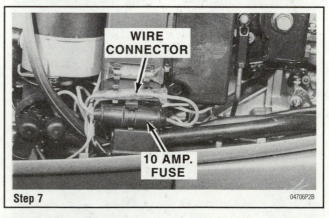

Step 7

V4 and V6 Powerheads

▶ **See accompanying illustrations**

1. Thread one of the mounting bolts through the coil and through the eye of the small Black lead connector. Install this bolt and the other bolt to secure the coil to the powerhead. Connect the White/Black leads with the numbered sleeves to the leads from each coil.

➡If the sleeves were lost and the leads not numbered as instructed during disconnecting, the correct firing order may be lost. There is no other way to determine which lead is for which cylinder other than the sleeves by tracing the leads back to the CDI unit and comparing it to the wiring diagram. These leads are encased in a network of plastic casings which will have to be destroyed in order to trace back the leads. If the leads are disconnected with no sleeves, and if the leads are not identified by markings or a piece of tape, then a trial and error method must be used to find the correct firing order for the powerhead. This might even work on a powerhead equipped with YMIS, because the knock sensor will pick up strange vibrations and send a signal to the microcomputer. At most, the timing will be retarded, but the powerhead will not be shut down.

2. Install the mounting bracket, with CDI unit and rectifier/regulator still

installed onto the powerhead. Refer to the appropriate illustration for correct lead connection to the screw terminals of the CDI unit and the terminals of the rectifier/regulator.

3. Position the rectifier/regulator in the mounting bracket. Install and tighten the two securing screws.

Position the CDI unit in the mounting bracket. Install and tighten the two securing screws.

4. Install the CDI unit cover with the attaching hardware. Tighten the screws securely.

5. Connect the spark plug leads to the spark plugs.

Install the plastic cover over the flywheel. Install the cowling to the powerhead.

Install both leads at the battery terminals, the Red lead to the positive terminal and the Black lead to the negative terminal.

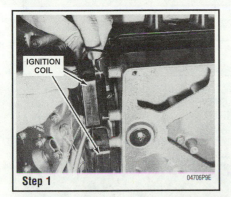

Step 1 04706P9E

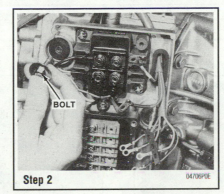

Step 2 04706P0E

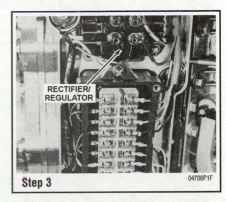

Step 3 04706P1F

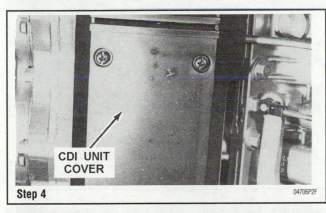

Step 4 04706P2F

Step 5 04706P3F

YAMAHA MICROCOMPUTER IGNITION SYSTEM (YMIS)

Description And Operation

The YMIS uses a microcomputer that analyzes signals sent from several sensors and switches to control ignition timing. The YMIS electronic system uses this detailed input to "custom fit" the timing to meet the needs of the motor in any given situation. This more detailed timing control offers the best performance and fuel economy possible under any set of circumstances. The YMIS primary input is the engine speed (rpm) and throttle position. These two inputs directly determine ignition timing. All other sensors just cause adjustments to the basic timing determined by the throttle position and engine speed.

Most engine problems are not caused by the computer. If ignition timing changes are noticed at the same time as an engine variation, the computer is probably just reacting to a carburetion or basic ignition system problem, not a computer problem. Always check the fuel system fully before troubleshooting the computer.

SYSTEM TYPES

The six different types of YMIS systems are shown in the chart below. The manual A & B connectors on the 220 and 225 allow for complete separation of the computer from the CDI systems. All other systems are automatic and will

jump into the fixed timing basic CDI bypass mode if a sensor, wiring, or supply voltage problem exists.

An intermittent problem can cause severe changes in ignition timing. For both types of systems, when the computer is bypassed, the ignition timing will be retarded and engine performance will be reduced. This will result in reduced fuel flow and any existing carburetion problem may not occur at this reduced fuel flow.

CONTROL UNIT

⬥ **See Figures 49 and 50**

The control unit is mounted on the aft end of the powerhead. It is a Black Box type unit, completely sealed to prevent moisture and tampering. A series of harness wires connect the control unit to engine sensors and circuits.

In addition to the circuits, the microcomputer contains a Central Processing Unit (CPU) an Input/Output (I/O) circuit and a memory map. The control unit is preprogrammed to send a specific set of instructions to the CDI unit after receiving certain signals from its sensors. The program or memory map is engraved in the control unit and differs for several models. Therefore, the microcomputer is not interchangeable between the models.

YMIS System Applications

Models	Computer/CDI	Computer Bypass	Ign. External Sensors	Ign. Internal Sensors	Other Sensors
60~90 Q~	Combined	Automatic	1	1	2 1 (C60, C80)
F40, F50X	Combined	Automatic	2	0	2
F80/F100 X	Combined	Automatic	4	0	3
220N~J/225H~F	Separate	"A" & "B" Connectors	4	0	2
150~225L U~X	Combined	Automatic	2	0	2
225D~T	Combined	Automatic	5	0	2
225X,S~U/250D~U	Combined	Automatic	6	0	2
225XV~X & 250V~X	Combined	Automatic	5	0	5
2.6 EFI X	Combined	Automatic	5	0	4

04706C19

Fig. 49 The control unit for the YMIS is mounted between the 2-cylinder banks

04706P4F

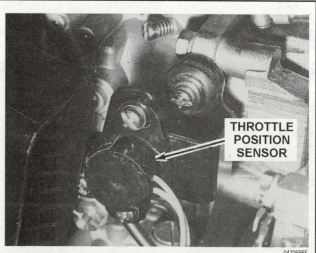

Fig. 50 The control unit is sealed with gel and is not serviceable. The unit can only be tested

04706P5F

THROTTLE POSITION SENSOR

▶ **See Figure 51**

The throttle position sensor is mounted port side on the top carburetor. The sensor is a small potentiometer. The body of the sensor is stationary with a small shaft emerging from the center of the sensor. This shaft is connected to the throttle shaft via a piece of plastic coupling. As the throttle shaft is rotated, the movement is transferred to the sensor and the resistance changes. Therefore, the variable voltage signal sent to the control unit is directly proportional to the throttle valve angle.

CRANKSHAFT POSITION SENSOR

▶ **See Figure 52**

The crank position sensor is mounted on the cylinder block and is positioned a critical (specified) distance from the outer rim of the flywheel. The inside face of the sensor has an electronic pickup device which is sensitive to changes in magnetic flux. The sensor counts the number of flywheel teeth passing the pickup in a specified time and is therefore able to calculate engine rpm. The sensor is also able to detect crank phase angle by counting the number of teeth which pass the pickup from a specified point on the flywheel.

Fig. 51 The throttle position sensor is usually located on the port side of the top carburetor

04706P6F

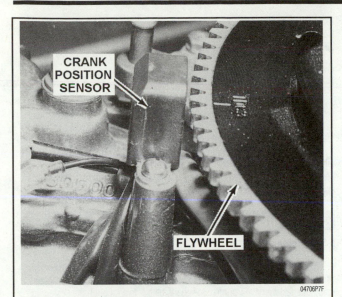

Fig. 52 The crankshaft position sensor is located on the cylinder block, adjacent to the flywheel and determines powerhead speed

KNOCK SENSOR

♦ See Figure 53

The knock sensor is threaded into the side cylinder head. The sensor is able to detect the frequency of vibrations associated with pre-ignition and detonation. If either of these conditions occur due to fuel of an insufficient octane rating (less than 90), or a sudden change in loading of the powerhead, the sensor would be activated. A signal would be sent to the microcomputer, which in turn would retard the ignition timing. If the knocking continues after the reduction in timing has taken place, the sensor will signal the control unit again and a further reduction will take place.

If no more knocking is detected, the ignition timing will gradually revert back to the original setting before the knocking occurred as determined by the control unit under the given operating conditions. The control unit will only take action on the input signal from the knock sensor if there is no accompanying signal from the throttle position sensor or the crank position sensor.

THERMO SENSOR

♦ See Figures 54 and 55

The thermosensor is located in the starboard cylinder head bank. This sensor consists of a Thermistor, an electronic device which acts in the exact opposite manner to a resistor. A resistor changes resistance with a variance in temperature.

If the powerhead temperature exceeds a specified level at a wide open throttle

setting, the thermosensor sends a signal to the control unit. In turn, the control unit sends two signals: one to the buzzer in the remote control box to sound the alarm and another signal to the CDI unit to misfire the cylinders and reduce engine rpm to a safer level. The buzzer continues to sound until the temperature drops to an acceptable level, but the signal to misfire the engine stays in effect until the throttle is backed off.

There is a distinct difference between a thermosensor and a thermoswitch. In the previous paragraph, the thermosensor was identified as a thermistor—an electronic device capable of detecting changes in temperature and transmitting these changes as voltage signals to the microcomputer. A thermoswitch is a bimetal type switch. It consists of two different type metals attached together in a small strip. Because each metal has a different coefficient of expansion—each will expand a different amount within a given temperature range, and the strip will bend rather than extend. If a contact arrangement were to be placed at the end, when heated, the end would bend away from the contact points breaking the electrical circuit. In this manner the bimetal strip serves as a switching device. As soon as a specific temperature is reached, electrical contact is broken.

The thermoswitch therefore only sends an ON or OFF signal, not a variable voltage as in the thermosensor signal. On powerheads covered in this manual, two thermoswitches are installed—one on each of the cylinder banks. A thermoswitch is required on each cylinder bank, because it is possible for the temperature of one bank to vary considerably from the other bank. The cause for such a difference may be due to blockage of a cooling passage or blockage of an oil hose leading to one cylinder. Either one of these conditions will contribute to increased friction, raising the temperature in or around a particular cylinder. The failure of a mechanical part within a cylinder, such as a broken ring, will cause added friction and increased temperature in the area.

Control Unit Functions

ENGINE START CONTROL

When the key is switched to the ON position, and the engine is cranked by the starter motor, a signal is sent from the starter relay to the control unit. The control unit sends back a signal to the CDI unit specifying the ideal setting for the engine to catch and start at cranking rpm.

ENGINE WARM UP CONTROL

From a cold start, the thermosensor detects and reports the engine temperature to the control unit. The throttle position sensor detects and reports the throttle opening to the control unit. When the control unit receives these two signals simultaneously, it overrides the throttle position sensor signal and sends a signal to the CDI unit specifying the ideal setting for ignition timing at a cool engine temperature.

The control unit disregards throttle opening in a cold start situation, but it does not and cannot change the throttle opening. As the engine temperature rises, the control unit readjusts the signal to the CDI unit to maintain the ideal ignition timing in relation to engine temperature.

During cranking of a warm powerhead, a different signal is sent to the control

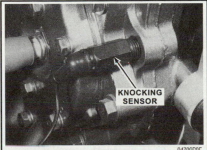

Fig. 53 The knock sensor is usually threaded into the port side of the cylinder head and detects powerhead damaging detonation

Fig. 54 The thermosensor is usually located on the starboard side cylinder bank

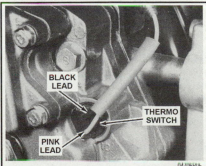

Fig. 55 A thermoswitch, different from the thermosensor, is installed on each cylinder bank

unit. It will take all factors into consideration and the throttle opening will affect the timing.

IDLE STABILIZING CONTROL

Should powerhead rpm be unusually low, on the verge of stalling, this condition would be detected and reported by the crank position sensor. If the throttle opening is too small—as detected by the throttle position sensor—the time delay in providing the engine with an adequate supply of fuel might be too long to prevent the engine from stalling. Therefore, when the control unit, receives information on engine condition from these two sensors (the crank position sensor and the throttle position sensor), the computer immediately advances the ignition timing for the duration of six crankshaft revolutions. This amount of time is usually sufficient for the engine to recover from a near stall condition.

IGNITION TIMING CONTROL

Under normal operating conditions, the ignition timing control is the most used. The throttle position sensor and the crank position sensor supply the control unit with information on throttle opening and powerhead rpm. The control unit sets the ignition timing which is ideal for the present conditions of operation, and alters the setting accordingly with variations in powerhead rpm. Signals from other sensors could be considered bad news, indicating a condition not favorable to powerhead efficiency. Therefore, the control unit will reevaluate and make corrections as required.

OVERHEATING CONTROL

If powerhead temperature exceeds a specified level at a wide open throttle setting, the thermosensor sends a signal to the control unit. In turn, the control unit sends two signals: one to the buzzer in the remote control box to sound the alarm and another signal to the CDI unit to misfire the cylinders and bring down powerhead rpm to a safer level. The buzzer continues to sound until the temperature drops to an acceptable level, but the signal to misfire the engine stays in effect until the throttle is backed off.

OVERREV CONTROL

If rough water or other conditions cause the propeller to rise out of the water, cavitation occurs. A no load situation at the propeller, or a propeller mismatch will cause the powerhead to overrev. Powerhead and lower unit life will be significantly shortened if overrevving for a prolonged period of time is allowed to occur. The crank position sensor detects and informs the control unit when powerhead rpm exceeds 6,000 rpm. In turn, this overrev condition will cause a command to be sent to the CDI unit to misfire the cylinders in sequence, until powerhead rpm falls to an acceptable level.

KNOCK CONTROL

Knocking in the engine usually takes the form of pre-ignition or detonation. Both these conditions are mechanically very damaging.

The knock sensor is able to detect the frequency of vibrations associated with pre-ignition and detonation. If either condition occurs due to fuel of an insufficient octane rating (less than 90), or a sudden change in loading of the powerhead, the sensor is activated. A signal is sent to the micro computer which in turn retards ignition timing.

If the knocking continues after the reduction in timing has taken place, the sensor will signal the control unit again and a further reduction will take place. If no more knocking is detected, the ignition timing will gradually revert back to the original setting before the knocking occurred as determined by the control unit under given operating conditions. The control unit will only take action on the input signal from the knock sensor if there is no accompanying signal from the throttle position sensor or the crank position sensor.

REVERSE DIRECTION CONTROL

If the operator attempts a sudden shift into reverse gear while at cruising speed, the inertial momentum of the propeller would force the crankshaft (and naturally the driveshaft) to abruptly stop and rotate counterclockwise for an instant. The crank position sensor detects and reports such a signal to the control unit. The control unit immediately sends a signal to the CDI unit to misfire all six cylinders until the powerhead stalls.

OPERATING VOLTAGE CONTROL

A minimum operating voltage of 7 volts is necessary for the control unit to function normally. If the voltage falls below this value because a battery cable becomes loose or disconnected, the control unit would be subjected to an on/off situation and could fluctuate powerhead speed by as much as 1,500 rpm.

Therefore, the YMIS control circuit upon receipt of a low (or excessively high) voltage signal limits the timing to 7° BTDC and sends a signal to the CDI unit to misfire the cylinders in sequence, until the powerhead rpm falls to an acceptable level; a maximum of 4,800 rpm.

Self Diagnosis

▶ See Figures 56, 57 and 58

The control unit on several powerheads includes a self-diagnosis system which constantly monitors circuits for shorted or open sensors. Powerheads using this feature have trouble code charts below. Even though the system is capable of monitoring the sensors, it may not indicate all possible sensor problems.

When a fault does occur, the control unit will set a trouble code which can be accessed using a special diagnostic flash harness available from Yamaha. There are several different harnesses, so check with your local dealer to determine which harness you need.

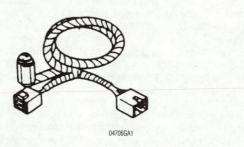

Fig. 56 Several diagnostic flash harnesses are available. The harness consists of three connectors, an LED light and a processor

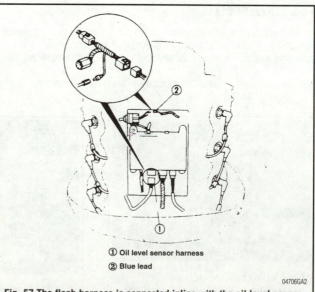

① Oil level sensor harness
② Blue lead

Fig. 57 The flash harness is connected inline with the oil level sensor harness. Another lead is connected to the lead (usually Blue) which activates diagnosis mode

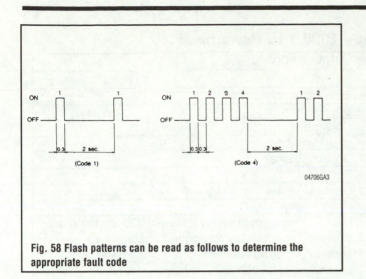

Fig. 58 Flash patterns can be read as follows to determine the appropriate fault code

➡On some systems, the most common trouble codes are Code 33 and Code 34. Most of the time these codes can be traced to a bad ground on the control unit.

1. Install the flash harness inline between the oil level sensor and the control unit. In addition, connect the additional lead (usually Blue) to activate the diagnosis readout.
2. Start the engine and allow it to reach operating temperature.
3. Read the LED on the flash harness and count the number of flashes.

➡If more than on problem is detected, the warning light flashes in the patter of the lower numbered problem. After that problem is corrected, the warning light flashes in the pattern of the next lowest numbered problem. This continues until all of the problems are detected and corrected.

4. Compare the number of flashes to the trouble code lists.
5. Once all codes are read and the associated problems corrected, the LED should flash a Code 1 (Normal Operation).

➡Codes are only present during the actual fault with the engine running and are not stored in memory.

Diagnosis Code Table—1990–95 250 and 1994–95 225

Code	Problem Area	Ignition Timing
1	Normal	Normal 10° ATDC ~ 32° BTDC
2	Crankshaft position sensor	Fixed 7° BTDC ~ 1° BTDC
3	Thermosensor	5° BTDC ~ 32° BTDC
4	Trim sensor	10° BTDC ~ 32° BTDC
5	Knock sensor	Fixed 7° BTDC ~ 1° BTDC
6	Throttle sensor	Fixed 7° BTDC ~ 1° BTDC
7	Fuel Enrichment Solenoid	Normal 10° ATDC ~ 32° BTDC
8	Shift cut switch	Normal 10° ATDC ~ 32° BTDC
9	Thermostat	2° BTDC ~ 32° BTDC
10	Trim angle sensor position	7° ATDC ~ 32° BTDC
11	Pulser coil	Fixed 7° BTDC ~ 1° BTDC

04706C21

Diagnosis Code Table—1996–98 150 and 200; 1996–97 225L

Code	Item	Source/Sensor	Symptom/Comment
1	Normal Condition		
12	Charge coil failure	Charge coil	Engine will not run - no spark
13	Pulser coil failure	Pulser coil	Engine will not run - no spark, or not running on all cylinders.
14	Crank position sensor failure	Crank position sensor	Engine only running on 4 cylinders.
15	Thermosensor failure	Thermosensor	Hard starting or stalling during warm up. No automatic timing advance when the engine is cold.
19	Battery failure	Yellow main power wire	Normal ignition operation if charge coil is working.
42	2000 rpm reduction system operating	Overheat or oil level sensor	Engine operates at 2000 rpm; buzzer may also operate.
43	Engine low on oil	Engine oil sender	Buzzer. Check oil system. Code only occurs when below 2000 rpm.
44	Engine stop lanyard switch	Engine stop lanyard switch	Engine will not run. Check that lanyard plate is installed and check switch.
Others	Internal ECU system	ECU	Many codes appear when various ECU systems are operating normally. Stop engine, check all connections and ground wires, then restart. If code still occurs, possibly ECU is bad.

04706C22

Diagnosis Code Table—1996 3.1L Powerhead

Code	Item	Output Source
1	Normal Condition	
12	Charge Coil	
13	Pulser Coil	Unusual signal
14	Crank position sensor failure	No signal
15	Thermosensor failure	Unusual signal
16	Thermosensor failure	Unusual signal
17	Knock sensor failure	No signal
18	Throttle sensor failure	Unusual signal
19	Battery voltage failure	Unusual signal
31~44	Internal ECU system	Many codes appear when various ECU systems are operating normally. Stop engine, check all connections and ground wires, then restart. If code still occurs, possibly the ECU is bad.

04706C23

Diagnosis Code Table—1997–98 3.1L Powerhead

Code	Item	Output Source
1	Normal Condition	
13	Pulser coil failure	Unusual signal
14	Crank position sensor failure	No signal
15	Thermosensor failure	Unusual signal
16	Thermosensor failure	Unusual signal
17	Knock sensor failure	No signal
18	Throttle sensor failure	Unusual signal
19	Battery voltage failure	Unusual signal
22	Atmospheric pressor sensor	Unusual signal (EFI models only)
23	Air temperature sensor	Unusual signal (EFI models only)
31~44	Internal ECU system	Many codes appear when various ECU systems are operating normally. Stop engine, check all connections and ground wires, then restart. If code still occurs, possibly the ECU is bad.

04706C24

Troubleshooting

The first objective of troubleshooting the YMIS system is to determine if the problem is ignition timing related. A weak spark or no spark is usually caused by the basic ignition components (stator, pulser, ignition coil, CDI, or wiring), not the computer system.

The Yamaha high voltage spark has different characteristics than the spark produced by some other manufacturer's engines. When looking for a spark, especially when in direct sunlight, the Yamaha spark may be hardly visible. If using an aftermarket spark checker, it is possible for electrical radio interference from this checker to interfere with proper computer operation and cause an erratic spark. If you are unsure of your test results, repeat the test in the shade using a resistor spark plug.

If the computer system is suspected, experience has shown that the problem is usually not the computer unit itself. Most computer problems are caused by either a bad sensor, poor connections or grounds or basic engine problems.

1992–98 60, C60, C80 AND 90 POWERHEADS

This system is unique in that there is only one pulser that controls cylinder #1 & #3. The ignition timing for cylinder #2 is entirely controlled by the computer. This means that when any problem occurs and the computer automati-

cally goes into the bypass mode, cylinder #2 will not fire and timing will be fixed.

This system is also the only YMIS system that has the throttle sensor incorporated into the main control unit. All electrical power is supplied by the charge coils and there are no connections to battery power.

Check for spark to #2. If there is no spark, check the yellow lead and crank position sensor. If there is spark, disconnect the linkage to the throttle sensor and check for timing changes while moving the throttle sensor.

1990–95 225 (2.6L) POWERHEAD

This is an updated version of the original YMIS system. The CDI and the computer were integrated into one component. The automatic bypass system will operate if a problem occurs or a sensor is disconnected. The knock sensor circuit was changed to eliminate the possible engine cycling. The new system will hold the retarded timing until the throttle is returned to idle.

Erratic operation at one throttle setting can be caused by a bad spot on the throttle sensor. Use an ohmmeter or voltmeter to check for a smooth change in the sensor readings as the sensor is moved from idle position to wide open throttle. If sensor voltage spikes or resistance is erratic, replace the sensor.

General erratic operation can be a symptom of ignition noise. Check resistor spark plugs and caps for condition. Replace spark plugs and caps if defective.

YMIS Sensor Characteristics

Sensor	Purpose	Failure Symptom	60~90	220, 225H-F	225D-(L)S,T	150~225L U-V	250, 225X)S-U	3.1L V~X, 2.6L X EFI	Notes
Crank Position	Crank position and RPM	Computer will not operate	X	X	X	X	X	X	Critical sensor but failure rare.
Throttle Sensor	Throttle opening - load	Erratic timing changes	X	X	X		X	X	Most common failure item. Located on CDI for 60~90
Knock Sensor	Detects engine vibrations caused by detonation	Retards timing		X	X		X	X	May operate because of mechanical problems. '84~'89 timing may cycle every 2 minutes. '90~ timing will stay retarded.
Thermo-sensor	Detects cold operation	Advanced timing at idle		X	X	X	X	X	Short to ground can interrupt computer operation
Oil Level Sensor	Detects oil level	2000 rpm operation	X	X	X	X	X	X	Oil System
Overheat Sensor	Detects engine overheat	2000 rpm operation	X	X	X	X	X	X	Warning System
Trim Sensor	Tilt angle (all V6 '90~'95)	Oil will not transfer 225XS/250 advanced timing at idle		X			X		All V6's ('90~'95)
Shift Cut Switch	Aids shifting	Hard shifting or #1 & #3					X	X	Not 2.6L EFI
Atmospheric Pressure Sensor	Detects atmospheric pressures	Richer at high altitude					X		
Atmospheric Temp. Sensor	Detects atmospheric Temperatures	Maximum speed not reached. Richer above 5°C (42°F)					X		
Oxygen Sensor	Detects exhaust oxygen density	Maximum speed not reached or surging.						X	Critical for fuel delivery

04706C20

If an extreme lack of power is noticed in an otherwise good running engine, suspect the throttle position sensor of failure. Check the circuit for open or short circuit and replace components as necessary.

A mild lack of power may result from the knock sensor retarding timing due to low quality fuel. The knock sensor will also retard timing if detonation is occurring due to a piston problem. Check the knock sensor for proper operation. If the knock sensor is functioning properly and all other possibilities have been ruled out, check the pistons for wear or damage.

Fast idle speed can be traced to the idle timing being too high. Check the thermosensor for proper resistance and replace as necessary.

1996–98 150–225L POWERHEADS

This is the latest system for the V6 carburetor line. The system uses a movable timer base, a crank position sensor, and only two pulsers to control all six cylinders. There is no throttle sensor or knock sensor. Basic ignition timing is controlled by the movable timer base, but the computer will adjust timing for some specific conditions; Like engine start and warm up. The computer includes a diagnosis system similar to the 250 system that uses a blinking light.

1990–95 250, 225X, 225U AND 1996–98 3.1L POWERHEADS

This is the most advanced YMIS system. The computer includes a self-diagnosis system. This system will check for shorted or open sensors, but will not indicate all possible sensor problems. The system also controls a fuel enriching system that includes valves on each carburetor. These valves and the feed pump have power all the time with the ground side control led by the computer.

Erratic operation at one throttle setting can be caused by a bad spot on the throttle sensor. Use an ohmmeter or voltmeter to check for a smooth change in the sensor readings as the sensor is moved from idle position to wide open throttle. If sensor voltage spikes or resistance is erratic, replace the sensor.

General erratic operation can be a symptom of ignition noise. Check resistor spark plugs and caps for condition. Replace spark plugs and caps if defective.

If an extreme lack of power is noticed in an otherwise good running engine, suspect a disconnected or shorted sensor. Check sensor circuits for open or short circuit and replace components as necessary.

Fast idle speed can be traced to the idle timing being too high. Check the thermosensor for proper resistance and replace as necessary.

A rough idle can be traced to a misfire on cylinders 1 and 3. This may be caused by a shift cut switch fault. Check the shift cut switch for proper operation and replace as necessary.

Hard shifting can also be traced the shift cut switch. Check the shift cut switch for proper operation and replace as necessary.

Testing

Nothing can be more frustrating than an intermittent failure of a component. The following resistance tests provide a procedure to test components in a laboratory situation mostly at room temperature in ideal working conditions. Unfortunately, this does not provide 100% reliable test results. The sensor, switch, wire harness, and the connector, are all subjected to vibration and temperature extremes during actual operation of the powerhead. If the component could be tested in these operating conditions it might register readings which are borderline with the specifications. If the heat or the vibration becomes excessive, the part may temporarily fail. Perhaps even if tested as outlined in the following section—Operational Testing, the conditions may not be severe enough to induce the part to fail. The best advice is to attempt to duplicate the conditions under which the part failed before troubleshooting can be successful.

CONTROL UNIT

No test exists, either in resistance values or operational performance for the microcomputer. If all the sensor signals are processed correctly, all the sensor signals are processed correctly, all engine control circuits function, and the timing is correct then the microcomputer is alive and well.

If the following tests and conditions have been performed or met:
All tests performed on the sensors.

All test performed on the switches.
Operational checks on the system have been conducted and are satisfactory.
All connectors have been checked and rechecked.
The battery is ample in size and power.

Then it might be best to take the complete outboard unit to the local Yamaha dealer for a second opinion before rushing out and buying a new, expensive, non-returnable microcomputer. A second opinion might be less expensive than a new microcomputer unit. If the sad verdict indicates the outboard does need a new microcomputer, the installation labor should be minimal, the work will most likely be guaranteed, the problem definitely solved, and the owner will have peace of mind.

YMIS POWER SUPPLY

▶ **See Figure 59**

1.   Obtain a voltmeter with probe leads, able to pierce through wire insulation in order to obtain a reading without disconnecting the leads or damaging the insulation. Select the V100 scale on the meter. Identify the Yellow lead from the microcomputer. Do not disconnect this lead. Make contact with the Red meter lead to the Yellow lead by probing through the insulation. Make contact with the Black meter lead to a suitable ground on the powerhead. Turn the key switch to the on position, but do not start the powerhead. The meter should register between 10 and 12 volts. If the required voltage is not obtained, trace the voltage path back from the Yellow lead through the 10 prong connector, to the harness, to the key switch and on back to the battery if necessary. Keep the Black meter lead in place and use the Red meter lead to probe all connections using the wiring diagram as a guide.

Fig. 59 Check the YMIS power supply by probing the yellow lead through the insulation. Do not disconnect the yellow lead

CRANK POSITION SENSOR

Gap

▶ **See Figure 60**

1.   Measure the gap between the inner face of the crank position sensor and the outer edge of the flywheel teeth. This distance should be between $1/32$–$1/16$ in. (0.5 and 1.5mm).
2.   If the distance is not as specified, loosen the two securing screws and adjust the gap. Tighten the two screws securely to hold this new position.

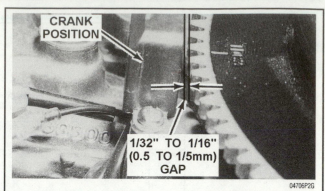

Fig. 60 Measure the gap between the inner face of the crank position sensor and the outer edge of the flywheel teeth

Resistance

▶ **See Figure 61**

1.   Disconnect the leads from the sensor at their harness connector.
2.   Using an ohmmeter measure the resistance across the two leads. On three wire sensors, measure resistance between the Green/White and Green/Blue wires on late model units or the Brown and Black wires on early model units.
3.   Resistance should be between 179–242 ohms at 70°F. If the reading is not within specification, the sensor is faulty.
4.   To replace the sensor, simply remove the two securing screws and remove the sensor. Install the new sensor and adjust.

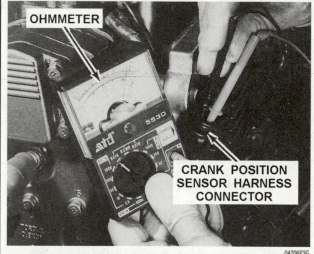

Fig. 61 Crankshaft position sensor resistance is checked at the sensor connector using an ohmmeter

Operational

▶ **See Figures 62 and 63**

1.   Start the powerhead and allow it to reach operating temperature.
2.   Verify the ignition timing is still within specification, with all sensors connected and the powerhead at idle rpm.
3.   Identify the harness connector from the crank position sensor.
4.   Disconnect the two halves of the connector. The powerhead should stall.
5.   The symptoms of a defective crank position sensor are: engine rpm surges and erratic timing shifts.
6.   To replace the sensor, simply remove the two securing screws and remove the sensor. Install the new sensor and adjust.

KNOCK SENSOR

Resistance

▶ See Figure 64

1. Disconnect the lead from the sensor at the harness connector.
2. Using an ohmmeter measure the resistance between the single lead and a good ground. Resistance should be infinite (no continuity). If the reading is less than infinity, there is a short in the sensor.
3. Adjustment or service of the sensor is not possible.
4. To replace the sensor, simply unscrew it from the powerhead.

Operational

▶ See Figure 65

1. Increase powerhead speed to maximum rpm. Aim a timing light at the timing pointer and note the number of degrees of advance.
2. The timing should be fully advanced. If the timing is not fully advanced, the knock sensor is defective and is giving a false reading. This may be because the octane rating of the fuel to too low or an internal problem exists in the powerhead.
3. To replace the sensor, simply unscrew it from the powerhead.

THERMOSWITCH TEST

Operational

▶ See Figure 66

1. Identify the leads (usually Pink and Black) from one of the two thermoswitches.
2. Disconnect the two leads at the quick disconnect fittings.
3. Increase engine speed to just above 2500 rpm.

4. Touch the two leads from the switch together. The warning buzzer should sound continuously and powerhead rpm should drop to 2000 rpm.
5. Reconnect the leads, back the throttle down to idle rpm and the buzzer should be silent.
6. Repeat this test for the second thermoswitch installed in the other cylinder bank.
7. If the thermoswitch does not operate as specified, either the switch or its circuit are faulty.

THERMOSENSOR

Resistance

▶ See Figure 67

➡ Resistance tests cannot be performed while the sensor is installed in the powerhead. Therefore, remove the sensor from the block.

1. Disconnect the wire harness connector, at the quick disconnect fitting.
2. The resistance of the sensor is monitored at different temperatures while heating the sensing end of the sensor in a body of water.
3. Place the container of water, at room temperature, on a stove. Secure the thermometer in the water in such a manner to prevent the bulb from contacting the sides or bottom of the pan.
4. Immerse the sensing ends of the sensor into the water up to the shoulder.
5. Check resistance across the sensor terminals. Resistance should be approximately 61.6 kilohms at 68°F (20°C) and 3.3 kilohms at 212°F (100°C).
6. Resistance should rise and fall evenly with temperature. Remember, the thermosensor is a thermistor which characteristically varies resistance (increases or decreases voltage) with a change in temperature.
7. If resistance is not within specification or does not fluctuate evenly, the sensor is faulty.
8. To replace the sensor, simply unscrew it from the powerhead.

Fig. 62 The crankshaft position sensor is located adjacent to the flywheel and can be identified by its two Blue wires

Fig. 63 Push back the solenoid boot and disconnect the main power lead to the starter motor from the starter relay

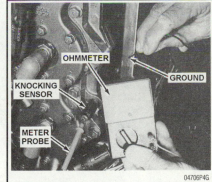

Fig. 64 Knock sensor should show infinite when tested with an ohmmeter

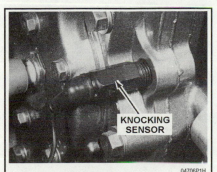

Fig. 65 Operational testing of the knock sensor is performed by check the ignition timing

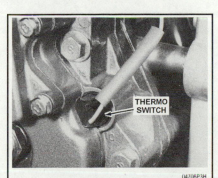

Fig. 66 With the leads of the thermoswitch connected, powerhead rpm should drop and a warning buzzer should sound

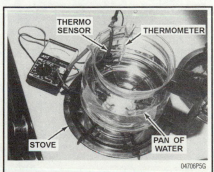

Fig. 67 Thermosensor resistance should increase smoothly as the temperature rises and fall smoothly as it decreases

Operational

◆ See Figures 68 and 69

1. Mount the engine in a test tank, or on a boat in a body of water.
2. Connect a timing light and tachometer to the powerhead.
3. Start the engine and allow it to warm to operating temperature.
4. Aim the timing light at the timing pointer and ensure the initial timing is at specification.
5. Disconnect the thermosensor wire harness at the quick disconnect fitting and use a small jumper cable and connect the two leads together. The timing should now retard and the engine rpm decrease.
6. Remove the thermosensor from the head. Reconnect the leads to the sensor and hold the sensing end of the sensor against an ice cube. The timing should now advance and the engine rpm increase.
7. To replace the sensor, simply unscrew it from the powerhead.

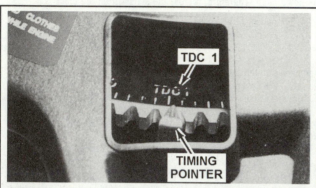

Fig. 68 Mark the timing locations on the flywheel prior to starting the thermosensor test

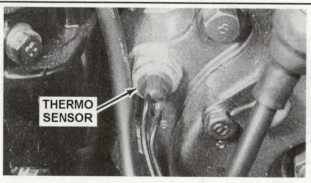

Fig. 69 The thermosensor is located on the cylinder head and can be identified by looking for the two Black wires

THROTTLE POSITION SENSOR

Adjustment

◆ See Figures 70 and 71

➠The throttle position sensor must be adjusted with the throttle plates fully closed. If it is necessary to disturb the setting of the throttle stop screw, adjust the throttle stop after the calibration of the sensor is complete. Readjust the setting on the throttle stop screw.

1. Loosen the throttle stop screw until the tip of the screw backs away from the throttle arm stopper. The throttle stop screw is located close to the throttle roller and is the only vertical screw equipped with a spring.

➠The meter used in this test must have probes capable of piercing through the insulation of the wires to make contact without disconnecting the leads or damaging the insulation of the leads.

2. Ensure the two mounting screws of the sensor are loose enough to permit the sensor to be rotated a few degrees either way but tight enough to still hold its position.
3. Turn the key to the ON position without starting the powerhead.
4. Connect the voltmeter between the sensor signal wire and ground (usually the Pink and Orange or Pink and Black wires). Voltage should be between 0.47–0.51 volts. If voltage is not within specification, rotate the sensor until correct voltage is obtained. Tighten the mounting screws on the sensor to hold this position.

With the voltmeter still connected, open and close the throttle valve a few times to be sure the output voltage fluctuates with different throttle angles. Also, check to see if the voltage reverts back to the specified level when the throttle valves are fully closed.

Tighten the throttle stop screw until it contacts the throttle arm stopper, then continue to tighten screw 1⅛ turns more, as a preliminary adjustment.

Resistance

◆ See Figure 71

1. Disconnect the leads from the sensor at their harness connector.
2. Using an ohmmeter measure the resistance across the sensor terminals (usually the Orange and Red wires).
3. Resistance should be between 4–6 kilohms at 68°F (20°C). If the reading is not within specification, the sensor is faulty.
4. To replace the sensor, simply remove the two securing screws and remove the sensor. Install the new sensor and adjust.

Operational

◆ See Figure 72

1. Identify the wire harness from the throttle position sensor.
2. Verify the ignition timing is correct with all sensors connected and the powerhead at idle rpm.
3. Disconnect the two halves of the harness plug. There should be no change in the timing or engine rpm.
4. Obtain a small jumper cable and connect the reference and signal wires together (usually the Pink and Red wires) in the connector leading from the sensor. The ignition timing should advance.

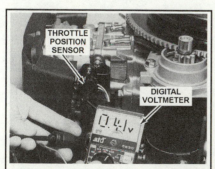

Fig. 70 Throttle position sensor output voltage is used to adjust the throttle position sensor properly

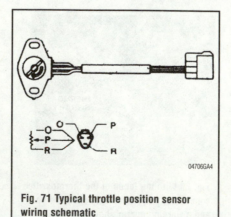

Fig. 71 Typical throttle position sensor wiring schematic

Fig. 72 The throttle position sensor can be identified by its adjustment bolts and three lead harness

TIMING AND SYNCHRONIZATION 7-2
INTRODUCTION 7-2
    TIMING 7-2
    SYNCHRONIZATION 7-2
    PREPARATION 7-2
2 HP MODEL 7-2
    IGNITION TIMING 7-2
    IDLE SPEED 7-3
3 HP MODEL 7-3
    IGNITION TIMING 7-3
    IDLE SPEED 7-3
4 HP AND 5 HP MODELS 7-4
    IGNITION TIMING 7-4
    IDLE SPEED 7-4
    THROTTLE LINKAGE
        ADJUSTMENT 7-4
6 HP AND 8 HP MODELS 7-4
    IGNITION TIMING 7-4
    IDLE SPEED 7-5
    THROTTLE LINKAGE
        ADJUSTMENT 7-5
9.9 HP AND 15 HP MODELS 7-5
    IGNITION TIMING 7-5
    THROTTLE LINKAGE
        ADJUSTMENT 7-6
    IDLE SPEED 7-7
C25 MODEL 7-7
    IGNITION TIMING 7-7
    CARBURETOR LINKAGE
        ADJUSTMENT 7-7
    THROTTLE LINKAGE
        ADJUSTMENT 7-7
    IDLE SPEED 7-7
25 HP MODEL 7-7
    IGNITION TIMING 7-7
    IDLE SPEED 7-8
    LINK ROD ADJUSTMENT 7-8
30 HP (2-CYLINDER) MODEL 7-9
    IGNITION TIMING 7-9
    IDLE SPEED 7-9
    THROTTLE CABLE 7-9
    THROTTLE CONTROL LINK 7-9
30 HP (3-CYLINDER) MODEL 7-9
    IGNITION TIMING 7-9
    CARBURETOR LINKAGE 7-10
    PICKUP TIMING 7-10
    IDLE SPEED 7-10
    THROTTLE CABLE
        ADJUSTMENT 7-11
    OIL PUMP LINK ADJUSTMENT 7-11
C40 (2-CYLINDER) MODEL 7-11
    DYNAMIC TIMING 7-11
    STATIC TIMING 7-12
    CARBURETOR LINK 7-12
    IDLE SPEED 7-13
    THROTTLE LINK 7-13
40 HP, 50 HP AND PRO 50
    MODELS 7-14
    IGNITION TIMING 7-14

    THROTTLE LINKAGE 7-14
    THROTTLE CABLE 7-14
    IDLE SPEED 7-14
    OIL PUMP LINK 7-14
C55 MODELS 7-14
    IGNITION TIMING 7-14
    CARBURETOR LINKAGE 7-15
    IDLE SPEED 7-15
PRO 60, 70 HP AND 90 HP
    MODELS 7-15
    TIMING PLATE POSITION 7-15
    IGNITION TIMING 7-15
    PICKUP TIMING 7-15
    THROTTLE SENSOR CONTROL
        LINK 7-15
    IDLE SPEED 7-16
    CARBURETOR LINKAGE 7-16
    OIL PUMP LINK 7-16
C75 HP AND C85 MODELS 7-16
    TIMING PLATE POSITION 7-16
    IGNITION TIMING 7-16
    PICKUP TIMING 7-17
    IDLE SPEED 7-17
    CARBURETOR LINKAGE 7-17
C115 MODELS 7-17
    TIMING PLATE POSITION 7-17
    IGNITION TIMING 7-17
    PICKUP TIMING 7-17
    IDLE SPEED 7-17
    CARBURETOR LINKAGE 7-18
V4 AND V6 EXCEPT YAMAHA
MICROCOMPUTER IGNITION SYSTEM
(YMIS) 7-18
    IGNITION TIMING 7-18
    CARBURETOR LINKAGE
        ADJUSTMENT 7-18
    CARBURETOR PICKUP TIMING
        ADJUSTMENT 7-18
    IDLE SPEED 7-19
    THROTTLE POSITION SENSOR (225
        HP ONLY) 7-19
    OIL PUMP LINK 7-19
V4 AND V6 WITH YAMAHA
MICROCOMPUTER IGNITION
SYSTEM (YMIS) 7-19
    CARBURETOR LINKAGE 7-19
    CARBURETOR PICKUP TIMING 7-19
    THROTTLE POSITION SENSOR 7-20
    IDLE SPEED 7-20
SPECIFICATIONS CHART
ENGINE TUNE-UP
    SPECIFICATIONS 7-21

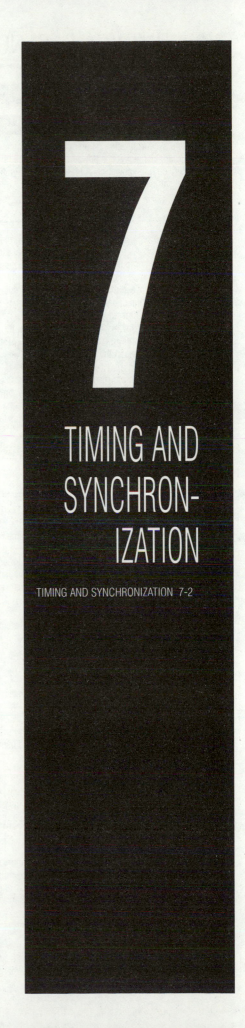

7

TIMING AND SYNCHRON-IZATION

TIMING AND SYNCHRONIZATION

Introduction

Timing and synchronization on an outboard engine is extremely important to obtain maximum efficiency. The powerhead cannot perform properly and produce its designed horsepower output if the fuel and ignition systems have not been precisely adjusted.

TIMING

All outboard powerheads have some type of synchronization between the fuel and ignition systems. All units covered in this manual except those equipped with Yamaha Micro-computer Ignition System (YMIS), are equipped with a mechanical advance type Capacitor Discharge Ignition (CDI) system and use a series of link rods between the carburetor and the ignition base plate assembly. At the time the throttle is opened, the ignition base plate assembly is rotated by means of the link rod, thus advancing the timing.

On models equipped with YMIS, the microcomputer decides when to advance or retard the timing, based on input from various sensors. Therefore, there is no link rod between the magneto control lever and the stator assembly.

Many models have timing marks on the flywheel and CDI base. A timing light is normally used to check the ignition timing dynamically—with the powerhead operating. An alternate method is to check the static timing—with the powerhead not operating. This second method requires the use of a dial indicator gauge.

Various models have unique methods of checking ignition timing. These differences are explained in detail later in this section.

SYNCHRONIZATION

In simple terms, synchronization is timing the carburetion to the ignition. As the throttle is advanced to increase powerhead rpm, the carburetor and the ignition systems are both advanced equally and at the same rate.

Any time the fuel system or the ignition system on a powerhead is serviced to replace a faulty part or any adjustments are made for any reason, powerhead timing and synchronization must be carefully checked and verified. For this reason the timing and synchronizing procedures have been separated from all others and presented alone in this section.

Before making adjustments with the timing or synchronizing, the ignition system should be thoroughly checked and the fuel system verified to be in good working order.

PREPARATION

Timing and synchronizing the ignition and fuel systems on an outboard motor are critical adjustments. The following equipment is essential and is called out repeatedly in this section. This equipment must be used as described, unless otherwise instructed by the equipment manufacturer. Naturally, the equipment is removed following completion of the adjustments.

Dial Indicator

Top dead center (TDC) of the No. 1 (top) piston must be precisely known before the timing adjustment can be made. TDC can only be determined through installation of a dial indicator into the No. 1 spark plug opening.

Timing Light

During many procedures in this section, the timing mark on the flywheel must be aligned with a stationary timing mark on the engine while the powerhead is being cranked or is running. Only through use of a timing light connected to the No. 1 spark plug lead, can the timing mark on the flywheel be observed while the engine is operating.

Tachometer

A tachometer connected to the powerhead must be used to accurately determine engine speed during idle and high-speed adjustment. Engine speed readings range from 0 to 6,000 rpm in increments of 100 rpm. Choose a tachometer with solid state electronic circuits which eliminates the need for relays or batteries and contribute to their accuracy.

A tachometer is installed as standard equipment on most powerheads covered in this manual. Due to local conditions, it may be necessary to adjust the carburetor while the outboard unit is running in a test tank or with the boat in a body of water. For maximum performance, the idle rpm should be adjusted under actual operating conditions. As conditions warrant, it might be necessary to attach a tachometer closer to the powerhead than the one installed on the control panel.

An auxiliary tachometer can be connected by attaching it to the tachometer leads in the control panel. These leads are usually Black and Green. Connect the Black lead to the ground terminal of the auxiliary tachometer and the Green lead to the input or hot terminal of the auxiliary tachometer.

Flywheel Rotation

The instructions may call for rotating the flywheel until certain marks are aligned with the timing pointer. When the flywheel must be rotated, always move the flywheel in a clockwise direction. If the flywheel should be rotated in the opposite direction, the water pump impeller tangs would be twisted backwards. Should the powerhead be started with the pump tangs bent back in the wrong direction, the tangs may not have time to bend in the correct direction before they are damaged. Even a small amount of damage to the water pump will severely restrict the cooling of the powerhead.

Test Tank

Since the engine must be operated at various times and engine speeds during some procedures, a test tank or moving the boat into a body of water, is necessary. If installing the engine in a test tank, outfit the engine with an appropriate test propeller. Test propeller specifications are given in the Tune-up Specifications chart.

✳✳ CAUTION

Water must circulate through the lower unit to the powerhead anytime the powerhead is operating to prevent damage to the water pump in the lower unit. Just five seconds without water will damage the water pump impeller.

➡**Remember the powerhead will not start without the emergency tether in place behind the kill switch knob.**

✳✳ CAUTION

Never operate the powerhead above a fast idle with a flush attachment connected to the lower unit. Operating the powerhead at a high rpm with no load on the propeller shaft could cause the powerhead to runaway causing extensive damage to the unit.

2 Hp Model

IGNITION TIMING

1990–94

◆ **See Figures 1 and 2**

1. Mount the engine in a test tank or move the boat to a body of water.
2. Remove the cowling and connect a tachometer to the powerhead.
3. Remove the flywheel.
4. Remove the spark plug.
5. Disconnect the magneto lead (usually white) from the connector and the stator lead (usually black) from the connector.
6. Check and adjust the breaker point gap as required.

7. Install a dial indicator in the spark plug hole.

8. Rotate the flywheel clockwise until the piston has reached TDC then reset the indicator to zero.

9. Connect an ohmmeter between the magneto wire and a good engine ground.

10. Slowly turn the flywheel clockwise until the ohmmeter indicates continuity. At this point, the indicator should read 0.039–0.048 in. (0.99–1.23mm) BTDC. If the gap is not within specification, loosen the points attaching screw and adjust the gap.

➡️**If the correct gap cannot be obtained by adjustment, the points should be replaced.**

1995–98

The ignition system on these models provides automatic ignition advance. Ignition timing is not adjustable.

IDLE SPEED

1990–94

Idle speed is not adjustable on these models.

1995–98

1. Mount the engine in a test tank or move the boat to a body of water.

2. Remove the cowling and connect a tachometer to the powerhead.

3. Start the engine and allow it to reach operating temperature.

4. Check idle speed. The powerhead should idle at the specified rpm in the Tune-up Specifications chart.

5. If adjustment is necessary, rotate the idle adjustment screw until the powerhead idles at the required rpm.

3 Hp Model

IGNITION TIMING

▶ **See Figure 3**

1. Mount the engine in a test tank or move the boat to a body of water.

2. Remove the cowling and connect a tachometer and a timing light to the powerhead.

3. Start the engine and allow it to warm to operating temperature. Place the engine in gear.

4. Check the idle speed and adjust as necessary.

5. Aim the timing light at the timing windows. If the timing mark can be seen through the left window at idle and the right window at full throttle, the timing is correct.

6. Timing cannot be adjusted. If timing is incorrect, a fault has occurred in the CDI system.

IDLE SPEED

▶ **See Figures 4 and 5**

1. Mount the engine in a test tank or move the boat to a body of water.

2. Remove the cowling and connect a tachometer to the powerhead.

3. Turn the pilot screw in until it lightly seats and then back out the specified number of turns, as indicated in the Tune-up Specifications chart.

4. Start the engine and allow it to warm to operating temperature. Place the engine in gear.

5. Check engine speed at idle. The powerhead should idle in at the rpm specified in the Tune-up Specifications chart.

6. Place the engine in gear and check engine trolling speed in the same manner.

7. If adjustment is necessary, rotate the idle adjustment screw (not the pilot screw) until the powerhead idles at the required rpm.

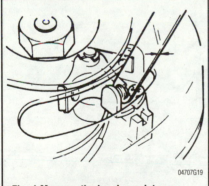

04707G19

Fig. 1 Measure the breaker point gap using a feeler gauge

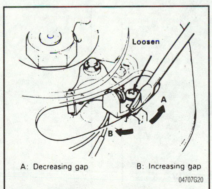

A: Decreasing gap   B: Increasing gap

04707G20

Fig. 2 Using a screwdriver, adjust the breaker point gap by rotating the points

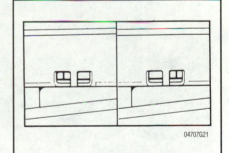

04707G21

Fig. 3 If the timing mark can be seen through the left window at idle and the right window at full throttle, the timing is correct

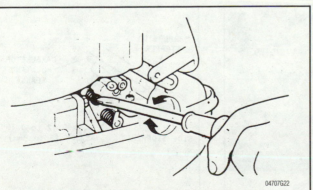

04707G22

Fig. 4 The pilot screw is located in a horizontal position on the carburetor

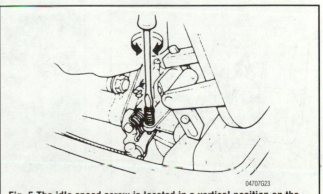

04707G23

Fig. 5 The idle speed screw is located in a vertical position on the carburetor

4 Hp and 5 Hp Models

IGNITION TIMING

♦ **See Figure 6**

The ignition system on these models provides automatic ignition advance. Ignition timing is not adjustable. However, ignition timing should be check periodically to ensure proper powerhead operation.

1. Mount the engine in a test tank or move the boat to a body of water.
2. Remove the cowling and connect a tachometer and a timing light to the powerhead.
3. Start the engine and allow it to warm to operating temperature. Place the engine in gear.
4. Aim the timing light at the timing windows. If the timing mark can be seen through the left window at with the powerhead operating between 1150 and 1700 rpm and the right window at approximately 4500, the timing is correct.
5. Timing cannot be adjusted. If timing is incorrect, a fault has occurred in the CDI system.

IDLE SPEED

♦ **See Figures 7 and 8**

1. Mount the engine in a test tank or move the boat to a body of water.
2. Remove the cowling and connect a tachometer to the powerhead.
3. Turn the pilot screw in until it lightly seats and then back out the specified number of turns, as indicated in the Tune-up Specifications chart.

4. Start the engine and allow it to warm to operating temperature. Place the engine in gear.
5. Check engine speed at idle. The powerhead should idle in at the rpm specified in the Tune-up Specifications chart.
6. Place the engine in gear and check engine trolling speed in the same manner.
7. If adjustment is necessary, rotate the idle adjustment screw (not the pilot screw) until the powerhead idles at the required rpm.

THROTTLE LINKAGE ADJUSTMENT

♦ **See Figures 9 and 10**

1. With the powerhead not operating, rotate the throttle grip to the wide-open throttle position. Verify the full open side stopper for the throttle valve makes contact with the stopper on the carburetor.
2. If the two stoppers fail to make contact before the throttle grip reaches the wide-open throttle position, loosen the screw on the barrel retaining end of the throttle cable and then adjust the length of the cable (wire) protruding from the barrel.
3. The cable should protrude beyond the barrel approximately 0.12–0.16 in. (3–4mm) with the throttle valve in the wide-open throttle position.

6 Hp and 8 Hp Models

IGNITION TIMING

♦ **See Figures 11, 12 and 13**

1. Mount the engine in a test tank or the boat in a body of water.
2. Remove the cowling and connect a tachometer and timing light to the powerhead.
3. Disconnect the link rod between the CDI magneto base and the magneto control lever at the ball joint.

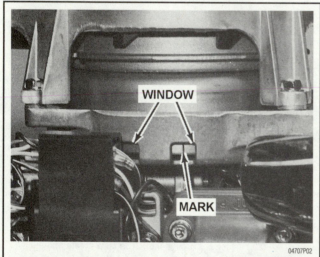

Fig. 6 View through the window showing the timing mark on the flywheel

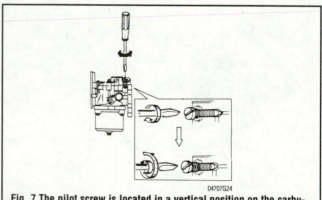

Fig. 7 The pilot screw is located in a vertical position on the carburetor

Fig. 8 The idle speed screw is located in a horizontal position on the carburetor

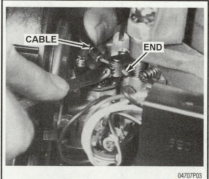

Fig. 9 Loosening the screw on the barrel retaining end of the throttle cable

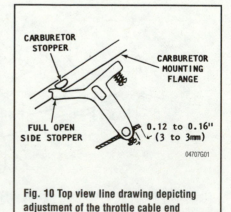

Fig. 10 Top view line drawing depicting adjustment of the throttle cable end

Fig. 11 Make sure the link rod remains disconnected until all adjustments have been completed

Fig. 12 Remove the cowling and connect a timing light to the powerhead as shown

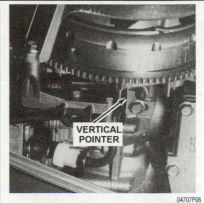

Fig. 13 When the magneto base is rotated counterclockwise until the stopper contacts the vertical timing pointer the full-advanced position is achieved

➡This link rod will remain disconnected until all adjustments have been completed.

4. Start the engine and allow it to reach operating temperature. Rotate the CDI magneto base counterclockwise until the base stopper on the left contacts the vertical timing pointer. This is the full-advanced position.

5. Aim the timing light at the vertical timing pointer. The pointer should align between the 34° BTDC and 36° BTDC embossed marks on the flywheel edge.

6. If the pointer does not align, as described, loosen the bolt on the vertical pointer bracket and move the pointer and the stopper on the magneto base plate together, until the vertical pointer is properly aligned. Hold the magneto base plate and the pointer together with the pointer on the mark and tighten the bolt.

7. Shut down the powerhead.

IDLE SPEED

1. Mount the engine in a test tank or move the boat to a body of water.

2. Remove the cowling and connect a tachometer to the powerhead.

3. Turn the pilot screw in until it lightly seats and then back out the specified number of turns, as indicated in the Tune-up Specifications chart.

4. Start the engine and allow it to warm to operating temperature. Place the engine in gear.

5. Check engine speed at idle. The powerhead should idle in at the rpm specified in the Tune-up Specifications chart.

6. Place the engine in gear and check engine trolling speed in the same manner.

7. If adjustment is necessary, rotate the idle adjustment screw (not the pilot screw) until the powerhead idles at the required rpm.

THROTTLE LINKAGE ADJUSTMENT

♦ See Figure 14

1. Twist the throttle grip to the wide-open throttle position.

2. Adjust the two locknuts on the outer throttle cable (wire) to bring the carburetor throttle lever into contact with the stopper.

3. Tighten both locknuts against the throttle wire stay to hold this position.

4. Bring the left magneto base stopper in contact with the vertical timing pointer.

5. Adjust the length of the link rod so that it snaps over the ball joint on the magneto control lever. Ensure the throttle lever still contacts the stopper and the magneto base stopper still contacts the vertical timing pointer.

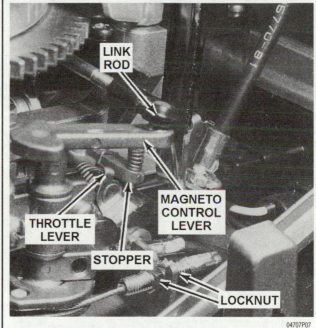

Fig. 14 Throttle linkage components–6Hp and 8Hp models

9.9 Hp and 15 Hp Models

IGNITION TIMING

♦ See Figures 15 thru 20

1. Shift the lower unit into **FORWARD** gear. Pry the link rod free from the ball joint on the magneto control lever.

2. Rotate the flywheel clockwise until the piston is at top dead center (TDC). Zero the needle on the gauge. Rotate the flywheel counterclockwise until the dial indicator gauge registers between 0.155 and 0.144 in. (3.95 and 4.49mm).

3. Rotate the CDI magneto base, under the flywheel, until the pointer on the base aligns between the Y and 30° on the flywheel.

4. Loosen the two bolts on top of the throttle cam. Move the stopper, located underneath the throttle cam, until the stopper makes contact with the crankcase stopper. Tighten both bolts to hold this adjustment.

Fig. 15 In order to set the ignition timing, the cylinder head must be removed and a dial indicator secured over the No. 1 piston dome

Fig. 16 The pointer on the base should align between the Y and 30° marks on the flywheel

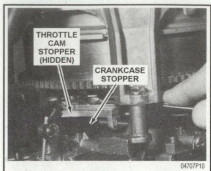

Fig. 17 Move the throttle cam stopper until it makes contact with the crankcase stopper

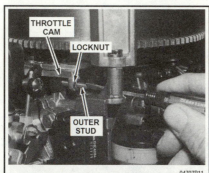

Fig. 18 The locknut is located on the outer adjustment stud on the right side of the throttle cam

Fig. 19 The roller should contact the high point of the throttle cam

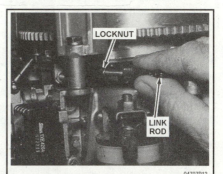

Fig. 20 Adjust the length of the rod so it snaps onto the ball joint without any movement

5. Rotate the flywheel clockwise until the dial indicator gauge registers Zero again. With the gauge at Zero, the piston will be at TDC.

6. Rotate the flywheel counterclockwise until the dial indicator registers between 0.003 and 0.007 in. (0.07 and 0.17mm). Loosen the locknut on the outer adjustment stud on the right side of the throttle cam. Rotate the CDI magneto base, under the flywheel, until the pointer on the base aligns between the 4° and 6° marks on the flywheel. Position the outer adjustment stud to just make contact with the crankcase stopper. Tighten the locknut to hold the adjustment.

7. Twist the throttle grip to the wide-open throttle position. Observe the location of the roller against the throttle cam. If necessary, move the throttle cam until the roller contacts the high point of the cam.

8. Loosen the locknut on the link rod. Adjust the length of the rod to enable the rod to snap onto the ball joint on the magneto control lever, without any movement at the other end of the rod. Tighten the locknut to hold this adjustment. Rotate the throttle grip from fast to the full-closed position.

9. Observe if crankcase stopper makes contact with the stopper beneath the throttle cam in the full-advanced position and then makes contact with the outer adjustment stud on the throttle cam in the fully retarded position.

THROTTLE LINKAGE ADJUSTMENT

▶ **See Figures 21 and 22**

1. Twist the throttle grip to the wide-open throttle position.
2. With the lower unit in **FORWARD** gear, loosen the joint link set screw.
3. Push down on the top of the joint link to bring the throttle lever into contact with the stopper and to position the throttle roller at the high point of the throttle cam.
4. Tighten the joint link set screw to hold the adjustment.
5. With the throttle grip still twisted the to the wide-open throttle position, pry off the link rod from the ball joint at the top of the magneto control lever.
6. Push in the lever until it makes contact with the stopper stay.

7. Loosen the locknut on the link rod and adjust the length of the rod until it can be snapped back into place on the ball joint of the magneto control lever, without any movement at the other end of the rod.
8. Tighten the locknut to hold the adjusted length.
9. Return the throttle grip to the full-closed position.

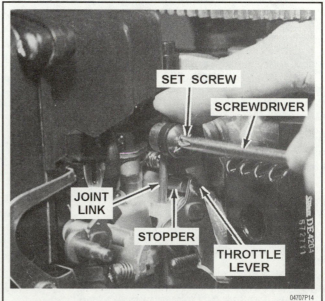

Fig. 21 Loosen the joint link set screw and bring the throttle lever into contact with the stopper

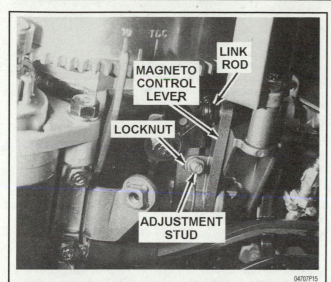

Fig. 22 Loosen the locknut on the link rod and adjust the length of the rod until it can be snapped back into place on the ball joint

IDLE SPEED

1. Mount the engine in a test tank or move the boat to a body of water.
2. Remove the cowling and connect a tachometer to the powerhead.
3. Turn the pilot screw in until it lightly seats and then back out the specified number of turns, as indicated in the Tune-up Specifications chart.
4. Start the engine and allow it to warm to operating temperature. Place the engine in gear.
5. Check engine speed at idle. The powerhead should idle in at the rpm specified in the Tune-up Specifications chart.
6. Place the engine in gear and check engine trolling speed in the same manner.
7. If adjustment is necessary, rotate the idle adjustment screw (not the pilot screw) until the powerhead idles at the required rpm.

C25 Model

IGNITION TIMING

1. Pry the link rod free from the ball joint on the magneto control lever.
2. Remove the park plug and install a dial indicator in the No. 1 cylinder spark plug hole.
3. Rotate the flywheel clockwise until the piston is at top dead center (TDC).
4. Check the timing pointer with the flywheel timing scale. If alignment is incorrect, loosen the timing pointer nut and move the pointer as required to align the pointer with the 0° mark on the flywheel.
5. Rotate the flywheel clockwise until the timing plate is aligned to the full advance timing as specified in the Tune-up Specifications chart.
6. Set the magneto base to the full-advanced position and set the stopper.
7. Loosen the locknut on the link rod and adjust the length of the rod until it can be snapped back into place on the ball joint of the magneto control lever, without any movement at the other end of the rod.

CARBURETOR LINKAGE ADJUSTMENT

1. Loosen the carburetor control link set screw.
2. Set the magneto control lever in the full-advanced position.
3. Adjust the guide collar so that the roller contacts the high point of the accelerator cam.
4. Hold down the control ring and tighten the set screw securely.

THROTTLE LINKAGE ADJUSTMENT

1. Place the lower unit in **FORWARD** gear and loosen the joint link set screw.
2. Adjust the accelerator control link rod so that the center to center length is 2.72 in. (69mm).

IDLE SPEED

1. Mount the engine in a test tank or move the boat to a body of water.
2. Remove the cowling and connect a tachometer to the powerhead.
3. Turn the pilot screw in until it lightly seats and then back out the specified number of turns, as indicated in the Tune-up Specifications chart.
4. Start the engine and allow it to warm to operating temperature. Place the engine in gear.
5. Check engine speed at idle. The powerhead should idle in at the rpm specified in the Tune-up Specifications chart.
6. Place the engine in gear and check engine trolling speed in the same manner.
7. If adjustment is necessary, rotate the idle adjustment screw (not the pilot screw) until the powerhead idles at the required rpm.

25 Hp Model

▶ See Figure 23

IGNITION TIMING

1. Place the lower unit in the **NEUTRAL** gear.
2. Remove the spark plug and install a dial indicator in the No. 1 cylinder spark plug hole.
3. Rotate the flywheel clockwise until the piston is at top dead center (TDC).
4. Check the timing pointer with the flywheel timing scale. If the pointer is not aligned with the TDC mark, loosen the timing pointer nut and move the pointer as required to align the pointer.
5. Remove the dial indicator.
6. Rotate the flywheel clockwise until the timing plate is aligned with to the full advance timing as specified in the Tune-up Specifications chart.
7. Set the magneto base to the full-advanced position (until it touches the stopper).
8. If the timing marks do not align, loosen the locknut on the link rod and adjust the length of the rod until it can be snapped back into place on the ball joint of the magneto control lever without any movement at the other end of the rod.
9. Rotate the flywheel clockwise and align the timing pointer with the idle timing mark as specified in the Tune-up Specifications chart.
10. Set the magneto base to the fully retarded position (until it touches the stopper).
11. If the timing marks do not align, loosen the stopper bolt locknut and adjust the bolt length as required. Tighten the locknut.

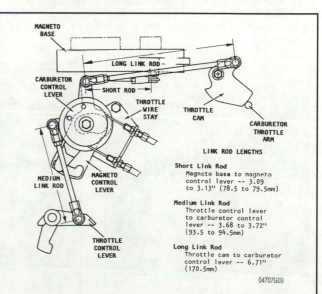

Fig. 23 Location and lengths of the three link rods used on the 25 Hp powerhead

IDLE SPEED

1. Mount the engine in a test tank or move the boat to a body of water.
2. Remove the cowling and connect a tachometer to the powerhead.
3. Turn the pilot screw in until it lightly seats and then back out the specified number of turns, as indicated in the Tune-up Specifications chart.
4. Start the engine and allow it to warm to operating temperature. Place the engine in gear.
5. Check engine speed at idle. The powerhead should idle in at the rpm specified in the Tune-up Specifications chart.
6. Place the engine in gear and check engine trolling speed in the same manner.
7. If adjustment is necessary, rotate the idle adjustment screw (not the pilot screw) until the powerhead idles at the required rpm.

LINK ROD ADJUSTMENT

♦ See Figures 24 thru 30

This model powerhead utilizes three different length link rods. One is short, one is long and the third is of medium length. Two of these rods are connected from the carburetor control lever to different points on the powerhead. The third rod is connected from the magneto control lever behind the carburetor control lever to another point on the powerhead. The carburetor control lever is actually a disc holding the ends of the throttle cables and ends of the rods.

The longest of the link rods is attached to a ball joint in front of the top arm of the carburetor control lever. This link rod extends behind one of the mounting legs of the hand rewind starter to the black plastic cam next to the carburetor. This longest rod activates the throttle cam. The throttle cam activates a roller controlling throttle opening. This link rod is called the throttle cam to the carburetor control lever link rod.

The medium length link rod is also attached to a ball joint in front of a side arm on the carburetor control lever. This rod extends downward and is attached to the ball joint on the throttle control lever. The purpose of this linkage and rod is to limit throttle opening any time the lower unit is in **NEUTRAL** gear. This link rod is called the throttle control to carburetor control lever link rod.

One end of the shortest rod is attached to the ball joint behind the magneto control lever. The other end of the short rod is attached to a ball joint on the underside of the CDI magneto base. This rod serves to advance the magneto base with increased throttle opening. This shortest rod is called the magneto base to magneto control lever link rod.

The fully retarded ignition timing is automatically adjusted when the full-advanced ignition timing is set correctly.

1. Pry off the three link rods at their ball joints at the carburetor control lever arms and at the magneto control lever arm.
2. Rotate the magneto base until the stopper on the base contacts the crankcase stopper. This action sets the base in the full-advanced position. Shift the lower unit into **FORWARD** gear and twist the throttle grip to the wide-open throttle position.

3. Loosen the locknut on the shortest link rod (the magneto base to magneto control lever link rod).
4. Adjust the length of the rod until the measurement from the ball joint center to the ball joint center is from 3.09 to 3.13 in. 78.5 to 79.5mm). After the measurement is satisfactory, snap the rod over the inside magneto control lever ball joint and tighten the locknut on the rod to hold this adjusted length.
5. Push down on the throttle roller until the throttle arm stopper contacts the wide open stopper. At the same time, rotate the throttle arm clockwise until the cam contacts the roller. Hold the roller and cam in this position for the next step.
6. Loosen the locknut on the longest link rod (the throttle cam to carburetor control lever link rod). Adjust the length of the rod until the measurement from the ball joint center to the ball joint center is 6.71 in. (170.5mm). After the measurement is satisfactory, snap the rod over the front upper arm of the carburetor control lever and tighten the locknut on the rod to hold the adjusted length.

Now, loosen the top locknut on the upper throttle wire and tighten the bottom locknut to take up the slack on the throttle wire. Loosen the top locknut on the lower throttle wire and tighten the bottom locknut to provide a deflection of 0.04 to 0.08 in. (1 to 2mm) at the mid point of the wire length.

7. Twist the throttle grip from the wide-open throttle position to the full-closed position. Check to verify the CDI magneto base stopper contacts the stoppers on the crankcase at the fully open and fully closed positions. If the stoppers fail to make contact, check the lengths of the two link rods as previously described.

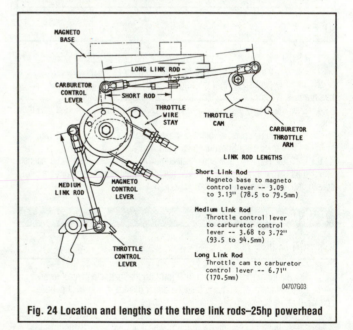

Fig. 24 Location and lengths of the three link rods–25hp powerhead

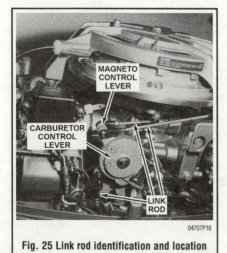

Fig. 25 Link rod identification and location

Fig. 26 Rotate the magneto base until the stopper on the base contacts the

Fig. 27 Push down on the throttle roller and rotate the throttle arm clockwise until the cam contacts the roller

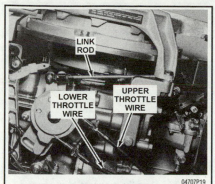

Fig. 28 The longest link rod is located just above the throttle wires

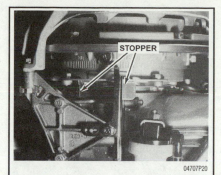

Fig. 29 Verify the CDI magneto base stopper contacts the stoppers on the crankcase at the fully open and fully closed positions

Fig. 30 Medium length link rod location on the powerhead

8. Loosen the locknut on the mid-length link rod (the throttle control to carburetor control lever link rod).

9. Adjust the length of the rod until the measurement from the ball joint center to the ball joint center is 3.68 to 3.72 in. (93.5 to 94.5mm). Snap the rod over the front lower arm of the carburetor control lever and tighten the locknut on the rod to hold the adjusted length.

30 Hp (2-Cylinder) Model

IGNITION TIMING

1. Mount the engine in a test tank or move the boat to a body of water.
2. Remove the cowling and connect a tachometer and a timing light to the powerhead.
3. Start the engine and allow it to warm to operating temperature. Place the lower unit in Neutral.
4. Increase engine speed to 4500–5500 and aim the timing light at the indicator on the starter case. It should align with the specified timing full throttle timing figure in the Tune-up Specifications chart.
5. If the timing mark is not aligned properly, stop the engine, shift the lower unit into **FORWARD** and rotate the flywheel until the timing marks align properly.
6. Rotate the magneto base and align the timing mark with the ignition mark on the rotor.
7. If the magneto base stopper is not in contact with the full open stopper on the cylinder body, loosen the holding bolts and adjust until proper contact is made.
8. Ensure the full open (T) mark on the accelerator cam aligns with the center of the cam roller.
9. If alignment is not as specified, loosen the accelerator cam bolts and align the full open (T) mark with the center of the carburetor throttle roller. Tighten the holding bolts.
10. Remove the starter.
11. Loosen the rod adjusting screw and adjust the rod so the throttle is fully open and the open stopper is pushed up against the stopper. Tighten the screw.
12. Install the starter.

IDLE SPEED

1. Mount the engine in a test tank or move the boat to a body of water.
2. Remove the cowling and connect a tachometer to the powerhead.
3. Turn the pilot screw in until it lightly seats and then back out the specified number of turns, as indicated in the Tune-up Specifications chart.
4. Start the engine and allow it to warm to operating temperature. Place the engine in gear.
5. Check engine speed at idle. The powerhead should idle in at the rpm specified in the Tune-up Specifications chart.
6. Place the engine in gear and check engine trolling speed in the same manner.

7. If adjustment is necessary, rotate the idle adjustment screw (not the pilot screw) until the powerhead idles at the required rpm.

THROTTLE CABLE

1. With the lower unit in **FORWARD** gear, twist the throttle grip to the wide-open throttle position.
2. The magneto base stopper should be in contact with the full open stopper.
3. If adjustment is necessary, loosen the adjust locknut on the pull side of the throttle cable. Turn the adjusting bolt until all slack is taken up and tighten the locknut.
4. Loosen the adjust locknut on the push side of the throttle cable. Turn the adjusting bolt until 0.12 in (3mm) slack is present with the throttle grip in the Slow position. Tighten the locknut.
5. Ensure the throttle shaft full open stopper contacts the full open stopper on the carburetor with the throttle in the wide-open throttle position.
6. If the throttle stopper is not a specified, loosen the locking screw and adjust it to specification.
7. Now adjust the throttle control link.

THROTTLE CONTROL LINK

➡The throttle cable must be adjusted prior to adjusting the throttle control link.

1. Twist the throttle grip to the wide-open throttle position.
2. With the lower unit in **FORWARD** gear, ensure the magneto base stopper is in contact with the stopper on the cylinder and the throttle control lever I in contact with the stopper on the bottom cowling.
3. If these condition do not exist, proceed as follows.
4. Disconnect the link rod between the CDI magneto base and the magneto control lever at the ball joint.
5. Rotate the magneto base plate until the stopper is in contact with the stopper on the cylinder.
6. Twist the throttle grip to the wide-open throttle position.
7. Adjust the connector on the end of the link rod so the center to center length is 1.81 in. (46mm).
8. Connect the link rod between the CDI magneto base and the magneto control lever at the ball joint without moving the magneto base.

30 Hp (3-Cylinder) Model

IGNITION TIMING

◆ See Figures 31, 32 and 33

1. Pry off the short link rod between the magneto control lever and the CDI magneto base at the base ball joint.
2. Remove the No. 1 (top) spark plug and install a dial indicator gauge into

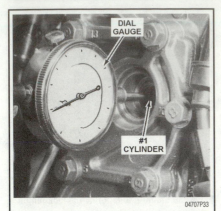
Fig. 31 Install a dial indicator gauge into the cylinder on top of the piston crown

Fig. 32 Check to verify the timing pointer is aligned with the TDC mark embossed on the flywheel

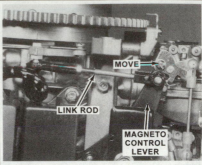
Fig. 33 Rotate the magneto base counter-clockwise to align the single line timing mark on the base with the TDC mark on the flywheel

the cylinder on top of the piston crown. Rotate the flywheel clockwise until the dial indicator registers TDC (top dead center).

3. Observe the timing plate on the port side of the powerhead. Check to verify the timing pointer is aligned with the TDC mark embossed on the flywheel. If the pointer is not aligned, loosen the timing plate set bolt beneath the pointer and move the pointer to the correct location. Tighten the bolt to hold the pointer aligned with the TDC mark.

4. Remove the dial indicator gauge and install the spark plug. Connect the high tension lead.

5. Rotate the flywheel clockwise until the timing pointer aligns with the 25° BTDC mark embossed on the flywheel.

6. Rotate the magneto base counterclockwise to align the single line timing mark on the base with the TDC mark on the flywheel. Check to verify the magneto base stopper makes contact with the crankcase stopper. If they do not make contact or if they do make contact but the TDC mark is not aligned with the single line mark on the base, loosen the base stopper set bolt, align the marks, bring the stoppers into contact and then tighten the bolt.

CARBURETOR LINKAGE

▶ See Figures 34, 35, 36 and 37

1. Loosen the throttle stop screw by turning clockwise until clearance develops between the screw and the throttle valve stop.
2. Close the throttle valves.
3. Loosen the throttle stop screws for the No. 1 and No. 2 carburetors .
4. Make sure all carburetor throttle valves are closed, then lightly depress the No. 2 carburetor
throttle roller and tighten the No. 1 and No. 2 throttle stop screws.
5. Adjust the idle speed.

PICKUP TIMING

▶ See Figures 34, 38 and 39

1. Mount the engine in a test tank or move the boat to a body of water.
2. Remove the cowling and connect a tachometer and a timing light to the powerhead.
3. Start the engine and allow it to warm to operating temperature. Place the lower unit in Neutral.
4. Aim the timing light at the timing pointer. Move the magneto control lever to the fully retarded position .
5. The timing mark specified in the Tune-up Specifications chart for carburetor pickup timing should align with the pointer.
6. If the timing mark and the pointer do not align, shut the engine OFF.
7. Disconnect the link rod from the magneto control lever ball stud. Loosen the locknut and adjust the plastic connector on the end of the link rod until it can be reconnected to the ball stud without changing the position of the linkage or timing marks.
8. Reconnect the link rod to the ball stud and tighten the locknut.
9. Loosen the throttle stop screw for the No. 2 carburetor . Lightly depress the No. 2 carburetor throttle roller and tighten the No. 2 throttle stop screw.

IDLE SPEED

▶ See Figures 40 and 41

1. Mount the engine in a test tank or move the boat to a body of water.
2. Remove the cowling and connect a tachometer to the powerhead.
3. Turn the pilot screw in until it lightly seats and then back out the specified number of turns, as indicated in the Tune-up Specifications chart.
4. Start the engine and allow it to warm to operating temperature. Place the engine in gear.
5. Check engine speed at idle. The powerhead should idle in at the rpm specified in the Tune-up Specifications chart.

Fig. 34 Throttle stop screw location on the carburetor

Fig. 35 Lightly press the carburetor throttle roller

Fig. 36 The throttle lever screws are left hand thread. Rotate them clockwise to loosen and counterclockwise to tighten

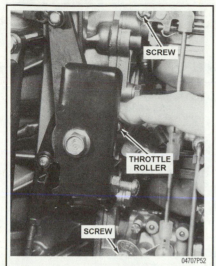

Fig. 37 Push down on the throttle roller again to keep the throttle valves closed while the screws are tightened

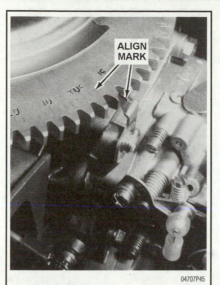

Fig. 38 The timing mark on the flywheel should align with the timing pointer

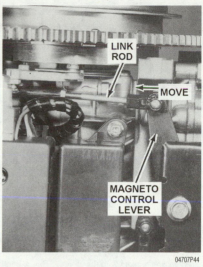

Fig. 39 Disconnect the link rod from the magneto control lever ball stud

Fig. 40 Turn the pilot screw in until it lightly seats and then back out the specified number of turns

Fig. 41 Rotate the idle adjustment screw (not the pilot screw) until the powerhead idles at the required rpm

6. Place the engine in gear and check engine trolling speed in the same manner.

7. If adjustment is necessary, rotate the idle adjustment screw (not the pilot screw) until the powerhead idles at the required rpm.

THROTTLE CABLE ADJUSTMENT

1. Shift the lower unit into **FORWARD** gear.

2. Rotate the throttle grip to the wide-open throttle position. At this point, the center of the throttle roller should align with the wide-open throttle mark on the throttle cam .

3. If the marks do not align, loosen the adjusting bolt locknut on the pull side of the throttle cable. Turn the adjusting bolt until all slack is removed, then tighten the locknut.

4. Loosen the adjusting bolt locknut on the push side of the throttle cable. Turn the adjusting bolt until the cable has approximately 0.12 in. (3 mm) slack, then tighten the locknut .

OIL PUMP LINK ADJUSTMENT

1. Rotate the throttle grip to the wide-open throttle position .

2. Turn the oil pump lever toward the wide open throttle position until it is against the wide-open stopper.

3. Loosen the locknut and adjust the plastic snap-on connector on the end of the link rod until

it can be reconnected to the ball stud without

changing the throttle or oil pump lever position.

4. Reconnect the link rod to the ball stud and tighten the locknut.

5. Rotate the throttle grip to the wide-open throttle position and make sure the throttle valve opens fully.

C40 (2-Cylinder) Model

DYNAMIC TIMING

▶ See Figures 42, 43 and 44

1. Mount the engine in a test tank or on a boat in a body of water.

2. Obtain a timing light and clip the pickup lead to the No. 1 spark plug lead.

3. Connect a tachometer to the powerhead per the instructions with the instrument.

4. Start the engine and allow it to warm to operating temperature.

5. Push the magneto control lever downward until the lower screw tip

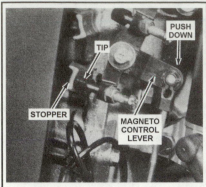

Fig. 42 Push the magneto control lever downward until the lower screw tip barely makes contact with the stopper

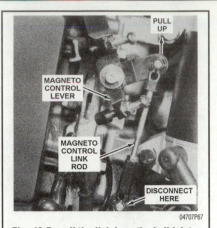

Fig. 43 Pry off the link from the ball joint at the magneto control lever ball joint

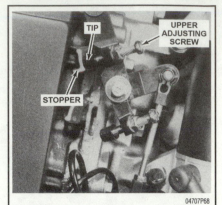

Fig. 44 Check to be sure the upper adjusting screw tip barely makes contact with the stopper

barely makes contact with the stopper. This action fully advances the timing. Allow the powerhead to operate at approximately 4,500 rpm.

6. Aim the timing light at the timing pointer. The pointer should align halfway between the 21–23° BTDC marks embossed on the flywheel. If the marks align, the full-advanced timing is correctly set.

7. Shut down the powerhead. Pry off the link from the ball joint at the magneto control lever ball joint. Restart the powerhead. Pull the magneto control lever all the way up. Aim the timing light at the timing pointer and use the free end of the link rod to rotate the magneto base until the timing pointer aligns properly.

8. Shut down the powerhead. Adjust the length of the link rod to snap back onto the ball joint of the magneto control lever without moving the magneto base or the magneto control lever. Snap the link rod back onto the ball joint of the magneto control lever.

9. Start the powerhead and allow it to idle. Check to be sure the upper adjusting screw tip barely makes contact with the stopper.

10. Aim the timing light at the timing pointer. The pointer should align half way between the 1–3° ATDC marks embossed on the flywheel. If the marks align, the fully retarded timing is correctly set and the timing procedures are completed. If the marks do not align, then proceed as follows: With the powerhead still running, continue to aim the timing light at the pointer and at the same time adjust the upper adjusting screw until the pointer aligns properly. Shut down the powerhead.

STATIC TIMING

Full Advance Adjustment

▶ See Figures 45, 46, 47 and 48

1. Remove all three spark plugs from the powerhead. Install a dial indicator into the No. 1 cylinder opening.

2. Rotate the flywheel clockwise until the dial indicator indicates the piston is at TDC (top dead center). Check the timing pointer to be sure it aligns with the TDC mark embossed on the flywheel. If the mark is misaligned, loosen the set screw on the timing plate and align the pointer with the flywheel mark. Tighten the screw to hold the adjustment.

3. Rotate the flywheel clockwise until the timing pointer aligns with 21–23° on the flywheel.

4. Rotate the lower adjustment screw until the tip contacts the stopper. Tighten the locknut to hold this new adjusted position.

Full Retard Adjustment

▶ See Figures 49 and 50

1. Rotate the flywheel clockwise until the timing pointer aligns with the 1–3° ATDC mark embossed on the flywheel.

2. Rotate the upper adjustment screw until the tip contacts the stopper. Tighten the locknut to hold this new adjusted position.

CARBURETOR LINK

▶ See Figures 51 and 52

1. Pull off the accelerator lever rod. This rod connects the three throttle levers together and is a set length. Loosen but do not remove the throttle valve screws on the top and center carburetors, by rotating the screws clockwise. Yes, they are rotated clockwise, because they have left hand threads. This fact is emphasized by the arrow and the word off embossed on each lever.

2. Loosen the idle speed adjustment screw. Snap on the accelerator rod over all three ball joints. Push down on the cam to close all throttle valves and then tighten the throttle valve screws on the top and center carburetor. This is accomplished by rotating the screws counterclockwise.

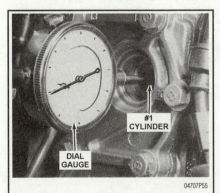

Fig. 45 Install a dial indicator into the No. 1 cylinder opening

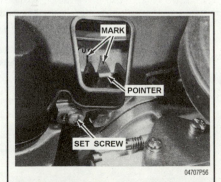

Fig. 46 Rotate the flywheel clockwise until the dial indicator indicates the piston is at TDC (top dead center)

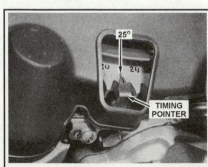

Fig. 47 Rotate the flywheel clockwise until the timing pointer aligns with 21–23° on the flywheel

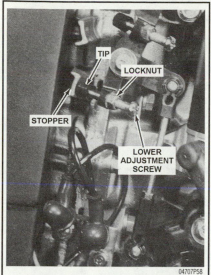

Fig. 48 Rotate the lower adjustment screw until the tip contacts the stopper

Fig. 49 There is no mark between TDC and 5° on the flywheel. Adjust the timing so the pointer falls just to the left of the 5° mark

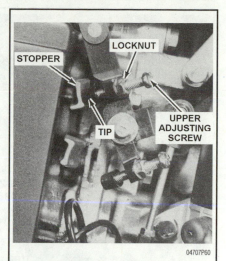

Fig. 50 Rotate the upper adjustment screw until the tip contacts the stopper and tighten the locknut

IDLE SPEED

▶ See Figure 53

1. Mount the engine in a test tank or move the boat to a body of water.
2. Remove the cowling and connect a tachometer to the powerhead.
3. Turn the pilot screw in until it lightly seats and then back out the specified number of turns, as indicated in the Tune-up Specifications chart.
4. Start the engine and allow it to warm to operating temperature. Place the engine in gear.
5. Check engine speed at idle. The powerhead should idle in at the rpm specified in the Tune-up Specifications chart.
6. Place the engine in gear and check engine trolling speed in the same manner.
7. If adjustment is necessary, rotate the idle adjustment screw (not the pilot screw) until the powerhead idles at the required rpm.

THROTTLE LINK

▶ See Figure 54

1. Disconnect the magneto control link .
2. Align the full-closed mark on the pulley with the mark on the bracket .
3. Rotate the magneto base clockwise until the full-closed side of the magneto base stopper No. 1 contacts the adjust bolt for the magneto base stopper No. 2 .
4. Adjust the plastic snap-on connector on the end of the link rod until it can be reconnected to the control lever ball stud without changing the position of the linkage or magneto base .
5. Align the wide-open throttle mark on the pulley with the mark on the throttle bracket .
6. Adjust the throttle link joint so the wide-open throttle mark on the throttle cam aligns with the center of the carburetor throttle roller .

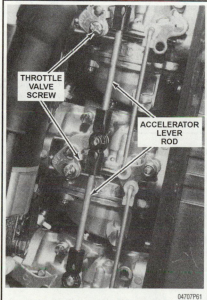

Fig. 51 Accelerator lever rod location adjacent to the throttle screws

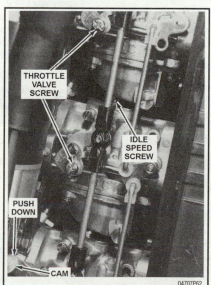

Fig. 52 Push down on the cam to close all throttle valves and then tighten the throttle valve screws by rotating them counterclockwise

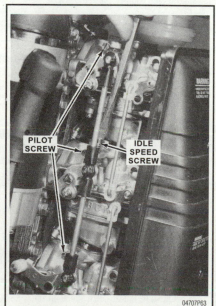

Fig. 53 Pilot and idle speed screw locations on the side of the powerhead

MAGNETO CONTROL LINK ROD

3-25/32" (96mm)

04707P64

Fig. 54 Magneto link control rod should be adjusted so that it can be reconnected to the control lever ball stud without changing the position of the linkage or magneto base

40 Hp, 50 Hp and Pro 50 Models

IGNITION TIMING

These models are equipped with an electronic ignition advance mechanism in place of a mechanical ignition advance system. Adjustment of the throttle linkage sets the timing.

THROTTLE LINKAGE

1. Turn the magneto control lever so that the adjust screw contacts the full-retard stopper.
2. Check the CDI indicator to see if it aligns with the full-retard timing specification as stated in the Tune-up Specifications chart.
3. Turn the magneto control lever so that the adjust screw contacts the full-advance adjusting screw .
4. Check the CDI indicator to see if it aligns with the full-advance timing specification as stated in the Tune-up Specifications chart.
5. To adjust full-retard and/or full advance, loosen the locknut and adjust the length of the full-retard screw to 20 mm (0.79 in. Tighten the locknut.
6. Loosen the control rod locknut and disconnect the control rod from the CDI unit.
7. Turn the magneto control lever so its adjusting screw contacts the full-retard stopper .
8. Adjust the control rod length so the CDI unit indicator aligns with the full-retard timing specification as stated in the Tune-up Specifications chart.
9. Connect the magneto control rod to the CDI unit.
10. Turn the magneto control lever so that it contacts the full-advance adjusting screw
11. Adjust the full-advance adjusting screw so that the CDI unit indicator aligns with the full-advance timing specification as stated in the Tune-up Specifications chart.
12. Adjust the throttle cable.

THROTTLE CABLE

1. Adjust the throttle link.
2. Shift the lower unit into **FORWARD** gear.
3. Rotate the throttle grip to the wide-open throttle position. At this point, the throttle valve lever
should contact the wide-open throttle stopper .
4. Ifit does not make contact, loosen the locknut and remove the clip.
5. Disconnect the cable joint from the magneto control lever
6. Rotate the throttle grip to the fully closed position.
7. Turn the magneto control lever so that its adjusting screw contacts the full-retard stopper .

➡ **The cable joint should be screwed into the fitting by more than 0.31 in. (8 mm).**

8. Adjust the position of the cable joint until its hole aligns with the set pin. Position the cable joint with the UP mark facing up and install it onto the set pin.
9. Install the clip and tighten the locknut .

IDLE SPEED

1. Mount the engine in a test tank or move the boat to a body of water.
2. Remove the cowling and connect a tachometer to the powerhead.
3. Turn the pilot screw in until it lightly seats and then back out the specified number of turns, as indicated in the Tune-up Specifications chart.
4. Start the engine and allow it to warm to operating temperature. Place the engine in gear.
5. Check engine speed at idle. The powerhead should idle in at the rpm specified in the Tune-up Specifications chart.
6. Place the engine in gear and check engine trolling speed in the same manner.
7. If adjustment is necessary, rotate the idle adjustment screw (not the pilot screw) until the powerhead idles at the required rpm.

OIL PUMP LINK

1. Rotate the throttle grip to the wide-open throttle position. At this point, the oil pump lever
should be approximately 0.04 in. (1.0 mm) off the wide-open throttle side stopper .
2. If adjustment is necessary, fully open the carburetor throttle valve. Set the oil pump lever 0.04 in. (1 mm) off the full open side stopper.
3. Loosen the locknut on the link joint, then disconnect the link rod from the oil pump lever ball stud. Adjust the plastic snap-on connector on the end of the link rod until its hole aligns with the oil pump set pin.
4. Connect the link joint and check that the throttle valve opens fully.
5. Reconnect the link rod to the ball stud and tighten the locknut.
6. Rotate the throttle grip to the wide-open throttle position and recheck the clearance.

C55 MODELS

IGNITION TIMING

1. Remove the standard propeller and install a test propeller.
2. Install the outboard in a test tank.
3. Connect a timing light and portable tachometer according to their manufacturer's instructions.
4. Shift the lower unit into NEUTRAL.
5. Start the engine and allow it to warm up for approximately 5 minutes.
6. Place the ignition in the full-retard position manually. .
7. Point the timing light at the timing pointer. The timing pointer should align with the full-retard timing specification as stated in the Tune-up Specifications chart.
8. If the timing pointer does not align, turn the adjusting screw and adjust the timing as necessary .
9. Manually move the magneto control lever to the wide-open throttle position (full-advanced ignition) and increase engine speed to more than 4,500 rpm.

10. Point the timing light at the timing pointer. It should align with the full-advance timing specification as stated in the Tune-up Specifications chart.

11. If the timing pointer does not align, loosen the locknut, turn the screw and adjust the timing as necessary. Tighten the locknut.

12. To adjust the pick-up timing, manually set the ignition to full-retard. Allow the engine to idle at idle speed. If necessary, adjust the idle speed as described in this section.

13. Bring the throttle cam to contact the throttle lever roller lightly The throttle valve should not open.

14. Loosen the locknut on the link joint, then disconnect the link rod from the oil pump lever ball stud. Adjust the plastic snap-on connector on the end of the link rod until its hole aligns with the set pin. Install the link joint.

CARBURETOR LINKAGE

1. Loosen the carburetor idle adjust screw .
2. Loosen the upper carburetor ball joint lock screw.
3. Pull up on the upper carburetor ball joint to remove play between the upper and lower carburetors then tighten the upper lock screw
4. Move the accelerator lever up and down several times to make sure the upper and lower carburetors open and close simultaneously.

IDLE SPEED

1. Mount the engine in a test tank or move the boat to a body of water.
2. Remove the cowling and connect a tachometer to the powerhead.
3. Turn the pilot screw in until it lightly seats and then back out the specified number of turns, as indicated in the Tune-up Specifications chart.
4. Start the engine and allow it to warm to operating temperature. Place the engine in gear.
5. Check engine speed at idle. The powerhead should idle in at the rpm specified in the Tune-up Specifications chart.
6. Place the engine in gear and check engine trolling speed in the same manner.
7. If adjustment is necessary, rotate the idle adjustment screw (not the pilot screw) until the powerhead idles at the required rpm.

Pro 60 Hp, 70 Hp and 90 Hp Models

TIMING PLATE POSITION

♦ **See Figure 55**

➡**This procedure must be performed prior to adjusting the ignition timing.**

1. Remove the spark plugs, and install a dial indicator in the No. 1 cylinder spark plug hole.
2. Slowly rotate the flywheel clockwise and stop when the piston reaches top dead center (TDC).
3. Check the timing plate alignment with the flywheel timing scale.
4. If the end of the timing plate is not aligned with the TDC mark on the CDI magneto rotor, loosen the timing plate set screw, align the timing plate end with the TDC mark, then tighten the screw.

IGNITION TIMING

♦ **See Figure 56**

➡**Check and adjust, if necessary, the timing plate position prior to checking and adjusting the timing.**

1. Remove the standard propeller and install a test propeller.
2. Install the outboard in a test tank.
3. Connect a timing light to the No. 1 cylinder and a portable tachometer according to the manufacturer's instructions.
4. Shift the lower unit into NEUTRAL.
5. Start the engine and allow it to warm up for approximately 5 minutes. Let the engine idle at specification.
6. Place the ignition in the full-retard position manually. .
7. Point the timing light at the timing pointer. The timing pointer should

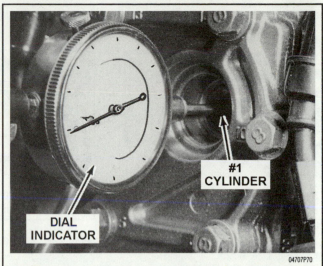

Fig. 55 Install a dial indicator in the No. 1 cylinder and slowly rotate the flywheel clockwise and stop when the piston reaches top dead center (TDC)

align with the full-retard timing specification as stated in the Tune-up Specifications chart.

8. If the timing pointer does not align, loosen the locknut on the upper adjusting screw and adjust the timing as necessary. Tighten the locknut

9. Manually move the magneto control lever to the wide-open throttle position (full-advanced ignition).

10. Increase engine to the maximum speed specified in the Tune-up Specifications chart.

11. Point the timing light at the timing pointer. The timing pointer should align with the full-advance timing specification as stated in the Tune-up Specifications chart.

12. If the timing pointer does not align, loosen the locknut on the lower adjusting screw and adjust the timing as necessary.

PICKUP TIMING

♦ **See Figures 57 and 58**

1. Place the ignition in the full-retard position manually..
2. Bring the throttle cam to contact the throttle lever roller lightly. The throttle valve should not open.
3. Loosen the locknut on the link joint, then disconnect the link rod from the oil pump lever ball stud. Adjust the plastic snap-on connector on the end of the link rod until its hole aligns with the set pin . Install the link joint.

THROTTLE SENSOR CONTROL LINK

1. Loosen the locknut on the throttle sensor control link and the throttle cam link joint, then disconnect the link rods from the lever ball stud.
2. Adjust the plastic snap-on connector on the end of the throttle sensor control link rod to the following dimensions:
   • Pro 60 and 70 hp: 128.5-129.5 5.10 in.
   • 90 hp: 3.66-3.70 in.
3. Adjust the plastic snap-on end of the throttle cam link rod to the following dimensions:
   • Pro 60 and 70 hp: 2.28 in.
   • 90 hp: 4.74 in.
4. Install the link joints and tighten the locknuts.

➡**The nut in the magneto control lever should be 0.08 in. (2 mm) from the end of the magneto control lever .**

5. Adjust the length of the full-retard adjusting screw so that when the full-retard adjusting screw contacts the stopper, the full-retard indication on the CDI unit aligns with the timing indicator.

6. Adjust the length of the full-advance adjusting screw so that when the

Fig. 56 The upper adjustment screw is used to set the fully retarded timing

Fig. 57 Bring the throttle cam to contact the throttle lever roller lightly

Fig. 58 The accelerator link rod is located just below the starter motor on this model

full-advance adjusting screw contacts the stopper, the full-advance indication on the CDI unit aligns with the timing indicator.

IDLE SPEED

1. Mount the engine in a test tank or move the boat to a body of water.
2. Remove the cowling and connect a tachometer to the powerhead.
3. Turn the pilot screw in until it lightly seats and then back out the specified number of turns, as indicated in the Tune-up Specifications chart.
4. Start the engine and allow it to warm to operating temperature. Place the engine in gear.
5. Check engine speed at idle. The powerhead should idle in at the rpm specified in the Tune-up Specifications chart.
6. Place the engine in gear and check engine trolling speed in the same manner.
7. If adjustment is necessary, rotate the idle adjustment screw (not the pilot screw) until the powerhead idles at the required rpm.

CARBURETOR LINKAGE

▶ **See Figure 59**

Pro 60 and 70 Hp Models

1. Loosen the carburetor idle adjust screw by turning them clockwise and close the throttle valve.
2. Loosen the throttle lever securing screws on the upper and middle carburetors.
3. While lightly pushing the throttle lever on the lower carburetor downward to the fully closed position, tighten the throttle lever securing screw on the upper and middle carburetors .

Fig. 59 To adjust the carburetor linkage, loosen the throttle lever securing screws

4. Move the accelerator lever up and down several times to make sure all carburetors open and close simultaneously.

90 Hp Models

1. Loosen the carburetor idle adjust screw by turning them clockwise and close the throttle valve.
2. Loosen the throttle lever securing screws on the upper and lower carburetors.
3. While lightly pushing the throttle lever on the middle carburetor downward to the fully closed position, tighten the throttle lever securing screw on the upper and lower carburetors .
4. Move the accelerator lever up and down several times to make sure all carburetors open and close simultaneously.

OIL PUMP LINK

1. Rotate the throttle grip to the wide-open throttle position.
2. At this point, the oil pump lever should be 0.04 in.(1 mm) off the wide-open throttle side stopper .
3. If adjustment is necessary, fully open the carburetor throttle valve. Set the oil pump lever 0.04 in. (1 mm) off the wide-open throttle side stopper.
4. Loosen the locknut on the link joint, then disconnect the link rod from the oil pump lever ball stud. Adjust the plastic snap-on connector on the end of the link rod until its hole aligns with the oil pump set pin.
5. Connect the link joint and check that the throttle valve opens fully.
6. Reconnect the link rod to the ball stud and tighten the locknut.
7. Rotate the throttle grip to the wide-open throttle position and recheck the clearance.

C75 and C85 Models

TIMING PLATE POSITION

➡**This procedure must be performed prior to adjusting the ignition timing.**

1. Remove the spark plugs, and install a dial indicator in the No. 1 cylinder spark plug hole.
2. Slowly rotate the flywheel clockwise and stop when the piston reaches top dead center (TDC).
3. Check the timing plate alignment with the flywheel timing scale.
4. If the end of the timing plate is not aligned with the TDC mark on the CDI magneto rotor, loosen the timing plate set screw, align the timing plate end with the TDC mark, then tighten the screw.

IGNITION TIMING

1. Remove the standard propeller and install a test propeller.
2. Install the outboard in a test tank.

➡The following dimensions are preliminary adjustments and will probably be changed to a different length during this procedure.

3. Perform a preliminary link length adjustment on all control links related to timing. Loosen the locknut on the links, then adjust the lengths as follows. Do not tighten the locknuts at this time.

- Stator control link rod—2.91 in. (74mm)
- Upper adjustment screw—1.38 in. (35mm)
- Lower adjustment screw—0.51 in. (13mm)
- Magneto control link rod—4.88 in. (124mm)

4. Connect a timing light and tachometer to the engine.
5. Start the engine and allow it to warm to operating temperature.
6. Increase engine speed to more than 4,000 rpm
7. Place the ignition in the full-retard position manually.
8. Point the timing light at the timing pointer. The timing pointer should align with the full-retard timing specification as stated in the Tune-up Specifications chart.
9. If the timing pointer does not align, loosen the locknut and turn the upper adjustment screw to adjust the timing. Tighten the locknut.
10. Manually move the magneto control lever to the wide-open throttle position (full-advanced ignition).
11. Maintain engine speed at more than 4,500 rpm.
12. Point the timing light at the timing pointer. The timing pointer should align with the full-advance timing specification as stated in the Tune-up Specifications chart.
13. If the timing pointer does not align, loosen the locknut and turn the lower adjustment screw to adjust the timing. Tighten the locknut.

PICKUP TIMING

1. Place the ignition in the full-retard position manually..
2. Bring the throttle cam to contact the throttle lever roller lightly. The throttle valve should not open.
3. Loosen the locknut on the link joint, then disconnect the link rod from the oil pump lever ball stud. Adjust the plastic snap-on connector on the end of the link rod until its hole aligns with the set pin . Install the link joint.

IDLE SPEED

1. Mount the engine in a test tank or move the boat to a body of water.
2. Remove the cowling and connect a tachometer to the powerhead.
3. Turn the pilot screw in until it lightly seats and then back out the specified number of turns, as indicated in the Tune-up Specifications chart.
4. Start the engine and allow it to warm to operating temperature. Place the engine in gear.
5. Check engine speed at idle. The powerhead should idle in at the rpm specified in the Tune-up Specifications chart.
6. Place the engine in gear and check engine trolling speed in the same manner.
7. If adjustment is necessary, rotate the idle adjustment screw (not the pilot screw) until the powerhead idles at the required rpm.

CARBURETOR LINKAGE

1. Loosen the carburetor idle adjust screw and close the throttle valve.

➡The throttle lever screws have left-hand threads. Turn the screws clockwise to loosen and counterclockwise to tighten.

2. Loosen the throttle lever securing screws on the upper and lower carburetors.
3. While lightly pushing the throttle lever on the middle carburetor downward to the full-closed position, tighten the throttle lever securing screw on the upper and lower carburetors.
4. Move the accelerator lever up and down several times to make sure all carburetors open and close simultaneously.

C115 MODELS

TIMING PLATE POSITION

➡This procedure must be performed prior to adjusting the ignition timing.

1. Remove all 4 spark plugs.
2. Install a dial indicator in the No. 1 cylinder spark plug hole.
3. Slowly rotate the flywheel clockwise and stop when the piston reaches 0.15 in. (3.91 mm) BTDC.
4. At this point the timing pointer should align with the full-advance timing specification as stated in the Tune-up Specifications chart. If alignment is incorrect, loosen the timing plate set screw and align the timing plate. Tighten the screw .

IGNITION TIMING

➡The timing plate position must be checked prior to adjusting the ignition timing.

1. Remove the standard propeller and install a test propeller.
2. Install the outboard in a test tank.
3. Set the preliminary link rod length on both the magneto control link and throttle cam control link as follows. Loosen the locknut on the links and adjust the center to center lengths. Do not tighten the locknuts at this time.
- Magneto control link length—2.36 in (60 mm).
- Throttle cam control link length—2.09 in. (53 mm).

4. Connect a timing light and tachometer to the engine.
5. Shift the lower unit into NEUTRAL.
6. Start the engine and allow it to warm to operating temperature. Ensure the engine is idling at the specification as stated in the Tune-up Specifications chart.
7. Place the ignition in the full-retard position manually
8. Point the timing light at the timing plate and the timing indicator. The timing pointer should align with the full-retard timing specification as stated in the Tune-up Specifications chart.
9. If the timing pointer does not align, loosen the locknut and turn the upper adjustment screw to adjust the timing. Tighten the locknut.
10. Manually move the magneto control lever to the wide-open throttle position (full-advanced ignition).
11. Increase engine speed to more than 4,500 rpm.
12. Point the timing light at the timing pointer. The timing pointer should align with the full-advance timing specification as stated in the Tune-up Specifications chart.
13. If the timing pointer does not align, loosen the locknut and turn the lower adjustment screw to adjust the timing. Tighten the locknut.

PICKUP TIMING

1. Disconnect the throttle cam control link .
2. Slowly rotate flywheel clockwise and stop when the timing plate is aligned with the 4° BTDC mark .
3. Align the mark on the pulser assembly arm with the timing mark on the flywheel rotor .
4. Loosen the roller adjusting screw and adjust so the mark on the throttle cam is centered on the roller. The throttle valve should not open.
5. Loosen the locknut on the throttle cam control link joint. Adjust the plastic snap-on connector on the end of the link rod until its hole aligns with the set pin. Install the link joint.

IDLE SPEED

1. Mount the engine in a test tank or move the boat to a body of water.
2. Remove the cowling and connect a tachometer to the powerhead.

3. Turn the pilot screw in until it lightly seats and then back out the specified number of turns, as indicated in the Tune-up Specifications chart.

4. Start the engine and allow it to warm to operating temperature. Place the engine in gear.

5. Check engine speed at idle. The powerhead should idle in at the rpm specified in the Tune-up Specifications chart.

6. Place the engine in gear and check engine trolling speed in the same manner.

7. If adjustment is necessary, rotate the idle adjustment screw (not the pilot screw) until the powerhead idles at the required rpm.

CARBURETOR LINKAGE

1. Loosen the roller adjusting screw and the throttle arm adjusting screw .

2. Loosen the carburetor idle adjust screw and completely close all throttle valves.

3. With the throttle valves on both carburetors fully closed, tighten the roller adjusting screw and the throttle arm adjusting screw.

4. Remove the play in the throttle link and throttle arm ball joint so that the upper and lower throttle valves open simultaneously.

5. Tighten the idle adjust screw into the original position.

6. Move the accelerator lever up and down several times to make sure all 3 carburetors open and close simultaneously.

7. Perform pick-up timing adjustment.

V4 and V6 Except Yamaha Microcomputer Ignition System (YMIS)

IGNITION TIMING

1. Place the lower unit in NEUTRAL.
2. Remove the spark plugs.
3. Install a dial indicator in the No. 1 cylinder spark plug hole.
4. Slowly rotate the flywheel clockwise and stop when the piston reaches the following position.

- 115 hp, Pro 115—0.15 in. (3.91mm) BTDC
- 130 hp, 140 hp, 175 hp, 200 hp—0.12 in. (3.05mm) BTDC
- 150 hp—0.14 in. (3.61mm) BTDC
- Pro 150—0.19 in. (4.88mm) BTDC
- Pro 200, 225—0.09 in. (2.53mm) BTDC

5. The timing pointer should align with the full-advanced timing specification as stated in the Tune-up Specifications chart.

6. Disconnect the magneto control link from the base assembly.

7. Move the magneto control lever to the full-advance position, until it touches the full-advance stopper.

8. Loosen the magneto control link locknut and adjust the length of the link until the mark on the flywheel aligns with the mark on the base assembly. Tighten the locknut and reinstall the control link.

9. Slowly rotate the flywheel clockwise and stop when the pointer aligns with the full-retarded timing specification as stated in the Tune-up Specifications chart.

10. Move the magneto control lever to the full-retard position, until it touches the full-retard stopper .

11. Adjust the full-retard stopper so the mark on the flywheel aligns with the mark on the base assembly

CARBURETOR LINKAGE ADJUSTMENT

▶ **See Figure 60**

➡ **Adjust the ignition timing prior to performing this procedure.**

1. Remove the air silencer.
2. Move the throttle link up and down and observe the opening and closing of the throttle valves .
3. Loosen the idle adjust screw and remove the screw from the throttle arm stopper .
4. Loosen the throttle valve screw by turning it clockwise and make sure the throttle valves are fully closed. Retighten the throttle valve screw.
5. Slowly tighten the idle adjust screw until it contacts the throttle arm stopper. From this position, tighten it another 1–1⅛ turns further.
6. Move the throttle link up and down several times to make sure the carburetors open and close simultaneously.
7. Adjust the oil pump control link.

➡ **On 225 hp models, adjust the throttle sensor.**

CARBURETOR PICKUP TIMING ADJUSTMENT

▶ **See Figures 61 and 62**

➡ **Adjust the ignition timing, carburetor linkage and idle speed prior to starting this procedure.**

1. Disconnect the throttle cam control link.
2. Slowly rotate the flywheel clockwise and stop when the timing plate is aligned with the 4° ATDC mark for 115 hp, Pro V 115, 130 hp engines and the 6° ATDC mark for all others.

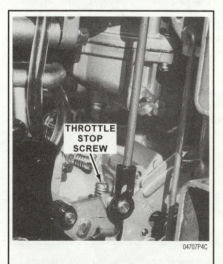

Fig. 60 Throttle stop screw location

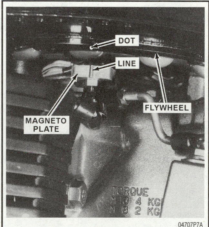

Fig. 61 Align the magneto control lever so the mark on the flywheel aligns with the mark on the pulser

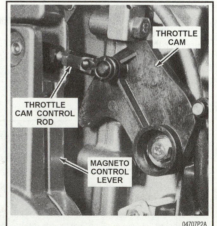

Fig. 62 The throttle cam control link is located between the throttle cam and the magneto control lever

3. Align the magneto control lever so the mark on the flywheel aligns with the mark on the pulser assembly.

4. Loosen the throttle roller adjusting screw .

5. Align the mark on the throttle cam with the center line on the throttle roller .

6. If alignment cannot be achieved, loosen the locknut and adjust the length of the throttle cam control link. Tighten the locknut.

7. Tighten the throttle roller adjust screw.

IDLE SPEED

♦ **See Figure 63**

1. Mount the engine in a test tank or move the boat to a body of water.

2. Remove the cowling and connect a tachometer to the powerhead.

3. Turn the pilot screw in until it lightly seats and then back out the specified number of turns, as indicated in the Tune-up Specifications chart.

4. Start the engine and allow it to warm to operating temperature. Place the engine in gear.

5. Check engine speed at idle. The powerhead should idle in at the rpm specified in the Tune-up Specifications chart.

6. Place the engine in gear and check engine trolling speed in the same manner.

7. If adjustment is necessary, rotate the idle adjustment screw (not the pilot screw) until the powerhead idles at the required rpm.

Fig. 63 Pilot screws on a big V6 engine

THROTTLE POSITION SENSOR (225 HP ONLY)

1. Loosen the idle adjustment screw and make sure the throttle valve is closed.

2. Disconnect the 3-pin harness from the throttle sensor and connect the appropriate test lead inline.

3. Connect the positive voltmeter lead to the Pink terminal and the negative lead to the Orange terminal.

4. Loosen the throttle sensor mounting screws and slowly turn the throttle sensor until 0.5 volts is obtained. Tighten the screws.

5. Adjust the idle speed.

OIL PUMP LINK

1. Remove the clip and washer and disconnect the control link from the oil pump.

2. Loosen the idle adjust screw and make sure the screw is not touching the throttle arm stopper . Make sure the throttle valves are fully closed.

3. Loosen the oil control link locknut .

4. HoLd the oil injection pump lever in the full-closed position, then adjust the control link length and reinstall it onto the oil pump. Tighten the locknut.

5. Adjust the carburetor linkage.

V4 and V6 With Yamaha Microcomputer Ignition System (YMIS)

➡**Powerheads equipped with Yamaha Microcomputer Ignition System (YMIS) do not require timing advance adjustment.**

CARBURETOR LINKAGE

♦ **See Figures 64 and 65**

1. Remove the air silencer.

2. Move the throttle control link up and down and make sure the throttle valves are completely closed when the throttle valve control lever is in the full-closed position. If not, continue with this procedure.

3. Loosen the throttle roller adjust screw by turning it clockwise.

4. Turn the starboard middle carburetor idle adjust screw counterclockwise until it does not touch the throttle linkage .

5. Disconnect the No. 1 and No. 2 accelerator links from the ball joints.

6. Disconnect the link joint, adjust the length to 5.571 in. (141.5 mm) from center-to-center and reconnect it.

7. Remove the oil pump joint link.

8. Loosen the throttle valve synchronization screw on each set of carburetors. Push on the throttle valve pivots with your fingers to make sure each of the throttle valves are completely closed.

9. With the throttle valves in the full-closed position, tighten the screws.

10. Connect the accelerator link to the ball joint.

11. Loosen the throttle valve synchronization screw. Keep pushing the point until all play is removed, then tighten the screw.

12. Hold the oil pump lever and oil pump control arm at the full-open position. Adjust the length of the oil pump control link to the correct length and reconnect it .

13. Slowly turn the No. 4 carburetor idle adjust screw clockwise until the throttle valve just starts to move . From this point, turn the screw an additional 1 1/2 turn.

14. Adjust the throttle roller so the roller contacts the accelerator cam at the alignment mark . Tighten the screw.

15. Adjust the length of the accelerator link to 1.97 in. (50 mm) from center-to center and reconnect it.

16. Move the throttle link up and down and make sure the throttle valves are completely closed when the throttle valve control lever is in the full-closed position.

17. Install the air silencer and the engine cover.

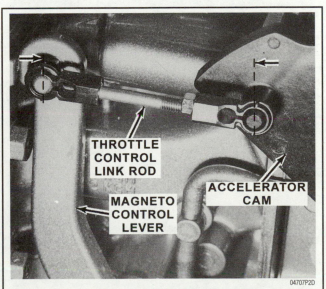

Fig. 64 Adjust the throttle control link rod length while measuring from center-to-center

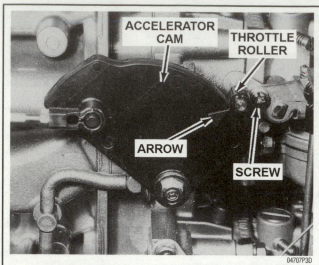

04707P3D

Fig. 65 Loosen the throttle roller adjust screw by turning it clockwise

CARBURETOR PICKUP TIMING

1. Loosen the throttle roller adjust screw by turning it clockwise.
2. Adjust the throttle roller so the roller contacts the accelerator cam at the alignment mark .
3. Tighten the throttle roller adjust screw.

THROTTLE POSITION SENSOR

1. Loosen the idle adjustment screw and make sure the throttle valve is closed.
2. Disconnect the 3-pin harness from the throttle sensor and connect the appropriate test lead inline.
3. Connect the positive voltmeter lead to the Pink terminal and the negative lead to the Orange terminal.
4. Loosen the throttle sensor mounting screws and slowly turn the throttle sensor until 0.5 volts is obtained. Tighten the screws.
5. Adjust the idle speed.

IDLE SPEED

1. Mount the engine in a test tank or move the boat to a body of water.
2. Remove the cowling and connect a tachometer to the power-head.
3. Turn the pilot screw in until it lightly seats and then back out the specified number of turns, as indicated in the Tune-up Specifications chart.
4. Start the engine and allow it to warm to operating temperature. Place the engine in gear.
5. Check engine speed at idle. The powerhead should idle in at the rpm specified in the Tune-up Specifications chart.
6. Place the engine in gear and check engine trolling speed in the same manner.
7. If adjustment is necessary, rotate the idle adjustment screw (not the pilot screw) until the powerhead idles at the required rpm.

Engine Tune-Up Specifications

Model	Years	NGK	Champion	Spark Plug Gap Inch(mm)	Magneto Point Gap Inch	Magneto Point Gap mm	Ignition	Full Retard	Carb Pickup	Full Advance	Pilot Top	Pilot Center	Pilot Bottom	Idle Neutral	Idle Trolling	Gear Oil Oz.(cc)	Tach Pole	Full Throttle RPM	Kent Moore Part No.	New Engine RPM
2	1990-98	B5HS	L90	0.024(0.6)	0.014	0.35		17-19		18-24		1.25		1100-1200	-	1.5(45)	-	4000-5000	-	-
3	1990-98	B6HS-10	L86C	0.039(1.0)			CDI	4-8		25-31		1.25		1200	1050	2.5(75)	-	4500-5500	-	-
4	1990-98	B7HS	L82C	0.024(0.6)			CDI	2-8		25-31		1.75		1150	1000	3.6(105)	-	4500-5500	-	-
5	1994-98	B7HS	L82C	0.039(1.0)			CDI	2-8		25-31		1.625		1150	1000	3.6(105)	4	4500-5500	-	-
6	1990-98	B7HS-10	L82C	0.039(1.0)			CDI	3-5		34-36		1.125		900	800	5.4(160)	4	4000-5000	-	-
8	1990-98	B7HS-10	L82C	0.039(1.0)			CDI	3-5		34-36		1.125		900	800	5.4(160)	4	4000-5000	-	-
9.9	1990-98	B7HS-10	L82C	0.039(1.0)			CDI	4-6		29-31		1.25		900	750	6.0(185)	4	4500-5500	YB-1619	5000-5200
9.9	1996-98	B7HS-10	L82C	0.039(1.0)			CDI	4-6	9-11	29-31		1.625		750	650	6.0(185)	4	4500-5501	YB-1619	5000-5200
15	1990-95	B7HS-10	L82C	0.039(1.0)			CDI	4-6	9-11	29-31		1.25		900	750	6.0(185)	4	4500-5500	YB-1619	5200-5400
15	1990-95	B7HS-10	L82C	0.039(1.0)			CDI	4-6		29-31		1.25		900	750	6.0(185)	4	4500-5500	YB-1619	5200-5400
15	1996-98	B7HS-10	L82C	0.039(1.0)			CDI	4-6		29-31		1.625		750	650	6.0(185)	4	4500-5500	YB-1619	5200-5400
20	1996-97	B7HS-11	L82C	0.039(1.0)			CDI	(a)6-(a)4	(a)1-1	24-26		2.5		750	600	12.7(375)	4	5000-6000	YB-1619	5500-5700
25	1990-98	B7HS-10	L82C	0.039(1.0)			CDI	(a)6-(a)4	(a)1-1	24-26		2.5		750	650	12.7(375)	4	5000-6000	YB-1619	5500-5700
25	1996-98	B7HS-10	L82C	0.039(1.0)			CDI	(a)6-(a)4		24-26		2		750	650	6.1(180)	6	4500-5500	YB-1621	5500-5700
25 (3CYL)	1996-98	B7HS	L82C	0.024(0.6)			CDI	(a)6-(a)4	(a)4-(a)2	24-26		0.75		750	650	6.8(200)	6	4500-5500	YB-1621	4500-5450
C25	1990-97	B7HS-10	L82C	0.039(1.0)			CDI	1-3		23-25	0.75	1.5(1)	1	950	850	6.1(180)	6	4500-5500	YB-1621	5250-5450
30 (3CYL)	1990-98	B7HS	L82C	0.024(0.6)			CDI	(a)6-(a)4	(a)3-(a)1	24-26		1.5		750	650	6.8(200)	6	4500-5500	YB-1621	5000-5200
C30	1990-92	B7HS	L82C	0.039(1.0)			CDI	(a)1-1	(a)1-1	24-26		1.25		900	800	10.8(320)	4	4500-5500	YB-1621	5250-5450
C30	1993-97	B8HS-10	L78C	0.039(1.0)			CDI	(a)4+0	(a)4+0	23-27		1.625		1150	950	14(415)	6	4500-5500	YB-1629	5250-5450
40	1990-94	B7HS-10	L82C	0.039(1.0)			CDI	(a)6-(a)4	(a)6-(a)4	24-26		1.25		800	600	14.5(430)	6	4500-5500	YB-1611	4900-5100
40 (3CYL)	1995-98	B7HS-10	L82C	0.039(1.0)			CDI	(a)6-(a)4	(a)6-(a)4	24-29		1.5		800	600	14.5(430)	6	4500-5500	YB-1611	4900-5100
C40 (3CYL)	1998-98	B7HS-10	L78C	0.039(1.0)			CDI	(a)6-(a)4	(a)6-(a)4	24-29		1.5		800	600	10.6(315)	6	4500-5500	YB-1611	4900-5100
C40	1990-97	B8HS	L78C	0.024(0.6)			CDI	1-3	5	21-23		1.75		1150	950	16.9(500)	4	4500-5500	YB-1611	4800-5000
E48	1995-98	B7HS	L82C	0.039(1.0)			CDI	3-5	3-5	19-21		1.375		1100	800	14(415)	4	4500-5500	YB-1611	5300-5500
50/P50	1990-94	B8HS-10	L78C	0.039(1.0)			CDI	(a)6-(a)4	(a)1	24-26		1.75		800	600	16.9(500)	6	4500-5500	YB-1611	5250-5450
50/P50	1995-98	B8HS-10	L78C	0.039(1.0)			CDI	(a)8-(a)6	(a)8-(a)6	23-28		1.625(2)		800	600	14.5(430)	6	4500-5500	YB-1611	5250-5450
C55	1990-95	B8HS-10	L78C	0.039(1.0)			CDI	(a)8-(a)6	(a)6-(a)4	25-27		2(3)		1100	800	16.9(500)	6	4500-5500	YB-1611	5300-5500
C60	1996-98	B8HS-10	L78C	0.039(1.0)			CDI	(a)8-(a)6	(a)8-(a)6	21-23		1.5		800	600	20.6(610)	4	4500-5500	YB-1620	4950-5150
E60	1995-98	B8HS-10	L78C	0.039(1.0)			CDI	(a)8-(a)6	(a)8-(a)6	18-20		1.5		800	600	20.6(610)	6	4500-5500	YB-1620	4950-5150
P60	1991	B8HS-10	L78C	0.039(1.0)			CDI	(a)7-(a)5	(a)7-(a)5	21-23		1.25		800	600	20.6(610)	6	4500-5500	YB-1620	4950-5150
P60	1992-98	B8HS-10	L78C	0.039(1.0)			CDI	(a)8-(a)6	(a)8-(a)6	21-23		1.5		800	600	20.6(610)	6	4500-5500	YB-1620	4950-5150
70	1990-91	B8HS-10	L78C	0.039(1.0)			CDI	(a)8-(a)6	(a)8-(a)6	21-23		1.5		800	600	20.6(610)	6	4500-5500	YB-1620	4950-5150
70	1992-98	B8HS-10	L78C	0.039(1.0)			CDI	(a)8-(a)6	(a)8-(a)6	19-21		1.375		800	600	20.6(610)	6	5000-6000	YB-1620	5250-5450
C75	1990-94	B8HS-10	L78C	0.039(1.0)			CDI	(a)8-(a)6	(a)8-(a)6	21-23		1.25		800	600	20.6(610)	12	4500-5500	YB-1620	4750-4950
C75	1994-96	B8HS-10	L78C	0.039(1.0)			CDI	6-8	6-8	21-23		1.375		800	600	20.6(610)	12	4500-5500	YB-1620	4750-4950
C75	1998-98	B8HS-10	L78C	0.039(1.0)			CDI	6-8	6-8	23-25		1.375		800	600	20.6(610)	12	4500-5500	YB-1620	4750-4950
E75	1995-96	B8HS-10	L78C	0.039(1.0)			CDI	1-3	1-3	21-23		1.25		800	600	20.6(610)	12	4500-5500	YB-1620	4750-4950
E75	1997-98	B8HS-10	L78C	0.039(1.0)			CDI	(a)3-(a)1	(a)3-(a)1	21-23		1.25		800	600	20.6(610)	12	4500-5500	YB-1620	4750-4950
P75	1996-98	B8HS-10	L78C	0.039(1.0)			CDI	(a)9-(a)7	(a)9-(a)7	19-21		1.375		800	570	25.7(760)	12	4500-5500	YB-1620	4750-4950
P75/S75	1997	B8HS-10	L78C	0.039(1.0)			CDI	(a)9-(a)7	(a)9-(a)7	19-21		1.375		700	570	25.7760(9)	12	4500-5500	YB-1620	4750-4950
C80	1996-98	B8HS-10	L78C	0.039(1.0)			CDI	(a)8-(a)6	(a)8-(a)6	23-25		1.125		700	575	33.1(980)(13)	12	4500-5500	YB-1620	5100-5300
C85	1990-91	B8HS-10	L78C	0.039(1.0)			CDI	(a)8-(a)6	(a)8-(a)6	21-23		1.125		800	600	(36)	12	4500-5500	YB-1620	5100-5300
90	1992-98	BR7HS C2[6]	RLB2C[6]	0.039(1.0)			CDI	(a)11-(a)9	(a)11-(a)9	21-23		1.5		800	600	(36)	12	5000-6000	YB-1620	4900-5100
90/B90/C90	1992-98	BR7HS C2[6]	RLB2C[6]	0.039(1.0)			CDI	(a)9-(a)7	(a)9-(a)7	19-23		1.25		730	575	(37)	12	5000-6000	YB-1620	5200-5400
115/B115/C115/P115	1990-95	B8HS-10 [4][6]	L78C [5][6]	0.039(1.0)			CDI	(a)6-(a)4	(a)7-(a)5	27-29(16)		(17)		(18)	575	33.1(980)	12	4500-5500	YB-1624	4900-5100
130L130/S130	1990-98	B9HS-10 [7][6]	L78C [8][6]	0.039(1.0)			CDI	(a)6-(a)4	(a)7-(a)5	21-23		1.5		700	575	33.1(980)	12	4500-5500	YB-1624	4900-5100
150	1994-95	B9HS-10 [10][6]	L78C [11][6]	0.039(1.0)			CDI	(a)8-(a)6	(a)7-(a)5	19-21		(21)		700	575	33.1(980)	12	5000-6000	YB-1624	4600-4800
150/D150/P150/S150/L150	1990-95	B9HS-10 [33][6]	RLB2C[34][6]	0.039(1.0)			CDI	(a)8-(a)6	(a)9-(a)5	20-25		1.25		750	650	33.1(980)	12	4500-5500	YB-1626	4600-4800
C150	1996-98	BR8HS-10 [6]	RLB2C[6]	0.039(1.0)			CDI	(a)9-(a)5	(a)9-(a)5	21-23		0.875		750	575	31.1(980)	12	4500-5500	YB-1626	4600-4800
DX150/L150/PX150/SX150	1999	B9HS-10	RL82C[6]	0.039(1.0)			CDI	(a)8-(a)6	(a)7-(a)5	21-23		1.25(12)		730	575	33.1(980)(23)	12	4500-5500	YB-1626	4600-4800
P150	1990-95	B8HS-10 [14][6]	L78C [15][6]	0.039(1.0)			CDI	(a)8-(a)6	(a)7-(a)5	24-26		(35)		700	575	33.1(980)	12	4500-5500	YB-1626	4900-5100
175	1990-95	B8HS-10 [19][6]	L78C [20][6]	0.039(1.0)			CDI	(a)8-(a)6	(a)7-(a)5	21-23		1		700	575	33.1(980)(41)	12	4500-5500	YB-1626	4900-5100
P175	1994-95	B8HS-10 [19][6]	L78C [20][6]	0.039(1.0)			CDI	(a)8-(a)6	(a)7-(a)5	23-25		1.125		700	575	30.5(870)(42)	12	5000-6000	YB-1624	5200-5400
P175/S175	1996-98	B8HS-10 [6]	QL78C [6]	0.039(1.0)			CDI	(a)7-(a)3	(a)7-(a)3	(39)		(38)		700	575	30.9(1150)(30)	12	4500-5500	YB-1626	4600-4800
200	1990-95	B9HS-10 [10][6]	L78C [11][6]	0.039(1.0)			CDI	(a)5-(a)1	(a)5-(a)1	21-25		1.375		730	575	40.5(1150)	12	4500-5500	YB-1626	4600-4800
P200	1991-95	B9HS-10 [24][6]	L78C [25][6]	0.039(1.0)			CDI	(a)5-(a)1	(a)5-(a)1	15-19		1.25		700	575	33.1(980)	12	4500-5500	YB-1626	5350-5500
P200/S200/L200	1996-98	B8HS-10 [6]	QL78C [6]	0.039(1.0)			CDI	(a)8-(a)6	(a)5-(a)1			(22)		700	575	33.1(980)	12	4500-5500	YB-1626	5350-5500
LX200/SX200	1999	B8HS-10 [6]	QL78C [6]	0.039(1.0)			CDI	(a)5-(a)1	(a)5-(a)1	13-22		1.375		730	625	31.1(980)	12	4500-5500	YB-1626	5300-5500
V200	1998	B9HS-10	QL77JC4	0.039(1.0)			CDI	(a)5-(a)1	(a)5-(a)1			(40)		730	625		12	4500-5500	YB-1626	5300-5500
225	1999	BR8HS-10 [6]	QL78C [6]	0.039(1.0)			CDI	(a)6(26)	(a)6(26)	22(26)				750	600	38.9(1150)(30)	12	5000-6000	YB-1626	5300-5500
225 (2.6L)	1990-93	BR9HS-10	QL78C	0.039(1.0)			CDI	(a)6(26)	(a)6(26)	20-22		1.125		750	600	33.1(980)	12	5000-6000	YB-1626	5450-5650
225 (2.6L)	1994-95	BR8HS-10	QL78C	0.039(1.0)			CDI	(a)6(26)	(a)6(26)	20-22		1.125		750	600	31.1(980)	12	5000-6000	YB-1626	5450-5650
225L	1996-98	BR9HS-10	QL78C	0.039(1.0)			CDI	(a)6(26)	(a)6(26)	22(26)		1.125		750	600	33.1(980)	12	5000-6000	YB-1626	5450-5650
225U (3.1L)	1994-95	B8HS-10	L78C	0.039(1.0)			CDI	(a)10(26)	(a)10(26)	(29)(26)		0.625		700	625	38.9(1150)(30)	12	4500-5500	YB-1626	5450-5650
225X	1994-95	B8HS-10	L78C	0.039(1.0)			CDI	(a)10(26)	(a)10(26)	(29)(26)		0.625		700	625	38.9(1150)(30)	12	4500-5500	YB-1626	5450-5650

04707C01

Engine Tune-Up Specifications

Model	Years	Spark Plug NGK	Spark Plug Champion	Spark Plug Gap Inch(mm)	Magneto Point Gap Inch	Magneto Point Gap mm	Ignition Timing Degrees (BTDC) Full Retard	Ignition Timing Degrees (BTDC) Carb Pickup	Ignition Timing Degrees (BTDC) Full Advance	Carb Pilot Screw Turns Out Top	Carb Pilot Screw Turns Out Center	Carb Pilot Screw Turns Out Bottom	Idle Speed RPM Neutral	Idle Speed RPM Trolling	Gear Oil Capacity Oz.(cc)	Tach Pole	Full Throttle RPM	Test Propeller Kent Moore Part Number	Test Propeller New Engine RPM
L225S/S225S/V225	1998-98	BR9HS-10	QL77JC4	0.039(1.0)	-	CDI	(a)5-(a)1	(a)5-(a)1	15-19	-	-	-	730	625	38.9(1150)(30)	12	4500-5500	-	-
S225X/S225U (3.1L)	1996	BR9HS-10	QL78C	0.039(1.0)	-	CDI	(a)6 (26)	(a)6 (26)	18 (26)	-	0.625	-	700	625	38.9(1150)(30)	12	4500-5500	-	-
S225X/S225U (3.1L)	1997	BR9HS-10	QL78C	0.039(1.0)	-	CDI	(a)8 (26)	(a)8 (26)	18 (26)	-	-	-	700	625	38.9(1150)(30)	12	4500-5500	-	-
250	1990-95	B8HS-10	L78C	0.039(1.0)	-	CDI	(a)6 (26)	(a)6 (26)	18(26)	-	0.75 (32)	-	700	625	38.9(1150)(30)	12	4500-5500	-	-
L250/S250	1998-98	BR9HS-10	QL77JC4	0.039(1.0)	-	CDI	(a)5-(a)1	-	14-18	-	-	-	730	625	38.9(1150)(30)	12	4500-5500	-	-
S250HP	1996	BR9HS-10	QL78C	0.039(1.0)	-	CDI	(a)6 (26)	(a)6 (26)	18	-	0.625	-	700	625	38.9(1150)(30)	12	5000-6000	YB-1626	5450-5650
S250HP	1997	BR8HS-10	QL78C	0.039(1.0)	-	CDI	(a)6 (26)	(a)6 (26)	18	-	0.625	-	700	625	38.9(1150)(30)	12	5000-6000	YB-1626	5450-5650

NOTE: It is recommended for optimum performance and engine life to adjust the wide open throttle engine speed to the top end of the recommended range

(a) After Top Dead Center (ATDC)
(1) 1993-95 1.75 turns out
(2) Manual Start, Electric Start 1.375 turns out
(3) 1995 2.25 turns out
(4) 1992-93 and C115, 1994-95 BR8HS-10
(5) 1992-93 and C115, 1994-95 QL78C
(6) Resistor spark plugs are standard equipment on 1994 and newer outboards (except C115) and are recommended as replacements for all years
(7) 1992-93, 1994-95 BR9HS-10
(8) 1992-93, 1994-95 QL77CJ4
(9) Right hand, Left hand 24.2 oz. (715 cc)
(10) 1992-93, 1994-95 BR8HS-10
(11) 1992-93, 1994-95 QL78C
(12) 1992-95 1 turn out
(13) Right hand, Left hand 29.4 oz. (870 cc)
(14) 1992-93, 1994-95 BR8HS-10
(15) 1992-93, 1994-95 QL78C
(16) 1992-93, 1994-95 17-19 degrees
(17) 1992 1.50 port, 1 starboard; 1992-93 1.25 port .75 starboard; 1994-95 1.375 turns out
(18) 1992-93 700 rpm, 1994-95 750 rpm
(19) 1992-93, 1994-95 BR9HS-10
(20) 1992-93, 1994-95 QL78C
(21) 1992-86 with TK carb 1.75 port, 1.125 starboard; 1992-95 with Nikki carb 1.375 turns out
(22) 1992-86 with TK carb 1.50 port, 1.125 starboard; 1992-89 with Nikki carb 1.25 port, .875 starboard; 1992-95 1.25 port, .750 starboard turns out
(23) Right hand, Left hand 30.4 oz. (900 cc)
(24) 1991-93, 1994-95 BR9HS-10
(25) 1991-93, 1994-95 QL77CJ4
(26) Computer system, timing not adjustable
(27) 1992 with TK carb 1.50; 1986 with Nikki carb 1.625 port, .75 starboard turns out
(28) 1992-89, 1992-95 0.50 volts
(29) Cylinders 1, 2, 5, and 6, 18 degrees; cylinders 3 and 4, 20 degrees
(30) Right hand, Left hand 33.8 oz. (1000 cc)
(31) 1992-94, 1995-95 0.48-0.51 volts
(32) 1992-92, 1993-95 0.625 turns out
(33) D150 Models BR9HS-10
(34) D150 Models QL82C
(35) 150 Models 1 turn, S150 and L150 1.25 turns, D150 and P150 1.0625 turn Port, 1.5625 Starboard
(36) Except D150 and L150 33.1 oz (980cc), D150 30.4 oz (900cc) and L150 29.4 oz (870cc)
(37) DX150 31.5 oz (900cc), LX150 30.5 oz (870cc), PX150 and SX150 34.5 oz (980cc)
(38) P175 1.125 turns, S175 1.125 Starboard and 1.625 Port
(39) 200 19-21 degrees, S200 and L200 19-23 degrees, P200 21-25 degrees
(40) 200 1.125 turns, S200 and L200 .625 turns Port and 1.125 turns Starboard, P200 .75 turns Port and 1.25 turns Starboard
(41) Right hand rotation, Left hand rotation 30.4 oz (870cc)
(42) LX, SX 34.5 oz (980cc)
(43) .75 turn Port, 1.25 turn Starboard

04707C02

POWERHEAD MECHANICAL 8-2
GENERAL INFORMATION 8-2
   INTRODUCTION 8-2
   REPAIR PROCEDURES 8-2
   TORQUE VALUES 8-2
   POWERHEAD COMPONENTS 8-2
   REED VALVE SERVICE 8-2
   CLEANLINESS 8-2
TWO-STROKE OPERATION 8-2
   INTAKE/EXHAUST 8-2
   LUBRICATION 8-2
   PHYSICAL LAWS 8-2
   POWER CYCLE 8-2
   TIMING 8-3
   CONCLUSION 8-3
ONE-CYLINDER 2 HP AND 3 HP
  MODELS 8-4
   REMOVAL & DISASSEMBLY 8-4
   CLEANING & INSPECTION 8-6
   ASSEMBLY & INSTALLATION 8-6
ONE-CYLINDER 4 HP AND 5 HP
  MODELS 8-9
   REMOVAL & DISASSEMBLY 8-9
   CLEANING & INSPECTION 8-12
   ASSEMBLY & INSTALLATION 8-12
TWO-CYLINDER 6 HP, 8 HP, 9.9 HP, 15
  HP, 25 HP AND 30 HP MODELS 8-15
   PREPARATION 8-15
   REMOVAL & DISASSEMBLY 8-16
   CLEANING & INSPECTION 8-20
   ASSEMBLY & INSTALLATION 8-20
THREE-CYLINDER POWERHEADS 8-28
   REMOVAL & DISASSEMBLY 8-28
   CLEANING & INSPECTION 8-32
   ASSEMBLY & INSTALLATION 8-32
V4 AND V6 POWERHEAD SERVICE 8-40
   REMOVAL & DISASSEMBLY 8-40
   CLEANING & INSPECTION 8-48
   ASSEMBLY & INSTALLATION 8-48
POWERHEAD REFINISHING 8-58
CLEANING AND INSPECTING 8-58
   REED BLOCK SERVICE 8-58
   EXHAUST COVER 8-58
   BLEED SYSTEM SERVICE 8-59
   CRANKSHAFT SERVICE 8-59
   CONNECTING ROD SERVICE 8-60
   PISTON SERVICE 8-61
   RING END-GAP CLEARANCE 8-62
   PISTON RING SIDE
    CLEARANCE 8-63
   OVERSIZE PISTONS & RINGS 8-63
   CYLINDER BLOCK SERVICE 8-63
   HONING CYLINDER WALLS 8-64
   BLOCK & CYLINDER HEAD
    WARPAGE 8-64
BREAK-IN PROCEDURES 8-66

SPECIFICATIONS CHARTS
ENGINE REBUILDING
  SPECIFICATIONS 8-67
ENGINE TORQUE
  SPECIFICATIONS 8-69

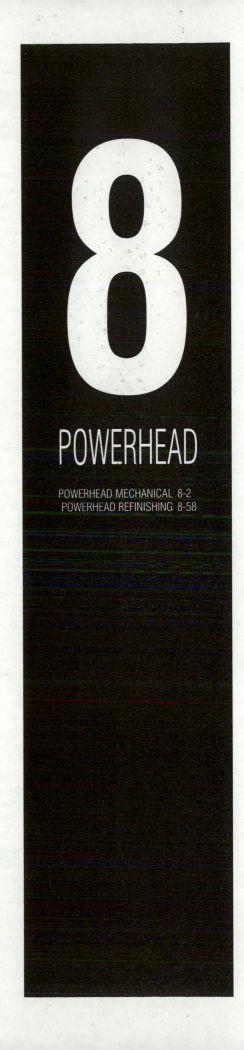

8
POWERHEAD

POWERHEAD MECHANICAL 8-2
POWERHEAD REFINISHING 8-58

POWERHEAD MECHANICAL

General Information

INTRODUCTION

The carburetion and ignition principles of two-stroke engine operation must be understood in order to perform proper service work on the outboard power-heads covered in this manual. The two-stroke powerhead differs in several ways from a four-stroke powerhead. Differences include the method by which the air/fuel mixture is delivered to the combustion chamber, the complete lubrication system, in most cases, the ignition system and the frequency of the power stroke.

Before commencing any work on the powerhead, an understanding of two-stroke engine operation will be most helpful. Therefore, it would be well worth the time to study the principles of two-stroke engines. A Polaroid, or equivalent instant-type camera is an extremely useful item, providing the means of accurately recording the arrangement of parts and wire connections before the disassembly work begins. Such a record is invaluable during assembling.

REPAIR PROCEDURES

Service and repair procedures will vary slightly between individual models, but the basic instructions are quite similar. Special tools may be called out in certain instances. These tools may be purchased from the local marine dealer.

TORQUE VALUES

All torque values must be met when they are specified. Required torque values for various parts of each powerhead are given in the Torque Specifications chart.

A torque wrench is essential to correctly assemble the powerhead. Never attempt to assemble a powerhead without a torque wrench. Attaching bolts must be tightened to the required torque value in three progressive stages, following the specified tightening sequence. Tighten all bolts to ⅓ the torque value, then repeat the sequence tightening to ⅔ the torque value. Finally, on the third and last sequence, tighten to the full torque value.

POWERHEAD COMPONENTS

Service procedures for the carburetors, fuel pumps, starter, and other power-head components are given in their respective Sections of this manual. See the Table of Contents.

REED VALVE SERVICE

The reeds on two-stroke powerheads covered in this manual are contained in an externally mounted reed valve block. Therefore, the powerhead need not be disassembled in order to replace a broken reed.

CLEANLINESS

▶ **See Figure 1**

Make a determined effort to keep parts and the work area as clean as possible. Parts must be cleaned and thoroughly inspected before they are assembled, installed, or adjusted. Use proper lubricants, or their equivalent, whenever they are recommended.

Two-Stroke Operation

INTAKE/EXHAUST

▶ **See Figures 2, 3 and 4**

Two-stroke engines utilize an arrangement of port openings to admit fuel to the combustion chamber and to purge the exhaust gases after burning has been completed. The ports are located in a precise pattern in order for them to be opened

Fig. 1 The exterior and interior of the powerhead must be kept clean, well lubricated and properly tuned for the owner to receive maximum enjoyment

and closed at an exact moment by the piston as it moves up and down in the cylinder. The exhaust port is located slightly higher than the fuel intake port. This arrangement opens the exhaust port first as the piston starts downward and therefore, the exhaust phase begins a fraction of a second before the intake phase.

Actually, the intake and exhaust ports are spaced so closely together that both open almost simultaneously. For this reason, the pistons of most two-stroke engines have a deflector-type top. This design of the piston top serves two purposes very effectively.

First, it creates turbulence when the incoming charge of fuel enters the combustion chamber. This turbulence results in more complete burning of the fuel than if the piston top were flat.

The second effect of the deflector-type piston crown is to force the exhaust gases from the cylinder more rapidly.

LUBRICATION

A two-stroke engine is lubricated by mixing oil with the fuel. Therefore, various parts are lubricated as the fuel mixture passes through the crankcase and the cylinder.

PHYSICAL LAWS

The two-stroke engine is able to function because of two very simple physical laws.

One: Gases will flow from an area of high pressure to an area of lower pressure. A tire blowout is an example of this principle. The high-pressure air escapes rapidly if the tube is punctured.

Two: If a gas is compressed into a smaller area, the pressure increases, and if a gas expands into a larger area, the pressure is decreased.

If these two laws are kept in mind, the operation of the two-stroke engine will be easier understood.

POWER CYCLE

Beginning with the piston approaching top dead center on the compression stroke: The intake and exhaust ports are closed by the piston, the reed valve is

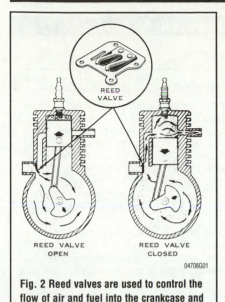

Fig. 2 Reed valves are used to control the flow of air and fuel into the crankcase and eventually into the cylinder

Fig. 3 The reeds are located in an externally mounted housing behind the intake manifold—two-cylinder powerhead shown

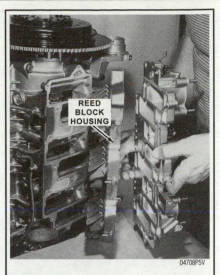

Fig. 4 The powerhead need not be disassembled to replace a broken reed—V4 and V6 powerheads shown

open, the spark plug fires, the compressed air/fuel mixture is ignited, and the power stroke begins. The reed valve was open because as the piston moved upward, the crankcase volume increased, which reduced the crankcase pressure to less than the outside atmosphere.

As the piston moves downward on the power stroke, the combustion chamber is filled with burning gases. As the exhaust port is uncovered, the gases, which are under great pressure, escape rapidly through the exhaust ports. The piston continues its downward movement. Pressure within the crankcase increases, closing the reed valves against their seats. The crankcase then becomes a sealed chamber. The air/fuel mixture is compressed ready for delivery to the combustion chamber. As the piston continues to move downward, the intake port is uncovered. A fresh air/fuel mixture rushes through the intake port into the combustion chamber striking the top of the piston where it is deflected along the cylinder wall. The reed valve remains closed until the piston moves upward again.

When the piston begins to move upward on the compression stroke, the reed valve opens because the crankcase volume has been increased, reducing crankcase pressure to less than the outside atmosphere. The intake and exhaust ports are closed and the fresh fuel charge is compressed inside the combustion chamber.

Pressure in the crankcase decreases as the piston moves upward and a fresh charge of air flows through the carburetor picking up fuel. As the piston approaches top dead center, the spark plug ignites the air/fuel mixture, the power stroke begins and one full cycle has been completed.

TIMING

▶ **See Figures 5 and 6**

The exact time of spark plug firing depends on engine speed. At low speed the spark is retarded, fires later than when the piston is at or beyond top dead center. Engine timing is built into the unit at the factory.

At high speed, the spark is advanced, fires earlier than when the piston is at top dead center. On all but the smallest, the 2 hp unit, the timing can be changed in the field to meet advance and retard factory specifications.

CONCLUSION

More than one phase of the cycle occurs simultaneously during operation of a two-stroke engine. On the downward stroke, power occurs above the piston while the ports are closed. When the ports open, exhaust begins and

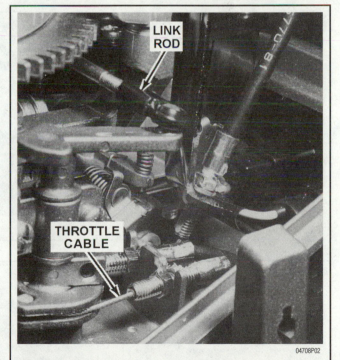

Fig. 5 Link rods rotate the stator plate under the flywheel to achieve advanced or retarded timing—single cylinder power head shown

intake follows. Below the piston, fresh air/fuel mixture is compressed in the crankcase.

On the upward stroke, exhaust and intake continue as long as the ports are open. Compression begins when the ports are closed and continues until the spark plug ignites the air/fuel mixture. Below the piston, a fresh air/fuel mixture is drawn into the crankcase ready to be compressed during the next cycle.

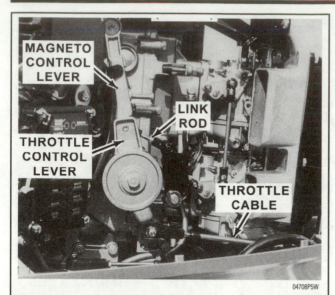

Fig. 6 Link rods rotate the stator plate under the flywheel to achieve advanced or retarded timing—three-cylinder power head shown

Labels on figure: MAGNETO CONTROL LEVER, LINK ROD, THROTTLE CONTROL LEVER, THROTTLE CABLE

04708P5W

One-Cylinder 2 Hp and 3 Hp Models

REMOVAL & DISASSEMBLY

♦ **See accompanying illustrations**

Remove the cowling, the hand starter, the flywheel, and the stator plate. Remove the carburetor and fuel tank.

1. Remove the four bolts securing the cylinder head to the block. Lift the fuel tank tray free of the powerhead.

2. Remove the cylinder head and the gasket. The head may have to be tapped lightly with a soft mallet to shock the gasket seal free of the powerhead. Remove the gasket material from the mating surfaces of the head and the block.

3. Remove the six bolts securing the powerhead to the intermediate housing.

4. Tap the side of the powerhead with a soft head mallet to shock the gasket seal, and then lift the powerhead from the intermediate housing.

5. Remove the gasket, plate, and a second gasket from the intermediate housing. Remove and Take care not to drop or lose the dowel pin seated in the intermediate housing.

6. Remove the four bolts securing the horseshoe bracket and reed valve housing to the powerhead. Separate the horseshoe bracket from the block.

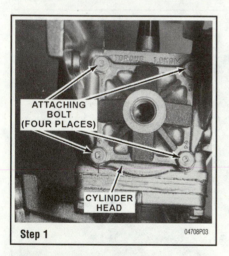

Labels: ATTACHING BOLT (FOUR PLACES), CYLINDER HEAD

Step 1 04708P03

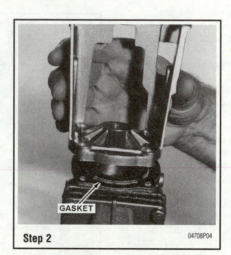

Labels: GASKET

Step 2 04708P04

Labels: ATTACHING BOLT (SIX PLACES)

Step 3 04708P05

Labels: POWERHEAD, INTERMEDIATE HOUSING

Step 4 04708P06

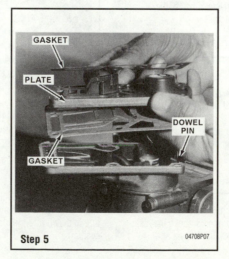

Labels: GASKET, PLATE, GASKET, DOWEL PIN

Step 5 04708P07

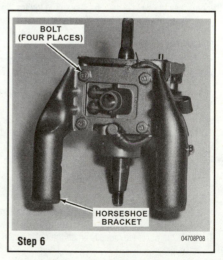

Labels: BOLT (FOUR PLACES), HORSESHOE BRACKET

Step 6 04708P08

7. Carefully lift off the valve reed housing and gasket. Note and remember the direction of the reeds as an aid during installation. It is possible to install this housing backwards by mistake.

8. After the reed housing has been removed, inspect the reed valve. If the valve is distorted or cracked, a proper seal cannot be obtained. Therefore, the reed valve must be replaced.

9. The reed stop is retained by two screws. If the reed valve must be removed, simply remove the reed stop and lift the valve out of the housing.

10. Remove the two bolts holding the two halves of the crankcase together. Note the position of the wire clip on one of these bolts as an aid during installation.

11. Separate the two crankcase halves. It may be necessary to shock one half with a soft headed mallet in order to jar the gasket sealing qualities loose. Slowly pull the two halves apart. The crankshaft will remain with one half, and the piston assembly will come out of the cylinder in the other half.

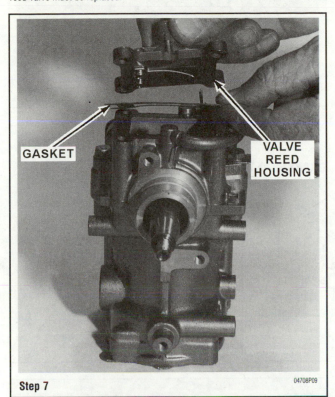

GASKET — VALVE REED HOUSING

Step 7

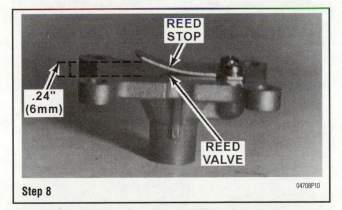

REED STOP — REED VALVE — .24" (6mm)

Step 8

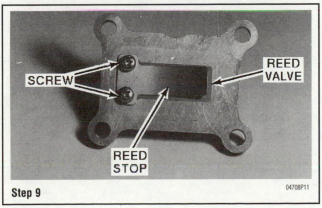

SCREW — REED VALVE — REED STOP

Step 9

WIRE CLIP

Step 10

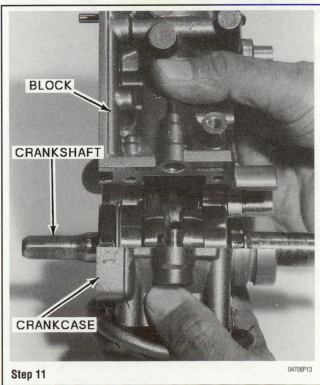

BLOCK — CRANKSHAFT — CRANKCASE

Step 11

12. Slide the upper and lower crankcase oil seals and the washer free of the crankshaft.

➡ **The piston pin lockrings are made of spring steel and may slip out of the pliers or pop out of the groove with considerable force. Therefore, wear eye protection glasses while removing the piston pin lockrings in the next step.**

13. Remove the G-lockring from both ends of the piston pin using a pair of needle nose pliers. Slide out the piston pin, and then the piston may be separated from the connecting rod. Push out the caged roller bearings from the small end of the connecting rod.

➡ **The rod and crank pin are pressed into the counterweights and can only be separated using a hydraulic press.**

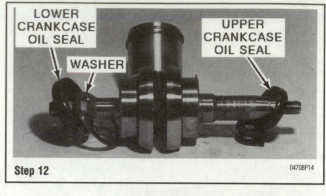

Step 12

Step 13

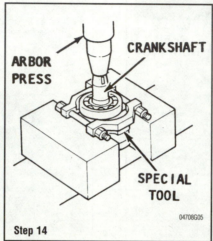

Step 14

Step 15

Slowly rotate both bearing races. If rough spots are felt, the bearings will have to be pressed free of the crankshaft.

14. Obtain special bearing separator tool, Yamaha P/N YB-06219 and an arbor press. Press each bearing from the crankshaft. Be sure the crankshaft is supported, because once the bearing breaks loose, the crankshaft is free to fall.

15. Gently spread the top piston ring enough to pry it out and up over the top of the piston. No special tool is required to remove the piston rings. Remove the lower ring in a similar manner. These rings are extremely brittle and have to be handled with care if they are intended for further service.

CLEANING & INSPECTION

♦ **See Figure 7**

Cleaning and inspecting the components is virtually the same for any two-stroke outboard. A section detailing the proper procedures is located later in this section.

ASSEMBLY & INSTALLATION

♦ **See accompanying illustrations**

1. Install a new set of piston rings onto the piston. No special tool is necessary for installation however, take care to spread the ring only enough to clear the top of the piston. The rings are extremely brittle and will snap if spread beyond their limit. Align the ring gap over the locating pin.

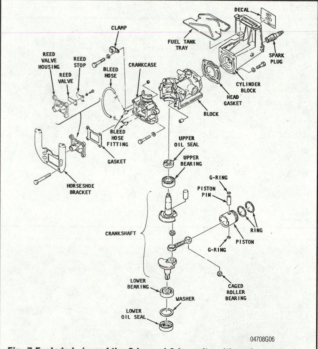

Fig. 7 Exploded view of the 2 hp and 3 hp units with major parts identified

2. If the main bearings were removed, support the crankshaft and press the bearings onto the shaft one at a time. Take note of the bearing size embossed on one side of the bearing. The side with the marking must face away from the crankshaft throw.

➡The piston pin lockrings are made of spring steel and may slip out of the pliers or pop out of the groove with considerable force. Therefore, wear eye protection glasses while installing the piston pin lockrings in the next step.

3. Apply a thin coating of Yamaha Grease A, or equivalent, to the inside surface of the upper end of the piston rod. Slide the caged roller bearings into the small end of the rod. Move the piston over the rod end with The word **UP** on the piston crown facing toward the tapered end of the crankshaft. Shift the piston to align the holes in the piston with the rod end opening. Slide the piston pin through the piston and connecting rod. Center the pin in the piston. Install a G-ring at each end of the piston pin.

4. Install the large washer onto the squared end of the crankshaft. Apply a light coating of Yamaha Grease A, or equivalent water resistant lubricant to both

LOCATING PIN

Step 1   04708P17

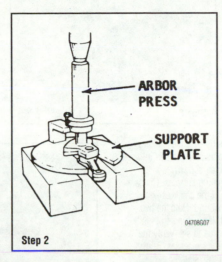

ARBOR PRESS

SUPPORT PLATE

Step 2   04708G07

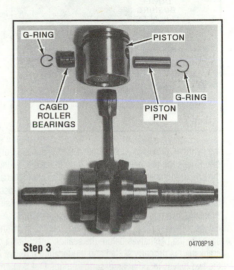

G-RING   PISTON

CAGED ROLLER BEARINGS   PISTON PIN   G-RING

Step 3   04708P18

LOWER CRANKCASE OIL SEAL

WASHER

UPPER CRANKCASE OIL SEAL

Step 4   04708P19

NOTCH

Step 6   04708P21

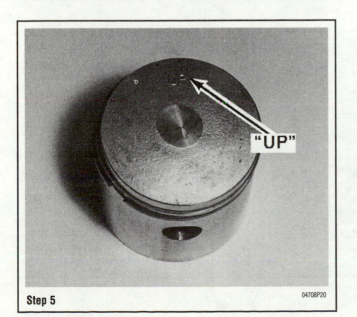

"UP"

Step 5   04708P20

seals before installation. Slide the lower crankshaft oil seal onto the squared end of the crankshaft with the lip facing toward the connecting rod. Slide the upper crankshaft oil seal onto the threaded end of the crankshaft with the lip of the seal facing toward the connecting rod.

5. The word **UP** is embossed on the piston crown. This word must face the threaded end of the crankshaft when the piston and rod assembly is installed into the cylinder.

6. Coat the piston and rings with engine oil. Check to be sure the ring gaps are centered over the locating pins. Lower the piston into the cylinder bore and seat the crankshaft assembly onto the crankcase. The rings will slide into

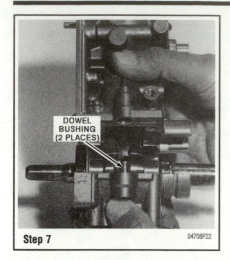

Step 7   04708P22

DOWEL BUSHING (2 PLACES)

Step 8   04708P23

TORQUE WRENCH

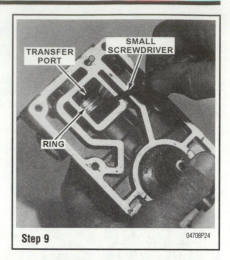

Step 9   04708P24

TRANSFER PORT   SMALL SCREWDRIVER   RING

the cylinder, provided each ring end-gap is centered properly over the locating pin. Rotate the two main bearings until the two indexing pins are recessed into the square notches at the mating surface of the crankcase, as shown.

7. Lay down a bead of Yamabond to the crankcase mating surfaces. Check to be sure the dowel bushings are in place on either side of the crankcase. Press the two halves together. Wipe away any excess Yamabond. Hold the two halves together and at the same time rotate the crankshaft. If any binding is felt, separate the two halves before the sealing agent has a chance to set. Verify the crankshaft is properly seated and the locating pins are in their recesses. Bring the two halves together as described in the first portion of this step.

8. Install the crankcase bolts. Install the bolt with the clip on the side of the crankcase which has the hose. Tighten the bolts alternately and evenly to the specified torque.

A torque wrench is essential to correctly assemble the powerhead. Never attempt to assemble a powerhead without a torque wrench. Attaching bolts must be tightened to the required torque value in three progressive stages, following the specified tightening sequence. Tighten all bolts to ⅓ the torque value, then repeat the sequence tightening to ⅔ the torque value. Finally, on the third and last sequence, tighten to the full torque value.

9. Check to be sure each piston ring has spring tension. This is accomplished by carefully pressing on each ring with a screwdriver extended through the transfer port. Take care not to burr the piston rings while checking for spring tension. If spring tension cannot be felt (the ring fails to return to its original position), the ring was probably broken during the piston and crankshaft installation process. Should this occur, new rings must be installed.

10. If the reed valve stop or reed valve was replaced, a new valve and stop should be positioned with the cut in the lower corner when the notch in the housing is facing up, as shown. Tighten the screws alternately to avoid warping the valve.

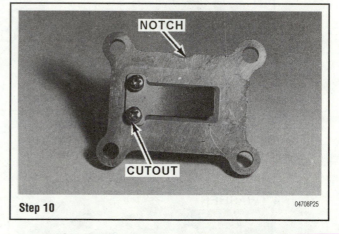

Step 10   04708P25

NOTCH   CUTOUT

11. Position a new gasket over the intake port and install the reed valve housing with the notch facing upward toward the threaded end of the crankshaft.

12. Place the horseshoe bracket over the housing. Install the four bolts and tighten alternately and evenly to the specified torque, in the sequence shown.

13. Install the two gaskets and the plate on top of the upper casing, as shown. Apply a small amount of Yamabond to both surfaces of each gasket as the gasket is positioned in place. Check to be sure the dowel pin is in place on the upper casing. Each gasket can only be fitted one way to prevent blocking of water passages.

Step 11   04708P26

VALVE REED HOUSING   GASKET

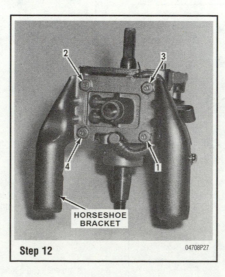

Step 12   04708P27

2   3   4   1   HORSESHOE BRACKET

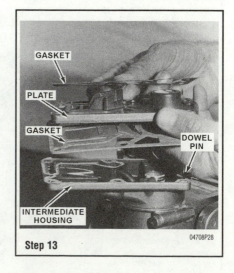

Step 13   04708P28

GASKET   PLATE   GASKET   DOWEL PIN   INTERMEDIATE HOUSING

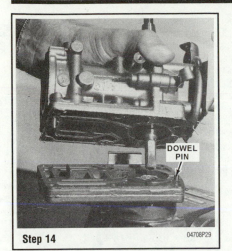

Step 14   04708P29

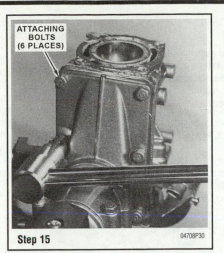

ATTACHING
BOLTS
(6 PLACES)

Step 15   04708P30

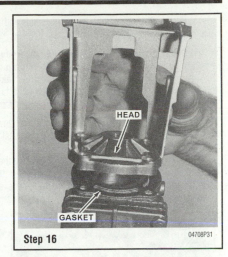

HEAD

GASKET

Step 16   04708P31

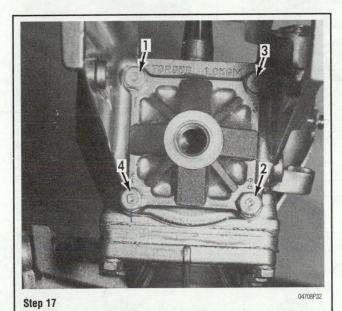

1   3

TORQUE 1.0KGM

4   2

Step 17   04708P32

14. Apply a coating of Yamaha Grease A, or an equivalent water resistant lubricant to the lower end of the driveshaft. Install the powerhead onto the intermediate housing, using the dowel pin to align the two surfaces. The propeller may have to be rotated slightly to permit the crankshaft to index with the driveshaft and allow the powerhead to seat properly.

15. Apply Loctite® to the threads of the six bolts securing the powerhead to the intermediate housing. Tighten the bolts in two stages starting with the center two bolts then the two on both ends. Tighten the bolts alternately and evenly to the specified torque.

16. Install a new head gasket without any sealing substance. Position the head in place over the gasket.

17. Coat the threads of the four attaching bolts with Loctite®. Install and tighten the bolts to two stages to the specified torque value, in the sequence shown. The sequence is also embossed on the head.

Install the flywheel.

Install the carburetor and fuel tank.

Install the hand rewind starter.

Install the cowling.

Mount the engine in a test tank, on a boat in a body of water, or connect a flush attachment to the lower unit.

Start the engine and check the completed work.

✳✳ WARNING

Water must circulate through the lower unit to the engine any time the engine is run to prevent damage to the water pump in the

lower unit. Just five seconds without water will damage the water pump.

Attempt to start and run the engine without the cowling installed. This will provide the opportunity to check for fuel and oil leaks, without the cowling in place.

After the engine is operating properly, install both halves of the cowling and secure them in place with the attaching hardware. Follow the break-in procedures with the unit on a boat and with a load on the propeller.

One-Cylinder 4 Hp and 5 Hp Models

REMOVAL & DISASSEMBLY

◆ See accompanying illustrations

Remove the cowling, the hand starter, the flywheel, and the stator plate, and the carburetor and fuel tank.

1. Loosen the outer nut on the cable to the starter and remove the cable end from the plastic barrel. Remove the three nuts shown in the accompanying illustration. Remove the metal and plastic brackets.

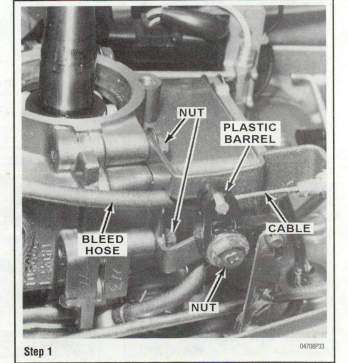

NUT

PLASTIC
BARREL

CABLE

BLEED
HOSE

NUT

Step 1   04708P33

2. Remove the seven bolts, four on one side and three on the other side, securing the powerhead to the intermediate housing.

➡ **Two dowel pins are used to mate the powerhead perfectly to the intermediate housing. These dowel pins may remain with the powerhead or they may stay with the intermediate housing. Take care when removing the powerhead, to prevent the dowel pins from falling down into the intermediate housing.**

3. Grasp the powerhead with both hands, pull upward, and make an attempt to rock the powerhead to break the gasket seal. Lift the powerhead clear of the intermediate housing.

4. Remove the two bolts and the two nuts, and then lift the reed valve housing clear of the two studs. NOTE and remember the direction of the reeds as an aid to installation. Remove and discard the gasket.

5. Remove the bolt and washer securing the oil seal housing over the lower end of the crankshaft. Remove and discard the O-ring.

6. Obtain bearing/oil seal puller tool Yamaha P/N YB6096. Secure the oil seal housing in a vise equipped with soft jaws.

Insert the expanding jaws of the tool under the edge of the oil seal. Tighten the top nut against the collar of the tool housing, and then rotate the center shaft to raise the jaws and pull the seal free.

7. Remove the four bolts securing the cylinder head cover to the block.

8. Lift off the cylinder head cover. Remove and discard the cover gasket.

9. Remove the nine bolts securing the exhaust cover to the powerhead.

10. Lift off the outer exhaust cover, the outer gasket, the thermostat, the inner exhaust cover, the inner gasket and finally the plastic thermostat insert.

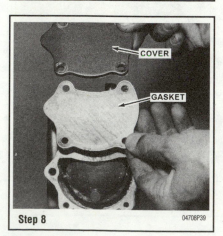

Step 2 — 04708G34

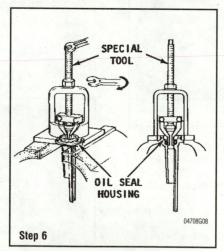

Step 3 — 04708P35

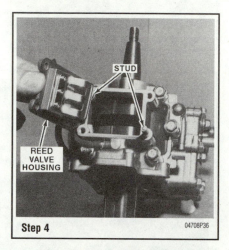

Step 4 — 04708P36

Step 5 — 04708P37

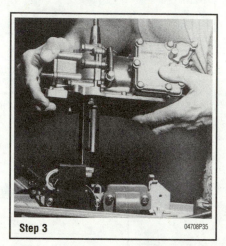

Step 6 — 04708G08

Step 7 — 04708P38

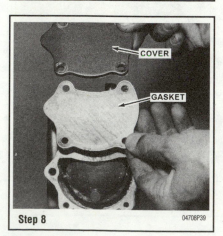

Step 8 — 04708P39

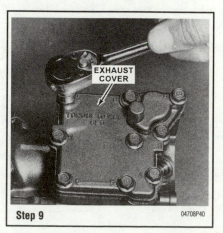

Step 9 — 04708P40

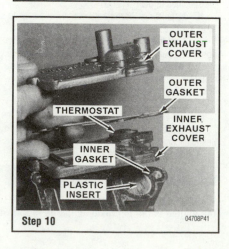

Step 10 — 04708P41

11. Remove the six bolts securing both halves of the crankcase together.

12. Insert two screwdrivers between the projections, provided for this purpose, on both sides of the crankcase. Pry on both sides at the same time to move the two crankcase halves apart. Take care not to lose the two dowel pins used to align the two halves perfectly.

13. Tap the crankshaft lightly with a soft head mallet to unseat it from the crankcase.

14. Lift out the crankshaft assembly from the cylinder block. The piston rod is an integral part of the crankshaft and cannot be separated.

15. Slide the upper and lower crankcase oil seals and the washer free of the crankshaft.

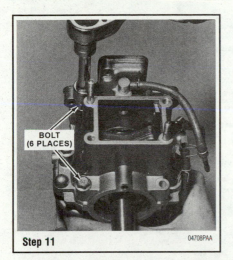

Step 11

Step 12

Step 13

Step 14

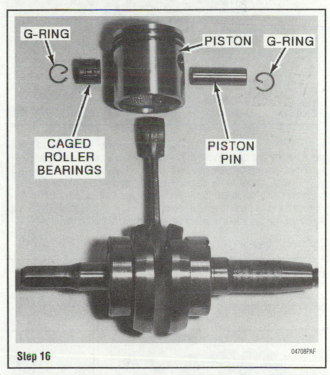

Step 16

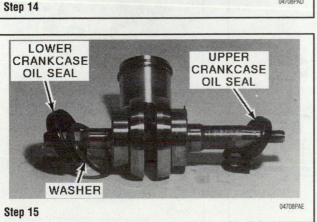

Step 15

➡The piston pin G-lockrings are made of spring steel and may slip out of the pliers or pop out of the groove with considerable force. Therefore, WEAR eye protection glasses while removing the piston pin lockrings in the next step.

16. Remove the G-lockrings from both ends of the piston pin using a pair of needle nose pliers. Slide out the piston pin, and then the piston may be separated from the connecting rod. Push the caged roller bearings free of the connecting rod end.

➡The rod and crank pin are pressed into the counterweights and can only be separated using a hydraulic press.

Slowly rotate both bearing races. If rough spots are felt, the bearings will have to be pressed free of the crankshaft.

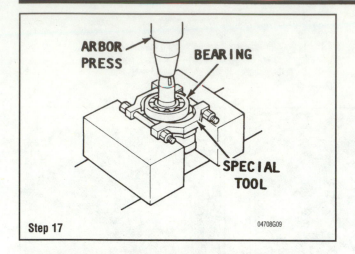

Step 17

04708G09

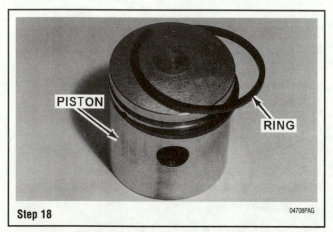

Step 18

04708PAG

17. Obtain special bearing separator tool, Yamaha P/N YB-06219 and an arbor press. Press each bearing from the crankshaft. Be sure the crankshaft is supported, because once the bearing breaks loose, the crankshaft is free to fall.

18. Gently spread the top piston ring enough to pry it out and up over the top of the piston. No special tool is required to remove the piston rings. Remove the lower ring in a similar manner. These rings are extremely brittle and have to be handled with care if they are intended for further service.

CLEANING & INSPECTION

▶ See Figure 8

Cleaning and inspecting the components is virtually the same for any two-stroke outboard. A section detailing the proper procedures is located later in this section.

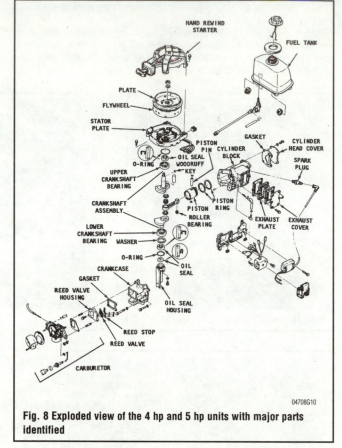

04708G10

Fig. 8 Exploded view of the 4 hp and 5 hp units with major parts identified

ASSEMBLY & INSTALLATION

▶ **See accompanying illustrations**

1. Install a new set of piston rings onto the piston. No special tool is necessary for installation. However, take care to spread the ring only enough to clear the top of the piston. The rings are extremely brittle and will snap if spread beyond their limit. Align the ring gap over the locating pin.

2. If the main bearings were removed, support the crankshaft and press the bearings onto the shaft one at a time. Take note of the bearing size embossed on one side of the bearing. The side with the marking must face away from the crankshaft throw.

➡**The piston pin lockrings are made of spring steel and may slip out of the pliers or pop out of the groove with considerable force. Therefore, wear eye protection glasses while installing the piston pin lockrings in the next step.**

Step 1

04708PAH

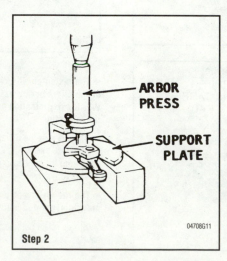

Step 2

04708G11

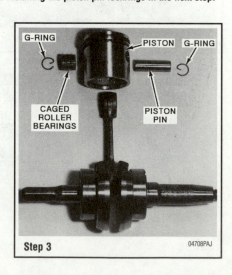

Step 3

04708PAJ

3. Apply a thin coating of Yamaha Grease A, or equivalent, to the inside surface of the upper end of the piston rod. Slide the caged roller bearings into the small end of the rod. Move the piston over the rod end with The word **UP** on the piston crown facing toward the tapered end of the crankshaft. Shift the piston to align the holes in the piston with the rod end opening. Slide the piston pin through the piston and connecting rod. Center the pin in the piston. Install a G-ring at each end of the piston pin.

4. Install the large washer onto the squared end of the crankshaft. Apply a light coating of Yamaha Grease A, or equivalent water resistant lubricant to both seals before installation. Slide the lower crankshaft oil seal onto the squared end of the crankshaft with the lip facing toward the connecting rod. Slide the upper crankshaft oil seal onto the threaded end of the crankshaft with the lip of the seal facing toward the connecting rod.

5. Coat the piston and rings with engine oil. Check to be sure the ring gaps are centered over the locating pins. Lower the piston into the cylinder bore and seat the crankshaft assembly onto the crankcase. The rings will slide into the cylinder, provided each ring end-gap is centered properly over the locating pin. Rotate the two main bearings until the two indexing pins are recessed into the square notches at the mating surface of the crankcase.

6. Check to be sure each piston ring has spring tension. This is accomplished by carefully pressing on each ring with a screwdriver extended through the transfer port. Take care not to burr the piston rings while checking for spring tension. If spring tension cannot be felt (the ring fails to return to its original position), the ring was probably broken during the piston and crankshaft installation process. Should this occur, new rings must be installed.

7. Lay down a bead of Yamabond to the crankcase mating surfaces. Check to be sure the dowel bushings on both halves of the crankcase are in place on either side of the crankshaft.

8. Press the two halves together. Wipe away any excess Yamabond. Hold the two halves together and at the same time rotate the crankshaft. If any binding is felt, separate the two halves before the sealing agent has a chance to set. Verify the crankshaft is properly seated and the locating pins are in their recesses. Bring the two halves together as described in the first portion of this step.

➡ **A torque wrench is essential to correctly assemble the powerhead. Never attempt to assemble a powerhead without a torque wrench. Attaching bolts must be tightened to the required torque value in two progressive stages, following the specified tightening sequence. Tighten all bolts to ½ the torque value, then repeat the sequence tightening to the full torque value.**

9. Install the drain hose onto the crankcase and position the metal bracket of the in-gear-protection system against bolt holes No. 1 and No. 5. Install and tighten the attaching bolts to the specified torque value.

10. Slide the plastic thermostat insert into the block. Install the following components in the order given: first, the inner gasket, then the inner plate, the thermostat, the outer gasket, and finally the outer cover.

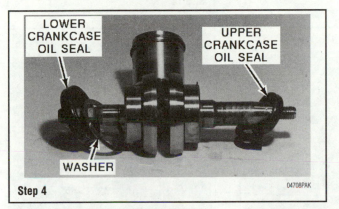

LOWER CRANKCASE OIL SEAL

UPPER CRANKCASE OIL SEAL

WASHER

Step 4   04708PAK

Step 5   04708P42

SCREWDRIVER

PISTON RING

Step 6   04708P43

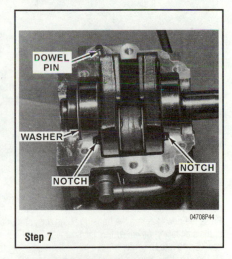

DOWEL PIN

WASHER

NOTCH

NOTCH

Step 7   04708P44

PIN

Step 8   04708P45

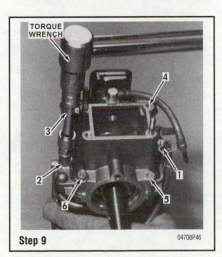

TORQUE WRENCH

3

4

2

6

5

1

Step 9   04708P46

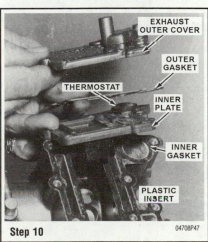

EXHAUST OUTER COVER

OUTER GASKET

THERMOSTAT

INNER PLATE

INNER GASKET

PLASTIC INSERT

Step 10   04708P47

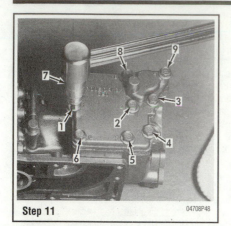

Step 11   04708P48

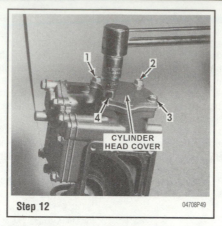

Step 12   04708P49

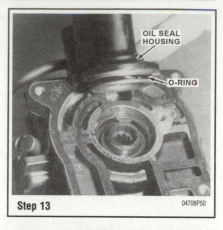

Step 13   04708P50

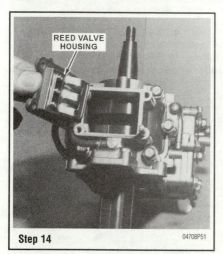

Step 14   04708P51

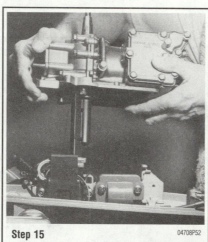

Step 15   04708P52

Step 16   04708P53

➡Three different length bolts are used to install the exhaust cover. Bolt No. 9 is 1.38 in. (35mm), bolt No. 3 is .63 in. (16mm), and the other seven are .98 in. (25mm). Be sure the proper bolt is installed in the proper location.

11. Install and tighten the exhaust cover bolts to the specified torque value.

12. Position a new cylinder head cover gasket in place, and then install the cover. Secure the cover with the four attaching bolts. Tighten the bolts to the specified torque value.

13. If the oil seal inside the oil seal housing was removed, coat the lip of a new seal with Yamaha all-purpose grease, or equivalent water resistant grease. Press the new seal into the housing using the appropriate mandrel, with the lip of the seal facing downward as the seal is pressed into the housing. Install a new O-ring into the outer groove of the housing. Coat the outer surface of the O-ring with the same grease as for the seal. Install the housing and tap it lightly with a soft head mallet to be sure it is fully seated. Secure the housing in place with the attaching bolt.

14. Position the reed valve housing onto the crankcase over the two studs. The reed valve opening must face the starboard side of the block. Install and tighten the two bolts and two nuts to specification.

15. Check to be sure the two dowel pins on the intermediate housing are in place forward and aft of the driveshaft area. Coat both sides of the powerhead gasket with Permatex®, or equivalent material. Position the gasket in place with the dowel pins passing up through the correct holes in the gasket.

Apply a coating of Yamaha Grease A, or an equivalent water resistant lubricant to the lower end of the driveshaft. Install the powerhead onto the upper casing using the dowel pin to align the two surfaces. The propeller may have to be rotated slightly to permit the crankshaft to index with the driveshaft and allow the powerhead to seat properly.

16. Apply Loctite® to the threads of the seven bolts securing the powerhead to the intermediate housing. Tighten the bolts in two stages starting with the center two bolts then the two on both ends. Tighten the bolts alternately and evenly to the specified torque value.

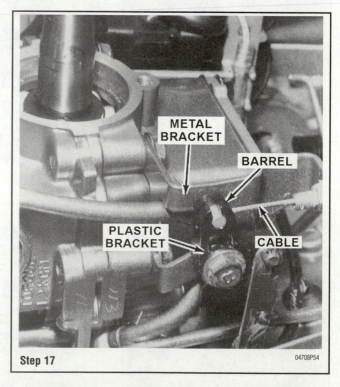

Step 17   04708P54

17. Install the plastic bracket to the metal bracket on the starboard side of the powerhead. Place the end of the cable from the starter into the plastic barrel. Slide the cable onto the metal retainer with the one lock cable nut on each side of the retainer.

Install the flywheel.

Install the carburetor and fuel tank.

Install the hand rewind starter. After the starter is installed, check the action of the no-start-in-gear protection system.

Mount the engine in a test tank, on a boat in a body of water, or connect a flush attachment to the lower unit.

Start the engine and check the completed work.

❊❊ WARNING

Water must circulate through the lower unit to the engine any time the engine is run to prevent damage to the water pump in the lower unit. Just five seconds without water will damage the water pump.

Attempt to start and run the engine without the cowling installed. This will provide the opportunity to check for fuel and oil leaks, without the cowling in place.

After the engine is operating properly, install the cowling. Follow the break-in procedures with the unit on a boat and with a load on the propeller.

Two-Cylinder 6 Hp, 8 Hp, 9.9 Hp, 15 Hp, 25 Hp and 30 Hp Models

PREPARATION

◆ **See accompanying illustrations**

Remove the cowling, the hand starter the flywheel, and the stator plate, disconnect the fuel line and remove the carburetor.

On models with electric cranking motor, remove the cranking motor and relay, disconnect the leads from the rectifier at the quick disconnect fittings, and remove the rectifier.

Procedural steps are given to remove and disassemble virtually all items of the powerhead. However, as the work moves along, if certain items (i.e. bearings, bushings, seals, etc.) are found to be fit for further service, simply skip the disassembly steps involved. Proceed with the required tasks to disassemble the necessary components.

1. On 6 hp and 8 hp models, remove the collar around the wire harness from the stator plate and the CDI unit. Disconnect all wires at their quick disconnect fittings and any ground wires which may be secured to the block.

Disconnect the two bolts securing the CDI unit to the powerhead and remove the CDI unit. Remove the two bolts securing the ignition coil to the powerhead and remove the coil.

Identify the ends of the two throttle cables and a matching identification on the stays the ends slip into.

2. On 6 hp and 8 hp models, loosen the two locknuts, one on each side of the two stays and lift each throttle cable free of the stays. Lift the ends of the cables up and out of the slots in the throttle control lever. Use a small screwdriver and pry the link free of the ball joint.

3. On 9.9 hp and 15 hp models, remove the hose from the exhaust cover. This hose may be moved out of the way while still attached to the pilot hole. Remove the bolts securing both the terminal cover and the CDI unit to the powerhead. Lift off the terminal cover and disconnect all wires leading to the CDI unit and the ignition coil. Remove the CDI unit.

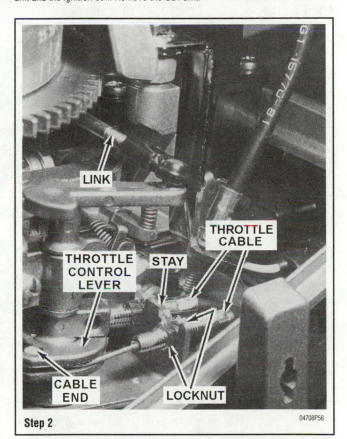

Step 2   04708P56

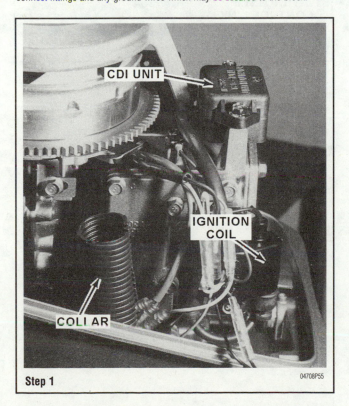

Step 1   04708P55

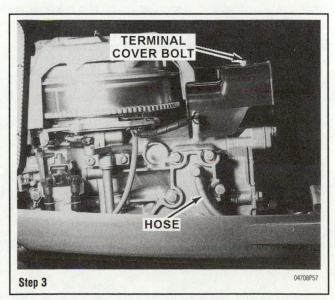

Step 3   04708P57

Step 4   04708P58

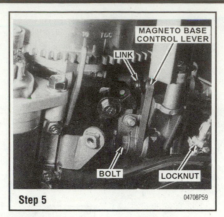

Step 5   04708P59

Step 6   04708P60

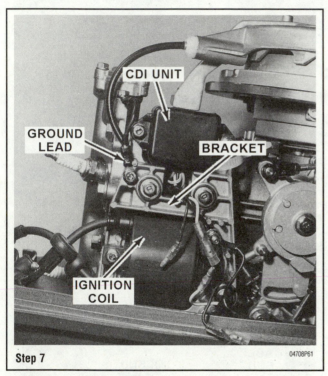

Step 7   04708P61

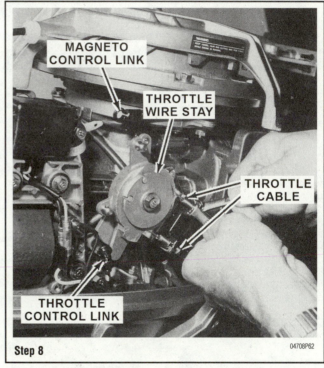

Step 8   04708P62

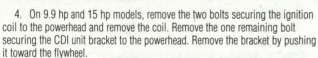

4. On 9.9 hp and 15 hp models, remove the two bolts securing the ignition coil to the powerhead and remove the coil. Remove the one remaining bolt securing the CDI unit bracket to the powerhead. Remove the bracket by pushing it toward the flywheel.

5. On 9.9 hp and 15 hp models, pry the link from the magneto control lever at the ball joint. Remove the bolt securing the magneto base control lever. Loosen the locknuts on the starter cable, and then remove the cable end from the bracket.

6. On 9.9 hp and 15 hp models, pry the link free of the ball joint at the top of the throttle control rod. Remove the inlet and outlet lines to the fuel filter. Plug both lines to prevent fuel spillage and contaminants from entering the lines. Fuel in the bottom of the cowling may attack grommets and rubber mounts. Remove the fuel filter.

7. On 25 hp and 30 hp models, disconnect all leads from the CDI unit and ignition coil at their quick disconnect fittings. Remove the attaching hardware, and then remove the CDI unit and the coil from the powerhead. Disconnect the ground lead from the powerhead to the CDI bracket. Remove the three bolts, and then remove the bracket.

8. On 25 hp and 30 hp models, pry the throttle cam, the magneto control, and the throttle control link rods free of their ball joints. Loosen the locknuts retaining the two throttle cables, and then lift their ends from the throttle wire stay. Remove the two bolts securing the throttle wire stay and magneto control lever, and then remove the stay and lever. Loosen the locknuts from the starter wire and remove the wire end from the bracket. Remove the attaching bolt, and then the bracket.

➡ **The powerhead preparation work is now complete for the various models. The following steps, in general, apply to all models. If differences should occur, the special task involved will be clearly indicated.**

REMOVAL & DISASSEMBLY

◆ **See accompanying illustrations**

1. Tilt the lower unit to the full up position and lock it in place. Remove the six bolts securing the powerhead to the intermediate housing. The powerhead

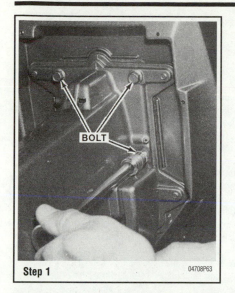

Step 1   04708P63

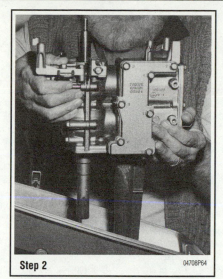

Step 2   04708P64

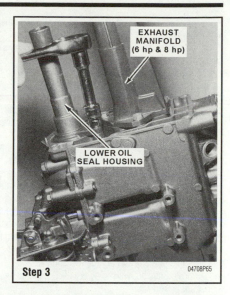

EXHAUST MANIFOLD (6 hp & 8 hp)

LOWER OIL SEAL HOUSING

Step 3   04708P65

may have to be rotated to gain access to the two front bolts. After the bolts have been removed, lower the unit to the full down position.

2. Lift the powerhead straight up and free of the intermediate housing.

✳✳ WARNING

If the unit is several years old, or if it has been operated in salt water, or has not had proper maintenance, or shelter, or any number of other factors, then separating the powerhead from the intermediate housing may not be a simple task. An air hammer may be required on the bolts to shake the corrosion loose, heat may have to be applied to the casting to expand it slightly, or other devices employed in order to remove the powerhead. One very serious condition would be the driveshaft frozen with the lower end of the crankshaft. In this case a circular plug type hole must be drilled and a torch used to cut the driveshaft.

A piece of wood may be inserted between the powerhead and the intermediate housing as a means of using leverage to force them apart.

Let's assume the powerhead will come free on the first attempt.

Take care not to lose the two dowel pins. The pins may come away with the powerhead or they may stay in the intermediate housing. Be especially careful not to drop them into the lower unit.

3. Remove the bolt securing the lower oil seal housing. Tap the housing lightly with a soft head mallet to jar it loose.

6 hp and 8 hp models, have a cylindrical exhaust manifold secured to the powerhead with three bolts. Remove the bolts and remove the manifold. It may be necessary to tap the manifold lightly with a soft head mallet to jar it loose.

4. Inspect the condition of the oil seals in the lower oil seal housing. Make a determination if they are fit for further service. If they are not, obtain slide

hammer P/N YB6096 with an expanding jaw attachment. Use the slide hammer and remove the oil seals from the lower oil seal housing.

6 hp and 8 hp models, have one large seal and one small seal behind the large seal.

9.9 hp 15 hp, 25 hp and 30 hp models, have one large seal and two identical small seals behind the large seal.

Remove and discard the outer O-ring.

5. On 6 hp, 8 hp, 25 hp & 30 hp models, remove the upper oil seal housing from the top of the crankshaft.

On 6 hp and 8 hp models, remove and discard the O-ring in the bottom recess.

On 25 hp and 30 hp models, remove and discard the gasket.

Inspect the condition of the oil seal in the upper oil seal housing. Make a determination if the seal is fit for further service. The seal will be destroyed during removal, therefore, remove it only if it is damaged and has lost its sealing qualities.

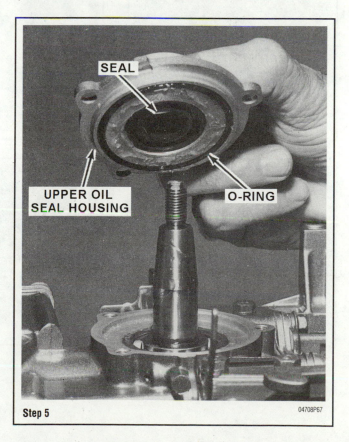

SEAL

UPPER OIL SEAL HOUSING

O-RING

Step 5   04708P67

LOWER OIL SEAL HOUSING   O-RING

OIL SEAL

Step 4   04708P66

To remove the seal, first obtain Yamaha slide hammer puller P/N YB6096 with expanding jaw attachment, and then pull the seal.

9.9 hp and 15 hp models do not have an upper oil seal housing. The upper crankshaft oil seal is contained in the stator plate.

6. On 6 hp and 8 hp models, remove the bolt and then the limited throttle opening device next to the timing pointer. Pry the link from the free acceleration lever. Remove the two Phillips head screws from the bracket retaining the magneto control lever. Remove the lever, the pulley and the free acceleration lever from the throttle wire stay. Remove the attaching hardware, and then the throttle wire stay.

7. On 9.9 hp, 15 hp, 25 hp and 30 hp models, remove the attaching bolts, and then the thermostat cover. If the cover is stuck fast, tap it lightly with a soft head mallet to jar it free. Lift out the thermostat and at the same time note the direction the thermostat faces as an aid during installation. Remove and discard the O-ring or washer.

Remove the cylinder head cover bolts, and then the cover. On the Model 6 hp and 8 hp, a hose stay is secured by one of the cover bolts. Remember which bolt as an aid during assembling. Remove and discard the gasket. If the cover is stuck to the cylinder head, insert a slotted screwdriver between the tabs provided for this purpose and pry the two surfaces apart. Never pry at gasket sealing surfaces. Such action would very likely damage the sealing surface of an aluminum powerhead.

8. On 6 hp and 8 hp models, remove the collar and thermostat from beneath the cylinder head cover.

➡The exhaust cover should always be removed during a powerhead overhaul. Many times water in the powerhead is caused by a leaking exhaust cover gasket or plate.

9. Remove the bolts and then the exhaust outer cover, the gasket, the exhaust inner cover, and another gasket. Discard all gaskets. If the cover is stuck to the powerhead, insert a slotted screwdriver between the tabs provided for this purpose and pry the two surfaces apart. Never pry at gasket sealing surfaces. Such action would very likely damage the sealing surface of an aluminum powerhead.

10. Take great care in the next step when handling reed valve assemblies. Once the assembly is removed, keep it away from sunlight, moisture, dust, and dirt. Sunlight can deteriorate valve seat rubber seals. Moisture can easily rust stoppers overnight. Dust and dirt—especially sand or other gritty material can break reed petals if caught between stoppers and reed petals.

Make special arrangements to store the reed valves to keep them isolated from the elements while further work is being performed on the powerhead.

11. On models 6 hp, 8 hp, 25 hp and 30 hp, remove the bolts and then the intake manifold. When removing the bolts—notice their lengths and locations as an aid during assembling. Remove and discard the gasket. Remove the reed valve assembly. Discard the gasket under the reed valve assembly. Model 25 hp and 30 hp have a wire stay attached by the middle left bolt and a fuel pipe clamp attached by the lower right bolt. Remember these locations as an aid during assembling.

Models 9.9 hp and 15 hp do not have an intake manifold. The carburetor is mounted directly onto the reed valve assembly.

Remove the upper right, middle left, and two lower outer bolts. Do not remove the upper left stud, middle right stud, or center lower bolt. Remove the reed valve assembly. Discard the gasket under the assembly.

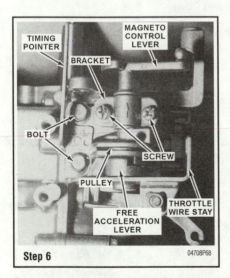

Step 6   04708P68

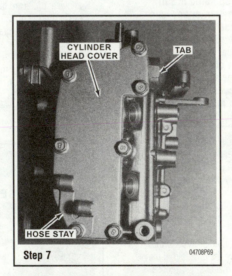

Step 7   04708P69

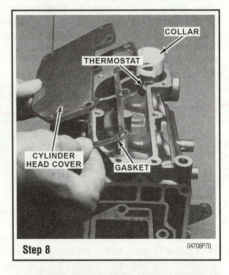

Step 8   04708P70

Step 9   04708P71

Step 10   04708P72

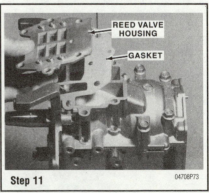

Step 11   04708P73

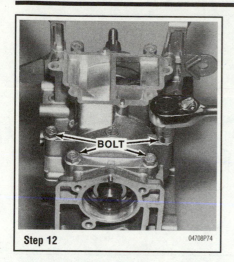

Step 12   04708P74

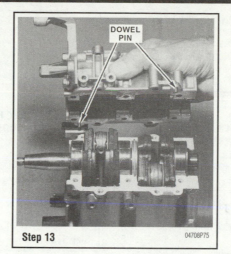

DOWEL PIN

Step 13   04708P75

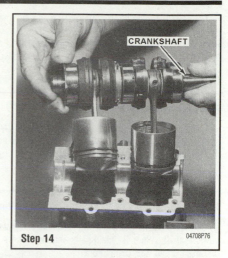

CRANKSHAFT

Step 14   04708P76

BOLT

12.   Remove the crankcase bolts. These bolts are of various sizes. Pay special attention to the locations and sizes of bolts during disassembly.

To remove the crankcase, insert a slotted screwdriver between the tabs provided for this purpose and pry the two surfaces apart. Never pry at gasket sealing surfaces. Such action would very likely damage the sealing surface of an aluminum powerhead.

13.   Separate the two halves of the crankcase. Take care not to lose the two dowel pins. These pins may remain in either half when the crankcase is separated.

14.   Tap the tapered end of the crankshaft, with a soft head mallet, to jar it free from the block. Slowly lift the crankshaft assembly straight up and out of the block.

15.   Slide the labyrinth seal circlips from the crankshaft, one at each end. Scribe a mark on the inside of the piston skirt to identify the top and bottom piston before removal from the connecting rod as described in the next step.

➡ **The piston pin C-lockrings are made of spring steel and may slip out of the pliers or pop out of the groove with considerable force. Therefore, wear eye protection glasses while removing the piston pin lockrings in the next step.**

Remove the C-lockring from both ends of the piston pin using a pair of needle nose pliers. Discard the C-lockrings. These rings stretch during removal and cannot be used a second time. The needle bearings and two retainers will fall away from the connecting rod small end.

➡ **New needle bearings should be installed in the connecting rods, even through they may appear to be in serviceable condition. New bearings will ensure lasting service after the overhaul work is completed. If it is necessary to install the used bearings, keep them separate and identified to ensure they will be installed onto the same crank pin throw and with the same connecting rod from which they were removed.**

Slowly rotate both bearing races. If rough spots are felt, the bearings will have to be pressed free of the crankshaft.

16.   Obtain special bearing separator tool, Yamaha P/N YB6219 and an arbor press. Press each bearing from the crankshaft. Be sure the crankshaft is supported, because once the bearing breaks loose, the crankshaft is free to fall.

➡ **Good shop practice dictates to replace the rings during a powerhead overhaul. However, if the rings are to be used again, expand them only enough to clear the piston and the grooves because used rings are brittle and break very easily.**

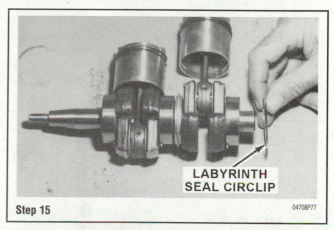

LABYRINTH SEAL CIRCLIP

Step 15   04708P77

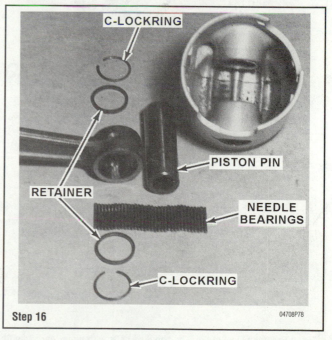

C-LOCKRING

PISTON PIN

RETAINER

NEEDLE BEARINGS

C-LOCKRING

Step 16   04708P78

17. Gently spread the top piston ring enough to pry it out and up over the top of the piston. No special tool is required to remove the piston rings. Remove the lower ring in a similar manner. These rings are extremely brittle and have to be handled with care if they are intended for further service.

CLEANING & INSPECTION

▶ See Figures 9, 10 and 11

Cleaning and inspecting the components is virtually the same for any two-stroke outboard. A section detailing the proper procedures is located later in this section.

ASSEMBLY & INSTALLATION

▶ See Figures 12, 13 and 14, and accompanying illustrations

Detailed procedures are given to assemble and install virtually all parts of the powerhead. Therefore, if certain parts were not removed or disassembled because the part was found to be fit for further service, simply skip the particu-

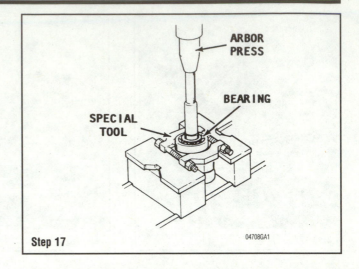

Step 17

04708GA1

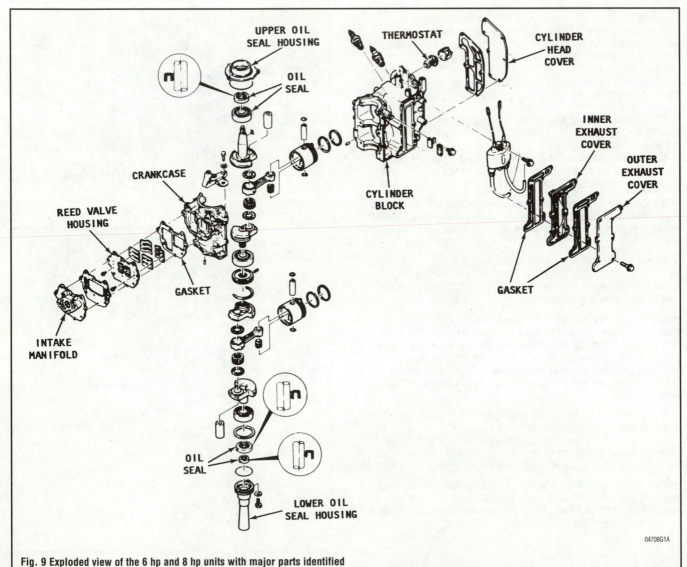

Fig. 9 Exploded view of the 6 hp and 8 hp units with major parts identified

04708G1A

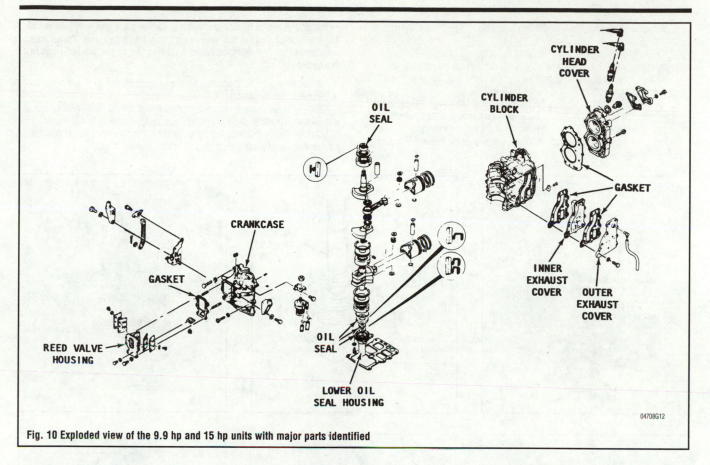

Fig. 10 Exploded view of the 9.9 hp and 15 hp units with major parts identified

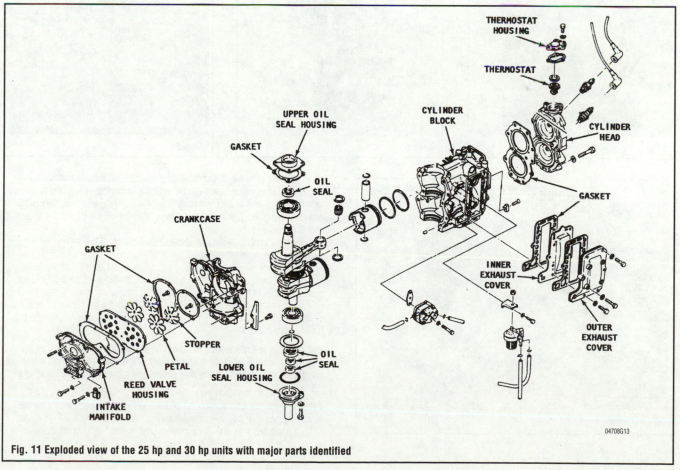

Fig. 11 Exploded view of the 25 hp and 30 hp units with major parts identified

lar step involved and continue with the required tasks to return the powerhead to operating condition.

1. Install a new set of piston rings onto the piston. No special tool is necessary for installation. However, take care to spread the ring only enough to clear the top of the piston. The rings are extremely brittle and will snap if spread beyond their limit. Align the ring gap over the locating pin.

2. If the main bearings were removed, support the crankshaft and press the bearings onto the shaft one at a time. Press only on the inner race. Pressing on the cage, the ball bearings, or the outer race may destroy the bearing.

Take note of the bearing size embossed on one side of the bearing. The side with the marking must face away from the crankshaft throw.

➡**The piston pin lockrings are made of spring steel and may slip out of the pliers or pop out of the groove with considerable force. Therefore, wear eye protection glasses while installing the piston pin lockrings in the next step.**

3. Select the set of needle bearings removed from the No. 1 piston or obtain a new set of bearings.

Coat the inner circumference of the small end of the No. 1 connecting rod with Yamaha A grease, or equivalent multipurpose water resistant lubricant. Position the needle bearings one by one around the circumference. Dab some lubricant on the sides of the rod and stick the retainers in place.

Step 1　　　04708P79

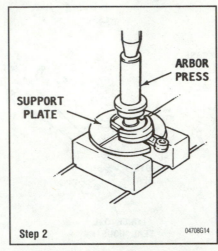

Step 2　　　04708G14

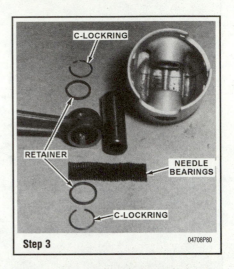

Step 3　　　04708P80

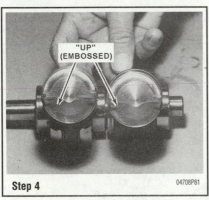

Step 4　　　04708P81

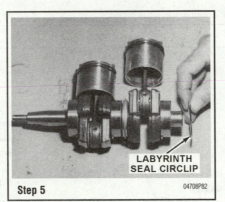

Step 5　　　04708P82

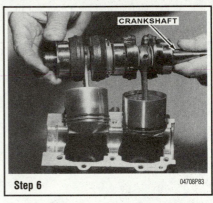

Step 6　　　04708P83

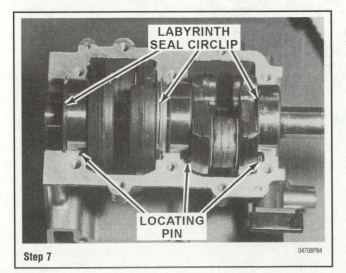

Step 7　　　04708P84

4. Position the end of the rod with the needle bearings and retainers in place up into the piston. The word **UP** on the piston crown must face toward the tapered (upper) end of the crankshaft. Slide the piston pin through the piston and connecting rod. Center the pin in the piston. Install the C-lockring at each end of the piston pin.

Perform the procedures in this step to install the No. 2 needle bearing set and the piston onto the No. 2 connecting rod.

5. Slide a labyrinth seal circlip on each end of the assembled crankshaft.

6. Coat the upper sides of each piston with 2-stroke engine oil. Hold the crankshaft at right angles to the cylinder bores and slowly lower one piston at a time into the appropriate cylinder. The upper edge of the each cylinder bore has a slight taper to squeeze in the rings around the locating pin and allow the piston to center the bore.

➡**If difficulty is experienced in fitting the piston into the cylinder, do not force the piston. Such action might result in a broken piston ring. Raise the crankshaft and make sure the ring end-gap is aligned with the locating pin.**

7. Push the crankshaft assembly down until it seats in the block. Fit the three labyrinth seal circlips into the grooves in the block. The center seal was never removed as it normally remains on the crankshaft. Rotate the upper, center, and lower bearings until their locating pins fit into the recesses in the block.

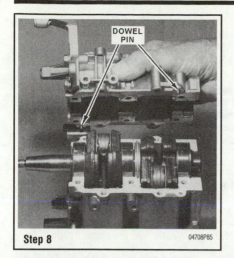

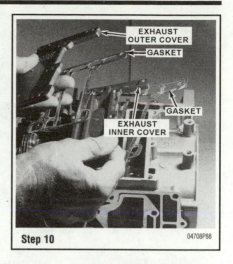

Step 8   04708P85

Step 9   04708P87

Step 10   04708P88

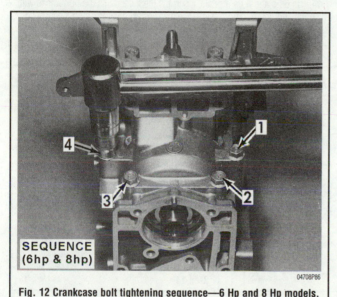

SEQUENCE
(6hp & 8hp)

04708P86

Fig. 12 Crankcase bolt tightening sequence—6 Hp and 8 Hp models.

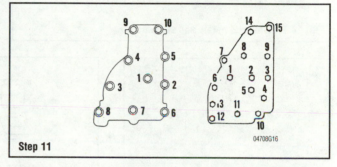

Step 11   04708G16

8. Apply a thin bead of Yamabond No. 4 Permatex® around both surfaces of the crankcase and block. Check to be sure the two dowel pins are in place and install the crankcase to the block.

Install and tighten the crankcase attaching bolts in the sequence shown in the accompanying illustration. Tighten the bolts in two rounds to the specified torque value.

Rotate the crankshaft by hand to be sure the crankshaft does not bind.

✶✶ WARNING

If binding is felt, it will be necessary to remove the crankcase and reseat the crankshaft and also to check the positioning of the labyrinth seal circlips and the bearing locating pins. If binding is still a problem after the crankcase has been installed a second time, the cause might very well be a broken piston ring.

9. Check to be sure each piston ring has spring tension. This is accomplished by carefully pressing on each ring with a screwdriver extended through the exhaust ports, as shown in the accompanying illustration. If spring tension cannot be felt (the spring fails to return to its original position), the ring was probably broken during the piston and crankshaft installation process. Take care not to burr the piston rings while checking for spring tension.

10. Install the following parts in the order given over the exhaust ports: the gasket, the inner exhaust cover, a second gasket, and finally the outer exhaust cover.

➡**The manufacturer recommends no sealing agent be applied to any of the gasket sealing surfaces.**

11. Install and tighten the exhaust cover attaching bolts in the sequence shown to the specified torque value.

On 6 hp and 8 hp models, install the following parts onto the intake port in the order given: the gasket, the reed valve housing, another gasket, and finally the intake manifold. Install and tighten the manifold attaching bolts in the sequence indicated in the accompanying illustration to the specified torque value.

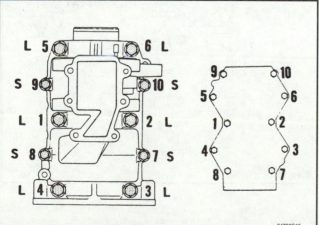

04708G15

Fig. 13 Crankcase bolt tightening sequence—9.9 Hp, 15 Hp, 25 Hp and 30 Hp models

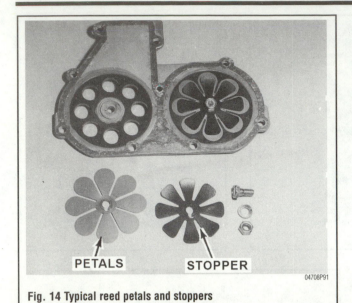

PETALS   STOPPER

04708P91

Fig. 14 Typical reed petals and stoppers

12. On 9.9 hp and 15 hp models, apply a light coating of Yamabond No. 4 or Permatex® to the upper portion only of the reed valve housing gasket. Install the gasket and reed valve housing to the intake port. Install and tighten the attaching bolts in a circular pattern to the specified torque value.

➡**If servicing a 6 hp, 8 hp, 25 hp, or 30 hp model, the manufacturer recommends no sealing agent be applied to the gasket sealing surfaces. However, the manufacturer does recommend Loctite® be applied to the threads of the intake manifold bolts on the Model 25 hp and 30 hp. No similar recommendations are made for the Model 6 hp and 8 hp units.**

13. On 25 hp and 30 hp models, install the following parts onto the intake port in the order given: the gasket with the narrow edges, the reed valve housing with the reeds facing toward the powerhead, the gasket with the wide edges, and finally the intake manifold. Install the various length bolts in the locations noted during disassembling. Install the wire stay on the middle left bolt and the fuel pipe clamp on the lower right bolt. Tighten the bolts in a circular pattern to the specified torque value.

14. On 6 hp and 8 hp models, insert the thermostat into the powerhead with the spring end going in first. Install the thermostat collar. Position a new head gasket in place on the powerhead. The manufacturer recommends no sealing agent whatsoever be used on either side of the gasket.

Step 12   04708P90

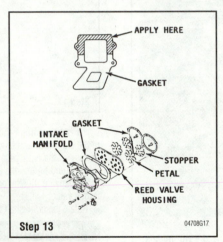

Step 13   04708G17

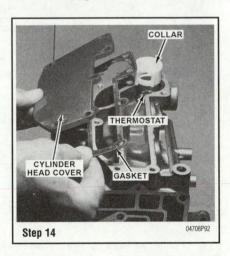

Step 14   04708P92

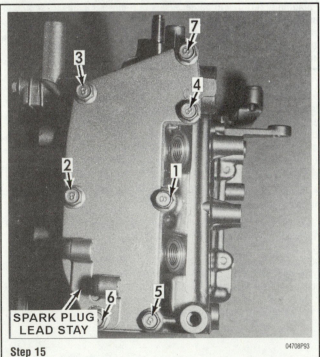

Step 15   04708P93

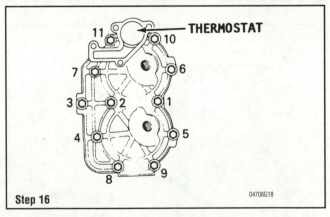

Step 16   04708G18

15. Start the seven attaching bolts. The spark plug lead stay is secured with the lower left bolt. Tighten the bolts in the sequence shown in the accompanying illustration to the specified torque value.

16. On 9.9 hp and 15 hp models, position a new head gasket in place on the cylinder head.

➡**The manufacturer recommends no sealing agent be used on either side of the thermostat gasket and the head gasket.**

Install the cylinder head cover and secure it with the eleven attaching bolts. Tighten the bolts in the sequence shown in the accompanying illustration to the specified torque value. Install the thermostat into the head cover with the spring end toward the cover. Position a new gasket in place, and then install the thermostat cover. Secure the cover with the four attaching bolts. Tighten the bolts in a circular pattern to the specified torque value.

17. On 25 hp and 30 hp models, position a new head gasket in place on the powerhead.

➡ **The manufacturer recommends no sealing agent be used on either side of the thermostat gasket and the head gasket.**

Install the cylinder head onto the powerhead. Apply Loctite® to the threads of the ten attaching bolts. Install the bolts and tighten them in the sequence shown in the accompanying illustration to the specified torque value.

Insert the thermostat into the powerhead with the spring end toward the powerhead. Position a new gasket in place, and then the thermostat cover. Secure the cover with the attaching bolts. Tighten the bolts in a circular pattern to the specified torque value.

➡ **Because of the high temperatures and pressures developed, the sealing surfaces of the cylinder head and the block are the most prone to water leaks. No sealing agent is recommended because it is almost impossible to apply an even coat of sealer. An even coat would be essential to ensure a air/water tight seal.**

Some head gaskets are supplied with a tacky coating on both surfaces applied at the time of manufacture. This tacky substance will provide an even coating all around. Therefore, no further sealing agent is required.

However, if a slight water leak should be noticed following completed assembly work and powerhead start up, do not attempt to stop the leak by tightening the head bolts beyond the recommended torque value. Such action will only aggravate the problem and most likely distort the head.

Furthermore, tightening the bolts, which are case hardened aluminum, may force the bolt beyond its elastic limit and cause the bolt to fracture. bad news, very bad news indeed. A fractured bolt must usually be drilled out and the hole retapped to accommodate an oversize bolt, etc. Avoid such a situation.

Probable causes and remedies of a new head gasket leaking are:
• Sealing surfaces not thoroughly cleaned of old gasket material. Disassemble and remove all traces of old gasket.
• Damage to the machined surface of the head or the block. The remedy for this damage is the same as for the next case.
• Permanently distorted head or block. Spray a light even coat of any type metallic spray paint on both sides of a new head gasket. Use only metallic paint—any color will do. Regular spray paint does not have the particle content required to provide the extra sealing properties this procedure requires.

Assemble the block and head with the gasket while the paint is till tacky. Install the head bolts and tighten in the recommended sequence and to the proper torque value and no more!

Allow the paint to set for at least 24 hours before starting the powerhead.

Consider this procedure as a temporary band aid type solution until a new head may be purchased or other permanent measures can be performed.

Under normal circumstances, if procedures have been followed to the letter, the head gasket will not leak.

18. On 6 hp and 8 hp models, install the throttle wire stay onto the block with the two bolts. Tighten the bolts to the specified torque value. Position the free acceleration lever and pulley onto the throttle wire stay. Insert the magneto control lever shaft into the free acceleration lever and pulley, and then install the magneto control lever between the bracket (installed with the embossed arrow pointing up), and the throttle wire stay. Install the joint link to the free acceleration lever. Slide the bolt through the limited throttle opening collar and arm, then thread it through the bolt hole next to the timing pointer. Tighten the bolt securely. Install the starter wire end (the end with the two locknuts), into the arm. Place the wire and two locknuts over the wire stay and tighten them temporarily to hold the wire in place.

19. On 6 hp, 8 hp, 25 hp, and 30 hp models, if the oil seal in the upper oil seal housing were removed during disassembling, install new oil seals in the housing using handle P/N YB6229 and the appropriate driver. Drive the seal in from the bottom of the housing with the lip facing up. After the housing is installed, the seal lip will actually face down, toward the powerhead. Pack the seal lip with Yamalube Grease, or equivalent water resistant lubricant.

➡ **When two seals are installed, the lips of both seals face in the same direction. Yamaha engineers have concluded it is better to have both seals face the same direction rather than have them back to back as directed by other outboard manufacturers. In this position, with both lips facing toward the water after oil seal installation, the engineers feel the seals will be more effective in keeping water out of the oil seal housing. Any lubricant lost will be negligible.**

9.9 hp and 15 hp models, do not have an upper oil seal housing. The upper crankshaft seal is installed in the stator plate. If this seal is damaged and must be replaced,

Pack the lips of the seal with Yamalube Grease, or an equivalent water resistant lubricant. Install the seal into the stator plate with the lips facing down toward the crankshaft. Install the seal using the appropriate driver and handle.

20. On 6 hp and 8 hp models, coat the O-ring and sealing surfaces of the upper oil seal housing with Yamalube Grease, or equivalent water resistant

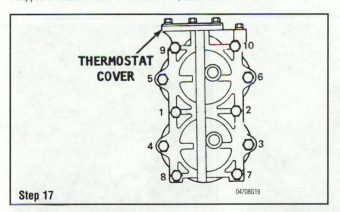

THERMOSTAT COVER

Step 17 04708G19

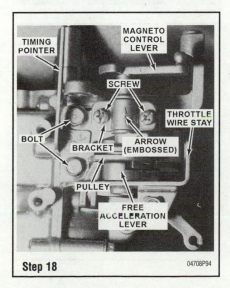

TIMING POINTER — MAGNETO CONTROL LEVER — SCREW — THROTTLE WIRE STAY — BOLT — BRACKET — ARROW (EMBOSSED) — PULLEY — FREE ACCELERATION LEVER

Step 18 04708P94

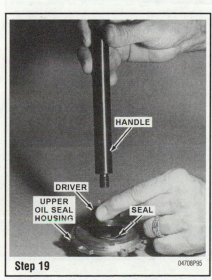

HANDLE — DRIVER — UPPER OIL SEAL HOUSING — SEAL

Step 19 04708P95

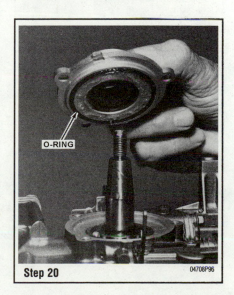

O-RING

Step 20 04708P96

lubricant. Install the O-ring into the recess of the housing and push the housing squarely into place over the crankshaft.

On 25 hp and 30 hp models, install a new gasket and the oil seal housing over the crankshaft. Seat the housing in the powerhead.

On 6 hp, 8 hp, 25 hp, and 30 hp models, the bolts are not installed at this time, but when the friction plate and retainer are installed.

If the oil seals in the lower oil seal housing were removed during disassembly, install new oil seals using a handle and appropriate driver.

21. Secure the lower oil seal housing in vice equipped with soft jaws. Pack the lips with Yamalube Grease, or equivalent water resistant lubricant. Drive the seals in from the top of the housing with the lip of each seal facing toward the lower unit.

➡**When two seals are installed, the lips of both seals face in the same direction. Yamaha engineers have concluded it is better to have both seals face the same direction rather than have them back to back as directed by other outboard manufacturers. In this position, with both lips facing toward the water after oil seal housing installation, the engineers feel the seals will be more effective in keeping water out of the oil seal housing. Any lubricant lost will be negligible.**

6 hp and 8 hp units use one small oil seal, installed first, then one large oil seal.

9.9 hp, 15 hp, 25 hp, and 30 hp models use two small oil seals, installed first, then one large oil seal. The lips of all three seals face in the same direction—toward the lower unit after the housing is installed.

22. Coat the sealing surfaces of the lower oil seal housing and a new O-ring with Yamaha Grease A, or equivalent water resistant lubricant. Install the new O-ring over the housing. Seat the housing into its recess in the powerhead. Rotate the housing until the bolt holes align. Install and tighten the bolts to the specified torque value.

On 6 hp and 8 hp models, these units have an exhaust manifold installed next to the oil seal housing. Install the manifold and tighten the attaching bolts to the specified torque value.

23. Check to be sure the two dowel pins on the intermediate housing are in place forward and aft of the driveshaft area.

On 9.9 hp and 15 hp models, apply Permatex®, or equivalent material to the gasket area shown in the accompanying illustration.

No sealing agent is required on the gasket.

Position the gasket in place with the dowel pins passing up through the correct holes in the gasket.

On 9.9 hp and 15 hp models, position the three rubber seals into the intermediate housing and bring the stator plate into contact with the stopper on the full open side. Set the throttle grip to the wide open position.

Apply a coating of Yamalube Grease, or equivalent water resistant lubricant to the lower end of the driveshaft. Install the powerhead onto the intermediate housing using the dowel pins to align the two surfaces. The propeller may have to be rotated slightly to permit the crankshaft to index with the driveshaft and allow the powerhead to seat properly.

24. Install the powerhead bolts. The outboard unit may have to be turned port or starboard to permit installation of the two front bolts. Tighten the bolts evenly and alternately to the specified torque value.

25. On 6 hp and 8 hp models, twist the throttle grip from slow to fast. Fit the shorter pulled cable end into the outer slot—the one close to the cowling edge. Fit the longer slack cable end into the inner slot—the one closest to the powerhead. Fit the wires down into the wire stay with the locknuts on both sides of the stay. Secure the locknuts in place. Snap the link over the ball joint.

26. On 6 hp and 8 hp models, install the ignition coil and CDI unit and secure them in place with the attaching hardware. Match the colors and connect the wires at their quick disconnect fitting. Ground the Black wires with eyes at their original locations. Tidy the wire harness and wrap the collar around it to keep it together neatly.

27. On 9.9 hp and 15 hp models, install the fuel filter. Connect the fuel lines leading to and from the filter according to the arrows embossed on top of the fittings. Secure the wire type clamps over the hoses. Snap the link over the ball joint on the throttle control rod.

Step 21   04708P97

Step 22   04708P98

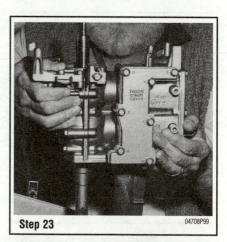

Step 23   04708P99

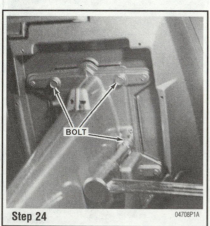

Step 24   04708P1A

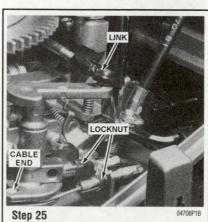

Step 25   04708P1B

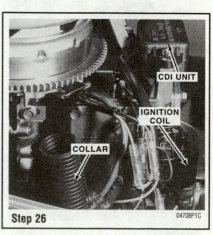

Step 26   04708P1C

28. On 9.9 hp and 15 hp models, install the starter cable end into the bracket. Push the cable into the wire stay with one locknut on each side of the stay. Tighten the nuts to secure the cable in place. Install the magneto base control lever and snap the link onto the ball joint.

29. On 9.9 hp and 15 hp models, install the CDI unit bracket. Seat the bracket by pushing it away from the flywheel. Install the CDI unit in the bracket. Install the ignition coil and secure the CDI unit and coil in place. Match colors and connect wires at their quick disconnect fittings. Ground any Black wires with eyes at their original locations. Install the cover over the CDI unit and tidy the wire harness.

30. On 9.9 hp and 15 hp models, install the hose from the pilot hole to the fitting on the exhaust cover.

31. On 25 hp and 30 hp models, install the starter wire stay bracket and arm. Insert the starter cable end into the arm and push the cable into the stay with a locknut on both sides of the stay. Tighten the locknuts to secure the cable in place. Install the bushing into the center of the throttle cable stay and magneto control lever. Secure the cable and lever to the block using a washer and bolts. Install the other retaining bolts located on the upper right of the circular throttle cable end retainer and tighten both bolts securely.

If servicing a 25 hp unit: install the long link rod from the throttle cam onto the front ball joint of the magneto control lever. Install the shorter link rod from the stator plate to the rear ball joint of the magneto control lever.

The 30 hp unit has only the short link rod from the stator plate. This rod attaches to the front ball joint of the magneto control lever.

The 25 hp and 30 hp units have the lower throttle control link rod attached to the throttle control lever.

➡When installing the various link rods, check to be sure the adjustable end is fully snapped onto the ball joints on the levers.

On 25 hp and 30 hp models, slide the throttle cable ends into their appropriate recesses in the circular throttle cable end retainer. Position the cables in the stays. Tighten the locknuts around the stays to secure the cables in place.

32. On 25 hp and 30 hp models, install the CDI unit bracket with the three attaching bolts. Connect the Black ground lead to the bracket. Install the CDI unit and the ignition coil. Match colors and connect wires at their quick disconnect fittings. Tidy the wire harness into the wire retainers.

Install the flywheel.

Install the carburetor and fuel tank.

Install the hand rewind starter. After the starter is installed, check the action of the no-start-in-gear protection system.

Mount the engine in a test tank, on a boat in a body of water, or connect a flush attachment to the lower unit.

Remember, the powerhead will not start without the emergency tether in place behind the kill switch knob.

Start the engine and check the completed work.

✳✳ WARNING

Water must circulate through the lower unit to the engine any time the engine is run to prevent damage to the water pump in the lower unit. Just five seconds without water will damage the water pump.

Attempt to start and run the engine without the cowling installed. This will provide the opportunity to check for fuel and oil leaks, without the cowling in place.

After the engine is operating properly, install the cowling. Follow the break-in procedures with the unit on a boat and with a load on the propeller.

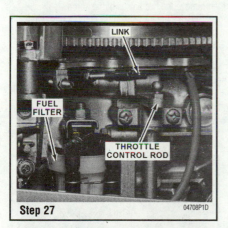

Step 27 04708P1D

Step 28 04708P1E

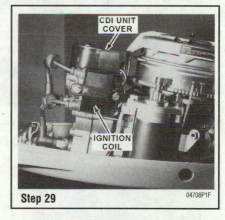

Step 29 04708P1F

Step 30 04708P1G

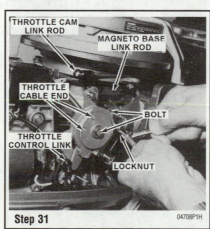

Step 31 04708P1H

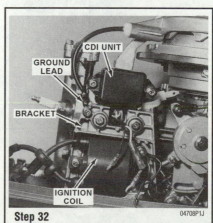

Step 32 04708P1J

Three-Cylinder Powerheads

REMOVAL & DISASSEMBLY

◆ **See accompanying illustrations**

Remove the cowling.
Remove the hand rewind starter or the electric cranking motor and relay.

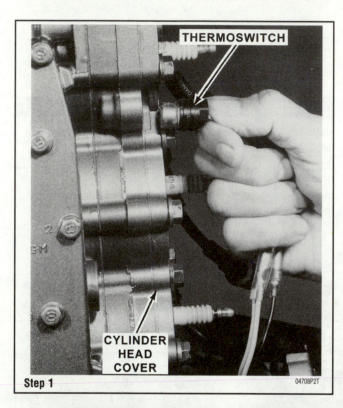

Step 1   04708P2T

Remove the flame arrestor, choke, and carburetors.
Remove the oil injection system.
Remove the CDI unit and the ignition coils.
Remove the flywheel and stator assembly.

1. Gently pull the thermoswitch from the cylinder head cover and set it aside. It is not necessary to disconnect the switch from the leads.

2. Pull the water drain hose free of the fitting at the bottom of the exhaust cover and set the hose aside.

3. On 30 hp model, remove the top and bottom bolt securing the fuel filter bracket. Do not remove the center bolt, because this center bolt only holds the arm assembly to the bracket, not the bracket to the powerhead. Remove the fuel filter bracket, and then remove the fuel pump.

On all other models, remove the nut on top of the fuel filter bracket and pull the filter down away from the bracket. Thread the nut back onto the stud for safe keeping. Remove the two attaching fuel pump bolts. Do not remove the screws on the fuel pump, because the fuel pump would fall apart. Disconnect the hose at the fuel joint to permit removal of the fuel filter and fuel pump as an assembly.

4. Pry the throttle control link rod free of the ball joint at the upper ball joint.

On 30 hp model, do not loosen or remove the front nut or the side screw on the magneto control lever cover. Remove the two bolts securing the mounting bracket to the powerhead. The throttle control lever, magneto control lever and cover will come free with the bracket.

5. On all other models, remove the single bolt securing the magneto control lever to the powerhead, and then remove the lever.

6. On 30 hp model, remove the two screws securing the apron around the lower cowling. Remove the apron.

7. On 40 hp and 50 hp models, remove the six attaching bolts from the inside of the cowling, and then remove the two halves of the apron.

On 70 hp and 90 hp models, remove the four attaching bolts from the inside of the cowling, and then remove the two halves of the apron.

8. Remove the bolts securing the powerhead to the intermediate housing.
Model 30 hp has six bolts, three on each side.
Model 40 hp and 50 hp units have eight bolts, four on each side.
Model 70 hp has eight bolts, three on each side, plus another two bolts at the forward end of the underside of the lower cowling.
Model 90 hp has eleven bolts, five on each side, plus one at the aft end of the underside of the lower cowling.

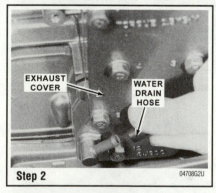

Step 2   04708G2U

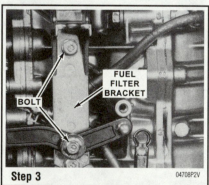

Step 3   04708P2V

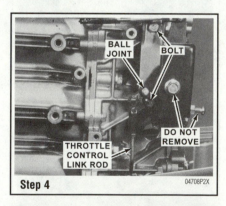

Step 4   04708P2X

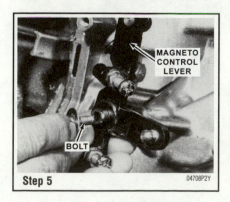

Step 5   04708P2Y

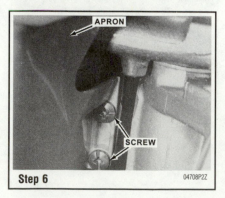

Step 6   04708P2Z

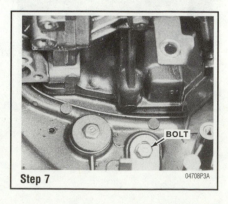

Step 7   04708P3A

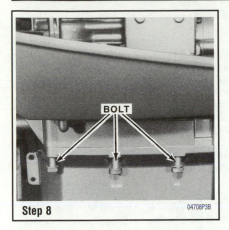

Step 8   04708P3B

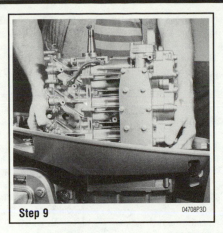

Step 9   04708P3D

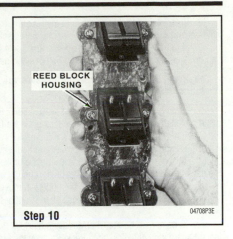

REED BLOCK HOUSING

Step 10   04708P3E

➡The powerhead may be difficult to dislodge from the intermediate housing because of a tight sealing gasket and joining compound. Prying up on the powerhead by using a long piece of wood and leverage on the edge of the lower cowling is an acceptable method by the manufacturer. If this method is employed, CARE must be exercised not to damage either the powerhead or the cowling. Once the powerhead has broken free of the intermediate housing, proceed to the next step.

✳✳ WARNING

If the unit is several years old, or if it has been operated in salt water, or has not had proper maintenance, or shelter, or any number of other factors, then separating the powerhead from the intermediate housing may not be a simple task. An air hammer may be required on the bolts to shake the corrosion loose, heat may have to be applied to the casting to expand it slightly, or other devices employed in order to remove the powerhead. One very serious condition would be the driveshaft frozen with the lower end of the crankshaft. In this case a circular plug type hole must be drilled and a torch used to cut the driveshaft.

Let's assume the powerhead will come free on the first attempt.

Take care not to lose the two dowel pins. The pins may come away with the powerhead or they may stay in the intermediate housing. Be especially careful not to drop them into the lower unit.

9. Raise the powerhead free of the intermediate housing. An alternate method, and easier on your back muscles, is to use a hook through the eye provided and a lifting device, such as a chain hoist.

Place the powerhead on a suitable work surface. Again, take care not to loose the alignment dowel pins. The pins may come away with the powerhead, or they may remain in the intermediate housing.

➡Take care in the next step when handling reed valve assemblies. Once the assembly is removed, keep it away from sunlight, moisture, dust, and dirt. Sunlight can deteriorate valve seat rubber seals. Moisture can easily rust stoppers overnight. Dust and dirt—especially sand or other gritty material can break reed petals if caught between stoppers and reed petals.

Make special arrangements to store the reed valves to keep them isolated from elements while further work is being performed on the powerhead.

10. Remove the bolts, and then the intake manifold. Remove and discard the gasket. Set the intake manifold aside, intact as a unit. Further work on the reed valves will be performed later in the Cleaning and Inspection section of this chapter.

➡The exhaust cover should always be removed during a powerhead overhaul. Many times, water in the powerhead is caused by a leaking exhaust cover gasket or plate.

➡If the inner or outer cover is stuck to the powerhead, insert a slotted screwdriver between the tabs provided for this purpose, and pry the two surfaces apart. Never pry at a gasket sealing surface. Such action would very likely damage the sealing surface of an aluminum powerhead.

11. Remove the bolts securing the outer cover, and then remove the cover and the gasket.

12. Remove the inner cover and gasket. Discard the outer and inner cover gaskets.

13. Remove the cylinder head cover bolts, and then remove the cover. Remove and discard the gasket. If the cover is stuck to the cylinder head, insert a slotted screwdriver between the tabs provided for this purpose and pry the two surfaces apart. Again, never pry at the gasket sealing surfaces, because the sealing surface of an aluminum powerhead could be damaged.

EXHAUST OUTER COVER

GASKET

Step 11   04708P3F

EXHAUST INNER COVER

GASKET

Step 12   04708P3G

CYLINDER HEAD COVER

GASKET

Step 13   04708P3H

14. Remove the attaching bolts, and then remove the thermostat cover. If the cover is stuck to the powerhead, tap it lightly with a soft head mallet to jar it free. Lift out the thermostat and at the same time, note the direction the thermostat faces, as an aid during installation. Remove and discard the gasket.

➡ **The Model 90 hp unit has a water pressure valve installed beneath the thermostat cover.**

15. Remove the cylinder head. If the head is stuck to the powerhead block, insert a slotted screwdriver between the tabs provided for this purpose and pry the two surfaces apart. Again, never pry at the gasket sealing surfaces, because the sealing surface of an aluminum powerhead could be damaged.

If the cylinder head is stubborn and cannot be broken free of the block, tap the head lightly with a soft head mallet to jar it free.

16. On the 40 hp, 50 hp and 90 hp models, remove the Phillips head screws, and then remove the two wedge shaped anodes located in the water jacket.

17. 30 hp and 70 hp model powerheads have two long anodes inserted into the starboard side of the cylinder block. Remove the bolts, covers and rubber plugs to gain access to these anodes.

18. Remove the bolts securing the lower oil seal housing. Some models have only one bolt, other models have more than one. Tap the housing lightly with a soft head mallet to jar it loose.

19. Inspect the condition of the oil seals in the lower oil seal housing. Make a determination if they are fit for further service. If they are not, obtain slide hammer P/N YB6096 with an expanding jaw attachment. Use the slide hammer and remove the oil seals from the lower oil seal housing.

30 hp, 40 hp, and 50 hp units have one large seal and two identical small seals behind the large seal.

70 hp and 90 hp units have one large seal and one small seal behind the large seal.

Remove and discard the outer O-ring.

20. Remove the upper oil seal housing from the top of the crankshaft. Remove and discard the O-ring around the housing.

Inspect the condition of the oil seal in the upper oil seal housing. Make a determination if the seal is fit for further service. The seal will be destroyed during removal. Therefore, remove the seal only if it is damaged and has lost its sealing qualities.

To remove the seal, first obtain Yamaha slide hammer puller P/N, YB6096 with expanding jaw attachment, and then pull the seal.

21. Remove the crankcase bolts. These bolts vary, depending on the unit being serviced, as follows:

Model 30 hp, 40 hp, 50 hp, and 70 hp have 14 bolts of two different sizes.

Model 90 hp has 20 bolts of two different sizes.

After all bolts have been removed, insert a slotted screwdriver between the tabs provided for this purpose and pry the two surfaces apart. Never pry at gasket sealing surfaces. Such action would very likely damage the sealing surface of an aluminum powerhead.

Separate the two halves of the crankcase. Take care not to lose the two dowel pins. These pins may remain in either half when the crankcase is separated.

22. On all models except the 90 hp, tap the tapered end of the crankshaft, with a soft head mallet, to jar it free from the block. Slowly lift the crankshaft assembly straight up and out of the block.

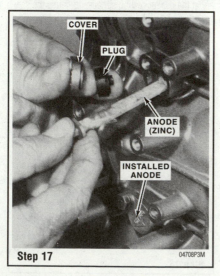

Step 14   04708P3J

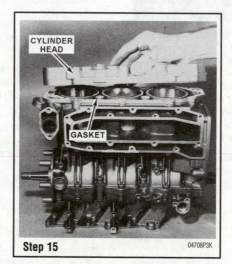

Step 15   04708P3K

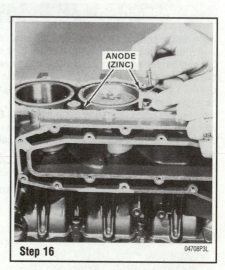

Step 16   04708P3L

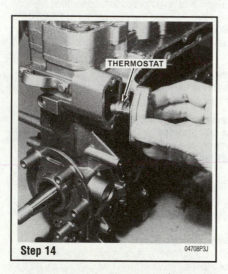

Step 17   04708P3M

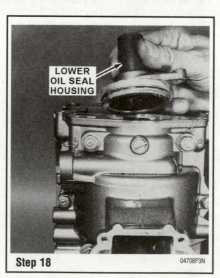

Step 18   04708P3N

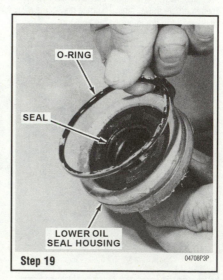

Step 19   04708P3P

Step 20

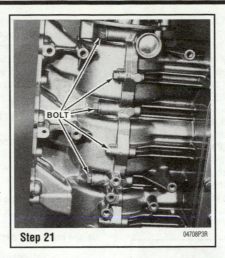

Step 21

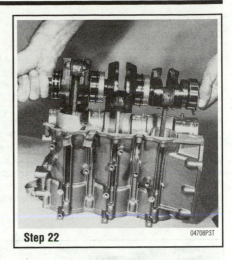

Step 22

23. Slide the labyrinth seal circlips from the two grooves in the crankcase.

24. Scribe a mark on the inside of the piston skirt to identify the top, center, and bottom piston before removal from the connecting rod.

25. On the 90 hp model, obtain a marker and identify both halves of each connecting rod to ensure the mating halves will be brought together—the cap in the original direction—during assembly and also to ensure each rod will be installed in its original location. Numbers such as 1 and 1, 2 and 2, 3 and 3 would be excellent.

Each rod cap must be kept with its connecting rod to ensure they remain as matched sets and the cap must be installed in its original direction—not 180° out.

If new parts are being used, the connecting rod and rod cap must be installed in the same direction from which they were separated when removed from the package.

Remove the connecting rod bolts and rod caps. Lift out both sets of caged needle bearings from around the crankshaft journal. Keep the bearings with the connecting rod cap to ensure they will be installed in their original locations.

Tap the crankshaft lightly with a soft head mallet to jar it free from the block. Lift the crankshaft out of the block.

Pull each piston and connecting rod assembly from the bottom—not through the top of the block. A ridge might have formed on the top of the cylinder bore. This ridge may have to be removed with a ridge reamer.

➡On 30 hp, 40 hp, 50 hp, and 70 hp models, the connecting rods are not normally removed from the crankshaft unless it is determined there is a problem in this area. Therefore, the following tasks will proceed with the crankshaft and connecting rods remaining as an assembly.

The connecting rod axial play and side clearance will be determined during cleaning and inspection.

If excessive clearances are found, then the occasion will arise when the connecting rod journal will be pressed from the crank-shaft throw in order to replace the connecting rod.

➡The piston pin C-lockrings are made of spring steel and may slip out of the pliers or pop out of the groove with considerable force. Therefore, wear eye protection glasses while removing the piston pin lockrings in the next step.

26. Remove the C-lockring from both ends of the piston pin using a pair of needle nose pliers. Discard the C-lockrings. These rings stretch during removal

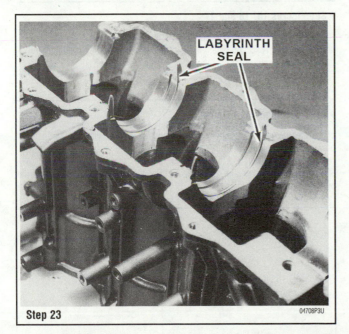

Step 23

Step 24

Step 25

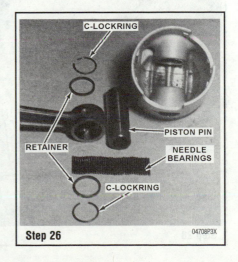

Step 26

and cannot be used a second time. The two retainers will fall away from the connecting rod small end.

Press the pin free of the piston using an arbor press. Be sure to catch all loose needle bearings as they fall free of the piston pin bore.

If an arbor press or holding block is not available, proceed as follows: Heat the piston with a small torch. Keep the torch moving to prevent overheating in any one area. Heating the piston will cause the metal to expand ever so slightly, but ease the task of driving the pin free. Assume a sitting position in a chair, on a box, whatever. Next lay a couple of towels over your legs. Hold your legs tightly together to form a cradle for the piston above your knees. Set the piston between your legs.

Now, drive the piston pin free using a drift pin with a shoulder. The drift pin and the shoulder will ride on the edge of the piston pin. Use sharp hard blows with a hammer. Your legs will absorb the shock without damaging the piston. If this method is used on a regular basis during the busy season, your legs will develop black and blue areas, but no problem, the marks will disappear in a few days.

Step 27   04708P4A

Step 28   04708P4B

➡ **New needle bearings should be installed in the connecting rods, even through they may appear to be in serviceable condition. New bearings will ensure lasting service after the overhaul work is completed. If it is necessary to install the used bearings, keep them separate and identified to ENSURE they will be installed onto the same crank pin throw and with the same connecting rod from which they were removed.**

On all models except 90 hp, slowly rotate both bearing races on the crankshaft. If rough spots are felt, the bearings will have to be pressed free of the crankshaft.

27. Obtain special bearing separator tool, Yamaha P/N YB6219 and an arbor press. Press each bearing from the crankshaft. Be sure the crankshaft is supported, because once the bearing breaks loose, the crankshaft is free to fall.

➡ **Good shop practice dictates replacing the rings during a powerhead overhaul. However, if the rings are to be used again, expand them only enough to clear the piston and the grooves, because used rings are brittle and break very easily.**

28. Gently spread the top piston ring enough to pry it out and up over the top of the piston. No special tool is required to remove the piston rings. Remove the middle and lower rings in a similar manner. These rings are extremely brittle and have to be handled with care if they are intended for further service.

CLEANING & INSPECTION

◆ **See Figures 15, 16 and 17**

Cleaning and inspecting the components is virtually the same for any two-stroke outboard. A section detailing the proper procedures is located later in this section.

ASSEMBLY & INSTALLATION

◆ **See accompanying illustrations**

Detailed procedures are given to assemble and install virtually all parts of the powerhead. Therefore, if certain parts were not removed or disassembled because the part was found to be fit for further service, simply skip the particular step involved and continue with the required tasks to return the powerhead to operating condition.

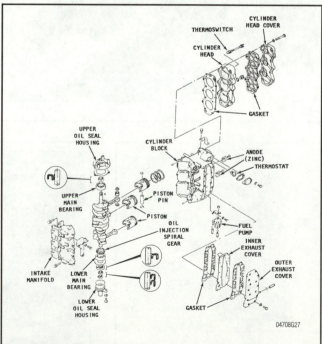

04708G27

Fig. 15 Exploded view of the 30 hp, 40 hp and 50 hp units with major parts identified

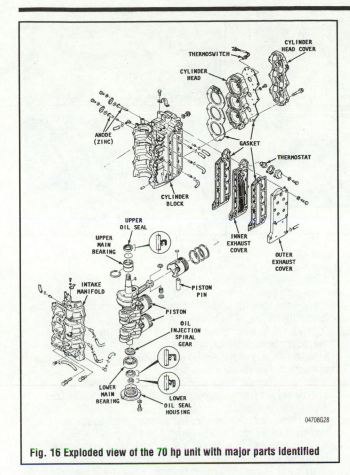

Fig. 16 Exploded view of the 70 hp unit with major parts identified

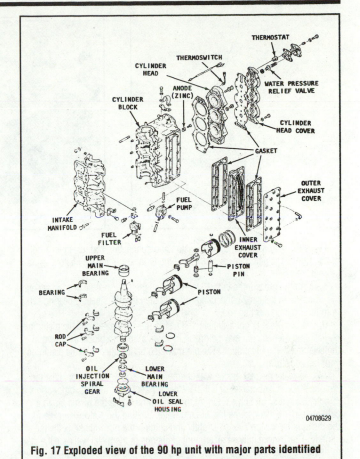

Fig. 17 Exploded view of the 90 hp unit with major parts identified

1. Install a new set of piston rings onto the piston, with the embossed marks facing up. No special tool is necessary for installation. However, take care to spread the ring only enough to clear the top of the piston. The rings are extremely brittle and will snap if spread beyond their limit. Align the ring gap over the locating pin.

2. On all models except 90 hp, if the main bearings were removed, support the crankshaft and press the bearings onto the shaft one at a time. Press only on the inner race. Pressing on the cage, the ball bearings, or the outer race may destroy the bearing.

Take note of the bearing size embossed on one side of the bearing. The side with the marking must face away from the crankshaft throw.

The piston pin lockrings are made of spring steel and may slip out of the pli-

ers or pop out of the groove with considerable force. Therefore, wear eye protection glasses while installing the piston pin lockrings in the next step.

3. Select the set of needle bearings removed from the No. 1 piston or obtain a new set of bearings.

Coat the inner circumference of the small end of the No. 1 connecting rod with Yamaha A grease, or equivalent multipurpose water resistant lubricant. Position the needle bearings one by one around the circumference. Dab some lubricant on the sides of the rod and stick the retainers in place.

Position the end of the rod with the needle bearings and retainers in place up into the piston. The word **UP** on the piston crown must face toward the tapered (upper) end of the crankshaft. Press the piston pin through the piston and connecting rod, using an arbor press.

Step 1

Step 2

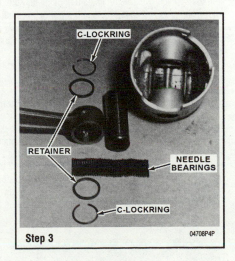

Step 3

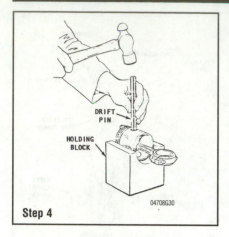

DRIFT PIN

HOLDING BLOCK

04708G30

Step 4

LABYRINTH SEAL

04708P4T

Step 5

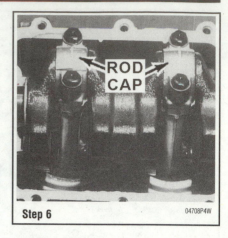

ROD CAP

04708P4W

Step 6

Press the piston pin through the piston and connecting rod, using an arbor press. Center the pin in the piston. Install the C-lockring at each end of the piston pin.

Perform the procedures in this step to install the No.2 needle bearing set and the piston onto the No.2 connecting rod, and then the No.3 needle bearing set onto the No.3 connecting rod.

If an arbor press is not available, the piston may be heated and the piston pin chilled, and then the pin may be driven in using a holding block, as shown in the accompanying illustration. The pin may also be installed with the piston on your lap as follows:

4. To make the task easier, with the holding block or in your lap, heat the piston, either in a container of boiling water for about 10 minutes, or for about a minute using a small bottle torch. At the same time, place the piston pin in a cold area, refrigerator, some ice, or cold water. Heating the piston will expand the metal in the piston ever so slightly and chilling the pin will shrink the metal slightly. This exceedingly small amount of change in the metal will ease the task of driving the pin into place. If a bottle torch is used to heat the piston, keep the torch moving to prevent excessive heating of any one area.

Before pressing the piston pin into place, hold the piston and rod assembly near the cylinder block and check to be sure both will be facing in the proper direction when they are installed.

Pack the piston pin needle bearing cage with needle bearing grease, or a good grade of petroleum jelly. Load the bearing cage with needles and insert it into the end of the rod.

Slide the rod into the piston boss and check a second time to be sure the piston is being installed correctly.

Now, assume a sitting position and lay a couple towels over your lap. Hold your legs tightly together to form a cradle for the piston above your knees. Set the piston between your legs. Drive the piston pin through the piston using a drift pin with a shoulder. The drift pin will fit into the hole through the piston pin and the shoulder will ride on the end of the piston pin. Use sharp hard blows with a hammer. Your legs will absorb the shock without damaging the piston. If this method is used on a regular basis during the busy season, your legs will develop black and blue areas, but no problem, the marks will disappear in a few days.

Continue to drive the piston pin through the piston until the groove in the piston pin for the lockring is visible at both ends. Install a C-lockring onto each end of the piston pin.

Repeat the procedure for the second and third piston.

5. On all model except 90 hp model, slide the labyrinth seal circlips into the two grooves of the crankcase.

On 90 hp models, coat the cylinder bores with a good grade of engine oil. Before installing the piston into the cylinder, make the following test.

Run your finger along the top rim of the cylinder. If the surface of the block and the surface of the bore have a sharp edge, the piston may be installed from the top. If the slightest groove or ridge is felt on the rim, the piston must be installed from the lower end of the cylinder. Attempting to install the piston from

the top will not be successful because the piston ring will bottom on the ridge. If force is used the ring may very well break.

For top installation, use a ring compressor to compress the aligned rings and then use the end of a wooden mallet handle to gently tap the piston down into the cylinder bore. The word **UP** embossed on the piston crown must face toward the flywheel end of the block.

Installation of the piston from the lower end of the cylinder bore is an easy matter and can be accomplished without the use of special tools. Verify the ring end-gaps are properly aligned and the word up, embossed on the piston crown, faces toward the flywheel end of the block.

Three hands are better than two for this task. Simply compress each ring, one by one and at the same time push the piston up into the cylinder bore.

Repeat either procedure for the other pistons.

After all three pistons have been installed, slide each piston up and down in the cylinder bore several times. Check for binding. Listen for scratching noises. Scratching (or any other spooky noise) may indicate a ring was broken during installation.

On models with bolt together connecting rods, place the lower half roller bearings in their original positions on the connecting rod caps. The locating pin hole for the first and third bearing outer race/cage should face upward, toward the tapered end of the crankshaft, when installed.

➡**If the old roller bearings are to be installed for further service, each must be installed in the same location from which it was removed.**

The tang on the bearing will slide into the groove in the crankshaft.

6. Position the crankshaft into place in the block. Pack the lip of the upper oil seal with Yamaha A Grease, or an equivalent water resistant grease. Install the upper bearing, with the seal installed, with the lip of the seal facing downward, towards the center of the crankshaft. Place the upper half of the roller bearings in their original positions, as recorded during disassembling, on the crankshaft journals. Place the connecting rod caps over the caged roller bearings in their original locations.

➡**The manufacturer does not recommend rod cap bolts be used a second time. Also, the manufacturer recommends a specific method of tightening the rod cap bolts, be followed as outlined in the next step.**

Work on just one rod at a time.

7. Thread in the new connecting rod cap bolts a few turns each. Now, tighten the cap bolts to the specified torque. Check to be sure the single mark on each rod cap end is centrally located between the two matching embossed marks on the rod end and on the cap, as shown in the accompanying illustration.

If the marks are aligned, as described and shown, loosen each bolt one half turn, and then tighten the bolt to the specified torque value.

If the marks are not aligned, as described and shown, remove the cap bolts, and then the upper caged roller bearing half. Install the upper caged roller bearing half again. Check the alignment. If the second attempt fails to align the marks as described and shown, the crankshaft must be removed and the lower caged roller bearing half checked for correct alignment.

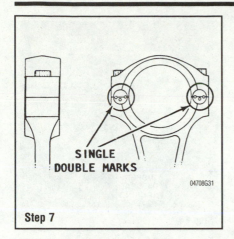

SINGLE
DOUBLE MARKS

04708G31

Step 7

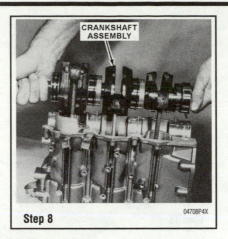

CRANKSHAFT
ASSEMBLY

04708P4X

Step 8

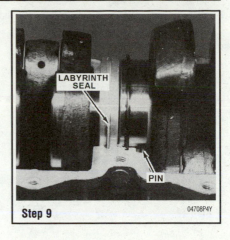

LABYRINTH
SEAL

PIN

04708P4Y

Step 9

CRANKCASE

DOWEL PIN
(2 PLCS)

04708P4Z

Step 10

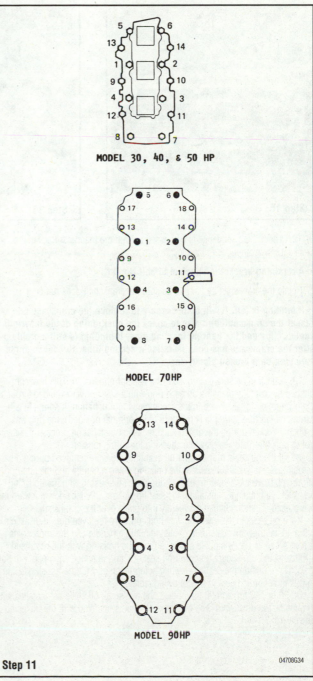

MODEL 30, 40, & 50 HP

MODEL 70HP

MODEL 90HP

04708G34

Step 11

8. On all models except 90 hp, coat the upper sides of each piston with 2-stroke engine oil. Hold the crankshaft at right angles to the cylinder bores and slowly lower one piston at a time into the appropriate cylinder. The upper edge of each cylinder bore has a slight taper to squeeze in the rings around the locating pin and allow the piston to center in the bore.

➡ **If difficulty is experienced in fitting the piston into the cylinder, do not force the piston. Such action might result in a broken piston ring. Raise the crankshaft and make sure the ring end-gap is aligned with the locating pin.**

9. Push the crankshaft assembly down until it seats in the block. Fit the labyrinth seal circlips into the grooves in the block. Rotate the four bearings until their locating pins fit into the recesses in the block.

10. Apply a thin bead of Yamabond No. 4 Permatex® around both surfaces of the crankcase and block. Check to be sure the two dowel pins are in place and install the crankcase to the block.

11. On 90 hp model, install and tighten the attaching bolts in the sequence shown in the accompanying illustrations. The numbering sequence is embossed around the matting surface of the crankcase on both sides of the block. Tighten the bolts in two rounds and to the proper torque specification.

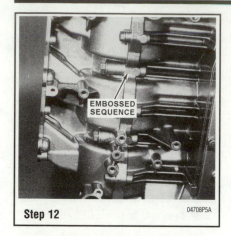

Step 12   04708P5A

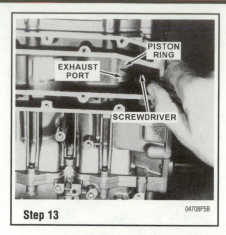

Step 13   04708P5B

Step 14   04708P5C

Step 15   04708P5E

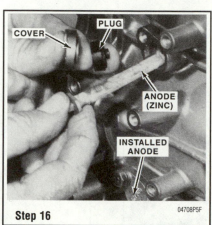

Step 16   04708P5F

Step 17   04708P5G

12. The tighten sequence is embossed around the mating surface of the crankcase on both sides of the block.

➡ **A retaining bracket is attached to bolt No. 11.**

Rotate the crankshaft by hand to be sure the crankshaft does not bind.

➡ **If binding is felt, it will be necessary to remove the crankcase and reseat the crankshaft and also to check the positioning of the labyrinth seal circlips and the bearing locating pins. If binding is still a problem after the crankcase has been installed a second time, the cause might very well be a broken piston ring.**

13. Check to be sure each piston ring has spring tension. This is accomplished by carefully pressing on each ring with a screwdriver extended through the exhaust ports, as shown in the accompanying illustration. If spring tension cannot be felt (the spring fails to return to its original position), the ring was probably broken during the piston and crankshaft installation process. Take care not to burr the piston rings while checking for spring tension.

14. If the oil seals in the upper oil seal housing were removed during disassembling, install new oil seals in the housing using a handle and the appropriate driver. Drive the seal in from the bottom of the housing with the lip facing up. After the housing is installed, the seal lip will actually face down, toward the powerhead. Push the housing squarely into place over the crankshaft.

If the oil seals in the lower oil seal housing were removed during disassembling, install new oil seals in the housing using a handle and the appropriate driver. All seals on all models are driven into the housing with the machined surface facing up. Secure the lower oil seal housing in a vice equipped with soft jaws. The direction the seal faces while being installed with the housing facing in this direction is given in the following table.

On 30 hp, 40 hp, and 50 hp models, the two small oil seals are installed with the lips facing downward. The one large oil seal is installed with the lip facing downward.

On 70 hp and 90 hp models, the one small oil seal is installed with the lip facing downward. The one large oil seal is installed with the lip facing downward.

When the lower oil seal housing is installed onto the powerhead, all seals will face in the correct direction, as installed.

Pack each seal lip with Yamalube Grease, or equivalent water resistant lubricant, as soon as the seal is installed.

➡ **When two seals are installed, the lips of both seals face in the same direction. Yamaha engineers have concluded it is better to have both seals face the same direction rather than have them back to back as directed by other outboard manufacturers. In this position, with both lips facing toward the water after oil seal housing installation, the engineers feel the seals will be more effective in keeping water out of the oil seal housing. Any lubricant lost will be negligible.**

Apply engine oil around the groove in the oil housing and around the new O-ring. Install the O-ring around the housing. Install the housing over the lower end of the crankshaft. Tap lightly around the circumference to seat the housing properly into the crankcase. Align the holes and install and tighten the securing bolts.

15. On 40 hp, 50 hp, and 90 hp models, insert the two wedge shaped anodes into the water jacket of the block. Secure the anodes with the two Phillips head screws. These anodes will only be visible and accessible the next time the powerhead is overhauled. Therefore, if the anodes show any sign of deterioration in this location, a new anode should be installed.

16. On 30 hp and 70 hp models, insert the two long anodes into the starboard side of the block. Cover each anode with a rubber plug. Install the covers. Tighten the cover attaching bolts to the specified torque value.

17. Position a new head gasket in place on the powerhead.

➡ **The manufacturer recommends no sealing agent be used on either side of the head gasket.**

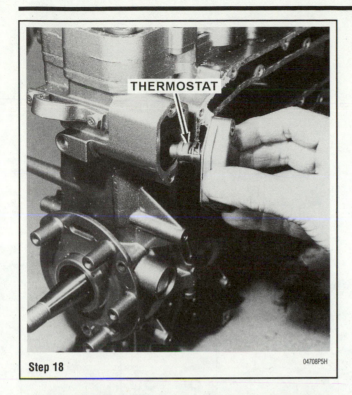

THERMOSTAT

Step 18   04708P5H

CYLINDER
HEAD COVER

GASKET

Step 19   04708P5J

Install the cylinder head onto the powerhead.

18. Insert the thermostat into the powerhead with the spring end going in first. The Model 90 hp also has a pressure relief valve installed next to the thermostat. Coat both sides of a new gasket with Permatex® and install the cover with the two attaching bolts. Tighten the bolts to the specified torque value.

19. Install a new cylinder head cover gasket, and then position the cylinder head cover over the gasket. The following table lists the recommended sealer to be applied to the head bolts and the torque value the bolts are to be tightened, for the powerhead being serviced.

20. Install the head bolts and tighten them to the specified torque value in the sequence shown in the accompanying illustrations.

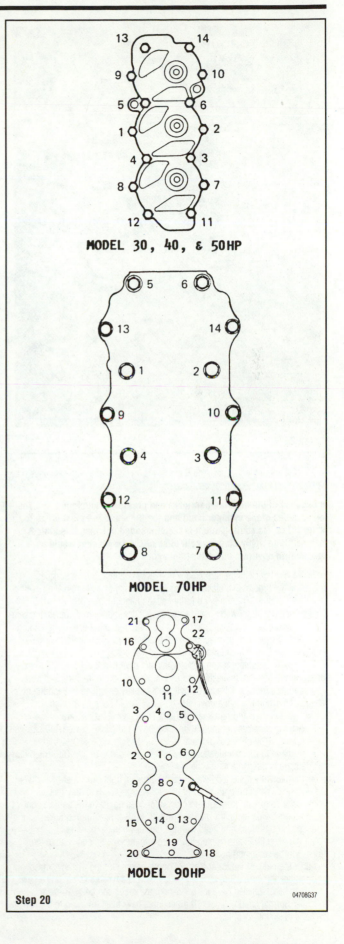

MODEL 30, 40, & 50HP

MODEL 70HP

MODEL 90HP

Step 20   04708G37

TORQUE VALVE

CYLINDER HEAD COVER

Step 21

04708P5K

21. On some models, the bolt dimensions and the tightening sequence may be embossed on the cylinder head cover.

➡**Because of the high temperatures and pressures developed, the sealing surfaces of the cylinder head and the block are the most prone to water leaks. No sealing agent is recommended because it is almost impossible to apply an even coat of sealer. An even coat would be essential to ensure a air/water tight seal.**

Some head gaskets are supplied with a tacky coating on both surfaces applied at the time of manufacture. This tacky substance will provide an even coating all around. Therefore, no further sealing agent is required.

However, if a slight water leak should be noticed following completed assembly work and powerhead start up, do not attempt to stop the leak by tightening the head bolts beyond the recommended torque value. Such action will only aggravate the problem and most likely distort the head.

Furthermore, tightening the bolts, which are case hardened aluminum, may force the bolt beyond its elastic limit and cause the bolt to fracture. Bad news, very bad news indeed. A fractured bolt must usually be drilled out and the hole retapped to accommodate an oversize bolt, etc. Avoid such a situation.

Probable causes and remedies of a new head gasket leaking are:
• Sealing surfaces not thoroughly cleaned of old gasket material. Disassemble and remove all traces of old gasket.
• Damage to the machined surface of the head or the block. The remedy for this damage is the same as for the next case.
• Permanently distorted head or block. Spray a light even coat of any type metallic spray paint on both sides of a new head gasket. Use only metallic paint—any color will do. Regular spray paint does not have the particle content required to provide the extra sealing properties this procedure requires.

Assemble the block and head with the gasket while the paint is till tacky. Install the head bolts and tighten in the recommended sequence and to the proper torque value and no more!

Allow the paint to set for at least 24 hours before starting the powerhead.

Consider this procedure as a temporary band aid type solution until a new head may be purchased or other permanent measures can be performed.

Under normal circumstances, if procedures have been followed to the letter, the head gasket will not leak.

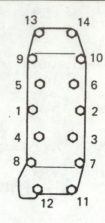

MODEL 30, 40 & 50HP

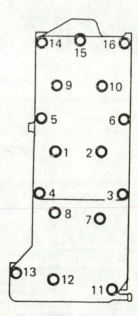

MODEL 70HP

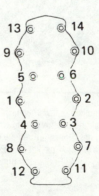

MODEL 90HP

Step 22

04708G40

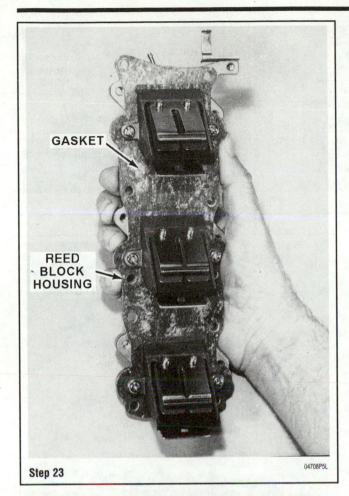

GASKET

REED
BLOCK
HOUSING

Step 23   04708P5L

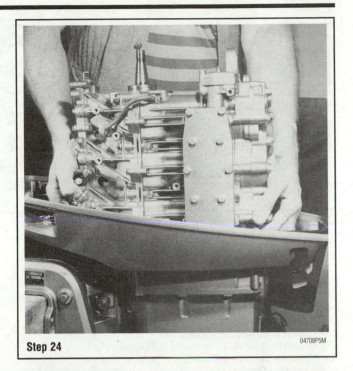

Step 24   04708P5M

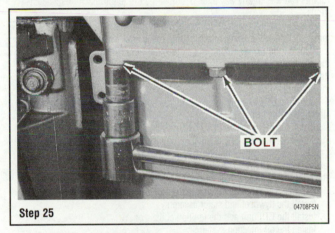

BOLT

Step 25   04708P5N

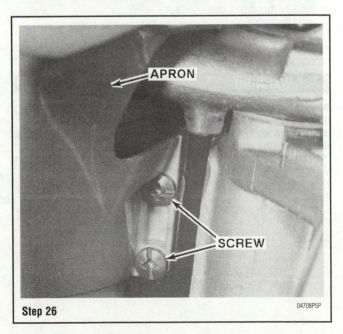

APRON

SCREW

Step 26   04708P5P

22. Obtain Very High Temperature (VHT) quick gasket maker. Apply this sealant to both sides of the two exhaust manifold gaskets. Quick Gasket is a silicone rubber based adhesive sealant recommended by the manufacturer for use where rubber gaskets are used next to metal surfaces.

Install the first gasket, the inner exhaust cover, the second gasket, and then the outer exhaust cover. Tighten the bolts to the specified torque values and in the sequence indicated in the accompanying illustration for the unit being serviced:

23. Install the intake manifold housing. The manufacturer recommends no sealant be applied to the gasket at this location. Install and tighten the attaching bolts to the specified torque value. Work from the center two bolts towards both ends alternately and evenly until all bolts are properly tightened.

24. Coat both sides of a new gasket with Permatex®, or equivalent material. Place the gasket in position on the intermediate housing surface. Check to be sure the two alignment dowel pins are in place. Carefully lower the powerhead onto the intermediate housing with the dowel pins indexing into the holes in the powerhead and the splines of the crankshaft indexing into the splines of the driveshaft. If the splines do not index, shift the lower unit into forward gear, have an assistant rotate the propeller just a whisker clockwise until the splines do index. Check to be sure the powerhead is fully down on the intermediate housing—the mating surfaces hard against each other.

25. Apply Loctite® to the bolts threads and install the bolts securing the powerhead to the intermediate housing.

Model 30 hp has six bolts, three on each side. Tighten the bolts alternately and evenly to the specified torque value.

Model Model 40 hp and 50 hp have eight bolts, four on each side. Tighten the bolts alternately and evenly to the specified torque value.

Model 70 hp has eight bolts, three on each side, and two at the forward end of the underside of the lower cowling. Tighten the bolts alternately and evenly to the specified torque value.

Model 90 hp has eleven bolts, five on each side and one on the aft end of the underside of the lower cowling. Tighten the bolts alternately and evenly to the specified torque value.

26. On 30 hp models, wrap the apron around the lower cowling. Snap it into the groove in the cowling and secure the two ends together with the two screws.

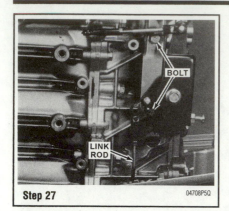

Step 27   04708P5Q

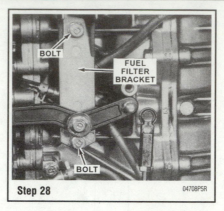

Step 28   04708P5R

Step 29   04708P5S

On 40 hp and 50 hp models, wrap the apron around the lower cowling. Secure the apron to the cowling with the six attaching bolts from the inside of the cowling. Tighten the bolts to the specified torque value.

On 70 hp and 90 hp models, wrap the two halves of the apron around the lower cowling. Secure both halves to the cowling with the four attaching bolts from the inside of the cowling. Tighten the bolts to the specified torque value.

27. On 30 hp models, install the bracket which secures the control lever covers to the powerhead. Secure the bracket in place with the two bolts. Tighten both bolts evenly and alternately to the specified torque value. Snap the link rod back onto the ball joint on the throttle control lever. If the length of this rod was in any way altered, adjust the rod length back to specifications.

On all models except 30 hp, install the magneto control lever onto the powerhead. Tighten the single attaching bolt to the specified torque value.

28. On the 30 hp model, install the fuel filter bracket to the powerhead with the two attaching bolts. Tighten the bolts to the specified torque value. Install the fuel pump onto the center carburetor and connect the fuel line.

On all models except 30 hp, install the fuel filter onto the fuel filter bracket and tighten the nut on the stud.

Install the fuel pump with the two attaching bolts onto the powerhead. Connect the inlet fuel line to the fuel joint on the lower cowling.

29. Push the water drain hose back onto the fitting on the base of the exhaust cover. Check to be sure the other end of the hose is firmly attached to the pilot hole fitting.

30. Insert the thermoswitch into the cylinder head cover until it seats.
Install the flywheel and stator assembly.
Install the CDI unit and the ignition coils.
Install the oil injection system.
Install the carburetors, choke, and flame arrestor.
Install the electric cranking motor or the hand rewind starter.

Move the outboard unit to a test tank or mount the unit on a boat in a body of water. Leave the cowling off to permit inspection and to make adjustments, if necessary.

⁂ WARNING

Water must circulate through the lower unit to the powerhead anytime the powerhead is operating to prevent damage to the water pump in the lower unit. Just five seconds without water will damage the water pump impeller.

Attempt to start and run the powerhead without the cowling installed. This will provide the opportunity to check for fuel and oil leaks, and to make adjustments, if required.

After the engine is operating properly, install the cowling. Follow the break-in procedures with the unit on a boat and with a load on the propeller.

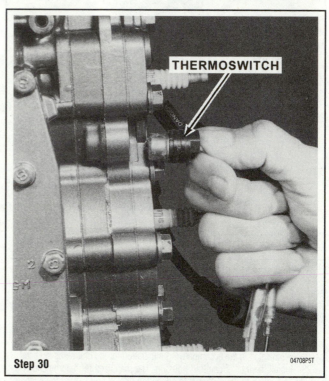

Step 30   04708P5T

V4 and V6 Powerhead Service

REMOVAL & DISASSEMBLY

▶ **See accompanying illustrations**

Remove the cowling.
Remove the electric cranking motor and relay.
Remove the flame arrestor, choke, and carburetors.
Remove the oil injection system.
Remove the Yamaha Microcomputer Ignition system control unit, the various sensors and switches (if equipped). Remember to MARK the exact location of the throttle position sensor in relation to its mounting bracket.

Next, remove the CDI unit, the control unit (on V6 only) and the ignition coils. Remove the flywheel and stator assembly.

The following instructions pickup the work after the preliminary tasks listed above have been accomplished.

1. Gently pull the two thermoswitches from the cylinder head covers and set them aside. It is not necessary to disconnect the switches from the leads.

2. Pull the water drain hose free of the fitting at the bottom of the exhaust cover and set the hose aside. On V6 models, snip the plastic clamp securing the water hose to the bypass cover, and then pull the hose free of the fitting on the cover.

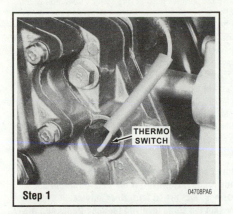

Step 1   04708PA6

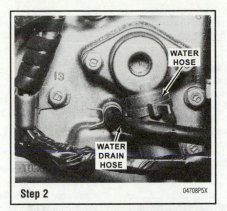

Step 2   04708P5X

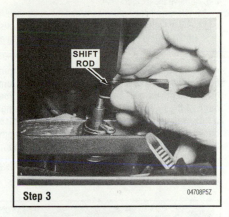

Step 3   04708P5Z

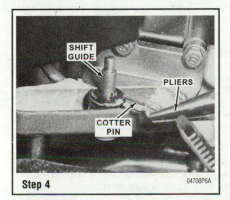

Step 4   04708P6A

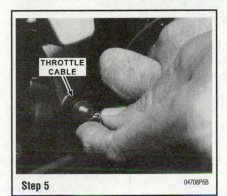

Step 5   04708P6B

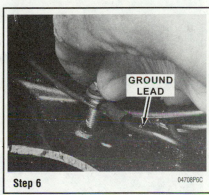

Step 6   04708P6C

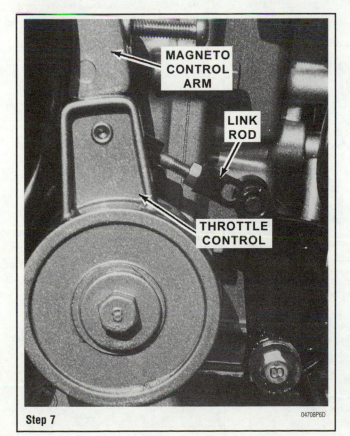

Step 7   04708P6D

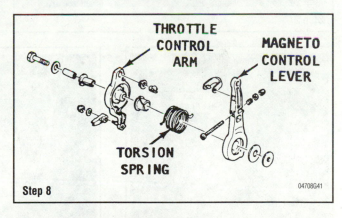

Step 8   04708G41

Remove the locknut and washer from the top of the shift rod.

3. Lift off the shift rod and set it aside.

4. Use a pair of needle nose pliers and pull out the cotter pin. Remove the shift guide from the block.

5. Remove the locknut and washer, and then lift off the throttle cable from the throttle arm.

6. Disconnect the ground leads attached to the lower cowling. Some leads are also attached to the exhaust cover.

7. Pry the link rods from the throttle control arm (on all models except those equipped with YMIS), and the magneto control arm. Try not to disturb the length of these rods.

8. Remove the center bolt from the throttle control arm, lift off the washer, the insert, and the plastic sleeve. Lift off the throttle control arm and torsion spring (on all models except those equipped with YMIS), then lift off the magneto control lever and two washers. Place these items in order on the workbench as they are removed, as an assist during assembling. Do not disturb any adjusting screw settings.

9. Remove the two bolts securing the front apron half around the lower cowling. Remove the forward apron half.

10. Remove the two bolts securing the aft apron half around the lower cowling. Remove the aft apron half.

11. Remove a total of ten bolts and two nuts securing the powerhead to the intermediate housing: six long bolts, two medium bolts and two short bolts. The nuts are located on the forward side of the intermediate housing, just below the lower cowling pan.

➡**The powerhead may be difficult to dislodge from the intermediate housing because of a tight sealing gasket and joining compound. Prying up on the powerhead by using a long piece of wood and leverage on the edge of the lower cowling is an acceptable method by the manufacturer. If this method is employed, care must be exercised not to damage either the powerhead or the cowling. Once the powerhead has broken free of the intermediate housing, proceed to the next step.**

If the unit is several years old, or if it has been operated in salt water, or has not had proper maintenance, or shelter, or any number of other factors, then

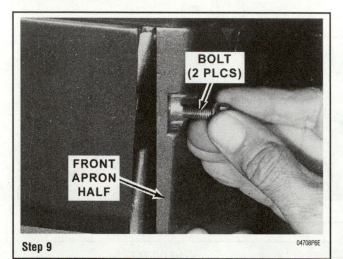

Step 9   04708P6E

separating the powerhead from the intermediate housing may not be a simple task. An air hammer may be required on the bolts to shake the corrosion loose, heat may have to be applied to the casting to expand it slightly, or other devices employed in order to remove the powerhead. One very serious condition would be the driveshaft frozen with the lower end of the crankshaft. In this case a circular plug type hole must be drilled and a torch used to cut the driveshaft.

Let's assume the powerhead will come free on the first attempt.

Take care not to lose the two dowel pins. The pins may come away with the powerhead or they may stay in the intermediate housing. Be especially careful not to drop them into the lower unit.

12. Raise the powerhead free of the intermediate housing. An alternate method, and easier on your back muscles, is to use a hook through the eye provided and a lifting device, such as a chain hoist.

Place the powerhead on a suitable work surface. Again, take care not to loose the alignment dowel pins. The pins may come away with the powerhead, or they may remain in the intermediate housing.

➡**The following procedures cover removal and installation of virtually all components of the powerhead. However, if the determination can be made certain seals, bearings, etc. are fit for further service, leave a sleeping dog lie, simply skip the steps involved for such items and proceed with the necessary work. In certain instances, the item would be destroyed or at least rendered unfit for service during the removal process.**

To avoid juggling the powerhead, the first component to be removed should be the lower oil seal housing leaving a fairly flat surface on the bottom of the powerhead. A couple of ½ inch pieces of wood wedged under the powerhead at strategic locations will stabilize the block.

13. Remove the four bolts securing the lower oil seal housing to the block.

14. Use a couple of screwdrivers and pry the housing away from the block or tap the housing lightly with a soft head mallet to jar it loose. Remove and discard the outer O-ring.

➡**Removal of the seals destroys their sealing qualities. Therefore, they cannot be installed a second time. Be absolutely sure a new seal is available before removing the old seal in the next step.**

15. Inspect the condition of the two seals in the lower oil seal housing. If the seals appear to be damaged and replacement is required, proceed with removal.

Step 10   04708P6F

Step 11   04708P6G

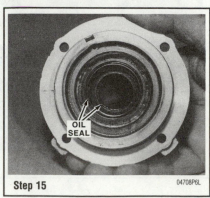

Step 12   04708P6H

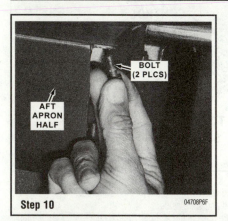

Step 13   04708P6J

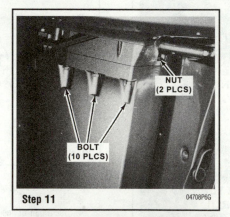

Step 14   04708P6K

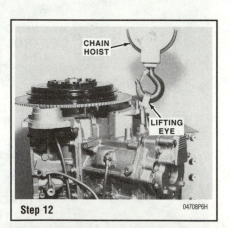

Step 15   04708P6L

Obtain special tool Yamaha P/N YB6096 slide hammer and jaw attachment and remove the seals.

Set the powerhead upright to perform the following work.

16. Identify the oil supply lines at each intake port, these lines are of different lengths. Remove the line retainer on the port side of the block and remove all the lines.

→Take care in the next step when handling reed valve assemblies. Once the assembly is removed, keep it away from sunlight, moisture, dust, and dirt. Sunlight can deteriorate valve seat rubber seals. Moisture can easily rust stoppers overnight. Dust and dirt—especially sand or other gritty material can break reed petals if caught between stoppers and reed petals.

Make special arrangements to store the reed valves to keep them isolated from elements while further work is being performed on the powerhead.

17. Remove the bolts securing the intake manifold/reed valve assembly to the block. Obtain a long wide screwdriver to separate both pieces from the block and from each other. Insert the screwdriver between the tabs provided for this purpose, and pry the two surfaces apart. Never pry at a gasket sealing surface. Such action would very likely damage the sealing surface of an aluminum powerhead.

18. Remove and discard the gasket. Set the reed valves aside. Further work on the reed valves will be performed later during cleaning and inspection.

→The exhaust cover should always be removed during a powerhead overhaul. Many times, water in the powerhead is caused by a leaking exhaust cover gasket or plate. If the inner or outer cover is stuck to the powerhead, insert a slotted screwdriver between the tabs provided for this purpose, and pry the two surfaces apart. Never pry at a gasket sealing surface. Such action would very likely damage the sealing surface of an aluminum powerhead.

19. Remove the bolts securing the outer cover.

20. Remove the cover and the gasket. Remove the inner cover and gasket. Discard the outer and inner cover gaskets.

Step 16   04708P6M

Step 17   04708P6N

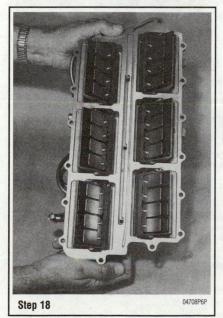

Step 18   04708P6P

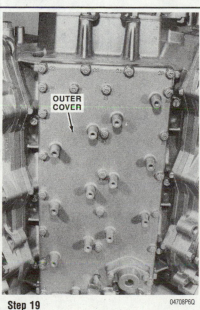

Step 19   04708P6Q

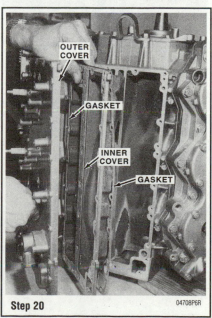

Step 20   04708P6R

21. On the V6 powerhead, remove the two bolts securing the bypass cover to the exhaust cover. Lift the cover up, and then remove the spring and water pressure valve. Observe how the short end of the insert faces upward, as an assist during assembling.

22. Remove the four bolts securing the thermostat cover to the cylinder head cover.

23. Remove the cover and the thermostat. If the cover is stuck to the power-head, tap it lightly with a soft head mallet to jar it free. Remove and discard the gasket. As an assist during assembling, observe how the spring end of the thermostat was inserted into the cylinder head.

On V4 powerheads, the water pressure relief valve is also located under the thermostat cover. Remove the spring and water pressure valve. As an assist during assembling, observe how the short end of the insert faces upward.

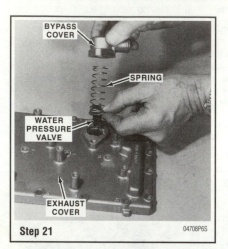
Step 21   04708P6S

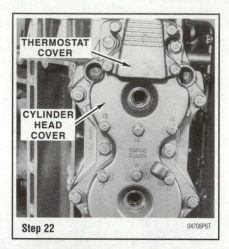
Step 22   04708P6T

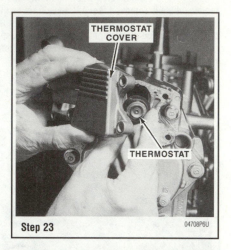
Step 23   04708P6U

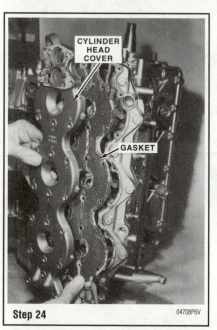
Step 24   04708P6V

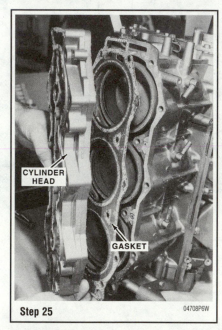
Step 25   04708P6W

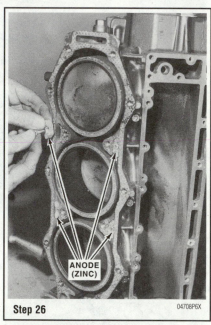
Step 26   04708P6X

Step 27   04708P6Y

24. Remove the cylinder head cover bolts, and then remove the cover. Remove and discard the gasket. If the cover is stuck to the cylinder head, insert a slotted screwdriver between the tabs provided for this purpose and pry the two surfaces apart. Again, never pry at the gasket sealing surfaces, because the sealing surface of an aluminum powerhead could be damaged.

25. Insert a long wide screwdriver between the tabs on the cylinder head and block. Pry the two surfaces apart using the tabs provided for this purpose. Never pry at a gasket sealing surface. Such action would very likely damage the sealing surface of an aluminum powerhead.

If the cylinder head is stubborn and cannot be broken free of the block, tap the head lightly with a soft head mallet to jar it free.

26. Remove the Phillips head screws, and then remove the wedge shaped anodes located in the water jacket.

27. Do not attempt to remove the upper oil seal housing, at this time. The housing must be removed from the crankshaft after the crankshaft has been lifted from the block. To attempt removal at this time would only damage the housing.

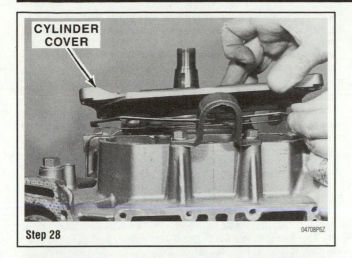

CYLINDER COVER

Step 28
04708P6Z

28. Remove the cylinder cover retaining bolts. Remove the cover, and then remove and discard the gasket.

29. Remove the crankcase bolts. These bolts vary, depending on the unit being serviced, as follows:
- V4 powerheads have 14 bolts of two different sizes.
- V6 powerheads have 20 bolts of two different sizes.

After all bolts have been removed, insert a slotted screwdriver between the tabs provided for this purpose and pry the two surfaces apart. Never pry at gasket sealing surfaces. Such action would very likely damage the sealing surface of an aluminum powerhead.

30. Separate the two halves of the crankcase. Take care not to lose the two dowel pins. These pins may remain in either half when the crankcase is separated.

31. Tap the edge of the oil seal housing with a soft head mallet to jar it free of the crankshaft. Remove the upper oil seal housing from the top of the crankshaft.

32. Remove and discard the two O-rings around the housing.

Inspect the condition of the oil seal in the upper oil seal housing. Make a determination if the seal is fit for further service. The seal will be destroyed during removal. Therefore, remove the seal only if it is damaged and has lost its sealing qualities.

To remove the seal, first obtain Yamaha slide hammer puller P/N YB6096 with expanding jaw attachment, and then pull the seal, or pry the seal free with a screwdriver.

➡ **Remove the roller bearing only if it is in question or is no longer fit for service.**

33. The roller bearing is pressed into the upper oil seal housing. To remove the bearing, first obtain Yamaha special tool P/N YB6205 bearing installer. Using the shaft of the installer, remove the bearing from the housing using a hydraulic press. Press the bearing downwards free of the housing.

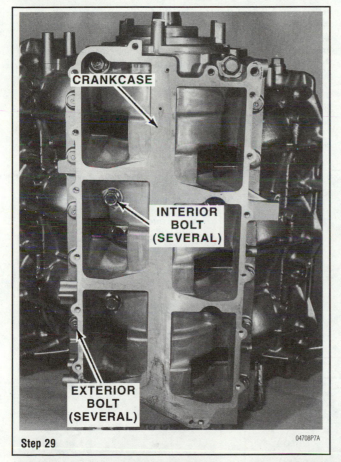

CRANKCASE

INTERIOR BOLT (SEVERAL)

EXTERIOR BOLT (SEVERAL)

Step 29
04708P7A

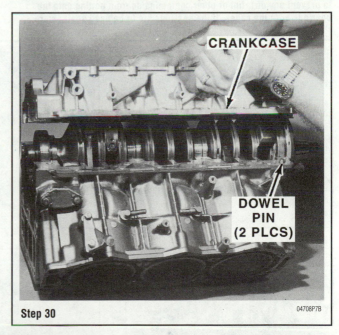

CRANKCASE

DOWEL PIN (2 PLCS)

Step 30
04708P7B

MALLET

UPPER OIL SEAL HOUSING

Step 31
04708P7C

OIL SEAL

UPPER OIL SEAL HOUSING

Step 32
04708P7D

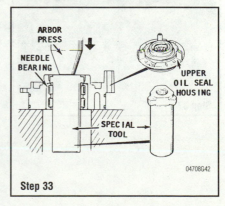

ARBOR PRESS

NEEDLE BEARING

SPECIAL TOOL

UPPER OIL SEAL HOUSING

Step 33
04708G42

34. Take time to mark the cylinder number on both halves of the connecting rod caps. This mark should be made with a marker, whiteout, paint, or any substance which will adhere to a metal surface. Under no circumstances should the mark be a series of notches, or gouges, or even scribed. All these can cause stress risers, and under heavy engine load can cause parts to crack and fail.

➡ **These connecting rods were cast as one piece. Holes were then drilled where they would normally separate, and then the two halves were physically broken apart. Therefore, each mating surface is unique, one of a kind. These rods can never be resized and can never be made to match another set.**

35. Obtain an 8mm 12 point socket, with very narrow sides—a rare animal—not in every one's tool kit.

➡ **Snap-on Tool Company markets such a socket. Without modification, this socket can be used successfully to remove the rod bolts. If this particular socket is not available, a 5/16 inch 12 point socket will suffice. The external diameter of most sockets, with the exception of the first one listed, will be too great to fit between the bolt and the cap.**

As a last resort, an 8mm or a 5/16 inch 12 point socket may be ground down to fit, but not without its disadvantages: First, grinding away material from the external wall will weaken the socket and the walls may break away. Upon installation, the rod bolts are tightened to the specified torque value. Secondly, if the grinding is not symmetrical, any high spots on the external socket wall may flake off when used and fall down into the cylinder bore.

36. Remove the connecting rod cap bolts. Lift off the cap and caged roller bearing beneath the cap. Slide the other half of the caged roller bearing around the journal and keep all three items together on the workbench.

➡ **Cleanliness is the password when handling roller bearings. Take care to prevent any dirt, lint or other contaminants from getting onto the bearings or in the cages. If the bearings are to be used again, store**

them in a numbered container to ensure they will be installed with the same rod and cap from which they were removed. Never intermix roller bearings from one rod to another. Never intermix used roller bearings with new bearings. If just one bearing is unfit for further service, the entire set must be replaced.

New bearings should be installed in the connecting rods, even though they may appear to be in serviceable condition. New bearings will ensure lasting service after the overhaul work is completed. If it is necessary to install the used bearings, keep them separate and identified to ensure they will be installed onto the same crank pin throw and with the same connecting rod from which they were removed.

Continue removing the rod caps and two bearing halves until all have been removed from the crankshaft.

37. Tap the crankshaft lightly with a soft head mallet to jar it free from the block. Lift the crankshaft out of the block.

38. Remove the large circlip from around each set of main bearings. Remove the two halves of the bearing shell and the two halves of the roller bearing. If the main bearings are to be reused, keep each set together, so they may be installed back into their original locations.

➡ **New main bearings should be installed in the connecting rods, even though they may appear to be in serviceable condition. New bearings will ensure lasting service after the overhaul work is completed. If it is necessary to install the used bearings, keep them separate and identified to ensure they will be installed in the same location from which they were removed.**

39. Pull each piston and connecting rod assembly from the bottom—not through the top of the block. A ridge might have formed on the top of the cylinder bore. This ridge may have to be removed with a ridge reamer.

Immediately after removing the piston and rod assembly, temporarily assemble the rod cap back onto the rod to keep it as a matched set.

Step 34   04708P7E

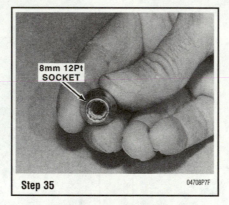

Step 35   04708P7F

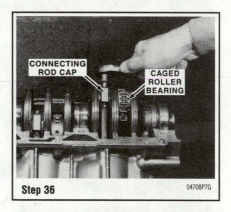

Step 36   04708P7G

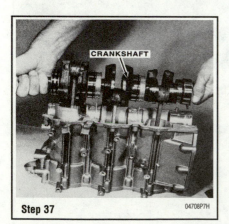

Step 37   04708P7H

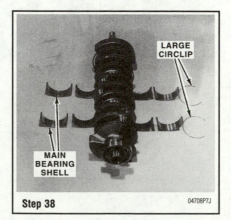

Step 38   04708P7J

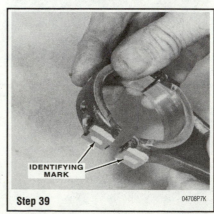

Step 39   04708P7K

40. Make an identifying mark on the outside edge of each rod I beam and a matching mark on the inside of each piston skirt. The identification mark must match the cylinder from which the piston and rod were removed.

This mark should be made with a marker, whiteout, paint or any substance which will adhere to a metal surface. Under no circumstances should the mark be a series of notches, or gouges, or even scribed. All these can cause stress risers, and under heavy engine load can cause parts to crack and fail.

➡The piston pin C-lockrings are made of spring steel and may slip out of the pliers or pop out of the groove with considerable force. Therefore,

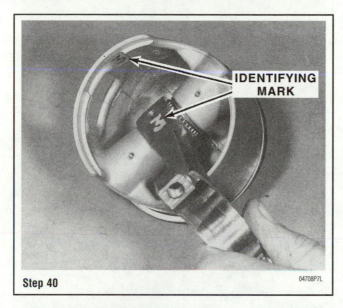

Step 40   04708P7L

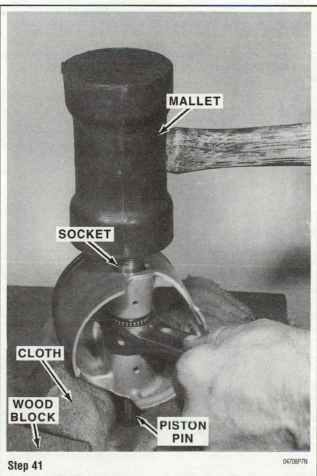

Step 41   04708P7N

wear eye protection glasses while removing the piston pin lockrings in the next step.

Remove the C-lockring from both ends of the piston pin using a pair of needle nose pliers or an awl. Discard the C-lockrings. These rings stretch during removal and cannot be used a second time.

41. Press the pin free of the piston using an arbor press or a long suitably sized socket, with the piston resting on a padded surface. Be sure to catch all the loose needle bearings and two small spacers as they fall free of the piston pin bore.

➡Good shop practice dictates to replace the rings during a powerhead overhaul. However, if the rings are to be used again, expand them only enough to clear the piston and the grooves, because used rings are brittle and break very easily.

42. Gently spread the top piston ring enough to pry it out and up over the top of the piston. No special tool is required to remove the piston rings. Remove the middle and lower rings in a similar manner. These rings are extremely brittle and have to be handled with care if they are intended for further service.

43. Inspect the bronze oil injection worm gear at the lower end of the crankshaft. If the gear needs to be replaced, the lower main bearing must be pulled from the crankshaft first. The bronze worm gear may then be pulled.

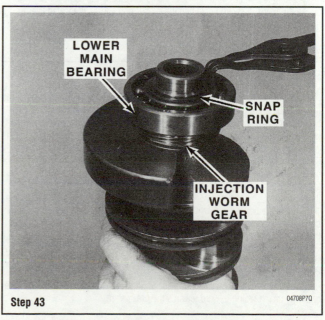

Step 42   04708P7P

Step 43   04708P7Q

Step 44   04708P7R

Slowly rotate the bearing race on the crankshaft. If rough spots are felt, the bearing will have to be pressed free of the crankshaft. Obtain a pair of snap-ring pliers. Remove the snap-ring around the lower end of the crankshaft.

44. Obtain special bearing separator tool, Yamaha P/N YB6219 and an arbor press. Press the bearing from the crankshaft. Be sure the crankshaft is supported, because once the bearing breaks loose, the crankshaft is free to fall. Relocate the bearing separator and press the bronze oil injection gear from the crankshaft.

45. Gently spread each of the crankshaft sealing rings enough to ease it out and up over the top of the groove and into a journal space. Then, once again separate the two ends enough to clear the journal, and lift the ring free. Take care not to scratch the highly polished journal surface as each ring is removed.

Remove all the rings in a similar manner. These rings are extremely brittle and have to be handled with care if they are intended for further service.

CLEANING & INSPECTION

Cleaning and inspecting the components is virtually the same for any two-stroke outboard. A section detailing the proper procedures is located later in this section.

ASSEMBLY & INSTALLATION

♦ **See accompanying illustrations**

Detailed procedures are given to assemble and install virtually all parts of the powerhead. Therefore, if certain parts were not removed or disassembled because the part was found to be fit for further service, simply skip the particular step involved and continue with the required tasks to return the powerhead to operating condition.

1. Install the crankshaft sealing rings by spreading each ring enough to clear the journal adjacent to its groove. Once the ring is around the journal, spread the ends gently again and slide it up and over the upper edges and into its groove.

Perform the next step only if the ball bearing was removed during disassembly. If the ball bearing was not disturbed, apply a coat of Yamalube to the inner bearing surfaces.

Install the bronze oil injection gear over the lower end of the crankshaft. Using an arbor press. Press the gear down until the gear seats against the shoulder on the shaft.

2. Position the ball bearing over the shaft with the embossed marks on the bearing surface facing upward towards the press shaft.

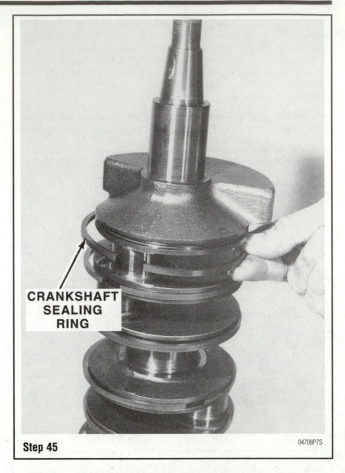

Step 45   04708P7S

Now, use a suitable mandrel and press against the inner bearing race.

➡**Take care to ensure the mandrel is pressing on the inner race and not on the outer race or the ball bearings. Such action would destroy the bearing.**

Continue to press the bearing into place until the bearing is seated against the oil injection gear.

Step 1   04708P8F

3. Using a pair of snap-ring pliers, install the snap-ring into the groove above the gear.

4. Install a new set of piston rings onto the piston, with the embossed marks facing up. No special tool is necessary for installation. However, take care to spread the ring only enough to clear the top of the piston. The rings are extremely brittle and will snap if spread beyond their limit. Align the ring gap over the locating pin.

✳✳ CAUTION

The piston pin lockrings are made of spring steel and may slip out of the pliers or pop out of the groove with considerable force. Therefore, wear eye protection glasses while installing the piston pin lockrings in the next step.

5. Gather all the components needed to assemble the piston for installation into No. 1 cylinder bore: the piston, two C-lockrings, two retainers, the piston pin, needle bearing set (30 by count), and the connecting rod.

6. Select the set of needle bearings removed from the No. 1 piston or obtain a new set of bearings.

Coat the inner circumference of the small end of the No. 1 connecting rod with Yamaha A grease, or equivalent multipurpose water resistant lubricant. Position the needle bearings one by one around the circumference.

7. Position the end of the rod with the needle bearings and retainers in place up into the piston with the word **Yamaha** facing the same direction as the word **UP** on the piston crown. The word **UP** must face toward the tapered (upper) end of the crankshaft.

Dab some lubricant on the sides of the rod and stick the retainers in place.

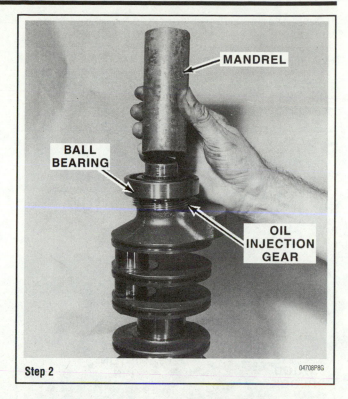

Step 2   04708P8G

Step 3   04708P8H

Step 4   04708P8J

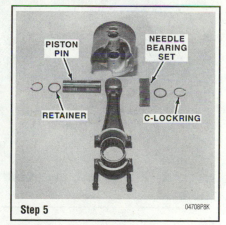

Step 5   04708P8K

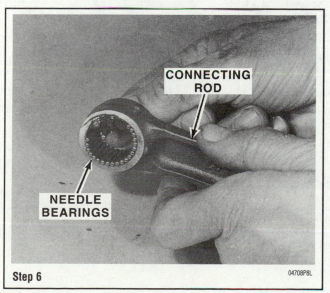

Step 6   04708P8L

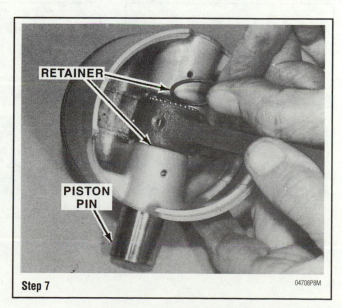

Step 7   04708P8M

8. Press the piston pin through the piston and connecting rod, using an arbor press or by just resting the piston on an open vise with plenty of padding under the piston. Center the pin in the piston.

9. Install the C-lockring at each end of the piston pin.

Perform the procedures in these last 5 steps to assemble the remaining connecting rods.

10. Coat the cylinder bores with a good grade of engine oil. Before installing the piston into the cylinder, make the following test:

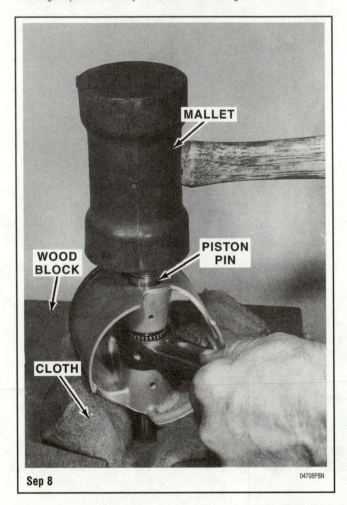

Sep 8

Run your finger along the top rim of the cylinder. If the surface of the block and the surface of the bore have a sharp edge, the piston may be installed from the top.

If the slightest groove or ridge is felt on the rim, the ridge must be removed using a ridge reamer, as shown in the accompanying illustration. Attempting to install the piston from the top without removing the ridge, will not be successful because the piston ring will bottom on the ridge. If force is used the ring may very well break.

11. Align each ring gap over its locating pin.

12. Obtain a ring compressor. Compress the aligned rings and then use the end of a wooden mallet handle to gently tap the piston down into the cylinder bore.

13. The word **UP** embossed on the piston crown must face toward the flywheel end of the block. The embossed letter **P** must face port side, and the embossed letter **S** must face starboard.

The piston pin is offset ever so slightly and for good reason. When the piston is correctly installed, having the pin slightly offset will reduce the thrust, commonly termed piston slap. This thrust is a frictional force on the cylinder walls. As the piston approaches TDC, the piston exerts a frictional force on one side of the cylinder wall due to the rod angle. This wall is considered the minor thrust wall. When the piston actually reaches TDC, the connecting rod pivots on the piston pin. Just a microsecond after TDC, the piston is forced downward in the cylinder under the pressure of combustion.

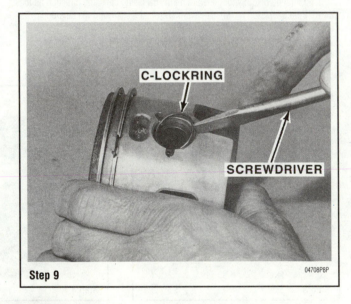

Step 9

Step 10

Step 11

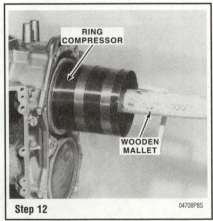

Step 12

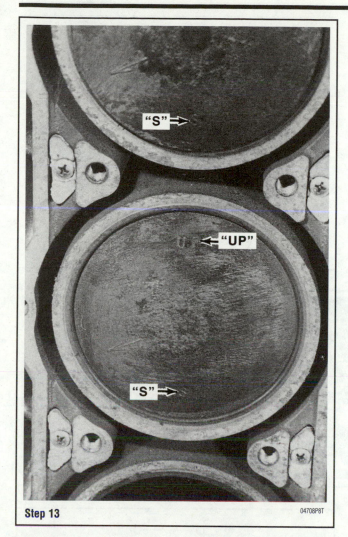

Step 13   04708P8T

During downward movement, the piston exerts a greater frictional force on the opposite cylinder wall. This side of the cylinder is referred to as the major thrust wall.

When the forces on the piston change, at TDC, the piston undergoes a tendency to tilt. The offset position of the piston pin towards the major thrust wall tends to:

• First, increase the piston-to-cylinder friction on the minor thrust wall during upward movement.

• Second, reduce the piston-to-cylinder friction on the major thrust wall during downward movement.

If the piston is installed incorrectly into the cylinder, the powerhead will still operate, but frictional forces on the minor thrust wall and the contacting wall of the piston will be far greater than normal. This friction will cause accelerated wear on both the piston and the cylinder wall and piston slap will increase to the point where it will be audibly noticeable.

Mechanics involved in racing units will sometimes purposely install the piston with the offset on the wrong side. This position will place the piston dome further up in the combustion chamber as TDC is approached. Result: increase in compression and therefore more horsepower. Under such conditions the powerhead will not last as long due to the extra friction created, but longevity is not the prime concern—if they win the race.

From the foregoing paragraphs, be advised, if the port and starboard pistons are inadvertently installed incorrectly, the piston assembly and the cylinder wall will be subjected to more than normal wear.

Repeat this procedure for the remaining pistons.

After all pistons have been installed, slide each piston up and down in the cylinder bore several times. Check for binding. Listen for scratching noises. Scratching, or any other spooky noise, may indicate a ring was broken during installation.

14. Obtain driver P/N YB6205. Support the upper oil seal housing in an arbor press with the O-ring end facing upward. Lower the needle bearing into the housing from the O-ring end. Install the bearing with the stamped mark on the bearing facing downward—away from the driver. Seat the bearing squarely into the bore, until the shoulder of the driver seats against the shoulder of the housing. The bearing will then be correctly seated in the housing. Invert the housing and leave it in place on the arbor press for the next step.

15. Pack the lips of the seal with Yamalube Grease, or equivalent water resistant lubricant.

Obtain driver P/N YB6198. Place the seal over the installed bearing with the lips of the seals facing downward toward the driver.

Lower the seal squarely into the top of the oil seal housing with the lip of the seal facing downward. Place the seal installer over the seal and actuate the press until the seal is fully seated.

➡ **If the old roller bearings are to be installed for further service, each must be installed in the same location from which it was removed.**

On a V4 crankcase there are center bearing locating holes between the No. 2 and No. 3 cylinders. On a V6 crankcase, these holes are located between the No. 2 and No. 3 cylinders, also between the No. 4 and No. 5 cylinders. These locating holes must match tangs on the main bearing shells during installation, or the crankcase will not seat properly.

16. Install two new O-rings around the housing and slide the housing over the tapered end of the crankshaft. Rotate the installed housing until the arrow embossed on the top points directly towards the small indent of the cylinder cover.

Step 14   04708P8U

Step 15   04708P8V

Step 16   04708P8W

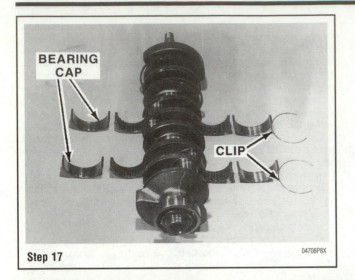

Step 17   04708P8X

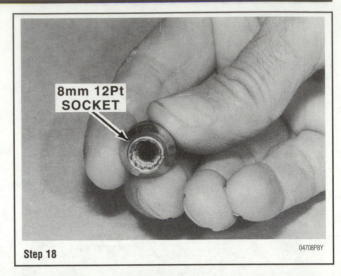

Step 18   04708P8Y

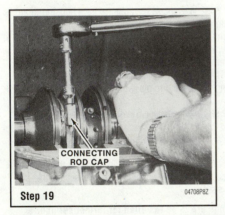

Step 19   04708P8Z

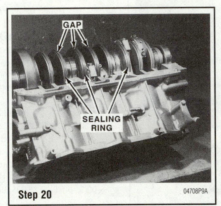

Step 20   04708P9A

Step 21   04708P9B

17. Place the lower half roller bearings in their original positions on the connecting rod caps.

Place the roller bearing, bearing caps and clips around the main journals of the crankshaft, hold them together while lowering the crankshaft down onto the connecting rod bearings.

Place the upper caged roller bearings and connecting rod caps in their original locations.

➡**The manufacturer does not recommend rod cap bolts be used a second time. Also, the manufacturer recommends a specific method of tightening the rod cap bolts be followed as outlined in the next step.**

Work on just one rod at a time.

18. Obtain an 8mm 12 point socket, with very narrow sides.

➡**Snap-on Tool Company markets such a socket. Without modification, this socket can be used successfully to install the rod bolts. If this particular socket is not available, a ⁵⁄₁₆ inch 12 point socket will suffice. The external diameter of most sockets, with the exception of the first one listed, will be too great to fit between the bolt and the cap.**

As a last resort, an 8mm or a ⁵⁄₁₆ inch 12 point socket may be ground down to fit, but not without its disadvantages: First, grinding away material from the external wall will weaken the socket and the walls may break away. During installation, the rod bolts are tightened to the specified torque value. Secondly, if the grinding is not symmetrical, any high spots on the external socket wall may flake off when used and fall down into the cylinder bore.

19. Thread in new connecting rod cap bolts a few turns each. Now, tighten the cap bolts to the specified torque. Check to be sure the single mark on each rod cap end is centrally located between the two matching embossed marks on the rod end and on the cap.

If the marks are aligned, as described, loosen each bolt one half turn, and then tighten the bolt to the specified torque.

If the marks are not aligned, as described, remove the cap bolts, and then the upper caged roller bearing half. Install the upper caged roller bearing half again.

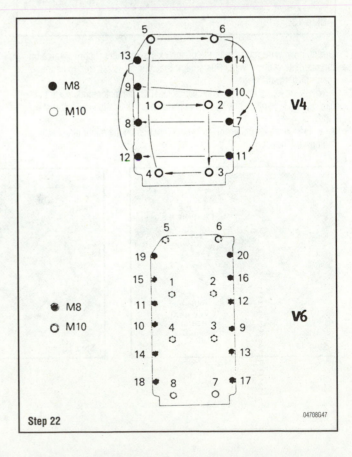

Step 22   04708G47

Check the alignment. If the second attempt fails to align the marks as described, the crankshaft must be removed and the lower caged roller bearing half checked for correct alignment.

20. Arrange the end-gaps of all the crankshaft sealing rings to face upward.

21. Apply a thin bead of Yamabond No. 4 Permatex® around both surfaces of the crankcase and block. Check to be sure the two dowel pins are in place and install the crankcase to the block.

22. Install and tighten the attaching bolts in the sequence shown. The numbering sequence is embossed around the mating surface of the crankcase on both sides of the block. Tighten the bolts to the specified torque value.

✳✳ WARNING

If binding is felt, it will be necessary to remove the crankcase and reseat the crankshaft and also to check the positioning of the crankshaft sealing rings and the bearing locating pins. If binding is still a problem after the crankcase has been installed a second time, the cause might very well be a broken piston ring.

23. Check to be sure each piston ring has spring tension. This is accomplished by carefully pressing on each ring with a screwdriver extended through the exhaust ports, as shown in the accompanying illustration. If spring tension cannot be felt (the spring fails to return to its original position), the ring was probably broken during the piston and crankshaft installation process. Take care not to burr the piston rings while checking for spring tension.

24. Verify the arrow embossed on the oil seal housing points directly towards the indent of the cylinder cover opening, as shown. Install the bolts securing the upper oil seal housing. Tighten the bolts alternately (across from each other), working in a clockwise direction around the housing. Tighten the bolts to the specified torque value.

25. Install a new gasket and then install the cylinder cover. Tighten the attaching bolts to the specified torque value.

26. Insert the wedge shaped anodes into the water jacket of the block. Secure the anodes with Phillips head screws. These anodes will only be visible and accessible the next time the powerhead is overhauled. Therefore, if the anodes show ANY sign of deterioration in this location, a NEW anode should be installed.

27. Position a new head gasket in place on the powerhead.

➡The manufacturer recommends no sealing agent be used on either side of the head gasket.

Install the cylinder head onto the powerhead.

28. Install and tighten the attaching bolts in the sequence shown. The numbering sequence is embossed around the mating surface of the head and block. Tighten the bolts in two rounds to the specified torque value.

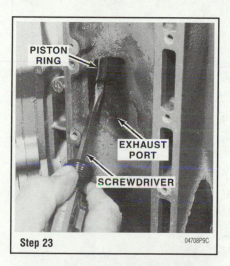

Step 23   04708P9C

Step 24   04708P9D

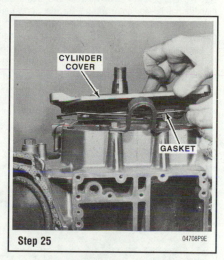

Step 25   04708P9E

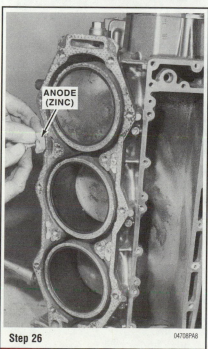

Step 26   04708PA8

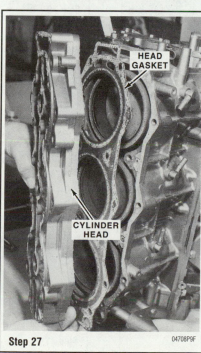

Step 27   04708P9F

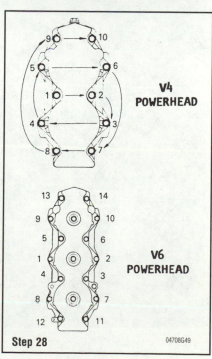

Step 28   04708G49

→Because of the high temperatures and pressures developed, the sealing surfaces of the cylinder head and the block are the most prone to water leaks. No sealing agent is recommended because it is almost impossible to apply an even coat of sealer. An even coat would be essential to ensure a air/water tight seal.

Some head gaskets are supplied with a tacky coating on both surfaces applied at the time of manufacture. This tacky substance will provide an even coating all around. Therefore, no further sealing agent is required.

However, if a slight water leak should be noticed following completed assembly work and powerhead start up, do not attempt to stop the leak by tightening the head bolts beyond the recommended torque value. Such action will only aggravate the problem and most likely distort the head.

Furthermore, tightening the bolts, which are case hardened aluminum, may force the bolt beyond its elastic limit and cause the bolt to fracture: bad news, very bad news indeed. A fractured bolt must usually be drilled out and the hole retapped to accommodate an oversize bolt. Avoid such a situation.

Probable causes and remedies of a new head gasket leaking are:

• Sealing surfaces not thoroughly cleaned of old gasket material. Disassemble and remove all traces of old gasket.

• Damage to the machined surface of the head or the block. The remedy for this damage is the same as for the next case.

• Permanently distorted head or block. Spray a light even coat of any type metallic spray paint on both sides of a new head gasket. Use only metallic paint—any color will do. Regular spray paint does not have the particle content required to provide the extra sealing properties this procedure requires.

Assemble the block and head with the gasket while the paint is till tacky. Install the head bolts and tighten in the recommended sequence and to the proper torque value and no more!

Allow the paint to set for at least 24 hours before starting the powerhead.

Consider this procedure as a temporary band aid type solution until a new head may be purchased or other permanent measures can be performed.

Under normal circumstances, if procedures have been followed to the letter, the head gasket will not leak.

29. Position a new head cover gasket in place on the cylinder head.

→The manufacturer recommends no sealing agent be used on either side of this gasket.

Install the head cover onto the head.

30. Install and tighten the attaching bolts in the sequence shown. The numbering sequence is embossed around the mating surface of the head and block. Tighten the bolts in two rounds to the specified torque value.

31. Insert the thermostat into the powerhead with the spring end going in first.

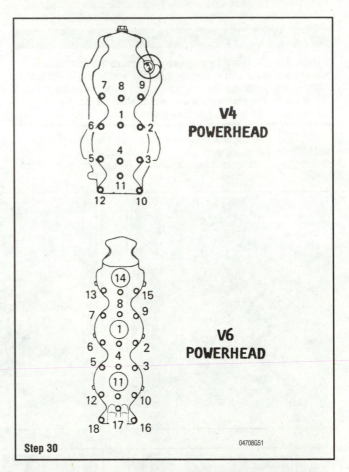

Step 30

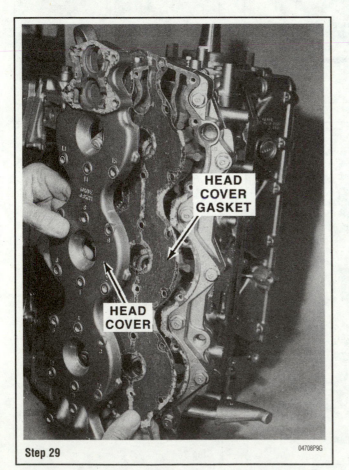

HEAD COVER GASKET

HEAD COVER

Step 29

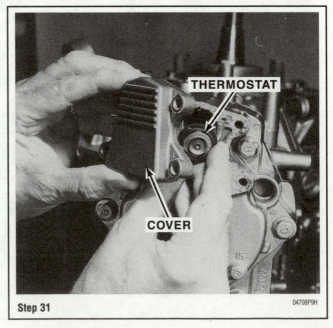

THERMOSTAT

COVER

Step 31

On V4 powerheads, the water pressure relief valve is also located under the thermostat cover. Install the longer end of the valve into the head. Place the spring over the short end of the valve. Coat both sides of a new gasket with Permatex® and install the cover with the four attaching bolts. Tighten the bolts to the specified torque value, starting with the lower right bolt and tightening the remaining three in a clockwise sequence.

32. On the V6 powerhead, install the pressure valve into the exhaust cover with the longer end of the valve being inserted into the cover. Place the spring over the short end of the valve. Install a new gasket and install the cover. Tighten the bolts securely.

33. Obtain Very High Temperature (VHT) quick gasket maker. Apply this sealant to both sides of the two exhaust manifold gaskets. Quick Gasket is a silicone rubber based adhesive sealant recommended by the manufacturer for use where rubber gaskets are used next to metal surfaces.

Install the first gasket, the inner exhaust cover, the second gasket, and then the outer exhaust cover.

34. Tighten the bolts to the specified torque values and in the sequence indicated.

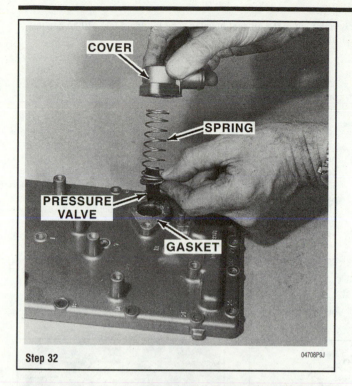

Step 32   04708P9J

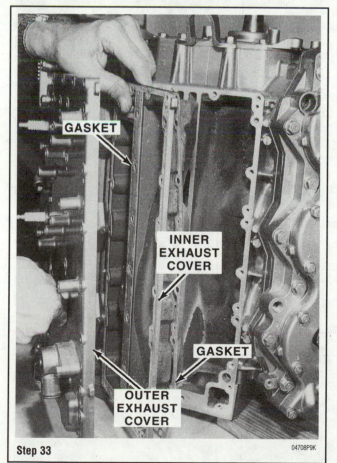

Step 33   04708P9K

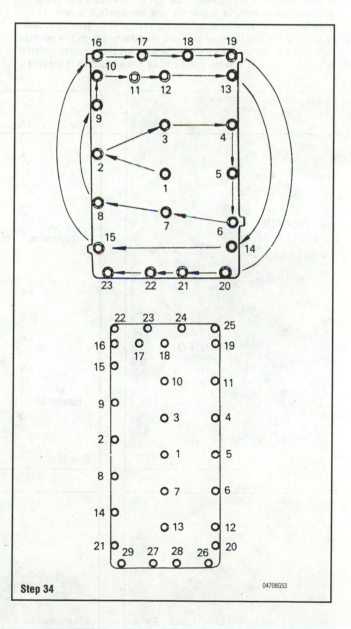

Step 34   04708G53

35. Install the intake manifold housing. The manufacturer recommends no sealant be applied to the gasket at this location.

36. Install and tighten the attaching bolts to the specified torque values and in the sequence indicated.

37. Route the oil injection supply lines between the retainers and the intake manifold. Slide the lines onto the fittings at each intake port.

38. If the oil seals in the lower oil seal housing were removed during disassembling, install new oil seals in the housing using a handle and driver Yamaha P/N YB6198. Both seals are driven into the housing with the machined surface facing up. Secure the lower oil seal housing in a vice equipped with soft jaws.

Both the large and the small seal are installed with lips facing downward.

When the lower oil seal housing is installed onto the powerhead, all seals will face in the correct direction, as installed.

Pack each seal lip with Yamalube Grease, or equivalent water resistant lubricant, as soon as the seal is installed.

➡ When two seals are installed, the lips of both seals face in the same direction. Yamaha engineers have concluded it is better to have both seals face the same direction rather than have them back to back as directed by other outboard manufacturers. In this position, with both lips facing toward the water after oil seal housing installation, the engineers feel the seals will be more effective in keeping water out of the oil seal housing. Any lubricant lost will be negligible.

Apply engine oil around the groove in the oil housing and around the new O-ring. Install the O-ring around the housing. Install the housing over the lower end of the crankshaft. Tap lightly around the circumference to seat the housing properly into the crankcase. Align the holes, and then install and tighten the securing bolts.

39. Coat both sides of a new gasket with Permatex®, or equivalent material. Place the gasket in position on the intermediate housing surface. Check to be sure the two alignment dowel pins are in place. Carefully lower the powerhead onto the intermediate housing with the dowel pins indexing into the holes in the powerhead. The splines of the crankshaft must also index into the splines of the driveshaft. If the splines do not index, shift the lower unit into forward gear, have an assistant slowly rotate the propeller just a whisker clockwise, and the splines should index. Check to be sure the powerhead is fully down on the intermediate housing—the mating surfaces hard against each other.

40. Apply Loctite® to the bolt threads and install the ten bolts of three different lengths and two nuts securing the powerhead to the intermediate housing. Tighten the bolts alternately and evenly to the specified torque value.

41. Wrap the aft half of the apron around the lower cowling. Secure the apron half to the cowling with the two attaching bolts at the outer edges of the apron. Tighten the bolts to the specified torque value.

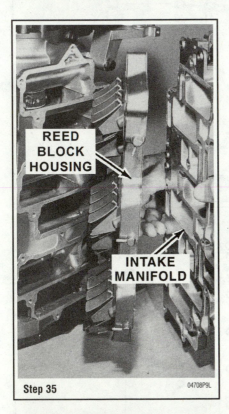

REED BLOCK HOUSING

INTAKE MANIFOLD

Step 35　04708P9L

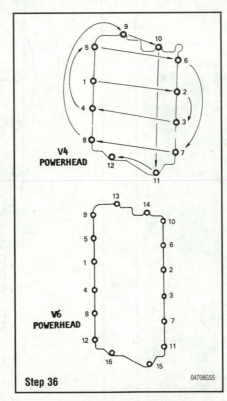

V4 POWERHEAD

V6 POWERHEAD

Step 36　04708G55

OIL SUPPLY LINE

Step 37　04708P9M

OIL SEAL

Step 38　04708P9N

CHAIN HOIST

LIFTING EYE

Step 39　04708P9Q

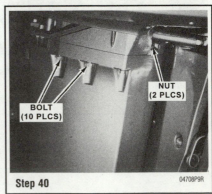

BOLT (10 PLCS)

NUT (2 PLCS)

Step 40　04708P9R

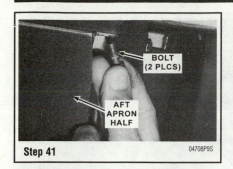

Step 41 04708P9S

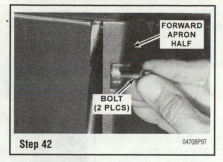

Step 42 04708P9T

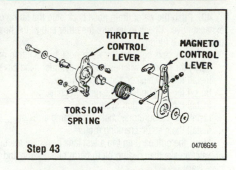

Step 43 04708G56

Step 44 04708P9U

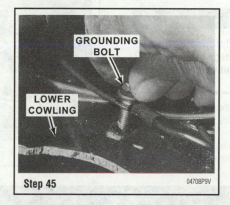

Step 45 04708P9V

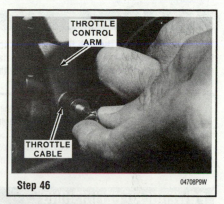

Step 46 04708P9W

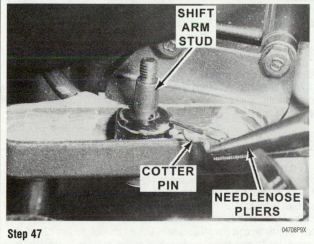

Step 47 04708P9X

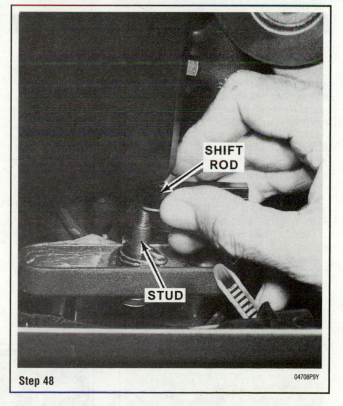

Step 48 04708P9Y

42. Wrap the forward half of the apron around the lower cowling. Secure both halves together with the two attaching screws. Tighten the screws securely.

43. On models without YMIS, place the bushing on the inside of the throttle control arm. Install the torsion spring on the magneto control lever and hook the throttle control lever onto the torsion spring. Twist the throttle control lever and snap it over the magneto control lever. Insert the bolt through the throttle control arm, slide the nylon washer on first, followed by the metal washer and install the assembly to the powerhead.

44. Install all the link rods onto both levers.
On models equipped with YMIS, slide the bolt through the magneto control arm, slide the nylon washer on first, followed by the metal washer and install the assembly to the powerhead.

45. Connect the ground leads attached to the lower cowling and a lower bolt on the exhaust cover.

46. Install the throttle cable onto the throttle arm. Secure the cable with a washer and a locknut.

47. Install the shift guide to the block, over the shift arm stud. Secure with attaching hardware. Using a pair of needle nose pliers, install the cotter pin through the hole in the stud.

48. Hook the shift rod over the stud.
Install the washer and locknut over the stud to retain the shift rod.

49. Push the water drain hose back onto the fitting on the base of the exhaust cover. Check to be sure the other end of the hose is firmly attached to the pilot hole fitting.

On V6 models connect the water hose to the fitting on the bypass cover.
Insert the thermoswitches into the cylinder head covers until they seat.
Install the flywheel and stator assembly.
Install the CDI unit and the ignition coils.
Install the oil injection system.
Install the carburetors, choke, and flame arrestor.
Install the electric cranking motor.

Move the outboard unit to a test tank or mount the unit on a boat in a body of water. Leave the cowling off to permit inspection and to make adjustments, if necessary.

❊❊ WARNING

Water must circulate through the lower unit to the powerhead any-time the powerhead is operating to prevent damage to the water pump in the lower unit. Just five seconds without water will damage the water pump impeller.

Attempt to start and run the powerhead without the cowling installed. This will provide the opportunity to check for fuel and oil leaks, and to make adjustments, if required.

After the engine is operating properly, install the cowling. Follow the break-in procedures with the unit on a boat and with a load on the propeller.

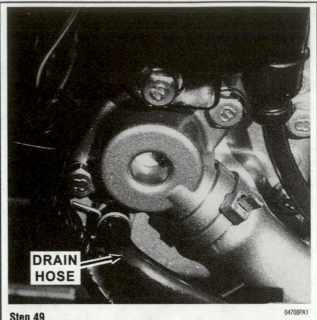

DRAIN HOSE

Step 49

04708PA1

POWERHEAD REFINISHING

Cleaning and Inspecting

The success of the overhaul work is largely dependent on how well the cleaning and inspecting tasks are completed. If some parts are not thoroughly cleaned, or if an unsatisfactory unit is allowed to be returned to service through negligent inspection, the time and expense involved in the work will not be justified with peak powerhead performance and long operating life. Therefore, the procedures in the following sections should be followed closely and the work performed with patience and attention to detail.

REED BLOCK SERVICE

♦ See Figures 18, 19 and 20

Disassemble the reed block housing by first removing the screws securing the reed stoppers and reed petals to the housing. After the screws are removed, lift the stoppers and petals from the housing.

Clean the gasket surfaces of the housing. Check the surfaces for deep grooves, cracks or any distortion which could cause leakage.

Replace the reed block housing if it is damaged. The reed petals should fit flush against their seats, and not be preloaded against their seats or bend away from their seats.

If the reed petal is distorted beyond its bending limit, rarely, if ever, can the petal be successfully straightened. Therefore, it must be replaced.

The valve stopper clearance is the distance between the bottom edge of the stopper and the top of the reed petal.

The valve stopper can sometimes be successfully bent to achieve the required clearance, if not, it must be replaced.

Do not remove the reed valves unless they, or the stoppers, are to be replaced. If servicing a 9.9 hp unit or larger, the reeds must be replaced in sets.

Apply Loctite® to the threads of the reed retaining screws. Tighten each screw to specification gradually, starting in the center and working outwards across the reed block.

EXHAUST COVER

The exhaust covers are one of the most neglected items on any outboard powerhead. Seldom are they checked and serviced. Many times a powerhead may be overhauled and returned to service without the exhaust covers ever having been removed.

One reason the exhaust covers are not removed is because the attaching bolts usually become corroded in place. This means they are very difficult to remove, but the work should be done. Heat applied to the bolt head and around the exhaust cover will help in removal. However, some bolts may still be broken. If the bolt is broken it must be drilled out and the hole tapped with new threads.

The exhaust covers are installed over the exhaust ports to allow the exhaust to leave the powerhead and be transferred to the exhaust housing. If the cover was the only item over the exhaust ports, they would become so hot from the

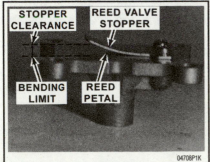

Fig. 18 A 2 hp reed valve housing with a single reed petal

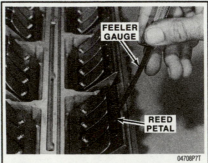

Fig. 19 Using a feeler gauge to measure the reed petal clearance

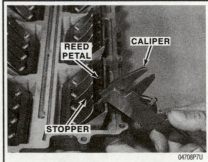

Fig. 20 Measuring the stopper clearance between the stopper and the reed petal

exhaust gases they might cause a fire or a person could be severely burned if they came in contact with the cover.

Therefore, an inner plate is installed to help dissipate the exhaust heat. Two gaskets are installed—one on either side of the inner plate. Water is channeled to circulate between the exhaust cover and the inner plate. This circulating water cools the exhaust cover and prevents it from becoming a hazard.

A thorough cleaning of the inner plate behind the exhaust covers should be performed during a major powerhead overhaul. If the integrity of the exhaust cover assembly is in doubt, replace the inner plate.

BLEED SYSTEM SERVICE

▶ **See Figures 21, 22, 23, 24 and 25**

The bleed system consists of one or more hoses depending on the model being serviced. These hoses transfer unburned fuel from one cylinder to another. The fuel is pulsed by crankcase vacuum. This system prevents accumulation of unburned fuel in the lower cylinder and transfers the fuel and oil mixture to the crankshaft upper main bearing for lubrication.

The accompanying illustrations show the routing of bleed hoses for most powerheads covered in this manual.

Check the condition of each rubber bleed hose. Replace the hose if it shows signs of deterioration or leakage. Check the operation of the check valves. The air/fuel mixture should be able to pass through the valve in only one direction.

Defective check valves cannot be serviced. If defective, they must be replaced.

CRANKSHAFT SERVICE

▶ **See Figures 26, 27, and 28**

Clean the crankshaft with solvent and wipe the journals dry with a lint free cloth. Inspect the main journals and connecting rod journals for cracks,

scratches, grooves, or scores. Inspect the crankshaft oil seal surface for nicks, sharp edges or burrs which might damage the oil seal during installation or might cause premature seal wear. Always handle the crankshaft carefully to avoid damaging the highly finished journal surfaces. Blow out all oil passages with compressed air. The oil passageway leads from the rod to the main bearing journal. Take care not to blow dirt into the main bearing journal bore.

Inspect the bronze oil injection worm gear at the lower end of the crankshaft, if equipped. If the gear needs to be replaced, the lower main bearing must be pulled from the crankshaft first. The bronze worm gear may then be pulled.

Inspect the internal splines at one end and threads at the other end for signs of abnormal wear. Check the crankshaft for run-out by supporting it on two V-blocks at the main bearing surfaces.

Install a dial indicator gauge above the main bearing journals. Rotate the crankshaft and measure the run-out (or the out-of-round) and the taper at both ends and in the two center journals (center journal on all two-cylinder models).

If V-blocks or a dial indicator are not available, a micrometer may be used to measure the diameter of the journal. Make a second measurement at right angles to the first. Check the difference between the first and second measurement for out-of-round condition. If the journals are tapered, ridged, or out-of-round by more than the specification allows, the journals should be reground, or the crankshaft replaced.

Any out-of-round or taper shortens bearing life. Good shop practice dictates new main bearings be installed with a new or reground crankshaft.

➡ **Normally the connecting rods would only be pressed from the crankshaft if either the crankshaft and/or the connecting rods were to be replaced. Therefore, the connecting rod axial play is checked at the piston end to determine the amount of wear at the crankshaft end of the connecting rod.**

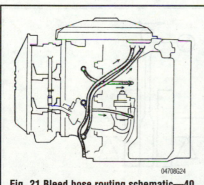

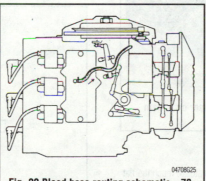

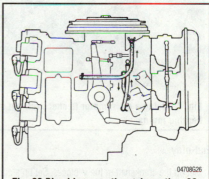

Fig. 21 Bleed hose routing schematic—40 hp and 50 hp powerheads

Fig. 22 Bleed hose routing schematic—70 hp powerhead

Fig. 23 Bleed hose routing schematic—90 hp powerheads

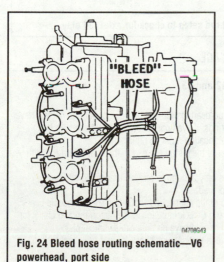

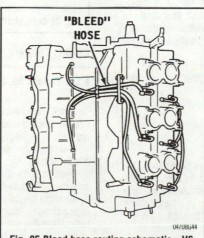

Fig. 24 Bleed hose routing schematic—V6 powerhead, port side

Fig. 25 Bleed hose routing schematic—V6 powerhead, starboard side

Fig. 26 The lower main bearing on some crankshafts secures the bronze oil injection gear

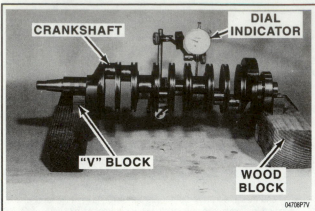

Fig. 27 Crankshaft set up with V-blocks and a dial indicator to measure run-out

Fig. 28 Using a micrometer to check run-out and taper on a main bearing journal

End-play

Set up the crankshaft in the V-blocks. Set up a dial indicator to touch the flat surface of the piston end of the rod. Now, hold the crankshaft steady in the V-blocks and at the same time, rock the piston end of the rod along the same axis as the crankshaft. If the dial indicator needle moves through more than 0.08 inch (2mm) for all two-stroke models covered in this manual, the play is considered excessive. The rod must be pressed from the crankshaft, the journal checked and a determination made as to whether the crankshaft and/or the rod must be replaced. A new rod may be purchased, but it must be pressed onto the crankshaft throw with a hydraulic press.

To check the connecting rod side clearance at the crankshaft, first insert a feeler gauge between the connecting rod and the counterweight of the crankshaft.

Side Clearance

EXCEPT BOLT TOGETHER RODS

▶ See Figure 29

1. If the measurement is not within specification, measure the distance from the outside edge of one counterweight to the outside edge of the other counterweight for the throw of the connecting rod involved. This measurement will give an indication if the counterweight is walking on the crank pin or if the clearance is due to worn parts. The connecting rod would wear before the edge of the counterweight because the rod is manufactured from a much softer material.

2. A new rod may be purchased, but it must be pressed onto the crankshaft throw with a hydraulic press.

BOLT TOGETHER RODS

1. Temporarily install the connecting rods, with matching caps, onto the crankshaft in their original locations, as recorded during disassembling.

2. Set up the crankshaft in a set of V-blocks.

3. Arrange a dial indicator to make contact with the flat surface of the piston end of the rod. Hold the crankshaft firmly in the V-blocks, and at the same time, rock the piston end of the rod along the same axis as the crankshaft axis.

4. If the dial indicator moves through more than 0.08 inch (2mm), the play is considered excessive. If only one rod is found to have excessive play, good shop practice dictates the entire set of rods be replaced. Rods are sold in sets.

5. To check the connecting rod side clearance, first insert a feeler gauge between the connecting rod and the crankshaft counterweight. If the clearance of only one rod is excessive, the complete set of rods should be replaced.

Inspect the crankshaft oil seal surfaces to be sure they are not grooved, pitted, or scratched. Replace the crankshaft if it is severely damaged or worn. Check all crankshaft bearing surfaces for rust, water marks, chatter marks, uneven wear, or overheating. Clean the crankshaft surfaces with 320-grit wet/dry sandpaper dampened with solvent. Never spin-dry a crankshaft ball bearing with compressed air.

Clean the crankshaft and crankshaft ball bearing with solvent. Dry the parts, but not the ball bearing, with compressed air. Check the crankshaft surfaces a second time. Replace the crankshaft if the surfaces cannot be cleaned properly for satisfactory service. If the crankshaft is to be installed for service, lubricate the surfaces with light oil. Do not lubricate the crankshaft ball bearing at this time.

After the crankshaft has been cleaned, grasp the outer race of the crankshaft ball bearing installed on the lower end of the crankshaft, and attempt to work the race back and forth. There should not be excessive play. A very slight amount of side play is acceptable because there is only about 0.001 inch (0.025mm) clearance in the bearing.

Lubricate the ball bearing with light oil. Check the action of the bearing by rotating the outer bearing race. The bearing should have a smooth action and no rust stains. If the ball bearing sounds or feels rough or catches, the bearing should be removed and discarded.

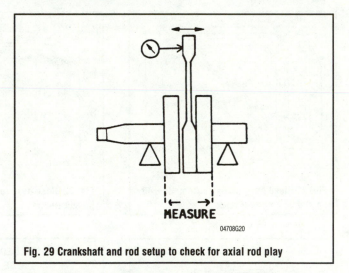

Fig. 29 Crankshaft and rod setup to check for axial rod play

CONNECTING ROD SERVICE

▶ See Figures 30, 31, 32 and 33

Inspect the connecting rod bearings for rust or signs of bearing failure. Never intermix new and used bearings. If even one bearing in a set needs to be replaced, all bearings at that location must be replaced.

Clean the inside diameter of the piston pin end of the connecting rod with crocus cloth.

Clean the connecting rod only enough to remove marks. Do not continue, once the marks have disappeared.

Assemble the piston end of the connecting rod with the loose needle bearings, piston pin, retainers, and C-lockrings. Insert the piston pin and check for vertical play. The piston pin should have no noticeable vertical play.

If the pin is loose or there is vertical play check for and replace the worn part/s.

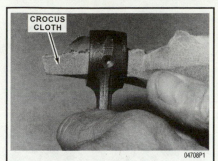

Fig. 30 Cleaning the piston end of a connecting rod with crocus cloth

Fig. 31 Checking the piston end of a connecting rod for vertical free-play using a piston pin

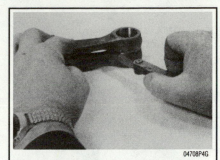

Fig. 32 Testing two rods for warpage at the piston end using a feeler gauge

Fig. 33 Testing two rods for warpage at the crankshaft end using a feeler gauge

Inspect the piston pin and matching rod end for signs of heat discoloration. Overheating is identified as a bluish bearing surface color and is caused by inadequate lubrication or by operating the powerhead at excessive high rpm.

On all bolt together connecting rods, check the bearing surface of the rod and rod cap for signs of chatter marks. This condition is identified by a rough bearing surface resembling a tiny washboard. The condition is caused by a combination of low-speed low-load operation in cold water. The condition is aggravated by inadequate lubrication and improper fuel.

Under these conditions, the crankshaft journal is hammered by the connecting rod. As ignition occurs in the cylinder, the piston pushes the connecting rod with tremendous force. This force is transferred to the connecting rod journal. Since there is little or no load on the crankshaft, it bounces away from the connecting rod. The crankshaft then remains immobile for a split second, until the piston travel causes the connecting rod to catch up to the waiting crankshaft journal, then hammers it. In some instances, the connecting rod crank pin bore becomes highly polished.

While the powerhead is running, a whir and/or chirp sound may be heard when the powerhead is accelerated rapidly—say from idle speed to about 1500 rpm, then quickly returned to idle. If chatter marks are discovered, the crankshaft and the connecting rods should be replaced.

Inspect the bearing surface of the rod and rod cap for signs of uneven wear and possible overheating. Overheating is identified as a bluish bearing surface color and is caused by inadequate lubrication or by operating the powerhead at excessive high rpm.

PISTON SERVICE

◗ See Figures 34 thru 39

Inspect each piston for evidence of scoring, cracks, metal damage, cracked piston pin boss, or worn pin boss. Be especially critical during inspection if the outboard unit has been submerged. If the piston pin is bent, the piston and pin must be replaced as a set for two reasons. First, a bent pin will damage the boss when it is removed. Secondly, a piston pin is not sold as a separate item.

Check the piston ring grooves for wear, burns distortion, or loose locating pins. During an overhaul, the rings should be replaced to ensure lasting repair and proper powerhead performance after the work is completed. Clean the piston dome, ring grooves, and the piston skirt. Clean carbon deposits from the ring grooves using the recessed end of a broken piston ring.

Never use a rectangular ring to clean the groove for a tapered ring, or use a tapered ring to clean the groove for a rectangular ring.

Never use an automotive type ring groove cleaner, because such a tool may loosen the piston ring locating pins.

Clean carbon deposits from the top of the piston using a soft wire brush, carbon removal solution or by sand blasting. If a wire brush is used, Take care not to burr or round machined edges. Clean the piston skirt with crocus cloth.

Install the piston pin through the first boss only. Check for vertical free-play. There should be no vertical free-play. The presence of play is an indication the piston boss is worn. The piston is manufactured from a softer material than the piston pin. Therefore, the piston boss will wear more quickly than the pin.

Fig. 34 This piston seized when the unit was operated at high rpm with the ignition timing not adjusted properly. The connecting rod ripped the lower part of the piston from the piston top

Fig. 35 The pitted damage to this piston is a result of foreign matter entering the cylinder

Fig. 36 Using part of a broken piston ring to clean the ring groove

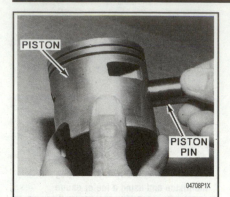

Fig. 37 There should be no play between the piston pin and the pin bore

Fig. 38 Using a micrometer to check the piston skirt diameter. Take several measurements to check for an out-of-round condition

Fig. 39 The rings on this piston became stuck due to lack of lubrication, incorrect timing or overheating. Notice the scoring on the piston

Excessive piston skirt wear cannot be visually detected. Therefore, good shop practice dictates the piston skirt diameter be measured with a micrometer.

Piston skirt diameter should be measured at right angles to the piston pin axis at a point 0.2 in. (5mm) for the 2 hp model and ⅜ inch (10mm) for all other models, above the bottom edge of the piston.

RING END-GAP CLEARANCE

▶ **See Figures 40 and 41**

Before the piston rings are installed onto the piston, the ring end-gap clearance for each ring must be determined. The purpose of the piston rings is to prevent the blow-by of gases in the combustion chamber. This cannot be achieved unless the correct oil film thickness is left on the cylinder wall.

This thin coating of oil acts as a seal between the cylinder wall and the face of the piston ring. An excessive end-gap will allow blow-by and the cylinder will lose compression. An inadequate end-gap will scrape too much oil from the cylinder wall and limit lubrication. Lack of adequate lubrication will cause excessive heat and wear.

Ideally the ring end-gap measurement should be taken after the cylinder bore has been measured for wear and taper and after any corrective work, such as boring or honing, has been completed.

If the ring end-gap is measured with a taper to the cylinder wall, the diameter at the lower limit of ring travel will be smaller than the diameter at the top of the cylinder.

If the ring is fitted to the upper part of a cylinder with a taper, the ring end-gap will not be great enough at the lower limit of ring travel. Such a condition could result in a broken ring and/or damage to the cylinder wall and/or damage to the piston and/or damage to the cylinder head.

If the cylinder is to be only honed, not bored, or if only cleaned, not honed, the ring end-gap should be measured at the lower limit of ring travel.

The manufacturer actually gives the precise depth the ring should be inserted into the cylinder—usually just above the ports—and assumes the cylinder walls are parallel with no taper.

Most piston rings are inserted from the bottom. Once the ring is in the proper position, measure the ring end-gap with a feeler gauge.

If the end-gap is greater than the amount listed, replace the entire ring set.

If the end-gap is less than the amount listed, carefully file the ends of the ring—just a little at a time—until the correct end-gap is obtained.

➡**Inspect the piston ring locating pins to be sure they are tight. There is one locating pin in each ring groove. If the locating pins are loose, the piston must be replaced.**

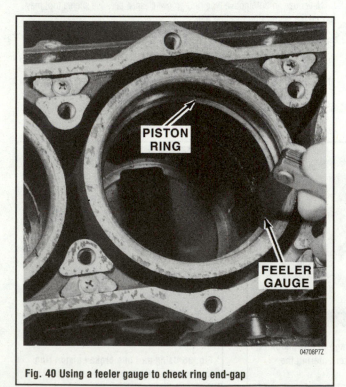

Fig. 40 Using a feeler gauge to check ring end-gap

Fig. 41 Cylinder wall taper drastically effects ring end-gap

PISTON RING SIDE CLEARANCE

After the rings are installed on the piston, the clearance in the grooves needs to be checked with a feeler gauge. Check the clearance between the ring and the upper land and compare your measurement with the specifications. Ring wear forms a step at the inner portion of the upper land. If the piston grooves have worn to the extent to cause high steps on the upper land, the step will interfere with the operation of new rings and the ring clearance will be too much. Therefore, if steps exist in any of the upper lands, the piston should be replaced.

On a plain ring this clearance may be measured either above or below the ring. On a Keystone ring—one with a taper at the top—the clearance must be measured below the ring.

OVERSIZE PISTONS & RINGS

Scored cylinder blocks can be saved for further service by boring and installing oversize pistons and piston rings. However, if the scoring is over 0.0075 inch (0.13mm) deep, the block cannot be effectively rebored for continued use.

Oversize pistons and rings are not available for all powerheads. Check with the parts department at your local Yamaha dealer for the model being serviced.

If oversize pistons are not available, the local marine shop may have the facilities to knurl the piston, making it larger.

A honed cylinder block is just surface finished. It is not parallel and therefore if an oversized or knurled piston is installed in this bore, the piston will soon seize-at the lower narrow end of the bore.

CYLINDER BLOCK SERVICE

◆ **See Figures 42, 43 and 44**

Inspect the cylinder block and cylinder bores for cracks or other damage. Remove carbon with a fine wire brush on a shaft attached to an electric drill or use a carbon remover solution.

❊❂❊ WARNING

If the cylinder block is to be submerged in a carbon removal solution, the crankcase bleed system must be removed from the block to prevent damage to hoses and check valves.

Use an inside micrometer or telescopic gauge and micrometer to check the cylinders for wear. Check the bore for out-of-round and/or oversize bore. If the bore is tapered, out-of-round or worn more than the wear limit specified by the manufacturer, the cylinders should be rebored—provided oversize pistons and rings are available.

Fig. 42 The walls of this cylinder were scored beyond repair when a piston ring broke and worked its way into the combustion chamber

Fig. 43 Checking the cylinder bore for taper using an inside micrometer. Once measurement should be taken near the top, a second in the middle and a third near the bottom

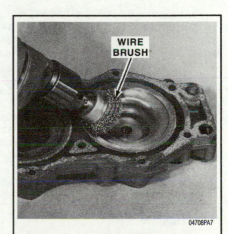

Fig. 44 Using a drill mounted wire brush to clean carbon deposits from the combustion area of the cylinder head

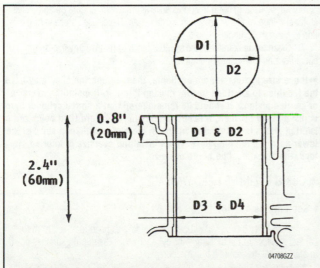

Fig. 45 Top view and cross section of a typical cylinder to indicate where measurements should be made for wear, taper and out of round

Check with the Yamaha dealer prior to boring. If oversize pistons and matching rings are not available, the block must be replaced.

➡**Oversize piston weight is approximately the same as a standard size piston. Therefore, it is not necessary to rebore all cylinders in a block just because one cylinder requires boring.**

Cylinder sleeves are an integral part of the die cast cylinder block and cannot be replaced. In other words, the cylinder cannot be sleeved.

Four inside cylinder bore measurements must be taken for each cylinder to determine an out-of-round condition, the maximum taper, and the maximum bore diameter.

In the accompanying illustration, measurements D1 and D2 are diameters measured at 0.8 inch (20mm) from the top of the cylinder at right angles to each other. Measurements D3 and D4 are diameters measured at 2.4 inch (60mm) from the top cf the cylinder at right angles to each other.

Out-of-Round

◆ **See Figure 45**

Measure the cylinder diameter at D1 and D2. The manufacturer requires the difference between the two measurements should be less than 0.002 inch (0.050mm) for all models.

Maximum Taper

▶ See Figure 41

Measure the cylinder diameter at D1, D2, D3, and D4. Take the largest of the D1 or D2 measurements and subtract the smallest measurement at D3 or D4. The answer to the subtraction—the cylinder taper—should be less than 0.003 inch (0.08mm) for all models.

Bore Wear Limit

▶ See Figure 41

The maximum cylinder diameter D1, D2, D3, and D4 must not exceed the bore wear limits indicated in the following table before the bore is rebored for the first time. These limits are only imposed on original parts because the sealing ability of the rings would be lost, resulting in power loss, increased powerhead noise, unnecessary vibration, piston slap, and excessive oil consumption.

The limits above the standard bore are usually 0.003 to 0.005 inch (0.08mm to 0.127mm) on all powerheads except V4 and V6 and 0.007 inch (0.1mm) on V4 and V6 powerheads.

Piston Clearance

▶ See Figure 41

Piston clearance is the difference between a maximum piston diameter and a minimum cylinder bore diameter. If this clearance is excessive, the powerhead will develop the same symptoms as for excessive cylinder bore wear—loss of ring sealing ability, loss of power, increased powerhead noise, unnecessary vibration, and excessive oil consumption.

Maximum piston diameter was described earlier in this section. Minimum cylinder bore diameter is usually determined by measurement D3 or D4 also described earlier in this section.

If the piston clearance exceeds the limits outlined in the following table, either the piston or the cylinder block must be replaced.

Calculate the piston clearance by subtracting the maximum piston skirt diameter from the maximum cylinder bore measurement and compare the results for the model being serviced.

HONING CYLINDER WALLS

▶ See Figure 46

Hone the cylinder walls lightly to seat the new piston rings, as outlined in this section. If the cylinders have been scored, but are not out-of-round or the bore is rough, clean the surface of the cylinder with a cylinder hone as described in the following procedures.

➡**If overheating has occurred, check and resurface the spark plug end of the cylinder block, if necessary. This can be accomplished with 240-grit sandpaper and a small flat block of wood.**

To ensure satisfactory powerhead performance and long life following the overhaul work, the honing work should be performed with patience, skill, and in the following sequence:

1. Follow the hone manufacturer's recommendations for use of the hone and for cleaning and lubricating during the honing operation. A Christmas tree hone may also be used.

Pump a continuous flow of honing oil into the work area. If pumping is not practical, use an oil can. Apply the oil generously and frequently on both the stones and work surface.

2. Begin the stroking at the smallest diameter. Maintain a firm stone pressure against the cylinder wall to assure fast stock removal and accurate results.

3. Expand the stones as necessary to compensate for stock removal and stone wear. The best cross hatch pattern is obtained using a stroke rate of 30 complete cycles per minute. Again, use the honing oil generously.

4. Hone the cylinder walls only enough to deglaze the walls.

5. After the honing operation has been completed, clean the cylinder bores with hot water and detergent. Scrub the walls with a stiff bristle brush and rinse thoroughly with hot water. The cylinders must be thoroughly cleaned to prevent any abrasive material from remaining in the cylinder bore. Such material will cause rapid wear of new piston rings, the cylinder bore, and the bearings.

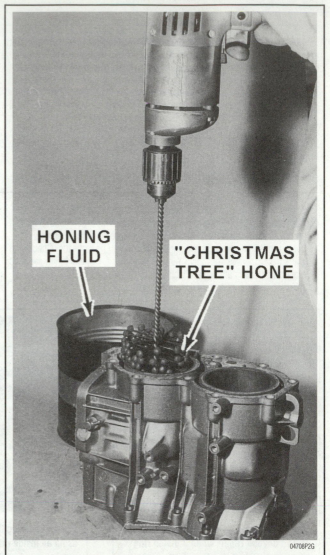

HONING FLUID

"CHRISTMAS TREE" HONE

04708P2G

Fig. 46 Refinishing the cylinder wall using a ball hone. Always keep the home moving and constantly flood the cylinder with honing oil

6. After cleaning, swab the bores several times with engine oil and a clean cloth, and then wipe them dry with a clean cloth. Never use kerosene or gasoline to clean the cylinders.

7. Clean the remainder of the cylinder block to remove any excess material spread during the honing operation.

➡**If oversize pistons are not available, the local marine shop may have the facilities to knurl the piston, making it larger. If installing oversize or knurled pistons, it should be remembered that a honed cylinder block is just surface finished. It is not parallel and therefore if an oversized or knurled piston is installed in this bore, the piston will soon seize at the lower narrow end of the bore. When installing oversize or knurled pistons, the block must be bored oversize.**

BLOCK & CYLINDER HEAD WARPAGE

▶ See Figures 47, 48, 49, 50 and 51

First, check to be sure all old gasket material has been removed from the contact surfaces of the block and the cylinder head. Clean both surfaces down to shiny metal, to ensure a true measurement.

Next, place a straightedge across the gasket surface. Check under the straightedge with a 0.004 inch (0.1mm) feeler gauge. Move the straightedge to at least eight different locations. If the feeler gauge can pass under the straightedge—anywhere contact with the other is made—the surface will have to be resurfaced.

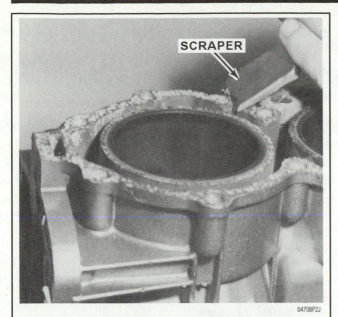

Fig. 47 All traces of gasket material must be removed to ensure accuracy when checking for warpage

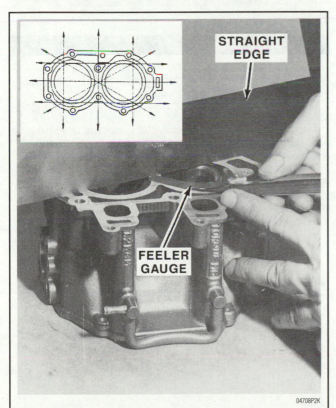

Fig. 48 Using a straightedge and feeler gauge to check the cylinder head-to-powerhead mating surfaces

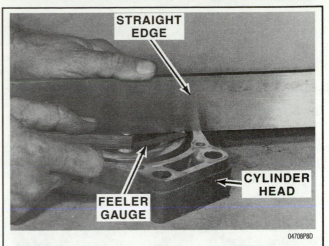

Fig. 49 Using a straightedge and feeler gauge to check for cylinder head warpage

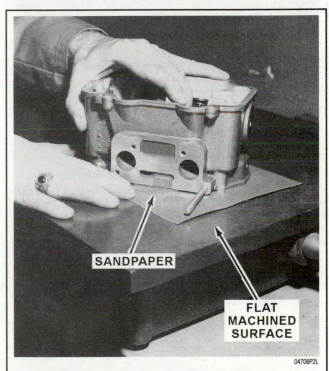

Fig. 50 Using a flat machined surface and sandpaper to correct warpage on a cylinder head. Do not attempt to do this on just any surface

The block or the cylinder head may be resurfaced by placing the warped surface on 400–600 grit wet sandpaper, with the sandpaper resting on a flat machined surface. If a machined surface is not available a large piece of glass or mirror may be used. Do not attempt to use a workbench or similar surface for this task. A workbench is never perfectly flat and the block or cylinder head will pickup the imperfections of the surface and the warpage will be made worse.

Sand—work—the warped surface on the wet sandpaper using large figure 8 motions. Rotate the block, or head, through 180° (turn it end for end) and spend an equal amount of time in each position to avoid removing too much material from one side.

If a suitable flat surface is not available, the next best method is to wrap 400–600 grit wet sandpaper around a large file. Draw the file as evenly as possible in one sweep across the surface. Do not file in one place. Draw the file in many, many directions to get as even a finish as possible.

As the work moves along, check the progress with the straightedge and feeler gauge. Once the 0.004 inch (0.1mm) feeler gauge will no longer slide under the straightedge, consider the work completed.

If the warpage cannot be reduced using one of the described methods, the block or cylinder head should be replaced.

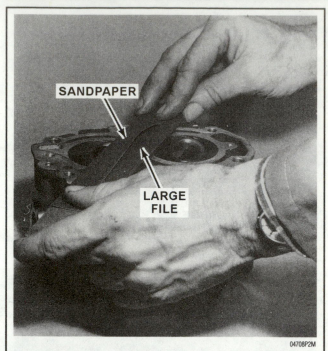

04708P2M

Fig. 51 When a flat machined surface is not available, a large flat file wrapped with sandpaper may be used

Assembling a Warped Cylinder Head or Block

If the warpage cannot be reduced and it is not possible to obtain new items—and the warped part must be assembled for further use—there is a strong possibility of a water leak at the head gasket. In an effort to prevent a water leak, follow the instructions outlined in the following paragraphs.

➡**Because of the high temperatures and pressures developed, the sealing surfaces of the cylinder head and the block are the most prone to water leaks. No sealing agent is recommended because it is almost impossible to apply an even coat of sealer. An even coat would be essential to ensure an air/water tight seal.**

Never, never, use automotive type head gasket sealer. The chemicals in the sealer will cause electrolytic action and eat the aluminum faster than you can get to the bank for money to buy a new cylinder block.

Some head gaskets are supplied with a tacky coating on both surfaces applied at the time of manufacture. This tacky substance will provide an even coating all around. Therefore, no further sealing agent is required.

However, if a slight water leak should be noticed following completed assembly work and powerhead start up, do not attempt to stop the leak by tightening the head bolts beyond the recommended torque value. Such action will only aggravate the problem and most likely distort the head.

Furthermore, tightening the bolts, which are case hardened aluminum, may force the bolt beyond its elastic limit and cause the bolt to fracture. bad news, very bad news indeed. A fractured bolt must usually be drilled out and the hole retapped to accommodate an oversize bolt, etc. Avoid such a situation.

Probable causes and remedies of a new head gasket leaking are:

a. Sealing surfaces not thoroughly cleaned of old gasket material. Disassemble and remove all traces of old gasket.

b. Damage to the machined surface of the head or the block. The remedy for this damage is the same as for the next case.

c. Permanently distorted head or block. Spray a light even coat of any type metallic spray paint on both sides of a new head gasket. Use only metallic paint—any color will do. Regular spray paint does not have the particle content required to provide the extra sealing properties this procedure requires.

Assemble the block and head with the gasket while the paint is till tacky. Install the head bolts and tighten in the recommended sequence and to the proper torque value and no more!

Allow the paint to set for at least 24 hours before starting the powerhead.

Consider this procedure as a temporary band aid type solution until a new head may be purchased or other permanent measures can be performed.

Under normal circumstances, if procedures have been followed to the letter, the head gasket will not leak.

Break-in Procedures

As soon as the engine starts, check to be sure the water pump is operating. If the water pump is operating, a fine stream will be discharged from the exhaust relief hole at the rear of the drive shaft housing.

Do not operate the engine at full throttle except for very short periods, until after 10 hours of operation as follows:

1. Operate at ½ throttle, approximately 2500 to 3500 rpm, for 2 hours.

2. Operate at any speed after 2 hours but not at sustained full throttle until another 8 hours of operation.

3. Mix gasoline and oil during the break-in period, total of 10 hours, at a ratio of 25:1.

4. While the engine is operating during the initial period, check the fuel, exhaust, and water systems for leaks.

Engine Rebuilding Specifications

Component	Standard (in.)	Metric (mm)
Cylinder head		
Warp limit	0.004	0.1
Cylinder Bore		
Diameter		
2 hp	1.535-1.536	39.00-39.02
3 hp	1.811-1.812	46.00-46.02
4 hp	1.9685-1.9697	50.00-50.02
5 hp	2.126-2.1268	54.00-54.02
6, 8 hp	1.9685-1.9697	50.00-50.02
9.9, 15 hp	2.2047-2.2055	56.00-56.02
C25, 25 hp	2.638-2.639	67.00-67.02
30 hp	2.34252.3444	59.5-59.52
C30	2.8346-2.8354	72.00-72.02
C40	2.953-2.954	75.00-75.02
40, 50 hp, Pro 50	2.638-2.639	67.00-67.02
C55, C75, C85, 90 hp	3.228-3.229	82.00-82.02
50, 60 hp	2.834-2.8354	72.00-72.02
V4 and V5	3.543-3.544	90.00-90.02
Taper limit	0.003	0.08
Out-of-round limit	0.002	0.05
Piston		
Diameter		
2 hp	1.5341-1.5349	38.967-38.969
3 hp	1.8096-1.8106	45.965-45.990
4 hp	1.9673-1.9685	49.97-50.00
5 hp	2.124-2.1260	53.97-54.00
6, 8 hp	1.9667-1.9677	49.955-49.980
9.9, 15 hp	2.2024-2.2041	55.940-55.985
C25	2.637-2.638	66.980-67.000
25 hp	2.636-2.637	66.960-66.980
30 hp	2.341-2.342	59.46-59.48
C30	2.8323-2.8331	71.94-71.96
C40	2.9506-2.9516	74.945-74.970
40, 50 hp Pro 50	2.6354-2.6378	66.940-67.000
C55, C75 C85, 90 hp	3.2258-3.2268	81.935-81.962
Pro 60, 70 hp	2.8325-2.8335	71.945-71.970
C115, 115 hp, P115, 130 hp, L130, 150 hp, L150, 175 hp, 200 hp, L200, Pro V 200, 225 hp	3.540-3.541	89.92-89.94
Pro V 15C, Pro V 175 225, L225, 250 hp, L250	3.539-3.540	89.91-89.93
76 Degree V6	3.5374-3.5382	89.850-89.870
Oversize Diameter		
2hp		
1st	1.545	39.25
2nd	1.555	39.5
3 hp	1.831	46.5
4, 5 hp	NA	NA
6, 8 hp		
1st	1.978	50.25
2nd	1.988	50.5
9.9, 15 hp		
1st	2.215	56.25
2nd	2.224	56.5
C25	NA	NA
25 hp	2.657	67.5
30 hp		
1st	2.352	59.75
2nd	2.362	60

04708C01

Engine Rebuilding Specifications

Component	Standard (in.)	Metric (mm)
Oversize Diameter		
C30, Pro 60, 70 hp		
1st	2.844	72.25
2nd	2.854	72.5
C40	2.972	75.5
40, 50 hp, Pro 50		
1st	2.648	67.25
2nd	2.657	67.5
C55, C75, C85, 90 hp		
1st	3.238	82.25
2nd	3.248	82.5
C115	NA	NA
115 hp, Pro 115, 130 hp, L130 150 hp, L150, Pro V150, 175 hp, Pro V 175, 200 hp, L200, Pro V 200, 225		
1st	3.553	90.25
2nd	3.563	90.5
225 hp, L225, 250 hp, L250, 76 Degree V6	3.557	90.36
Off Set		
2, 3 hp	–	–
4, 5, 6, 8 hp	0.02	0.5
9.9, 15 hp	0.04	1.0
C25, 25, 30 hp, C30	–	–
C40, C55, C75, C85	0.059	1.5
40, 50 hp, Pro 50	–	–
Pro 60, 70 hp	0.02	0.5
90 hp	0.04	1.0
V4 and V6	–	–
Piston Ring End Gap		
2, 3 hp	0.004-0.012	0.10-0.30
4, 5, 6, 8 hp, 9.9, 15 hp	0.006-0.014	0.15-0.35
C25, 25 hp	0.016-0.023	0.40-0.60
30 hp	0.006-0.012	0.15-0.30
C30	0.008-0.014	0.20-0.35
C40, Pro 60, 70 hp	0.012-0.020	0.30-0.50
40, 40 hp, Pro 50, C55, C75, C85, 90 hp	0.006-0.023	0.40-0.60
V4 and V6	0.012-0.016	0.30-0.40
Piston Ring Side Clearance		
2 hp	0.001-0.003	0.03-0.07
3, 6, 8 hp		
Top	0.0008-0.0024	0.02-0.06
2nd	0.001-0.003	0.03-0.07
4.5 hp	0.0008-0.0024	0.02-0.06
9.9, 15 hp		
Top	0.0008-0.0024	0.02-0.06
2nd	0.0016-0.0024	0.04-0.08
C25		
Top	0.002-0.0020	0.03-0.05
2nd	0.001-0.003	0.03-0.07
Piston Ring Side Clearance		
25 hp, C40		
Top	0.0008-0.0024	0.02-0.06
2nd	0.0012-0.0028	0.03-0.07
30 hp	0.002-0.004	0.05-0.09
40, 50 hp, Pro 50	NA	NA
Top	0.0016-0.0031	0.04-0.08
2nd	0.0012-0.0028	0.03-0.07

04708C02

Engine Rebuilding Specifications

Component	Standard (in.)	Metric (mm)
Piston Ring Side Clearance		
C55, C75, C85		
Top	0.0012-0.0026	0.03-0.065
2nd	0.001-0.003	0.03-0.07
Pro 60, 70 hp	0.001-0.003	0.03-0.07
90 hp	0.001-0.0024	0.03-0.06
V4 and V6	0.0008-0.0024	0.02-0.06
Seal ring clearance wear limit		
V4 and V6	0.004	0.10
Crankshaft		
Maximum Run-out		
2 hp	0.0008	0.02
3 hp	0.001	0.03
4, 5, 6, 8 hp	0.001	0.03
9.9, 15 hp	0.001	0.03
C25	0.001	0.03
25, 30 hp	0.001	0.03
C30	0.001	0.03
C40	0.001	0.03
40, 50, Pro 50	0.0008	0.02
C55	0.001	0.03
Pro 60, 70 hp	0.0008	0.02
C75, C85	0.001	0.03
90 hp	0.0008	0.02
V4 and 90 Degree V6	0.002	0.05
76 Degree V6		
Distance Between Outside Edge Of Crankshaft Throws		
2 hp	0.012-0.024	0.30-0.60
3 hp	0.012-0.024	0.30-0.60
4, 5, 6, 8 hp	0.008-0.028	0.20-0.70
9.9, 15 hp	NA	NA
C25	0.075-0.082	1.90-2.10
25, 30 hp	0.008-0.028	0.20-0.70
C30	0.008-0.028	0.20-0.70
C40	NA	NA
40, 50, Pro 50	0.008-0.028	0.20-0.70
C55	NA	NA
Pro 60, 70 hp	0.008-0.028	0.20-0.70
C75, C85	NA	NA
90 hp	0.005-0.010	0.12-0.26
V4 and 90 Degree V6	NA	NA
76 Degree V6	0.005-0.010	0.12-0.26
Connecting Rod		
Crank End Diameter		
2 hp	1.098-1.100	27.90-27.95
3 hp	1.098-1.100	35.00-36.00
4, 5, 6, 8 hp	1.571-1.573	39.90-39.95
9.9, 15 hp	1.846-1.848	46.90-46.95
C25	2.122-2.124	53.90-53.95
25, 30 hp	1.965-1.967	49.90-49.95
C30	2.240-2.242	56.90-56.95
C40	2.372-2.382	60.25-60.50
40, 50, Pro 50	2.122-2.124	53.90-53.95
C55	NA	NA
Pro 60, 70 hp	2.280-2.281	57.90-57.95
C75, C85	2.280-2.282	57.90-57.96
90 hp	2.280-2.281	57.90-57.95
V4 and 90 Degree V6		
76 Degree V6		

04708C03

Engine Rebuilding Specifications

Component	Standard (in.)	Metric (mm)
Side Clearance		
2, 3 hp	0.012-0.024	0.30-0.60
4, 5, 6, 8 hp	0.008-0.028	0.20-0.70
9.9, 15 hp		
C25	0.075-0.082	1.90-2.10
25, 30 hp, C30	0.008-0.028	0.20-0.70
C40, C55, C75, C85		
40, 50 hp, Pro 50, Pro 60, 70 hp	0.008-0.028	0.20-0.70
90 hp	0.005-0.010	0.12-0.26
C115	0.008-0.0126	0.20-0.32
V4 and V6	0.005-0.010	0.12-0.26
Small end free play limit		
76 degree V6	0.002	0.5
All other engines	0.08	2

NA - Not Applicable

04708C04

Engine Torque Specifications

Component	Standard (ft. lbs.)	Metric (Nm)
Connecting Rod Bolts		
C40, C55, C75, C85, C115	25	35
115-130hp V4, 150-225hp 90" V6	27	37
225-250hp, 76" V6	32	45
Crankcase-to-cylinder block bolts		
2hp	7	10
3hp	8	11
4, 5hp	9	12
6, 8hp	8	11
9.9, 15hp		
6 mm bolts	9	12
8 mm bolts	22	30
C25	20	28
25, 30hp		
6 mm bolts	8	11
8 mm bolts	20	28
C30	19	27
C40, C55		
6 mm bolts	8	12
10 mm bolts	29	40
40, 50hp, Pro 50		
6 mm bolts	8	12
8 mm bolts	20	28
Pro 60, 70hp, 90hp		
6 mm bolts	8	12
8 mm bolts	14	20
10 mm bolts	29	40
C75, C85		
6 mm bolts	8	12
10 mm bolts	29	40
C115		
8 mm bolts	13	18
10 mm bolts	29	40
115-130hp, V4, 150-225hp, 90" V6		
8 mm bolts	13	18
10 mm bolts	29	40
225-250hp, 76" V6		
6 mm bolts	5	8
10 mm bolts	29	40
Cylinder head bolts		
2hp	7	10
3, 4, 5, 6, 8hp	8	11
9.9, 15hp	12	17
C25, 25, 30hp	20	28
C30	19	27
C40, 55hp	22	30
40, 50, Pro	20	28
50 Pro 60, 70hp, 90hp	23	32
C75, C85, C115, 115-130hp, V4, 150-225hp 90" V6	22	30
225-250hp 76" V6	20	28
Cylinder head cover bolts		
4, 5hp	7	9
6, 8hp	6	8
C30	19	27
115-250 V4 and V6	6	8

04708C05

Engine Torque Specifications

Component	Standard (ft. lbs.)	Metric (Nm)
Exhaust cover (or manifold)		
2hp, 3hp	6	8
4, 5, 6, 8hp	7	9
9.9, 15hp	9	12
C25, 25hp, 30hp, C30	7	9
C40	5	7
40, 50, Pro 50, C55	7	9
Pro 60, 70hp, 90hp		
6 mm bolt	6	8
8 mm bolt	13	18
C75, C85, 115-250hp V4 and V6	6	8
Flywheel nut		
2, 3, 4, 5, 6, 8hp	32	45
9.9, 15hp	85	115
C25, 25hp	73	100
30, 40, 50hp, Pro 50	81	110
C30	103	140
C40, C55, Pro 60, 70hp, 90hp, C75, C85, C115	118	160
115-250 V4 and V6	140	190
Intake Manifold		
2, 3hp	7	9
4, 5hp	6	9
6, 8hp	8	11
9.9, 15hp, C25, 25hp, 30hp, C30	7	9
C40	15	21
40hp, 50hp, Pro 50, C55, Pro 60, 70hp	7	9
90hp, C75, C85	9	12
115-225hp V4 and 90" V6	6	8
225-250hp 76" V6	7	10
Lower oil seal housing		
All engines	4-5	6-8
Powerhead mounting bolts		
2, 3, 4, 5, 9.9, 15hp	6	8
C25, 25hp, C40	15	21
C30, 30hp	20	28
All others	15	21
Spark plug		
All engines	14	20
Thermostat cover		
	6	8

04708C06

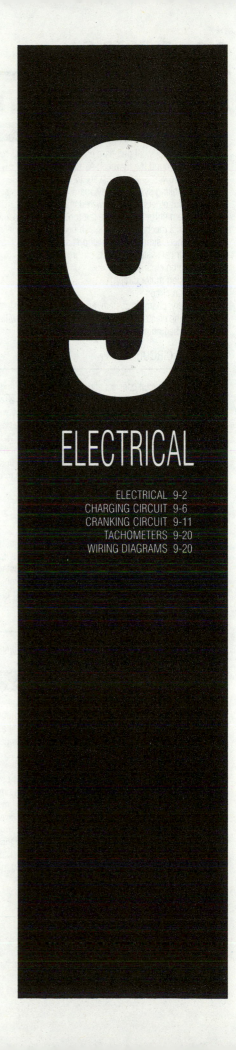

ELECTRICAL 9-2
DESCRIPTION AND OPERATION 9-2
   CHARGING CIRCUIT 9-2
   CRANKING MOTOR CIRCUIT 9-2
   IGNITION CIRCUIT 9-2
BATTERIES 9-2
   MARINE BATTERIES 9-2
   BATTERY CONSTRUCTION 9-2
   BATTERY RATINGS 9-3
   BATTERY LOCATION 9-3
   BATTERY SERVICE 9-3
   BATTERY TERMINALS 9-5
   BATTERY AND CHARGING SAFETY
    PRECAUTIONS 9-5
   BATTERY CHARGERS 9-5
   REPLACING BATTERY CABLES 9-5
   STORAGE 9-6
CHARGING CIRCUIT 9-6
SINGLE-PHASE CHARGING SYSTEM 9-8
   DESCRIPTION AND OPERATION 9-8
   TROUBLESHOOTING 9-8
   SERVICING 9-8
THREE-PHASE CHARGING SYSTEM 9-8
   DESCRIPTION AND OPERATION 9-8
   TROUBLESHOOTING 9-9
   SERVICING 9-9
V76 CHARGING SYSTEM 9-9
   WATER-COOLED RECTIFIER/
    REGULATOR 9-9
   BATTERY CABLE DISCONNECT
    WARNING 9-9
   TROUBLESHOOTING 9-9
   SERVICING 9-11
CRANKING CIRCUIT 9-11
DESCRIPTION AND OPERATION 9-11
   MAINTENANCE 9-11
   FAULTY SYMPTOMS 9-11
CRANKING MOTOR CIRCUIT 9-11
   TROUBLESHOOTING 9-11
CRANKING MOTOR RELAY 9-12
   DESCRIPTION AND OPERATION 9-12
   REMOVAL 9-13
   TESTING 9-13
   INSTALLATION 9-14
CRANKING MOTOR 9-14
   DESCRIPTION 9-14
1- AND 2-CYLINDER POWERHEAD
  CRANKING MOTOR 9-14
   REMOVAL 9-14
   INSTALLATION 9-15
3-CYLINDER POWERHEAD CRANKING
  MOTOR 9-16
   REMOVAL 9-16
   INSTALLATION 9-17
V4 AND V6 POWERHEAD CRANKING
  MOTORS 9-18
   DESCRIPTION 9-18
   REMOVAL 9-18
   INSTALLATION 9-19

TACHOMETERS 9-20
   TACHOMETER CONNECTIONS 9-20
WIRING DIAGRAMS 9-20

9

ELECTRICAL

ELECTRICAL 9-2
CHARGING CIRCUIT 9-6
CRANKING CIRCUIT 9-11
TACHOMETERS 9-20
WIRING DIAGRAMS 9-20

ELECTRICAL

Description and Operation

In the early days, all outboard engines were started by simply pulling on a rope wound around the flywheel. As time passed and owners were reluctant to use muscle power, it was necessary to replace the rope starter with some form of power cranking system. Today, many small engines are still started by pulling on a rope, but others have a powered cranking motor installed.

The system utilized to replace the rope method was an electric cranking motor coupled with a mechanical gear mesh between the cranking motor and the powerhead flywheel, similar to the method used to crank an automobile engine.

The electrical system consists of three circuits:
- Charging circuit
- Cranking motor circuit
- Ignition circuit

The battery, charging system, and the cranking system are considered subsystems of the electrical system. Each of these units will be covered in detail in this section beginning with the battery.

CHARGING CIRCUIT

The charging circuit consists of permanent magnets and a stator located within the flywheel, a lighting coil installed on the stator plate, a rectifier located elsewhere on the powerhead, an external battery, and the necessary wiring to connect the units. The negative side of the rectifier is grounded. The positive side of the rectifier passes through the internal harness plug to the battery. The negative side of the battery is connected, through the connector, to a good ground on the engine.

The alternating current generated in the stator windings passes to the rectifier. The rectifier changes the alternating current (AC) to direct current (DC) to charge the 12-volt battery.

CRANKING MOTOR CIRCUIT

The cranking motor circuit consists of a cranking motor and a starter-engaging mechanism. A starter relay is used as a heavy-duty switch to carry the heavy current from the battery to the cranking motor. On most models, the starter relay is actuated by depressing the start button. On boats equipped with a remote control shift box, the ignition key is turned to the start position.

IGNITION CIRCUIT

The ignition circuit is covered extensively in the "Ignition" section of this manual.

Batteries

The battery is one of the most important parts of the electrical system. In addition to providing electrical power to start the engine, it also provides power for operation of the running lights, radio, and electrical accessories.

Because of its job and the consequences (failure to perform in an emergency), the best advice is to purchase a well-known brand, with an extended warranty period, from a reputable dealer.

The usual warranty covers a pro-rated replacement policy, which means the purchaser would be entitled to a consideration for the time left on the warranty period if the battery should prove defective before its time.

Do not consider a battery of less than 70- amp/hour or 100-minute reserve capacity. If in doubt as to how large the boat requires, make a liberal estimate and then purchase the one with the next higher amp rating. Outboards equipped with an onboard computer, commonly referred to as YMIS (Yamaha Microcomputer Ignition System), should be equipped with a battery of at least 100 to 105 amp/hour capacity.

MARINE BATTERIES

▶ See Figure 1

Because marine batteries are required to perform under much more rigorous conditions than automotive batteries, they are constructed differently than those used in automobiles or trucks. Therefore, a marine battery should always be the No. 1 unit for the boat and other types of batteries used only in an emergency.

Fig. 1 A fully charged battery, filled to the proper level with electrolyte, is the heart of the ignition and electrical systems. Engine cranking and efficient performance of electrical items depend on a full rated battery

Marine batteries have a much heavier exterior case to withstand the violent pounding and shocks imposed on it as the boat moves through rough water and in extremely tight turns. The plates are thicker and each plate is securely anchored within the battery case to ensure extended life. The caps are spill proof to prevent acid from spilling into the bilges when the boat heels to one side in a tight turn, or is moving through rough water. Because of these features, the marine battery will recover from a low charge condition and give satisfactory service over a much longer period of time than any type intended for automotive use.

✶✶ WARNING

Never use an automotive type Maintenance-free battery with an outboard unit. The charging system is not regulated as with automotive installations and the battery may be quickly damaged.

BATTERY CONSTRUCTION

▶ See Figure 2

A battery consists of a number of positive and negative plates immersed in a solution of diluted sulfuric acid. The plates contain dissimilar active materials

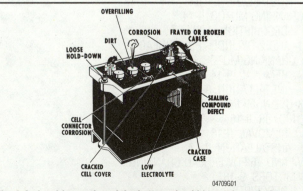

Fig. 2 A visual inspection of the battery should be made each time the boat is used. Such a quick check may reveal a potential problem in its early stages. A dead battery in a busy waterway or far from assistance could have serious consequences

and are kept apart by separators. The plates are grouped into elements. Plate straps on top of each element connect all of the positive plates and all of the negative plates into groups.

The battery is divided into cells holding a number of the elements apart from the others. The entire arrangement is contained within a hard plastic case. The top is a one-piece cover and contains the filler caps for each cell. The terminal posts protrude through the top where the battery connections for the boat are made. Each of the cells is connected to its neighbor in a positive-to-negative manner with a heavy strap called the cell connector.

BATTERY RATINGS

▶ **See Figure 3**

Three different methods are used to measure and indicate battery electrical capacity:
- Amp/hour rating
- Cold cranking performance
- Reserve capacity

The amp/hour rating of a battery refers to the battery's ability to provide a set amount of amps for a given amount of time under test conditions at a constant temperature. Therefore, if the battery is capable of supplying 4 amps of current for 20 consecutive hours, the battery is rated as an 80 amp/hour battery. The amp/hour rating is useful for some service operations, such as slow charging or battery testing.

Cold cranking performance is measured by cooling a fully charged battery to 0°F (-17°C) and then testing it for 30 seconds to determine the maximum current flow. In this manner the cold cranking amp rating is the number of amps available to be drawn from the battery before the voltage drops below 7.2 volts.

The illustration depicts the amount of power in watts available from a battery at different temperatures and the amount of power in watts required of the engine at the same temperature. It becomes quite obvious—the colder the climate, the more necessary for the battery to be fully charged.

Reserve capacity of a battery is considered the length of time, in minutes, at 80°F (27°C), a 25 amp current can be maintained before the voltage drops below 10.5 volts. This test is intended to provide an approximation of how long the engine, including electrical accessories, could operate satisfactorily if the stator assembly or lighting coil did not produce sufficient current. A typical rating is 100 minutes.

If possible, the new battery should have a power rating equal to or higher than the unit it is replacing.

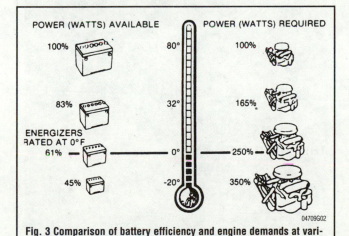

Fig. 3 Comparison of battery efficiency and engine demands at various temperatures

BATTERY LOCATION

Every battery installed in a boat must be secured in a well protected, ventilated area. If the battery area lacks adequate ventilation, hydrogen gas, which is given off during charging, is very explosive. This is especially true if the gas is concentrated and confined.

BATTERY SERVICE

▶ **See Figures 4, 5 and 6**

Batteries require periodic servicing and a definite maintenance program will ensure extended life. If the battery should test satisfactorily but still fails to perform properly, one of four problems could be the cause.

1. An accessory might have accidentally been left on overnight or for a long period during the day. Such an oversight would result in a discharged battery.

2. Using more electrical power than the stator assembly or lighting coil can replace would result in an undercharged condition.

3. A defect in the charging system. A faulty stator assembly or lighting coil, defective rectifier, or high resistance somewhere in the system could cause the battery to become undercharged.

4. Failure to maintain the battery in good order. This might include a low level of electrolyte in the cells, loose or dirty cable connections at the battery terminals or possibly an excessively dirty battery top.

Fig. 4 Explosive hydrogen gas is normally released from the cells under a wide range of circumstances. This battery exploded when the gas ignited from someone smoking in the area when the caps were removed. Such an explosion could also be caused by a spark from the battery terminals

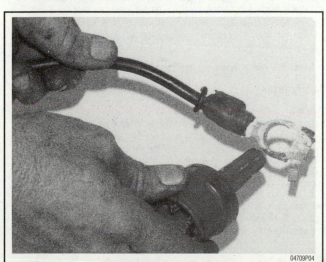

Fig. 5 A two part battery cable cleaning tool will do an excellent job of cleaning the inside of the cable connectors

Fig. 6 The second part of the battery cable cleaning tool contains a brush for cleaning the battery terminals

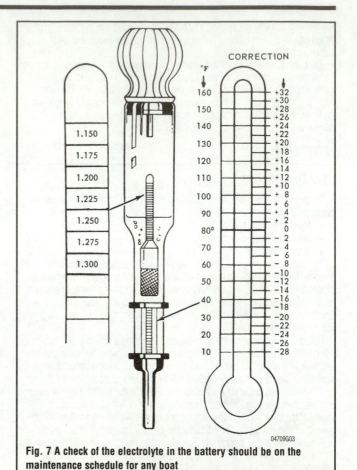

Fig. 7 A check of the electrolyte in the battery should be on the maintenance schedule for any boat

Electrolyte Level

▶ See Figures 7 and 8

The most common procedure for checking the electrolyte level in a battery is to remove the cell caps and visually observe the level in the cells. The bottom of each cell has a split vent which will cause the surface of the electrolyte to appear distorted when it makes contact. When the distortion first appears at the bottom of the split vent, the electrolyte level is correct.

During hot weather and periods of heavy use, the electrolyte level should be checked more often than during normal operation. Add distilled water to bring the level of electrolyte in each cell to the proper level. Take care not to overfill, because adding an excessive amount of water will cause loss of electrolyte and any loss will result in poor performance, short battery life, and will contribute quickly to corrosion.

➡Never add electrolyte from another battery. Use only distilled water.

Battery Testing

A hydrometer is a device to measure the percentage of sulfuric acid in the battery electrolyte in terms of specific gravity. When the condition of the battery drops from fully charged to discharged, the acid leaves the solution and enters the plates, causing the specific gravity of the electrolyte to drop.

It may not be common knowledge, but hydrometer floats are calibrated for use at 80°F (27°C). If the hydrometer is used at any other temperature, hotter or colder, a correction factor must be applied.

➡Remember, a liquid will expand if it is heated and will contract if cooled. Such expansion and contraction will cause a definite change in the specific gravity of the liquid, in this case the electrolyte.

A quality hydrometer will have a thermometer/temperature correction table in the lower portion, as shown in the accompanying illustration. By knowing the air temperature around the battery and from the table, a correction factor may be applied to the specific gravity reading of the hydrometer float. In this manner, an accurate determination may be made as to the condition of the battery.

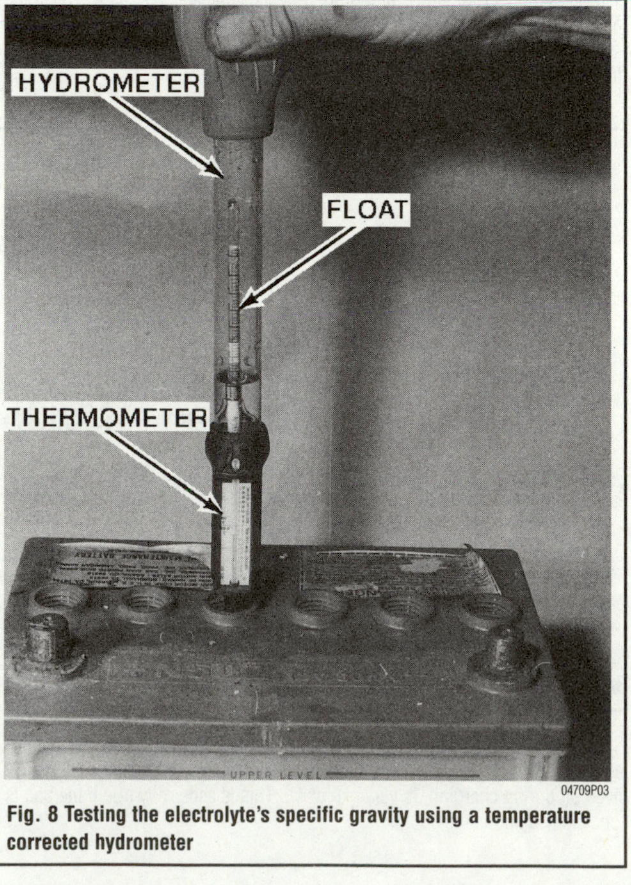

Fig. 8 Testing the electrolyte's specific gravity using a temperature corrected hydrometer

When using a hydrometer, pay careful attention to the following points:

1. Never attempt to take a reading immediately after adding water to the battery. Allow at least ¼ hour of charging at a high rate to thoroughly mix the electrolyte with the new water. This time will also allow for the necessary gases to be created.

2. Always be sure the hydrometer is clean inside and out as a precaution against contaminating the electrolyte.

3. If a thermometer is an integral part of the hydrometer, draw liquid into it several times to ensure the correct temperature before taking a reading.

4. Be sure to hold the hydrometer vertically and suck up liquid only until the float is free and floating.

5. Always hold the hydrometer at eye level and take the reading at the surface of the liquid with the float free and floating.

6. Disregard the slight curvature appearing where the liquid rises against the float stem. This phenomenon is due to surface tension.

7. Do not drop any of the battery fluid on the boat or on your clothing, because it is extremely caustic. Use water and baking soda to neutralize any battery liquid that does accidentally drop.

8. After drawing electrolyte from the battery cell until the float is barely free, note the level of the liquid inside the hydrometer. If the level is within the Green band range for all cells, the condition of the battery is satisfactory. If the level is within the white band for all cells, the battery is in fair condition.

9. If the level is within the Green or white band for all cells except one, which registers in the red, the cell is shorted internally. No amount of charging will bring the battery back to satisfactory condition.

10. If the level in all cells is about the same, even if it falls in the Red band, the battery may be recharged and returned to service. If the level fails to rise above the Red band after charging, the only solution is to replace the battery.

Cleaning

Dirt and corrosion should be cleaned from the battery as soon as it is discovered. Any accumulation of acid film or dirt will permit current to flow between the terminals. Such a current flow will drain the battery over a period of time.

Clean the exterior of the battery with a solution of diluted ammonia or a paste made from baking soda to neutralize any acid which may be present. Flush the cleaning solution off with clean water.

➡ **Take care to prevent any of the neutralizing solution from entering the cells, by keeping the caps tight.**

A poor contact at the terminals will add resistance to the charging circuit. This resistance will cause the voltage regulator to register a fully charged battery, and thus cut down on the stator assembly or lighting coil output adding to the low battery charge problem.

Scrape the battery posts clean with a suitable tool or with a stiff wire brush. Clean the inside of the cable clamps to be sure they do not cause any resistance in the circuit.

BATTERY TERMINALS

At least once a season, the battery terminals and cable clamps should be cleaned. Loosen the clamps and remove the cables, negative cable first. On batteries with top mounted posts, the use of a puller specially made for this purpose is recommended. These are inexpensive and available in most parts stores.

Clean the cable clamps and the battery terminal with a wire brush, until all corrosion, grease, etc., is removed and the metal is shiny. It is especially important to clean the inside of the clamp thoroughly (a wire brush is useful here), since a small deposit of foreign material or oxidation there will prevent a sound electrical connection and inhibit either starting or charging. It is also a good idea to apply some dielectric grease to the terminal, as this will aid in the prevention of corrosion.

After the clamps and terminals are clean, reinstall the cables, negative cable last, do not hammer the clamps onto battery posts. Tighten the clamps securely, but do not distort them. Give the clamps and terminals a thin external coating of grease after installation, to retard corrosion.

Check the cables at the same time that the terminals are cleaned. If tho insulation is cracked or broken, or if its end is frayed, that cable should be replaced with a new one of the same length and gauge.

BATTERY AND CHARGING SAFETY PRECAUTIONS

Always follow these safety precautions when charging or handling a battery:

• Wear eye protection when working around batteries. Batteries contain corrosive acid and produce explosive gas a byproduct of their operation. Acid on the skin should be neutralized with a solution of baking soda and water made into a paste. In case acid contacts the eyes, flush with clear water and seek medical attention immediately.

• Avoid flame or sparks that could ignite the hydrogen gas produced by the battery and cause an explosion. Connection and disconnection of cables to battery terminals is one of the most common causes of sparks.

• Always turn a battery charger **OFF**, before connecting or disconnecting the leads. When connecting the leads, connect the positive lead first, then the negative lead, to avoid sparks.

• When lifting a battery, use a battery carrier or lift at opposite corners of the base.

• Ensure there is good ventilation in a room where the battery is being charged.

• Do not attempt to charge or load-test a maintenance-free battery when the charge indicator dot is indicating insufficient electrolyte.

• Disconnect the negative battery cable if the battery is to remain in the boat during the charging process.

• Be sure the ignition switch is **OFF** before connecting or turning the charger **ON**. Sudden power surges can destroy electronic components.

• Use proper adapters to connect charger leads to batteries with non-conventional terminals.

BATTERY CHARGERS

Before using any battery charger, consult the manufacturer's instructions for its use. Battery chargers are electrical devices that change Alternating Current (AC) to a lower voltage of Direct Current (DC) that can be used to charge a marine battery. There are two types of battery chargers—manual and automatic.

A manual battery charger must be physically disconnected when the battery has come to a full charge. If not, the battery can be overcharged, and possibly fail. Excess charging current at the end of the charging cycle will heat the electrolyte, resulting in loss of water and active material, substantially reducing battery life.

➡ **As a rule, on manual chargers, when the ammeter on the charger registers half the rated amperage of the charger, the battery is fully charged. This can vary, and it is recommended to use a hydrometer to accurately measure state of charge.**

Automatic battery chargers have an important advantage—they can be left connected (for instance, overnight) without the possibility of overcharging the battery. Automatic chargers are equipped with a sensing device to allow the battery charge to taper off to near zero as the battery becomes fully charged. When charging a low or completely discharged battery, the meter will read close to full rated output. If only partially discharged, the initial reading may be less than full rated output, as the charger responds to the condition of the battery. As the battery continues to charge, the sensing device monitors the state of charge and reduces the charging rate. As the rate of charge tapers to zero amps, the charger will continue to supply a few milliamps of current—just enough to maintain a charged condition.

REPLACING BATTERY CABLES

Battery cables don't go bad very often, but like anything else, they can wear out. If the cables on your boat are cracked, frayed or broken, they should be replaced.

When working on any electrical component, it is always a good idea to disconnect the negative (ñ) battery cable. This will prevent potential damage to many sensitive electrical components

Always replace the battery cables with one of the same length, or you will increase resistance and possibly cause hard starting. Smear the battery posts with a light film of dielectric grease, or a battery terminal protectant spray once you've installed the new cables. If you replace the cables one at a time, you won't mix them up.

➥Any time you disconnect the battery cables, it is recommended that you disconnect the negative (ñ) battery cable first. This will prevent you from accidentally grounding the positive (+) terminal when disconnecting it, thereby preventing damage to the electrical system.

Before you disconnect the cable(s), first turn the ignition to the **OFF** position. This will prevent a draw on the battery which could cause arcing. When the battery cable(s) are reconnected (negative cable last), be sure to check all electrical accessories are all working correctly.

STORAGE

If the boat is to be laid up for the winter or for more than a few weeks, special attention must be given to the battery to prevent complete discharge or possible damage to the terminals and wiring. Before putting the boat in storage, discon-

nect and remove the batteries. Clean them thoroughly of any dirt or corrosion, and then charge them to full specific gravity reading. After they are fully charged, store them in a clean cool dry place where they will not be damaged or knocked over, preferably on a couple blocks of wood. Storing the battery up off the deck, will permit air to circulate freely around and under the battery and will help to prevent condensation.

Never store the battery with anything on top of it or cover the battery in such a manner as to prevent air from circulating around the fillercaps. All batteries, both new and old, will discharge during periods of storage, more so if they are hot than if they remain cool. Therefore, the electrolyte level and the specific gravity should be checked at regular intervals. A drop in the specific gravity reading is cause to charge them back to a full reading.

In cold climates, care should be exercised in selecting the battery storage area. A fully-charged battery will freeze at about 60 degrees below zero. A discharged battery, almost dead, will have ice forming at about 19 degrees above zero.

CHARGING CIRCUIT

♦ **See Figures 9, 10 and 11**

For many years, single-phase, full-wave charging systems were the dominant design. Most manufacturers used single-phase systems because they were simple and reliable. The drawback to these systems is low output. A typical single-phase lighting coil system is capable of only 10 to 15 amps. On many larger

rigs, the electrical demand is more than 15 amps. New electronic and electrical devices are arriving on the market every day, so the demand for higher amperage output continues to rise.

In response to higher electrical demands, three-phase systems were introduced on the larger Yamaha outboards in 1990. These systems produce 25 to 35 amps. At the heart of a three-phase charging system is an interconnected

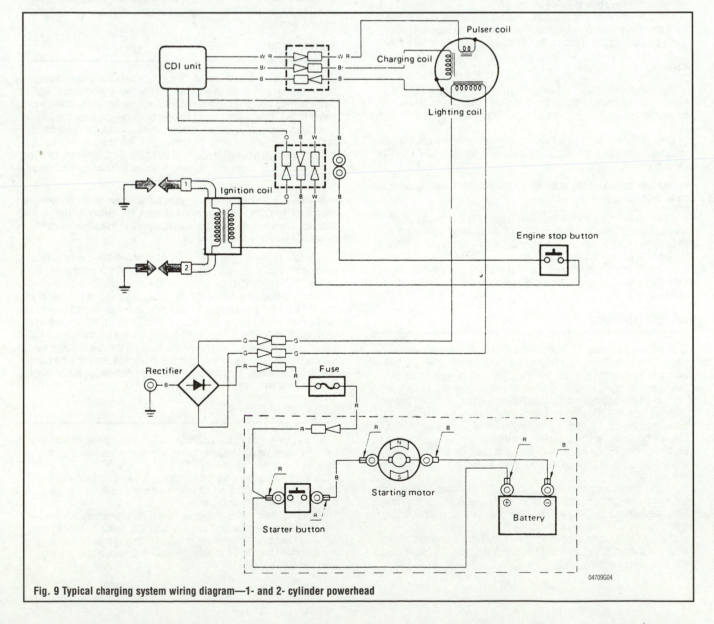

Fig. 9 Typical charging system wiring diagram—1- and 2- cylinder powerhead

04709G04

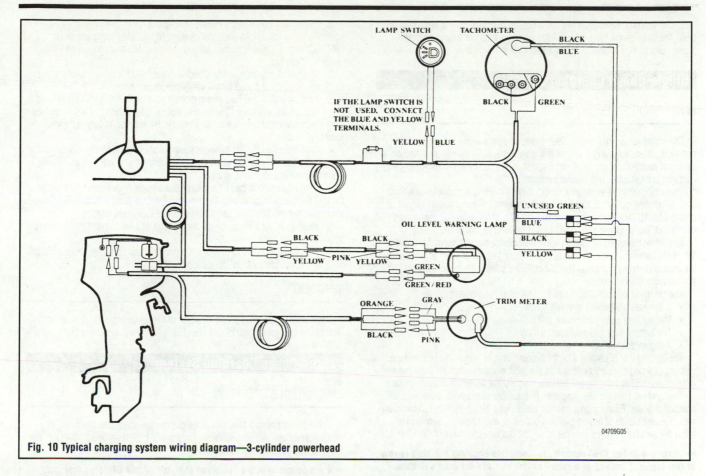

Fig. 10 Typical charging system wiring diagram—3-cylinder powerhead

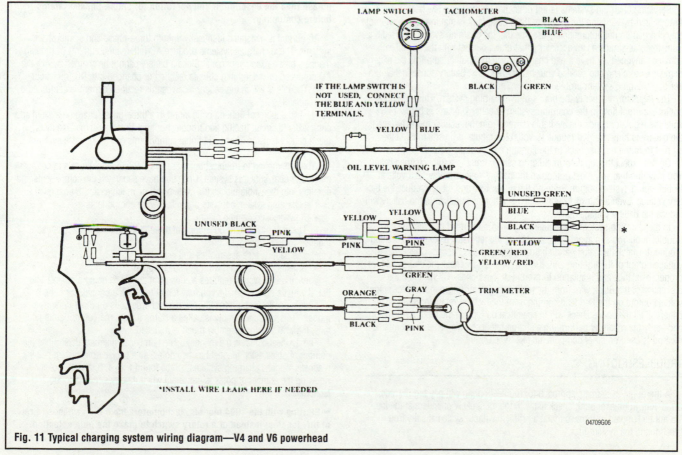

Fig. 11 Typical charging system wiring diagram—V4 and V6 powerhead

three coil winding. By using three coils instead of one, output is more than doubled. The three-phase rectifier/regulator works in a similar way to the single-phase system. The difference is the addition of more diodes.

Single-phase Charging System

DESCRIPTION & OPERATION

The single-phase charging system found on inline engines provides basic battery maintenance. Single-phase, full wave systems like these are found on a variety of products. Many outboard engines, water vehicles, motorcycles, golf cars and snowmobiles use similar systems.

This charging system produces electricity by moving a magnet past a fixed coil. Alternating current is produced by this method. Since a battery cannot be charged by AC (alternating current), the AC current produced by the lighting coil is rectified or changed into DC (direct current) to charge the battery.

To control the charging rate an additional device called a regulator is used. When the battery voltage reaches approximately 14.6 volts the regulator sends the excess current to ground. This prevents the battery from overcharging and boiling away the electrolyte.

The charging system consists of the following components:
- A flywheel containing magnets
- The lighting coil or alternator coil
- The battery, fuse assembly and wiring
- A regulator/rectifier

The lighting coil is usually a bright exposed copper wire with a lacquer-type coating. Lighting coils are built in with the ignition charge coils on some models. If the charge coil or lighting coil fails the whole stator assembly must be replaced.

The flywheel contains the magnets. The number of magnets determines the number of poles. Each magnet has two poles, so a 4-pole system has two magnets. Yamaha builds charging systems with 4, 6, and 12 poles. You need to know the number of poles in order to set the tachometer correctly.

➡**Starting with the 1994 models, tachometers have dip switches (a row of tiny toggles) instead of a rotary switch to make the pole selection.**

Servicing charging systems is not difficult if you follow a few basic rules. Always start by verifying the problem. If the complaint is that the battery will not stay charged do not automatically assume that the charging system is at fault. Something as simple as an accessory that draws current with the key off will convince anyone they have a bad charging system. Another culprit is the battery. Remember to clean and service your battery regularly. Battery abuse is the number one charging system problem.

The regulator/rectifier is the brains of the charging system. This assembly controls current flow in the charging system. If battery voltage is below 14.6 volts the regulator sends the available current from the rectifier to the battery. If the battery is fully charged (about 15 volts) the regulator diverts most of the current from the rectifier back to the lighting coil through ground.

Do not expect the regulator/rectifier to send current to a fully charged battery. You may find that you must pull down the battery voltage below 12.5 volts to test charging system output. Running the power trim and tilt will reduce the battery voltage. Even a pair of 12 volt sealed beam lamps hooked to the battery will reduce the battery voltage quickly.

In the charging system the regulator/rectifier is the most complex item to troubleshoot. You can avoid troubleshooting the regulator/rectifier by checking around it. Check the battery and charge or replace it as needed. Check the AC voltage output of the lighting coil. If AC voltage is low check the charge coil for proper resistance and insulation to ground. If these check OK measure the resistance of the Black wire from the rectifier/regulator to ground and for proper voltage output on the Red lead coming from the rectifier/regulator going to the battery. If all the above check within specification replace the rectifier/regulator and verify the repair by performing a charge rate test. This same check around method is used on other components like the CDI unit.

TROUBLESHOOTING

A thorough, systematic approach to troubleshooting will pay big rewards. Build your troubleshooting check list with the most likely offenders at the top. Do not be tempted to throw parts at a problem without systematically troubleshooting the system first.

1. Do a visual check of the battery, wiring and fuses. Are there any new additions to the wiring? An excellent clue might be, "Everything was working OK until I added that live well pump." With a comment like this you would know where to check first.

2. Test the battery thoroughly. Check the electrolyte level, the wiring connections and perform a load test to verify condition.

3. Perform a fuse and Red wire check with the voltmeter. Verify the ground at the rectifier. Do you have 12 volts and a good fuse? While you are at the Red wire, check alternator output with an ammeter. Be sure the battery is down around 12 volts.

4. Do a draw test if it fits the symptoms. Many times a battery that will not charge overnight or week-to-week. Put a test lamp or ammeter in the line with everything off and look for a draw.

5. A similar problem can be a system that is simply overdrawn. The electrical system cannot keep up with the demand. Do a consumption survey. More amps out than the alternator can return requires a different strategy.

6. Next, go to the source. Check the lighting coil for correct resistance and shorts to ground.

7. If all these tests fail to pinpoint the problem and you have verified low or no output to the battery then replace the rectifier.

SERVICING

The charging system is an integral part of the ignition system. For information on service procedures, please refer to the "Ignition" section of this manual.

Three-Phase Charging System

DESCRIPTION & OPERATION

Three-phase systems have two more coils in the stator and one more wire than single-phase charging systems. They create higher amperage output than single-phase in nearly the same space.

➡**If you do not have a solid grasp of single-phase charging systems, please read the description and operation for single-phase systems before continuing.**

AC current is generated identically in both three-phase and single-phase systems. These charging systems produce AC (alternating current) by moving magnets past a fixed set of coils. Since a battery cannot be charged by AC, the AC produced by the lighting coils is rectified or changed into DC (direct current). The rate at which the battery receives this rectified current is controlled by the regulator.

The two additional lighting coils found in a three-phase charging system add complexity to circuit tracing and troubleshooting. Some systems also incorporate a battery isolator. These additional components can make these systems intimidating.

When attempting to troubleshoot these systems, apply a divide and conquer method to demystify this system. Once you have separated the components and circuitry into digestible blocks the system will be much easier to understand.

The charging system consists of the following components:
- A flywheel containing magnets
- The stator assembly, consisting of three individual lighting coils tied together in a "Y" configuration
- The battery, fuse assemblies and wiring
- A battery isolator and wiring, if so equipped

Servicing this system requires a consistent approach using a reliable checklist. If you are not systematic you may forget to check a critical component.

Lighting coils are built together with the charge coils on most V4 and V6 models. This whole assembly is called a stator. If a charge coil or lighting coil fails, the whole stator assembly must be replaced.

The flywheel contains the magnets. The number of magnets determines the number of poles. Each magnet has two poles, so a twelve pole system has six magnets. Yamaha charging systems can be found with 4, 6, and 12 poles. Knowing the number of poles is important when it comes to setting the tachometer.

➡**Starting with the 1994 models, tachometers have dip switches (a row of tiny toggles) instead of a rotary switch to make the pole selection.**

TROUBLESHOOTING

Servicing three-phase charging systems is not difficult if you follow a few basic rules. Always start by verifying the problem.

• Do not automatically assume that the charging system is at fault.

• A small draw with the key off, a battery with a low electrolyte level, or an overdrawn system can cause the same symptoms.

• It has become common practice on V4 and V6 engines to overload the electrical system with accessories. This places an excessive demand on the charging system. If the system is "overdrawn at the amp bank" then no amount of parts changing will fix it.

When troubleshooting a three-phase charging system use the following procedure:

1. The regulator/rectifier assembly is the brains of the charging system. The regulator controls current flow in the charging system. If battery voltage is below about 14.6 volts the regulator sends the available current to the battery. If the battery is fully charged (about 14.5 to 15 volts) the regulator diverts the current/amps to ground.

2. Do not expect the regulator to send current to a fully charged battery. Check the battery for a possible draw with the key off. This draw may be the cumulative effect of several radio and/or clock memories. If these accessories are wired to the cranking battery then a complaint of charging system failure may really be excessive draw. Draw over about 25 milliamps should arouse your suspicions. The fuel management gauge memory and speedometer clock draw about 10 milliamps each. Remember that a milliamp is $\frac{1}{1000}$ of an amp. Check battery condition thoroughly because it is the #1 culprit in charging system failures.

3. Do not forget to check through the fuse and Red wire back to the battery. It can be embarrassing to overlook a blown fuse or open Red wire.

4. You must pull the battery voltage down below 12.5 volts to test charging system output. Running the power trim and tilt will reduce the battery voltage. A load bank or even a pair of 12-volt sealed-beam headlamps hooked to the battery can also be used to reduce the battery voltage.

5. Once the battery's good condition is verified and it has been reduced to below 12.5 volts you can test further.

6. Install an ammeter to check actual amp output. Several tool manufacturers produce a shunt adapter that will attach to your multi-meter and allow you to read the amp output. Verify that the system is delivering sufficient amperage. Too much amperage and a battery that goes dry very quickly indicates that the rectifier/regulator should be replaced.

7. If the system does not put out enough amperage, then test the lighting coil. Isolate the coil and test for correct resistance and short to ground.

8. During these test procedures the regulator/rectifier has not been bench checked. Usually it is advisable to avoid troubleshooting the regulator/rectifier directly. The procedures listed so far have focused on checking around the rectifier/regulator. If you verify that the battery, Black lead, Red lead, and stator are good then what is left in the system to cause the verified problem? The process of elimination has declared the rectifier/regulator bad.

9. This check around method is also useful on other components that can not be checked directly or involve time-consuming test procedures. This is the same method suggested for checking the capacitor discharge ignition box.

SERVICING

The charging system is an integral part of the ignition system. For information on service procedures, please refer to the "Ignition" section of this manual.

V76 Charging System

The V76 series has the highest output three-phase charging system in the Yamaha product line. In addition, the V76 has several other charging system features. The following paragraphs detail the differences between a normal three-phase system and the V76 system.

WATER-COOLED RECTIFIER/REGULATOR

The V76 has cooling water running behind the rectifier/regulator. This cooling water removes the heat produced by the charging system. On the V76, this cooling water runs through a plate bolted next to the rectifier/regulator. From here the water exits through the pilot tube. The plate acts as a heat sink for the rectifier/regulator.

The design of the rectifier/regulator allows it to be removed without disconnecting the water hoses.

The rectifier/regulator assembly has four Red wires, three Green wires and one Black wire. The three Green wires are from the stator. Note that the Red wires combine into two pairs. This extra set of Red wires is for the battery isolator system. Remember to keep these wires from touching each other.

The V76 rectifier incorporates a battery isolator. By using three extra diodes, this unit can independently charge two batteries. Both batteries are electrically isolated from each other. If one battery is drained, it will not discharge the other.

The rectifier prioritizes charging current to the battery with the lowest state of charge. When the charge states of both batteries are equal, output is divided equally to both batteries until they are both charged. When both batteries are fully charged, the regulator shunts unneeded current to ground.

➡**Follow battery wiring instructions carefully when rigging boats or installing batteries to reduce the risk of fire. The negative cable between two batteries must be of a type equivalent to the main battery cables.**

BATTERY CABLE DISCONNECT WARNING

Starting in 1990, the V76, V4, and V6 models have a warning system to signal if a battery cable is loose. If a battery cable is loose, a special electronic circuit senses that charging current isn't reaching the battery. This circuitry is connected through the computer. Once the circuitry is activated, it activates the rpm reduction system to reduce rpm to 2,000 and sound the buzzer. All three oil warning indicators will flash on and off together.

TROUBLESHOOTING

There are several conditions you can find when troubleshooting a three-phase charging system:

1. Normal—In a normal system the charge rate is correct. There could be a problem elsewhere, such as an electrical short, too many accessories or a bad battery. Whatever the problem, there is no need to work on the charging system. It is working correctly!

2. Overcharging—The charging system continues to supply current to the battery even after the battery is fully charged. Usually this is caused by a bad regulator portion of the rectifier.

3. Undercharging—The charging system is not producing current at all or is producing it at a reduced rate.

4. Battery drain during non-use—Isolate the battery draw to the motor or to the boat accessories by removing loads one at a time. Although it is rare, one of the diodes in the rectifier can short and slowly drain the battery.

Keep the above possibilities in mind when troubleshooting. By simplifying your troubleshooting approach you may get to the solution more quickly.

The first step in testing a charging system is to confirm there is a charging problem.

The real problem may be too many accessories or a draw with the key off. The charging system may really be OK, but if the draw on the system exceeds the charging output, the charging system will appear faulty.

There are two methods for checking three-phase charging systems, the DC amp check and the DC voltage check. The DC amp check method is usually preferred, but both methods are useful.

DC Amperage Check

1. Eliminate the battery as the problem by using a known good one. Now check for any amperage drain on the battery with an ammeter. Connect the ammeter between the positive battery cable and the positive post on the battery. Take your first reading with the key switch **OFF**. Your reading should be zero. Then take a reading with the key switch **ON**. This reading will vary according to how many accessories are connected to key-on power. Record the amperage reading.

2. Determine actual DC amperage output from the alternator. To determine alternator output, subtract the key-on/engine-off amperage draw from the maximum alternator output. Start this process by disconnecting the isolator lead from the accessory battery and protect it from grounding out. Next, connect a DC ammeter (0-40 amps) in series with the rectifier/regulator output lead at the starter solenoid. (Motor should be in the water for this test to provide adequate cool water supply).

3. Now, start and rev the motor to 3000 rpm. Observe the alternator output.

➡When making the DC amperage output check, do not use a fully charged battery! A fully charged battery will not receive full system output. It may only show half the expected amperage output. Reduce the battery state of charge by operating the trim/tilt motor through several cycles. This reduces the charge on the battery and permits higher alternator output.

DC Voltage Check

1. The DC voltage check begins just like the DC amperage check. Begin the DC voltage check by establishing the condition of the battery and by checking for any key-off amperage draw.
2. Verify that you have 12 volts through the fuse and Red wire. Reading voltage through the fuse establishes continuity and fuse condition.
3. Check the system carefully for good grounds at all the ground points for the Black wires. Remember that there are several splices within the harness that can corrode and create high resistance.
4. At this point move to the lighting coil Green wires and disconnect the connector. Crank the engine and check the AC voltage output among the three wires. The voltage should be above battery voltage at idle and rise with engine rpm. Check each leg to ground. The AC reading should be nearly the same from

each leg to ground. If not, shut off the engine, switch the meter to ohms and look for a coil leg that is open or shorted to ground.
5. The rectifier/regulator is purposely left for last. In reality, these checks aren't usually necessary. By the process of elimination you can decide if the rectifier is bad. If the stator, battery and fuse are all good, and if the Red and Black wires are OK, the only thing left is the rectifier/regulator assembly. Since you can't disassemble the unit to fix it, replace it.

Charging System Checks

EXCESSIVE CHARGING

There is really only one cause for this type of failure, the regulator is not working. It isn't controlling charging output to the battery. Since there is no repair of this part, replace it.

UNDERCHARGING

If there is an undercharge condition after running the DC amperage check at the fuse assembly, then disconnect the stator coupling from the harness and perform AC voltage checks between the three stator leads. Check between two stator leads at a time. There are three volt checks done to cover all possible combinations.

CHARGING SYSTEM CHECKS

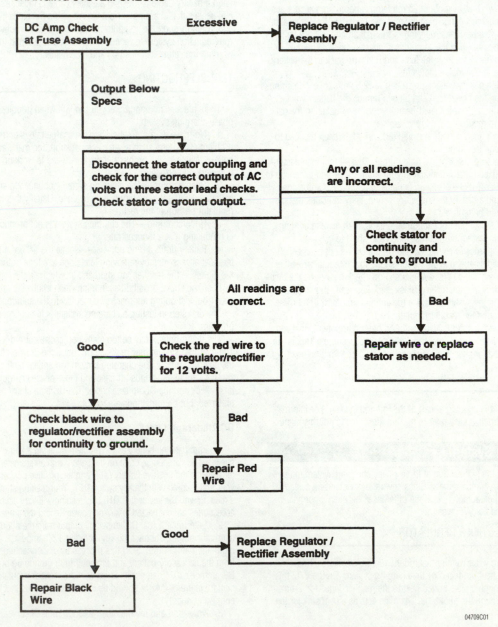

04709C01

At idle, there is typically 14+ volts on each test. It can be higher if the idle is higher. All three readings should be equal, within a volt or two. Stator shorts to ground can be checked by doing a voltage test between one stator lead and ground, engine running. There should be roughly half the normal stator voltage check reading.

If the readings are all within specification, the stator is working correctly. Proceed to the Red wire and Black wire checks.

If any or all readings are below normal, turn the engine **OFF** and check the stator windings using an ohmmeter. An isolated continuity check and a short to ground check should be done. If the stator is bad, replace it since it can't be repaired.

CRANKING CIRCUIT

Description and Operation

As the name implies, the sole purpose of the cranking motor circuit is to control operation of the cranking motor to crank the powerhead until the engine is operating. The circuit includes a solenoid or magnetic switch to connect or disconnect the motor from the battery. The operator controls the switch with a key switch.

A neutral safety switch is installed into the circuit to permit operation of the cranking motor only if the shift control lever is in neutral. This switch is a safety device to prevent accidental engine start when the engine is in gear.

The cranking motor is a series wound electric motor which draws a heavy current from the battery. It is designed to be used only for short periods of time to crank the engine for starting. To prevent overheating the motor, cranking should not be continued for more than 30-seconds without allowing the motor to cool for at least three minutes. Actually, this time can be spent in making preliminary checks to determine why the engine fails to start.

Power is transmitted from the cranking motor to the powerhead flywheel through a Bendix drive. This drive has a pinion gear mounted on screw threads. When the motor is operated, the pinion gear moves upward and meshes with the teeth on the flywheel ring gear.

When the powerhead starts, the pinion gear is driven faster than the shaft, and as a result, it screws out of mesh with the flywheel. A rubber cushion is built into the Bendix drive to absorb the shock when the pinion meshes with the flywheel ring gear. The parts of the drive must be properly assembled for efficient operation. If the drive is removed for cleaning, take care to assemble the parts as shown in the accompanying illustrations in this section. If the screw shaft assembly is reversed, it will strike the splines and the rubber cushion will not absorb the shock.

The sound of the motor during cranking is a good indication of whether the cranking motor is operating properly or not. Naturally, temperature conditions will affect the speed at which the cranking motor is able to crank the engine. The speed of cranking a cold engine will be much slower than when cranking a warm engine. An experienced operator will learn to recognize the favorable sounds of the powerhead cranking under various conditions.

MAINTENANCE

The cranking motor does not require periodic maintenance or lubrication. If the motor fails to perform properly, the checks outlined in the previous paragraph should be performed. The frequency of starts governs how often the motor should be removed and reconditioned. The manufacturer recommends removal and reconditioning every 1000 hours. Naturally, the motor will have to be removed if corrective actions do not restore the motor to satisfactory operation.

FAULTY SYMPTOMS

If the cranking motor spins, but fails to crank the engine, the cause is usually a corroded or gummy Bendix drive. The drive should be removed, cleaned, and given an inspection.

If the cranking motor cranks the engine too slowly, the following are possible causes and the corrective actions that may be taken:
• Battery charge is low. Charge the battery to full capacity.
• High resistance connections at the battery, solenoid, or motor. Clean and tighten all connections.
• Undersize battery cables. Replace cables with sufficient size.
• Battery cables too long. Relocate the battery to shorten the run to the solenoid.

As the chart shows, this is a complete check of the whole system. A problem in the system can be found if the chart is followed. Don't jump around the chart! With some practice, this troubleshooting procedure will become second nature.

SERVICING

The charging system is an integral part of the ignition system. For information on service procedures, please refer to the "ignition" section of this manual.

Cranking Motor Circuit

▶ See Figure 12

Before wasting too much time troubleshooting the cranking motor circuit, the following checks should be made. Many times, the problem will be corrected.
• Battery fully charged.
• Shift control lever in neutral.
• Main 20-amp fuse located at the base of the fuse cover is good (not blown).
• All electrical connections clean and tight.
• Wiring in good condition, insulation not worn or frayed.

Two more areas may cause the powerhead to crank slowly even though the cranking motor circuit is in excellent condition: a tight or frozen powerhead and water in the lower unit. The following troubleshooting procedures are presented in a logical sequence, with the most common and easily corrected areas listed first in each problem area. The connection number refers to the numbered positions in the accompanying illustrations.

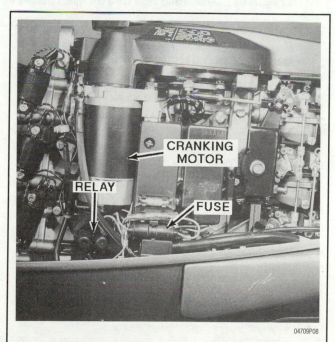

Fig. 12 Typical location of the cranking motor, relay and fuse

TROUBLESHOOTING

▶ See Figure 13

1. Cranking Motor Rotates Slowly
   a. Battery charge is low. Charge the battery to full capacity.
   b. Electrical connections corroded or loose. Clean and tighten.
   c. Defective cranking motor. Perform an amp draw test. Lay an amp draw-gauge on the cable leading to the cranking motor. Turn the key on and

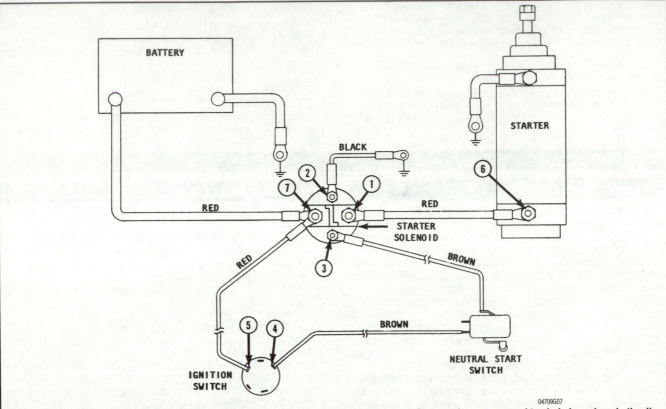

Fig. 13 Perform the troubleshooting steps using this typical cranking motor system diagram. Step numbers correspond to circled numbers in the diagram

attempt to crank the engine. If the gauge indicates an excessive amperage draw, the cranking motor must be replaced or rebuilt.

2. Cranking Motor Fails To Crank Powerhead

a. Disconnect the cranking motor lead from the solenoid to prevent the powerhead from starting during the testing process.

➡**This lead is to remain disconnected from the solenoid during tests No. 2–6.**

b. Disconnect the Black ground wire from the No. 2 terminal.

c. Connect a voltmeter between the No. 2 terminal and a common engine ground.

d. Turn the key switch to the start position.

e. Observe the voltmeter reading. If there is the slightest amount of reading, check the Black ground wire connection or check for an open circuit.

3. Test Cranking Motor Solenoid

a. Connect a voltmeter between the engine common ground and the No. 3 terminal.

b. Turn the ignition key switch to the start position.

c. Observe the voltmeter reading. If the meter indicates more than 0.3 volt, the solenoid is defective and must be replaced.

4. Test Neutral Start Switch

a. Connect a voltmeter between the common engine ground and the No. 4. Turn the ignition key switch to the start position.

b. Observe the voltmeter. If there is any indication of a reading, the neutral start switch is open or the brown wire lead is open between the No. 3 and No. 4.

5. Test for Open Wire

a. Connect a voltmeter between the common engine ground and No. 5.

b. The voltmeter should indicate (12-volts. If the meter needle flickers (fails to hold steady), check the circuit between No. 5 and common engine ground. If meter fails to indicate voltage, replace the positive battery cable.

6. Further Tests for Solenoid

a. Connect the voltmeter between the common engine ground and No. 1.

b. Turn the ignition key switch to the start position.

c. Observe the voltmeter. If there is no reading, the cranking motor solenoid is defective and must be replaced.

7. Test Large Red Cable

a. Connect the Red cable to the cranking motor solenoid.

b. Connect the voltmeter between the engine common ground and No. 6.

c. Turn the ignition key switch to the start position, or depress the start button.

d. Observe the voltmeter. If there is no reading, check the Red cable for a poor connection or an open circuit. If there is any indication of a reading, and the cranking motor does not rotate, the cranking motor must be replaced.

Cranking Motor Relay

DESCRIPTION AND OPERATION

The cranking motor relay is actually a switch between the battery and the powerhead. The switch cannot be serviced. Therefore, if troubleshooting indicates the switch to be faulty, it must be replaced.

Before beginning any work on the relay, disconnect the positive (+) lead from the battery terminal. Remove the cowling from the powerhead.

Check to be sure the battery cables are disconnected from the battery.

✳ WARNING

Disconnecting the battery leads is most important because the cranking motor relay lead will be disconnected and allowed to hang free. The other end of this lead is connected to the battery. If the leads are not disconnected from the battery and the free relay end should happen to come in contact with any metal part on the powerhead, sparks would fly and the end of the lead burned.

REMOVAL

◆ See accompanying illustrations

1. Push down the boots from the two large Red leads at the relay. Take time to make a note of leads and to which terminal they are connected, and then remove the leads. Disconnect the small Brown lead at the quick disconnect fitting.

2. Slide the relay from its mounting bracket. Remove the grounding bolt on the bracket behind the relay to release the Black relay grounding wire.

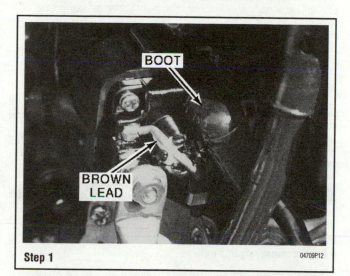

Step 1   04709P12

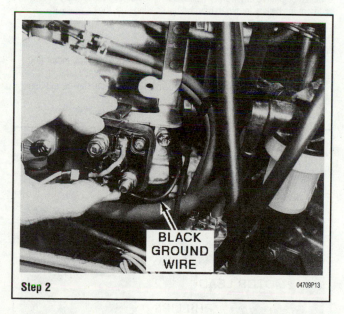

Step 2   04709P13

TESTING

◆ See accompanying illustrations

➡**The following tests must be conducted with the relay removed from the powerhead.**

1. Obtain an ohmmeter. Make contact with the Black meter lead to the Black relay lead and the Red meter lead to the Brown relay lead. The meter should

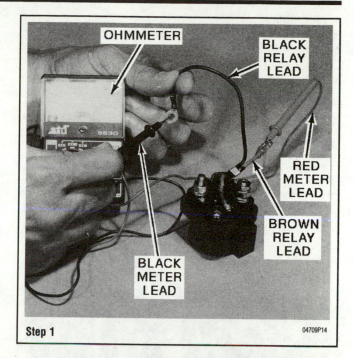

Step 1   04709P14

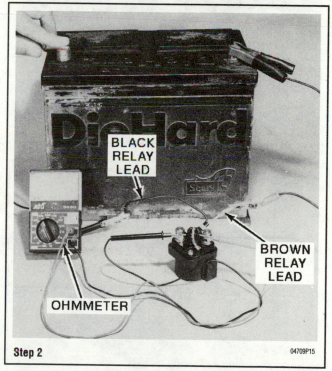

Step 2   04709P15

indicate continuity. If the meter registers no continuity, the relay is defective and must be replaced. No service or adjustment is possible.

2. Connect one test lead of the ohmmeter to each of the large relay terminals. Connect the positive (+) lead from a fully charged 12-volt battery to the Brown lead. Momentarily make contact with the ground lead from the battery to the Black lead. If a loud click sound is heard, and the ohmmeter indicates continuity, the solenoid is in serviceable condition. If, however, a click sound is not heard, and/or the ohmmeter does not indicate continuity, the solenoid is defective and must be replaced only with a marine type solenoid.

INSTALLATION

♦ **See accompanying illustrations**

1. Slide the relay back onto its mounting bracket. Secure the Black lead behind the relay by installing the grounding bolt on the bracket.

2. Connect the Brown lead at the quick disconnect fitting.

Connect the two large Red leads to the front of the cranking motor relay. The lead on the right is from the hot terminal on the cranking motor. The lead on the left is also hot coming from the positive battery terminal. This lead also has a small Red lead attached to the relay terminal.

Install the elbow boots onto both relay leads.

If the work is complete, then reconnect the battery terminals. If further work

is to be carried out on the cranking system, then leave the battery cables disconnected until the work is complete.

Cranking Motor

DESCRIPTION

One type cranking motor is used on the powerheads covered in this manual. The exterior appearance of the cranking motor may vary. Therefore, the accompanying illustrations may differ slightly from the unit being serviced, but the procedures and maintenance instructions are valid for all cranking motors on most Yamaha powerheads.

As an example, the collar on the 90hp cranking motor has been modified to provide an escape route for any water trapped around the pinion gear.

Marine cranking motors are very similar in construction and operation to the units used in the automotive industry.

All marine cranking motors use the inertia type drive assembly. This type assembly is mounted on an armature shaft with external spiral splines which mate with the internal splines of the drive assembly.

Never operate a cranking motor for more than 30 seconds without allowing it to cool for at least three minutes. Continuous operation without the cooling period can cause serious damage to the cranking motor.

1- and 2-Cylinder Powerhead Cranking Motor

REMOVAL

♦ **See accompanying illustrations**

Before beginning any work on the cranking motor, disconnect the positive (+) lead from the battery terminal. Remove the cowling from the power-head.

1. Disconnect the cranking motor lead by removing the Phillips screw from the relay. The terminal on the cranking motor is not accessible. Therefore, the lead will come off with the motor.

2. Remove the mounting bolts and washers from the cranking motor housing. One of the bolts is partially under the flywheel. However, by rotating the flywheel until a cutout is directly over the bolt head, the bolt may be wiggled out.

BLACK GROUND

Step 1   04709P16

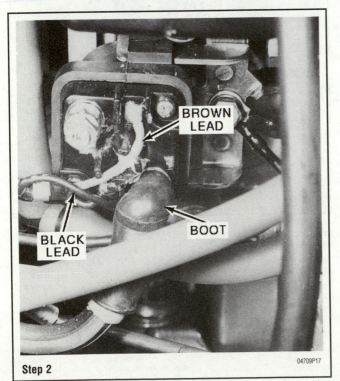

BROWN LEAD

BLACK LEAD

BOOT

Step 2   04709P17

CRANKING MOTOR LEAD

PHILLIPS HEAD SCREW (HIDDEN)

Step 1   04709P18

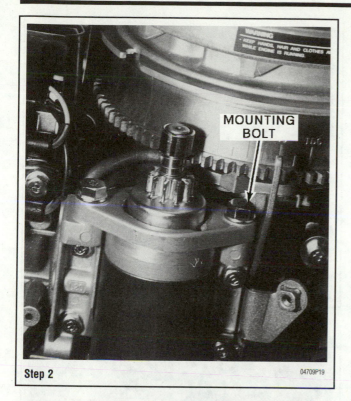

MOUNTING BOLT

Step 2   04709P19

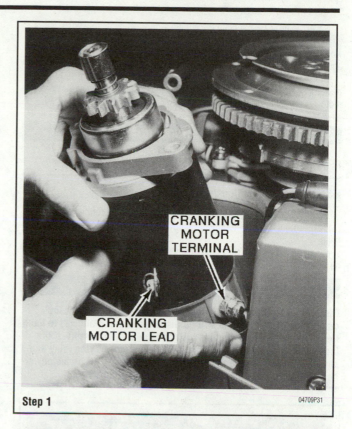

CRANKING MOTOR TERMINAL

CRANKING MOTOR LEAD

Step 1   04709P31

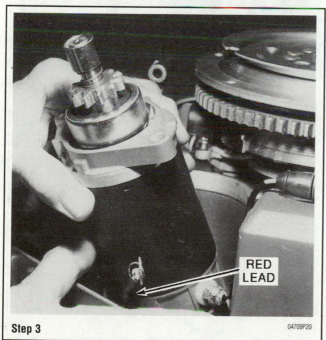

RED LEAD

Step 3   04709P20

CRANKING MOTOR LEAD

SCREW

Step 2   04709P32

3. Remove the cranking motor from the powerhead. Disconnect the large Red lead from the motor.

INSTALLATION

◆ See accompanying illustrations

1. Move the cranking motor close to position on the powerhead. Connect the Red lead to the cranking motor terminal. Now, position the cranking motor against the mounting bracket. Secure the motor in place with the two bolts and washers. One of the bolts goes into place partially under the flywheel. However, by rotating the flywheel, a cutout in the flywheel can be positioned directly over the bolt hole allowing the bolt to be wiggled into place and the threads started. Tighten the mounting bolts to a torque value of 13 ft. lbs. (18 Nm).

2. Connect the cranking motor lead to the relay with the Phillips head screw.

Mount the outboard unit in a test tank, on the boat in a body of water, or connect a flush attachment and hose to the lower unit.

✳✳ CAUTION

Water must circulate through the lower unit to the engine any time the engine is run to prevent damage to the water pump in the lower unit. Just five seconds without water will damage the water pump.

Never, again, never operate the engine at high speed with a flush device attached. The engine, operating at high speed with such a device attached, would runaway from lack of a load on the propeller, causing extensive damage.

Crank the powerhead with the cranking motor and start the unit. Shut the powerhead down and start it several times to check operation of the cranking motor.

3-Cylinder Powerhead Cranking Motor

REMOVAL

◆ **See accompanying illustrations**

Before beginning any work on the cranking motor, disconnect the positive (+) lead from the battery terminal. Remove the cowling from the powerhead.

1. Check to be sure the battery cables are disconnected from the battery.

✳✳ CAUTION

Disconnecting the battery leads is most important because the cranking motor relay lead will be disconnected and allowed to hang free. The other end of this lead is connected to the battery. If the leads are not disconnected from the battery and the free relay end should happen to come in contact with any metal part on the power-head, sparks would fly and the end of the lead burned.

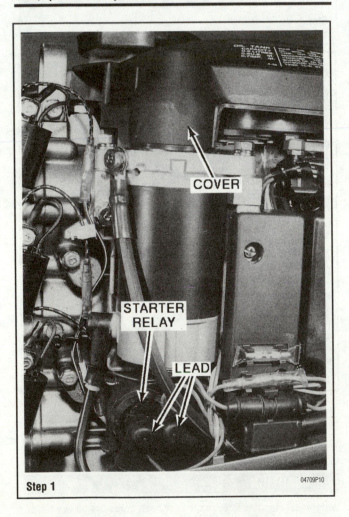

Step 1   04709P10

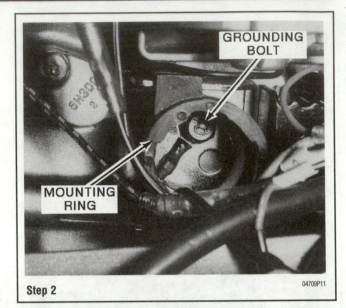

Step 2   04709P11

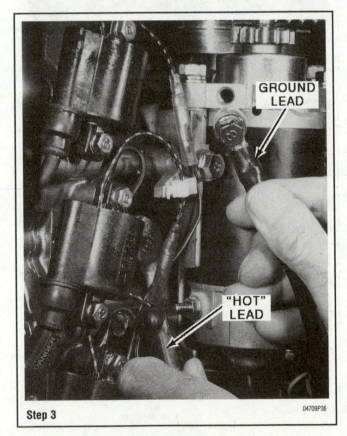

Step 3   04709P36

Lift off the plastic flywheel cover which serves as a shroud for the pinion gear. Disconnect both large Black cables from the cranking motor relay.

2. Pull the starter relay free from its rubber mounting ring. Disconnect the Brown lead at its quick disconnect fitting. Reach inside the rubber mounting ring and disconnect the Black lead with the eye connector from its grounding bolt securing the cranking motor bracket. The bracket to the rubber mounting ring will come away with the grounding bolt.

3. Disconnect both the lower hot lead and the upper ground lead from the cranking motor.

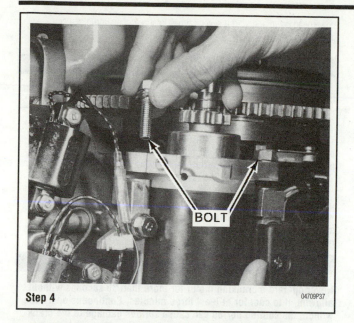

Step 4

04709P37

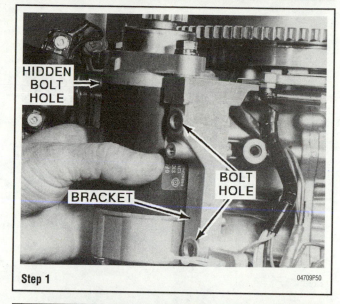

Step 1

04709P50

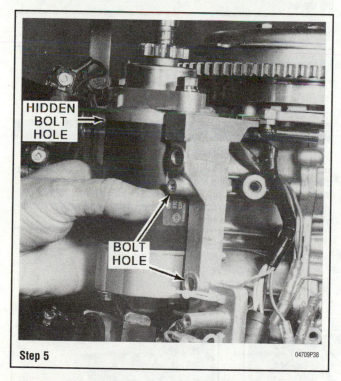

Step 5

04709P38

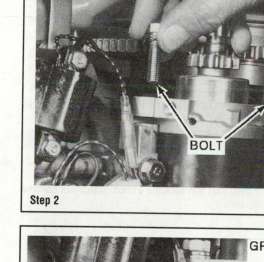

Step 2

04709P51

4. Remove the bolts securing the cranking motor to the top of the mounting bracket and lift the motor free of the bracket.

5. Insure the hidden bolt behind the starter is removed before removing the starter.

INSTALLATION

▶ **See accompanying illustrations**

1. Install the cranking motor and bracket to the powerhead with the three attaching bolts. The top forward bolt is longer than the other two bolts. Tighten the bolts to a torque value of 13 ft. lbs. (18 Nm).

2. Place the cranking motor in position over the mounting bracket and install the two securing bolts. Tighten the bolts to a torque value of 13 ft. lbs. (18 Nm).

3. Connect the upper ground lead to the case of the cranking motor. Connect the lower hot lead to the terminal of the motor. Slip the elbow boots over the installed leads.

Step 3

04709P52

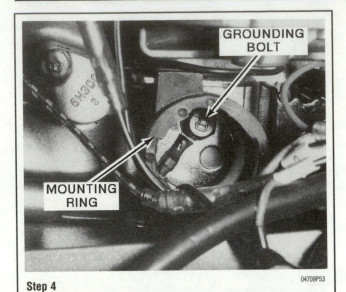

Step 4   04709P53

4. Position the rubber mounting ring in place. Slip the Black ground lead with the eye connector through the bolt and then through the backing plate of the mounting ring. Secure both the lead and the mounting ring to the cranking motor bracket. Tighten the bolt to a torque value of 5.8 ft. lbs. (8 Nm). Connect the Brown lead at its quick connect fitting and push the cranking motor relay into the rubber mounting ring.

Connect the two large Black leads to the front of the cranking motor relay. The lead on the left is the one from the hot terminal on the cranking motor. The lead on the right is also hot coming from the positive battery terminal.

Install the elbow boots onto both relay leads. Install the plastic flywheel cover over the pinion gear. Connect the electrical leads to the battery.

Mount the outboard unit in a test tank, on the boat in a body of water, or connect a flush attachment and hose to the lower unit.

✳✳ CAUTION

Water must circulate through the lower unit to the powerhead anytime the powerhead is operating to prevent damage to the water pump in the lower unit. Just five seconds without water will damage the water pump impeller.

Never, again, never operate the engine at high speed with a flush device attached. The engine, operating at high speed with such a device attached, would runaway from lack of a load on the propeller, causing extensive damage.

Crank the powerhead with the cranking motor and start the unit. Shut the powerhead down and start it several times to check operation of the cranking motor.

V4 and V6 Powerhead Cranking Motors

DESCRIPTION

One type cranking motor is used on the powerheads covered in this manual. The exterior appearance of the cranking motor may vary. Therefore, the accompanying illustrations may differ slightly from the unit being serviced, but the procedures and maintenance instructions are valid for all cranking motors on all Yamaha powerheads covered in this manual.

Marine cranking motors are very similar in construction and operation to the units used in the automotive industry.

All marine cranking motors use the inertia type drive assembly. This type assembly is mounted on an armature shaft with external spiral splines which mate with the internal splines of the drive assembly.

✳✳ WARNING

Never operate a cranking motor for more than 30 seconds without allowing it to cool for at least three minutes. Continuous operation without the cooling period can cause serious damage to the cranking motor.

REMOVAL

◆ **See accompanying illustrations**

Before beginning any work on the cranking motor, disconnect the positive (+) lead from the battery terminal. Remove the cowling from the powerhead.

1. Check to be sure the battery cables are disconnected from the battery.

✳✳ WARNING

Disconnecting the battery leads is most important because the cranking motor relay lead will be disconnected and allowed to hang free. The other end of this lead is connected to the battery. If the leads are not disconnected from the battery and the free relay end should happen to come in contact with any metal part on the powerhead, sparks would fly and the end of the lead burned.

Disconnect both large cables from the cranking motor relay.

2. Disconnect the upper ground lead from the cranking motor.
3. Disconnect the lower hot lead from the cranking motor.
4. Remove the three bolts securing the cranking motor to the powerhead.
5. Lift the motor free.

Step 1   04709P66

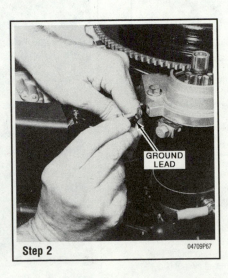

Step 2   04709P67

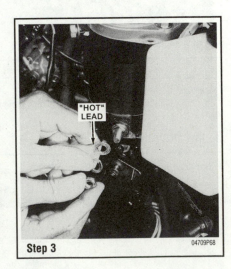

Step 3   04709P68

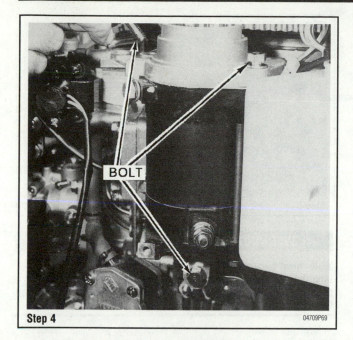

BOLT

Step 4　　04709P69

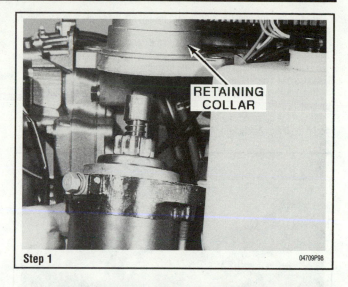

RETAINING COLLAR

Step 1　　04709P98

Step 5　　04709P70

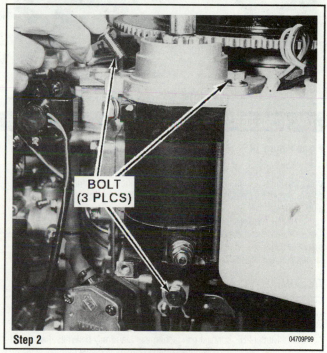

BOLT (3 PLCS)

Step 2　　04709P99

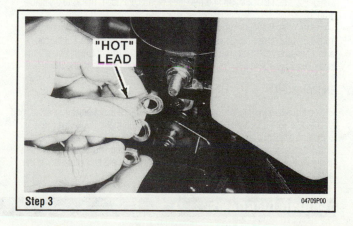

"HOT" LEAD

Step 3　　04709P00

INSTALLATION

▶ **See accompanying illustrations**

1. Slide the cranking motor up into the retaining collar.
2. Start the three mounting bolts. Tighten these bolts to a torque value of 22 ft. lbs. (30 Nm) in the following order. Tighten the lower bolt first, then the upper aft bolt and finally the upper forward bolt.
3. Connect the lower hot load to the terminal of the motor.

4. Connect the upper ground lead to the case of the cranking motor. Slip the elbow boots over the installed leads.

5. Connect the two large Red leads to the front of the cranking motor relay. The lead on the right is the one from the hot terminal on the cranking motor. The lead on the left is also hot coming from the positive battery terminal. This lead also has a small Red lead attached to the relay terminal.

Install the elbow boots onto both relay leads. Connect the electrical leads to the battery.

Mount the outboard unit in a test tank, on the boat in a body of water, or connect a flush attachment and hose to the lower unit.

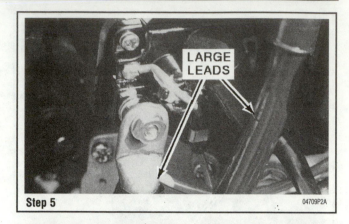

Step 5   04709P2A

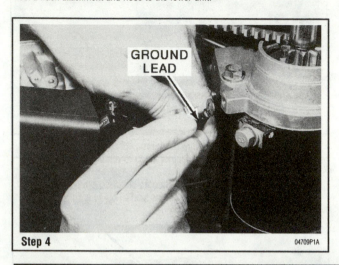

Step 4   04709P1A

✳✳ WARNING

Water must circulate through the lower unit to the powerhead anytime the powerhead is operating to prevent damage to the water pump in the lower unit. Just five seconds without water will damage the water pump impeller.

Never, again, never operate the engine at high speed with a flush device attached. The engine, operating at high speed with such a device attached, would runaway from lack of a load on the propeller, causing extensive damage.

Crank the powerhead with the cranking motor and start the unit. Shut the powerhead down and start it several times to check operation of the cranking motor.

TACHOMETERS

◆ See Figure 14

An accurate tachometer can be installed on any engine. Such an instrument provides an indication of engine speed in revolutions per minute (rpm). This is accomplished by measuring the number of electrical pulses per minute generated in the primary circuit of the ignition system.

The meter readings range from 0 to 6,000 rpm, in increments of 100. Tachometers have solid-state electronic circuits which eliminate the need for relays or batteries and contribute to their accuracy. The electronic parts of the tachometer, susceptible to moisture, are coated to prolong their life.

TACHOMETER CONNECTIONS

Manual Start

For the Model 2HP, connect one tachometer lead (may be White, Red, or Yellow, depending on the manufacturer), to the primary negative terminal of the coil (usually a small Black lead), and the other tachometer lead, Black, to a suitable ground.

For all other models, connect the two tachometer leads to the two Green leads from the stator. These two Green leads are encased inside a sheath, but the connecting ends are exposed. The leads are connected to a pair of Green female leads. Either tachometer lead may be connected to either Green lead from the stator.

Electric Start

The following instructions apply to a model without a tachometer installed, or for a model with a tachometer installed, but a second meter is needed to assist in making adjustments.

Inside the control box, the Green lead with the female end connector is input or signal lead. The Black lead with either a male or female end connector is the tachometer return or ground lead.

Connect the tachometer to these two leads per the instructions with the meter, input and ground.

➡ Some powerheads use a CDI system firing a twin lead ignition coil twice for each crankshaft revolution. If an induction tachometer is installed to measure powerhead speed, the tachometer will probably indicate double the actual crankshaft rotation. Check the instructions with the tachometer to be used. Some tachometer manufacturers have allowed for the double reading and others have not.

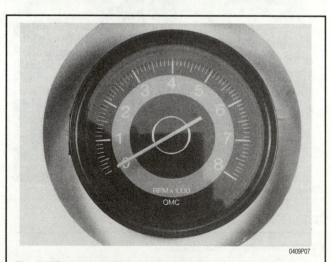

0409P07

Fig. 14 Maximum engine performance can only be obtained through proper tuning using a tachometer

WIRING DIAGRAMS

The following wiring diagrams represent the most common models of outboard engines covered in this manual. Models with accessory options may not be depicted here.

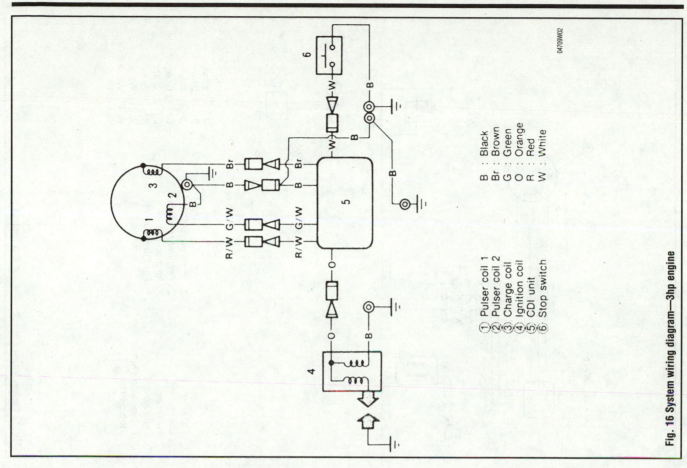

04709W02

B :	Black
Br :	Brown
G :	Green
O :	Orange
R :	Red
W :	White

① Pulser coil 1
② Pulser coil 2
③ Charge coil
④ Ignition coil
⑤ CDI unit
⑥ Stop switch

Fig. 16 System wiring diagram—3hp engine

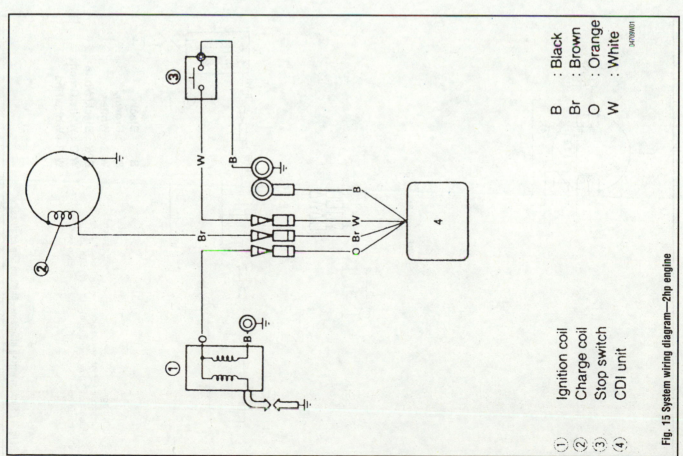

04709W01

B	: Black
Br	: Brown
O	: Orange
W	: White

① Ignition coil
② Charge coil
③ Stop switch
④ CDI unit

Fig. 15 System wiring diagram—2hp engine

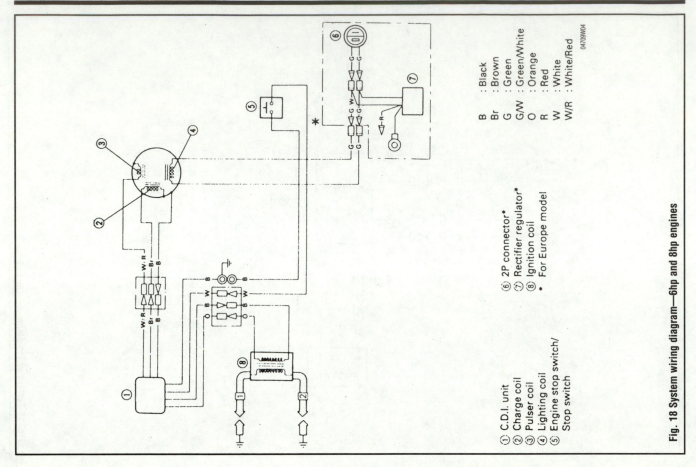

B : Black
Br : Brown
G : Green
G/W : Green/White
O : Orange
R : Red
W : White
W/R : White/Red

⑥ 2P connector*
⑦ Rectifier regulator*
⑧ Ignition coil
* For Europe model

① C.D.I. unit
② Charge coil
③ Pulser coil
④ Lighting coil
⑤ Engine stop switch/ Stop switch

Fig. 18 System wiring diagram—6hp and 8hp engines

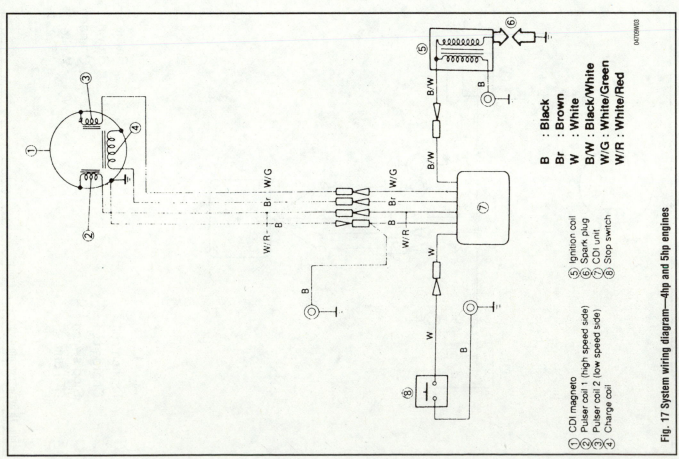

B : Black
Br : Brown
W : White
B/W : Black/White
W/G : White/Green
W/R : White/Red

① CDI magneto
② Pulser coil 1 (high speed side)
③ Pulser coil 2 (low speed side)
④ Charge coil

⑤ Ignition coil
⑥ Spark plug
⑦ CDI unit
⑧ Stop switch

Fig. 17 System wiring diagram—4hp and 5hp engines

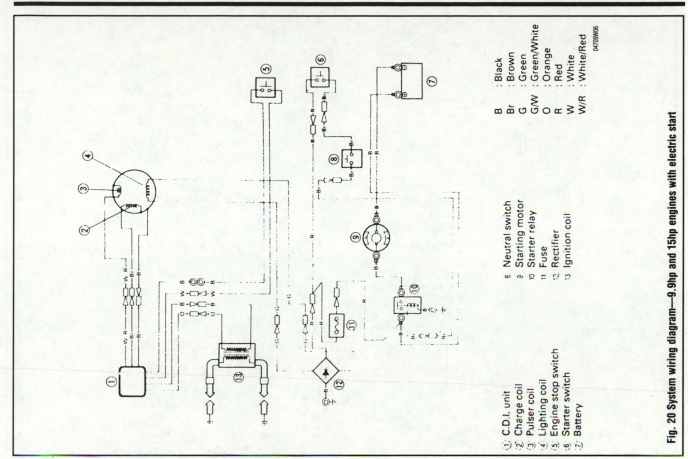

B	: Black	
Br	: Brown	
G	: Green	
G/W	: Green/White	
O	: Orange	
R	: Red	
W	: White	
W/R	: White/Red	

① C.D.I. unit   ⑧ Neutral switch
② Charge coil   ⑨ Starting motor
③ Pulser coil   ⑩ Starter relay
④ Lighting coil   ⑪ Fuse
⑤ Engine stop switch   ⑫ Rectifier
⑥ Starter switch   ⑬ Ignition coil
⑦ Battery

Fig. 20 System wiring diagram—9.9hp and 15hp engines with electric start

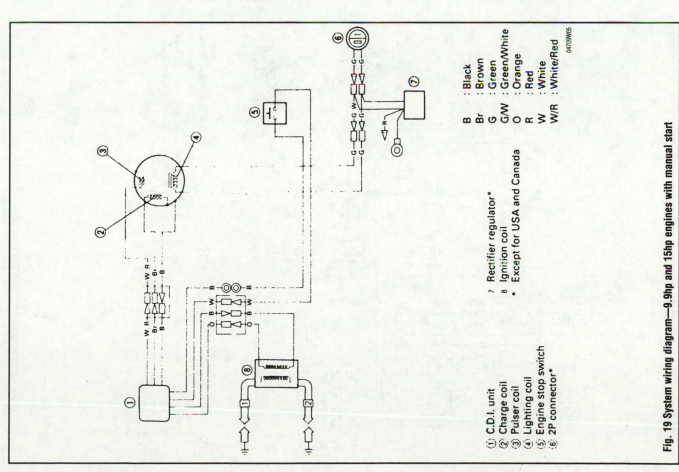

B	: Black	
Br	: Brown	
G	: Green	
G/W	: Green/White	
O	: Orange	
R	: Red	
W	: White	
W/R	: White/Red	

① C.D.I. unit
② Charge coil
③ Pulser coil
④ Lighting coil
⑤ Engine stop switch
⑥ 2P connector*

⑦ Rectifier regulator*
⑧ Ignition coil
* Except for USA and Canada

Fig. 19 System wiring diagram—9.9hp and 15hp engines with manual start

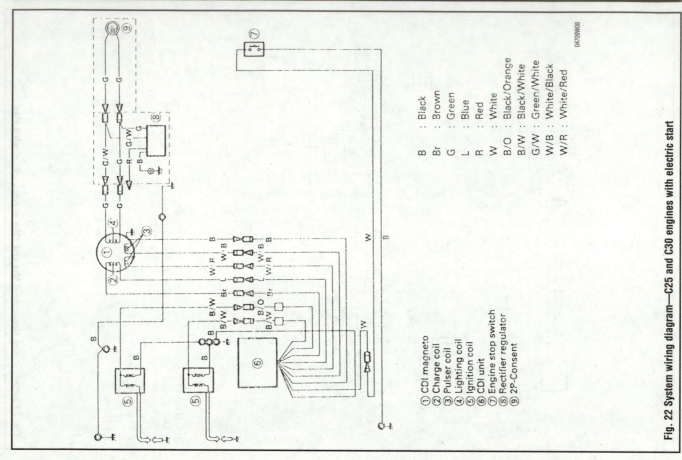

B : Black
Br : Brown
G : Green
L : Blue
R : Red
W : White
B/O : Black/Orange
B/W : Black/White
G/W : Green/White
W/B : White/Black
W/R : White/Red

① CDI magneto
② Charge coil
③ Pulser coil
④ Lighting coil
⑤ Ignition coil
⑥ CDI unit
⑦ Engine stop switch
⑧ Rectifier regulator
⑨ 2P-Consent

Fig. 22 System wiring diagram—C25 and C30 engines with electric start

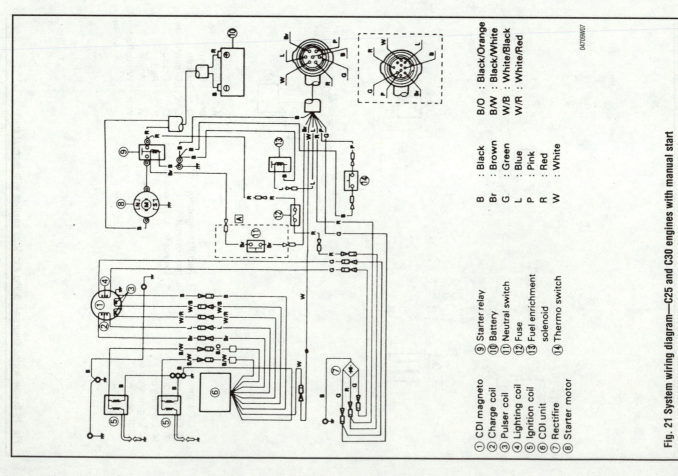

B/O : Black/Orange
B/W : Black/White
W/B : White/Black
W/R : White/Red

B : Black
Br : Brown
G : Green
L : Blue
P : Pink
R : Red
W : White

① CDI magneto
② Charge coil
③ Pulser coil
④ Lighting coil
⑤ Ignition coil
⑥ CDI unit
⑦ Rectifire
⑧ Starter motor

⑨ Starter relay
⑩ Battery
⑪ Neutral switch
⑫ Fuse
⑬ Fuel enrichment solenoid
⑭ Thermo switch

Fig. 21 System wiring diagram—C25 and C30 engines with manual start

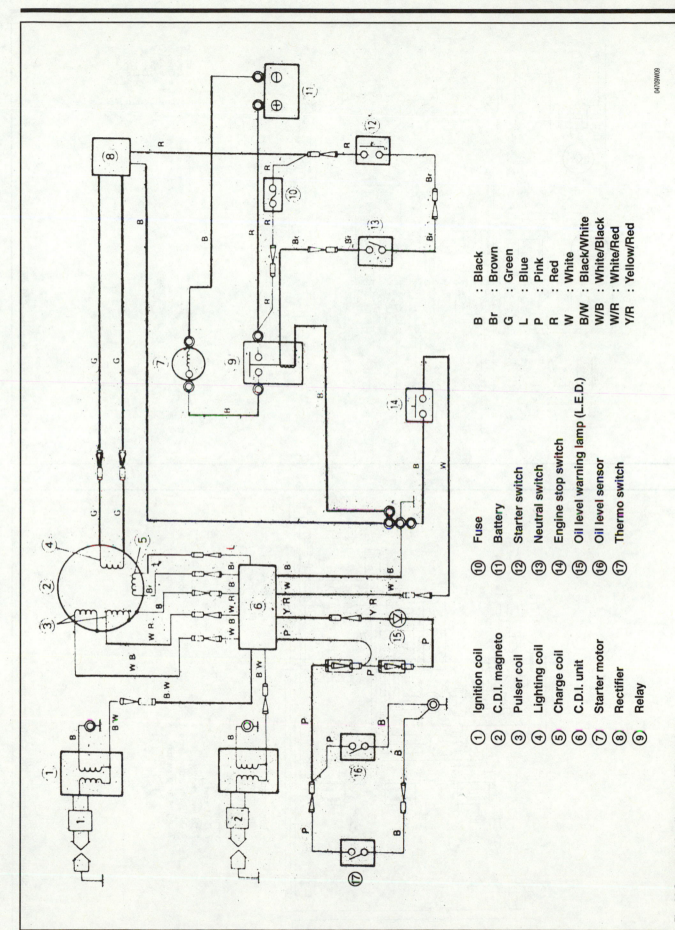

04709W09

Fig. 23 System wiring diagram—25hp engine

B	: Black
Br	: Brown
G	: Green
L	: Blue
P	: Pink
R	: Red
W	: White
B/W	: Black/White
W/B	: White/Black
W/R	: White/Red
Y/R	: Yellow/Red

①	Ignition coil
②	C.D.I. magneto
③	Pulser coil
④	Lighting coil
⑤	Charge coil
⑥	C.D.I. unit
⑦	Starter motor
⑧	Rectifier
⑨	Relay
⑩	Fuse
⑪	Battery
⑫	Starter switch
⑬	Neutral switch
⑭	Engine stop switch
⑮	Oil level warning lamp (L.E.D.)
⑯	Oil level sensor
⑰	Thermo switch

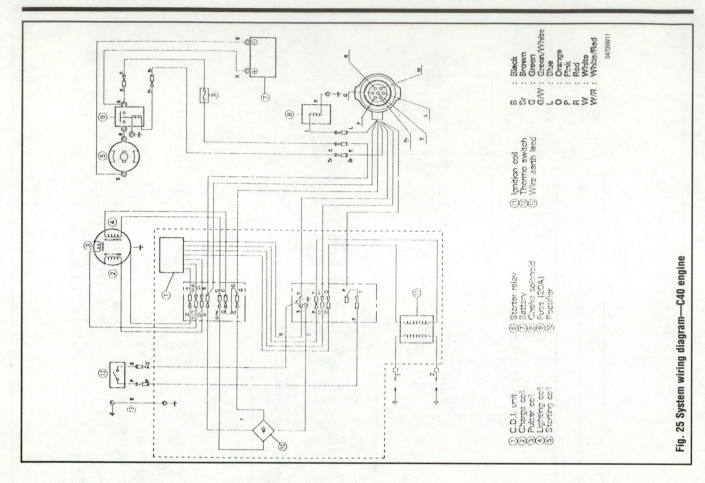

Fig. 25 System wiring diagram—C40 engine

① C.D.I. unit
② Charge coil
③ Pulser coil
④ Lighting coil
⑤ Starting coil

⑥ Starter relay
⑦ Battery
⑧ Choke solenoid
⑨ Fuse (20A)
⑩ Rectifier

⑪ Ignition coil
⑫ Thermo switch
⑬ Wire earth lead

B : Black
Br : Brown
G : Green
G/W : Green/White
L : Blue
O : Orange
P : Pink
R : Red
W : White
W/R : White/Red

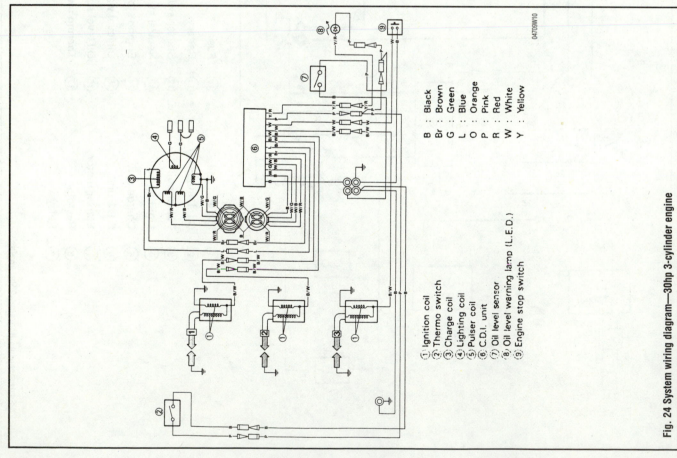

Fig. 24 System wiring diagram—30hp 3-cylinder engine

① Ignition coil
② Thermo switch
③ Charge coil
④ Lighting coil
⑤ Pulser coil
⑥ C.D.I. unit
⑦ Oil level sensor
⑧ Oil level warning lamp (L.E.D.)
⑨ Engine stop switch

B : Black
Br : Brown
G : Green
L : Blue
O : Orange
P : Pink
R : Red
W : White
Y : Yellow

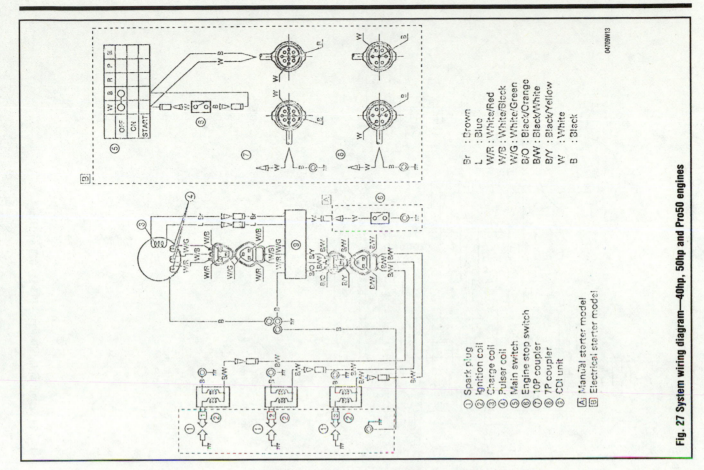

04709W13

Br : Brown
L : Blue
W/R : White/Red
W/B : White/Black
W/G : White/Green
B/O : Black/Orange
B/W : Black/White
B/Y : Black/Yellow
W : White
B : Black

① Spark plug
② Ignition coil
③ Charge coil
④ Pulser coil
⑤ Main switch
⑥ Engine stop switch
⑦ 10P coupler
⑧ 7P coupler
⑨ CDI unit
Ⓐ Manual starter model
Ⓑ Electrical starter model

Fig. 27 System wiring diagram—40hp, 50hp and Pro50 engines

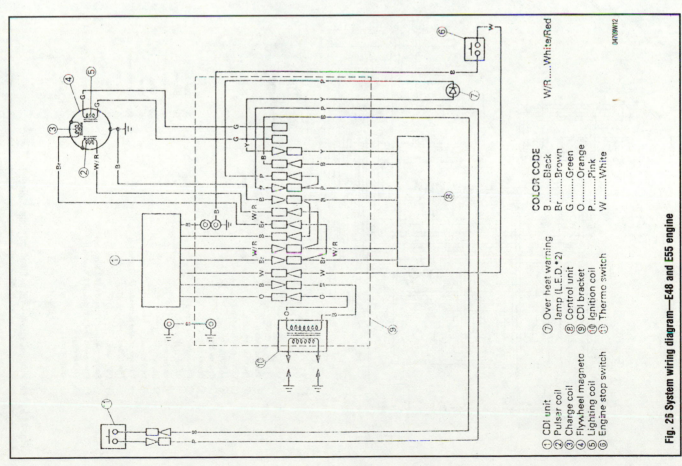

04709W12

W/R .....White/Red

COLOR CODE
B ......Black
Br......Brown
G ....Green
O ......Orange
P ....Pink
W ......White

① CDI unit
② Pulsar coil
③ Charge coil
④ Flywheel magneto
⑤ Lighting coil
⑥ Engine stop switch
⑦ Over heat warning lamp (L.E.D. *2)
⑧ Control unit
⑨ CDI bracket
⑩ Ignition coil
⑪ Thermo switch

Fig. 26 System wiring diagram—E48 and E55 engine

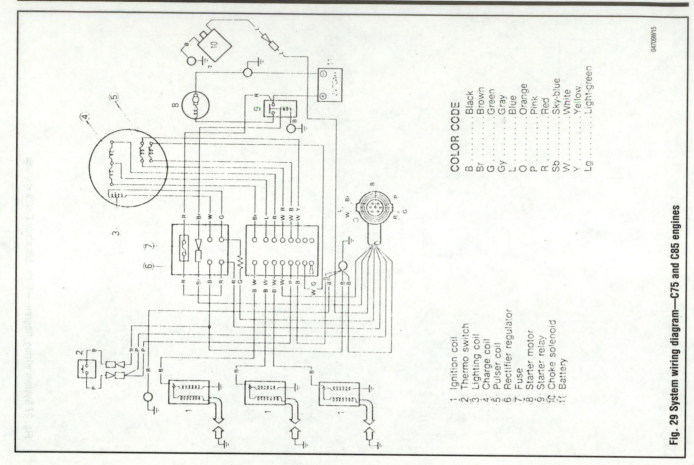

COLOR CODE

B .... Black
Br .... Brown
G .... Green
Gy .... Gray
L .... Blue
O .... Orange
P .... Pink
R .... Red
Sb .... Sky-blue
W .... White
Y .... Yellow
Lg .... Light-green

① Ignition coil
② Thermo switch
③ Lighting coil
④ Charge coil
⑤ Pulser coil
⑥ Rectifier regulator
⑦ Fuse
⑧ Starter motor
⑨ Starter relay
⑩ Choke solenoid
⑪ Battery

Fig. 29 System wiring diagram—C75 and C85 engines

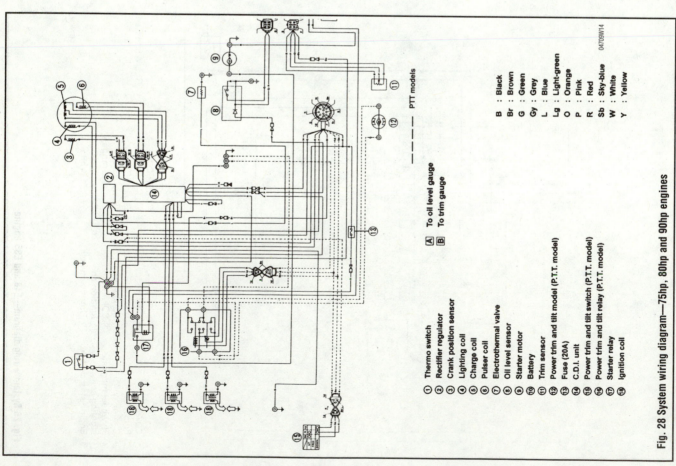

① Thermo switch
② Rectifier regulator
③ Crank position sensor
④ Lighting coil
⑤ Charge coil
⑥ Pulser coil
⑦ Electrothermal valve
⑧ Oil level sensor
⑨ Starter motor
⑩ Battery
⑪ Trim sensor
⑫ Power trim and tilt model (P.T.T. model)
⑬ Fuse (20A)
⑭ C.D.I. unit
⑮ Power trim and tilt switch (P.T.T. model)
⑯ Power trim and tilt relay (P.T.T. model)
⑰ Starter relay
⑱ Ignition coil

Ⓐ To oil level gauge
Ⓑ To trim gauge

- - - - - PTT models

B : Black
Br : Brown
G : Green
Gy : Grey
L : Blue
Lg : Light-green
O : Orange
P : Pink
R : Red
Sb : Sky-blue
W : White
Y : Yellow

Fig. 28 System wiring diagram—75hp, 80hp and 90hp engines

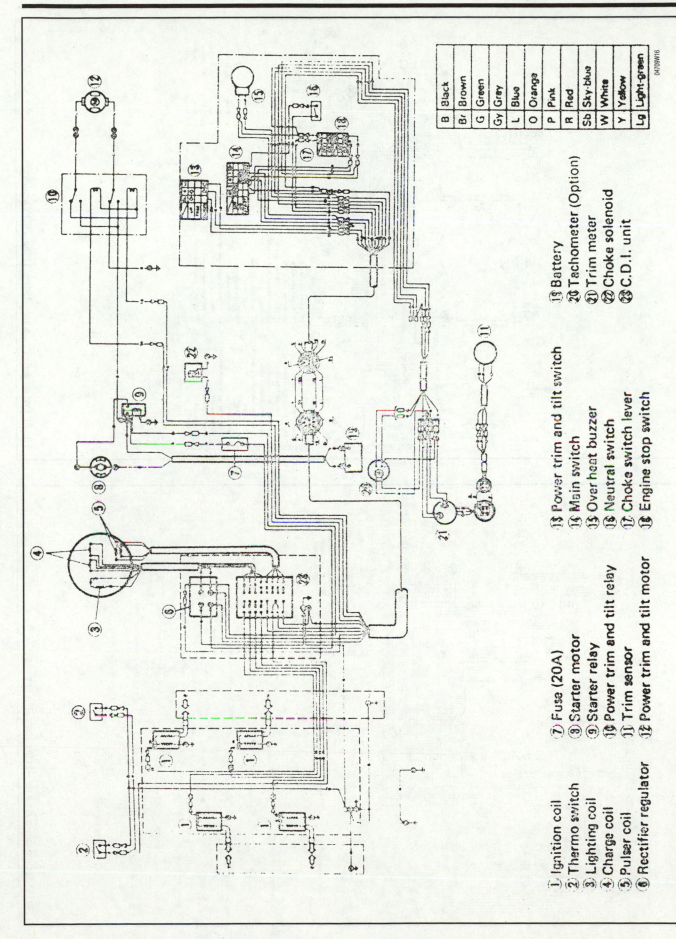

B	Black
Br	Brown
G	Green
Gy	Grey
L	Blue
O	Orange
P	Pink
R	Red
Sb	Sky-blue
W	White
Y	Yellow
Lg	Light-green

04709W16

① Ignition coil
② Thermo switch
③ Lighting coil
④ Charge coil
⑤ Pulser coil
⑥ Rectifier regulator
⑦ Fuse (20A)
⑧ Starter motor
⑨ Starter relay
⑩ Power trim and tilt relay
⑪ Trim sensor
⑫ Power trim and tilt motor
⑬ Power trim and tilt switch
⑭ Main switch
⑮ Over heat buzzer
⑯ Neutral switch
⑰ Choke switch lever
⑱ Engine stop switch
⑲ Battery
⑳ Tachometer (Option)
㉑ Trim meter
㉒ Choke solenoid
㉓ C.D.I. unit

Fig. 30 System wiring diagram—C115 engine

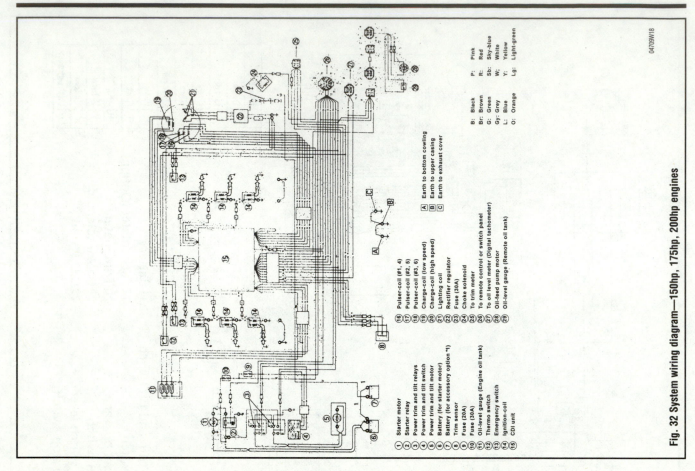

Fig. 32 System wiring diagram—150hp, 175hp, 200hp engines

B : Black	P : Pink	
Br : Brown	R : Red	
G : Green	Sb : Sky-blue	
Gy : Grey	W : White	
L : Blue	Y : Yellow	
O : Orange	Lg : Light-green	

- ① Starter motor
- ② Starter relay
- ③ Power trim and tilt relays
- ④ Power trim and tilt switch
- ⑤ Power trim and tilt motor
- ⑥ Battery (for starter motor)
- ⑦ Battery (for accessory option *)
- ⑧ Trim sensor
- ⑨ Fuse (20A)
- ⑩ Fuse (30A)
- ⑪ Oil-level gauge (Engine oil tank)
- ⑫ Thermo switch
- ⑬ Emergency switch
- ⑭ Ignition-coil
- ⑮ CDI unit
- ⑯ Pulser-coil (#1, 4)
- ⑰ Pulser-coil (#2, 5)
- ⑱ Pulser-coil (#3, 6)
- ⑲ Charge-coil (low speed)
- ⑳ Charge-coil (high speed)
- ㉑ Lighting coil
- ㉒ Rectifier regulator
- ㉓ Choke solenoid
- ㉔ To trim meter
- ㉕ To trim meter
- ㉖ To remote control or switch panel
- ㉗ To oil level meter (Digital tachometer)
- ㉘ Oil-feed pump motor
- ㉙ Oil-level gauge (Remote oil tank)

- Ⓐ Earth to bottom cowling
- Ⓑ Earth to upper casing
- Ⓒ Earth to exhaust cover

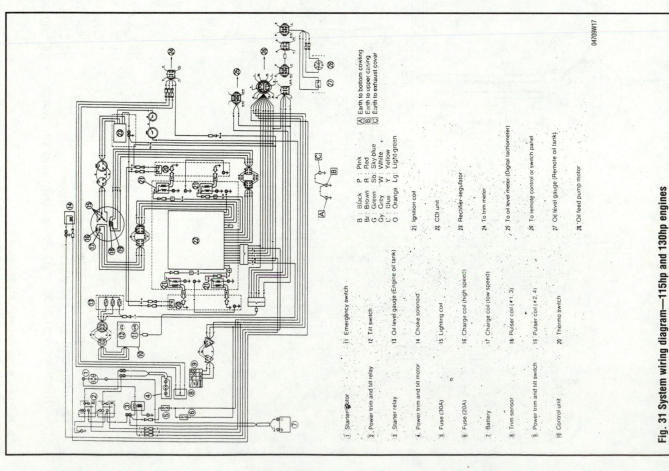

Fig. 31 System wiring diagram—115hp and 130hp engines

B : Black	P : Pink	
Br : Brown	R : Red	
G : Green	Sb : Sky-blue	
Gy : Grey	W : White	
L : Blue	Y : Yellow	
O : Orange	Lg : Light-green	

- ① Starter motor
- ② Power trim and tilt relay
- ③ Starter relay
- ④ Power trim and tilt motor
- ⑤ Fuse (30A)
- ⑥ Fuse (20A)
- ⑦ Battery
- ⑧ Trim sensor
- ⑨ Power trim and tilt switch
- ⑩ Control unit
- ⑪ Emergency switch
- ⑫ Tilt switch
- ⑬ Oil level gauge (Engine oil tank)
- ⑭ Choke solenoid
- ⑮ Lighting coil
- ⑯ Charge coil (high speed)
- ⑰ Charge coil (low speed)
- ⑱ Pulser coil (#1, 3)
- ⑲ Pulser coil (#2, 4)
- ⑳ Thermo switch
- ㉑ Ignition coil
- ㉒ CDI unit
- ㉓ Rectifier-regulator
- ㉔ To trim meter
- ㉕ To oil level meter (Digital tachometer)
- ㉖ To remote control or switch panel
- ㉗ Oil level gauge (Remote oil tank)
- ㉘ Oil feed pump motor

- Ⓐ Earth to bottom cowling
- Ⓑ Earth to upper casing
- Ⓒ Earth to exhaust cover

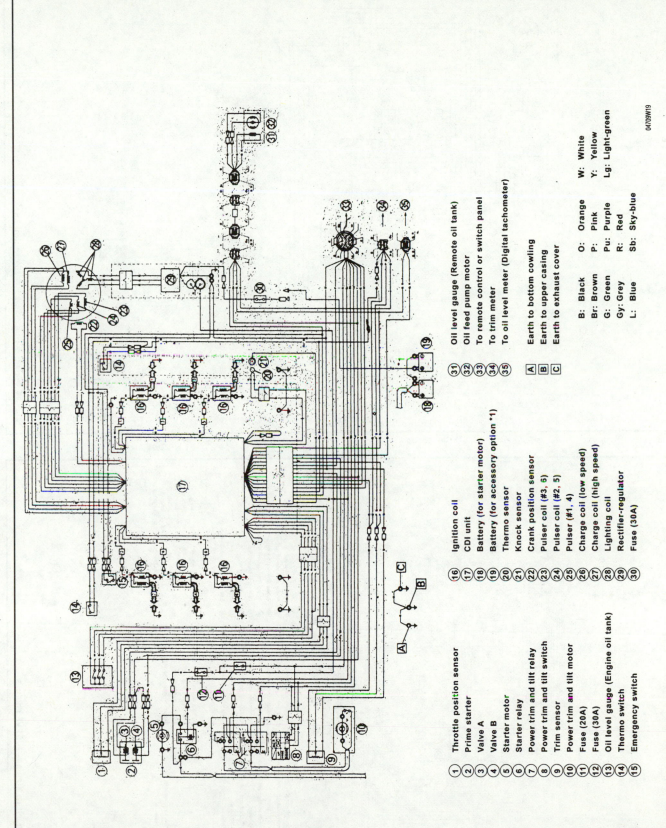

① Throttle position sensor
② Prime starter
③ Valve A
④ Valve B
⑤ Starter motor
⑥ Starter relay
⑦ Power trim and tilt relay
⑧ Power trim and tilt switch
⑨ Trim sensor
⑩ Power trim and tilt motor
⑪ Fuse (20A)
⑫ Fuse (30A)
⑬ Oil level gauge (Engine oil tank)
⑭ Thermo switch
⑮ Emergency switch

⑯ Ignition coil
⑰ CDI unit
⑱ Battery (for starter motor)
⑲ Battery (for accessory option *1)
⑳ Thermo sensor
㉑ Knock sensor
㉒ Crank position sensor
㉓ Pulser coil (#3, 6)
㉔ Pulser coil (#2, 5)
㉕ Pulser (#1, 4)
㉖ Charge coil (low speed)
㉗ Charge coil (high speed)
㉘ Lighting coil
㉙ Rectifier-regulator
㉚ Fuse (30A)

㉛ Oil level gauge (Remote oil tank)
㉜ Oil feed pump motor
㉝ To remote control or switch panel
㉞ To trim meter
㉟ To oil level meter (Digital tachometer)

Ⓐ Earth to bottom cowling
Ⓑ Earth to upper casing
Ⓒ Earth to exhaust cover

B: Black	O: Orange	W: White
Br: Brown	P: Pink	Y: Yellow
G: Green	Pu: Purple	Lg: Light-green
Gy: Grey	R: Red	
L: Blue	Sb: Sky-blue	

04709W19

Fig. 33 System wiring diagram—90° V6 engines

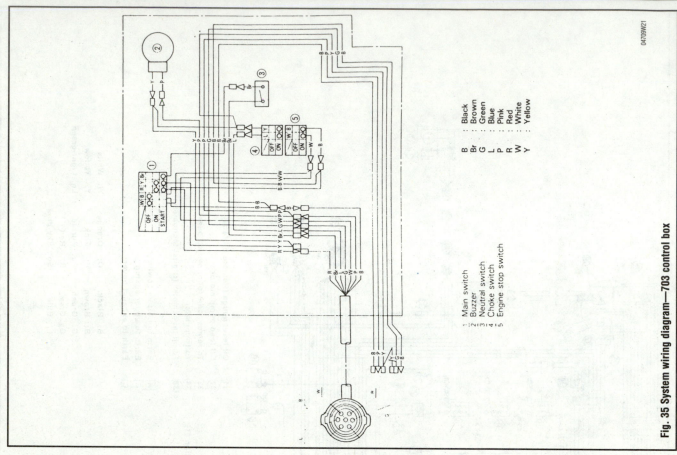

04709W21

Fig. 35 System wiring diagram—703 control box

B : Black
Br : Brown
G : Green
L : Blue
P : Pink
R : Red
W : White
Y : Yellow

1 Main switch
2 Buzzer
3 Neutral switch
4 Choke switch
5 Engine stop switch

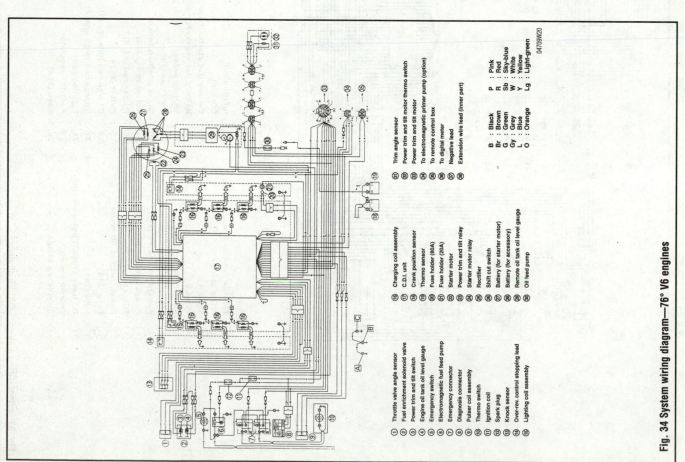

04709W20

Fig. 34 System wiring diagram—76° V6 engines

1 Throttle valve angle sensor
2 Fuel enrichment solenoid valve
3 Power trim and tilt switch
4 Engine oil tank oil level gauge
5 Emergency switch
6 Electromagnetic fuel feed pump
7 Emergency connector
8 Diagnosis connector
9 Pulser coil assembly
10 Thermo switch
11 Ignition coil
12 Spark plug
13 Knock sensor
14 Over-rev. control stopping lead
15 Lighting coil assembly
16 Charging coil assembly
17 C.D.I. unit
18 Crank position sensor
19 Thermo sensor
20 Fuse holder (80A)
21 Fuse holder (20A)
22 Starter motor
23 Power trim and tilt relay
24 Starter motor relay
25 Rectifier
26 Shift cut switch
27 Battery (for starter motor)
28 Battery (for accessory)
29 Remote oil tank oil level gauge
30 Oil feed pump
51 Trim angle sensor
52 Power trim and tilt motor thermo switch
53 Power trim and tilt motor
54 To electromagnetic primer pump (option)
55 To remote control box
56 To digital meter
57 Negative lead
58 Extension wire lead (inner part)

B : Black
Br : Brown
G : Green
Gy : Grey
L : Blue
O : Orange
P : Pink
R : Red
Sb : Sky-blue
W : White
Y : Yellow
Lg : Light-green

LOWER UNIT 10-2
GENERAL INFORMATION 10-2
SHIFTING PRINCIPLES 10-2
   STANDARD ROTATING UNIT 10-2
   COUNTERROTATING UNIT 10-3
EXHAUST GASES 10-4
TROUBLESHOOTING 10-4
LOWER UNIT SERVICE 10-5
PROPELLER 10-5
   REMOVAL 10-5
   INSTALLATION 10-6
LOWER UNIT—NO REVERSE GEAR 10-7
   REMOVAL 10-7
   INSTALLATION 10-8
LOWER UNIT—WITH REVERSE
  GEAR 10-9
   REMOVAL 10-9
   INSTALLATION 10-10
LOWER UNIT OVERHAUL 10-11
1–2 CYLINDER POWERHEAD WITHOUT
  REVERSE GEAR 10-11
   DISASSEMBLY 10-11
   CLEANING AND INSPECTING 10-12
   ASSEMBLY 10-13
1–2 CYLINDER POWERHEAD WITH
  REVERSE GEAR 10-16
   DISASSEMBLY 10-16
   CLEANING AND INSPECTING 10-22
   ASSEMBLY 10-23
EXCEPT 1–2 CYLINDER POWERHEAD
  10-33
   DISASSEMBLY 10-33
   CLEANING AND INSPECTING 10-40
   ASSEMBLY 10-43
   CLUTCH DOG 10-47
LOWER UNIT SERVICE JET DRIVE 10-54
   DESCRIPTION AND
    OPERATION 10-54
   MODEL IDENTIFICATION AND SERIAL
    NUMBERS 10-54
   REMOVAL & DISASSEMBLY 10-55
   CLEANING AND INSPECTING 10-56
   ASSEMBLING 10-57
JET DRIVE ADJUSTMENTS 10-61
   ADJUSTMENT 10-61
   TRIM ADJUSTMENT 10-62

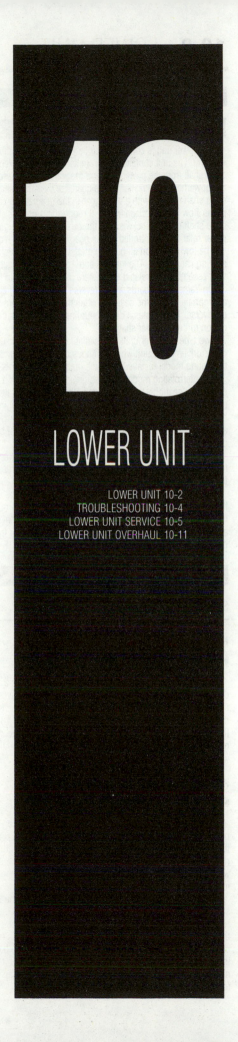

10

LOWER UNIT

LOWER UNIT 10-2
TROUBLESHOOTING 10-4
LOWER UNIT SERVICE 10-5
LOWER UNIT OVERHAUL 10-11

LOWER UNIT

General Information

The lower unit is considered to be the part of the outboard below the exhaust housing. The unit contains the propeller shaft, the driven and pinion gears, the drive shaft from the powerhead and the water pump. Torque is transferred from the powerhead's crankshaft to the gearcase by a driveshaft. A pinion gear on the drive shaft meshes with a drive gear in the gearcase to change the vertical power flow into a horizontal flow through the propeller shaft. The power head drive shaft rotates clockwise continuously when the engine is running, but propeller rotation is controlled by the gear train shifting mechanism.

The lower units on all but one model, the 2 hp model, are equipped with shifting capabilities. The forward and reverse gears together with the clutch, shift assembly and related linkage are all housed within the lower unit.

On Yamaha outboards with a reverse gear, a sliding clutch engages the appropriate gear in the gearcase when the shift mechanism is placed in forward or reverse. This creates a direct coupling that transfers the power flow from the pinion to the propeller shaft.

Two types of lower units are available. The first type is a conventional propeller driven lower unit which includes both the standard model and the counterrotating model installed on some outboards.

Counterrotating models are designated with an "L" in front of the horsepower model designation. On these models, the propeller rotates in the opposite direction than on regular models and is used when dual engines are mounted in the boat to equalize the propeller's directional churning force on the water. This allows the operator to maintain a true course instead of being pulled off toward one side while underway.

The second type is a jet drive propulsion system. Water is drawn in from the forward edge of the lower unit and forced out under pressure to propel the boat forward.

The lower unit can be removed without removing the entire outboard from the boat. Each part of this section is presented with complete detailed instructions for removal, disassembly, cleaning and inspecting, assembling, adjusting and installation of only one unit. Each part is complete from removal of the first item to final test operation.

Shifting Principles

STANDARD ROTATING UNIT

Non-Reverse Type

♦ See Figure 1

A non-reversing type lower unit is used only on the 2 hp model. It is a direct drive unit—the pinion gear on the lower end of the driveshaft is in constant mesh with the forward gear. Reverse action of the propeller is accomplished by the operator swinging the engine with the tiller handle 180° and holding it in this position while the boat moves sternward. When the operator is ready to move forward again, they simply swing the tiller handle back to the normal forward position.

Reverse Type

♦ See Figures 2, 3, 4 and 5

The standard lower unit is equipped with a clutch dog permitting operation in neutral, forward and reverse. When the unit is shifted from neutral to reverse, the shift rod is rotated. This action moves the plunger and clutch dog toward the reverse gear. When the unit is shifted from reverse to neutral and then to forward gear, the rotation of the shift rod is reversed and the clutch dog is moved toward the forward gear.

The shift mechanism design consists of a cam on the shift rod, a shifter, a shift slide, a compression spring and six steel balls: two small, two medium and two large. The shift slide is a hollow tube, closed at one end. The closed end of this tube is necked and the head or knob of the tube fits into the shifter. The shifter has a vertical hole all the way through it. The shift rod passes through this hole in the shifter. The cam in the shift rod engages the shifter at the side notch, so any rotating movement in the shift rod will translate to a back and forth movement in the shifter and the shift slide.

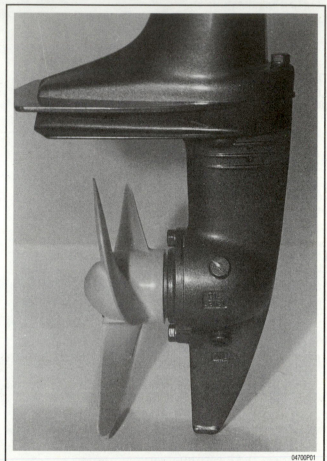

04700P01

Fig. 1 Non reversing lower unit used on the 2 hp powerhead

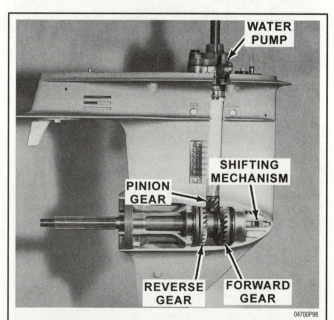

04700P98

Fig. 2 Cutaway view of a lower unit with major parts, including the shift mechanism and water pump, identified. Note how the forward, reverse and pinion gears are all bevel cut

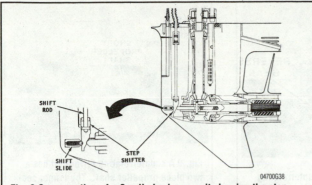

Fig. 3 Cross section of a 3-cylinder lower unit showing the step shifter

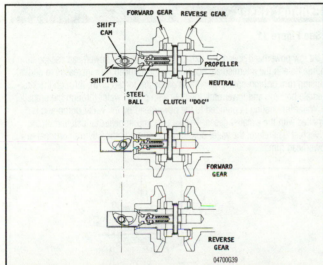

Fig. 4 Cross section of a 3-cylinder lower unit shift mechanism. The dog is shown in the neutral, forward and reverse positions

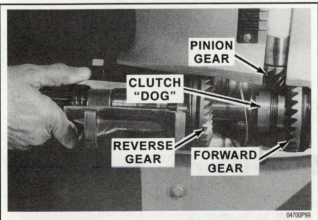

Fig. 5 Cut away view of a standard rotation lower unit with major parts identified

The shift slide rests inside the propeller shaft. If the shift slide were to be inserted into the propeller shaft without any of the six balls, it would be a snug fit. But, there are grooves in the internal recess of the propeller shaft and there are holes drilled into the shift slide at strategic locations.

The six balls inside the shift slide are held under tension by the compression spring and arranged to protrude from the holes drilled in the slide. As the shift slide moves back and forth within the propeller shaft, four of the balls seat themselves in the grooves of the propeller shaft, to hold a certain gear position.

In the neutral position, the cam is centered in the shifter and the two medium steel balls are settled in internal grooves in the recess of the propeller shaft.

When the lower unit is shifted into forward gear, the shift cam rotates in a counterclockwise direction and pulls on the shifter and shift slide. Because the shifter and shift slide are connected, they are moved out of the propeller shaft—moving the clutch dog toward the forward gear. The steel balls are forced out of their grooves and apply a torsional force on the shift slide. The shift into forward gear is complete.

When the lower unit is shifted into reverse gear, the unit first moves into the neutral position. The shift cam rotates in a clockwise direction. The cam pushes the shifter and the shift slide in toward the propeller shaft. The clutch dog moves toward the reverse gear and two steel balls are moved past their detent groove and on to the other side. This action applies a torsional force on the shift slide. The shift movement to reverse gear is complete.

The pinion gear on the lower end of the driveshaft is in constant mesh with both the forward and reverse gear. These three gears constantly rotate anytime the powerhead is operating.

A sliding clutch dog is mounted on the propeller shaft. A shifting motion at the control box will translate into a back and forth motion at the clutch dog via a series of shift mechanism components. When the clutch dog is moved forward, it engages with the forward gear. Because the clutch is secured to the propeller shaft with a pin, the shaft rotates at the same speed as the clutch. The propeller is thereby rotated to move the boat forward.

When the clutch dog is moved aft, the clutch engages only the reverse gear. The propeller shaft and the propeller are thus moved in the opposite direction to move the boat sternward.

When the clutch dog is in the neutral position, neither the forward nor reverse gear is engaged with the clutch and the propeller shaft does not rotate.

From this explanation, an understanding of wear characteristics can be appreciated. The pinion gear and the clutch dog receive the most wear, followed by the forward gear, with the reverse gear receiving the least wear. All three gears, the forward, reverse and pinion, are spiral bevel type gears.

A mixture of ball bearings, tapered roller bearings and caged or loose needle bearings is used in each unit. The type bearing used is clearly indicated in the procedures.

COUNTERROTATING UNIT

▶ **See Figures 6, 7, 8, 9 and 10**

As mentioned earlier in this section a single design shifting mechanism is employed on both the standard and counterrotating units, with the counterrotating shift mechanism being a mirror image of the standard shift mechanism.

The main physical differences lie in the shifting mechanism (mirror image) and the propeller shaft. The counterrotating unit has a two piece propeller shaft. Another difference regards nomenclature: what would be the forward gear on a standard unit becomes the reverse gear on a counterrotating unit and what would normally be the reverse gear on a standard unit, becomes the forward gear on a counterrotating unit. The pinion gear remains the same and driveshaft rotation remains the same as on a standard lower unit.

Mirror image shifting mechanisms produce counter rotation of the propeller shaft. This type lower unit consists of the same major identical components as the standard unit (with the exception of the two piece propeller shaft).

Fig. 6 Cutaway view of a counterrotating lower unit with the clutch dog in the neutral position

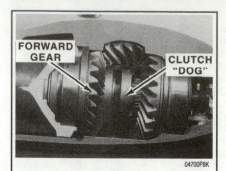

Fig. 7 Cutaway view of a counterrotating lower unit with the clutch dog in the forward position

Fig. 8 Cutaway view of a counterrotating lower unit with the clutch dog in the reverse position

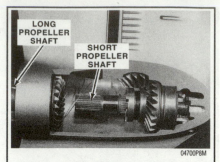

Fig. 9 A counterrotating lower unit has a two piece propeller shaft. The longer section is attached to the propeller, the shorter section is internal

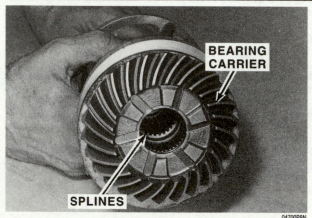

Fig. 10 Bearing carrier of a counterrotating lower unit with the internal splines for the short section of the propeller shaft clearly visible

On a standard lower unit, the cam on the shift shaft is located on the starboard side of the shifter. Therefore, when the rod is rotated counterclockwise, the clutch dog is pulled forward and the forward gear is engaged.

On a counterrotating lower unit, the cam on the shift rod is located on the port side of the shifter. Therefore, when the rod is rotated counterclockwise, the clutch dog is pushed back and the gear in the aft end of the housing (which normally is the reverse gear) is engaged. In this manner, the rotation of the propeller shaft is reversed. The same logic applies to the selection of reverse gear.

→ Counterrotational shifting is accomplished without modification to the shift cable at the shift box. The normal setup is essential for correct shifting. The only special equipment the counterrotating unit requires is the installation of a left-hand propeller.

TROUBLESHOOTING

▶ See accompanying illustrations

Troubleshooting must be done before the unit is removed from the powerhead to permit isolating the problem to one area. Always attempt to proceed with troubleshooting in an orderly manner. The shot-in the-dark approach will only result in wasted time, incorrect diagnosis, frustration and unnecessary replacement of parts.

Exhaust Gases

▶ See Figure 11

At low powerhead speed, the exhaust gases from the powerhead escape from an idle hole in the intermediate housing. As powerhead rpm increases to normal cruising rpm or high-speed rpm, these gases are forced down through the intermediate housing and lower unit, then out with cycled water through the propeller.

Water for cooling is pumped to the powerhead by the water pump and is expelled with the exhaust gases. The water pump impeller is installed on the driveshaft. Therefore, the water output of the pump is directly proportional to powerhead rpm.

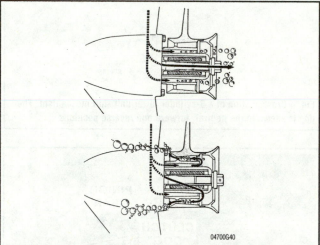

Fig. 11 Cross section of the lower unit showing route of the exhaust gases with the unit in forward (top) and reverse (bottom) gears

The following procedures are presented in a logical sequence with the most prevalent, easiest and less costly items to be checked listed first.

Check the propeller and the rubber hub. See if the hub is shredded. If the propeller has been subjected to many strikes against underwater objects, it could slip on its hub. If the hub appears to be damaged, replace it with a new hub. Replacement of the hub must be done by a propeller rebuilding shop equipped with the proper tools and experience for such work.

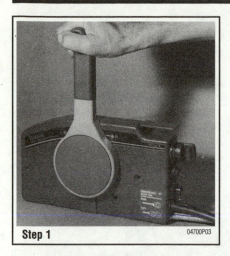

Step 1 04700P03

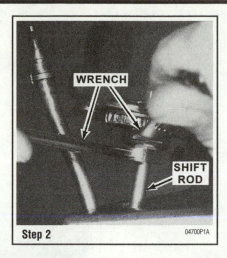

Step 2 04700P1A

Step 3 04700P8Q

1. Verify the ignition switch is **OFF**, to prevent possible personal injury, should the engine start. Shift the unit into reverse gear and at the same time have an assistant turn the propeller shaft to ensure the clutch is fully engaged.

2. If the shift handle is hard to move, the trouble may be in the lower unit shift rod, requiring an adjustment, or in the shift box.

Disconnect the remote control cable at the engine and then remove the remote control shift cable. Operate the shift lever. If shifting is still hard, the problem is in the shift cable or control box.

3. If the shifting feels normal with the remote control cable disconnected, the problem must be in the lower unit. To verify the problem is in the lower unit, have an assistant turn the propeller and at the same time move the shift cable back and forth. Determine if the clutch engages properly.

LOWER UNIT SERVICE

Propeller

REMOVAL

♦ **See accompanying illustrations**

1. Straighten the cotter pin and pull it free of the propeller shaft. Remove the castle nut, washer and outer spacer. Never pry on the edge of the propeller. Any small distortion will affect propeller performance.

2. If the nut is frozen, place a block of wood between one blade of the propeller and the anti-cavitation plate to keep the shaft from turning. Use a socket and breaker bar to loosen the castle nut. Remove the nut, washer, outer spacer and then the propeller and inner spacer.

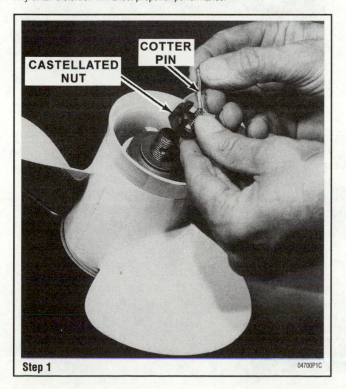

Step 1 04700P1C

Step 2 04700P8S

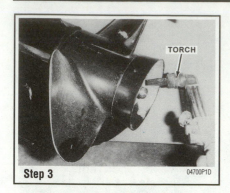

Step 3   04700P1D

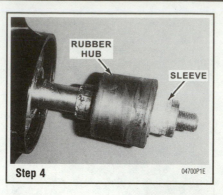

Step 4   04700P1E

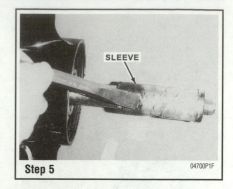

Step 5   04700P1F

3. If the propeller is frozen to the shaft, heat must be applied to the shaft to melt out the rubber inside the hub. Using heat will destroy the hub, but there is no other way. As heat is applied, the rubber will expand and the propeller will actually be blown from the shaft. Therefore, stand clear to avoid personal injury.

4. Use a knife and cut the hub off the inner sleeve.

5. The sleeve can be removed by cutting it with a hacksaw, or it can be removed with a puller. Again, if the sleeve is frozen, it may be necessary to apply heat. Remove the thrust hub from the propeller shaft.

INSTALLATION

▶ **See accompanying illustrations**

➡**An anti-seize compound will prevent the propeller from freezing to the shaft and permit propeller removal, without difficulty, the next time the propeller needs to be pulled.**

Apply Yamalube Grease, or equivalent anti-seize compound, to the propeller shaft.

1. Install the inner spacer onto the propeller shaft

2. Install the propeller.

3. Install the outer spacer, washer and the castle nut. Place a block of wood between one of the propeller blades and the anti-cavitation plate to prevent the propeller from rotating. Tighten the nut to specification, then back off the nut until the cotter pin may be inserted through the nut and the hole in the propeller shaft. Bend the arms of the cotter pin around the nut to secure it in place.

Remove the block of wood. Connect the spark plug wires to the spark plugs. Connect the electrical lead to the battery terminal.

4. The trim tab is held in place by a hidden bolt. Position the trim tab so the helmsperson is able to handle the boat with equal ease to starboard and port at normal cruising speed. If the boat seems to turn more easily to starboard, loosen the mounting bolt and move the trim tab trailing edge to the starboard. Move the trailing edge of the trim tab to the left if the boat tends to turn more easily to port.

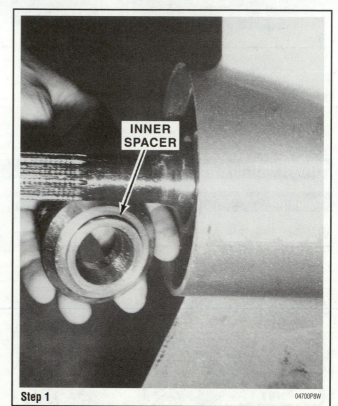

Step 1   04700P8W

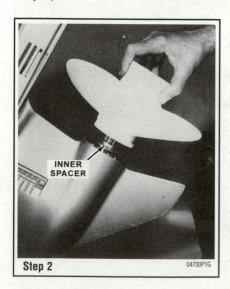

Step 2   04700P1G

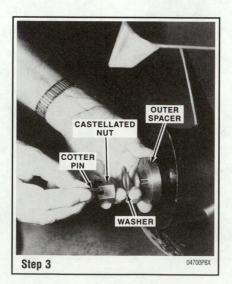

Step 3   04700P8X

Step 4   04700P8Z

Lower Unit—No Reverse Gear

REMOVAL

♦ **See accompanying illustrations**

The following procedures present complete instructions to remove, disassemble, assemble and adjust the lower unit of the 2 hp unit.

➡ **In order to remove the water pump impeller, the driveshaft must be removed from the lower unit. The impeller and pump housing can only be removed from the lower end of the driveshaft. Therefore, the circlip securing the pinion gear to the driveshaft must first be removed. This can only be accomplished by removing the lower unit bearing carrier cap and removing the propeller shaft.**

Before purchasing a lower unit gasket replacement kit, take time to establish the year of manufacture for the unit being serviced. On some units the cap gasket has been replaced with an O-ring.

1. Position a suitable container under the lower unit and then remove the oil plug and the oil level screw. Allow the gear lubricant to drain into the container. As the lubricant drains, catch some with your fingers from time to time and rub it between your thumb and finger to determine if any metal particles are present. If metal is detected in the lubricant, the unit must be completely disassembled,

inspected and the damaged parts replaced. Check the color of the lubricant as it drains. A whitish or creamy color indicates the presence of water in the lubricant. Check the drain pan for signs of water separation from the lubricant. The presence of any water in the gear lubricant is bad news. The unit must be completely disassembled, inspected and the cause of the problem determined and corrected.

After the lubricant has drained, temporarily install both the drain and oil level screws.

2. Straighten the cotter pin and then pull it free of the propeller with a pair of pliers or a cotter pin removal tool. Remove the propeller and then push the shear pin out of the propeller shaft.

3. Remove the two bolts securing the bearing carrier cap.

4. Rotate the cap through 90° and then gently tap the bearing carrier cap to break it free from the lower unit.

5. Remove the cap from the lower unit. Remove and discard the gasket, as required. Remove and discard the O-ring, if equipped.

➡ **Perform the previous step only if the seal has been damaged and is no longer fit for service. Removal of the seal destroys its sealing qualities and it cannot be installed a second time. Therefore, be absolutely sure a new seal is available before removing the old seal in the next step.**

6. Obtain a slide hammer with jaw expander attachment and use it to remove the oil seal from the cap.

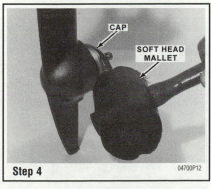

Step 1 — 04700P09

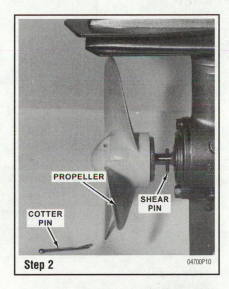

Step 2 — 04700P10

Step 3 — 04700P11

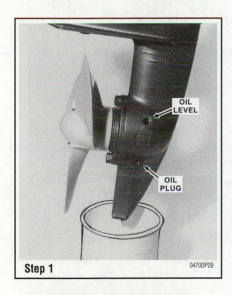

Step 4 — 04700P12

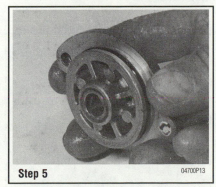

Step 5 — 04700P13

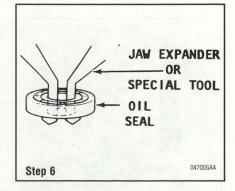

Step 6 — 04700GAA

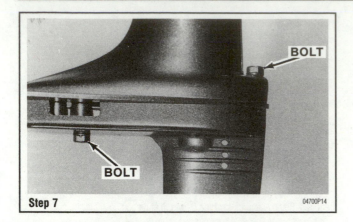

Step 7   04700P14

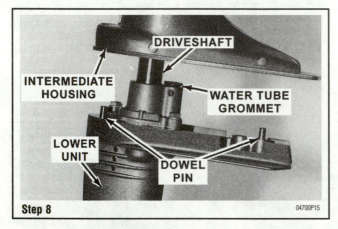

Step 8   04700P15

7. Remove the two attaching bolts securing the lower unit to the intermediate housing.

8. Separate the lower unit from the intermediate housing. Watch for and save the two dowel pins when the two units are separated. The water tube will come out of the grommet and remain with the intermediate housing. The driveshaft will remain with the lower unit.

INSTALLATION

♦ See accompanying illustrations

1. Apply just a dab of Yamalube Grease or an equivalent water resistant lubricant, to the indexing pin on the mating surface of the lower unit. Install the

anti-cavitation plate onto the lower surface of the intermediate housing. Begin to bring the intermediate housing and the lower gear housing together. As the two units come closer, rotate the propeller shaft slightly to index the upper end of the lower driveshaft tube with the upper rectangular driveshaft. At the same time, feed the water tube into the water tube seal. Push the lower gear housing and the intermediate housing together. The pin on the upper surface of the lower unit will index with a matching hole in the lower surface of the anti-cavitation plate.

2. Apply Loctite® to the threads of the two bolts used to secure the lower unit to the intermediate housing. Install and tighten the two bolts to a torque value of 5.8 ft. lbs. (8Nm).

Apply Yamaha All Purpose Grease, or equivalent anti-seize compound to the propeller shaft.

➡**The compound will prevent the propeller from freezing to the shaft and permit the propeller to be removed, without difficulty, the next time removal is required.**

3. Install a new shear pin through the propeller shaft. Guide the propeller onto the pin. Insert a new cotter pin into the hole and bend the ends of the cotter pin in opposite directions.

4. Remove the oil level plug and the oil plug. Fill the lower unit with Yamalube gearcase lubricant until the lubricant flows from the top hole. Install both plugs and clean any excess fluid from the lower unit.

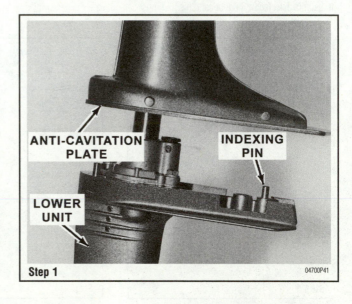

Step 1   04700P41

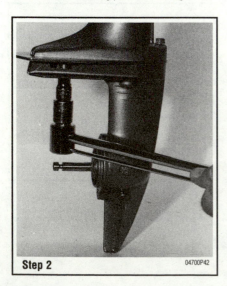

Step 2   04700P42

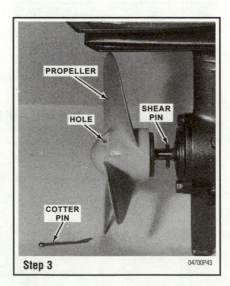

Step 3   04700P43

Step 4   04700P44

Lower Unit—With Reverse Gear

REMOVAL

♦ **See accompanying illustrations**

The following procedures present complete instructions to remove, disassemble, assemble and adjust the lower unit. When the standard and counterrotating units differ, special instructions are given for each unit.

Because so many different models are covered in this manual, it would not be feasible to provide an illustration of each and every unit. Therefore, the accompanying illustrations are of a typical unit. The unit being serviced may differ slightly in appearance due to engineering or cosmetic changes but the procedures are valid. If a difference should occur, the models affected will be clearly identified.

1. Mark the position of the trim tab, as an aid to installing it back in its original location.

2. Remove the plastic cap above the trim tab and then using the correct size socket and a long extension, remove the bolt and the trim tab.

3. Position a suitable container under the lower unit and then remove the oil screw and the oil level screw.

4. Allow the gear lubricant to drain into the container. As the lubricant drains, catch some with your fingers from time to time and rub it between your thumb and finger to determine if any metal particles are present. If metal is detected in the lubricant, the unit must be completely disassembled, inspected and the damaged parts replaced.

Check the color of the lubricant as it drains. A whitish or creamy color indicates the presence of water in the lubricant. Check the drain pan for signs of water separation from the lubricant. The presence of any water in the gear lubricant is bad news. The unit must be completely disassembled, inspected, the cause of the problem determined and then corrected.

After the lubricant has drained, temporarily install both the drain and oil level screws.

➡ **On counterrotating models, the first few times lower unit lubricant is drained, a discoloration may be noticed. This condition is quite normal and is no cause for alarm unless accompanied by the presence of metal chips. The discoloration is due to the use of molybdenum-disulfide assembly grease at the factory.**

On 4 hp and 5 hp models, straighten the cotter pin and then pull it free of the propeller with a pair of pliers or a cotter pin removal tool. Remove the propeller and then push the shear pin out of the propeller shaft.

5. Straighten the cotter pin and then pull it free of the castle nut with a pair of pliers or a cotter pin removal tool. Remove the castle propeller nut by first placing a block of wood between one of the propeller blades and the anti-cavitation plate to prevent the propeller from rotating and then remove the nut. Remove the washer and the outer spacer. Remove the outer thrust hub from the propeller shaft. If the thrust hub is stubborn and refuses to budge, use two padded pry bars on opposite sides of the hub and work the hub loose. Take care not to damage the lower unit.

Remove the propeller. All models have a spacer between the bearing carrier and the propeller. Slide this spacer free of the propeller shaft.

Remove the inner thrust hub. If this hub is also stubborn, use padded pry bars and work the hub loose. Again, take care not to damage the lower unit.

Remove the large grommet in the intermediate housing.

Shift the lower unit into reverse gear. If shifting is difficult, rotate the flywheel counterclockwise as an aid in shifting.

Step 1   04700P8Z

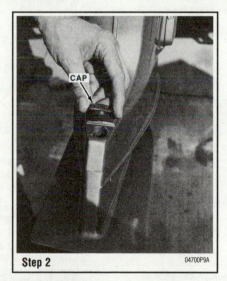

Step 2   04700P9A

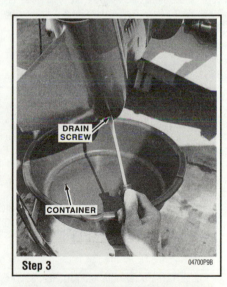

Step 3   04700P9B

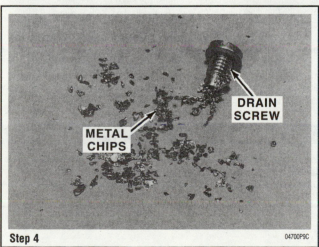

Step 4   04700P9C

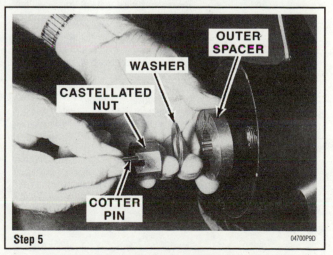

Step 5   04700P9D

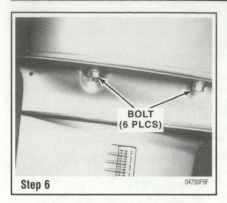

BOLT
(6 PLCS)

Step 6   04700P9F

BOLT

TRIM TAB
REMOVED

Step 7   04700P9G

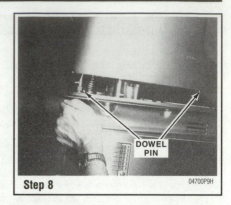

DOWEL
PIN

Step 8   04700P9H

Snip the band retaining the pilot tube to the swivel bracket and gently pull the two ends of the tube apart, at their connector.

As required, loosen but do not remove the shift rod locknut

Separate the lower and upper shift rod by rotating the shift rod connecting rod joint nut upward.

Tilt and lock the outboard unit in the raised position.

➡**Check to be sure the lower unit is in neutral gear.**

6. Remove the external bolts securing the lower unit to the intermediate housing.

7. One bolt securing the lower unit to the intermediate housing is located under the trim tab.

8 Separate the lower unit from the intermediate housing. Watch for and save the two dowel pins when the two units are separated. The water tube will come out of the grommet and remain with the intermediate housing. The driveshaft will remain with the lower unit.

The upper and lower driveshafts will automatically disengage as the unit separates.

INSTALLATION

1. Apply a dab of Yamalube Grease, or equivalent water resistant lubricant to the splines at the upper end of the driveshaft.

➡**An excessive amount of lubricant on top of the driveshaft to crankshaft splines will be trapped in the clearance space. This trapped lubricant will not allow the driveshaft to fully engage with the crankshaft.**

Apply some of the same lubricant to the end of the water tube in the intermediate housing.

Apply a dab of Yamalube Grease, or equivalent water resistant lubricant, to the indexing pin on the mating surface of the lower unit. Check to see if the lower unit is in neutral gear position. Then push the shift lever on the powerhead into the neutral gear position.

Begin to bring the intermediate housing and lower gear housing together.

➡**The next step takes time and patience. Success will probably not be achieved on the first attempt. Three items must mate at the same time before the lower unit can be seated against the intermediate housing.**

• The top of the driveshaft on the lower unit indexes with the lower end of the crankshaft.

• The water tube in the intermediate housing slides into the grommet on the water pump housing.

• The top splines of the lower shift rod in the lower unit slide into the internal splines of the upper shift rod in the intermediate housing.

2. As the two units come closer, rotate the propeller shaft slightly to index the upper end of the lower driveshaft tube with the crankshaft. At the same time, feed the water tube into the water tube grommet and feed the lower shift rod into the upper shift rod.

Push the lower unit housing and the intermediate housing together. The pin on the upper surface of the lower unit will index with a matching hole in the lower surface of the anti-cavitation plate.

Tighten the bolt on the connector to secure the two shift rods together or secure the joint nut onto the lower shift rod at least five turns and lock it in place with the lower locknut.

➡**If all items appear to mate properly, but the lower unit seems locked in position about 4 inches (10cm) away from the intermediate housing and it is not possible, with ease, to bring the two housings closer, the driveshaft has missed the cylindrical lower oil seal housing leading to the crankshaft.**

Move the lower unit out of the way. Shine a flashlight up into the intermediate housing and find the oil seal housing. Now, on the next attempt, find the edges of the oil seal housing with the driveshaft before trying to mate anything else—the water tube and the top of the shift rod. If the driveshaft can be made to enter the oil seal housing, the driveshaft can then be easily indexed with the crankshaft.

3. Apply Loctite® to the threads of the six bolts used to secure the lower unit to the intermediate housing. Remember, one bolt passes through the area covered by the trim tab. Install and tighten the bolts to a torque value of 29 ft. lbs. (40Nm).

4. Apply Loctite® to the threads of the bolt located under the trim tab, install and tighten this bolt to the same torque specification as given in the previous step.

Install and secure the trim tab with the attaching hardware.

5. Slide the two ends of the pilot tube together at the push-on fitting. Secure the tube to the swivel bracket using a new band retainer.

6. Operate the shift lever through all gears. The shifting should be smooth and the propeller should rotate in the proper direction when the flywheel is rotated by hand in a clockwise direction. Naturally the propeller should not rotate when the unit is in neutral.

➡**An anti-seize compound will prevent the propeller from freezing to the shaft and permit propeller removal, without difficulty, the next time the propeller needs to be pulled.**

7. Apply Yamalube Grease, or equivalent anti-seize compound, to the propeller shaft. Install the propeller.

Remove the block of wood. Connect the spark plug wires to the spark plugs. Connect the electrical lead to the battery terminal.

8. The trim tab should be positioned to enable the helmsperson to handle the boat with equal ease to starboard and port at normal cruising speed. If the boat seems to turn more easily to starboard, loosen the socket head screw and move the trim tab trailing edge to the right. Move the trailing edge of the trim tab to the left if the boat tends to turn more easily to port.

Shift the unit into forward gear, release the tilt lock lever and lower the outboard to the normal operating position.

9. Remove the oil level plug and the drain plug. Fill the lower unit with Yamalube gearcase lubricant or Hypoid gear oil 90 weight until the lubricant flows from the top hole. Install both plugs and clean any excess lubricant from the lower unit.

Mount the engine in a test tank or body of water.

❊❊ CAUTION

Water must circulate through the lower unit to the powerhead anytime the powerhead is operating to prevent damage to the water pump in the lower unit. Just five seconds without water will damage the water pump impeller.

Start the engine and check the completed work for satisfactory operation, shifting and no leaks.

LOWER UNIT OVERHAUL

1–2 Cylinder Powerhead Without Reverse Gear

DISASSEMBLY

◆ **See accompanying illustrations**

1. Pull the driveshaft tube free of the driveshaft.

2. Remove the two bolts securing the water pump housing cover to the lower unit.

3. Raise the water pump cover a bit to clear the indexing pin. Leave the water pump cover in this position at this time.

4. Pry the circlip free from the end of the driveshaft with a thin screwdriver. This clip holds the pinion gear onto the driveshaft. The clip may not come free on the first try, but have patience and it will come free. With one hand, remove driveshaft up and out of the lower unit housing and at the same time, with the other hand, catch the pinion gear and save any shim material from behind the gear. The shim material is critical to obtaining the correct backlash during installation. Using the old shim material will save considerable time, starting with no shim material.

With the driveshaft on the workbench, remove the oil seal protector (a white plastic cap), the insert cartridge (a metal cup) and the water pump impeller. Check the condition of the impeller carefully and replace with a new one if there is any question as to its condition for satisfactory service. Never turn the impeller over in an attempt to gain further life from the impeller.

Remove the pin from the driveshaft and slide the water pump housing cover and cartridge outer plate free of the shaft.

Remove the O-ring from atop the water pump housing.

➡ Removal of the seal destroys its sealing qualities and it cannot be installed a second time. Therefore, remove the seal only if it is unfit for further service and be absolutely sure a new seal is available before removing the old seal.

Obtain a slide hammer with jaw expander attachment and use it remove the oil seal from the housing cover.

5. Remove the propeller shaft from the lower unit housing. The forward gear will come out with the shaft. Watch for and save any shim material from the back side of the forward gear. The shim material is critical to obtaining the correct backlash during installation. Using the old shim material will save considerable time, starting with no shim material.

6. Inspect the condition of the upper seal in the lower unit housing. If replacement is required, use the same slide hammer and jaw attachment to remove the seal.

Three driveshaft bushings are used in the lower unit housing. These bushings need not be removed unless the determination is made they are no longer fit for service. Each bushing may be removed using bushing driver to drive the bushing free.

Forward Propeller Shaft Bearing

◆ **See accompanying illustrations**

➡ Removal of the forward propeller shaft bearing in the next step will destroy the bearing. Therefore, remove the bearing only if it is no longer fit for service and be absolutely sure a replacement bearing is available prior to removal.

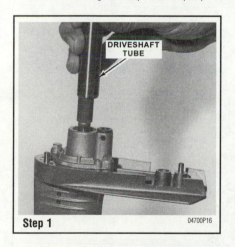

Step 1   04700P16

Step 2   04700P17

Step 3   04700P18

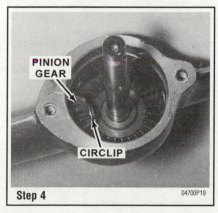

Step 4   04700P19

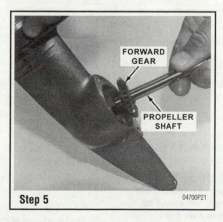

Step 5   04700P21

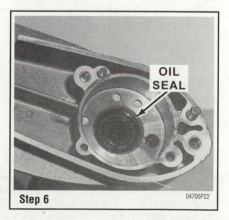

Step 6   04700P22

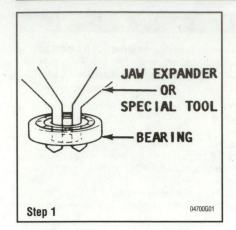

Step 1   04700G01

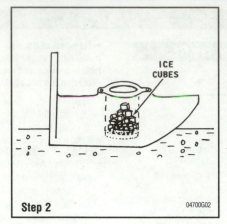

Step 2   04700G02

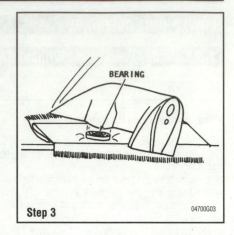

Step 3   04700G03

Rotate the forward propeller shaft bearing. If any roughness is felt, the bearing must be removed and a new one installed.

1. Removal of the bearing is accomplished using a slide hammer with jaw expander attachment.

The following two steps are to be performed only if the forward propeller shaft bearing must be removed and a suitable bearing puller is not available. The procedure will change the temperature between the bearing retainer and the housing substantially, hopefully about 80°F (50°C). This change will contract one metal—the bearing retainer and expand the other metal—the housing, giving perhaps as much as .003 inch (.08mm) clearance to allow the bearing to fall free. Read the complete steps before commencing the work because three things are necessary: a freezer, refrigerator, or ice chest; some ice cubes or crushed ice; and a container large enough to immerse about 1-½ in. (3.8cm) of the forward part of the lower gear housing in boiling water.

After all parts, including all seals, grommets, etc., have been removed from the lower gear housing, place the gear housing in a freezer, preferably overnight. If a freezer is not available try an electric refrigerator or ice chest. The next morning, obtain a container of suitable size to hold about 1-½ in. (3.8cm) of the forward part of the lower gear housing. Fill the container with water and bring to a rapid boil. While the water is coming to a boil, place a folded towel on a flat surface for padding.

2. After the water is boiling, remove the lower gear housing from its cold storage area. Fill the propeller shaft cavity with ice cubes or crushed ice. Hold the lower gear housing by the trim tab end and the lower end of the housing. Now, immerse the lower unit in the boiling water for about 20 or 30 seconds.

3. Quickly remove the housing from the boiling water; dump the ice; and with the open end of the housing facing downward, slam the housing onto the padded surface. Presto, the bearing should fall out.

If the bearing fails to come free, try the complete procedure a second time. Failure on the second attempt will require the use of a bearing puller.

CLEANING AND INSPECTING

◆ **See Figures 12, 13 and 14**

Clean all water pump parts with solvent and then dry them with compressed air. Inspect the water pump cover and base for cracks and distortion. If possible, always install a new water pump impeller while the lower unit is disassembled. A new impeller will ensure extended satisfactory service and give peace of mind to the owner. If the old impeller must be returned to service, never install it in reverse to the original direction of rotation. Installation in reverse will cause premature impeller failure.

Inspect the ends of the impeller blades for cracks, tears and wear. Check for a glazed or melted appearance, caused from operating without sufficient water. If any question exists, as previously stated, install a new impeller if at all possible.

➡ **If an old impeller is installed be sure the impeller is installed in the same manner from which it was removed—the blades will rotate in the same direction. Never turn the impeller over thinking it will extend its life. On the contrary, the blades would crack and break after just a short time of operation.**

Inspect the bearing surface of the propeller shaft. Check the shaft surface for pitting, scoring, grooving, imbedded particles, uneven wear and discoloration.

Check the straightness of the propeller shaft with a set of V-blocks. Rotate the propeller on the blocks

Good shop practice dictates installation of new O-rings and oil seals regardless of their appearance.

Clean the pinion gear and the propeller shaft with solvent. Dry the cleaned parts with compressed air.

Check the pinion gear and the drive gear for abnormal wear.

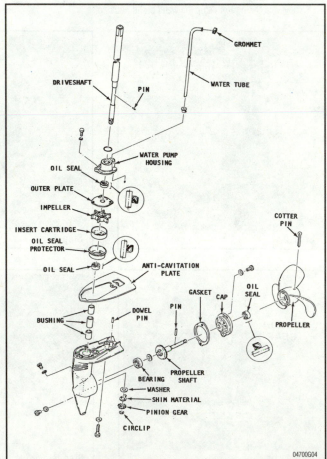

Fig. 12 Exploded view of the non-reversing lower unit used on the 2 hp powerhead. Major parts are identified

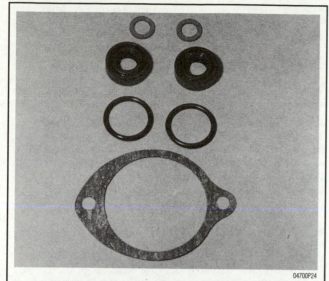

Fig. 13 Typical parts included in a lower unit gasket replacement kit

04700P24

Fig. 14 typical parts included in a water pump repair kit for a 2 hp powerhead

04700P25

gear housing to be immersed. While the water is coming to a boil, place a folded towel on a flat surface for padding. Immerse the forward part of the gear housing in the boiling water for about a minute.

2.   Quickly remove the lower gear housing from the boiling water and place it on the padded surface with the open end facing upward. At the same time, have an assistant bring the bearing from the cold storage area. Continue working rapidly. Carefully place the bearing squarely into the housing as far as possible, with the embossed side facing outward. Push the bearing into place. Obtain a blunt punch or piece of tubing to bear on the complete circumference of the retainer. Carefully tap the bearing retainer all the way into its forward position—until it bottoms-out. Tap evenly around the outer perimeter of the retainer, shifting from one side to the other to ensure the bearing is going squarely into place. The bearing must be properly installed to receive the forward end of the propeller shaft.

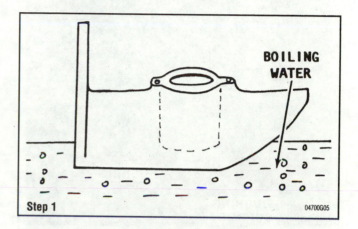

Step 1

04700G05

Step 2

04700P27

ASSEMBLY

Forward Propeller Shaft Bearing

♦ See accompanying illustrations

This first section applies only if the forward propeller shaft bearing was removed from the housing.

Place the propeller shaft forward bearing squarely into the housing with the side embossed with the bearing size facing outward. Drive the bearing into the housing until it is fully seated.

1.   Place a new forward propeller shaft bearing in a freezer, refrigerator, or ice chest, preferably overnight. The next morning, boil water in a container of sufficient size to allow about 1-½ in. (3mm) of the forward part of the lower

Driveshaft Bushing

♦ See accompanying illustration

➡The following step is to be performed if any one or all three of the driveshaft bushings were removed. Three short bushings are used instead of one long bushing to facilitate installation and still provide the required amount of bearing surface.

1.   Lower a long threaded bushing installer, Yamaha P/N YB6029, into the lower unit from the top until the threads protrude into the lower cavity of the lower unit, as shown. Now, thread the nut provided with the tool down onto the installer tool until the nut is snug against the plate. Slide the first bushing over the threads at the lower end of the driveshaft and then install the bushing retainer onto the threads. Tighten the bushing installer from the upper end of the tool using the proper size wrench. Continue rotating the bushing installer until the bushing is drawn up into the lower unit and seats properly. Install the second and third bushing in the same manner.

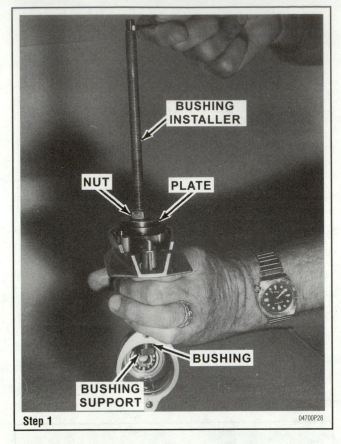

Step 1 04700P28

Oil Seal

1. Obtain a seal installer. Place the oil seal over the end of the installer with the lip facing upward.

➡ **The seal must be installed with the lip facing upward to prevent water from entering and contaminating the lubricant in the lower unit.**

Lower the seal installer and the seal squarely into the seal recess. Tap the end of the handle with a hammer until the seal is fully seated. After installation, pack the seal with Yamaha Grease A or equivalent water resistant lubricant.

Propeller shaft

◆ **See accompanying illustration**

1. Place the shim material saved during disassembly onto the propeller shaft ahead of the forward gear. The shim material should give the same amount

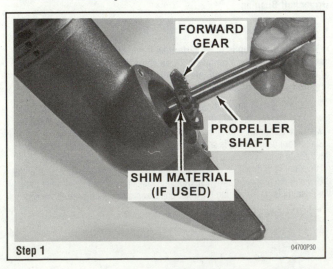

Step 1 04700P30

of backlash between the pinion and forward gear as before disassembling. Insert the propeller shaft into the lower unit housing. Push the propeller shaft into the forward propeller shaft bearing as far as possible.

Water Pump

◆ **See accompanying illustrations**

Obtain seal installer tool Yamaha P/N YB6025 and handle P/N YB6229.

➡ **After installation of the water pump housing cover, the oil seal lip faces downward to prevent water in the water pump from contaminating the lubricant around the driveshaft. However, to install the seal, the water pump cover is turned upside down on the work surface. In this position, the lip of the seal must face upward.**

Using the seal installer and handle, install the seal. After installation, pack the seal with Yamaha Grease A or equivalent water resistant lubricant.

Install a new O-ring atop the water pump housing.

Slide the water pump housing cover over the splined end of the driveshaft. Apply a coating of Yamabond #4, or equivalent adhesive to both sides of the water pump plate. Next, install the plate with the hole in the plate indexed over the pin on the water pump housing. Dab some Yamaha Grease A, or equivalent water resistant lubricant, onto the dowel pin and insert it into the hole in the driveshaft. Slide the water pump impeller onto the driveshaft with the notch in the impeller indexed over the dowel pin. Slide the metal cup over the impeller and then the plastic cup over the metal cup.

1. Lower the assembled driveshaft into the lower unit but do not mate the cover with the lower unit surface at this time. Leave some space, as shown. The splines on the lower end of the driveshaft will protrude into the lower unit cavity.

2. Slide the thrust washer and any shim material saved during disassembly onto the lower end of the driveshaft. Slide the pinion gear up onto the end of the driveshaft. The splines of the pinion gear will index with the splines of the driveshaft and the gear teeth will mesh with the teeth of the forward gear. Rotating the pinion gear slightly will permit the splines to index and the gears to mesh.

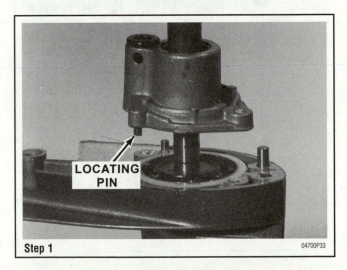

Step 1 04700P33

Step 2 04700P34

Now, comes the hard part. Snap the circlip into the groove on the end of the driveshaft to secure the pinion gear in place. If the first attempt is not successful, try again. Take a break, have a cup of coffee, tea, whatever, then give it another go. With patience, the task can be accomplished.

3. Apply some Loctite, or equivalent, to the two water pump cover retaining bolts. Tighten the bolts alternately and evenly to a torque value of 3.2 fit lbs. (4.4 Nm).

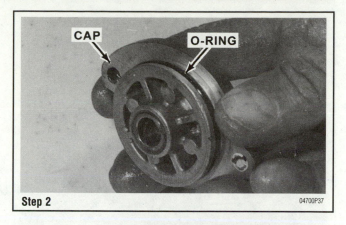

Step 2   04700P37

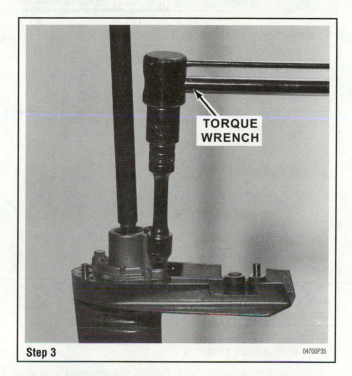

Step 3   04700P35

Bearing Carrier

♦ **See accompanying illustrations**

1. Place the bearing carrier cap on the work surface with the painted side facing upward. Install the oil seal with the lip facing downward. In this position the seal with prevent water from entering and contaminating the lubricant in the lower unit. Coat the seal lip with Yamaha Grease A, or equivalent water resistant lubricant.

➡ **Apply a coating of Yamabond #4 to the gasket or O-ring and to its mating surface.**

2. Install the bearing carrier cap to the lower unit and make sure the cap is seated evenly all the way around.

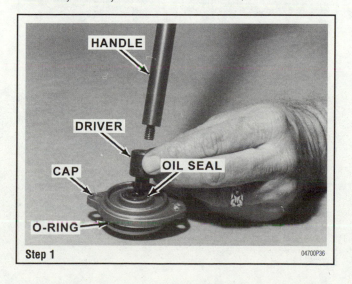

Step 1   04700P36

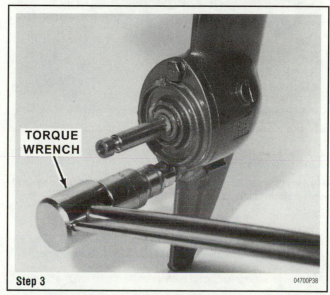

Step 3   04700P38

3. Apply Loctite, or equivalent, to the threads of the bearing carrier attaching bolts. Install and tighten the bolts alternately and evenly to a torque value of 5.8 ft. lbs. (8 Nm).

Gear Backlash

♦ **See accompanying illustrations**

Backlash between two gears is the amount of movement one gear will make before turning its mating gear when either gear is rotated back and forth.

1. Remove the anode, if it is installed. The hole for the anode retaining bolt will be used for the indicator gauge setup. Obtain a backlash plate, Yamaha P/N YB7003. Secure the plate on the anti-cavitation plate using a suitable bolt and nut with the bolt passing through the anode bolt hole.

Secure the backlash indicator gauge, Yamaha P/N YB6154 or YB6265, to the propeller shaft. If the hose clamp is too large to fit the propeller shaft snugly, insert some kind of packing into the clamp to allow it to be tightened. The clamp must be secure to permit no movement of the indicator on the shaft.

Obtain a dial gauge and magnetic base with a holder. Set up the dial gauge with the stem making contact with the 30A mark on the indicator.

Now, with one hand hold the driveshaft to prevent the shaft from rotating. With the other hand gently push in on the propeller shaft while at the same time slowly rock the shaft back and forth. When a click is felt, stop the rocking motion and note the maximum deflection of the dial gauge needle.

The amount of backlash is determined by dividing the maximum deflection by 1.57 as expressed in the following simple formula: Backlash = Maximum Deflection/1.57

The manufacturer gives 0.003–0.01 in. (0.08–0.3mm) as acceptable backlash.

If the backlash is greater than the figures given, the propeller shaft must be pulled and the amount of shim material behind the forward gear increased.

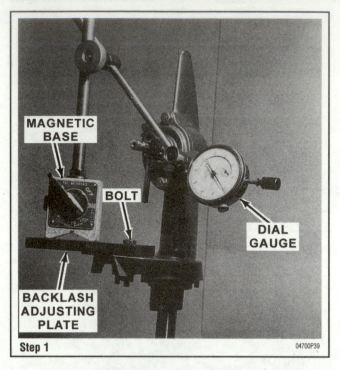

MAGNETIC BASE

BOLT

DIAL GAUGE

BACKLASH ADJUSTING PLATE

Step 1   04700P39

If the backlash is less than the figures given, remove some of the shim material behind the forward gear.

➠**In summary, adding or removing shim material will affect the forward gear backlash as follows:**

Adding shim material decreases backlash.
Removing shim material increases backlash.
If the correct backlash cannot be obtained by adding or removing shim material, it may be necessary to replace either the pinion gear, the forward gear, or the forward gear bearing.
After the backlash measurement is complete, remove the gauge, plate, etc. and install the anode.

2. Apply a small amount of Yamaha Grease, or equivalent water resistant lubricant to the squared section at the upper end of the driveshaft.

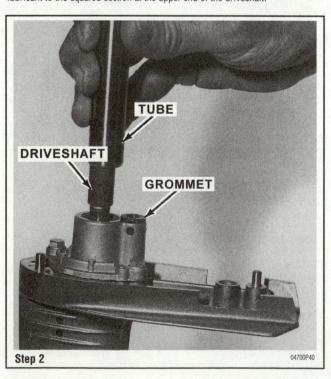

TUBE

DRIVESHAFT

GROMMET

Step 2   04700P40

➠An excessive amount of lubricant on top of the driveshaft to crankshaft splines will be trapped in the clearance space. This trapped lubricant will not allow the driveshaft to fully engage with the crankshaft.

Slide the tube over the driveshaft and push a new grommet in place where the water tube enters the water pump housing cover.

1–2 Cylinder Powerhead With Reverse Gear

DISASSEMBLY

Water Pump
♦ **See Figure 15**

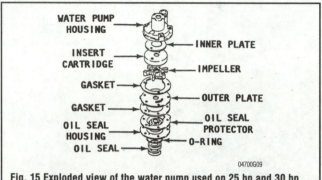

WATER PUMP HOUSING — INNER PLATE
INSERT CARTRIDGE — IMPELLER
GASKET — OUTER PLATE
GASKET — OIL SEAL PROTECTOR
OIL SEAL HOUSING — O-RING
OIL SEAL

04700G09

Fig. 15 Exploded view of the water pump used on 25 hp and 30 hp models. This pump is of a different design than other pumps depicted in this manual

♦ **See accompanying illustrations**

1. Remove the four bolts and washer securing the two plates on both sides of the water pump housing.

➠**The model 25 hp and 30 hp units do not have these plates. Model 9.9 hp and 15 hp have an extra retaining plate on top of the water pump housing. This plate is secured in place with two separate Phillips head screws.**

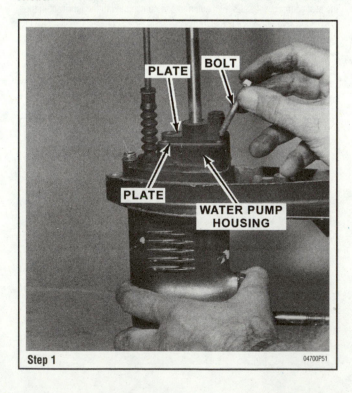

PLATE **BOLT**

PLATE

WATER PUMP HOUSING

Step 1   04700P51

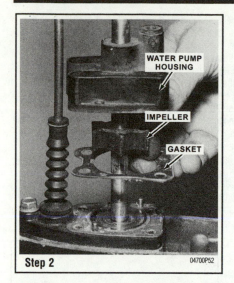

Step 2   04700P52

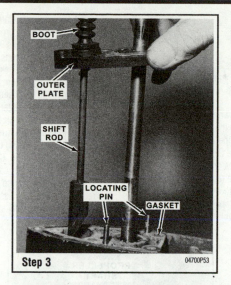

Step 3   04700P53

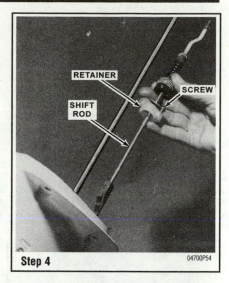

Step 4   04700P54

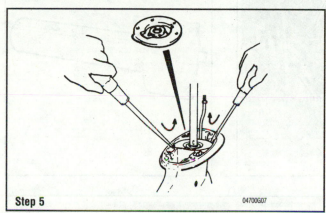

Step 5   04700G07

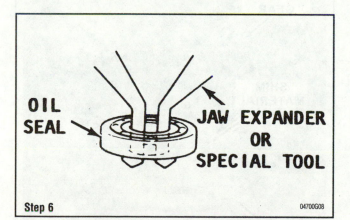

Step 6   04700G08

under the housing. The shift rod and boot will come away with the outer plate. Take care not to lose the two locating pins in the bearing housing.

4. On 9.9 hp, 15 hp, 25 hp and 30 hp models, remove the outer plate and the gasket under the plate. Remove the oil seal housing and the gasket under the housing. Loosen but do not remove the small Phillips screw on the white plastic shift rod retainer. Pull out the shift rod and boot assembly.

5. On 25 hp and 30 hp models, use two screwdrivers and lift out the oil seal protector and then remove the oil seal housing and O-ring in the housing.

➡ **Removal of the seal destroys its sealing qualities and it cannot be installed a second time. Therefore, remove the seal only if it is unfit for further service and be absolutely sure a new seal is available before removing the old seal.**

6. Obtain a slide hammer with jaw expander attachment. On 4 hp and 5 hp models, use the tool to remove the oil seals from the lower unit housing. On all other models, use the tool to remove the oil seals from the oil seal housing.

Oil Seal Housing Bushing

♦ **See accompanying illustration**

1. On 6 hp, 8 hp, 9.9 hp and 15 hp models, The only tool required is handle P/N YB6071. Obtain this tool. Use the appropriate tool for the unit being serviced and drive the bushing free of the oil seal housing.

The direction the bushing is to be driven out does not matter, UNLESS the bushing has a shoulder. In this case, drive the bushing from the flush side.

2. Slide the following components upward and free of the driveshaft: First, the water pump housing. On models 4 hp and 5 hp, the indexing pin may now be removed from the driveshaft. Next, slide the inner plate up and free of the driveshaft on the models 25 hp and 30 hp. Now, slide the water pump impeller and the insert cartridge free of the driveshaft. Remove and save the small Woodruff key on all models except the 4 hp and 5 hp. These two models have the indexing pin. Remove the water pump gasket. Pull out the water tube grommet from atop the water pump housing.

3. On 4 hp, 5 hp, 6 hp and 8 hp models, lift up the outer plate and the gasket beneath it. The 6 hp and 8 hp units have an oil seal housing and a gasket

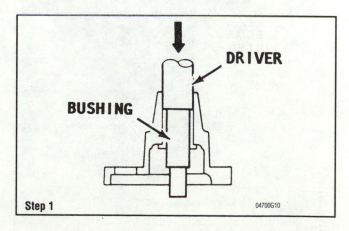

Step 1   04700G10

Bearing Carrier Cap

♦ **See accompanying illustrations**

1. On 4 hp and 5 hp models, remove the two bolts securing the bearing carrier cap. Rotate the cap 90° (¼ turn) and then gently tap the bearing carrier cap to break it free from the lower unit. Remove the cap from the lower unit. Remove and discard the O-ring.

2. On 6 hp, 8 hp, 9.9 hp and 15 hp models, use two small screwdrivers, one on each side and simultaneously pry the cap from the lower unit. Take care not to mar the gasket sealing surfaces. Pull out the propeller shaft and then remove the cap from the shaft. Remove and discard the O-ring.

3. On 25 hp and 30 hp models, straighten the tabs on the lockwasher bent over the ring nut. Note the word **OFF** embossed on the ring nut. Rotate the ring in the direction indicated. Rotate the ring nut counterclockwise until the nut is free. Remove the lockwasher. Attempt to remove the propeller shaft. If the shaft and the bearing carrier will not come out easily, they will have to be pulled.

4. On stubborn carriers, first remove the two bolts and washers from the front of the bearing carrier. Obtain a universal puller, Yamaha P/N YB6234. Hook the ends of the J-bolts into the bearing carrier ribs across from each other. Insert the threaded ends through the puller and then install the washers and nuts to take up the slack. Rotate the center threaded shaft clockwise to separate the bearing carrier from the lower unit.

Remove the tools and withdraw the propeller shaft with the bearing carrier, reverse gear and washer still on the shaft.

On 25 hp and 30 hp models, take care not to lose the small key fitted into the side of the bearing carrier.

Remove the bearing carrier from the propeller shaft. Remove the washer.

5. On 4 hp, 5 hp, 6 hp, 8 hp, 9.9 hp and 15 hp models, remove the reverse gear from the bearing carrier. Watch for and save any shim material from the back side of the reverse gear. The shim material is critical in obtaining the correct backlash during assembling. Using the old shim material will save considerable time, especially starting with no shim material.

Step 1　　04700P55

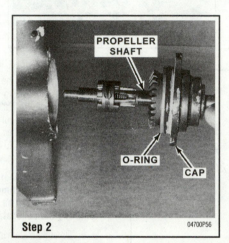

Step 2　　04700P56

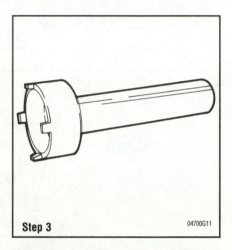

Step 3　　04700G11

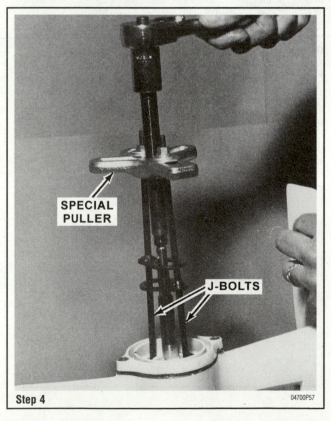

SPECIAL PULLER

J-BOLTS

Step 4　　04700P57

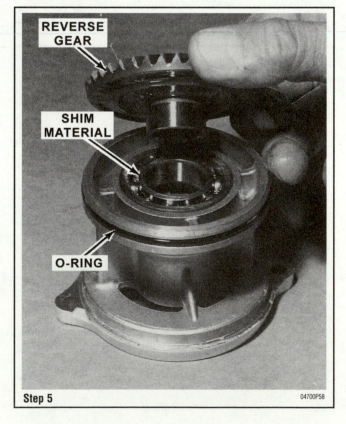

REVERSE GEAR

SHIM MATERIAL

O-RING

Step 5　　04700P58

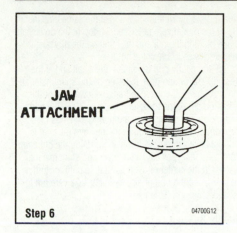

JAW ATTACHMENT

Step 6   04700G12

BALL BEARING
BEARING SEPARATOR

Step 7   04700G13

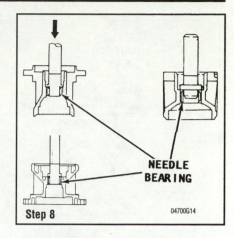

NEEDLE BEARING

Step 8   04700G14

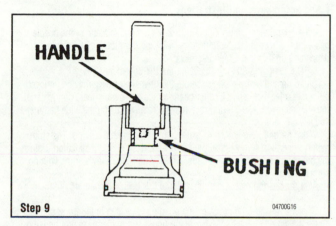

HANDLE

BUSHING

Step 9   04700G16

On 25 hp and 30 hp models, the reverse gear and ball bearing assembly is pressed into the bearing carrier on these models. The ball bearing is pressed onto the back of the reverse gear and must be separated using a slide hammer with jaw expander attachment.

The ball bearing or the ball bearing and reverse gear together must be pulled from the bearing carrier.

Obtain a slide hammer with jaw expander attachment and pull the bearing or the bearing and reverse gear from the bearing carrier. When using the tool check to be sure the jaws are hooked onto the inner race.

6. Inspect the condition of the two seals in the bearing carrier cap for the 4 hp and 5 hp models, or in the bearing carrier for all other models. If the seals appear to be damaged and replacement is required, use the same slide hammer and jaw attachments to remove the seals.

7. On 25 hp and 30 hp models, the ball bearing is pressed onto the back of the reverse gear. To remove this bearing, first obtain a universal bearing separator tool and then press on the inner race to separate the bearing from the gear.

Watch for and save any shim material from the back side of the reverse gear. The shim material is critical in obtaining the correct backlash during assembling. Using the old shim material will save considerable time, especially starting with no shim material.

8 On all models except 4 hp, 5 hp, 6 hp and 8 hp, the caged needle bearing set is pressed into the bearing carrier. To remove the bearing set, first obtain Yamaha Handle P/N YB6071 and Driver P/N YB6081. Drive the needle bearing set free of the bearing carrier. Note the direction to drive out the needle bearing. The direction is different for different model lower units.

9. On the 6 hp and 8 hp models, obtain Yamaha Handle P/N YB6071. Use the handle to drive the bushing free of the bearing carrier. The direction the bushing is to be driven out does not matter, unless the bushing has a shoulder. In this case, drive the bushing from the flush side.

Driveshaft

♦ **See accompanying illustrations**

Before the driveshaft can be removed, the pinion gear at the lower end of the shaft must be removed. The pinion gear may be secured to the driveshaft with a simple circlip, as on the 4 hp, 5 hp, 6 hp and 8 hp models, or with a nut, as on all other models.

1. On 4 hp, 5 hp, 6 hp and 8 hp models, pry the circlip free from the end of the driveshaft with a thin screwdriver. This clip holds the pinion gear onto the lower end of the driveshaft. The clip may not come free on the first try, but have patience and it will come free. With one hand, lift the driveshaft up and out of the lower unit housing and at the same time, with the other hand, catch the pinion gear and SAVE any shim material from behind the gear. The shim material is critical to obtaining the correct backlash during installation. Using the old shim material will save considerable time, especially starting with no shim material.

➡ **In most cases, when working with tools, a nut is rotated to remove or install it to a particular bolt, shaft, etc. In the next two steps, the reverse is required because there is no room to move a wrench inside the lower unit cavity. The nut on the lower end of the driveshaft is held steady and the shaft is rotated until the nut is free.**

2. Obtain pinion nut wrench Yamaha P/N YB6078. This wrench is used to prevent the nut from rotating while the driveshaft is rotated.

On 9.9 hp and 15 hp models, obtain driveshaft tool Yamaha P/N YB6228. On 25 hp and 30 hp models, obtain driveshaft tool, Yamaha P/N YB6079

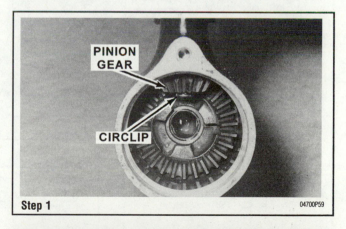

PINION GEAR

CIRCLIP

Step 1   04700P59

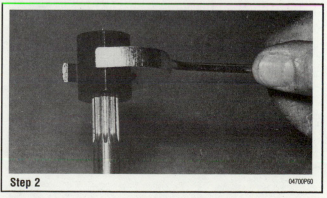

Step 2   04700P60

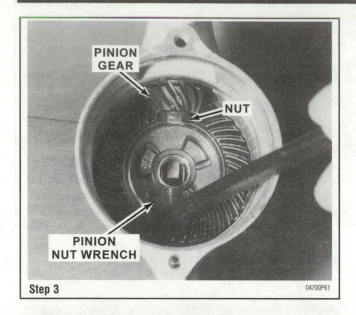

Step 3   04700P61

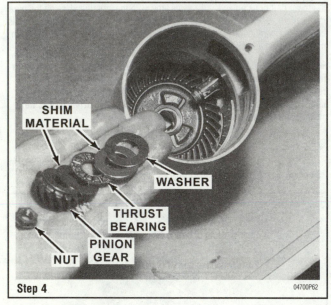

Step 4   04700P62

3. Now, hold the pinion nut steady with the tool and at the same time install the proper driveshaft tool, for the model being serviced, on top of the driveshaft. With both tools in place, one holding the nut and the other on the driveshaft, rotate the driveshaft counterclockwise to break the nut free.

4. Remove the pinion nut and gently pull up on the driveshaft and at the same time rotate the driveshaft. The pinion gear, followed by the shim material, washer, thrust bearing and a washer will come free from the lower end of the driveshaft. Pull the driveshaft up out of the lower unit housing. Keep the parts from the lower end of the driveshaft in order, as an aid during assembling.

Save any shim material from behind the pinion gear. The shim material is critical to obtaining the correct backlash during installation. Using the old shim material will save considerable time, especially starting with no shim material.

If the tapered roller bearing in the center of the driveshaft is unfit for further service, press the bearing free using the proper size mandrel. Take care not to bend or distort the driveshaft because of its length.

Driveshaft Bushing/Needle Bearing

▶ **See accompanying illustrations**

If the driveshaft bushing, upper or lower, on some models, or the needle bearing on other models, is unfit for service, perform the following steps, depending on the model being serviced.

1. On 25 hp and 30 hp models, lift out the driveshaft sleeve.

On 25 hp and 30 hp models, before the driveshaft sleeve may be removed the upper driveshaft tapered roller bearing race and pinion gear shim material must be removed. The bearing race may be removed using the slide hammer and jaw attachment.

Watch for and save any shim material from behind the bearing. The shim material is critical to obtaining the correct backlash during installation. Using the old shim material will save considerable time, especially starting with no shim material.

After the bearing race and shim material has been removed, lift out the driveshaft sleeve.

2. On 4 hp and 5 hp models, one bushing is located in the lower unit just above the pinion gear and another at the upper end of the lower unit housing. Obtain Yamaha P/N YB6027. Insert the tool from the top of the lower unit and drive the lower bushing down and free. Attach bushing remover P/N YB6178 to a slide hammer. Remove the upper bushing out the top of the housing.

On 6 hp and 8 hp models, these two models have only one bushing in the lower unit just above the pinion gear. Obtain driver Yamaha P/N YB6028. Attach the driver to handle Yamaha P/N YB6229. Insert the tool from the top of the lower unit and drive the bushing down and free.

3. Two small caged needle bearing sets are used at the lower end of the driveshaft, on the model 9.9 hp and 15 hp. One small needle bearing set is used at the lower end of the driveshaft on the model 25 hp, 30 hp. Attach the appropriate driver to handle Yamaha P/N YB6229. Insert the tool from the top of the lower unit and drive the needle bearing/s down and free.

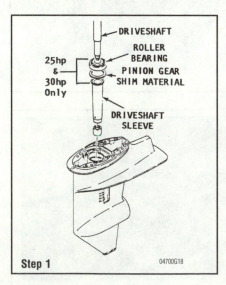

Step 1   04700G18

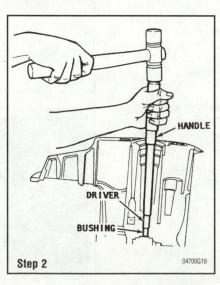

Step 2   04700G19

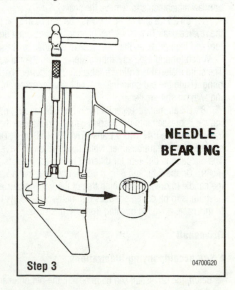

Step 3   04700G20

Forward Gear

♦ **See accompanying illustrations**

1. On 4 hp and 5 hp models, remove the forward gear from the lower unit.
2. If the forward ball bearing is no longer fit for service, proceed as follows: Obtain slide hammer and jaw attachment Yamaha P/N YB6096. Pull the ball bearing set from the lower unit.

Step 1   04700P63

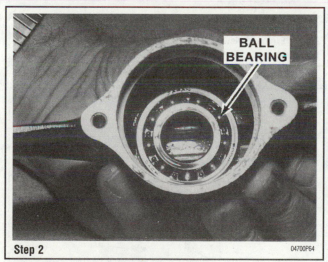

Step 2   04700P64

3. On all other models, lift out the forward gear and the tapered roller bearing.

➡ **If a two piece bearing is to be replaced, the bearing and the race must be replaced as a matched set. Remove the bearing only if it is unfit for further service.**

4. Position a bearing separator between the forward gear and the tapered roller bearing. Using a hydraulic press, separate the gear from the bearing.
5. Obtain a slide hammer with a jaw attachment. Use the this tool to pull the bearing race from the lower unit housing. Be sure to hold the slide hammer at right angles to the driveshaft while working the slide hammer. Watch for and save any shim material found behind the forward gear. The shim material is critical to obtaining the correct backlash during installation. Using the old shim material will save considerable time, especially starting with no shim material.

Clutch Dog

♦ **See accompanying illustrations**

1. Insert an awl under the end loop of the cross pin ring and pry the ring free of the clutch dog.

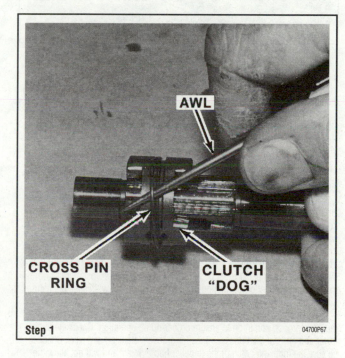

Step 1   04700P67

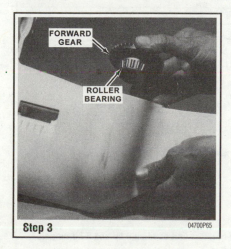

Step 3   04700P65

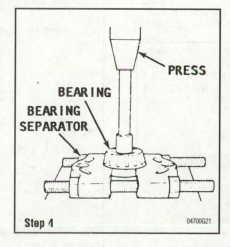

Step 4   04700G21

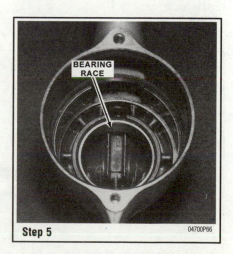

Step 5   04700P66

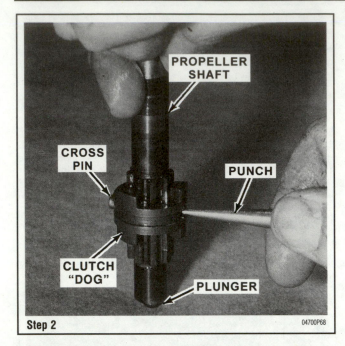

Step 2

04700P68

2. Use a long pointed punch and press out the cross pin. Remove the plunger and spring from the end of the propeller shaft. Slide the clutch dog from the shaft. Observe how the clutch dog was installed. It must be installed in the same direction.

CLEANING AND INSPECTING

◆ **See Figures 16, 17, 18, 19 and 20**

Good shop practice requires installation of new O-rings and oil seals regardless of their appearance.

Clean all water pump parts with solvent and then dry them with compressed air. Inspect the water pump housing and oil seal housing for cracks and distortion, possibly caused from overheating. Inspect the inner and outer plates and water pump cartridge for grooves and/or rough surfaces. If possible, always install a new water pump impeller while the lower unit is disassembled. A new impeller will ensure extended satisfactory service and give peace of mind to the owner. If the old impeller must be returned to service, never install it in reverse to the original direction of rotation. Installation in reverse will cause premature impeller failure.

If installation of a new impeller is not possible, check the seal surfaces. All must be in good condition to ensure proper pump operation. Check the upper, lower and ends of the impeller vanes for grooves, cracking and wear. Check to be sure the indexing notch of the impeller hub is intact and will not allow the impeller to slip.

Clean around the Woodruff key or impeller pin. Clean all bearings with solvent, dry them with compressed air and inspect them carefully. Be sure there is

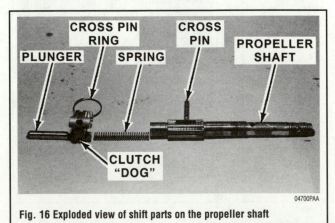

Fig. 16 Exploded view of shift parts on the propeller shaft

04700PAA

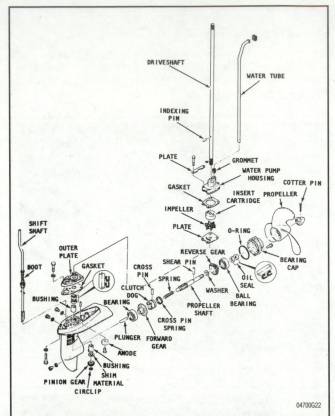

Fig. 17 Exploded view of lower unit used on 4 hp and 5 hp models with major parts identified

04700G22

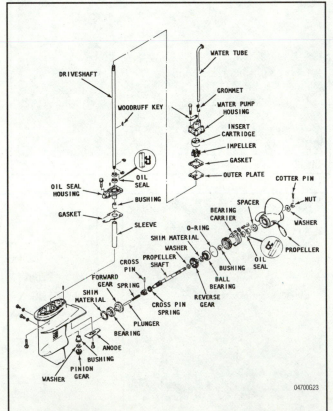

Fig. 18 Exploded view of lower unit used on 6 hp and 8 hp models with major parts identified

04700G23

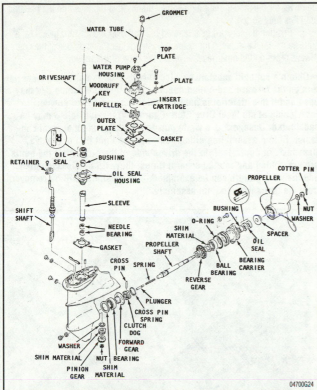

Fig. 19 Exploded view of lower unit used on 9.9 hp and 15 hp models with major parts identified

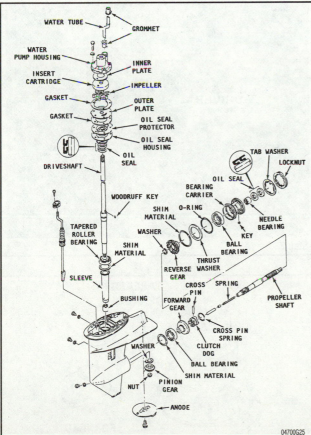

Fig. 20 Exploded view of lower unit used on 25 hp and 30 hp models with major parts identified

no water in the air line. Direct the air stream through the bearing. Never spin a bearing with compressed air. Such action is highly dangerous and may cause the bearing to score from lack of lubrication. After the bearings are clean and dry, lubricate them with Formula 50 oil, or equivalent. Do not lubricate tapered bearing cups until after they have been inspected.

Inspect all ball bearings for roughness, scratches and bearing race side wear. Hold the outer race and work the inner bearing race in-and-out, to check for side wear.

Determine the condition of tapered bearing rollers and inner bearing race, by inspecting the bearing cup for pitting, scoring, grooves, uneven wear, imbedded particles and discoloration caused from overheating. Always replace tapered roller bearings as a set.

Clean the forward gear with solvent and then dry it with compressed air. Inspect the gear teeth for wear. Under normal conditions the gear will show signs of wear but it will be smooth and even.

Clean the bearing carrier or cap with solvent and then dry it with compressed air. Never spin bearings with compressed air. Such action is highly dangerous and may cause the bearing to score from lack of lubrication. Check the gear teeth of the reverse gear for wear. The wear should be smooth and even.

Check the clutch dogs to be sure they are not rounded-off , or chipped. Such damage is usually the result of poor operator habits and is caused by shifting too slowly or shifting while the engine is operating at high rpm. Such damage might also be caused by improper shift rod adjustments.

Rotate the reverse gear and check for catches and roughness. Check the bearing for side wear of the bearing races.

Inspect the roller bearing surface of the propeller shaft. Check the shaft surface for pitting, scoring, grooving, embedded particles, uneven wear and discoloration caused from overheating.

Clean the driveshaft with solvent and then dry it with compressed air. Never spin bearings with compressed air. Such action is dangerous and could damage the bearing. Inspect the bearing for roughness, scratches, or side wear. If the bearing shows signs of such damage, it should be replaced. If the bearing is satisfactory for further service coat it with oil.

Inspect the driveshaft splines for excessive wear. Check the oil seal surfaces above and below the water pump drive pin or Woodruff key area for grooves. Replace the shaft if grooves are discovered.

Inspect the driveshaft bearing surface above the pinion gear splines for pitting, grooves, scoring, uneven wear, embedded metal particles and discoloration caused by overheating.

Inspect the propeller shaft oil seal surface to be sure it is not pitted, grooved, or scratched. Inspect the roller bearing contact surface on the propeller shaft for pitting, grooves, scoring, uneven wear, embedded metal particles and discoloration caused from overheating.

Inspect the propeller shaft splines for wear and corrosion damage. Check the propeller shaft for straightness.

Inspect the following parts for wear, corrosion, or other signs of damage:
- Shift shaft boot
- Shift shaft retainer
- Shift cam
- Check the circlip to be sure it is not bent or stretched. If the clip is deformed, it must be replaced.
- Clean all parts with solvent and then dry them with compressed air.
- Inspect:
- All bearing bores for loose fitting bearings.
- Gear housing for impact damage.
- Cover nut threads on the 25 hp and 30 hp models for cross-threading and corrosion damage.
- Check the pinion nut corners for wear or damage. This nut is a special locknut. Therefore, do not attempt to replace it with a standard nut. Obtain the correct nut from an authorized Yamaha dealer.

ASSEMBLY

Procedural steps are given to assemble and install virtually all items in the lower unit. However, if certain items, i.e. bearings, bushings, seals, etc. were found fit for further service and were not removed, simply skip the assembly steps involved. Proceed with the required tasks to assemble and install the necessary components.

Clutch Dog

◆ **See accompanying illustrations**

1. During installation on the propeller shaft, the F embossed on the clutch dog must face the forward gear.

2. Slide the spring down into the propeller shaft. Insert a narrow screwdriver into the slot in the shaft and compress the spring until approximately ½ in. (12mm) is obtained between the top of the slot and the screwdriver.

Hold the spring compressed and at the same time, slide the clutch dog over the splines of the propeller shaft with the hole in the dog aligned with the slot in the shaft. The letter F embossed on the dog must face toward the forward gear.

Insert the cross pin into the clutch dog and through the space held open by the screwdriver. Center the pin and then remove the screwdriver allowing the spring to pop back into place.

Fit the cross pin ring into the groove around the clutch dog to retain the crosspin in place.

Insert the flat end of the plunger into the propeller shaft, with the rounded end protruding to permit the plunger to slide along the cam of the shift rod.

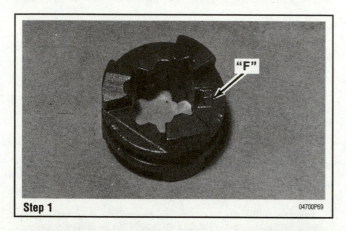

Step 1   04700P69

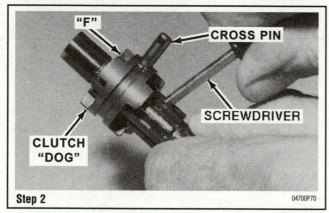

Step 2   04700P70

Forward Gear Ball Bearing

◆ **See accompanying illustrations**

The next three steps apply only if the forward gear ball bearing was removed. If the bearing was not disturbed.

1. On 4 hp and 5 hp models, obtain driver P/N YB6014 and handle P/N YB6071. Place the propeller shaft forward bearing squarely into the housing with the side embossed with the bearing size facing outward. Drive the bearing into the housing until it is fully seated.

2. On 9.9 hp, 15 hp, 25 hp, 30 hp models, obtain driver p/n yb6085 driver and handle p/n yb6071. On 6 hp and 8 hp models, obtain driver p/n yb6167 and handle p/n yb6071.

Insert the shim material saved during disassembly into the lower unit bearing race cavity. The shim material should give the same amount of backlash between the pinion gear and the forward gear as before disassembling. Insert the bearing race squarely into the lower unit housing and then use the appropri-

ate driver for the model unit being serviced and drive the race into the housing until it is fully seated.

3. Position the forward gear tapered bearing over the forward gear. Use a suitable mandrel and press the bearing flush against the shoulder of the gear. Always press on the inner race, never on the cage or the rollers.

➡ **Obtain a suitable substance which can be used to indicate a wear pattern on the forward and pinion gears as they mesh. Machine dye may be used and if this material is not available, Desenex® Foot Powder (obtainable at the local Drug Store/Pharmacy), or equivalent may be substituted. Desenex® is a white powder available in an aerosol container. Before assembling either gear, apply a light film of the dye, Desenex®, or equivalent, to the driven side of the gear. After the gears are assembled and rotated several times, they will be disassembled and the wear pattern can be examined. The substance will be removed from the gears prior to final assembly.**

Step 1   04700P71

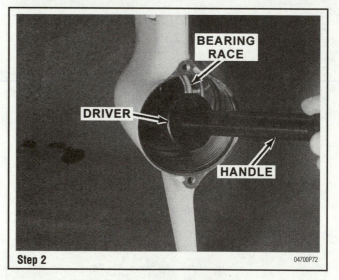

Step 2   04700P72

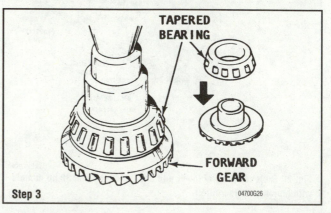

Step 3   04700G26

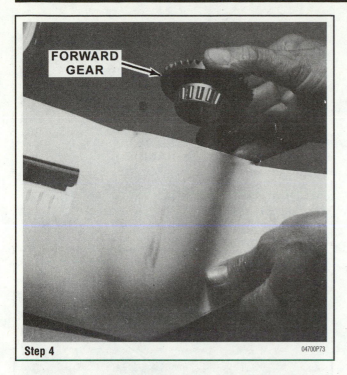

Step 4   04700P73

4. Position the forward gear assembly into the forward bearing race.

Driveshaft Bushing And Bearing

♦ **See accompanying illustrations**

Perform the next two or three steps only if the bushings and/or bearings were removed during disassembly. If these items were not disturbed.

1. 4 hp and 5 hp models have two bushings for the driveshaft. One is located at the top of the lower unit housing and the other just above the pinion gear at the lower end.

Obtain driver P/N YB6025 and handle P/N YB6071 and drive the upper bushing into place from the top until it seats.

On 4 hp and 5 hp models or 6 hp and 8 hp with single lower bushing, obtain driver P/N YB6028, plate P/N YB6169 and bushing installer P/N YB6029. Position the plate on top of the lower unit. Lower the long threaded bushing installer into the lower unit from the top until the threads protrude into the lower unit cavity, as shown.

Now, thread the nut provided with the tool down onto the installer tool until the nut is snug against the plate. Slide the first bushing over the threads at the lower end of the tool and then install the bushing retainer onto the threads. Tighten the bushing installer from the upper end of the tool, using the proper size wrench. Continue rotating the bushing installer until the bushing is drawn up into the lower unit and seats properly.

2. On 9.9 hp and 15 hp These models use two needle bearings at the lower end of the driveshaft just above the pinion gear.

Obtain driver P/N YB6230, handle P/N YB6229 and guide plate P/N YB6229. Slide the guide plate onto the driver with the stamped mark facing upward. Install the driver onto the threaded end of the handle. Use the guide plate to center the handle in the hole and then install the first needle bearing with the stamp mark on the bearing facing upward toward the driver.

Remove the driver and guide plate from the handle. Install the guide plate back onto the handle, this time with the stamped mark facing downward. Install the driver and then install the second needle bearing into the hole with the stamp mark on the bearing facing upward.

3. 25 hp and 30 hp models have a single needle bearing at the lower end of the driveshaft just above the pinion gear.

Obtain driver P/N YB6081, handle P/N YB6079 and guide plate P/N YB6169. Slide the guide plate onto the driver with the stamped mark 30A facing upward. Install the driver onto the threaded end of the handle. Use the guide plate to center the handle in the hole and then install the needle bearing with the stamped mark on the bearing facing upward toward the driver.

4. On all models except 4 hp and 5 hp, slide the driveshaft sleeve into the upper end of the lower unit with the notch in the lower flange facing AFT. Model 4 hp and 5 hp units do not have this sleeve.

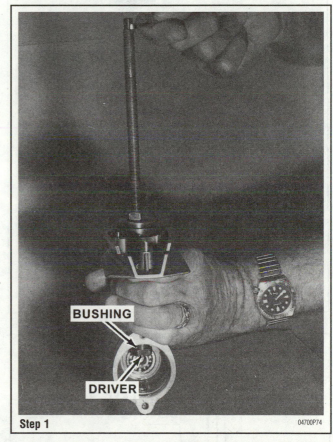

Step 1   04700P74

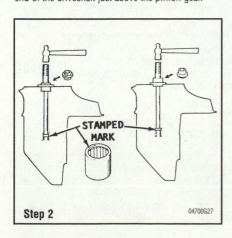

Step 2   04700G27

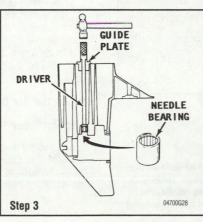

Step 3   04700G28

Step 4   04700G29

Oil Housing Bushing

♦ See accompanying illustrations

1. On all units except 4 hp, 5 hp, 25 hp and 30 hp, obtain driver P/N YB6028 and handle P/N YB6229. Drive the bushing into place until the shoulder seats on the housing.

2. On 25 hp and 30 hp models, press a new tapered roller bearing onto the driveshaft with the pinion end facing toward the tapered end of the bearing. Because of the driveshaft length, Take care not to bend or distort the driveshaft while the bearing is being pressed on.

Obtain driver P/N YB6167 and handle P/N YB6071.

Install the shim material saved during disassembly. Install the tapered roller bearing race over the shim material. Drive the race in squarely until it seats.

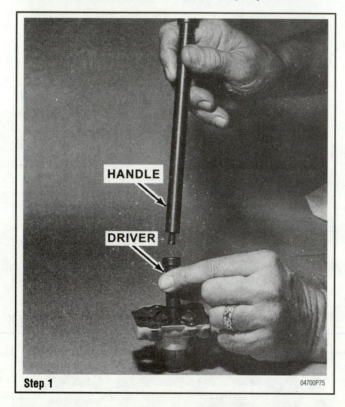

Step 1   04700P75

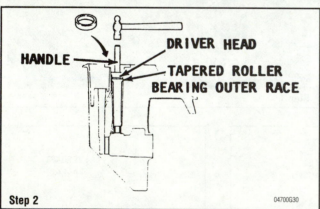

Step 2   04700G30

Driveshaft Oil Seals

♦ See accompanying illustration

➡ Two seals are installed into the top of the lower unit housing on the Model 4 hp and 5 hp units. On all other units, the oil seals are installed into the oil seal housing. These seals on all models are installed with the lip of both seals facing upward. Yamaha engineers have concluded

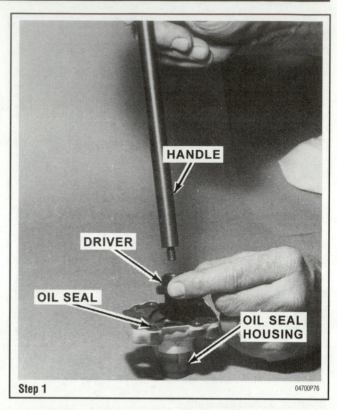

Step 1   04700P76

it is better to have both seals face the same direction rather than have them back to back as directed by other outboard manufacturers.

1. On 4 hp and 5 hp models, obtain driver P/N YB6014 and handle P/N YB6229.

Lower the seal installer and the first seal squarely into the seal recess on top of the lower unit, with the lip of the seal facing upward. Tap the end of the handle with a hammer until the seal is fully seated. After installation, pack the seal with Yamaha Grease A, or equivalent water resistant lubricant.

Install the second seal in the same manner, with the seal lip facing upward. Pack the second seal with grease.

On 6 hp and 8 hp models, obtain oil seal driver P/N YB6021 and handle P/N YB6071.

On 9.9 hp and 15 hp models, obtain oil seal driver P/N YB6022 and handle P/N YB6071.

On 25 hp and 30 hp models, obtain oil seal driver P/N YB6015 and handle P/N YB6071.

Lower the seal installer and first seal squarely into the oil seal housing recess, with the lip of the seal facing upward. Tap the end of the handle with a hammer until the seal is fully seated. After installation, pack the seal with Yamaha Grease A or equivalent water resistant lubricant.

Install the second seal in the same manner, with the seal lip facing upward. Pack the second seal with grease.

On all models except 4 hp, 5 hp, 25 hp and 30 hp, install the gasket and oil seal housing into the top of the lower unit over the driveshaft sleeve, to index with the dowel pin. Install two more dowel pins on the top surface of the oil seal housing.

4 hp and 5 hp models do not have an oil seal housing.

The oil seal housing on the 25 hp and 30 hp models is not installed until the backlash adjustment has been completed.

Pinion Gear And Driveshaft

♦ See accompanying illustrations

1. Lower the driveshaft down through the sleeve in the upper end of the lower unit. Coat the pinion gear with a fine spray of Desenex®, as instructed in the plan ahead paragraph prior to assembling. Handle the gear carefully to prevent disturbing the powder.

Hold the driveshaft in place with one hand and at the same time assemble the parts onto the lower end of the driveshaft with the other hand in the same order as they were removed. Hopefully they were kept in order on the work surface.

First, the washer goes on, followed by the thrust bearing. Next, install the same amount of shim material removed during disassembling. After the shim material is in place, slide on the washer and then the pinion gear. It may be necessary to rotate the driveshaft slightly to allow the splines on the driveshaft to index with the internal splines of the pinion gear. The teeth of the pinion gear will index with the teeth of the forward gear.

On 4 hp, 5 hp, 6 hp and 8 hp models, secure the pinion gear in place with the circlip. Slipping the circlip into the groove on the end of the driveshaft is not an easy task, but have patience and success will be the reward.

On all other models, once the pinion gear is in place, then start the threads of the pinion gear nut. Tighten the nut as much as possible by rotating the driveshaft with one hand and holding the nut with the other hand. The next step tightens the nut.

   2. Tighten the pinion gear nut as follows:

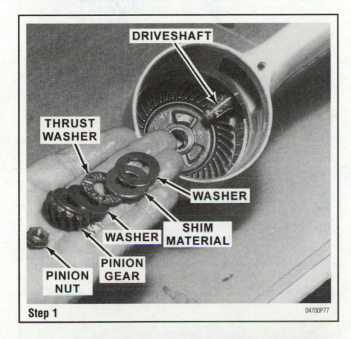

Step 1   04700P77

Step 2   04700P78

   On 9.9 hp and 15 hp models, obtain driveshaft tool P/N YB6228 and pinion nut wrench P/N YB6078.

   On 25 hp and 30 hp models, obtain driveshaft tool P/N YB6079 and pinion nut wrench P/N YB6078.

   Now, place the proper tool over the splines on the upper end of the driveshaft. Position a socket and torque wrench on the tool. Reach into the lower unit cavity and hold the pinion gear nut steady with the wrench. Rotate the driveshaft clockwise until the torque wrench indicates the following values for the models listed:

- 9.9 hp and 15 hp—19 ft. lbs. (26Nm)
- 25 hp and 30 hp—25 ft. lbs. (35Nm)

Pinion Gear Depth

◆ **See accompanying illustration**

➡**The proper amount of pinion gear depth (pinion gear engagement with the forward gear), is critical for proper operation of the lower unit and long life of the internal parts.**

➡**On 9.9 hp and 15 hp models, the pinion gear depth is measured and determined with the lower unit housing inverted (upside down). For all other units the measurement is made with the lower unit housing in the normal upright position.**

   1. Grasp the driveshaft and pull up or pull down (depending on the model being serviced as described in the previous paragraph). At the same time, check the pinion gear tooth engagement with the forward gear teeth to be sure contact is made the full length of the tooth. This can be accomplished by using a flashlight and looking into the lower unit opening. If the pinion gear depth is not correct, the amount of shim material behind the pinion gear must be adjusted. The addition or removal of shim material behind the pinion gear will not affect the forward gear backlash procedures.

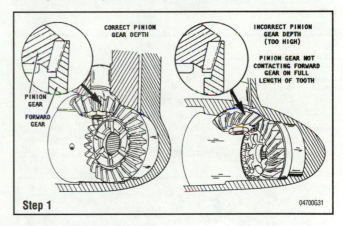

Step 1   04700G31

Bearing Carrier Cap

◆ **See accompanying illustration**

➡**Two seals are installed into the bearing carrier cap. These seals on 4 hp and 5 hp models are installed with the lip of both seals facing downward. Yamaha engineers have concluded it is better to have both seals face the same direction rather than have them back to back as directed by other outboard manufacturers. In this position, with both lips facing outward toward the water, after cap installation, the engineers feel the seals will be more effective in keeping water out of the lower unit. Any lubricant lost will be negligible.**

   1. On 4 hp and 5 hp models, obtain driver P/N YB6023 and handle YB6071. Place the bearing carrier cap on the work surface with the painted side facing upward. Install the first oil seal, using the driver and handle, with the lip facing downward. After the seal is installed, coat the seal lip with Yamalube Grease, or equivalent water resistant lubricant from the propeller side of the cap.

   Coat the lip of the second seal with grease. Install the second seal in the same manner, with the lip of the seal facing downward.

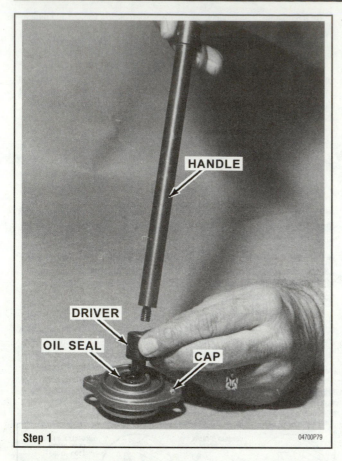

Step 1   04700P79

Reverse Gear Ball Bearing

▸ **See accompanying illustration**

1. On 4 hp and 5 hp models, obtain driver P/N YB6016 and handle P/N YB6071. Using the driver and handle, install the reverse gear ball bearing squarely into the carrier cap with the embossed letters facing OUTWARD. Stretch a new outer O-ring around the cap and coat the outside perimeter with Yamalube Grease, or equivalent water resistant lubricant.

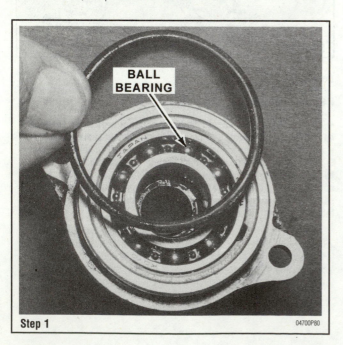

Step 1   04700P80

Bearing Carrier Bushing

▸ **See accompanying illustration**

1. On 6 hp and 8 hp models, obtain handle P/N YB6071. Install the bushing into the bearing carrier from the oil seal side with the shoulder of the bushing facing the handle.

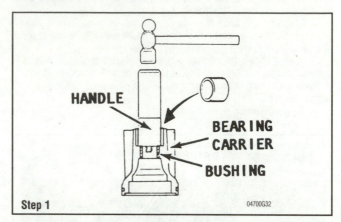

Step 1   04700G32

Bearing Carrier Needle Bearing

▸ **See accompanying illustration**

On 9.9 hp, 15 hp, 25 hp and 30 hp models, obtain driver P/N YB6081 and handle P/N YB6071.

On 9.9 hp and 15 hp models, lower the needle bearing into the bearing carrier from the propeller end of the carrier.

On 25 hp 30 hp models, lower the needle bearing into the bearing carrier from the lower unit end of the carrier.

1. In all cases, install the bearing with the stamped mark on the bearing facing upward toward the driver. Seat the bearing squarely into the bore, until the shoulder of the driver seats against the shoulder of the bearing housing. The bearing will then be correctly seated in the bearing carrier.

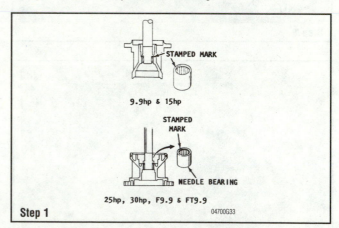

Step 1   04700G33

Bearing Carrier Oil Seal

▸ **See accompanying illustration**

On 6 hp, 8 hp, 25 hp and 30 hp models, obtain driver P/N YB6021 and handle P/N YB6229

9.9 hp and 15 hp models, obtain driver P/N YB6022 and handle P/N YB6071.

Pack the lips of both seals with Yamalube Grease, or equivalent water resistant lubricant.

➥**Two seals are installed into bearing carrier on all models except the 4 hp and 5 hp units. After installation of the bearing carrier to the lower unit, the lips of both seals face toward the propeller. Yamaha engineers** have concluded it is better to have both seals face the same direction rather than have them back to back as directed by other outboard manufacturers. In this position, with both lips facing outward toward the water after bearing carrier installation, the engineers feel the seals will be more effective in keeping water out of the lower unit. Any lubricant lost will be negligible.

1. The direction of installation into the bearing carrier varies depending on the model being serviced.

On 6 hp, 8 hp, 25 hp and 30 hp models, both seals are driven into the bearing carrier from the lower unit end of the carrier with the lips of the seals facing downward away from the driver.

On 9.9 hp and 15 hp models, both seals are driven into the bearing carrier from the propeller end of the carrier with the lips of the seals facing upward toward the driver.

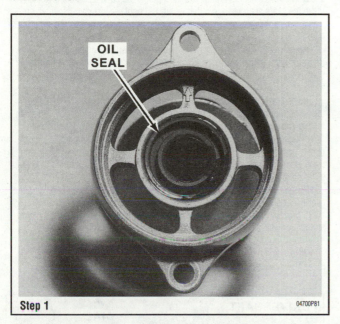

Step 1   04700P81

Reverse Gear Ball Bearing

♦ **See accompanying illustrations**

The reverse gear ball bearing is pressed into the bearing carrier on some models. On other models the reverse gear is pressed onto the reverse gear. If the reverse gear is a press fit do not forget to install any shim material removed from behind the reverse gear during disassembling. This shim material and, in some cases, a thrust washer, must be installed between the reverse gear and the ball bearing assembly in order to ensure proper mesh between the reverse gear and the pinion gear.

On 4 hp, 5 hp, 6 hp and 8 hp models, obtain driver P/N YB6016 and handle P/N YB6071.

On 9.9 hp and 15 hp models, obtain driver P/N YB6105 and handle P/N YB6071.

1. Install the ball bearing into the bearing carrier with the marks embossed on the bearing facing upward toward the driver.

Install the same amount of shim material saved during disassembly. Install the reverse gear.

2. On 25 hp, 30 hp models, position the reverse gear on a press with the gear teeth facing down. Place the same amount of shim material saved from disassembling, on the back of the gear. If servicing a Model 25 hp or 30 hp unit, install the thrust washer on top of the shim material.

Position the ball bearing assembly on top of the shim material, or the thrust washer, as the case may be, with the embossed marks on the bearing facing upward toward the press shaft.

Now, use a suitable mandrel and press against the inner bearing race.

➡ **Take care to ensure the mandrel is pressing on the inner race and not on the outer race or the ball bearings. Such action would destroy the bearing.**

Continue to press the bearing into place until the bearing, thrust washer, shim material and back of the reverse gear are all seated against each other.

Leave the assembled unit in place on the press and install the bearing carrier over the ball bearing. This is accomplished by using a suitable mandrel which will contact the inner hub of the bearing carrier and does not apply pressure on the ribs.

Continue to press until the outer race of the bearing seats against the bearing carrier surface.

3. Install a new O-ring into the outer groove of the bearing carrier. Apply a coating of Yamabond #4 to the O-ring and to its mating surface.

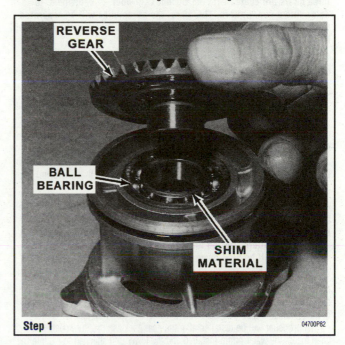

Step 1   04700P82

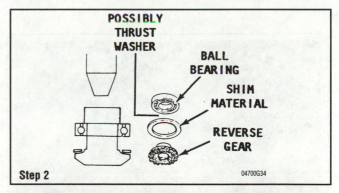

Step 2   04700G34

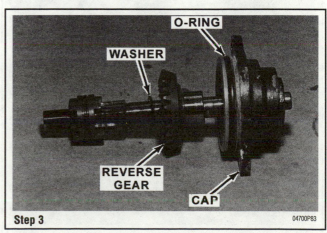

Step 3   04700P83

Coat the teeth of the reverse gear with a fine spray of Desenex®, as instructed in the Plan Ahead paragraph prior to assembling. Handle the gear carefully to prevent disturbing the powder.

Place the washer over the reverse gear. Slide the threaded end of the assembled propeller shaft into the bearing carrier.

4. Install the propeller shaft and bearing carrier into the gearcase.

On all models except 25 hp and 30 hp, install the two bolts and lockwashers. Tighten the bolts to a torque value of 5.8 ft. lbs. (8Nm).

➡**Assembling of parts at this time is not to be considered as final. The three gears are coated with the Desenex® powder, or equivalent, to determine a gear pattern. Therefore, the assemblies will be separated to check the pattern. During final installation the two mounting bolts will be coated with Loctite, or equivalent.**

If the assembler has omitted the application of the Desenex® powder and does not have plans to check the gear pattern, then this step may be considered as the final assembly of the bearing carrier. Loctite, or equivalent, should be applied to the threads of the bearing carrier attaching bolts.

On 25 hp and 30 hp models, align the keyway in the lower unit housing with the keyway in the bearing carrier. Insert the key into both grooves and then push the bearing carrier into place in the lower unit housing. Install the ring nut with the embossed marks facing outward, away from the bearing carrier.

Obtain special bearing carrier holding tool P/N YB6075. Tighten the locknut, using the tool and a torque wrench, to a torque value of 65 ft. lbs. (90Nm) in the direction indicated by the embossed on mark.

➡**Assembling of parts at this time is not to be considered as final. The three gears are coated with the Desenex® powder, or equivalent, to determine a gear pattern. Therefore, the assemblies will be separated to check the pattern. During final installation, one or more of the lock washer tabs will be bent down over the locknut.**

If the assembler has omitted the application of Desenex® powder and does not have plans to check the gear pattern, then this step may be considered as the final assembly of the bearing carrier. If such is the case, bend one or more of the lockwasher tabs down over the locknut to secure it in place.

The propeller will be installed after the gear backlash measurements have been made, the water pump installed and the lower unit attached to the intermediate housing.

Backlash

♦ **See accompanying illustration**

1. The lower unit backlash is measured with the unit in the upright position for 6 hp, 8 hp, 25 hp and 30 hp models. The backlash is measured with the lower unit inverted (upside down) for the 9.9 hp and 15 hp models.

➡**The manufacturer does not give backlash specification for the 4 hp and 5 hp models. Therefore, the next lengthy and detailed section may be omitted for these two models.**

Backlash is the acceptable clearance between two meshing gears, in order to take into account possible errors in machining, deformation due to load, expansion due to heat generated in the lower unit and center-to-center distance tolerances. A no backlash condition is unacceptable, as such a condition would mean the gears are locked together or are too tight against each other which would cause phenomenal wear and generate excessive heat from the resulting friction.

Excessive backlash which cannot be corrected with shim material adjustment indicates worn gears. Such worn gears must be replaced. Excessive backlash is usually accompanied by a loud whine when the lower unit is operating in neutral gear.

The backlash is measured at this time before the water pump is installed. If the amount of backlash needs to be adjusted, the lower unit must be disassembled to change the amount of shim material behind one of the gears.

As a general rule, if the lower unit was merely disassembled, cleaned and then assembled with only a new water pump impeller, new gaskets, seals and O-rings, there is no reason to believe the backlash would have changed. Therefore, it is safe to say this next section may be skipped.

However, if any one or more of the following components were replaced, the gear backlash should be checked for possible shim adjustment:

• New lower unit housing—check forward and reverse gear shim material and pinion gear depth.
• New forward gear tapered roller bearing—check forward gear backlash.
• New pinion gear—check pinion gear depth.
• New forward gear—check forward gear backlash.

BEARING CARRIER

Step 4   04700P84

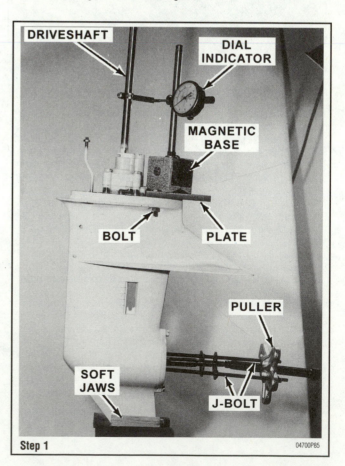

DRIVESHAFT — DIAL INDICATOR — MAGNETIC BASE — BOLT — PLATE — PULLER — SOFT JAWS — J-BOLT

Step 1   04700P85

- New reverse gear—check reverse gear backlash.
- New bearing carrier—check reverse gear backlash.
- New thrust washer on the 25 hp and 30 hp models—check reverse gear backlash.

FORWARD GEAR BACKLASH

Install the bearing carrier puller and J bolts onto the ribs of the carrier. With the bearing carrier attaching bolts or the bearing carrier locknut secured, the puller locks the shaft and prevents rotation in any direction. The puller will also lock the lower unit in forward gear.

Obtain backlash adjusting plate P/N YB7003. Secure the plate over the top of the lower unit with the nut and bolt provided with the tool.

Secure a dial indicator to the plate.

Obtain and install backlash indicator gauge P/N YB6265 onto the driveshaft. Adjust the end of the dial indicator to rest on the 30A mark on the gauge.

➡**On 9.9 hp and 15 hp models, after the dial indicator is in place and all is secure, invert the lower unit (turn the lower unit upside down). The forward gear and reverse gear backlash for these models is measured with the lower unit in this position.**

➡**On 6 hp, 8 hp, 25 hp and 30 hp models, after the dial indicator is in place and all is secure, leave the lower unit in the upright (normal) position. The forward gear and reverse gear backlash is measured for these models with the lower unit in this position.**

BACKLASH MEASUREMENT

Push down on the driveshaft, if the lower unit is upright, or pull down if the lower unit is inverted and at the same time slowly rotate the shaft, rocking the shaft back and forth through about a 25° to 30° arc.

As soon as a click is felt, stop all motion and observe the maximum deflection of the dial indicator needle. Acceptable backlash is as follows for the models listed:

- 6 hp & 8 hp   0.010–0.030 in. (0.25–0.75mm)
- 9.9 hp & 15 hp   0.009–0.027 in. (0.23–0.69mm)
- 25 hp & 30 hp 0.008–0.020 in. (0.20–0.50mm)

Remove or add shim material behind the forward gear to bring the backlash within specifications.

Forward gear—adding shim material decreases backlash.
Forward gear—removing shim material increases backlash.

➡**To determine how much shim material that must be moved to obtain the desired backlash, the manufacturer gives a very simple formula:**

A constant (a number depending on the unit being serviced) minus the backlash measurement and then the answer multiplied by two. This may sound complicated but it is not.

Formula: (Constant—measurement) x 2.

On 6 hp and 8 hp models, the constant is 0.5 if measuring in millimeters and 0.020 if measuring in inches. Therefore: Assuming the measurement was 0.008 in. and we needed 0.010 in. (0.020–0.008) x 2 = 0.024.

To increase backlash remove 0.024 in. shim material.
To decrease backlash add 0.024 in. shim material.

If measuring in millimeters use the same formula with the millimeter constant, then add or remove shim material as required.

On 9.9 hp and 15 hp models, the constant is 0.46 if measuring in millimeters and 0.018 if measuring in inches.

On 25 hp and 30 hp models, the constant is 0.35 if measuring in millimeters and 0.014 if measuring in inches.

➡**If the backlash specification cannot be reached by adding and removing shim material, the gears may have to be replaced.**

Remove the bearing carrier puller and J bolts from the propeller shaft.

REVERSE GEAR BACKLASH

Temporarily install the shift rod and the propeller. Push the shift rod into the lower unit a notch to shift the unit into neutral. Move the dial indicator out of the way temporarily and check to be sure when the driveshaft is rotated in either direction, the propeller shaft does not rotate. Now, push the shift rod into the lower unit one more notch to shift the lower unit into reverse gear. Rotate the driveshaft clockwise and check to be sure the propeller shaft rotates counterclockwise.

This is a test to see if the clutch mechanism was properly assembled and functions correctly.

Move the shift rod out from the lower unit one notch to shift the lower unit back into neutral. Rotate the driveshaft clockwise 20° to 30° with the other hand. This action will pre-load the reverse gear. Push the shift rod into the lower unit one notch to shift the unit into reverse gear. Hold the propeller with one hand to prevent it from turning and push in on the driveshaft with the other hand. Continue to hold the propeller immobile and while still pushing in on the driveshaft, rotate the driveshaft back and forth through about 20° to 30°. When a click is felt, stop all motion and observe the maximum deflection on the dial indicator.

Acceptable reverse gear backlash is as follows for the models listed.

- 6 hp & 8 hp   0.010–0.030 in. (0.25–0.75mm)
- 9.9 hp & 15 hp   0.031–0.045 in. (0.80–1.15mm)
- 25 hp & 30 hp 0.030–0.040 in. (0.70–1.00mm)

Remove or add shim material behind the reverse gear to bring the backlash to within specifications.

Reverse gear—adding shim material increases backlash.
Reverse gear—removing shim material decreases backlash.

➡**To determine how much shim material must be moved to obtain the desired backlash, the manufacturer gives a very simple formula:**

A constant (a number depending on the unit being serviced) minus the backlash measurement and then the answer multiplied by two. This may sound complicated but it is not.

Formula: (Constant – measurement) x 2.

On 6 hp, 8 hp models, the constant is 1.00 if measuring in millimeters and 0.039 if measuring in inches. Therefore: Assuming the measurement was 0.020 in. and we needed 0.031 in. (0.039 – 0.020) x 2 = 0.038.

To increase backlash add 0.016 in. shim material.
To decrease backlash remove 0.016 in. shim material.

If measuring in millimeters use the same formula with the millimeter constant, then add or remove shim material as required.

- 9.9 hp and 15 hp—0.038 in. (0.98mm)
- 25 hp and 30 hp—0.034 in. (0.85mm).

➡**If the backlash specification cannot be reached by adding and removing shim material, the pinion gear and/or the reverse gear may have to be replaced.**

Remove the shift rod and the propeller.

➡**25 hp and 30 hp models have a thrust washer between the shim material and the reverse gear. The thrust washer absorbs backlash. Therefore, it may be possible to replace the thrust washer and again check the backlash. The cost of a new thrust washer is minimal compared to the cost of a pinion gear and a reverse gear.**

After the proper amount of backlash and pinion gear depth has been obtained, check the gear mesh pattern.

Gear Mesh Pattern

◆ **See accompanying illustration**

All models to be held with the lower unit in the upright (normal) position.

Grasp the driveshaft and pull upward. At the same time, rotate the propeller shaft counterclockwise through about six or eight complete revolutions. This action will establish a wear pattern on the gears with the Desenex® powder.

1. Disassemble the unit and compare the pattern made on the gear teeth with the accompanying illustrations. The pattern should almost be oval on the drive side and be positioned about halfway up the gear teeth.

If the pattern appears to be satisfactory, clean the dye or powder from the gear teeth and assemble the unit one final time.

If the pattern does not appear to be satisfactory, add or remove shim material, as required. Adding or removing shim material will move the gear pattern towards or away from the center of the teeth.

After the gear mesh pattern is determined to be satisfactory, assemble the bearing carrier one final time. For all units except the 25 hp or 30 hp model apply Loctite to the threads of the attaching bolts. Tighten the bolts to a torque value of 5.8 ft. lbs. (8Nm).

If servicing a 25 hp or 30 hp unit, install the bearing carrier and then bend down one or more lockwasher tabs over the locknut.

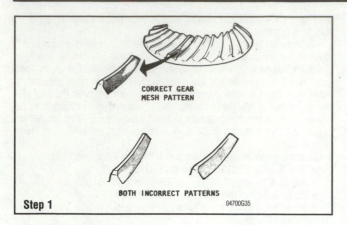

Step 1   04700G35

Water Pump Installation

♦ See accompanying illustrations

Installation of the water pump varies for the different models covered in this manual.

1. On 4 hp and 5 hp models, install the gasket and the base plate with the shift rod over the driveshaft. Index the gasket and plate over the two dowel pins. Secure the plate to the lower unit with the one bolt next to the shift rod. Seat the boot well onto the plate.

2. On 25 hp and 30 hp models, install a new O-ring into the oil seal housing. Slide the housing over the driveshaft and into the lower unit. Check to be sure the projection on the housing fits into the recess in the lower unit.

Install the two dowel pins on the top surface of the oil seal housing. Install the following parts over the driveshaft and index each over the two dowel pins, the oil seal protector, the gasket and then the outer plate cartridge.

Fit the Woodruff key into the driveshaft. Just a dab of grease on the key will help to hold the key in place. Slide the water pump impeller over the driveshaft with the rubber membrane on the top side and the keyway in the impeller indexed over the Woodruff key. Take care not to damage the membrane. Coat the impeller blades with Yamalube Grease, or equivalent water resistant lubricant.

Install the insert cartridge, the inner plate and finally the water pump housing over the driveshaft. Rotate the insert cartridge counterclockwise over the impeller to tuck in the blades. Seat all parts over the two dowel pins and secure the water pump housing with the three washers and bolts. Tighten the bolts to a torque value of 5.8 ft. lbs. (8Nm).

3. On 4 hp, 5 hp, 6 hp, 9.9 hp and 15 hp models, install a new water tube grommet into the water pump housing. Slide the gasket and the outer plate over the driveshaft. Fit the Woodruff key into place in the driveshaft. Just a dab of grease on the key will help to hold the key in place. The 4 hp and 5 hp models have an indexing pin.

Slide the water pump impeller onto the driveshaft with the keyway in the impeller indexed over the Woodruff key, or the indexing pin. Coat the impeller blades with Yamalube Grease, or equivalent water resistant lubricant.

Install the insert cartridge over the driveshaft. Rotate the cartridge counterclockwise over the impeller to tuck in the blades. Install another gasket and finally the water pump housing over the driveshaft. Check to be sure all parts are indexed over the two dowel pins.

4. On 4 hp, 5 hp, 6 hp, 9.9 hp and 15 hp models, position the left and right side plates over the water pump housing and secure them in place with the four washers and bolts. Tighten the bolts to a torque value of 5.8 ft. lbs. (8Nm).

9.9 hp and 15 hp models have an extra retaining plate on top of the water pump housing. This extra plate is secured in place with two Phillips head screws.

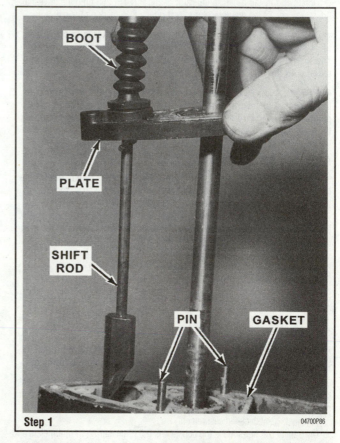

Step 1   04700P86

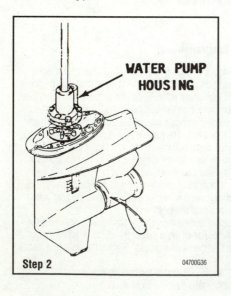

Step 2   04700G36

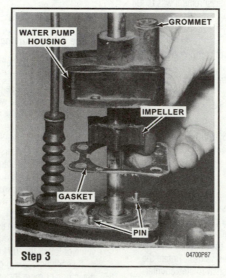

Step 3   04700P87

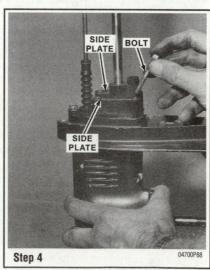

Step 4   04700P88

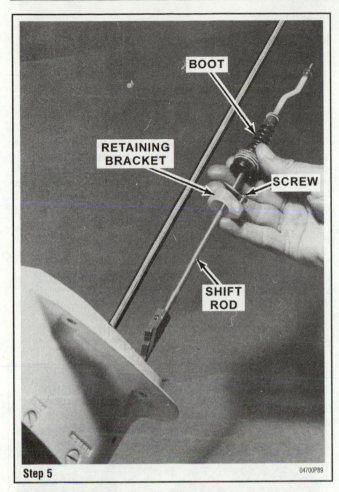

Step 5   04700P89

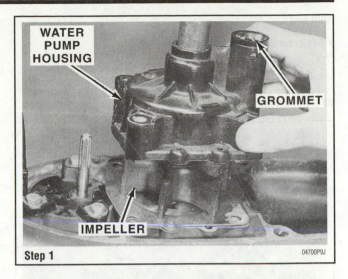

Step 1   04700P9J

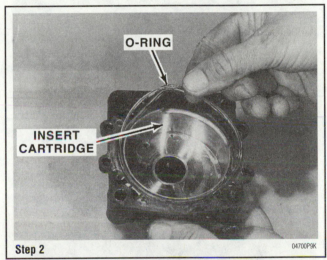

Step 2   04700P9K

5. On 4 hp, 5 hp, 6 hp, 9.9 hp and 15 hp models, install the shift rod and retaining bracket into the lower unit with the cam lobe facing toward the propeller shaft. Secure the rod in place by tightening the Phillips head screws into the retaining bracket. Fit the boot over the bracket.

Except 1–2 Cylinder Powerhead

The overhaul procedure for 3-cylinder, V4 and V6 units is essentially the same. Differences between the units have been called out in the procedures as necessary.

DISASSEMBLY

Water Pump

◗ **See accompanying illustrations**

1. Remove the four bolts and washers securing the water pump housing. Slide the water pump housing upward and free of the driveshaft. Pull out the water tube grommet from atop the water pump housing. Slide the impeller upward and free of the driveshaft. Remove and save the small Woodruff key.

2. Pull out the insert cartridge from the water pump housing. Remove and discard the O-ring.

3. Remove the outer plate and then the gasket beneath the plate. Slide both pieces upward and off the driveshaft.

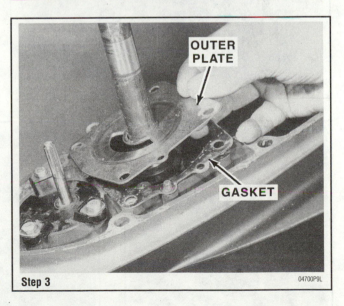

Step 3   04700P9L

Shift Rod

♦ **See accompanying illustrations**

1. Check to ensure the lower unit is in neutral gear. The shift rod cannot be removed if the unit is in forward or reverse.

2. Remove the three bolts and washers securing the shift rod cover and then pull the rod and cover off the lower unit.

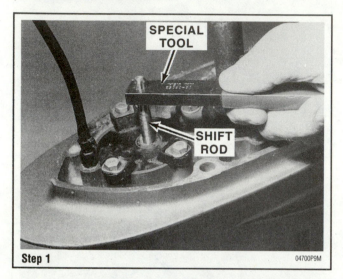

Step 1   04700P9M

Step 2   04700P9N

Oil Seal Housing

♦ **See accompanying illustrations**

1. Remove the four bolts securing the oil seal housing.

2. Using two screwdrivers, gently pry up on both sides of the oil seal housing. Lift the housing up and free of the driveshaft. If the housing is stubborn and cannot be removed at this time, proceed with the work. The housing will be removed in a later step when the driveshaft is pulled from the lower unit.

3. Remove and discard the O-ring around the oil seal housing.

➥**Removal of the seals and caged needle bearing destroys the sealing qualities of the seals and distorts the needle bearing cage. Therefore, once removed, these parts are unfit for further service and cannot be installed a second time. Remove the seals and bearing only if they need to be replaced and be absolutely certain new seals and bearing are available before removing the old parts.**

Obtain a slide hammer with jaw expander attachment. Use the tool to remove the oil seals one by one from the oil seal housing.

Obtain a suitable driver. Use the tool and the driver to drive the bearing from the oil seal through the top of the housing.

4. Watch for and save any shim material installed around the driveshaft. The shim material is critical in obtaining the correct backlash during assembling. Using the old shim material will save considerable time, especially starting with no shim material.

Lift out the shim material, thrust washer and thrust bearing. Slide all the pieces upward and off the driveshaft.

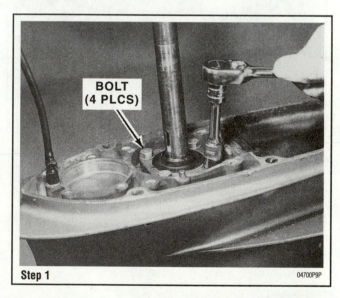

Step 1   04700P9P

Step 2   04700P9Q

Step 3   04700P9R

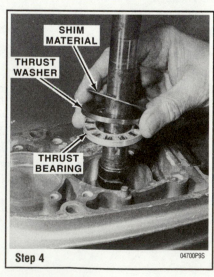

Step 4   04700P9S

Bearing Carrier

◆ **See accompanying illustrations**

1. Straighten the tabs on the lockwasher bent over the ring nut.

2. Note the word **OFF** embossed on the ring nut. Install the tool into the ring and rotate the ring in the direction indicated. Continue rotating the ring nut until the nut is free.

3. Remove the ring nut and the tabbed washer behind the nut.

4. Obtain a slide hammer with jaw expander attachment and pull the bearing carrier free.

5. Remove the bearing carrier. Take care not to lose the tiny key in the groove at the bottom of the lower unit. On counterrotating lower units, one half of the propeller shaft will come away with the bearing carrier, the other half will remain in the lower unit.

6. Watch for and save any shim material from the back side of the reverse gear. Be advised, on counterrotating units, this gear is the forward gear. The shim material is critical in obtaining the correct backlash during assembling. Using the old shim material will save considerable time, especially starting with no shim material.

7. Remove the spacer washer from the front of the reverse gear (forward gear on counterrotating units).

8. Remove and discard the O-ring around the bearing carrier.

➡ The reverse gear and ball bearing assembly is pressed into the bearing carrier. The ball bearing is pressed onto the back of the reverse gear and must be separated using a slide hammer with jaw expander attachment.

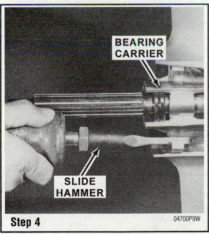

Step 1   04700P9T

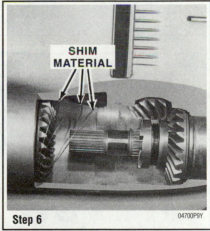

Step 2   04700P9U

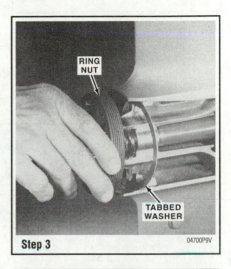

Step 3   04700P9V

Step 4   04700P9W

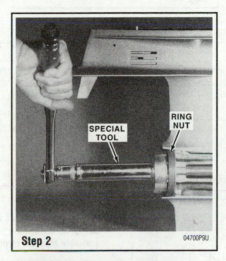

Step 5   04700P9X

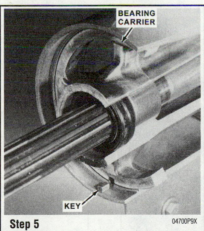

Step 6   04700P9Y

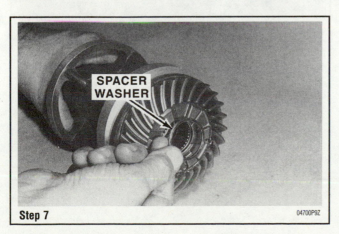

Step 7   04700P9Z

Step 8   04700P0A

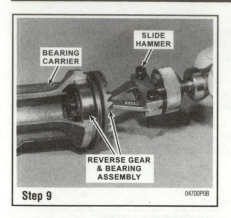

BEARING CARRIER • SLIDE HAMMER • REVERSE GEAR & BEARING ASSEMBLY

Step 9 04700P0B

REVERSE GEAR & BEARING ASSEMBLY • BEARING SEPARATOR

Step 10 04700P0C

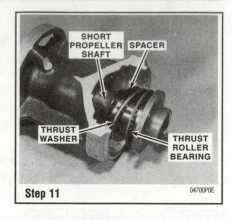

SHORT PROPELLER SHAFT • SPACER • THRUST WASHER • THRUST ROLLER BEARING

Step 11 04700P0E

The ball bearing or the ball bearing and reverse gear together must be pulled from the bearing carrier. For counterrotating lower units, these special words apply to the forward, not the reverse gear.

9. Obtain a slide hammer with jaw expander attachment and pull the bearing or the bearing and reverse gear from the bearing carrier. When using the tool, check to be sure the jaws are hooked onto the inner race.

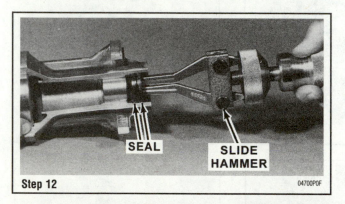

SEAL • SLIDE HAMMER

Step 12 04700P0F

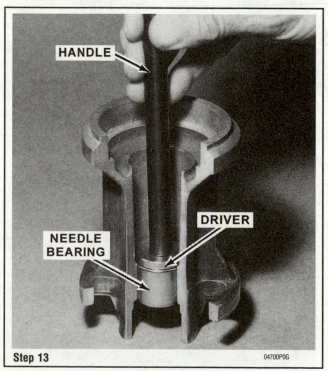

HANDLE • DRIVER • NEEDLE BEARING

Step 13 04700P0G

10. The ball bearing is pressed onto the back of the reverse gear. To remove this bearing, first obtain a universal bearing separator tool and then press on the inner race to separate the bearing from the gear.

On counterrotating lower units, obtain a universal bearing separator. Separate the forward gear from the bearing carrier. Remove the large thrust washer and the thrust roller bearing.

➡**Perform the following half of this step only if the needle bearing in question is no longer fit for service.**

The caged needle bearing set is pressed into the bearing carrier. To remove the bearing set, first obtain Yamaha Handle P/N YB6071 and Driver P/N YB6196. Drive the needle bearing set free of the bearing carrier.

11. On counterrotating lower units, pull the short propeller shaft from the bearing carrier. Remove the spacer, large thrust washer and thrust bearing.

➡**Removing the seals destroys their sealing qualities. Therefore, they cannot be installed a second time. Be absolutely sure a new seal is available BEFORE removing the old seal in the next step.**

12. Inspect the condition of the two seals in the bearing carrier. If the seals appear to be damaged and replacement is required, obtain a slide hammer and jaw attachment. Use these tools to remove the seals.

13. The caged needle bearing set is pressed into the bearing carrier. To remove the bearing set, first obtain Yamaha Handle P/N YB6071 and Driver P/N YB6196. Drive the needle bearing set free of the bearing carrier.

Propeller Shaft

◆ **See accompanying illustration**

1. Pull the propeller shaft, clutch and shifter assembly straight back and free of the lower unit.

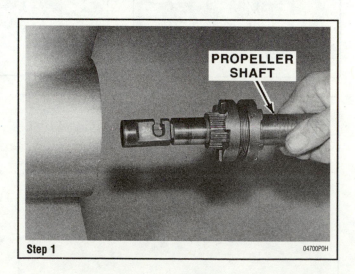

PROPELLER SHAFT

Step 1 04700P0H

Clutch Dog

▶ **See accompanying illustrations**

1. Insert an awl under the end loop of the cross pin ring and pry the ring free of the clutch dog.

2. Use a long pointed punch and press out the cross pin. Slide the clutch dog from the propeller shaft. Notice how both shoulders of the dog are an equal width, therefore the dog may be reinstalled either way, usually with the least worn side facing the forward gear. Remember this fact, as an aid during assembling.

➡ **As the work proceeds in the disassembly of the shift slide, six ball bearings will be found. A set of two small balls, two medium balls and two large balls. Take care to store these balls separately to avoid confusion during assembly.**

3. Unhook the shifter from the head or knob on the end of the shift slide. Pull out the shift slide. Take care not to lose the two medium ball bearings wedged between the shift slide and the propeller shaft.

4. Pry out the two medium balls from the shift slide.

5. Continue to pull out the shift slide until two more smaller balls appear. Pry out these balls from the shift slide.

6. Remove one large ball, a compression spring and another large ball from the shift slide.

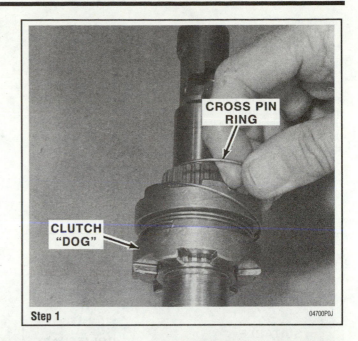

Step 1   04700P0J

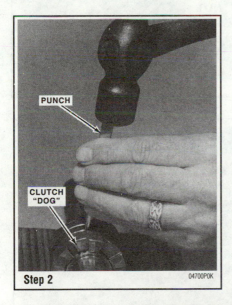

Step 2   04700P0K

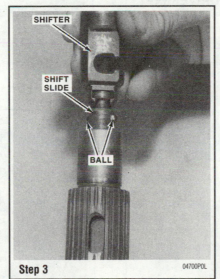

Step 3   04700P0L

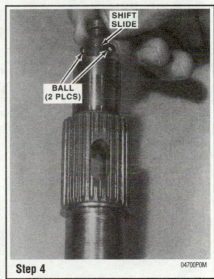

Step 4   04700P0M

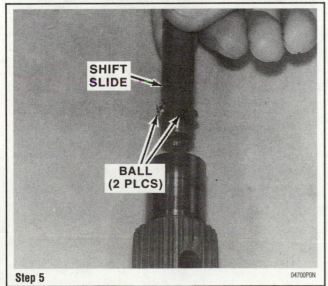

Step 5   04700P0N

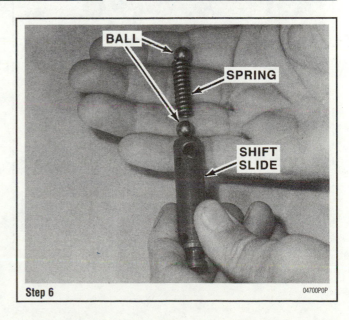

Step 6   04700P0P

Driveshaft

◆ **See accompanying illustrations**

Before the driveshaft can be removed, the pinion gear at the lower end of the shaft must be removed. The pinion gear is secured to the driveshaft with a nut.

➡**In most cases, when working with tools, a nut is rotated to remove or install it to a particular bolt, shaft, etc. In the next two steps, the reverse is required because there is no room to move a wrench inside the lower unit cavity. The nut on the lower end of the driveshaft is held steady and the shaft is rotated until the nut is free.**

1. Obtain driveshaft tool Yamaha P/N YB6201 and a suitable size wrench with which to rotate the tool.

2. Obtain a 22mm size socket. This socket will be used to prevent the nut from rotating while the driveshaft is rotated.

Now, hold the pinion nut steady with the socket and at the same time install the driveshaft tool on top of the driveshaft. With both tools in place, one holding the nut and the other on the driveshaft, use muscle to rotate the driveshaft counterclockwise and break the nut free.

3. Remove the pinion nut.

4. Gently pull up on the driveshaft and at the same time rotate the driveshaft. The pinion gear will come free from the lower end of the driveshaft.

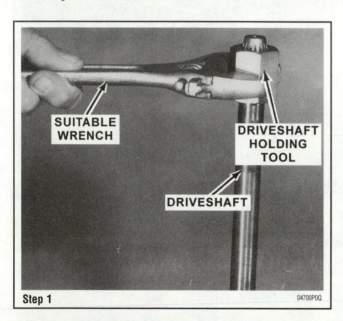

Step 1   04700P0Q

Step 3   04700P0S

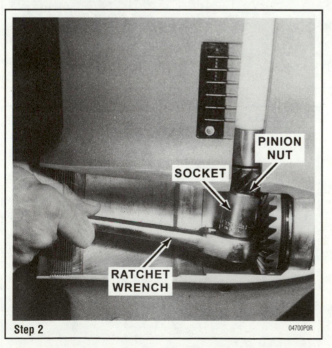

Step 2   04700P0R

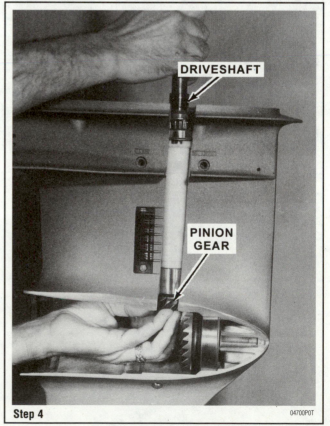

Step 4   04700P0T

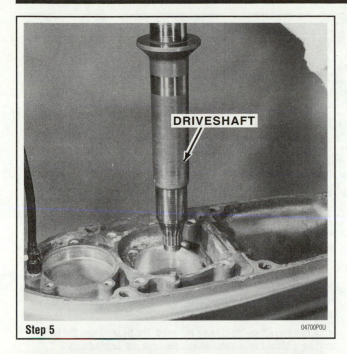

Step 5

DRIVESHAFT

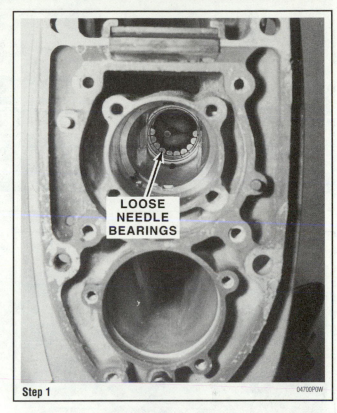

Step 1

LOOSE
NEEDLE
BEARINGS

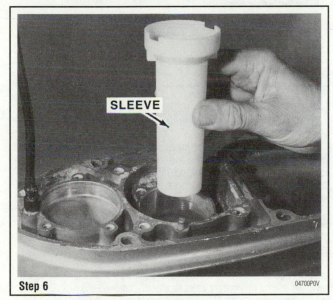

Step 6

SLEEVE

the needle bearings. They can be held in place with grease while the driveshaft is installed later. If any of the needle bearings are lost—bad news, the cage must be driven out and an entire new bearing set installed.

Forward Gear

♦ **See accompanying illustrations**

1. On standard lower units, lift out the forward gear and the tapered roller bearing.

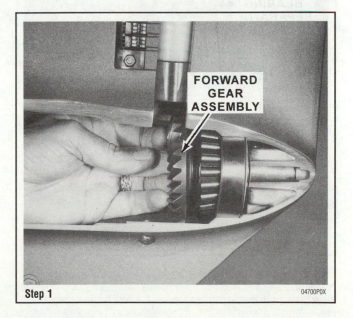

Step 1

FORWARD
GEAR
ASSEMBLY

5. Pull the driveshaft up out of the lower unit housing.

If the oil seal housing and the components beneath it were not removed the housing at this point will still be on the driveshaft and can now be easily removed. Go back and perform the steps which were omitted.

6. Lift out the driveshaft sleeve.

Driveshaft Needle Bearing

♦ **See accompanying illustration**

1. The loose needle bearing set is pressed into the driveshaft housing. To remove the bearing set, first obtain Yamaha Handle P/N YB6071 and Driver P/N YB6194. Drive the needle bearing set downward free of the bearing carrier.

Even if the entire bearing is not to be replaced, there is a good chance, when the driveshaft was removed some of the needle bearings fell away from the cage. This is not an indication the entire cage and needle set must be replaced. Save

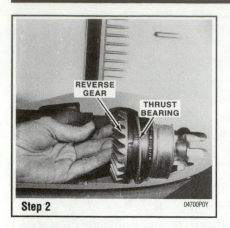

REVERSE GEAR

THRUST BEARING

Step 2   04700P0Y

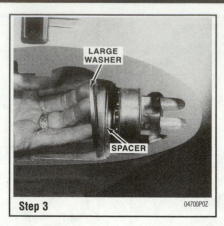

LARGE WASHER

SPACER

Step 3   04700P0Z

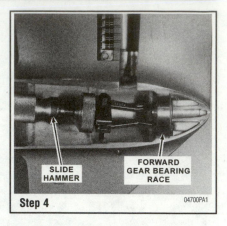

SLIDE HAMMER

FORWARD GEAR BEARING RACE

Step 4   04700PA1

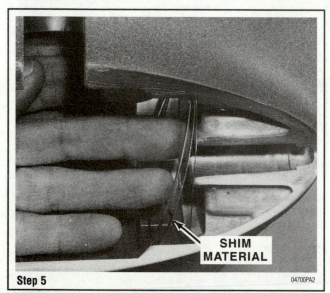

SHIM MATERIAL

Step 5   04700PA2

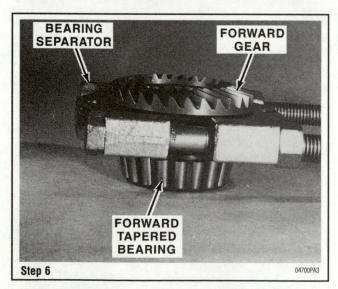

BEARING SEPARATOR

FORWARD GEAR

FORWARD TAPERED BEARING

Step 6   04700PA3

4. Obtain a slide hammer with expanding jaw attachment to pull the bearing race from the lower unit housing. Be sure to hold the slide hammer at right angles to the driveshaft while working the slide hammer.

5. Watch for and save any shim material found behind the forward gear (reverse gear on counterrotating units). The shim material is critical to obtaining the correct backlash during installation. Using the old shim material will save considerable time, especially starting with no shim material.

➡ **If a two piece bearing is to be replaced, the bearing and the race must be replaced as a matched set. Remove the bearing only if it is unfit for further service.**

6. Position a bearing separator between the forward gear (reverse gear on counterrotating units) and the tapered roller bearing. Using a hydraulic press, separate the gear from the bearing.

CLEANING AND INSPECTING

♦ **See Figures 21 thru 34**

Good shop practice requires installation of new O-rings and oil seals regardless of their appearance.

Clean all water pump parts with solvent and then dry them with compressed air. Inspect the water pump housing and oil seal housing for cracks and distortion, possibly caused from overheating. Inspect the plate and water pump cartridge for grooves and/or rough surfaces. If possible, always install a new water pump impeller while the lower unit is disassembled. A new impeller will ensure extended satisfactory service and give peace of mind to the owner. If the old impeller must be returned to service, never install it in reverse to the original direction of rotation. Installation in reverse will cause premature impeller failure.

If installation of a new impeller is not possible, check the seal surfaces. All must be in good condition to ensure proper pump operation. Check the upper, lower and ends of the impeller vanes for grooves, cracking and wear. Check to be sure the indexing notch of the impeller hub is intact and will not allow the impeller to slip.

Clean around the Woodruff key. Clean all bearings with solvent, dry them with compressed air and inspect them carefully.

Be sure there is no water in the air line. Direct the air stream through the bearing. Never spin a bearing with compressed air. Such action is highly dangerous and may cause the bearing to score from lack of lubrication. After the bearings are clean and dry, lubricate them with Formula 50 oil, or equivalent. Do not lubricate tapered bearing cups until after they have been inspected.

Inspect all ball bearings for roughness, scratches and bearing race side wear. Hold the outer race and work the inner bearing race in and out, to check for side wear.

Determine the condition of tapered bearing rollers and inner bearing race, by inspecting the bearing cup for pitting, scoring, grooves, uneven wear, imbedded particles and discoloration caused from overheating. Always replace tapered roller bearings as a set.

Clean the forward gear with solvent and then dry it with compressed air. Inspect the gear teeth for wear. Under normal conditions the gear will show signs of wear but it will be smooth and even.

Clean the bearing carrier with solvent and then dry it with compressed air. Never spin bearings with compressed air. Such action is highly dangerous and

2. On counterrotating lower units, lift out the reverse gear and tapered roller bearing assembly, then lift out the thrust bearing. Take care not to confuse this thrust bearing with the one previously removed. If these thrust bearing are to be reused, they must be installed in their original locations, because each develops a unique wear pattern. If a bearing is installed in a different location, the wear on the individual tiny roller bearings would be greatly accelerated and lead to premature failure of the bearing.

3. Lift out the large thrust washer and spacer.

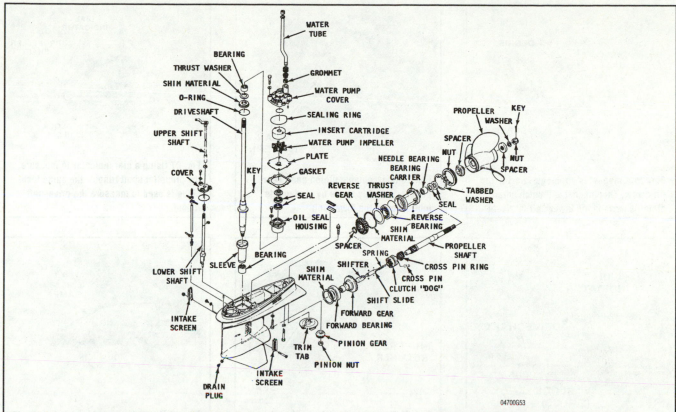

Fig. 21 Exploded view of a standard rotation lower unit with major parts identified. The internal mechanism of the counterrotating lower unit is shown vividly with photographs throughout this section

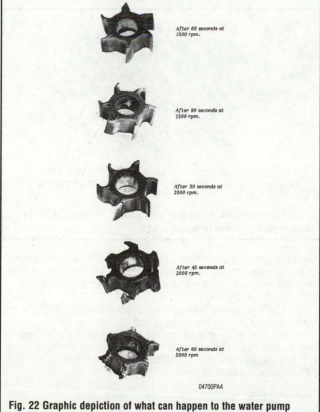

After 60 seconds at 1500 rpm.

After 90 seconds at 1500 rpm.

After 30 seconds at 2000 rpm.

After 45 seconds at 2000 rpm.

After 60 seconds at 2000 rpm

Fig. 22 Graphic depiction of what can happen to the water pump impeller if water is not circulated through the lower unit to the engine when the engine is running

Fig. 23 Grooves on the cross pin or marked wear patterns on the outer roller bearing races are evidence of premature failure of these or associated parts

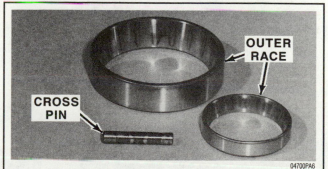

Fig. 24 A new needle bearing (left) along side a used needle bearing after the bearing was removed using the bigger hammer method

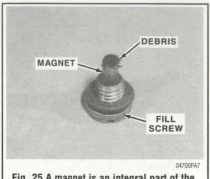

Fig. 25 A magnet is an integral part of the fill screw. This magnet will catch small metallic parts in the lower unit lubricant

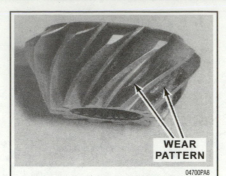

Fig. 26 Unacceptable pinion gear wear pattern, probably cause by inadequate lubrication in the lower unit

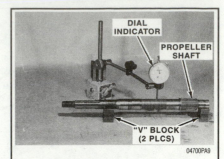

Fig. 27 Using a dial indicator to measure the propeller shaft runout. the same technique is used to measure the driveshaft runout

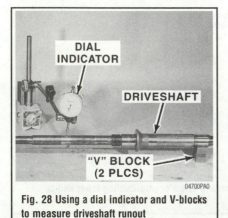

Fig. 28 Using a dial indicator and V-blocks to measure driveshaft runout

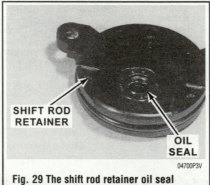

Fig. 29 The shift rod retainer oil seal should not be removed unless it is unfit for further service

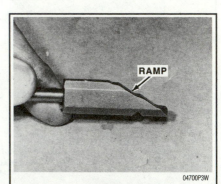

Fig. 30 The ramp should be carefully inspected. Any grooves, chips or other damage will affect the shift operation

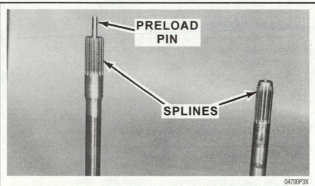

Fig. 31 a 90 hp driveshaft with preload pin (left) along side a driveshaft for other models covered in this manual. Check the condition of the splines and the return action of the preload pin

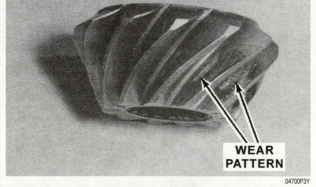

Fig. 32 Unacceptable pinion gear wear pattern, probably cause by inadequate lubrication in the lower unit

may cause the bearing to score from lack of lubrication. Check the gear teeth of the reverse gear for wear. The wear should be smooth and even.

Check the clutch dogs to be sure they are not rounded-off, or chipped. Such damage is usually the result of poor operator habits and is caused by shifting too slowly or shifting while the engine is operating at high rpm. Such damage might also be caused by improper shift rod adjustments.

Rotate the reverse gear and check for catches and roughness. Check the bearing for side wear of the bearing races.

Clean the driveshaft with solvent and then dry it with compressed air.

Inspect the driveshaft splines for excessive wear. Check the oil seal surfaces above and below the water pump drive pin or Woodruff key area for grooves. Replace the shaft if grooves are discovered.

Inspect the driveshaft bearing surface above the pinion gear splines for pitting, grooves, scoring, uneven wear, embedded metal particles and discoloration caused by overheating.

Inspect the propeller shaft oil seal surface to be sure it is not pitted, grooved, or scratched. Inspect the roller bearing contact surface on the propeller shaft for pitting, grooves, scoring, uneven wear, embedded metal particles and discoloration caused from overheating.

Inspect the propeller shaft splines for wear and corrosion damage. Check the propeller shaft and driveshaft for runout.

Place each shaft on V blocks and measure the runout with a dial indicator gauge at a point midway between the V blocks. The maximum acceptable runout for the propeller shaft is 0.0008 in. (0.02mm). The maximum acceptable runout for the driveshaft is 0.02 in. (0.5mm).

Inspect:
All bearing bores for loose fitting bearings.
Gear housing for impact damage.
Cover nut threads for cross-threading and corrosion damage.
Check the pinion nut corners for wear or damage. This nut is a special lock-

nut. Therefore, do not attempt to replace it with a standard nut. Obtain the correct nut from an authorized Yamaha dealer.

If the lower unit case is to be repainted. Mask off the threads engaging the cover nut. If this nut is installed against painted threads, a false torque value will be obtained upon tightening the nut and it is possible the nut could back off with continued use.

ASSEMBLY

Procedural steps are given to assemble and install virtually all items in the lower unit. However, if certain items, i.e. bearings, bushings, seals, etc. were found fit for further service and were not removed, simply skip the assembly steps involved. Proceed with the required tasks to assemble and install the necessary components.

Tapered Bearing

◆ See accompanying illustrations

The next two steps apply only if the ball bearing race was removed.

1. Insert the same amount of shim material saved during disassembly into the lower unit bearing race cavity. The shim material should give the same amount of backlash between the pinion gear and the gear, as before disassembling.

2. Obtain driver P/N YB6199 for V4 units or YB6258 for V6 units and handle P/N YB6071. Insert the bearing race squarely into the lower unit housing and then use the driver and drive the race into the housing until it is fully seated.

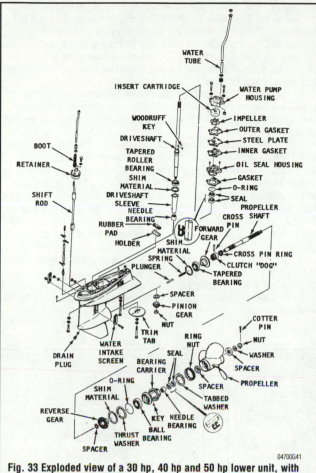

Fig. 33 Exploded view of a 30 hp, 40 hp and 50 hp lower unit, with major parts identified

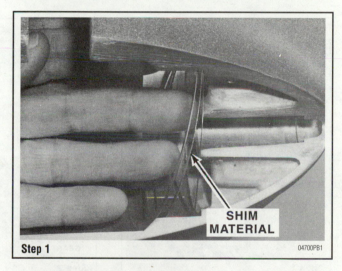

Step 1

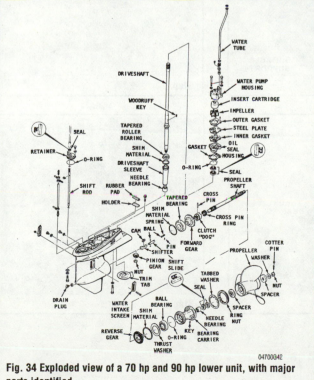

Fig. 34 Exploded view of a 70 hp and 90 hp lower unit, with major parts identified

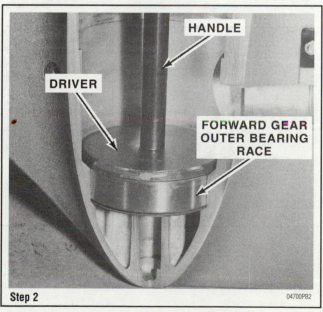

Step 2

Driveshaft Bushing and Bearing

♦ **See accompanying illustrations**

Perform the next step only if the needle bearing set was removed during disassembly. If the needle bearing set was not disturbed, apply a coat of Yamalube to the inner bearing surfaces and check to be sure all the needle bearings are still in place.

1. A single needle bearing is used at the lower end of the driveshaft just above the pinion gear. The installation procedure differs for V4 and V6 units.

On V4 units, obtain driver P/N YB6194, handle P/N YB6071 and guide plate P/N YB6213. Apply a coat of Yamalube around the inside of the bearing to help keep the needle bearings in place during installation. Slide the guide plate onto the driver with the stamped mark facing upward. Install the driver onto the threaded end of the handle. Use the guide plate to center the handle in the hole and then install the needle bearing with the stamped mark on the bearing facing upward toward the driver until the shoulder of the handle seats against the guide plate. This position places the needle bearing at a predetermined location in the lower unit.

On V6 units, obtain bearing installation tool P/N YB6029, driver P/N YB6246 and plate P/N YB6169. Apply a coat of Yamalube around the inside of the bearing to help keep the needle bearings in place during installation. Hold the bearing with the embossed numbers facing upward. Insert the driver into the bearing from the bottom and move the bearing into position into the torpedo housing of the lower unit. The bearing will be pulled up into place. Insert the bearing installation tool down into the driveshaft cavity, with the centering plate (sup-

plied with the tool), resting on the cavitation plate. Lower the long bolt through the bearing and driver. Slide the special plate up over the end of the bolt and install and tighten the lockwasher and nut. Place a wrench on the bolt head of the installing tool and tighten the bolt to seat the bearing. This action will draw the bearing upward to a predetermined location in the lower unit.

Slide the driveshaft sleeve into the upper end of the lower unit with the notch in the upper flange facing AFT

2. Position the forward gear (reverse gear on counterrotating models), tapered bearing over the gear. Use a suitable mandrel and press the bearing flush against the shoulder of the gear. Always press on the inner race, never on the cage or the rollers.

3. Obtain a suitable substance which can be used to indicate a wear pattern on the forward and pinion gears as they mesh. Machine dye may be used and if this material is not available, Desenex® Foot Powder (obtainable at the local Drug Store/Pharmacy), or equivalent may be substituted. Desenex® is a white powder available in an aerosol container. Before assembling either gear, apply a light film of the dye, Desenex®, or equivalent, to the driven side of the gear. After the gears are assembled and rotated several times, they will be disassembled and the wear pattern can be examined. The substance will be removed from the gears prior to final assembly.

4. On counterrotating lower units, insert the spacer and large thrust washer to rest up against the reverse gear bearing race.

5. Insert the thrust bearing and reverse gear assembly.

6. On standard lower units, position the forward gear assembly into the forward bearing race.

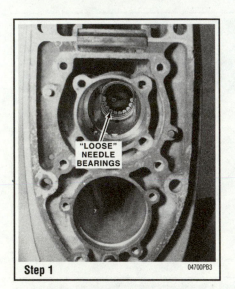

Step 1   04700PB3

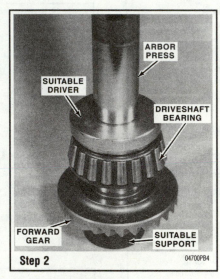

Step 2   04700PB4

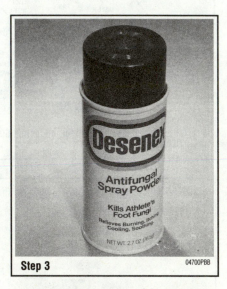

Step 3   04700PBB

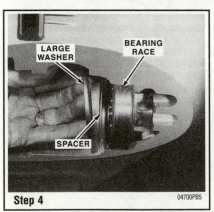

Step 4   04700PB5

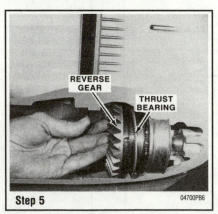

Step 5   04700PB6

Step 6   04700PB7

Pinion Gear and Driveshaft

◆ **See accompanying illustrations**

1. Lower the driveshaft down through the sleeve in the upper end of the lower unit.

Coat the pinion gear with a fine spray of Desenex®. Handle the gear carefully to prevent disturbing the powder.

2. Raise the pinion gear to allow the driveshaft to pass through the pinion gear. It may be necessary to rotate the driveshaft slightly to allow the splines on the driveshaft to index with the internal splines of the pinion gear. The teeth of the pinion gear will index with the teeth of the forward gear.

3. Once the pinion gear is in place, start the threads of the pinion gear nut. Tighten the nut as much as possible by rotating the driveshaft with one hand and holding the nut with the other hand. The next step tightens the nut.

4. Tighten the pinion gear nut as follows: Obtain driveshaft tool P/N YB6151 and a socket the same size as the pinion gear nut. Now, place the tool over the splines on the upper end of the driveshaft.

5. Position another socket and torque wrench on the tool. Reach into the lower unit cavity and hold the pinion gear nut steady with the proper size socket. Rotate the driveshaft clockwise until the proper torque is reached.

- 30 hp—36 ft. lbs. (49Nm)
- 40 hp—54 ft. lbs. (73Nm)
- 50 hp—54 ft. lbs. (73Nm)
- All others—68 ft. lbs. (95Nm)

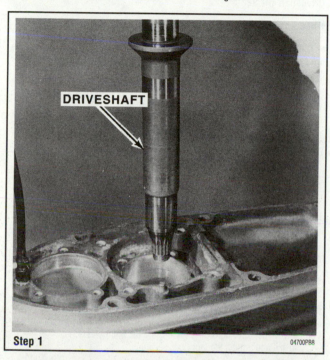

DRIVESHAFT

Step 1   04700PB8

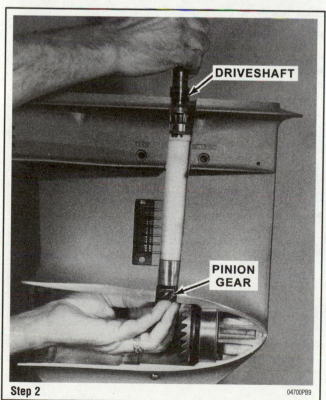

DRIVESHAFT

PINION GEAR

Step 2   04700PB9

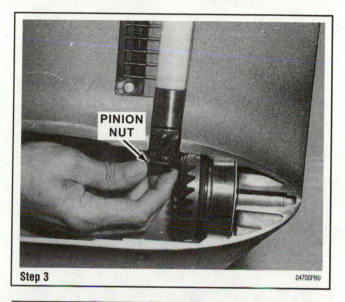

PINION NUT

Step 3   04700PB0

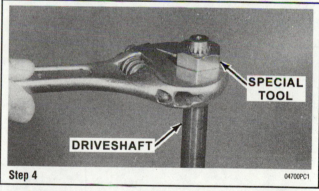

SPECIAL TOOL

DRIVESHAFT

Step 4   04700PC1

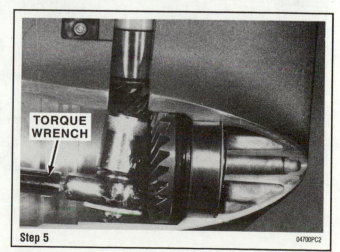

TORQUE WRENCH

Step 5   04700PC2

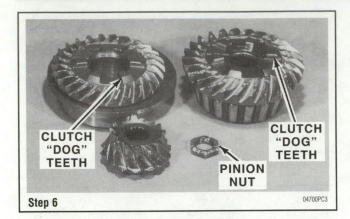

CLUTCH "DOG" TEETH

CLUTCH "DOG" TEETH

PINION NUT

Step 6   04700PC3

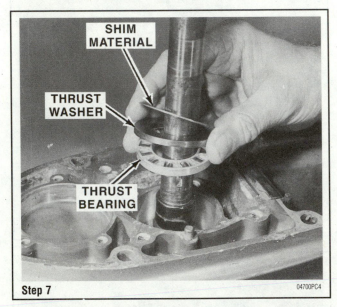

SHIM MATERIAL

THRUST WASHER

THRUST BEARING

Step 7   04700PC4

6. The damage to this gear set could possibly have been caused by failure to tighten the pinion gear nut to the required torque value. The pinion nut may have shaken loose, allowing the pinion gear to lower, drastically changing the backlash and gear mesh pattern. Notice the clutch dog engaging teeth were not affected, indicating the gear damage was not caused by a speed shift.

7. Slide the thrust bearing and then the thrust washer over the driveshaft. Next, install the same amount of shim material saved during disassembly. The shim material should give the same backlash between the pinion gear and the other two gears as was obtained prior to disassembling.

➡ Perform the next step only if the needle bearing set or oil seals were removed from the oil seal housing during disassembly. If the needle bearing set was not disturbed: apply a coat of Yamalube to the inner bearing surfaces, check to be sure all the needle bearings are still in place.

Driveshaft Oil Seals

◗ See accompanying illustrations

➡ Yamaha engineers have concluded it is better to have both seals face the same direction rather than back to back as directed by other outboard manufacturers.

1. Place the oil seal housing on a suitable surface, such as a small block of wood, in the same position with the correct end facing up (as it is positioned after installation).
Obtain driver P/N YB6196 and handle P/N YB6071. Insert the driver into the top of the bearing, with the numbers embossed on the bearing facing upward. Attach the handle to the driver and tap the bearing into the oil seal housing until it seats.
If servicing a V4 unit, obtain handle P/N YB6071 and seal installer P/N YB6016. If servicing a V6 unit, obtain P/N YB6196.
Lower the first seal squarely into the top of oil seal housing recess, with the lip of the seal facing upward. Place the seal installer over the seal and attach the handle. Tap the end of the handle with a hammer until the seal is fully seated. After installation, pack the seal with Yamaha Grease A or equivalent water resistant lubricant.
Install the second seal in the same manner, with the seal lip facing upward. Pack the second seal with grease.
Install a new O-ring around the oil seal housing. Coat the O-ring with Yamalube All Purpose Grease.

2. Lower the oil seal housing down over the driveshaft. Tap it lightly to seat it properly in the lower unit. Check to be sure the bolt holes align.

3. Install and tighten the four bolts securely.

Pinion Gear Depth

◗ See accompanying illustration

➡ The proper amount of pinion gear depth (pinion gear engagement with the forward gear), is critical for proper operation of the lower unit and long life of the internal parts.

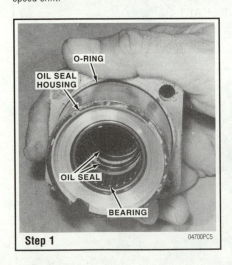

O-RING

OIL SEAL HOUSING

OIL SEAL

BEARING

Step 1   04700PC5

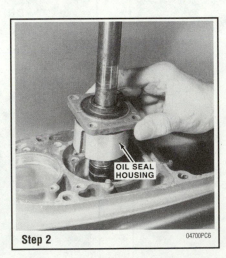

OIL SEAL HOUSING

Step 2   04700PC6

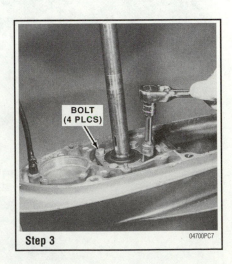

BOLT (4 PLCS)

Step 3   04700PC7

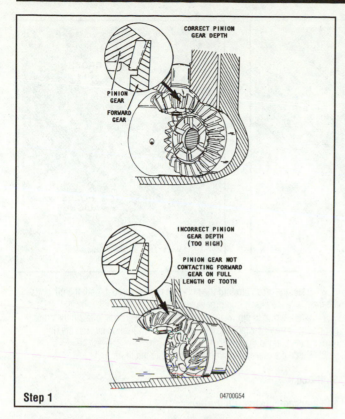

Step 1 04700G54

1. Grasp the driveshaft and pull up. At the same time, check the pinion gear tooth engagement with the forward gear teeth (reverse gear on a counterrotating lower unit), to be sure contact is made the full length of the tooth. This can be accomplished by using a flashlight and looking into the lower unit opening. If the pinion gear depth is not correct, the amount of shim material behind the pinion gear must be adjusted. The addition or removal of shim material behind the pinion gear will not affect the gear backlash procedures.

CLUTCH DOG

♦ **See accompanying illustrations**

1. Insert one large ball bearing, the compression spring and the other large ball bearing into the shift slide.

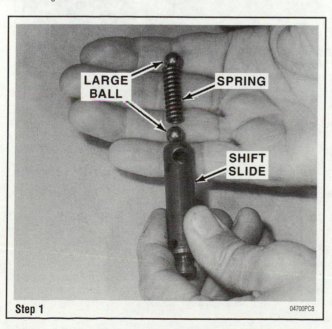

Step 1 04700PC8

2. Apply just a dab of grease to the two smallest balls to help keep them in place and then insert them into the holes nearest the open end of the shift slide. Insert the shift slide into the propeller shaft with the large hole in the slide aligned with the slot in the propeller shaft. Continue to insert the shift slide into the propeller shaft until both small balls enter the shaft—then stop.

3. Apply a dab of grease to the medium size balls to help keep them in place and then insert them into the holes nearest the necked end of shift slide. Continue to insert the shift slide into the propeller shaft until both medium balls are about to enter the shaft—then stop.

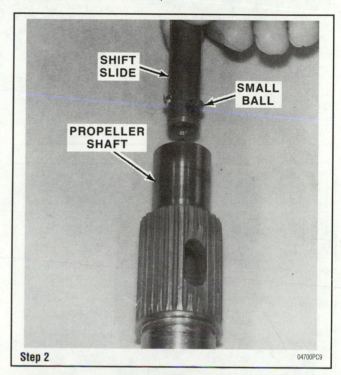

Step 2 04700PC9

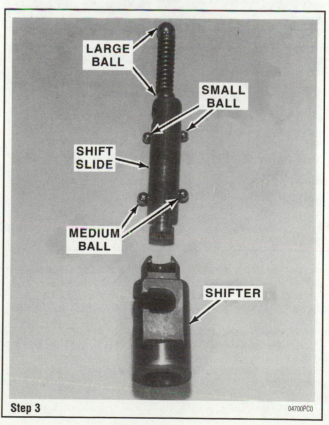

Step 3 04700PC0

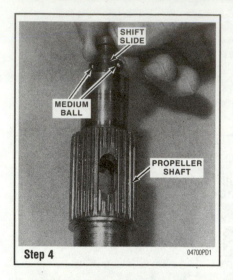

Step 4   04700PD1

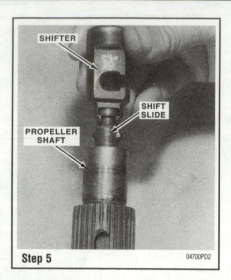

Step 5   04700PD2

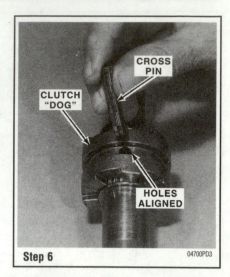

Step 6   04700PD3

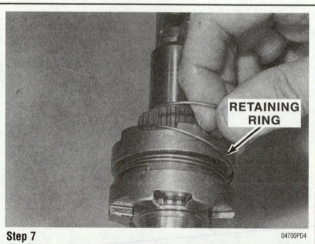

Step 7   04700PD4

6. Insert the cross pin into the hole and push it through until the pin ends are flush with the clutch dog groove surface.

7. Wrap the cross pin retaining ring around the groove to retain the cross pin. The ring may be wrapped in either direction. Check to be sure the ring turns do not overlap one another.

8. Guide the assembled propeller shaft into the lower unit.

Shift Rod

♦ **See accompanying illustration**

1. Lower the shift rod down into the lower unit and through the hole in the shifter. On standard lower units, the cam on the shift rod must face to starboard, on counterrotating lower units, this cam must face to port.

Install and tighten the three securing bolts.

Step 1   04700PD6

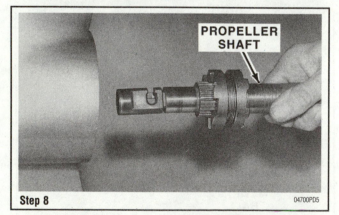

Step 8   04700PD5

4. Hook the shifter onto the knob on the end of the shift slide. Push in the shift slide until the medium balls enter the propeller shaft and seat themselves into internal grooves inside the shaft. Stop the action when a click is heard, indicating the two small balls have moved into the neutral groove in the propeller shaft. There is only one groove, so wiggle the slide back and forth until the ball is definitely seated in the groove.

5. Slide the clutch dog onto the propeller shaft, with the hole in the dog aligned with the two holes (hopefully already aligned), of the shaft and shift slide. Notice how both shoulders of the dog are an equal width, therefore the dog may be installed either way, usually with the least worn side facing the forward gear.

Bearing Carrier Needle Bearing And Oil Seal

♦ **See accompanying illustration**

1. Obtain driver P/N YB6196 and handle P/N YB6071.

Lower the needle bearing into the bearing carrier from the propeller end of the carrier.

In all cases, install the bearing with the stamped mark on the bearing facing upward toward the driver. Seat the bearing squarely into the bore, until the shoulder of the driver seats against the shoulder of the bearing housing. The

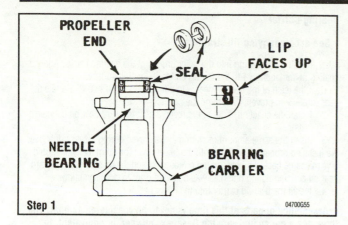

PROPELLER END · SEAL · LIP FACES UP · NEEDLE BEARING · BEARING CARRIER

Step 1   04700G55

bearing will then be correctly seated in the bearing carrier. Use the same tools and install both oil seals.

Pack the lips of both seals with Yamalube Grease, or equivalent water resistant lubricant.

➡ **Two seals are installed into the bearing carrier. After installation of the bearing carrier into the lower unit, the lips of both seals face toward the propeller. Yamaha engineers have concluded it is better to have both seals face the same direction rather than back to back as directed by other outboard manufacturers. In this position, with both lips facing outward toward the water after bearing carrier installation, the engineers feel the seals will be more effective in keeping water out of the lower unit. Any lubricant lost will be negligible.**

Obtain driver P/N YB6195 and handle P/N YB6071.

Both seals are driven into the bearing carrier from the propeller end of the carrier with the lips of the seals facing downward toward the driver.

Lower the first seal squarely into the bearing carrier with the lip of the seal facing downward. Place the seal installer over the seal and attach the handle. Tap the end of the handle with a hammer until the seal is fully seated. After installation, pack the seal with Yamaha Grease A or equivalent water resistant lubricant.

Install the second seal in the same manner, with the seal lip facing downward. Pack the second seal with grease.

Reverse Gear Ball Bearing—Standard Lower Units

◆ **See accompanying illustrations**

The reverse gear ball bearing is pressed onto the reverse gear, because the reverse gear is a press fit. Do not forget to install the thrust washer, between the reverse gear and the ball bearing assembly. This thrust washer will ensure proper mesh between the reverse gear and the pinion gear.

1. Position the reverse gear on a press with the gear teeth facing down. Install the thrust washer on top of the reverse gear.

Position the ball bearing assembly on top of the thrust washer, with the embossed marks on the bearing facing upward toward the press shaft.

Now, use a suitable mandrel and press against the inner bearing race.

➡ **Take care to ensure the mandrel is pressing on the inner race and not on the outer race or the ball bearings. Such action would destroy the bearing.**

Continue to press the bearing into place until the bearing, thrust washer and back of the reverse gear are all seated against each other.

2. Place the bearing carrier on the press with the lower unit end facing up, as shown. Fit the reverse gear ball bearing into the top of the bearing carrier. Obtain a suitable mandrel which will rest only on the inner hub of the reverse gear. Do not use a mandrel which would apply pressure on the gear teeth.

Continue to press until the outer race of the bearing seats against the bearing carrier surface.

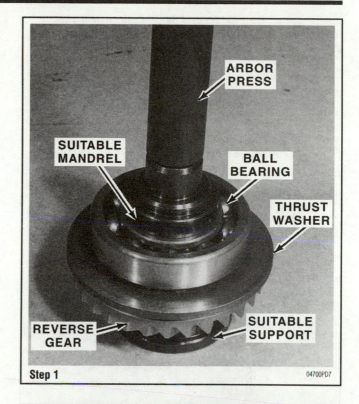

ARBOR PRESS · SUITABLE MANDREL · BALL BEARING · THRUST WASHER · REVERSE GEAR · SUITABLE SUPPORT

Step 1   04700PD7

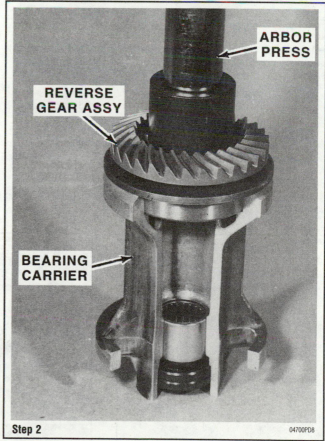

ARBOR PRESS · REVERSE GEAR ASSY · BEARING CARRIER

Step 2   04700PD8

Short Propeller Shaft and Forward Gear—Counterrotating Lower Units

◆ **See accompanying illustration**

1. Slide the thrust bearing, large thrust washer and spacer onto the short propeller shaft. Insert the shaft into the bearing carrier.

Position the forward gear on a press with the gear teeth facing down. Install the thrust bearing and then the large thrust washer on top of the reverse gear.

Position the ball bearing assembly on top of the thrust washer, with the embossed marks on the bearing facing upward—toward the press shaft.

Now, use a suitable mandrel and press against the inner bearing race.

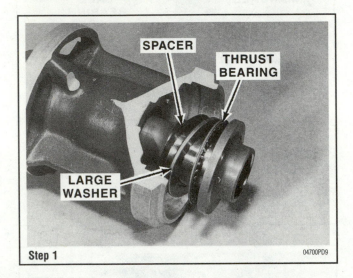

SPACER
THRUST BEARING
LARGE WASHER

Step 1   04700PD9

➡ **Take care to ensure the mandrel is pressing on the inner race and not on the outer race or the ball bearings. Such action would destroy the bearing.**

Continue to press the bearing into place until the ball bearing, thrust bearing, thrust washer and back of the forward gear are all seated against each other.

Place the bearing carrier on the press with the lower unit end facing up, with the short propeller shaft inserted. Fit the forward gear ball bearing into the top of the bearing carrier. Obtain a suitable mandrel which will rest only on the inner hub of the forward gear. Do not use a mandrel which would apply pressure on the gear teeth.

Continue to press until the outer race of the bearing seats against the bearing carrier surface.

Bearing Carrier

◆ **See accompanying illustrations**

1. Install a new O-ring into the outer groove of the bearing carrier. Apply a coating of Yamabond #4 to the O-ring and to its mating surface.

Coat the teeth of the reverse gear with a fine spray of Desenex®. Handle the gear carefully to prevent disturbing the powder.

2. Install the spacer in front of the reverse gear (forward gear on counterrotating units).

3. Insert the same amount of shim material saved during disassembly over the installed propeller shaft and into the lower unit. The shim material should give the same backlash between the pinion gear and the reverse gear (forward gear on counterrotating units) as was obtained prior to disassembling.

4. Install the bearing carrier into the lower unit.

➡ **Assembling of parts at this time is not to be considered as final. The three gears are coated with the Desenex® powder, or equivalent, to determine a gear pattern. Therefore, the assemblies will be separated to check the pattern. During final installation the two mounting bolts will be coated with Loctite, or equivalent.**

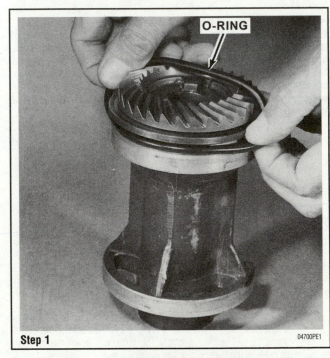

O-RING

Step 1   04700PE1

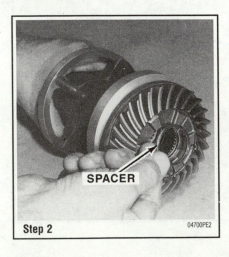

SPACER

Step 2   04700PE2

SHIM MATERIAL

Step 3   04700PE3

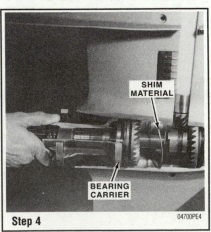

SHIM MATERIAL
BEARING CARRIER

Step 4   04700PE4

Step 5   04700PE6

Step 6   04700PE7

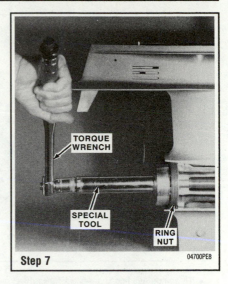

Step 7   04700PE8

If the assembler has omitted the application of the Desenex® powder and does not have plans to check the gear pattern, then this step may be considered as the final assembly of the bearing carrier. Loctite, or equivalent, should be applied to the threads of the bearing carrier attaching bolts.

5. Align the keyway in the lower unit housing with the keyway in the bearing carrier. Insert the key into both grooves and then push the bearing carrier into place in the lower unit housing.

6. Install a tabbed washer against the bearing carrier and then install the ring nut with the embossed marks facing outward, away from the bearing carrier.

7. Obtain special bearing carrier holding tool from your local Yamaha dealer. These tools are model specific. Tighten the locknut, in the direction indicated by the embossed on mark to the following specification.

- 30 hp—65 ft. lbs. (90Nm)
- 40 hp and 50 hp—95 ft. lbs. (130Nm)
- V6—140 ft. lbs. (190Nm)
- All others—105 ft. lbs. (145Nm)

➡**Assembling of parts at this time is not to be considered as final. The three gears are coated with the Desenex® powder, or equivalent, to determine a gear pattern. Therefore, the assemblies will be separated to check the pattern. During final installation, one or more of the lock washer tabs will be bent down over the locknut.**

If the assembler has omitted the application of Desenex® powder and does not have plans to check the gear pattern, then this step may be considered as the final assembly of the bearing carrier. If such is the case, bend one or more of the tabbed washer tabs down over the locknut to secure it in place.

Propeller

The propeller will be installed after the gear backlash measurements have been made, the water pump installed and the lower unit attached to the intermediate housing.

Gear Mesh Pattern

◆ See accompanying illustration

This step is only necessary if Desenex®, or similar material, was applied to the three gears prior to assembling.

Grasp the driveshaft and pull upward. At the same time, rotate the propeller shaft counterclockwise through about six or eight complete revolutions. This action will establish a wear pattern on the gears with the Desenex® powder.

1. Disassemble the unit and compare the pattern made on the gear teeth with the accompanying illustrations. The pattern should almost be oval on the drive side and be positioned about halfway up the gear teeth.

If the pattern appears to be satisfactory, clean the dye or powder from the gear teeth and assemble the unit one final time.

If the pattern does not appear to be satisfactory, add or remove shim material, behind the pinion gear, as required. Adding or removing shim material will move the gear pattern towards or away from the center of the teeth.

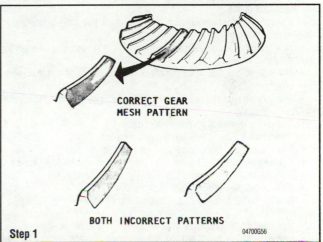

CORRECT GEAR MESH PATTERN

BOTH INCORRECT PATTERNS

Step 1   04700G56

After the gear mesh pattern is determined to be satisfactory, assemble the bearing carrier again to check for backlash, as described in the following paragraphs.

Backlash

GENERAL INFORMATION

◆ See Figure 35

Backlash is the acceptable clearance between two meshing gears, in order to take into account possible errors in machining, deformation due to load, expansion due to heat generated in the lower unit and center-to-center distance tolerances. A no backlash condition is unacceptable, as such a condition would mean the gears are locked together or are too tight against each other which would cause phenomenal wear and generate excessive heat from the resulting friction.

Excessive backlash which cannot be corrected with shim material adjustment indicates worn gears. Such worn gears must be replaced. Excessive backlash is usually accompanied by a loud whine when the lower unit is operating in neutral gear.

The backlash is measured at this time before the water pump is installed. If the amount of backlash needs to be adjusted, the lower unit must be disassembled to change the amount of shim material behind one of the gears.

As a general rule, if the lower unit was merely disassembled, cleaned and then assembled with only a new water pump impeller, new gaskets, seals and O-rings, there is no reason to believe the backlash would have changed. Therefore, it is safe to say this next section may be skipped.

However, if any one or more of the following components were replaced, the gear backlash should be checked for possible shim adjustment:

Fig. 35 Wear pattern on a gear set sprayed with Desenex® foot powder

• New lower unit housing—check forward and reverse gear shim material and pinion gear depth.
• New forward gear tapered roller bearing—check forward gear backlash (on standard lower units).
• New reverse gear tapered roller bearing—check reverse gear backlash (on counter-rotating units).
• New reverse gear ball bearing—check reverse gear backlash (on standard lower units).
• New forward gear ball bearing—check forward gear backlash (on counter-rotating lower units).
• New pinion gear—check pinion gear depth.
• New forward gear—check forward gear backlash.
• New reverse gear—check reverse gear backlash.
• New bearing carrier—check reverse gear backlash (on standard lower units), check forward gear backlash (on counterrotating lower units).
• New drive shaft—check pinion gear depth.
• New driveshaft thrust bearing, thrust washer or spacer—check pinion gear depth.
• New driveshaft oil seal housing—check pinion gear depth.
• New forward gear thrust bearing, thrust washer or spacer—check forward gear backlash.
• New reverse gear thrust bearing, thrust washer or spacer—check reverse gear backlash.

STANDARD LOWER UNIT—FORWARD GEAR BACKLASH MEASUREMENT COUNTERROTATING LOWER UNIT—REVERSE GEAR BACKLASH MEASUREMENT

♦ See accompanying illustration

1. Install the bearing carrier puller and J bolts onto the ribs of the carrier. With the bearing carrier attaching bolts or the bearing carrier locknut secured, the puller locks the shaft and prevents rotation in any direction. The puller will also lock the lower unit in forward gear (on standard lower units) or reverse gear (on counterrotating lower units).
Obtain backlash adjusting plate P/N YB7003. Secure the plate over the top of the lower unit with the nut and bolt provided with the tool.
Secure a dial indicator to the plate.
Obtain and install backlash indicator gauge P/N YB6265 onto the driveshaft. Adjust the end of the dial indicator to rest on the mark on the gauge.

➡After the dial indicator is in place and all is secure, leave the lower unit in the upside-down position. The forward gear and reverse gear backlash is measured for these models with the lower unit in this position.

Slowly rotate the driveshaft, rocking the shaft back and forth through about a 25° to 30° arc, without any rotation of the propeller shaft. At the outer limits of the arc, a click will be heard. This click sound occurs when the pinion gear tooth contacts one face of the driven gear tooth. Another click is heard when the pinion gear swings back and the pinion tooth contacts the face of the adjacent driven gear tooth. The arc between the two clicks represents the backlash, or free play, between the gears.

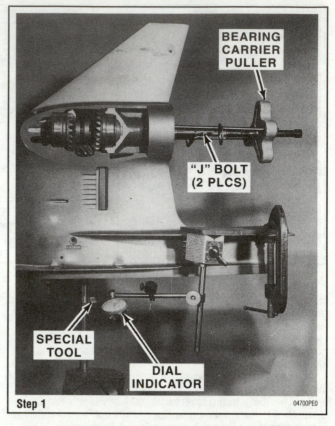

Step 1

Zero the dial indicator gauge at the first click. As soon as the second click is heard, stop all motion and observe the maximum deflection of the dial indicator needle. Acceptable backlash measurement is as follows for the models listed:

• 30 hp   0.008–0.020 in. (0.2–0.5mm)
• 40 hp and 50 hp   0.003–0.010 in. (0.09–0.26mm)
• 70 hp and 90 hp   0.004–0.011 in. (0.09–0.28mm)
• V4 units   0.013–0.018 in. (0.32–0.45mm)
• V6 units   0.011–0.015 in. (0.28–0.39mm) w/standard lower unit.
• V4 and V6   0.038–0.049 in. (0.97–1.25mm) w/counterrotating lower unit.

Remove or add shim material behind the forward gear (on standard lower units) or reverse gear (on counterrotating lower units), to bring the backlash within specifications.
On the forward gear of standard lower units, adding shim material decreases backlash and removing shim material increases backlash.
On the reverse gear of counterrotating lower units, adding shim material decreases backlash and removing shim material increases backlash.

➡The actual measurement and the amount of shim material to be added or removed are related but not equal. Therefore, some very simple arithmetic must be performed.

To determine how much shim material must be moved to obtain the desired backlash, the manufacturer gives a very simple formula:
A constant (a number depending on the unit being serviced) minus the backlash measurement and then the answer multiplied by a multiplying factor. This may sound complicated but it is not.
Formula:
(Measurement – constant) x factor.
If the constant has a greater value than the measurement, the formula becomes:
(Constant – measurement) x factor.
The constant and the multiplying factor vary, depending on the model hp unit being serviced. No problem! The following list indicates the exact constant and multiplying factor for each of the powerheads covered in this manual.

Model	Constant Inches (mm)	Multiplying Factor
• 30 hp	0.014 (0.35)	1.0
• 40 hp and 50 hp	0.007 (0.18)	1.14
• 70 hp and 90 hp	0.0075 (0.19)	1.07

• V4	0.015 (0.39)	1.25
• V6	0.013 (0.34)	1.45

➡**The millimeter answer should be the same if the original measurement was made in millimeters and the millimeter constant used, instead of the measurement being made in inches.**

STANDARD LOWER UNIT—REVERSE GEAR BACKLASH MEASUREMENT COUNTERROTATING LOWER UNIT—FORWARD GEAR BACKLASH MEAUREMENT

▸ **See accompanying illustration**

1. Shift the lower unit into reverse gear. Rotate the driveshaft clockwise and check to be sure the propeller shaft rotates in the correct direction, counterclockwise on standard lower units and clockwise on counter rotating lower units. This is a test to see if the clutch mechanism was properly assembled and functions correctly. Operate the shift rod to shift the lower unit back into neutral. Rotate the driveshaft clockwise 20° to 30° with the other hand. This action will preload the reverse gear.

Hold the propeller to prevent the propeller shaft from turning. At the same time, rock the driveshaft back and forth through about a 25° to 30° arc, without any rotation of the propeller shaft. At the outer limits of the arc, a click sound will be heard. This click sound occurs when the pinion gear tooth contacts one face of the driven gear tooth. Another click is heard when the pinion gear swings back and the pinion tooth contacts the face of the adjacent driven gear tooth. The arc between the two clicks represents the backlash, or free play, between the gears.

Zero the dial indicator gauge at the first click. As soon as the second click is heard, stop all motion and observe the maximum deflection of the dial indicator needle. Acceptable backlash measurement is as follows for the models listed:

- 30 hp   0.028–0.039 in. (0.7–1.0mm)
- 40 hp and 50hp   0.028–0.035 in. (0.7–0.88mm)

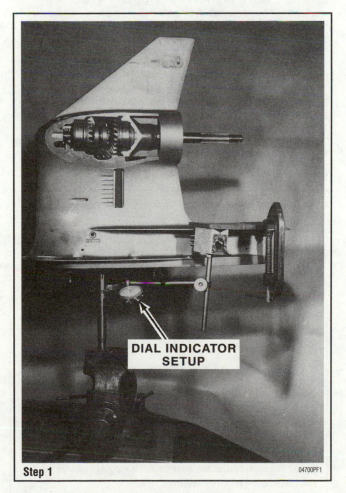

DIAL INDICATOR SETUP

Step 1   04700PF1

- 70 hp and 90 hp   0.030–0.044 in. (0.75–1.13mm)
- V4 units   0.031–0.044 in. (0.80–1.12mm)
- V6 units   0.038–0.049 in. (0.97–1.25mm) w/standard lower unit.
- V4 and V6   0.011–0.015 in. (0.28–0.39mm) w/counterrotating lower unit.

Remove or add shim material behind the gear to bring the backlash to within specifications.

On the forward gear of counterrotating lower units, adding shim material decreases backlash and removing shim material increases backlash.

On the reverse gear of standard lower units, adding shim material decreases backlash and removing shim material increases backlash.

➡**The actual measurement and the amount of shim material to be added or removed are related but not equal. Therefore, some very simple arithmetic must be performed.**

To determine how much shim material must be moved to obtain the desired backlash, the manufacturer gives a very simple formula:

A constant (a number depending on the unit being serviced) minus the backlash measurement and then the answer multiplied by a multiplying factor. This may sound complicated but it is not.

Formula:

(Measurement – constant) x factor.

If the constant has a greater value than the measurement, the formula becomes:

(Constant – measurement) x factor.

The constant and the multiplying factor vary, depending on the model hp unit being serviced. No problem! The following list indicates the exact constant and multiplying factor for each of the powerheads covered in this manual.

Model	Constant Inches (mm)	Multiplying Factor
• 30 hp	0.033 (0.85)	1.0
• 40 hp and 50 hp	0.031 (0.79)	1.14
• 70 hp and 90 hp	0.037 (0.94)	1.07
• V4	0.043 (1.11)	1.45
• V6	0.038 (0.96)	1.25

➡**The millimeter answer should be the same if the original measurement was made in millimeters and the millimeter constant used, instead of the measurement being made in inches.**

Water Pump

▸ **See accompanying illustrations**

1. Place a new gasket and the outer plate over the driveshaft and onto the oil seal housing with the holes in the plate and gasket indexed over the two pins in the housing.

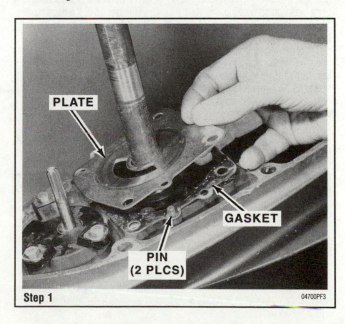

PLATE

GASKET

PIN (2 PLCS)

Step 1   04700PF3

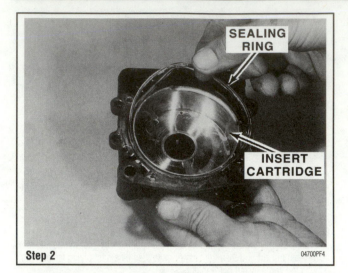

Step 2

04700PF4

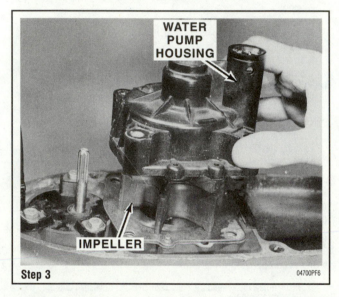

Step 3

04700PF6

2. Fit the insert cartridge into the water pump housing. Push the water tube grommet into place in the housing. Apply a coat of Yamalube to the sealing ring of the water pump housing and place the ring in the groove of the housing.

Fit the Woodruff key into the driveshaft. Just a dab of grease on the key will help to hold the key in place.

3. Slide the water pump impeller over the driveshaft with the rubber membrane on the top side and the keyway in the impeller indexed over the Woodruff key. Take care not to damage the membrane. Coat the impeller blades with Yamalube Grease or equivalent water resistant lubricant.

Rotate the insert cartridge counterclockwise over the impeller to tuck in the vanes.

Seat all parts over the two locating pins and secure the water pump housing with the four washers and bolts. Tighten the bolts to a torque value of 5.8 ft. lbs. (8Nm).

Lower Unit Service Jet Drive

DESCRIPTION AND OPERATION

♦ See Figure 36

The jet drive unit is designed to permit boating in areas prohibited to a boat equipped with a conventional propeller drive system. The housing of the jet drive barely extends below the hull of the boat allowing passage in ankle deep water, white water rapids and over sand bars or in shoal water which would foul a propeller drive.

04700P6L

Fig. 36 Jet drive mounted to the intermediate housing of a 40 hp powerhead

The jet drive provides reliable propulsion with a minimum of moving parts. Simply stated, water is drawn into the unit through an intake grille by an impeller driven by a driveshaft off the crankshaft of the powerhead. The water is immediately expelled under pressure through an outlet nozzle directed away from the stern of the boat.

As the speed of the boat increases and reaches planing speed, the jet drive discharges water freely into the air and only the intake grille makes contact with the water.

The jet drive is provided with a gate arrangement and linkage to permit the boat to be operated in reverse. When the gate is moved downward over the exhaust nozzle, the pressure stream is reversed by the gate and the boat moves sternward.

Conventional controls are used for powerhead speed, movement of the boat, shifting and power trim and tilt.

MODEL IDENTIFICATION AND SERIAL NUMBERS

♦ See Figure 37

A model letter identification is stamped on the rear, port side of the jet drive housing. A serial number for the unit is stamped on the starboard side of the jet drive housing, as indicated in the accompanying illustration.

Since their introduction by Yamaha in 1984, jet drive units have been installed on certain 3-cylinder and V4 and V6 units.

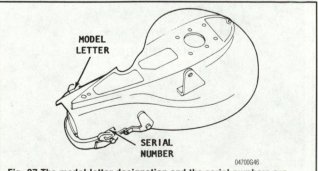

04700G46

Fig. 37 The model letter designation and the serial numbers are embossed on the jet drive housing

Four different size jet drives are used with the outboard units covered in this manual: Model Z and Model Y, Model AA4 and AA6. These letters are embossed on the port side of the jet drive housing.

Model Z is used with Jet Power 28 and 35 (Model 40 hp and 50 hp). Model Y is used with . Model AA4 is used on the larger V4 and Model AA6 is used on V6 units.

For the most part, jet drive units are identical in design, function and operation. Differences lie in size and securing hardware.

REMOVAL & DISASSEMBLY

▶ **See accompanying illustrations**

1. Remove the two bolts and retainer securing the shift cable to the shift cable support bracket.

2. Remove the locknut, bolt and washer securing the shift cable to the shift arm. Try not to disturb the length of the cable.

3. Remove the six bolts securing the intake grille to the jet casing. Ease the intake grille from the jet drive housing.

4. Pry the tab or tabs of the tabbed washer away from the nut to allow the nut to be removed.

5. Loosen and then remove the nut.

6. Remove the tabbed washer and spacers. Make a careful count of the spacers behind the washer. If the unit is relatively new, there could be as many as eight spacers stacked together. If less than eight spacers are removed from behind the washer, the others will be found behind the jet impeller, which is removed in the following step. A total of eight spacers will be found.

7. Remove the jet impeller from the shaft. If the impeller is frozen to the shaft, obtain a block of wood and a hammer. Tap the impeller in a clockwise direction to release the shear key.

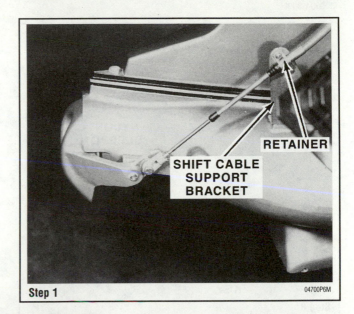

Step 1

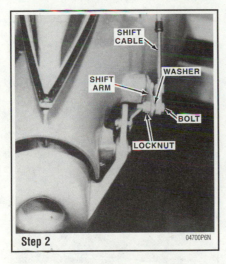

Step 2

Step 3

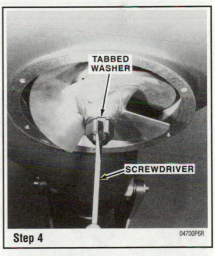

Step 4

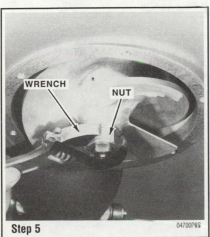

Step 5

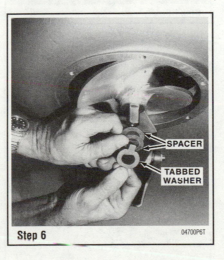

Step 6

Step 7

8. Slide the nylon sleeve and shear key free of the driveshaft and any spacers found behind the impeller. Make a note of the number of spacers at both locations—behind the impeller and on top of the impeller, under the nut and tabbed washer.

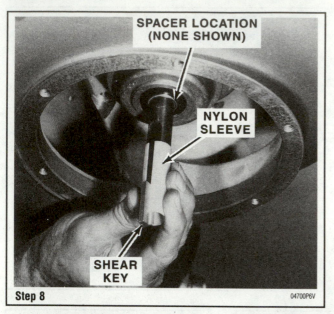

SPACER LOCATION (NONE SHOWN)

NYLON SLEEVE

SHEAR KEY

Step 8   04700P6V

9. One external bolt and four internal bolts are used to secure the jet drive to the intermediate housing. The external bolt is located at the aft end of the anti-cavitation plate.

10. The four internal bolts are located inside the jet drive housing, as indicated in the accompanying illustration. Remove the five attaching bolts.

11. Lower the jet drive from the intermediate housing. Remove the locating pin from the forward starboard side (or center forward, depending on the model being serviced) of the upper jet housing.

➡ **There will be a total of six locating pins to be removed in the following steps. Make careful note of the size and location of each when they are removed, as an assist during assembling.**

12. Remove the locating pin from the aft end of the housing. This pin and the one removed in the previous step should be of identical size.

13. Remove the four bolts and washers from the water pump housing.

Pull the water pump housing, the inner cartridge and the water pump impeller, up and free of the driveshaft. Remove the Woodruff key from its recess in the driveshaft. Next, remove the outer gasket, the steel plate and the inner gasket.

14. Remove the two small locating pins and lift the aluminum spacer up and free of the driveshaft.

Remove the driveshaft and bearing assembly from the housing.

➡ **Model Z installed has two #10–24x⅝ in. screws and lockwashers securing the driveshaft assembly to the housing. Model Y has four ¼–20x⅞ in. bolts and lockwashers securing the driveshaft assembly to the housing.**

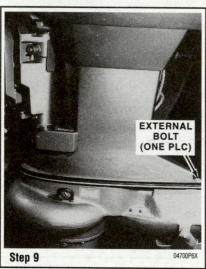

EXTERNAL BOLT (ONE PLC)

Step 9   04700P6X

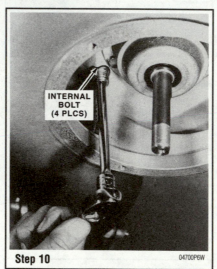

INTERNAL BOLT (4 PLCS)

Step 10   04700P6W

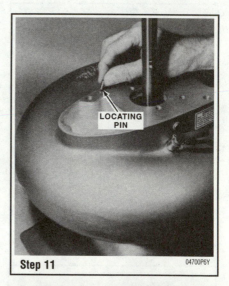

LOCATING PIN

Step 11   04700P6Y

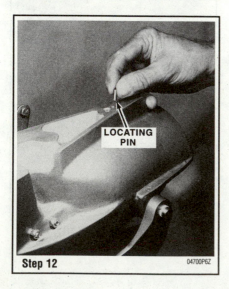

LOCATING PIN

Step 12   04700P6Z

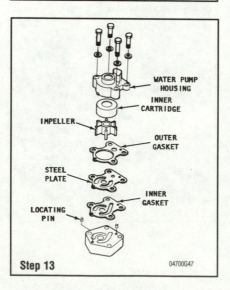

WATER PUMP HOUSING

INNER CARTRIDGE

IMPELLER

OUTER GASKET

STEEL PLATE

INNER GASKET

LOCATING PIN

Step 13   04700G47

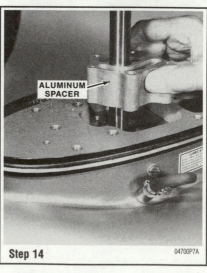

ALUMINUM SPACER

Step 14   04700P7A

Remove the large thick adaptor plate from the intermediate housing. This plate is secured with seven bolts and lock-washers. Lower the adaptor plate from the intermediate housing and remove the two small locating pins, one on the forward port side and another from the last aft hole in the adaptor plate. Both pins are identical size.

CLEANING AND INSPECTING

▶ **See Figures 38 and 39**

Wash all parts, except the driveshaft assembly, in solvent and blow them dry with compressed air. Rotate the bearing assembly on the driveshaft to inspect the bearings for rough spots, binding and signs of corrosion or damage.

Saturate a shop towel with solvent and wipe both extensions of the driveshaft.

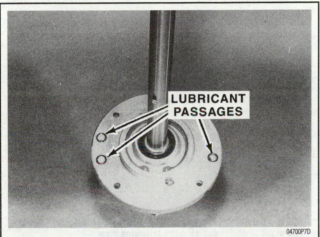

Fig. 38 Take extra precautions to prevent solvent from entering the lubrication passages

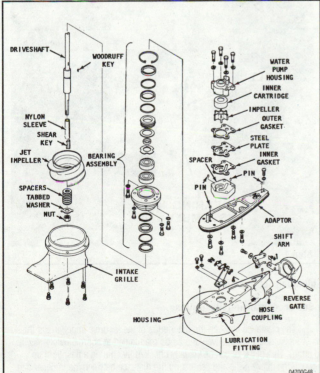

Fig. 39 Exploded view of a typical jet drive lower unit with major parts identified

Bearing Assembly

▶ **See Figure 40**

Lightly wipe the exterior of the bearing assembly with the same shop towel. Do not allow solvent to enter the three lubricant passages of the bearing assembly. The best way to clean these passages is not with solvent—because any solvent remaining in the assembly after installation will continue to dissolve good useful lubricant and leave bearings and seals dry. This condition will cause bearings to fail through friction and seals to dry up and shrink—losing their sealing qualities.

The only way to clean and lubricate the bearing assembly is after installation to the jet drive—via the exterior lubrication fitting.

If the old lubricant emerging from the hose coupling is a dark, dirty, gray color, the seals have already broken down and water is attacking the bearings. If such is the case, it is recommended the entire driveshaft bearing assembly be taken to the dealer for service of the bearings and seals.

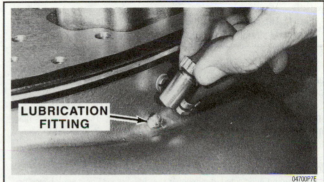

Fig. 40 Cleaning and lubricating the bearing assembly is best accomplished by completely replacing the old lubricant

Dismantling Bearing Assembly

A complicated procedure must be followed to dismantle the bearing assembly including torching off the bearing housing. Naturally, excessive heat might ruin the seals and bearings. Therefore, the best recommendation is to leave this part of the service work to the experts at your local Yamaha dealership.

Driveshaft and Associated Parts

Inspect the threads and splines on the driveshaft for wear, rounded edges, corrosion and damage.

Carefully check the driveshaft to verify the shaft is straight and true without any sign of damage.

Inspect the jet drive housing for nicks, dents, corrosion, or other signs of damage. Nicks may be removed with No. 120 and No. 180 emery cloth.

Reverse Gate

Inspect the gate and its pivot points. Check the swinging action to be sure it moves freely the entire distance of travel without binding.

Inspect the slats of the water intake grille for straightness. Straighten any bent slats, if possible. Use the utmost care when prying on any slat, as they tend to break if excessive force is applied. Replace the intake grille if a slat is lost, broken, or bent and cannot be repaired. The slats are spaced evenly and the distance between them is critical, to prevent large objects from passing through and becoming lodged between the jet impeller and the inside wall of the housing.

Jet Impeller

▶ **See Figure 41**

The jet impeller is a precisely machined and dynamically balanced aluminum spiral. Observe the drilled recesses at exact locations to achieve this delicate balancing. Some of these drilled recesses are clearly shown in the accompanying illustration.

Excessive vibration of the jet drive may be attributed to an out-of-balance condition caused by the jet impeller being struck excessively by rocks, gravel or cavitation burn.

Fig. 41 The slats of the grille must be carefully inspected and any bent slats straightened for maximum performance of the jet drive

The term cavitation burn is a common expression used throughout the world among people working with pumps, impeller blades and forceful water movement.

Burns on the jet impeller blades are caused by cavitation air bubbles exploding with considerable force against the impeller blades. The edges of the blades may develop small dime size areas resembling a porous sponge, as the aluminum is actually eaten by the condition just described.

Excessive rounding of the jet impeller edges will reduce efficiency and performance. Therefore, the impeller should be inspected at regular intervals.

If rounding is detected, the impeller should be placed on a work bench and the edges restored to as sharp a condition as possible, using a file. Draw the file in only one direction. A back-and-forth motion will not produce a smooth edge. Take care not to nick the smooth surface of the jet impeller. Excessive nicking or pitting will create water turbulence and slow the flow of water through the pump.

Inspect the shear key. A slightly distorted key may be reused although some difficulty may be encountered in assembling the jet drive. A cracked shear key should be discarded and replaced with a new key.

Water Pump

♦ **See Figure 42**

Clean all water pump parts with solvent and then blow them dry with compressed air. Inspect the water pump housing for cracks and distortion, possibly caused from overheating. Inspect the steel plate, the thick aluminum spacer and the water pump cartridge for grooves and/or rough spots. If possible always install a new water pump impeller while the jet drive is disassembled. A new water pump impeller will ensure extended satisfactory service and give peace of

Fig. 42 The edges of the jet impeller should be kept as sharp as possible for maximum jet drive efficiency

mind to the owner. If the old water pump impeller must be returned to service, never install it in reverse of the original direction of rotation. Installation in reverse will cause premature impeller failure.

If installation of a new water pump impeller is not possible, check the sealing surfaces and be satisfied they are in good condition. Check the upper, lower and ends of the impeller vanes for grooves, cracking and wear. Check to be sure the indexing notch of the impeller hub is intact and will not allow the impeller to slip.

ASSEMBLING

♦ **See accompanying illustration**

Identify the two small locating pins used to index the large thick adaptor plate to the intermediate housing. Insert one pin into the last hole aft on the top-side of the plate. Insert the other pin into the hole forward toward the port side, as shown.

Lift the plate into place against the intermediate housing with the locating pins indexing with the holes in the intermediate housing. Secure the plate with the five (or seven) bolts.

➡**On the five bolt model, one of the five bolts is shorter than the other four. Install the short bolt in the most aft location.**

Tighten the long bolts to a torque value of 22 ft. lbs. (30Nm). Tighten the short bolt to a torque value of 11 ft. lbs. (15Nm).

1. Place the driveshaft bearing assembly into the jet drive housing. Rotate the bearing assembly until all bolt holes align. There is only one correct position.

Model Z has two securing screws and lockwasher. Tighten these screws just good and snug by hand.

Model Y has four securing bolts and lockwasher. Tighten these four bolts to a torque value of 5 ft. lbs. (7Nm).

➡**If installing a new jet impeller, place all eight spacers at the lower or nut end of the impeller and skip the following step.**

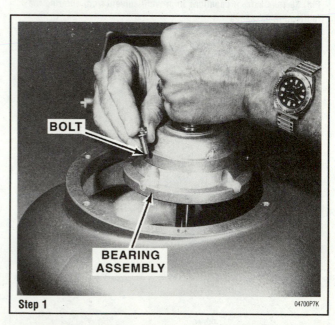

Step 1

Shimming Jet Impeller

♦ **See accompanying illustrations**

1. The clearance between the outer edge of the jet drive impeller and the water intake housing cone wall should be maintained at approximately $\frac{1}{32}$ in. (0.8mm). This distance can be visually checked by shining a flashlight up through the intake grille and estimating the distance between the impeller and the casing cone, as indicated in the accompanying illustrations. It is not humanly possible to accurately measure this clearance, but by observing closely and estimating the clearance, the results should be fairly accurate.

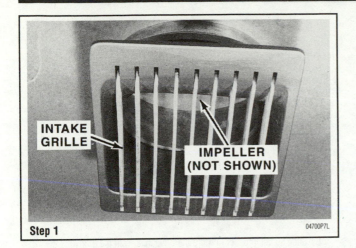

Step 1

04700P7L

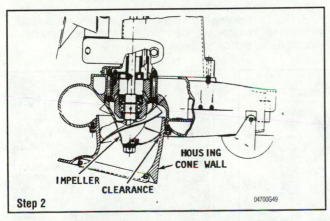

Step 2

04700G49

After continued use, the clearance will increase. The spacers previously removed are used to position the impeller along the driveshaft with a desired clearance of 1/32 in. (0.8mm) between the jet impeller and the housing wall.

2. A total of either eight (Model Z, Model AA4 and Model AA6) or nine (Model Y) spacers are used depending on the model being serviced. When new, all spacers are located at the tapered (or nut) end of the impeller. As the clearance increases, the spacers are transferred from the tapered (nut) end and placed at the wide (intermediate housing) end of the jet impeller.

This procedure is best accomplished while the jet drive is removed from the intermediate housing.

Secure the driveshaft with the attaching hardware. Installation of the shear key and nylon sleeve is not vital to this procedure. Place the unit on a convenient work bench. Shine a flashlight through the intake grille into the housing cone and eyeball the clearance between the jet impeller and the cone wall, as indicated in the accompanying line drawing. Move spacers one-at-a-time from the tapered end to the wide end to obtain a satisfactory clearance. Dismantle the driveshaft and note the exact count of spacers at both ends of the bearing assembly. This count will be recalled later during assembly to properly install the jet impeller.

Water Pump Assembling

♦ **See accompanying illustrations**

1. Place the aluminum spacer over the driveshaft with the two holes for the indexing pins facing upward. Fit the two locating pins into the holes of the spacer.

➡️**The manufacturer recommends no sealant be used on either side of the water pump gaskets.**

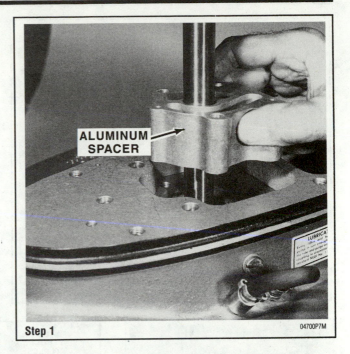

Step 1

04700P7M

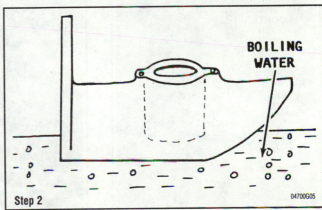

Step 2

04700G05

2. Slide the inner water pump gasket (the gasket with two curved openings) over the driveshaft. Position the gasket over the two locating pins. Slide the steel plate down over the driveshaft with the tangs on the plate facing downward and with the holes in the plate indexed over the two locating pins.

Check to be sure the tangs on the plate fit into the two curved openings of the gasket beneath the plate. Now, slide the outer gasket (the gasket with the large center hole) over the driveshaft. Position the gasket over the two locating pins.

Fit the Woodruff key into the driveshaft. Just a dab of grease on the key will help to hold the key in place. Slide the water pump impeller over the driveshaft with the rubber membrane on the top side and the keyway in the impeller indexed over the Woodruff key. Take care not to damage the membrane. Coat the impeller blades with Yamalube Grease or equivalent water resistant lubricant.

Install the insert cartridge, the inner plate and finally the water pump housing over the driveshaft. Rotate the insert cartridge counterclockwise over the impeller to tuck in the impeller vanes. Seat all parts over the two locating pins.

➡️**On some models, two different length bolts are used at this location. The Model Y uses special D shaped washers. The Model Z uses plain washers.**

Tighten the four bolts to a torque value of 11 ft. lbs. (15Nm).

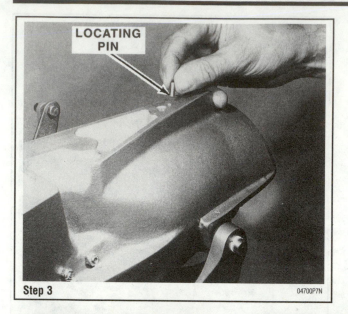

LOCATING PIN

Step 3   04700P7N

3. Install one of the small locating pins into the aft end of the jet drive housing.

Jet Drive Installation

▶ **See accompanying illustrations**

1. Install the other small locating pin into the forward starboard side (or center forward end, depending on the model being serviced).

2. Raise the jet drive unit up and align it with the intermediate housing, with the small pins indexed into matching holes in the adaptor plate. Install the four internal bolts.

3. Install the one external bolt at the aft end of the anti-cavitation plate. Tighten all bolts to a torque value of 11 ft. lbs. (15Nm).

4. Place the required number of spacers up against the bearing housing. Slide the nylon sleeve over the driveshaft and insert the shear key into the slot of the nylon sleeve with the key resting against the flattened portion of the driveshaft.

5. Slide the jet impeller up onto the driveshaft, with the groove in the impeller collar indexing over the shear key.

6. Place the remaining spacers over the driveshaft. The number of spacers will be nine less the number used in previous step, for the Model Y and eight minus the number used during jet drive installation.

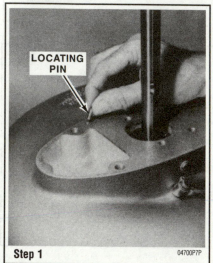

LOCATING PIN

Step 1   04700P7P

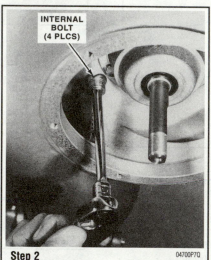

INTERNAL BOLT (4 PLCS)

Step 2   04700P7Q

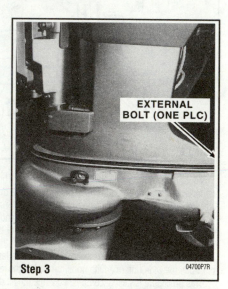

EXTERNAL BOLT (ONE PLC)

Step 3   04700P7R

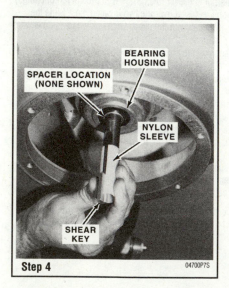

SPACER LOCATION (NONE SHOWN)

BEARING HOUSING

NYLON SLEEVE

SHEAR KEY

Step 4   04700P7S

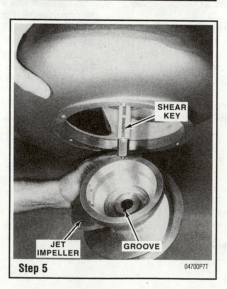

SHEAR KEY

JET IMPELLER

GROOVE

Step 5   04700P7T

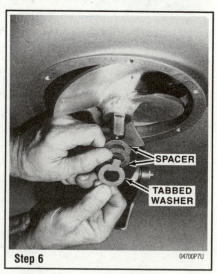

SPACER

TABBED WASHER

Step 6   04700P7U

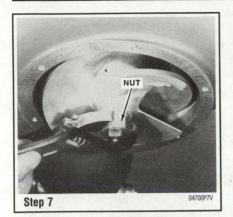

NUT

Step 7   04700P7V

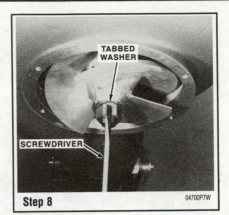

TABBED
WASHER

SCREWDRIVER

Step 8   04700P7W

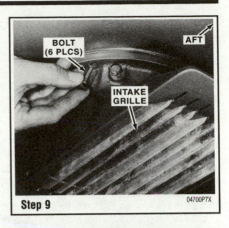

BOLT
(6 PLCS)

AFT

INTAKE
GRILLE

Step 9   04700P7X

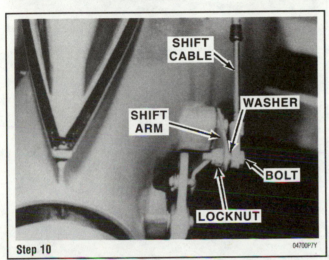

SHIFT
CABLE

WASHER

SHIFT
ARM

BOLT

LOCKNUT

Step 10   04700P7Y

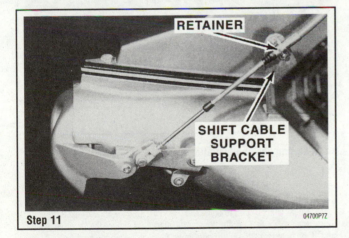

RETAINER

SHIFT CABLE
SUPPORT
BRACKET

Step 11   04700P7Z

7. Tighten the nut to a torque value of 17 ft. lbs. (23Nm). If neither of the two tabs on the tabbed washer aligns with the sides of the nut, remove the nut and washer. Invert the tabbed washer. Turning the washer over will change the tabs by approximately 15°. Install and tighten the nut to the required torque value. The tabbed washer is designed to align with the nut in one of the two positions described.

8. Bend the tabs up against the nut to prevent the nut from backing off and becoming loose.

9. Install the intake grille onto the jet drive housing with the slots facing aft. Install and tighten the six securing bolts. Tighten ¼ in. bolts to a torque value of 5 ft. lbs. (7Nm). Tighten 5⁄16 in. bolts to 11 ft. lbs. (15Nm).

10. Slide the bolt through the end of the shift cable, washer and into the shift arm. Install the locknut onto the bolt and tighten the bolt securely.

11. Install the shift cable against the shift cable support bracket and secure it in place with the two bolts.

Jet Drive Adjustments

ADJUSTMENT

Cable Alignment And Free Play

▶ **See accompanying illustrations**

1. Move the shift lever downward into the forward position. The leaf spring should snap over on top of the lever to lock it in position.

2. Remove the locknut, washer and bolt from the threaded end of the shift cable. Push the reverse gate firmly against the rubber pad on the underside of the jet drive housing.

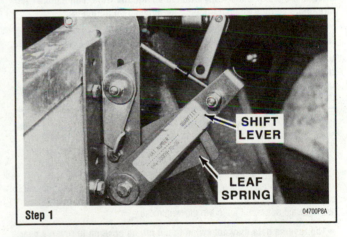

SHIFT
LEVER

LEAF
SPRING

Step 1   04700P8A

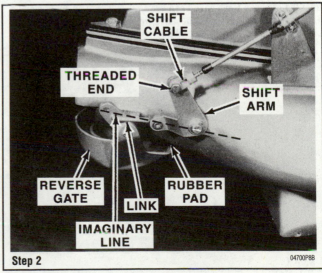

SHIFT
CABLE

THREADED
END

SHIFT
ARM

REVERSE
GATE

LINK

RUBBER
PAD

IMAGINARY
LINE

Step 2   04700P8B

Check to be sure the link between the reverse gate and the shift arm is hooked into the LOWER hole on the gate.

Hold the shift arm up until the link rod and shift arm axis form an imaginary straight line, as indicated in the accompanying illustration. Adjust the length of the shift cable by rotating the threaded end, until the cable can be installed back onto the shift arm without disturbing the imaginary line. Pass the nut through the cable end, washer and shift arm. Install and tighten the locknut.

Neutral Stop Adjustment

◆ **See accompanying illustrations**

In the forward position, the reverse gate is neatly tucked underneath and clear of the exhaust jet stream.

In the reverse position, the gate swings up and blocks the jet stream deflecting the water in a forward direction under the jet housing to move the boat sternward.

In the neutral position, the gate assumes a happy medium—a balance between forward and reverse when the powerhead is operating at IDLE speed. Actually, the gate is deflecting some water to prevent the boat from moving forward, but not enough volume to move the boat sternward.

❈❈ WARNING

The gate must be properly adjusted for safety of boat and passengers. Improper adjustment could cause the gate to swing up to the reverse position while the boat is moving forward causing serious injury to boat or passengers.

1. Loosen, but do not remove the locknut on the neutral stop lever. Check to be sure the lever will slide up and down along the slot in the shift lever bracket.

➡ **The following procedure must be performed with the boat and jet drive in a body of water. Only with the boat in the water can a proper jet stream be applied against the gate for adjustment purposes.**

❈❈ CAUTION

Water must circulate through the lower unit to the powerhead anytime the powerhead is operating to prevent damage to the water pump in the lower unit. Just five seconds without water will damage the water pump impeller.

2. Start the powerhead and allow it to operate only at IDLE speed. With the neutral stop lever in the down position, move the shift lever until the jet stream forces on the gate are balanced. Balanced means the water discharged is divided in both directions and the boat moves neither forward nor sternward. The gate is then in the neutral position with the powerhead at idle speed.

3. Move the neutral stop lever up against the shift lever until the stop lever barely makes contact with the shift lever. Tighten the locknut to maintain this new adjusted position. Shut down the powerhead.

➡ **The reverse gate may not swing to the full up position in reverse gear after the previous steps have been performed. Do not be concerned. This condition is acceptable, because water pressure in reverse will close the gate fully under normal operation.**

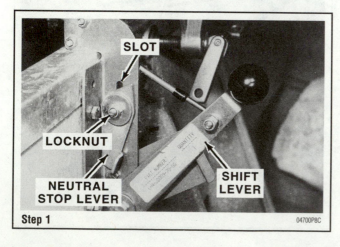

Step 1   04700P8C

NEUTRAL POSITION

Step 2   04700P8D

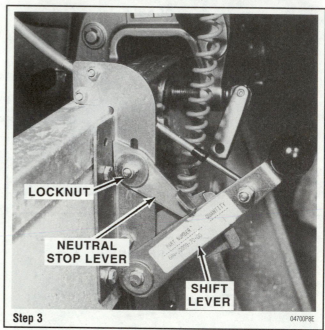

LOCKNUT

NEUTRAL STOP LEVER

SHIFT LEVER

Step 3   04700P8E

TRIM ADJUSTMENT

◆ **See accompanying illustration**

1. During operation, if the boat tends to pull to port or starboard, the flow fins may be adjusted to correct the condition. These fins are located at the top and bottom of the exhaust tube.

If the boat tends to pull to starboard, bend the trailing edge of each fin approximately 1/16 in. (1.5mm) toward the starboard side of the jet drive. Naturally, if the boat tends to pull to port, bend the fins toward the port side.

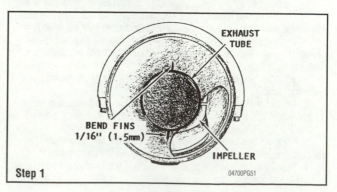

EXHAUST TUBE

BEND FINS 1/16" (1.5mm)

IMPELLER

Step 1   04700PG51

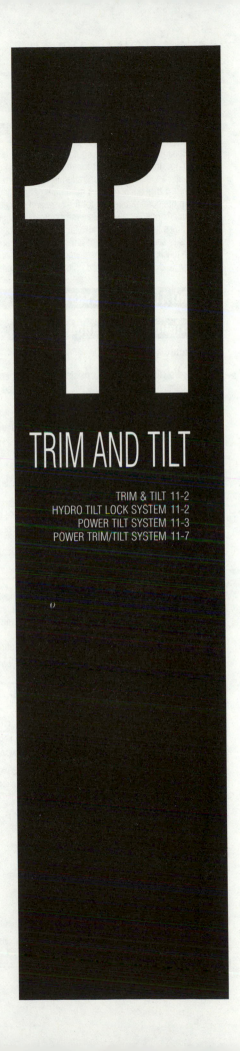

TRIM & TILT 11-2
INTRODUCTION 11-2
HYDRO TILT LOCK SYSTEM 11-2
DESCRIPTION & OPERATION 11-2
   RAISING OUTBOARD UNIT 11-2
   LOWERING OUTBOARD UNIT 11-2
   UNDERWATER STRIKE 11-2
SERVICING 11-2
POWER TILT SYSTEM 11-3
DESCRIPTION & OPERATION 11-3
   TILT UP OPERATION 11-3
   TILT DOWN OPERATION 11-3
   MANUAL OPERATION 11-4
   SHOCK ABSORBER ACTION 11-4
MAINTENANCE 11-4
   CHECKING HYDRAULIC FLUID
     LEVEL 11-4
   PURGING AIR FROM THE
     SYSTEM 11-4
TROUBLESHOOTING 11-5
   ELECTRICAL TESTING 11-5
   HYDRAULIC TESTING 11-5
TILT RELAY 11-5
   TESTING 11-5
TILT SWITCH 11-6
   TESTING 11-6
TILT MOTOR 11-6
   TESTING 11-6
SERVICING 11-7
POWER TRIM/TILT SYSTEM 11-7
DESCRIPTION & OPERATION 11-7
   TRIM UP 11-7
   TRIM DOWN 11-8
   TILT UP 11-8
   TILT DOWN 11-8
   SHOCK ABSORBER ACTION 11-8
MAINTENANCE 11-8
   PURGING AIR FROM SYSTEM 11-8
TROUBLESHOOTING 11-9
   MANUAL OPERATION 11-9
   PRELIMINARY INSPECTION 11-9
   SYMPTOM DIAGNOSIS 11-9
   HYDRAULIC TESTING 11-10
TRIM/TILT RELAY 11-10
   TESTING 11-10
POWER TRIM/TILT SWITCH 11-11
   TESTING 11-11
TRIM/TILT MOTOR 11-11
   TESTING 11-11
TRIM SENSOR 11-12
   ADJUSTMENT 11-12
   TESTING 11-12
SERVICING 11-12
   PRELIMINARY TASKS 11-12
   DISASSEMBLY 11-12
   CLEANING & INSPECTION 11-14
   ASSEMBLY 11-15
   CLOSING TASKS 11-17

11

TRIM AND TILT

TRIM & TILT 11-2
HYDRO TILT LOCK SYSTEM 11-2
POWER TILT SYSTEM 11-3
POWER TRIM/TILT SYSTEM 11-7

TRIM & TILT

Introduction

All outboard installations are equipped with some means of raising or lowering (pivoting), the complete unit for efficient operation under various load, boat design, water conditions, and for trailering to and from the water.

The correct trim angle ensures maximum performance and fuel economy as well as a more comfortable ride for the crew and passengers.

The most simple form of tilt is a mechanical tilt adjustment consisting of a series of holes in the transom mounting bracket through which an adjustment pin passes to secure the outboard unit at the desired angle.

Such a mechanical arrangement works quite well for the smaller units, but with larger (and heavier) outboard units a power system is required. The power system for these larger outboards is hydraulically operated and electrically controlled from the helmperson's position.

All trim and tilt systems are installed between the two large clamp brackets. The power trim/tilt relay is usually mounted in the upper cowling pan where it is fairly well protected from moisture.

All power trim/tilt systems use a manual release valve to permit movement of the outboard unit in the remote event the trim/tilt system develops a malfunction, either hydraulic or electrical, preventing use of power.

This section covers three different types of trim/tilt units which may be installed on Yamaha outboards. Each system is described in a separate section. Troubleshooting, filling the system with hydraulic fluid and purging (bleeding) procedures are included.

HYDRO TILT LOCK SYSTEM

Description & Operation

♦ See Figure 1

The Hydro Tilt Lock system consists of a single shock absorber. The shock absorber contains a high pressure gas chamber located in the upper portion of the cylinder bore above the piston assembly.

The piston contains a down relief valve and an absorber relief valve. Below the piston assembly, the lower cylinder bore contains an oil chamber. This lower chamber is connected to the upper chamber above the piston by a hydraulic line with a manual check valve. This check valve is located about half way down the hydraulic line.

This manual check valve is activated by the tilt lever, when the lever is rotated from the lock (down) position to the tilt (up) position. The check valve cam rotates and pushes the manual check valve push rod against the check valve. This action opens the check valve and allows hydraulic fluid to flow from the lower chamber through the hydraulic line, past the open manual check valve and into the upper gas chamber.

RAISING OUTBOARD UNIT

When the outboard unit is tilted up, the volume below the piston decreases, and at the same time, the volume above the piston increases until the piston has reached the bottom of its stroke. In this position all fluid is contained above the piston.

The tilt lever is then rotated to the lock (down) position to engage with the clamp bracket. When the tilt lever is in the lock position, the manual valve push rod rests on a flat spot of the manual valve cam and releases pressure on the check valve. Releasing pressure on the check valve closes off the hydraulic line and the flow of hydraulic fluid. The outboard unit is now in the trailering position.

LOWERING OUTBOARD UNIT

To lower the outboard unit from the full up and locked position, the tilt lever is again rotated from the lock (down) position to the tilt (up) position. The manual check valve cam rotates and pushes the manual check valve push rod against the check valve and opens the valve.

➡ When the manual check is open, the valve will allow hydraulic fluid to flow in only. One direction—from the lower chamber to the upper chamber.

As the outboard unit is tilted down, the piston moves up and compresses the fluid in the upper chamber. The fluid pressure overcomes the down relief valve spring and opens the relief valve. The valve in the open position permits hydraulic fluid to flow through the piston from the upper chamber to the lower chamber.

During normal cruising, the tilt lever is set in the lock (down) position. The manual check valve is closed to prevent the outboard unit from being tilted up by water pressure against the propeller when the unit is in reverse gear. When the unit is in forward gear, the outboard is held in position by the tilt pin through the swivel bracket.

UNDERWATER STRIKE

In the event the outboard lower unit should strike an underwater object while the boat is underway, the piston would be forced down. The hydraulic fluid below the piston would be under pressure with no escape because the manual check valve is closed. The valve is closed because the tilt lever is in the lock (down) position.

To prevent rupture of the hydraulic line, a safety relief valve is incorporated in the piston. This relief valve permits fluid to pass through the piston from the lower chamber to the upper chamber through the absorber relief valve. After the outboard has passed the obstacle, the fluid returns to the lower chamber through the piston and the down relief valve, because the piston is pushed up.

Servicing

Service procedures for the Hydro Tilt Lock system are confined to removal of the end cap, removing the piston and replacing the O-rings.

A spanner wrench is required to remove the end cap. Even with the tool, removal of the end cap is not a simple task. The elements, especially if the unit has been used in a salt water atmosphere, will have their corrosive affect on the threads. The attempt with the special tool to break the end cap loose may very likely elongate the two holes provided for the tool. Once the holes are damaged, all hope of removing the end are lost. The only solution in such a case is to replace the unit.

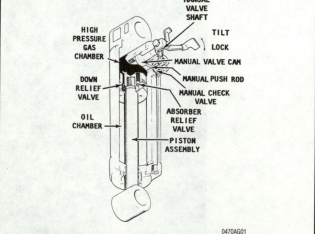

0470AG01

Fig. 1 Cutaway view of a hydro tilt lock system with major parts identified

POWER TILT SYSTEM

Description & Operation

♦ See Figures 2, 3 and 4

The one-cylinder power tilt system incorporates a single tilt hydraulic cylinder and piston. This unit is used only for tilt purpose only. The system consists of an electric motor mounted on top of a gear driven hydraulic pump, a small fluid reservoir (which is an integral part of the pump) and a single hydraulic piston and cylinder used to move the outboard unit up or down, as required.

Unlike other power trim and tilt units, all hydraulic circuits are routed inside the unit.

➡**Three safety relief valves are incorporated into the hydraulic passageways as protection against excessive pressurization. Each of these valves has a different pressure release factor. The valves are not interchangeable. The up relief valve and the down relief valve are located, one on each side of the pump. The third, main relief valve, is located above the main valve assembly.**

Each valve is secured in place with an Allen head screw accessible from the exterior of the pump. The distance the Allen head screws are sunk into the pump housing is critical. Therefore, do not remove and examine the valves without good cause. If a valve is accidentally removed, see "Troubleshooting".

TILT-UP OPERATION

When the up portion of the tilt switch on the remote control handle is depressed, the electric motor rotates in a clockwise direction. The drive gear, on the end of the motor shaft, indexed with the driven gear act as an oil pump. This action is very similar to the action in an automobile oil circulation pump.

The hydraulic fluid is forced through a series of valves into the lower chamber of the cylinder. The fluid fills the lower chamber and forces the piston upward and the outboard unit rises. As the piston continues to extend, oil in the upper chamber is routed back through the suction side of the pump until the tilt piston reaches the top of its stroke.

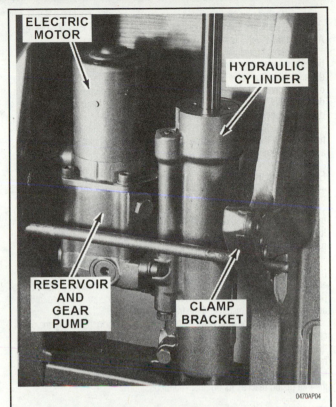

Fig. 3 Power tilt unit with major parts identified

Fig. 2 Power tilt unit installed on a 40 hp outboard

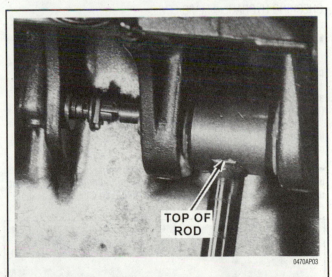

Fig. 4 Mounting for the upper piston end of the power tilt unit

TILT DOWN OPERATION

When the down portion of the tilt switch on the remote control handle is depressed, the electric motor rotates counterclockwise. The drive gear on the end of the motor shaft indexed with the driven gear are now rotating in the opposite direction. This action forces the fluid into the upper cylinder chamber under pressure causing the piston to retract, and the outboard unit is lowered. The fluid under pressure beneath the piston is routed back through a series of valves to the pump until the tilt piston reaches the bottom of its stroke and the outboard unit is in the full down position.

MANUAL OPERATION

The outboard unit may be raised or lowered manually should the battery fail to provide sufficient current to operate the electric motor or for any other reason. A manual relief valve is provided to permit manual operation.

This manual relief valve is located on the lower end of the gear pump beneath the electric motor facing aft. The valve has an Allen head and left hand threads. When the valve is rotated clockwise with an Allen wrench, the valve is opened. Opening the valve releases pressure in both the upper and lower cylinder chambers. With a complete loss of pressure, the piston may be moved up or down in the cylinder without resistance.

After the outboard unit has been moved to the desired position, the Allen head valve is rotated counterclockwise to close the valve and lock the outboard against movement.

SHOCK ABSORBER ACTION

The lower end of the tilt piston is capped with a free piston. This free piston normally moves up and down with the tilt piston. In the event the outboard lower unit should strike an underwater object while the boat is underway, the tilt piston would be suddenly and forcibly moved upward.

The free piston also moves upward but at a much slower rate than the tilt piston. The action of the tilt piston separating from the free piston causes two actions. First, the hydraulic fluid in the upper chamber above the piston is compressed and pressure builds in this area. Second, a vacuum is formed in the area between the tilt piston and the free piston.

This vacuum in the area between the two pistons sucks fluid from the upper chamber. The fluid fills the area slowly and the shock of the lower unit striking the object is absorbed. After the object has been passed, the weight of the outboard unit tends to retract the piston. The fluid between the tilt piston and the free piston is compressed and forced through check valves to the reservoir until the free piston reaches its original neutral position.

Maintenance

CHECKING HYDRAULIC FLUID LEVEL

♦ See Figure 5

The following procedures are to be performed if the only task is to check and possibly add fluid to the system.

If one of the hydraulic valves has been removed, or the system opened for any other reason, the system must be purged of any trapped air. To purge (bleed) the system see "Purging Air From The System".

Begin by rotating the manual release valve clockwise to release pressure from the cylinder. Remember, the valve has left hand threads. Next, move the outboard unit to the full down position.

➡ Never check the fluid level or add fluid with the outboard unit in the up position. Adding fluid to the system to bring the fluid level to the bottom of the screw threads with the unit up, and then closing the manual

Fig. 5 Two different types of manual relief valves are used. Some of the newer valves (left) have a left handed thread

0470AP05

release valve and installing the fill plug would cause excessive internal pressure and damage the main valve assembly when the unit was lowered.

Replenish the system using Yamalube Power Trim/Tilt Fluid, or any brand name automatic transmission fluid, Dexron or Type F. Never mix brand name fluids.

Install the fill plug, and then close the manual release valve by rotating the valve counterclockwise.

PURGING AIR FROM THE SYSTEM

♦ See Figure 6

Air must be purged (bled) from the system if any of the following conditions exist:

    a. Erratic motion is felt during operation of the system.
    b. Fluid brands have been mixed.
    c. Fluid has been contaminated with moisture or other foreign material.
    d. A component in the system has been replaced.
    e. The system has been opened for any reason.
    f. The outboard unit has been left in the full up position and lowers slowly over a period of time.

Begin by moving the outboard unit to the full down position. Check the fluid level in the reservoir.

➡ Do not install the fill plug until the purging process has been completed.

Clean the area around the fill plug to prevent contaminants entering the system when the plug is removed. Remove the fill plug. The fluid level should be even with the bottom of the screw threads.

Open the manual release valve by rotating the Allen head of the valve clockwise until it stops. Remember, this valve has left hand threads. Slowly pull the outboard upward, extending the tilt piston. Extending the tilt piston in the cylinder will permit fluid to be drawn down into the lower chamber.

With the outboard unit in the up position, add hydraulic fluid through the fill

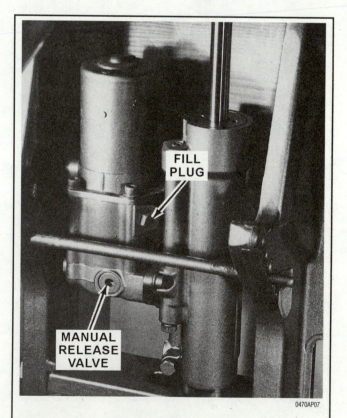

FILL PLUG

MANUAL RELEASE VALVE

0470AP07

Fig. 6 Location of the fill plug and the manual relief valve on a power tilt system

opening, but do not install the plug. Close the manual release valve by rotating the Allen head counterclockwise, until it stops.

Place a suitable shop cloth under the fill opening to catch excess fluid forced out of the system. Slowly push down on the outboard unit to retract the tilt cylinder. As the piston is retracted, fluid will be forced into the upper chamber.

Slowly move the outboard unit up and down and at the same time observe air bubbles escaping at the fill opening each time the unit is lowered.

Continue movement of the outboard unit until bubbles fail to appear at the opening, indicating air has been purged from the system.

The last time the unit is lowered check to be sure the fluid level reaches the bottom of the plug threads, and then install the plug.

Troubleshooting

♦ **See Figures 7 and 8**

ELECTRICAL TESTING

If an operational problem develops and the determination is made the trouble is in the hydraulic system, only a few simple checks may be made. Valves, check valves, and relief valves, are all an integral part of the tilt unit.

Before assuming a serious fault in the system exists, make the checks listed below. Conduct an operational performance after each check has been completed for possible correction of the problem.

1. Check the quantity and quality of the hydraulic fluid in the reservoir. With the outboard unit in the full down position, the level of fluid should reach to the bottom of the fill plug threads. Add fluid, as required. If the fluid is murky drain all fluid from the system through the two drain plug openings. Fill the system with Yamalube Power Trim/Tilt Fluid or a good grade of automatic transmission fluid (Dexron or Type F). Purge the system of air.

2. Check the manual release valve to verify it is just snug counterclockwise. Remember, the threads are left hand.

3. Check the battery for a full charge.

4. Verify the quick disconnect plugs on the up/down relay are tight and making good contact. The relay is mounted in the bottom cowling pan, starboard side, next to the cranking motor relay.

5. Verify the wires are matched properly, color to color.

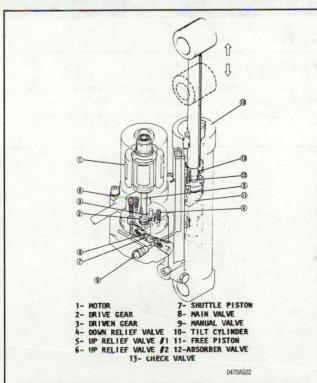

1-	MOTOR	7-	SHUTTLE PISTON
2-	DRIVE GEAR	8-	MAIN VALVE
3-	DRIVEN GEAR	9-	MANUAL VALVE
4-	DOWN RELIEF VALVE	10-	TILT CYLINDER
5-	UP RELIEF VALVE #1	11-	FREE PISTON
6-	UP RELIEF VALVE #2	12-	ABSORBER VALVE
		13-	CHECK VALVE

0470AG02

Fig. 7 Cutaway drawing of the power tilt unit with flow direction indicated and major parts identified

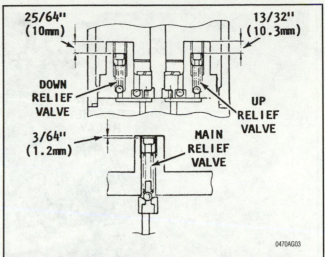

0470AG03

Fig. 8 Detailed drawing showing the depth measurement for each of the three Allen head screws holding the relief valves

➡Three safety relief valves are incorporated in the hydraulic passageways as protection against excessive pressurization. Each valve has a different pressure release factor. The valves are not interchangeable. The up relief valve and the down relief valve are located one on each side of the pump. The third, main relief valve, is located above the main valve assembly.

Each valve is secured in place with an Allen head screw accessible from the exterior of the pump. The distance the Allen head screws are sunk into the pump housing is critical. Therefore, do not remove and examine the valves without good cause.

6. Check the depth of the three Allen head screws holding the three relief valves. The distance measured from the top of the boss to the screw head should be as follows:
- Down relief valve—$^{25}/_{64}$ in. (10mm)
- Up relief valve—$^{13}/_{32}$ in. (10.3mm)
- Main relief valve—$^{3}/_{64}$ in. (1.2mm)

7. Test the up/down relay, the electric motor, and tilt button.

If the above listed areas have been checked and verified to be in proper condition, the best advice at this point is to remove the unit and seek the services of a shop with the proper test equipment and trained personnel with the expertise to rebuild high pressure hydraulic units. An alternative solution is to replace the unit.

HYDRAULIC TESTING

1. Remove the tilt cylinder drain bolts and install a Yamaha Pressure Gauge P/N YB6175, or equivalent. Connect the pressure gauge between the hydraulic motor and the piston as per the manufacturer's instructions.

2. Check the pump fluid hydraulic level.

3. Move the tilt switch to the UP position and allow the outboard to raise up as far as it will go. The pressure should read 500–750 psi (72.5–108.8 kPa). Move the tilt switch to the DOWN position and allow the outboard to lower as far as it will go. The pressure should read 430–500 psi (62.4–72.5 kPa).

4. If the pressure gauge does not read as specified, the hydraulic unit is faulty and must be serviced.

Tilt Relay

TESTING

♦ **See Figure 9**

The relay used on most models is a one piece unit, which incorporates the up circuit and the down circuit in a single relay. The relay is located on the starboard side of the powerhead inside the lower cowling.

1. Disconnect the six leads: the White female, Black eyelet, Sky Blue male,

Fig. 9 Using an ohmmeter to test the power trim/tilt relay

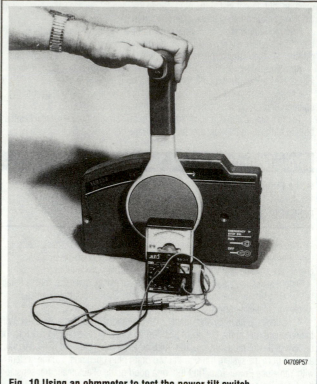

Fig. 10 Using an ohmmeter to test the power tilt switch

Red eyelet, Light Green male, and the Black female leads, from the relay at their quick disconnect or eyelet fittings.

2. Obtain a 12 volt battery and an ohmmeter. Connect the Black eyelet lead to the negative battery terminal. Connect the Light Green lead to the positive battery terminal. Connect the Red meter lead to the Red eyelet lead from the relay, and connect the Black meter lead to the Black female lead from the relay. The meter should indicate continuity.

3. Connect the Sky Blue relay lead to the positive battery terminal, keeping the Black eyelet lead connected to the negative battery lead. Connect the Black meter lead to the White relay lead and keep the Red meter lead connected to the Red eyelet lead from the relay. The meter should indicate continuity.

4. If the relay should fail one or both resistance tests, the unit should be replaced. No service or adjustment is possible.

Tilt Switch

TESTING

▶ See Figure 10

The power tilt switch is located at the top of the remote control handle. The harness from the switch is routed down the handle to the base of the control box, and then into the box through a hole. The control box cover must be removed to gain access to the quick disconnect fittings and permit testing of the switch.

An auxiliary tilt switch is sometimes mounted on the exterior surface of the starboard side lower cowling pan. This switch is convenient for performing tests on the tilt unit, when the need to observe the unit in operation is required.

1. Disconnect the three leads from the switch: the Red, Light Green, and Sky Blue, leads at their quick disconnect fittings. Connect the Red ohmmeter lead to the Red switch lead, and keep this connection for the following two resistance tests. Connect the Black meter lead to the Sky Blue switch lead. Depress the upper portion of the toggle switch. The meter should indicate continuity. Release the switch to the neutral position. The meter should indicate no continuity. Depress the lower portion of the switch. The meter should still indicate no continuity.

2. With the Red meter lead still connected to the Red switch lead, move the Black meter lead to make contact with the Light Green switch lead. Depress the

lower portion of the toggle switch. The meter should indicate continuity. Release the switch to the neutral position. The meter should indicate no continuity. Depress the upper portion of the switch. The meter should still indicate no continuity.

3. If the switch fails one or both resistance tests, replace the switch.

Tilt Motor

TESTING

▶ See Figure 11

Check to be sure the manual release valve is in the manual tilt position. This means it is rotated approximately three full turns from the power tilt position, as evidenced by the embossed words and directional arrow on the housing.

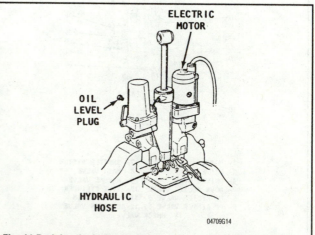

Fig. 11 Draining the hydraulic system prior to removing the electric motor for testing and/or servicing

1. Disconnect the Black lead and the White lead from the tilt motor at their quick disconnect fittings. Momentarily make contact with the two disconnected leads to the posts of a fully charged battery. Make the contact only as long as necessary to hear the electric motor rotating.

2. Reverse the leads on the battery posts and again listen for the sound of the motor rotating. The motor should rotate with the leads making contact with the battery in either direction.

3. If the motor fails to operate in one or both directions, remove the electric motor. First, place a suitable container under the unit to catch the hydraulic fluid as it drains. Next, disconnect the two lower hydraulic lines from the bottom of the housing and remove the fill plug from the reservoir. Permit the fluid to drain into the container. After the fluid has drained, disconnect the electrical leads at the harness plug, and then remove the electric motor through the attaching hardware.

4. This motor is very similar in construction and operation to a cranking motor. The arrangement of the brushes differ to allow the trim/tilt motor to operate in opposite directions, but otherwise, it is almost identical to the cranking motor.

Servicing

Service procedures for the power tilt system are confined to basic maintenance and some minor rebuilding. Rebuilding the unit involves removal of the end cap, removing the piston and replacing the O-rings.

A spanner wrench is required to remove the end cap. Even with the tool, removal of the end cap is not a simple task. The elements, especially if the unit has been used in a salt water atmosphere, will have their corrosive affect on the threads. The attempt with the special tool to break the end cap loose may very likely elongate the two holes provided for the tool. Once the holes are damaged, all hope of removing the end are lost. The only solution in such a case is to replace the unit.

POWER TRIM/TILT SYSTEM

Description & Operation

♦ **See Figures 12, 13 and 14**

The multi-cylinder power trim/tilt system consists of a housing with an electric motor, gear driven hydraulic pump, hydraulic reservoir, two trim cylinders, and one tilt cylinder attached. The tilt cylinder performs a double function as tilt cylinder and also as a shock absorber, should the lower unit strike an underwater object while the boat is underway.

The necessary valves, check valves, relief valves, and hydraulic passageways are incorporated internally and externally for efficient operation. A manual release valve is provided, on the starboard side of the housing, to permit the outboard unit to be raised or lowered should the battery fail to provide the necessary current to the electric motor or if a malfunction should occur in the hydraulic system.

The gear driven pump operates in much the same manner as an oil circulation pump installed on motor vehicles. The gears may revolve in either direction, depending on the desired cylinder movement, up or down. One side of the pump is considered the suction side, and the other the pressure side, when the gears rotate in a given direction. These sides are reversed, the suction side becomes the pressure side and the pressure side becomes the suction side when gear movement is changed to the opposite direction.

Depending on the model, one or two relays for the electric motor are located at the bottom cowling pan, where they are fairly well protected from moisture.

➡ **Yamaha engineers have been constantly working to improve the operational performance of the trim and tilt system installed on their outboard units. Therefore, many of the units will appear to be quite similar but internal hydraulic passages and check valves have been changed as well as the external routing of hydraulic lines.**

The basic principles described apply to all multi-cylinder power trim/tilt units, but the specific location and number of components, may vary, and the routing of hydraulic lines may not be exactly as viewed on the unit being serviced.

TRIM UP

♦ **See Figure 15**

When the up portion of the trim/tilt switch on the remote control handle is depressed, the up circuit, through the relay, is closed and the electric motor rotates in a clockwise direction. As a convenience, an auxiliary trim/tilt switch is installed on the exterior of the starboard side lower cowling on some models.

The pump sucks in fluid from the reservoir through a check valve and forces the fluid out the pressure side of the pump.

From the pump, the pressurized fluid passes through a series of valves to the lower chamber of both trim cylinders and the pistons are extended. The outboard unit raises. The fluid in the upper chamber of the pistons is routed back to the reservoir as the piston is extended. When the desired position for trim is obtained, the switch on the control handle is released and the outboard is held stationary.

A trim sender unit is installed on the port side clamp bracket. This unit sends a signal to an indicator on the control panel to advise the helmperson of the relative position of the outboard unit.

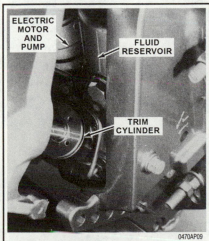

Fig. 12 Power trim/tilt system installed on a 90 hp outboard

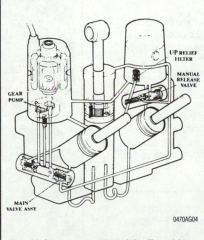

Fig. 13 Cutaway drawing of the Type 01 trim/tilt unit with major parts identified

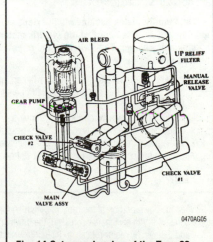

Fig. 14 Cutaway drawing of the Type 03 trim/tilt unit with major parts identified

Fig. 15 Close-up of the auxiliary trim/tilt control switch on the exterior cowling of some outboards

If the switch is not released when the trim cylinders are fully extended, the tilt cylinder will continue to move the outboard unit upward.

TRIM DOWN

When the down portion of the trim/tilt switch on the remote control handle, or the auxiliary switch, is depressed, the down circuit, through the relay, is closed and the electric motor rotates counterclockwise. The pressure side of the pump now becomes the suction side and the original suction side becomes the pressure side.

Fluid is forced through a series of check valves to the upper chamber of each trim cylinder and the pistons begin to retract, moving the outboard unit downward. Fluid from the lower chamber of each trim cylinder is routed back through the pump and a relief valve to the reservoir.

TILT UP

The first phase of the tilt up movement is the same as for the trim up function.

When the pistons of the trim cylinders are fully extended, fluid is forced through the system to the lower chamber of the tilt cylinder. Pressure increases in the lower chamber and the piston is extended, raising the outboard unit.

As fluid pressure in the upper chamber of the tilt cylinder increases, the fluid is routed through check valves back to the pump and the reservoir.

When the tilt piston is fully extended, fluid pressure in the lower chamber of the trim cylinders increases. This increase in pressure opens an up relief valve and the fluid is routed to the reservoir.

➡ **When the tilt piston becomes fully extended, the outboard is in the full up position. The sound of the electric motor and the pump will have a noticeable change. The switch on the remote control handle should be released immediately.**

If the switch is not released, the motor will continue to rotate, the pump will continue to pump, but the up relief valve will open and the pressurized fluid will be routed to the reservoir.

If the boat is underway when the tilt cylinder is extended and powerhead rpm is increased beyond a very slow speed, the forward thrust of the propeller will increase the pressure on the tilt piston. This increase in pressure will cause the up relief valve to open and the outboard unit will begin a downward movement.

TILT DOWN

When the down portion of the trim/tilt switch on the remote control handle, or the auxiliary trim/tilt switch, is depressed, the down circuit is closed through the relay and the electric motor rotates counterclockwise, as in the case of Trim Down.

The hydraulic pump sucks fluid from the reservoir. Fluid, under pressure is then routed to the upper chamber of the tilt cylinder and the piston begins to retract and the outboard unit moves downward.

Fluid in the lower chamber of the tilt cylinder is routed through the lower

chamber of each trim cylinder and then back to the pump. When the outboard unit makes physical contact with the ends of the trim cylinders, the trim cylinders also retract until the outboard is in the full down position.

SHOCK ABSORBER ACTION

The lower end of the tilt piston is capped with a free piston. This free piston normally moves up and down with the tilt piston—goes along for the ride.

In the event the outboard lower unit should strike an underwater object while the boat is underway, the tilt piston would be suddenly and forcibly extended, moved upward.

The free piston also moves upward but at a much slower rate than the tilt piston. The action of the tilt piston separating from the free piston causes two actions. First, the hydraulic fluid in the upper chamber above the piston is compressed and pressure builds in this area. Second, a vacuum is formed in the area between the tilt piston and the free piston.

This vacuum in the area between the two pistons sucks fluid from the upper chamber. The fluid fills the area slowly and the shock of the lower unit striking the object is absorbed. After the object has been passed the weight of the outboard unit tends to retract the piston. The fluid between the tilt piston and the free piston is compressed and forced through check valves to the reservoir until the free piston reaches its original neutral position.

Maintenance

PURGING AIR FROM SYSTEM

▶ **See Figure 16**

Air must be purged (bled) from the system if any of the following conditions exist.

    a. Erratic motion is felt during operation of the system.
    b. Fluid brands have been mixed.

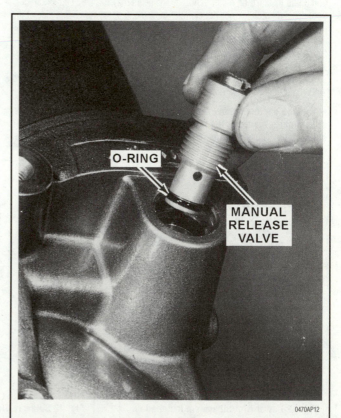

Fig. 16 Some manual relief valves used on the power trim/tilt system have left hand threads

c. Fluid has been contaminated with moisture or other foreign material.
d. A component in the system has been replaced.
e. The system has been opened for any reason.
f. The outboard unit has been left in the full up position and lowers slowly over a period of time.

➡ **If the unit has been removed, disassembled, and serviced on the work bench, a separate set of purging procedures must be performed.**

1. Operate the system until the outboard unit is in the full up position.
2. Open the manual release valve to the manual tilt position by rotating the screw approximately three full turns clockwise from the POWER tilt position.

➡ **The words power tilt and manual tilt in addition to a directional arrow for the manual position are embossed on the housing.**

3. Permit the outboard unit to move to the full down position under its own weight.
4. Close the manual release valve to the power tilt position by rotating the head counterclockwise approximately three full turns.
5. Perform steps 1–4 two or three times.
6. Move the outboard to the full up position.
7. Clean the area around the fill plug to prevent contaminants entering the system when the plug is removed. Remove the fill plug. Check the fluid level in the reservoir. The fluid should reach the lower edge of the fill opening. Replenish the system using Yamalube Power Trim/Tilt Fluid, or any brand name automatic transmission fluid (Dexron or Type F). Never mix brand name fluids.
8. Install and tighten the fill plug.

Troubleshooting

➡ **When moving through the listed troubleshooting procedures, always stop and check the system after each task. The problem may have been corrected, intentionally, or not.**

MANUAL OPERATION

If the battery is dead, or sufficient power cannot be supplied to the electric motor to drive the hydraulic pump for any number of reasons, the outboard unit may be raised or lowered manually, by opening the manual release valve. This is accomplished by rotating the manual release valve approximately three full turns clockwise from the power tilt position. Words and a directional arrow embossed on the housing indicate proper direction.

❈❈ WARNING

If outboard unit is in the up position when the manual release valve is opened, the outboard will drop to the full down position rapidly. Therefore, ensure all persons stand clear.

PRELIMINARY INSPECTION

1. Check to be sure the manual release head is tightened snugly clockwise, approximately three full turns from the power tilt position.
2. Verify the hydraulic reservoir is filled with fluid. The level of fluid should reach to the lower edge of the fill opening. Replenish as required with Yamalube Power Trim/Tilt Fluid, or any brand name automatic transmission fluid (Dexron or Type F). Never mix brand name fluids.

❈❈ WARNING

Trim system is pressurized! Do not remove fill screw unless outboard unit is raised to full up position. Tighten fill screw securely before lowering outboard.

3. Inspect the hydraulic system, lines and fittings, for leaks. If an external leak is discovered, correct the condition.
4. Purge air from the system, if there is any indication the hydraulic fluid contains air.
To check for air in the system, first check to be sure the manual release valve is snug in the power tilt position. Next, activate the up circuit and raise the outboard slightly with the trim cylinders. Now, exert a heavy, steady, downward force on the lower unit.
If the trim pistons retract into the trim cylinders more than ⅛ in. (3.2mm) there is air in the system.
Purge (bleed) air from the system.
5. If the system fails to hold the outboard unit in the full tilted (trailering) position, service the tilt cylinder.
6. If the system fails to hold the outboard unit in the desired trim position, service the trim cylinders.
7. If the hydraulic pump whines during operation, there is probably air in the system. Purge air from the system.
8. If the electric motor makes strange sounds or seems to be laboring, the electric motor may require service.

➡ **If a problem is encountered with the trim/tilt system, it is important to determine, if possible, whether the malfunction is in the hydraulic system or in an electrical circuit.**

SYMPTOM DIAGNOSIS

Symptoms of a Hydraulic Problem

The most common problem in the hydraulic system is failure of an O-ring to hold pressure.

- **Outboard Behaves Abnormally**—Ensure the battery is adequately charged; the fluid level in the reservoir reaches the lower edge of the fill opening, with the outboard fully raised; the hydraulic fluid is not contaminated (murky color); the system does not contain air; the unit does not physically bind somewhere due to an accident.
- **Outboard Fails to Trim Up or Down**—Ensure the unit has adequate fluid in the reservoir; manual release valve is tightened counterclockwise snugly to the power tilt position, approximately three full turns from the manual tilt position. Once cause may be hydraulic pump failure; O-rings in trim cylinders failing to hold pressure; trim cylinders damaged due to accident.
- **Outboard Trims/Tilts Up but Fails to Trim/Tilt Down**—Manual release valve is leaking; O-rings in trim cylinder or in the tilt cylinder failing to hold pressure; main valve has sticky or damaged shuttle piston; sticky or contaminated check valves; down relief valve has weak spring; damaged check ball or seat; or contamination is holding a valve open.
- **Outboard Trims/Tilts Down but Fails to Trim/Tilt Up**—Manual release valve is leaking; O-rings in trim cylinders or tilt cylinder failing to hold pressure; shuttle piston in main valve assembly is sticking; contaminated check valves; up relief valve has damaged seat or contamination holds the valve open.
- **Outboard Shudders When Shifted From One Gear to Another**—Hydraulic system contaminated with air or foreign matter; internal cylinder leaks—O-rings failing to hold pressure.
- **Outboard Fails to Hold Set Trim or Tilt Position**—O-rings in trim and/or tilt cylinder failing to hold pressure; check valves in tilt piston contaminated requiring cleaning; external leak—fitting or part; manual release valve damaged; shuttle piston in main valve assembly sticking or contaminated check valve; up relief valve damaged or contaminated causing a slow leak.
- **Outboard Tilts Up When Unit In Reverse Gear**—Tilt piston has leaky absorber valve or metering valve; main valve assembly has sticky or damaged shuttle piston or leaky check valves; manual release valve is leaking; O-rings in tilt piston failing to hold pressure.
- **Outboard Makes Excessive Noise**—Hydraulic fluid level is low; fluid is contaminated with air.
- **Outboard Begins To Trail Out When Throttle Backed Off at High Speed**—Manual release valve not tightened snugly counterclockwise to power tilt position; O-rings in tilt cylinder failing to hold pressure.
- **Outboard Fails to Hold Trim Position When Unit Operating In Reverse**—Manual release valve not tightened snugly counterclockwise to power tilt position; O-rings in trim cylinders failing to hold pressure.
- **Outboard Moves With Jerky Motion**—System contaminated with air; internal leaks in cylinders.
- **Outboard Fails to Reach Full Down Position**—System contaminated with air or internal leaks in cylinders.

Symptoms of an Electrical Problem

If any of the following problems are encountered, troubleshoot the electrical system.

- Outboard trims up and down, but the electrical motor grinds.
- Outboard will not trim up or down.
- Outboard trims up, but will not trim down.
- Outboard trims down, but will not trim up.

HYDRAULIC TESTING

Except 76° V6 Models

1. Turn the manual release valve toward to the tilt position until it stops and place a suitable container under the fittings to catch any spilled hydraulic fluid.

2. Disconnect the hydraulic line from the bottom of the reservoir and upper chamber of the tilt cylinder. Install the pressure gauge P/N YB6181, or equivalent to the reservoir and the reservoir and tilt cylinder fittings.

3. Turn the manual valve to the power tilt position and immediately operate the trim/tilt switch to tilt the outboard motor up and then down.

4. Turn the manual valve toward the manual tilt position until it stops. This will bleed any air from the system. Return the switch to the power tilt position.

5. Check the hydraulic fluid level and top off as necessary.

6. Operate the trim/tilt switch to tilt the unit up, noting the pressure gauge reading. The gauge should read 0–71 psi (0–489 kPa) during the upward movement and 1351–1636 psi (9.3–11.3 kPa) once the outboard motor has reached the full up position.

7. Return the outboard engine to the full down position, noting the pressure gauge readings. The gauge should read 85–156 psi (586–1,075 kPa) once the outboard engine has reached the full down position.

8. Remove the pressure gauge, reconnect the hydraulic line to the reservoir and tilt cylinder upper chamber and repeat the test on the lower chambers of the tilt/trim cylinder.

9. Operate the trim/tilt switch to drive the outboard motor up, noting the pressure gauge readings. The gauge should read 0–71 psi (0–489 kPa) during the upward movement and 0 psi once the unit has reached the full up position.

10. Return the unit to the full down position, noting the pressure gauge readings. The gauge should read 583–782 psi (4,019–5,391 kPa) once the unit has reached the full down position.

11. Remove the pressure gauge and reconnect the hydraulic line to the trim and tilt cylinder chambers and tighten the fittings securely. Bleed and refill the reservoir with Dexron II automatic transmission fluid (ATF).

76° V6 Models

1. Turn the manual valve to the power tilt position and immediately operate the trim/tilt switch to drive the outboard motor up and then down. Operate the trim/tilt switch to tilt the outboard motor up and then down.

2. Check the hydraulic fluid level and top off as necessary.

3. Turn the manual release valve toward the manual tilt position until it stops.

4. Place a suitable container under the fittings to be removed in the following steps to catch any hydraulic fluid that leaks out. Disconnect both hydraulic lines from the reservoir and chamber of the tilt cylinder. Install both sets of pressure gauges, P/N YB-6181 or equivalent.

5. Operate the trim/tilt switch to drive the outboard motor to the full down position, noting the pressure gauge readings. The "A" gauge should read 683–697 psi (4.7–4.8 kPa) and the "B" gauge should read 0 psi once the outboard motor has reached the full down position.

6. Operate the trim/tilt switch to drive the outboard motor to the full up position, noting the pressure gauge readings. The "A" gauge should read 0 psi and the "B" gauge should read 1636–1920 psi (11.3–13.2 kPa) once the outboard motor has reached the full up position.

7. Remove both sets of pressure gauges and reconnect the hydraulic lines to the trim and tilt cylinder chambers. Tighten the fittings securely. Bleed and refill the reservoir with Dexron II automatic transmission fluid (ATF).

Trim/Tilt Relay

TESTING

Except V4 and V6 Powerheads

♦ See Figure 17

Two different trim/tilt relay designs are installed on the powerheads covered in this manual. Normally two identical solenoids are used, an up solenoid and a down solenoid. These units are similar in appearance to those used as electric cranking motor solenoids. Testing this type solenoid/relay is exactly the same as for testing solenoids used on cranking motors.

The relay installed on some models is a one piece unit, incorporating the up circuit and the down circuit in a single relay. The relay is located on the starboard side of the powerhead inside the lower cowling.

1. Disconnect the six leads: the White female, Black eyelet, Sky Blue male, Red eyelet, Light Green male, and the Black female leads, from the relay at their quick disconnect or eyelet fittings.

2. Obtain a 12 volt battery and an ohmmeter. Connect the Black eyelet lead to the negative battery terminal. Connect the Light Green lead to the positive battery terminal. Connect the Red meter lead to the Red eyelet lead from the relay, and connect the Black meter lead to the Black female lead from the relay. The meter should indicate continuity.

3. Connect the Sky Blue relay lead to the positive battery terminal, keeping the Black eyelet lead connected to the negative battery lead. Connect the Black meter lead to the White relay lead and keep the Red meter lead connected to the Red eyelet lead from the relay. The meter should indicate continuity.

4. If the relay should fail one or both resistance tests, the unit should be replaced. No service or adjustment is possible.

POWER TRIM/TILT RELAY

04709P56

Fig. 17 Using an ohmmeter to test the power trim/tilt relay

V4 and V6 Powerheads

♦ See Figure 18

Two identical solenoids are used, an up solenoid and a down solenoid. These units are similar in appearance to those used as electric cranking motor

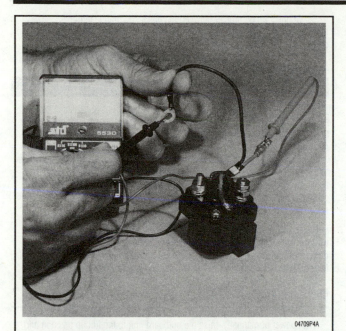

Fig. 18 The trim/tilt relay can be tested on or off the powerhead. Simple resistance tests determine if the relay is functional

solenoids. Testing this type solenoid/relay is exactly the same as for testing solenoids used on cranking motors.

1. When testing these two relays, the Sky Blue and Light Green leads take the place of the Brown lead in the tests outlined for the cranking motor relay.

2. If the relay should fail one or both resistance tests, the unit should be replaced. No service or adjustment is possible.

Power Trim/Tilt Switch

TESTING

▶ See Figure 19

The power trim/tilt switch is located at the top of the remote control handle. The harness from the switch is routed down the handle to the base of the control box, and then into the box through a hole. The control box cover must be removed to gain access to the quick disconnect fittings and permit testing of the switch.

An auxiliary trim/tilt switch is mounted on the exterior surface of the starboard side lower cowling pan. This switch is most convenient, while performing tests on the trim/tilt unit, when the need to observe while operating the system is required.

1. Disconnect the three leads from the switch: the Red, Light Green, and Sky Blue, leads at their quick disconnect fittings. Obtain an ohmmeter and select the 1000 ohm scale. Connect the Red meter lead to the Red switch lead, and keep this connection for the following two resistance tests. Connect the Black meter lead to the Sky Blue switch lead. Depress the upper portion of the toggle switch. The meter should indicate continuity. Release the switch to the neutral position. The meter should indicate no continuity. Depress the lower portion of the switch. The meter should still indicate no continuity.

2. With the Red meter lead still connected to the Red switch lead, move the Black meter lead to make contact with the Light Green switch lead. Depress the lower portion of the toggle switch. The meter should indicate continuity. Release the switch to the neutral position. The meter should indicate no continuity. Depress the upper portion of the switch. The meter should still indicate no continuity.

3. If the switch fails one or both resistance tests, replace the switch.

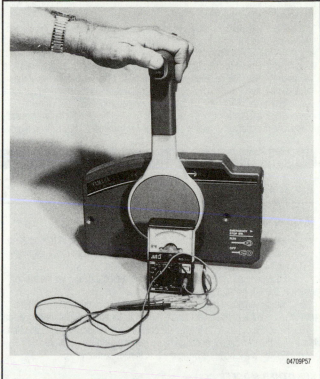

Fig. 19 Using an ohmmeter to test the power trim/tilt switch

Trim/Tilt Motor

TESTING

▶ See Figure 20

Check to be sure the manual release valve is in the manual tilt position. This means rotated approximately three full turns from the power tilt position, as evidenced by the embossed words and directional arrow on the housing.

1. Disconnect the Black lead and the White lead from the tilt motor at their quick disconnect fittings. Momentarily make contact with the two disconnected leads to the posts of a fully charged battery. Make the contact only as long as necessary to hear the electric motor rotating.

2. Reverse the leads on the battery posts and again listen for the sound of

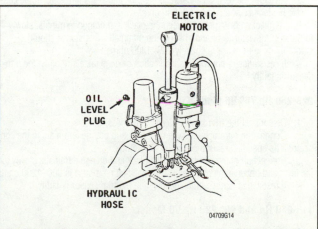

Fig. 20 Draining the hydraulic system prior to removing the electric motor for testing and/or servicing

the motor rotating. The motor should rotate with the leads making contact with the battery in either direction.

3.   If the motor fails to operate in one or both directions, remove the electric motor. First, place a suitable container under the unit to catch the hydraulic fluid as it drains. Next, disconnect the two lower hydraulic lines from the bottom of the housing and remove the fill plug from the reservoir. Permit the fluid to drain into the container. After the fluid has drained, disconnect the electrical leads at the harness plug, and then remove the electric motor through the attaching hardware.

4.   This motor is very similar in construction and operation to a cranking motor. The arrangement of the brushes differ to allow the trim/tilt motor to operate in opposite directions, but otherwise, it is almost identical to the cranking motor.

Trim Sensor

ADJUSTMENT

60–90 HP & 76° 225–250 HP V6 MODELS

1.   Raise the outboard to the full tilt position and support it in this position.
2.   Loosen the 2 screws securing the trim sensor so it can move slightly.
3.   Fully tilt the outboard to the full down position.
4.   If disconnected, connect the outboard to the battery and set the main switch to the **ON** position.
5.   With the outboard in the down position, use a screwdriver and adjust the trim sensor so only one segment on the trim indicator on the digital meter goes on.
6.   Raise the outboard to the full tilt position and support it in this position. Make sure the trim sensor does not move from the original position.
7.   Tighten the 2 bolts securing the trim sensor securely.

ALL OTHER MODELS

1.   Raise the outboard to the full tilt position and support it in this position.
2.   Manually move the trim sender lever to the full DOWN position. The trim sender gauge should read full DOWN. Manually move the trim sender lever to full UP position. The trim sender gauge should read full UP.
3.   If the sender gauge is not in agreement with the lever position, loosen the trim sender attaching screws and position the sender unit to achieve the correct gauge alignment. When adjustment is correct, the outboard will trim upward a maximum 50.5 inches.

TESTING

60–90 hp Models

➡**This test is best accomplished using an analog ohmmeter or a digital ohmmeter with an oscilloscope screen.**

1.   Disconnect the trim sensor electrical connector.
2.   Measure the resistance between the pink and black terminals in the connector Resistance should be 360–540 ohms.
3.   Connect an ohmmeter between the black and orange terminals, slowly turn the trim sensor lever and observe the ohmmeter. Resistance should smoothly raise from approximately 800–1200 ohms.
4.   If resistance is not within specification or does raise smoothly, the trim sensor is faulty.

225-250 Hp 76° V6 Models

1.   Disconnect the trim sensor electrical harness.
2.   Connect an ohmmeter between the pink and orange terminals in the connector. The specified resistance is 494–741 ohms.
3.   Connect an ohmmeter between the black and orange terminals, slowly turn the lever and observe the ohmmeter. The specified resistance is 800–1200 ohms.
4.   If resistance is not within specification the trim sensor is faulty.

115-220 Hp and 90° 225 Hp V6 Models

1.   Disconnect the trim sensor electrical harness.
2.   Connect an ohmmeter between the pink and black terminals in the connector. The specified resistance is 489–735 ohms.

3.   Connect an ohmmeter between the black and orange terminals, slowly turn the lever and observe the ohmmeter. The specified resistance is 300–1200 ohms.
4.   If resistance is not within specification the trim sensor is faulty.

Servicing

The following procedures provide detailed instructions to service most accessible parts of the power trim/tilt system. Many of the instructions require the end cap of the tilt cylinder and/or the end caps of the trim cylinders to be removed. As explained in the previous paragraphs, this is not an easy task.

If the attempt to remove the end cap is not successful, the unit must be taken to a shop with the proper test equipment and trained personnel with the expertise to service a high pressure hydraulic unit. If the holes provided in the end cap for the special tool are damaged, the trim/tilt unit will probably have to be replaced.

➡**Some of the accompanying illustrations were made with the trim/tilt unit on the work bench for photographic clarity. However, the work described, with the exception of the tilt cylinder removal, may be performed without removing the unit from the clamp bracket.**

PRELIMINARY TASKS

With power or manually, raise the outboard unit to the full up position and lock it in place.

Obtain a suitable container to receive the hydraulic fluid from the trim/tilt system.

Remove the two lines from the bottom of the trim/tilt housing.

Remove the fill plug from the reservoir and allow the hydraulic fluid to drain into the container.

After the fluid has drained, replace the drain plug as an assist in preventing contamination from entering the reservoir.

DISASSEMBLY

◆ **See accompanying illustrations**

Make an attempt to keep parts identified as they are removed. Many parts may appear similar, but components should be installed into the same location from which they are removed.

1.   Obtain Yamaha special tool P/N YB6175. Observe the pattern of pins and the words etched on each side of the special tool. The side with the three pins and the word TRIM is used to remove/install the end cap on the trim cylinders. The side with the four pins and the word tilt is used for the end cap on the tilt cylinder.

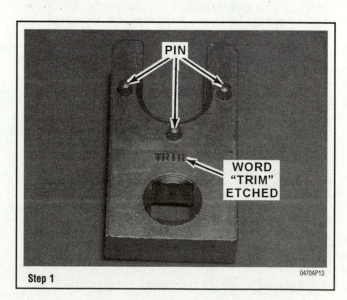

PIN

WORD "TRIM" ETCHED

Step 1

0470AP13

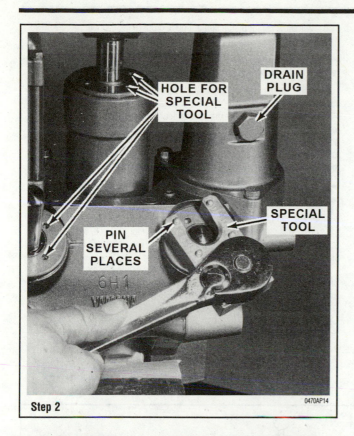

HOLE FOR SPECIAL TOOL

DRAIN PLUG

PIN SEVERAL PLACES

SPECIAL TOOL

6H1

Step 2   0470AP14

TRIM ROD

Step 4   0470AP16

END CAP

SPRING

Step 3   0470AP15

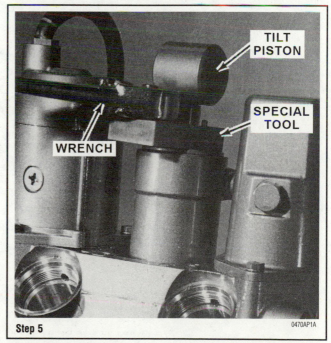

TILT PISTON

SPECIAL TOOL

WRENCH

Step 5   0470AP1A

2. Using the trim side of the special tool, index the pins into the recess holes provided in the end cap. Index a socket wrench adaptor into the square hole in the tool and remove the end cap from the trim cylinder to be serviced. This is not an easy task, but under certain favorable conditions it can be accomplished.

3. Remove the end cap and spring. Early models may not have the spring. The spring is partially attached to the end cap and will come free with the cap.

4. Withdraw the trim piston straight up and out of the cylinder. Repeat Steps 2–4 to remove the other trim piston.

➡ If the tilt piston must be removed from the cylinder for servicing, the trim/tilt unit must be removed from the clamp bracket assembly. This task is accomplished by first removing the end caps from both ends of the pivot pin, and then removing the pin. The pin can only be removed from the port side out the starboard side. After the pin is free, remove the attaching hardware securing the trim/tilt assembly in the clamp

bracket, and remove the assembly. Clamp the unit in a vise equipped with soft jaws or pad the jaws with a couple pieces of wood. The vise will provide stability and access to almost all parts.

5. After the trim/tilt unit has been removed from the clamp bracket and clamped in a vise, as described in the previous paragraph, the tilt end cap may be removed. Using the tilt side of the same tool as for the trim cylinder end cap, index the pins into the recess holes provided in the end cap. Remove the end cap in the same manner with a socket adaptor and wrench as was used for the end cap of the trim cylinders.

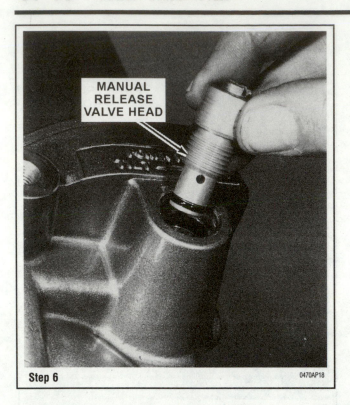

MANUAL RELEASE VALVE HEAD

Step 6

0470AP18

6. Withdraw the tilt piston straight up and out of the cylinder.
7. Remove the circlip and then remove the manual release head.

➡**Threads of the release head are left hand. Turn the head clockwise to remove and counterclockwise to install.**

The inner parts of the manual release valve, the ball, release rod, seat, spring, and pin, are all secured by the valve seat screw.

Removal of this screw is extremely difficult. Without good cause, an attempt to remove the seat screw should not be made. Individual replacement parts are not available for the items behind the screw. Therefore, the only gain in removing them would be cleaning. In most cases replacement of the O-ring in the lower groove of the manual release head will solve a problem in this area.

➡**In the majority of cases, service of the hydraulic items removed thus far will solve any rare problems encountered with the trim/tilt system.**

The reservoir can be removed through the attaching hardware and cleaned if the system was considered contaminated with foreign material, which is highly unlikely, because the system is a closed system. The only route for entry of foreign material would be through the fill opening.

Further disassembly and service to the system would best be left to a shop properly equipped with the proper test equipment and trained personnel with the expertise to work with high pressure hydraulic systems.

CLEANING & INSPECTION

▸ **See Figure 21**

Keep the work area as clean as possible to prevent contamination through foreign material entering the system on the parts to be installed.

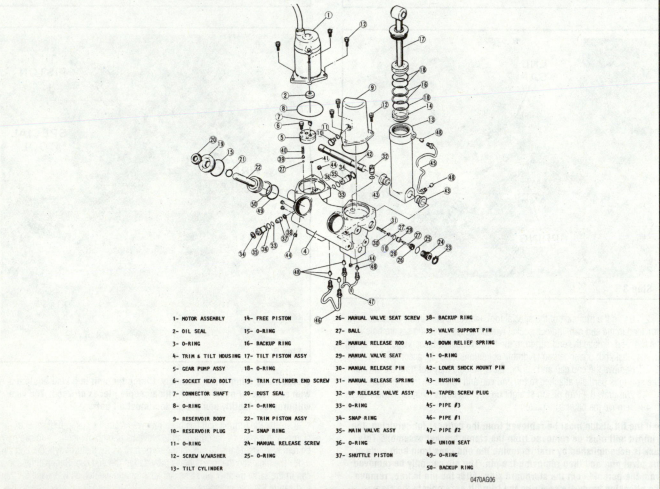

1- MOTOR ASSEMBLY	14- FREE PISTON	26- MANUAL VALVE SEAT SCREW	38- BACKUP RING
2- OIL SEAL	15- O-RING	27- BALL	39- VALVE SUPPORT PIN
3- O-RING	16- BACKUP RING	28- MANUAL RELEASE ROD	40- DOWN RELIEF SPRING
4- TRIM & TILT HOUSING	17- TILT PISTON ASSY	29- MANUAL VALVE SEAT	41- O-RING
5- GEAR PUMP ASSY	18- O-RING	30- MANUAL RELEASE PIN	42- LOWER SHOCK MOUNT PIN
6- SOCKET HEAD BOLT	19- TRIM CYLINDER END SCREW	31- MANUAL RELEASE SPRING	43- BUSHING
7- CONNECTOR SHAFT	20- DUST SEAL	32- UP RELEASE VALVE ASSY	44- TAPER SCREW PLUG
8- O-RING	21- O-RING	33- O-RING	45- PIPE #3
9- RESERVOIR BODY	22- TRIM PISTON ASSY	34- SNAP RING	46- PIPE #1
10- RESERVOIR PLUG	23- SNAP RING	35- MAIN VALVE ASSY	47- PIPE #2
11- O-RING	24- MANUAL RELEASE SCREW	36- O-RING	48- UNION SEAT
12- SCREW W/WASHER	25- O-RING	37- SHUTTLE PISTON	49- O-RING
13- TILT CYLINDER			50- BACKUP RING

0470AG06

Fig. 21 Exploded view of a typical power trim/tilt system with major parts identified. Some changes have been made to the internal routing of the hydraulic fluid and the number and location of internal check valves on various models

Clean all parts thoroughly with solvent and blow them dry with compressed air.

Carefully inspect the trim pistons and the tilt piston for any sign of damage.

Purchase, if available, new O-rings and discard the old items, but only after the replacement O-ring is verified as correct for the intended installation.

ASSEMBLY

♦ **See accompanyinmg illustrations**

The following procedures outline the steps required to install the parts removed in disassembly. Make every effort to keep the parts as clean as possible during the installation work to prevent contaminating the system.

Good shop practice dictates new O-rings be installed anytime the unit is disassembled and the rings are exposed.

1. Coat a new O-ring with Yamalube Power Trim and Tilt Fluid or a good grade of automatic transmission fluid, and then install the O-ring into the groove in the manual release head. The accompanying illustration shows two different type heads used on the trim/tilt units installed on the outboard units

covered in this manual. As mentioned several times, the manual release valve is one area of constant engineering changes.

2. Insert and thread the head into the manual release valve opening. Remember some units are standard right hand threads and others have left hand threads. Tighten the head just snug because it will be rotated for power tilt and manual tilt operation.

3. Secure the head in the trim/tilt housing with a circlip or Tru-arc snapring, depending on the trim/tilt unit being serviced.

4. Check to be sure the back-up rings are in place in the groove of the tilt piston and the free piston, or install the rings if they were removed. Apply a coating of Yamalube Power Trim and Tilt Fluid to new O-rings, and then install the O-rings into the grooves of the tilt piston, free piston, and the tilt piston end cap.

With the piston rod facing up the O-ring of the free piston must be installed under the back-up ring. The O-ring of the tilt piston must be installed on top of the back-up ring.

MANUAL RELEASE VALVE

Step 1   0470AP19

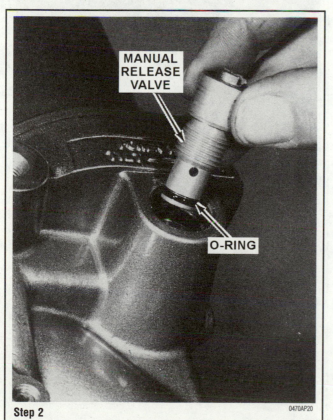

MANUAL RELEASE VALVE

O-RING

Step 2   0470AP20

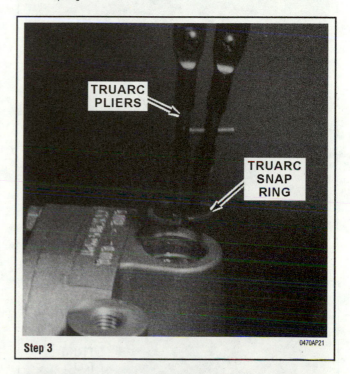

TRUARC PLIERS

TRUARC SNAP RING

Step 3   0470AP21

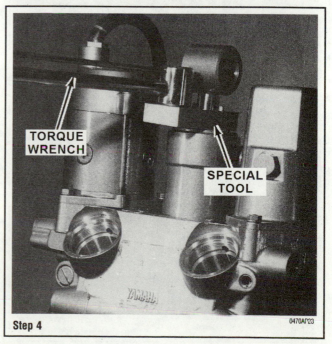

TORQUE WRENCH

SPECIAL TOOL

Step 4   0470AP23

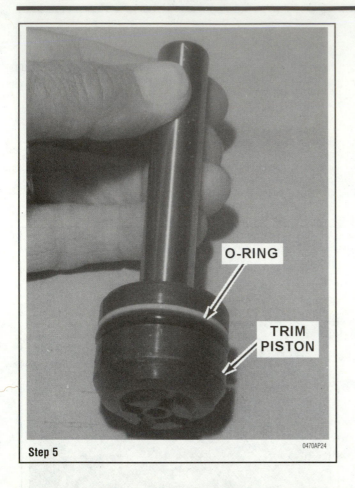

O-RING

TRIM PISTON

Step 5   0470AP24

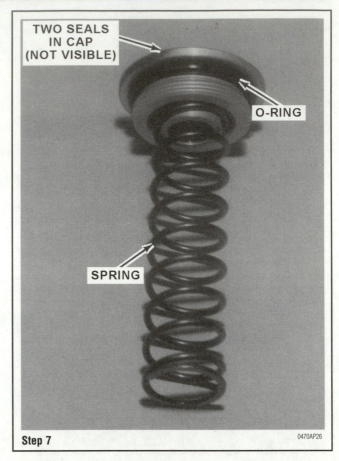

TWO SEALS IN CAP (NOT VISIBLE)

O-RING

SPRING

Step 7   0470AP26

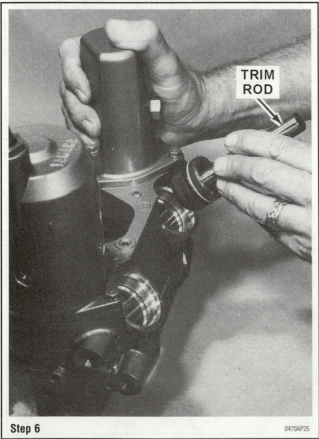

TRIM ROD

Step 6   0470AP25

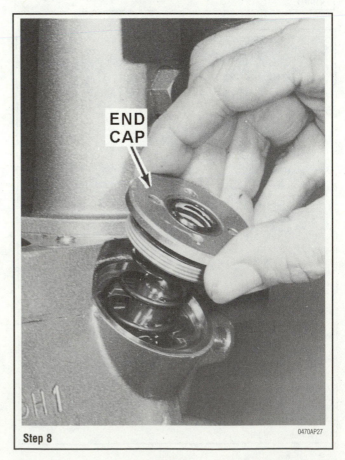

END CAP

Step 8   0470AP27

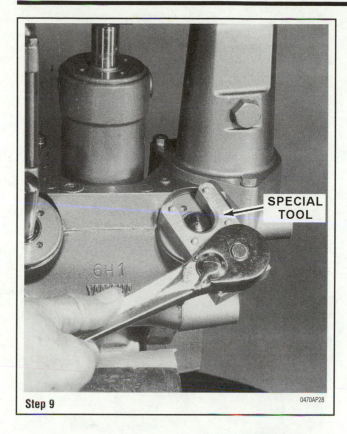

Step 9   0470AP28

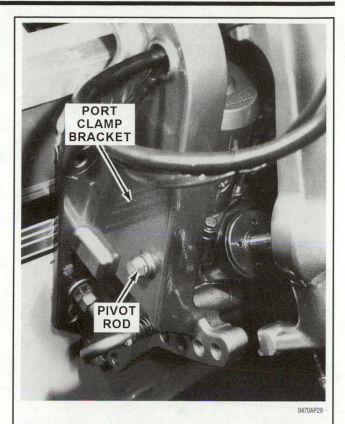

0470AP29

Fig. 22 Port view of a power trim/tilt system showing the pivot rod and clamp bracket

Insert the tilt piston into the piston and thread the end cap into the housing.

5. Clamp the trim/tilt housing in a vise equipped with soft jaws or pad the jaws with a couple pieces of wood. Using the tilt side of Yamaha special tool YB6175 with the pins indexed into the recess holes of the end cap, tighten the end cap to 61 ft. lbs. (85Nm).

6. Check to be sure the back-up ring is properly installed in the trim piston groove, or install the ring if it was removed. Coat a new O-ring with Yamalube Power Trim and Tilt Fluid, and then install the O-ring into the groove of the trim piston. With the trim piston rod facing up, the O-ring must be installed UNDER the back-up ring.

7. Insert the trim piston straight down into the cylinder. Push the piston as far down as possible. Repeat Steps 6 and 7 for the other trim piston.

8. Coat a new O-ring with Yamalube Power Trim and Tilt Fluid, and then install the O-ring into the groove of the trim end cap. On early models, check to be sure the spring is properly seated. If the two seals in the end cap were removed, coat new seals with hydraulic fluid, and then insert them into the individual grooves of the end cap.

9. Slide the spring down over the trim piston rod, and then thread the end cap into the trim/tilt housing.

Using the trim side of Yamaha special tool YB6175 with the pins indexed into the recess holes of the end cap, tighten the end cap to 61 ft. lbs. (85Nm).

Repeat Steps 8–10 for the other trim cylinder.

CLOSING TASKS

♦ **See Figures 22 and 23**

If the trim/tilt unit was not removed from the clamp brackets, fill the system with Yamalube Power Trim/Tilt Fluid or a good grade of automatic transmission fluid. Purge the system of air.

If the trim/tilt unit was removed from the clamp bracket, the system is filled and purged with the unit on the bench. Fill the system with Yamalube Power Trim/Tilt Fluid or a good grade of automatic transmission fluid.

Purge air from the system by first pulling the tilt cylinder to its fully extended position. Check the fluid level and add fluid as required to bring the level up to the bottom of the fill opening.

Next, rotate the manual release valve to the power tilt position, approximately three full turns from the manual position.

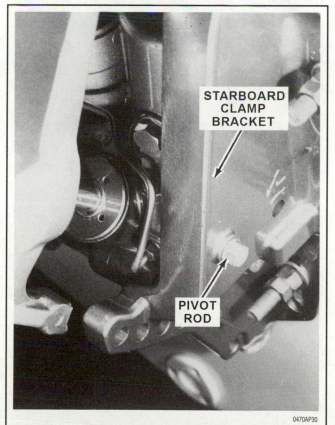

0470AP30

Fig. 23 Starboard view of a power trim/tilt system showing the pivot rod and clamp bracket

Now, obtain a 12 volt battery and connect the Blue lead from the trim/tilt unit to the positive lead from the battery. Now, momentarily make contact with the Black lead from the unit to the negative post of the battery.

The trim cylinders should move to the fully extended position. Check the fluid level and add fluid, as required.

Finally, connect the Green lead from the unit to the positive post on the battery. Momentarily make contact with the Black lead from the trim/tilt unit to the negative post of the battery. The trim cylinders and the tilt cylinder should retract to the full down position.

Repeat the extension and retraction of the cylinders two or three times.

To check for air in the system, extend the tilt cylinder, and then apply a downward heavy force manually to the end of the piston. The piston should feel solid. If the piston retracts more than about 1/8 in. (3.2mm), the system still contains air. Perform the purging sequence until the tilt cylinder is solid.

Install the unit between the clamp bracket. Begin by checking to be sure the sleeve for the piston rod end is in place, and the insert in both port and starboard bracket arms are in place. Coat the inside surfaces of the sleeve and inserts with Yamalube Grease or equivalent water resistant grease.

Position the trim/tilt in place and insert the pivot pin. Remember, the pin could only be removed in one direction. Now, the reverse is true, it must be installed from the starboard side, through the piston rod end, and then through the port side clamp bracket arm.

Secure the trim/tilt housing with the attaching hardware.

Install the end caps onto both ends of the pivot pin.

Perform an operational check of the system.

REMOTE CONTROLS 12-2
REMOTE CONTROL BOX 12-2
   DESCRIPTION & OPERATION 12-2
CHOKE SWITCH 12-2
   TESTING 12-2
LOW OIL WARNING BUZZER 12-2
   TESTING 12-2
NEUTRAL SAFETY SWITCH 12-2
   TESTING 12-2
START BUTTON 12-3
   TESTING 12-3
KILL SWITCH 12-3
   TESTING 12-3
CONTROL BOX ASSEMBLY 12-3
   REMOVAL 12-3
   DISASSEMBLY 12-4
   CLEANING & INSPECTION 12-7
   ASSEMBLY 12-8

12

REMOTE CONTROLS

REMOTE CONTROLS 12-2

REMOTE CONTROLS

Remote Control Box

DESCRIPTION & OPERATION

▶ See Figures 1 and 2

The remote control unit allows the helmsperson to control throttle operation and shift movements from a location other than where the outboard unit is mounted.

In most cases, the remote control box is mounted approximately halfway forward (midship) on the starboard side of the boat.

The control unit houses a key switch, a choke switch, a kill switch, a neutral safety switch, a warning horn, and the necessary wiring and cable hardware to connect the control box to the outboard unit.

A safety feature is incorporated in the unit. The control arm can be shifted out of the **NEUTRAL** position if and only if the neutral lever is squeezed into the control arm. This feature prevents the arm from being accidentally moved from Neutral into either forward or reverse gear. Unintentional movement of the shift lever could be dangerous, resulting in personal injury to the operator, passengers, or the boat.

Starting from the upright **NEUTRAL** position, when the control arm is moved forward to about 30° from the vertical position, the unit shifts into forward gear. At this point the throttle plate is fully closed. As the control arm is moved past the 30° position, forward and downward, the throttle will open, until the wide open position, approximately 90° from the vertical position, is reached.

To shift into reverse gear, the control arm is first returned to the full upright position (Neutral) momentarily. From the upright position, the control arm is moved aft about 30°, and the unit shifts in reverse gear. At this point, the throttle plate is fully closed. If the arm is moved further aft and downward, the throttle will be opened until the wide open position is reached at about 60°.

The remote control unit is equipped with a free acceleration lever. This lever can be moved up to open the throttle and down to close the throttle. This lever is utilized only during powerhead startup and when the control arm is in the full upright (Neutral) position. When the free acceleration lever is not in the full down, idling position, the control lever cannot be moved from the **NEUTRAL** position.

Complete, detailed, and illustrated procedures to disassemble, service, and assemble the control box are included in this chapter.

Choke Switch

TESTING

▶ See Figure 3

➡ On some late model control boxes, the choke switch is integrated into the main switch for easier operation.

The choke switch is a spring loaded toggle type switch located in the forward side of the control box. The control box must be opened to gain access to the switch leads.

1. Disconnect the Blue and Yellow leads from the choke switch at the nearest quick disconnect fitting.
2. Select the 1000 ohm scale on the meter. Make contact with the meter leads, one to each of the disconnected leads.
3. In the normal **OFF** position the meter should indicate no continuity. Move the switch to the **ON** position. The meter should indicate continuity.
4. If the switch fails either of these two tests, it must be replaced. The switch cannot be serviced or adjusted.

Low Oil Warning Buzzer

TESTING

The buzzer is a warning device to indicate low oil in the reservoir, an over rev. condition, or overheating of the powerhead. The buzzer is located inside the control box.

1. Remove the control box cover and identify the two leads from the buzzer, one is Yellow and the other is Pink.
2. Disconnect these two leads at their quick disconnect fittings, and ease the buzzer out from between the four posts which anchor it in place.
3. Obtain a 12 volt battery. Connect the Yellow buzzer lead to the negative battery terminal. Momentarily make contact with the Pink buzzer lead to the positive battery terminal.
4. As soon as the Pink buzzer lead makes contact with the positive battery terminal, the buzzer should sound. If the buzzer is silent, or the sound emitted does not capture the helmperson's attention immediately, the buzzer should be replaced. Service or adjustment is not possible.
5. If the sound is satisfactory and immediate, install the buzzer between the four posts and connect the two leads matching color to color. Tuck the leads to prevent them from making contact with any moving parts inside the control box. Replace the cover.

Neutral Safety Switch

TESTING

▶ See Figures 4 and 5

➡ **Remember this is a safety switch. A faulty switch may allow the powerhead to be started with the lower unit in gear—an extremely dangerous situation for persons aboard and the boat.**

1. Trace the neutral safety switch leads from the switch to their nearest quick disconnect fitting. Both of these leads are usually Brown, but may vary for different models. Refer to the wiring diagram in the Appendix for the proper color identification.
2. Disconnect the two leads and connect an ohmmeter across the two disconnected leads. When the shift lever is in the **NEUTRAL** position, the meter should register continuity.

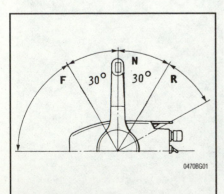

Fig. 1 Shift lever position for the remote control unit

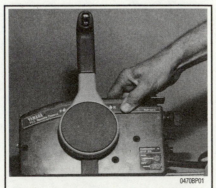

Fig. 2 Remote control box removed from the boat and ready for service

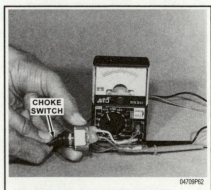

Fig. 3 Using an ohmmeter to test the choke switch

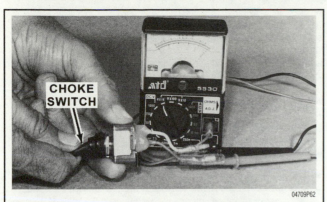

Fig. 4 Using an ohmmeter to test the neutral safety switch

Fig. 5 The neutral safety switch is sometimes hidden, but is usually located on the axis of the shift lever just inside the lower cowling pan

3. When the lower unit is shifted to either forward or reverse, the meter should register no continuity.

4. The switch must pass all three tests to indicate the safety switch is functioning properly. If the switch fails any one of the tests, the switch must be replaced.

Start Button

TESTING

▶ **See Figures 6 and 7**

1. Trace the start button harness containing two wires from the switch to their nearest quick disconnect fitting. The colors may vary for different models.

2. Disconnect the two leads and connect an ohmmeter across the discon-

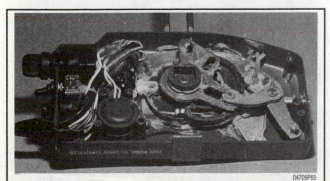

Fig. 6 The most difficult task involving testing of the remote control box is stuffing the electrical leads back into the box in an orderly manner

Fig. 7 Using an ohmmeter to test the start button

nected leads. Depress the start button. The meter should register continuity. Release the button and the meter should now register no continuity.

3. Both tests must be successful. If the tests are not successful, the start button must be replaced. The start button is a one piece sealed unit and cannot be serviced.

Kill Switch

TESTING

1. Trace the kill switch button harness containing two wires from the switch to their nearest quick disconnect fitting. The colors may vary for different models, but the hot wire is usually White/Black.

Disconnect the two leads and connect an ohmmeter across the disconnected leads. Verify the emergency tether is in place behind the kill switch button. Select the 1000 ohm scale on the meter.

2. Depress the kill button. The meter should register continuity. Release the button. The meter should now register no continuity.

3. Both tests must be successful. If the switch fails either test, the switch is defective and must be replaced. The switch is a one piece sealed unit and cannot be serviced.

Control Box Assembly

REMOVAL

Removal of the control box is accomplished by first disconnecting the throttle and shift cables at the powerhead, and then disconnecting the main wiring harness at the quick disconnect fitting. Next, the three mounting screws are removed securing the control box to the boat.

DISASSEMBLY

♦ **See accompanying illustrations**

1. Move the control arm to the full upright (Neutral) position. Remove the five Phillips head screws securing the upper and lower parts of the back plate.

2. Pry off the circlip retaining the throttle cable end to the throttle arm and the circlip retaining the shift cable end to the shift arm. Take care not to lose these two small circlips. Lift off the cable ends from the arms and be careful not to alter their length at the turnbuckles. Remove both cable ends from the box.

➥**One of the most difficult tasks during assembling of the control unit is attempting to return all the wires back into their original positions.**

Some wires are tucked neatly under switches, others are routed into neat bundles secured with plastic retainers, some are looped and double back, but believe-it-or-not, with patience and some good words, they all fit into one side of the box away from moving parts.

Therefore, it would be most advantageous to take a Polaroid picture of the unit as an aid during assembling.

3. Remove the retaining nuts on the main key switch, the electric choke switch, and the kill switch on the side of the control box. Ease these three switches out of their grommets and holes. Disconnect the following leads at their quick disconnect fittings:

The Pink and Yellow leads to the neutral safety switch, and for models with trim/tilt.

The Yellow, Green, and Black leads encased in a small harness leading to the up/down button on the upper control arm.

The entire harness, switches, and horn may now be lifted free of the control box, as shown. The horn is not secured with hardware, but is simply retained between four bosses.

4. Lift out the throttle arm, consisting of three pieces hinged together. A plastic bushing will probably remain on the underneath side of the throttle arm. This bushing was indexed with the throttle friction bands.

5. Remove the two Phillips head screws securing the neutral switch, and

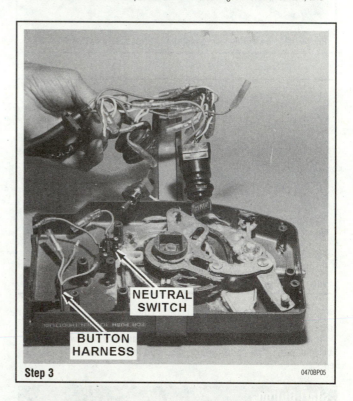

Step 3   0470BP05

NEUTRAL SWITCH

BUTTON HARNESS

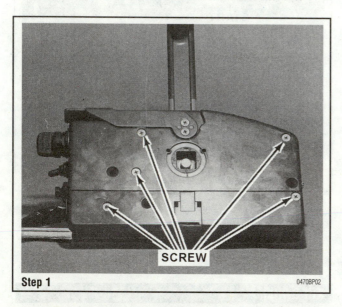

SCREW

Step 1   0470BP02

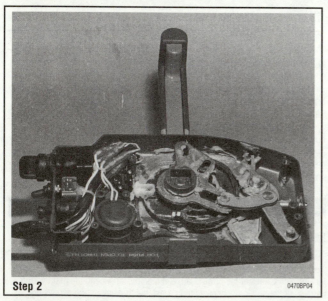

Step 2   0470BP04

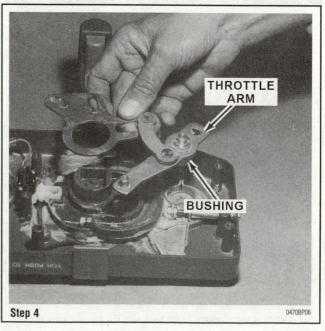

THROTTLE ARM

BUSHING

Step 4   0470BP06

then remove the switch. Remove the Phillips head screw and switch arm from the gear.

6. Lift the two halves of the throttle friction band up and out of the control box. The throttle friction screw, with the circlip attached, will come away with the band.

Lift out the small wavy washer from the center of the shift arm.

7. Remove the Phillips screw securing the spring retainer, and then remove the spring retainer. Grasp one end of the leaf spring pack with a pair of needle nose pliers.

Pull up on the pack and at the same time allow the pack to straighten to release tension on the springs. Lift out the detent roller from under the gear.

8. Loosen the bolt in the center of the gear ½ turn only. After the center bolt has been loosened, lightly tap on the bolt to free it from the gear. Now, remove the bolt.

9. Turn the control box over. Three things are now to be performed, almost simultaneously. Support the gear—now underneath—with one hand and at the same time unsnap the bottom harness cover from the front plate, as the control arm is lifted from the box. Remove the attaching screws, and then the **NEUTRAL** position plate.

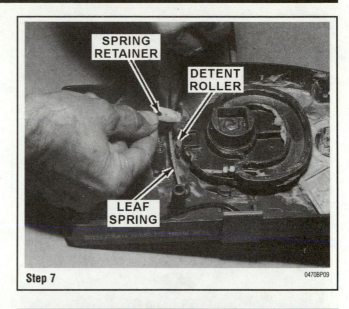

Step 7   0470BP09

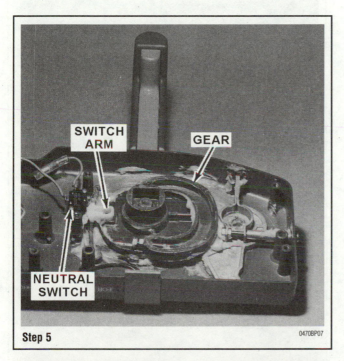

Step 5   0470BP07

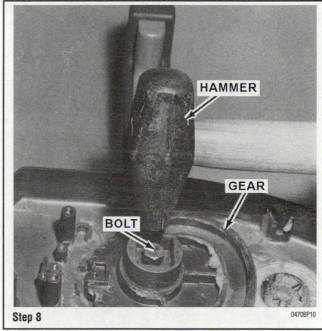

Step 8   0470BP10

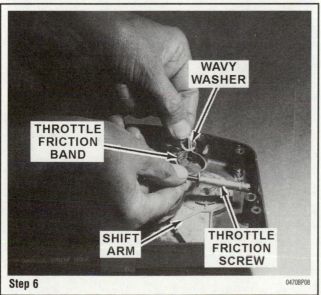

Step 6   0470BP08

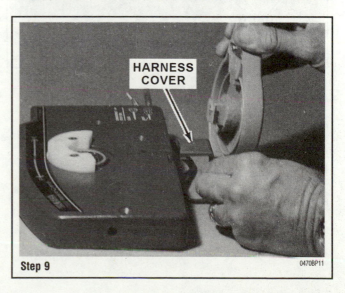

Step 9   0470BP11

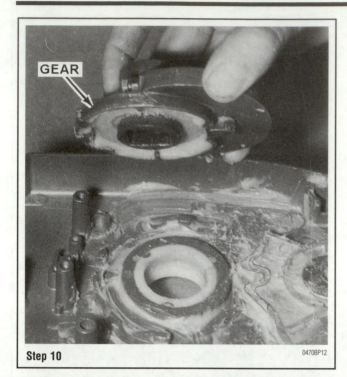

GEAR

Step 10 0470BP12

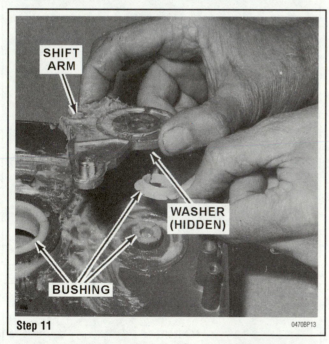

SHIFT ARM

WASHER (HIDDEN)

BUSHING

Step 11 0470BP13

10. Support the gear and at the same time turn the control box over, and then lift the gear free of the box.

11. Lift off the shift arm, a large flat washer, and two bushings from the front plate. This step concludes the disassembly of the inside of the front plate.

Acceleration Lever

▶ See accompanying illustrations

1. Place the upper back plate on the work bench with the lever facing down. Remove the Phillips screw and lift off the detent roller retainer.

2. Pry out the detent roller from the free acceleration disc.

3. Turn the back plate over and remove the two Phillips screws securing the free acceleration lever to the disc. Lift off the lever and the wavy washer under the lever.

Turn the back plate over again, and then lift off the free acceleration disc and another wavy washer.

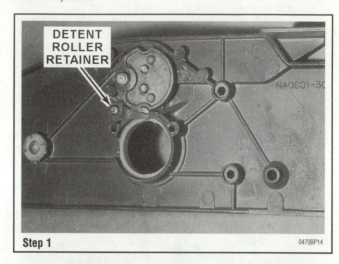

DETENT ROLLER RETAINER

Step 1 0470BP14

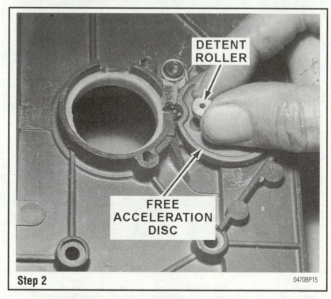

DETENT ROLLER

FREE ACCELERATION DISC

Step 2 0470BP15

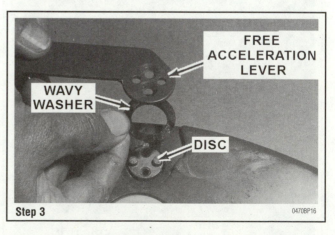

FREE ACCELERATION LEVER

WAVY WASHER

DISC

Step 3 0470BP16

4. Remove the **NEUTRAL** position lever retainer and slide the lever from the arm. Remove the small spring between the top of the lever and the top of the arm.

5. Remove the two small Phillips screws securing the handle to the control arm.

6. Pry up on the front disc and separate the disc from the control lever arm. Unthread the harness, to the up/down button, from the cavity of the arm.

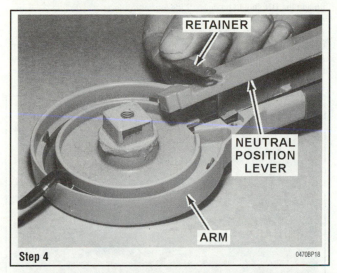

Step 4   0470BP18

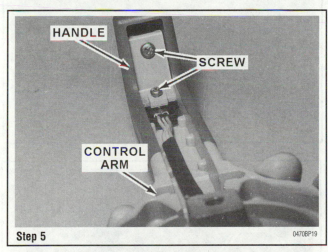

Step 5   0470BP19

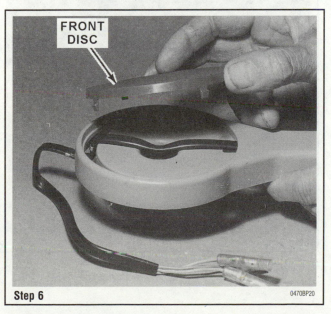

Step 6   0470BP20

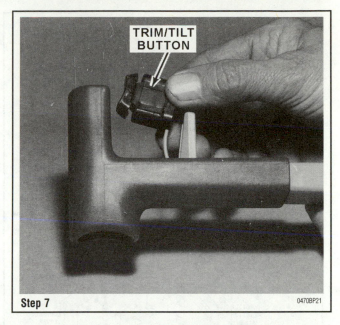

Step 7   0470BP21

7. Grasp the handle in one hand and the shaft of the control arm in the other. Gently slide them apart about 2 inches (5cm) or until the trim/tilt button with the harness attached can be removed from the handle.

CLEANING & INSPECTION

▶ See Figures 8 and 9

Clean all metal parts with solvent, and then blow them dry with compressed air.

Never allow nylon bushings, plastic washers, nylon retainers, wiring harness retainers, and the like, to remain submerged in solvent more than just a few

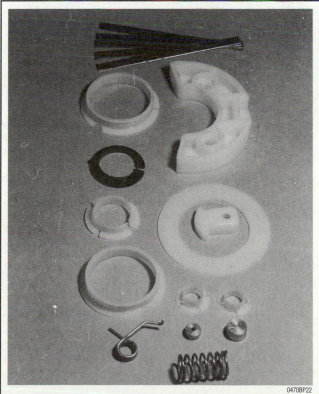

0470BP22

Fig. 8 Just some of the small metal and nylon parts from the interior of a remote control box

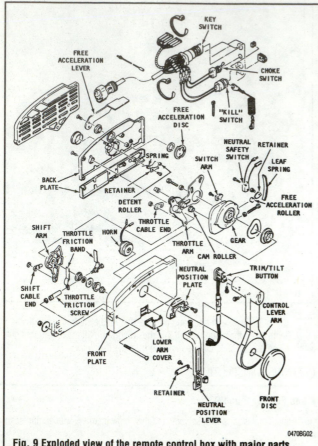

Fig. 9 Exploded view of the remote control box with major parts identified

Trim/Tilt Button And Harness

♦ **See Accompanying Illustrations**

1. Feed the harness wires for the power tilt/trim button down from the top in between the handle and the arm. Push the face of the button into the handle and observe the button from the operator's position. The word **UP** should be up and the **DN** should be down. Slide the control lever arm up into the handle.

2. Continue to feed the harness wires along the length of the arm—in and out of the cavity of the arm. Check to be sure the harness lies flat with no kinks. A kink in the wire will damage the harness over a period of time. Snap the front disc over the cavity.

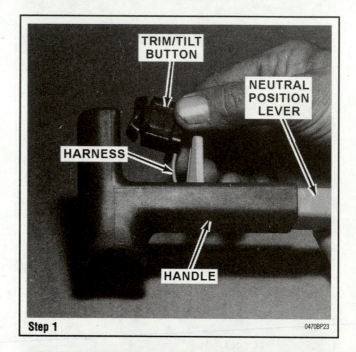

Step 1

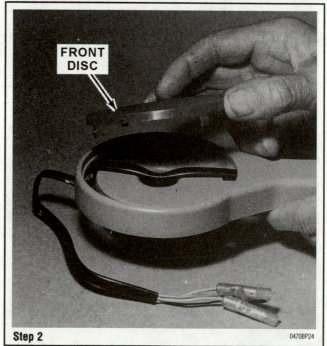

Step 2

moments. The solvent will cause these type parts to expand slightly. They are already considered a tight fit and even the slightest amount of expansion would make them very difficult to install. If force is used, the part is most likely to be distorted.

Inspect the control housing plastic case for cracks or other damage that would allow moisture to enter and cause problems with the mechanism.

Carefully check the teeth on the gear and shift arm for signs of wear. Inspect all ball bearings for nicks or grooves which would cause them to bind and fail to move freely.

Closely inspect the condition of all wires and their protective insulation. Look for exposed wires caused by the insulation rubbing on a moving part, cuts and nicks in the insulation and severe kinking which could cause internal breakage of the wires.

Inspect the bosses on both ends of the leaf spring. If either end shows signs of failure, the front plate must be replaced.

Inspect the edges of the cut-out in the **NEUTRAL** position plate. Replace this plate if the corners of the cut-out show any sign of rounding. If rounded, a slight pressure on the **NEUTRAL** position lever could throw the lower unit into gear. Check and double check all components of the **NEUTRAL** position system from the spring at the top of the lever down to the extension at the bottom of the lever which indexes into the cut-out of the **NEUTRAL** position plate.

ASSEMBLY

The following procedures provide complete detailed instructions to assemble all parts of the remote control unit. If certain areas were not disturbed during disassembling, simply bypass the steps involved and proceed with the work.

3. Secure the arm to the handle with the two Phillips head screws.

4. Hold the return spring in place in the recess at the top of the **NEUTRAL** position lever and at the same time slide the lever along the length of the arm up into the handle. Install the lever retainer across the lever and secure it to the arm with the two small Phillips head screws.

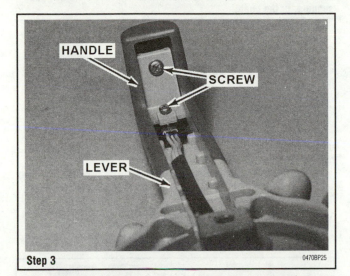

Step 3   0470BP25

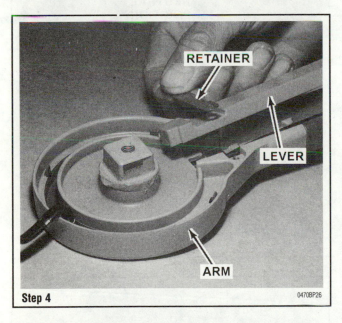

Step 4   0470BP26

Free Acceleration Lever

♦ **See Accompanying Illustrations**

Apply just a dab of Yamalube to the wavy washer and the free acceleration disc. Place the wavy washer and the free acceleration disc over the smaller hole in the inside of the top back plate. The single large post on the disc must face away from the notch cut in the plate for the free acceleration arm.

Hold the washer and disc (the Yamalube will help), in place—from falling away—and at the same time, turn the plate over on the work bench.

1. Place another wavy washer and the free acceleration arm over the installed disc.

➥ **The arm can only be installed one way because of the groove cut into the face of the upper back plate to accommodate the arm. If the free acceleration disc has been installed correctly in the previous step, the**

two beveled holes in the arm will align with the two threaded holes in the disc. Also, the two round holes in the arm will index over the two posts on the disc.

Install and tighten the two Phillips head screws. Turn the plate over again with the inside facing upward.

2. Install the upturned portion of the spring between the installed disc and the center boss, as shown. Hook the coiled part of the spring over the threaded post and at the same time direct the free end of the spring to anchor between the threaded and plain posts.

The detent roller must be positioned over the upturned end of the spring and be seated into the curved notch of the free acceleration disc. A small screwdriver inserted along the spring under the disc may aid in pushing the end into place to allow the roller to drop down over the spring end and against the disc.

3. Install the retainer over the detent roller. Secure the roller in place with the Phillips head screw threaded into the post with the spring around it.

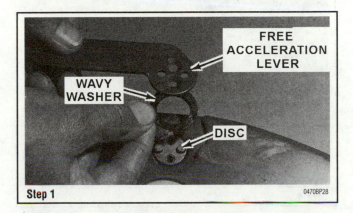

Step 1   0470BP28

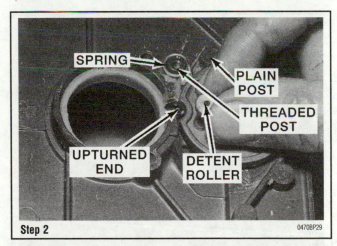

Step 2   0470BP29

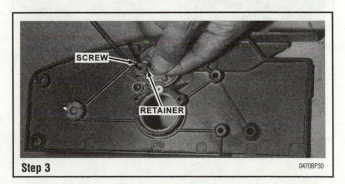

Step 3   0470BP30

4. Place the small bushing onto the shift arm boss on the inside back plate. Next, place the large bushing onto the same boss. The small and large bushing must be installed face-to-face. After both bushings are in position, slide the large flat washer onto the boss. Now, install the shift arm over the flat washer with the post for the shift cable facing upward—pointed toward the lower part of the case.

5. Lower the shift gear into the case with the post indexing into the notch in the shift gear. Support the shift gear inside the cover and turn the front plate over.

6. Place the **NEUTRAL** position plate onto the front plate and secure it in place with the two Phillips head screws. Position the control arm over the front plate with the **NEUTRAL** position lever indexed into the cutout of the **NEUTRAL** position plate.

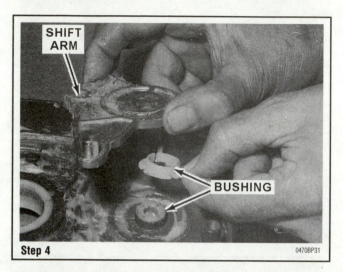

Step 4   0470BP31

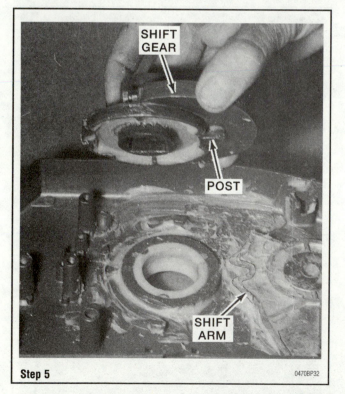

Step 5   0470BP32

If the NEUTRAL position lever is not sealed properly, a slight pressure on the handle could shift the lower unit into geaar—forward or reverse. Such action coould cause serious injury to the crew, passengers, or the boat.

Guide the wire harness into the groove below the arm and snap on the lower arrm cover to secure the harness in place.

7. Support the control arm and turn the front plate over. Install the washer and bolt into the square recess of the gear. Tighten the bolt to a torque value of 5.8 ft. lbs. (8Nm).

8. Slide the free acceleration roller into the center left notch in the shift gear. Grasp the pack of leaf springs with a pair of needle nose pliers. Insert one end of the pack into the lower boss. Bend the pack around the roller. Guide the other end into the upper boss. Install the small metal leaf spring retainer onto the threaded post to the left of the leaf spring. Secure the retainer in place with a phillips head screw.

9. Install the throttle friction band over the shift arm. Move the two ends of the band into the boss on the front plate. Center the opening of the band squarely over the shift arm. Insert a wavy washer into the center of the band on the shift arm.

10. Install the neutral safety switch with the tab on the switch facing toward the shift gear. Secure the switch in place with the two phillips head screws. Position the white plastic switch arm into the slot provided on the

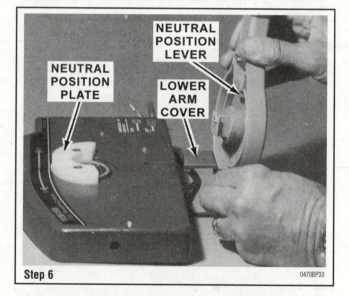

Step 6   0470BP33

Step 7   0470BP34

shift gear. Install and tighten the phillips head screw to secure the arm to the gear.

11. Install the throttle arm. Try not to disturb the wavy washer in the center of the throttle friction band when the bushing on the underneath side of the throttle arm indexes with the band.

➡**If you think some of the other assembling procedures were tricky on this unit, stand by! This next one will put you to the test.**

12. Connect the neutral safety switch leads, pink and yellow (male) at the quick disconnect fittings—color to color. Models with power trim/tilt: connect the button harness leads yellow (female), green and black at the quick disconnect fittings—color to color. Position the horn between the four tall posts next to the neutral safety switch. Install the main key switch, the electric choke switch, and the kill switch into their respective openings on the side of the remote control box. Arrange the mess of wires neatly.

Remember, some wires are tucked neatly under switches, others are routed into neat bundles secured with plastic retainers, and some are looped then doubled back. Believe-it-or-not, with patience and some good words, they will all fit into one side of the box. The wires must be clear of moving parts.

13. Secure the electrical switches to the side of the box with the retaining nuts. Slide the rubber boot over the choke switch. If possible, secure a tie-wrap around the bundle of wires to prevent loose wires from rubbing against and interfering with moving parts.

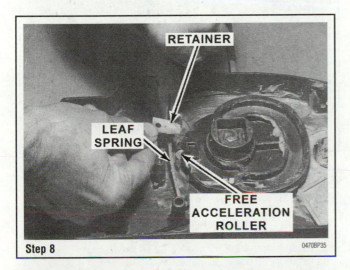

Step 8   0470BP35

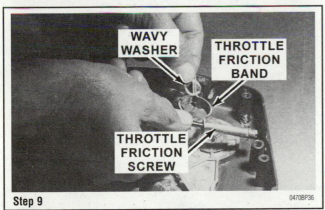

Step 9   0470BP36

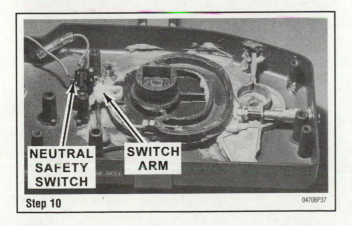

Step 10   0470BP37

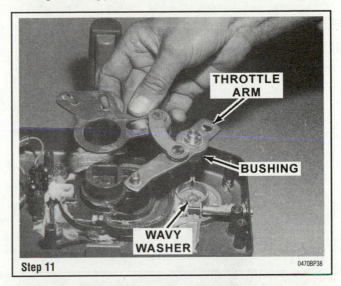

Step 11   0470BP38

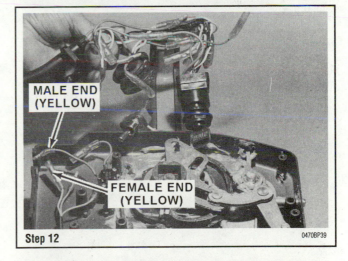

Step 12   0470BP39

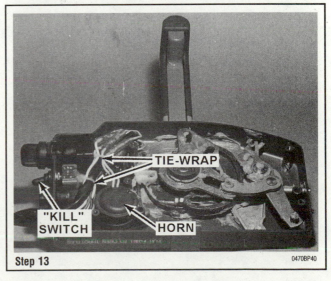

Step 13   0470BP40

14. Thread the cable joint 0.3 in. (8mm) onto the shift cable. Hold the joint to prevent it from rotating and at the same time hook the cable end onto the shift arm post. Secure the cable joint with the restraining circlip.

Install the throttle cable in the same manner as the shift cable. Bring both halves of the back plate together with the front plate. Secure it all together with the five phillips head screws.

15. Check operation of the remote control lever to and between each of the three positions—neutral, forward, and reverse. The lever should move smoothly and with a definite action. The shift cable and the throttle cable should move in and out of the sheathing without any indication of binding. The movement can be checked at the powerhead end of the cable.

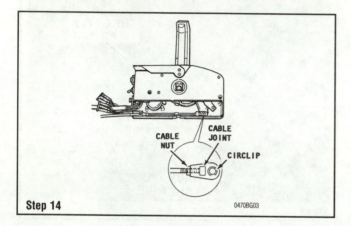

Step 14   0470BG03

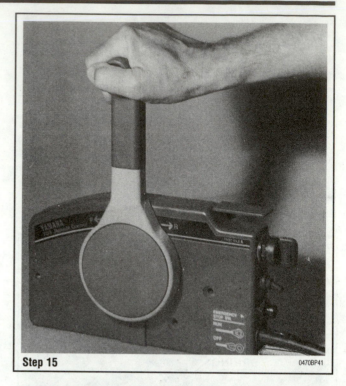

Step 15   0470BP41

Control Box

1. Guide the cables along a selected path and secure them in place with the retainers. Do not bend any cable into a diameter smaller than 16 in. (40cm).

2. Connect the shift cable to the shift lever on the powerhead. Insert the outer throttle cable wire into the throttle cable bracket. Connect the cable joint onto the throttle control attachment.

3. Do not confuse the cables. If in doubt, operate the control lever on the control box. The cable moving first is the shift cable. Tilt the outboard unit from full up to the full down position, and from hard over starboard to hard over port, to verify the cables move smoothly without binding, bending, or buckling.

4. Align the mark on the wire harness plug with the mark on the coupler plug, and then connect the plugs.

5. Install the safety tether to the back of the kill switch button.

6. Remember, the powerhead will not start without the tether in place.

HAND REWIND STARTER 13-2
INTRODUCTION 13-2
2 HP POWERHEADS 13-2
    REMOVAL & DISASSEMBLY 13-2
    CLEANING & INSPECTION 13-3
    ASSEMBLY & INSTALLATION 13-3
EXCEPT 2 HP POWERHEADS 13-6
    REMOVAL & DISASSEMBLY 13-6
    CLEANING & INSPECTION 13-7
    ASSEMBLING & INSTALLATION 13-7
    ADJUSTMENT 13-9

13

HAND REWIND STARTER

HAND REWIND STARTER 13-2

HAND REWIND STARTER

Introduction

Two different hand rewind starters are used on Yamaha outboards. The first unit is installed on the single cylinder, 2 hp units only. The second unit is used on the all other units offering a hand rewind starter. Because the second starter is used on numerous outboard models, slight variations in appearance and design may be noted. However, the procedures outlined in this chapter are valid.

2 hp Powerheads

REMOVAL & DISASSEMBLY

♦ **See accompanying illustrations**

1. Remove the screw on one half of the spark plug cover. Remove four more screws securing one-half of the cowling. Separate the cowling half from which the screws were removed. Remove the four screws securing the other half of the cowling and remove it from the engine. The spark plug cover will remain attached to one of the cowling halves.

➡ **Observe the different length screws used to secure the cowling halves to the powerhead. Remember their location as an aid during assembling.**

2. Remove the three mounting bolts securing the legs of the hand rewind starter to the powerhead.

➡ **A no start-in-gear protection device is not incorporated on single-cylinder powerheads.**

3. Lift the hand rewind starter free of the powerhead.

4. Rotate the starter sheave to align the notch in the sheave with the starter handle. With the sheave in this position, pull the rope out a little and hook it into the notch. Carefully allow the sheave to unwind clockwise until the spring has lost all its tension. Control the rotation with the rope secured in the notch to prevent the sheave from free wheeling.

5. Invert the hand starter and remove the sheave retainer bolt with the proper size socket.

COWLING

Step 1   0470CP01

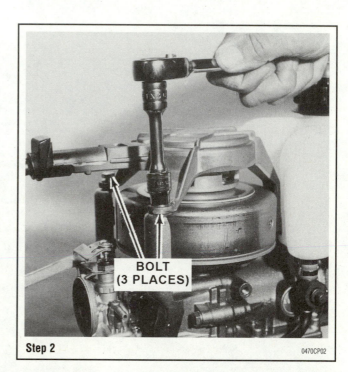

BOLT
(3 PLACES)

Step 2   0470CP02

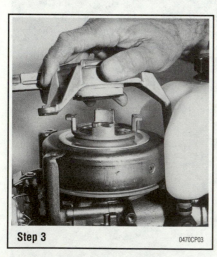

Step 3   0470CP03

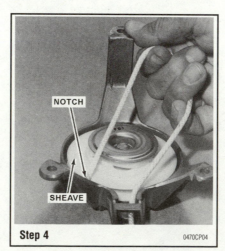

NOTCH

SHEAVE

Step 4   0470CP04

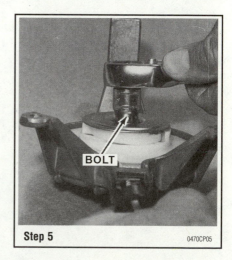

BOLT

Step 5   0470CP05

6. Lift the starter housing shaft free of the drive pawl. The drive pawl spring will remain attached to the starter housing shaft. Observe how the drive pawl spring was indexed over the peg on the drive pawl.

7. Using a small screwdriver, hold the back of the return spring to allow the drive pawl to be removed.

8. Carefully note, and mark the recess holding the return spring before removing the spring.

➥The recess must be marked to ensure proper installation. There are two recesses which appear to be identical, but actually are mirror images of each other.

After marking the recess, lift out the spring.

❊❊ WARNING

The rewind spring is a potential hazard. The spring is under tremendous tension when it is wound—a real tiger in a cage! If the spring should accidentally be released, severe personal injury could result from being struck by the spring with force. Therefore, the following steps must be performed with care to prevent personal injury to self and others in the area.

Do not attempt to remove the spring unless it is unfit for service and a new spring is to be installed.

9. Carefully lift the sheave free of the starter housing, leaving the rewind spring still wound tightly inside the housing.

10. Obtain two pieces of wood, a short 2–4 in. (5–10cm) will work fine. Place the two pieces of wood approximately 8 in. (20 cm) apart on the floor. Stand the housing on its legs between the two pieces of wood with the spring side facing down.

➥The accompanying illustration shows the spring being released from the same type, but different model rewind unit. Therefore, the principle is exactly the same. The procedure outlined in this step may be followed with safety.

Stand behind the wood, keeping away from the openings as the spring unwinds with considerable force and the housing will jump off the floor. Tap the housing a moderate blow with a soft mallet. The spring will fall and unwind almost instantly and with much force.

11. If the rope is to be replaced, first push the rope back through the opening in the sheave, and then untie the knot and pull the rope free.

CLEANING & INSPECTION

▶ **See Figure 1**

Wash all parts except the rope and the handle in solvent, and then blow them dry with compressed air.

Remove any trace of corrosion and wipe all metal parts with an oil dampened cloth.

Inspect the rope. Replace the rope if it appears to be weak or frayed. If the rope is frayed, check the holes through which the rope passes for rough edges or burrs. Remove the rough edges or burrs with a file and polish the surface until it is smooth. Inspect the starter spring end hooks. Replace the spring if it is weak, corroded or cracked. Inspect the inside surface of the sheave rewind recess for grooves or roughness. Grooves may cause erratic rewinding of the starter rope.

Coat the entire length of the used rewind spring (a new spring will be coated with lubricant from the package), with low-temperature lubricant.

ASSEMBLY & INSTALLATION

The authors, the manufacturers, and almost anyone else who has handled the spring from this type rewind starter strongly recommend a pair of safety goggles or a face shield be worn while the spring is being installed. As the work progresses a tiger is being forced into a cage—over 14 ft. (4.3 m) of spring steel

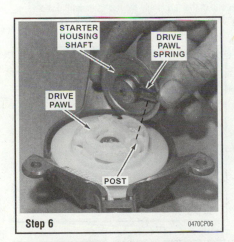

Step 6   0470CP06

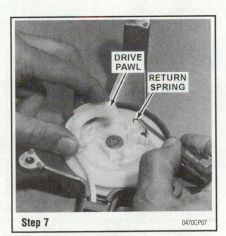

Step 7   0470CP07

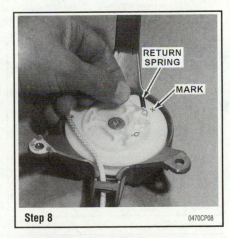

Step 8   0470CP08

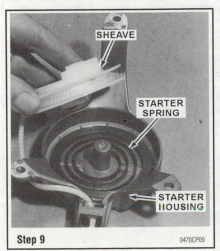

Step 9   0470CP09

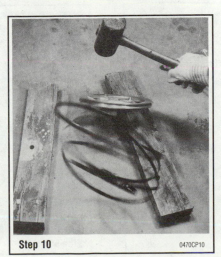

Step 10   0470CP10

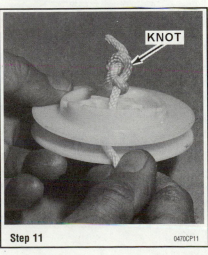

Step 11   0470CP11

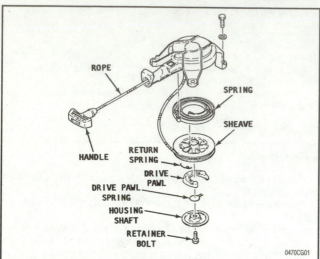

ROPE

SPRING

SHEAVE

HANDLE

RETURN
SPRING

DRIVE
PAWL

DRIVE PAWL
SPRING

HOUSING
SHAFT

RETAINER
BOLT

0470CG01

Fig. 1 Exploded view of the hand rewind starter used on a 2 hp powerhead. Major parts are identified

wound into about 4 in. (10.2cm) circumference. If the spring is accidentally released, it will lash out with tremendous ferocity and very likely could cause personal injury to the installer or other persons nearby.

➡**The rewind starter may be assembled with a new rewind spring or a used one. Procedures for assembling are not the same because the new spring will arrive held in a steel hoop already wound, lubricated, and ready for installation. The used spring must be manually wound into its recess.**

The situation may arise when it is only necessary to replace a broken spring. The following few procedures outline the tasks required to replace the spring. A new spring is already properly wound and will arrive in a special hoop. This hoop is designed to be used as an aid to installing the new spring.

New Spring

Hook the outer end of the spring onto the insert in the starter housing, then place the spring into the housing. Seat the spring and then carefully remove the steel hoop.

Used Spring

◗ **See accompanying illustrations**

A used spring naturally will not be wound. Therefore, special instructions are necessary for installation.

➡**Wear a good pair of gloves while winding and installing the spring. The spring will develop tension and the edges of the spring steel are extremely sharp. The gloves will prevent cuts to the hands and fingers.**

1. Loop the spring loosely into a coil, as shown, to enable it to be handled and fed into its recess safely.

2. Insert the hook on the end of the spring into the notch of the recess. Feed the spring around the inner edge of the recess and at the same time rotate the housing counterclockwise. The spring will be slippery with lubrication. Work slowly and with definite movements to prevent losing control of the spring. Proceed with great care. Guide the spring into place.

3. Thread one end of the rope through the sheave and tie a figure 8 knot, as shown. Thread the other end of the rope through the starter handle and again tie a figure 8 knot in the end.

4. Wind the rope 2-½ turns in a counterclockwise direction around the sheave. Position the rope at the notch on the outer edge. Lower the sheave into the starter housing.

5. Insert a small screwdriver or an awl into the access window of the sheave and push the inner end of the spring into the recess under the sheave. This is not an easy task and may not be accomplished on the first try. If too

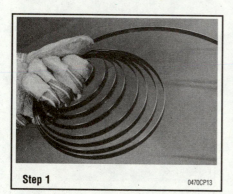

Step 1 0470CP13

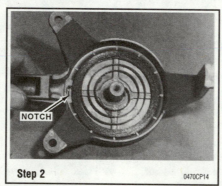

NOTCH

Step 2 0470CP14

FIGURE "8"
KNOT

Step 3 0470CP15

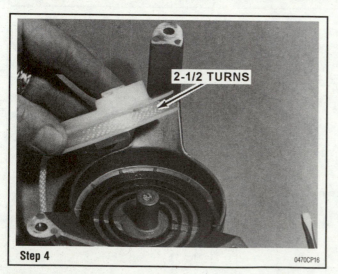

2-1/2 TURNS

Step 4 0470CP16

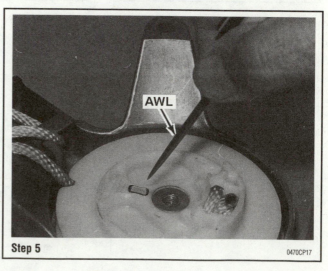

AWL

Step 5 0470CP17

Step 6   0470CP18

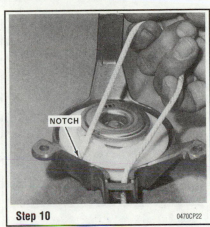

Step 7   0470CP19

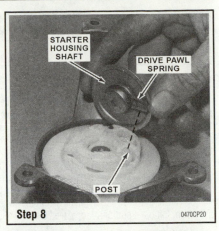

Step 8   0470CP20

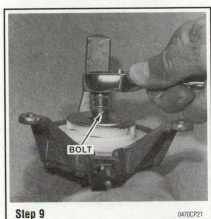

Step 9   0470CP21

Step 10   0470CP22

Step 11   0470CP23

Step 12   0470CP24

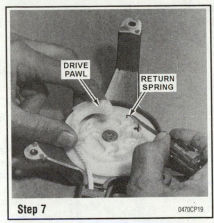

Step 13   0470CP25

Step 14   0470CP26

much trouble is encountered, take a break, have a cup of coffee, cup of tea, whatever, and then try again. With patience, much patience, it can be done.

6. Congratulations on performing Step 5 successfully! Now, insert the return spring into the recess of the sheave which was previously marked during Step 8 of removal. If the recess was not marked during removal, rotate the sheave until both recesses are on the right and insert the spring into the upper one.

7. Hold back the return spring with a small screwdriver and at the same time install the drive pawl.

8. Place the starter housing shaft, with the drive pawl spring attached, over the drive pawl. Check to be sure the spring is centered over the post of the drive pawl.

9. Install and tighten the center bolt to a torque value of 5.8 ft. lbs. (8Nm).

10. Pick up the slack in the rope, and then hold the rope firmly in the notch of the sheave. While the rope is being firmly held in the notch, wind the sheave counterclockwise until it can be wound no further. Now, ease the sheave just a little at a time until the notch in the sheave aligns with the starter handle. Slowly release the sheave and allow the rope to feed around the sheave as it unwinds, pulling in the slack rope.

Check the action of the rewind starter before proceeding with the installation. If all the rope is not taken in around the sheave as the spring unwinds, repeat this step, and then check again.

11. Position the rewind starter on top of the powerhead with the legs in place on the three bracket arms.

12. Secure the three starter legs with the attaching bolts. Tighten the bolts to a torque value of 5.9 ft. lbs. (8Nm).

13. Install the two halves of the cowling around the powerhead.

14. Secure the cowling with the attaching screws. Eight screws hold the cowling halves in place plus one more for the spark plug cover.

➡ **As noted during disassembling, the screws are different lengths. Ensure the proper size is used in the correct location.**

Except 2 hp Powerheads

REMOVAL & DISASSEMBLY

♦ **See accompanying illustrations**

1. Unscrew the plastic nut and pull the shift interlock cable free of the starter housing. Remove the plunger and spring from the cable end, because they are easily lost.

2. Remove the three bolts securing the starter legs to the powerhead, and then remove the starter.

3. Place the starter assembly upside down on a suitable work surface.

4. Pry the circlip from the pawl post using a narrow slotted screwdriver.

5. Lift the pawl, with the spring attached free of the sheave.

6. Rotate the sheave to align the slot in the sheave with the starter handle, as shown. Lift out a portion of rope, feed the rope into the slot and with a con-trolled motion allow the sheave to rotate in a clockwise direction until the tension on the rewind spring is completely released. Do not allow the sheave to spin without control.

7. Pry the seal from the handle and push out the knot in the end of the rope. Untie the knot and pull the handle free of the rope.

8. Remove the bolt and washer from the center of the sheave.

9. Remove the sheave bushing and starter housing shaft from the sheave.

➡ **If the only work to be performed on the hand rewind starter is to replace the rope, it is best not to disturb the sheave and spring beneath the sheave.**

Hold the sheave against the starter housing to prevent the spring from disengaging from the sheave and carefully rotate the sheave to allow the rope hole to align with the starter handle. Pull the knotted end out of the sheave until all of the rope is free.

If either the sheave or the starter rewind spring is to be replaced the rope may be left in place until the sheave is removed from the starter housing.

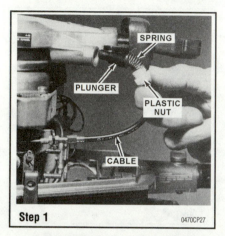

Step 1   0470CP27

Step 2   0470CP28

Step 3   0470CP29

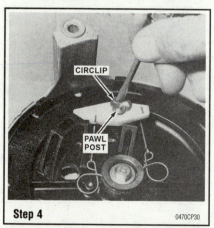

Step 4   0470CP30

Step 5   0470CP31

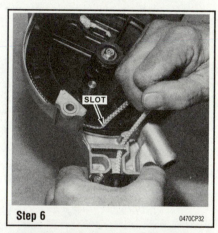

Step 6   0470CP32

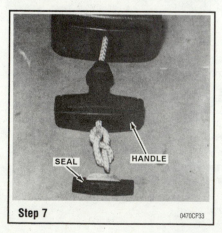

Step 7   0470CP33

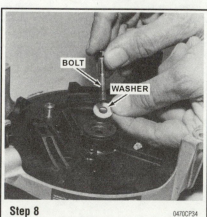

Step 8   0470CP34

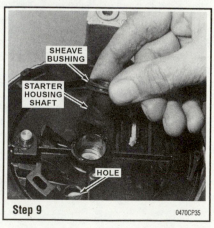

Step 9   0470CP35

Step 10   0470CP37

➡ **Wear a good pair of heavy gloves and safety glasses while performing the following tasks.**

✳✳ WARNING

The rewind spring is a potential hazard. The spring is under tremendous tension when it is wound—a real tiger in a cage! If the spring should accidentally be released, severe personal injury could result from being struck by the spring with force. Therefore, the following steps must be performed with care to prevent personal injury to self and others in the area.

Do not attempt to remove the spring unless it is unfit for service and a new spring is to be installed.

Insert a screwdriver into the hole in the sheave, push down on the section of spring visible through the hole. At the same time gently lift up on the sheave and hold the spring down to confine it in the housing and prevent it from escaping uncontrolled. If the rope has not been removed from the sheave, remove it at this time.

➡ **The accompanying illustration shows the spring being released from the same type but different model rewind spring. Therefore, the principle is exactly the same. The procedure outlined in the next step may be followed with safety.**

10. Obtain two pieces of wood, a short 2–4 in. (5–10cm) will work fine. Place the two pieces of wood approximately 8 in. (20 cm) apart on the floor. Center the housing on top of the wood with the spring side facing down. Check to be sure the wood is not touching the spring.

Stand behind the wood, keeping away from the openings as the spring unwinds with considerable force. Tap the sheave with a soft mallet. The spring retainer plate will drop down releasing the spring. The spring will fall and unwind almost instantly and with force.

CLEANING & INSPECTION

▸ **See Figure 2**

Wash all parts except the rope and the handle in solvent, and then blow them dry with compressed air.

Remove any trace of corrosion and wipe all metal parts with an oil dampened cloth.

Inspect the rope. Replace the rope if it appears to be weak or frayed. If the rope is frayed, check the holes through which the rope passes for rough edges or burrs. Remove the rough edges or burrs with a file and polish the surface until it is smooth. Inspect the starter spring end hooks. Replace the spring if it is weak, corroded or cracked. Inspect the inside surface of the sheave rewind recess for grooves or roughness. Grooves may cause erratic rewinding of the starter rope.

Coat the entire length of the used rewind spring (a new spring will be coated with lubricant from the package), with low-temperature lubricant.

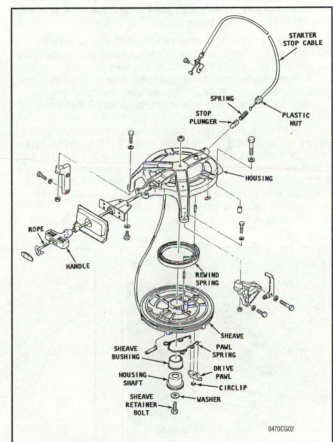

0470CG02

Fig. 2 Exploded view of the hand rewind starter used on a 2 hp powerhead. Major parts are identified

ASSEMBLING & INSTALLATION

➡ **If the rewind spring or the sheave was not removed, proceed directly to Step 6.**

Wear a good pair of gloves while winding and installing the spring. The spring will develop tension and the edges of the spring steel are extremely sharp. The gloves will prevent cuts to the hands and fingers.

New Spring

Apply a light coating of Yamaha All-Purpose Grease, or equivalent anti-seize lubricant to the inside surface of the starter housing.

A new spring will be wound and held in a steel hoop. Hook the outer end of the new spring onto the starter housing post, and then place the spring inside the housing. Carefully remove the steel hoop. The spring should unwind slightly and seat itself in the housing.

Old Spring

♦ **See accompanying illustrations**

➡The authors, the manufacturers, and almost anyone else who has handled the spring from this type rewind starter strongly recommend a pair of safety goggles or a face shield be worn while the spring is being installed. As the work progresses a tiger is being forced into a cage—over 14 ft. (4.3 m) of spring steel wound into about 4 in. (10.2cm) circumference. If the spring is accidentally released, it will lash out with tremendous ferocity and very likely could cause personal injury to the installer or other persons nearby.

1. Apply a light coating of Yamaha All-Purpose Grease, or equivalent anti-seize lubricant to the inside surface of the starter housing. Wind the old spring loosely in one hand in a clockwise direction, as shown.

2. Hook the outer end of the spring onto the starter housing post. Rotate the sheave clockwise and at the same feed the spring into the housing in a counterclockwise direction. Continue working the spring into the housing until the entire length has been confined.

3. Insert one end of the rope through the hole in the starter sheave. Tie a figure 8 knot in the end of the rope leaving about one inch (2.5cm) beyond the knot. Tuck the end of the rope beyond the knot into the groove next to the knot.

Wind the rope in a clockwise direction 1-½ turns around the sheave, ending at the slot in the sheave. Lower the sheave into the starter housing. At the same time, use a small screwdriver through the hole to guide the inner loop of the spring onto the post on the underneath side of the sheave.

4. On units with spring and sheave undisturbed, align the hole in the edge of the sheave with the starter handle. Thread the rope through the hole and up through the top side. Tie a figure 8 knot in the end which was just brought through, leaving about one inch (25cm). Tuck the short free end into the groove next to the hole.

5. Without rotating the sheave, feed the rope between the sheave and the edge of the starter housing in a clockwise direction. Push the rope into place with a narrow screwdriver. Continue feeding and tucking the rope for 1-½ turns, ending with the rope at the slot of the sheave.

Slide the sheave bushing into the starter housing shaft. Insert the shaft and bushing into the center of the sheave.

6. Coat the threads of the center bolt with Loctite®. Install the washer and bolt. Tighten the bolt to a torque value of 5.8 ft. lbs. (8Nm).

7. Thread the rope through the starter handle housing and through the handle. Tie a figure 8 knot in the rope as close to the end as practical. Pull the knot back into the handle recess, and then install the seal in the handle to hide the rope knot.

8. Lift up a portion of rope, and then hook it into the slot of the sheave. Hold the handle tightly and at the same time rotate the sheave counterclockwise until the spring beneath is wound tight. This will take about three complete turns of the sheave. Slowly release the tension on the sheave and allow it to rewind clockwise while the rope is taken up as it feeds around the sheave.

9. With the beveled end of the pawl facing to the left, hook each end of the pawl spring into the two small holes in the pawl, from the underneath side of the pawl, and with the pattern of the spring, as shown. The short ends of the spring will then be on the upper surface of the pawl. Move the spring up against the center of the sheave shaft, and then slide the center of the pawl onto the pawl post, as indicated in the accompanying illustration.

10. Snap the circlip into place over the pawl post to secure the pawl in place.

11. Check the action of the rewind starter before further installation work proceeds. Pull out the starter rope with the handle, then allow the spring to slowly rewind the rope. The starter should rewind smoothly and take up all the rope to lightly seat the handle against the starter housing.

12. Position the rewind starter in place on the powerhead. Apply Loctite® to the threads of the three attaching bolts. Secure the starter legs to the powerhead with the bolts, and tighten them to a torque value of 5.8 ft. lbs. (8Nm).

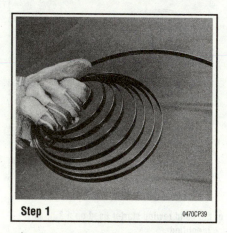

Step 1 0470CP39

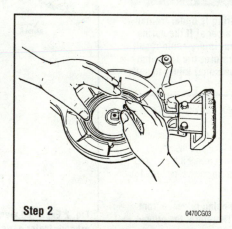

Step 2 0470CG03

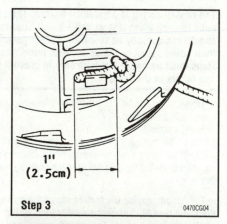

Step 3 0470CG04

1"
(2.5cm)

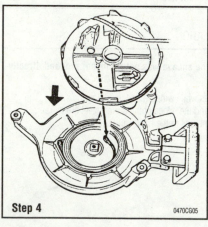

Step 4 0470CG05

SHEAVE BUSHING

STARTER HOUSING SHAFT

Step 5 0470CP40

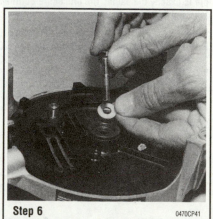

Step 6 0470CP41

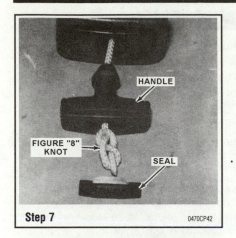

Step 7 — HANDLE, FIGURE "8" KNOT, SEAL

0470CP42

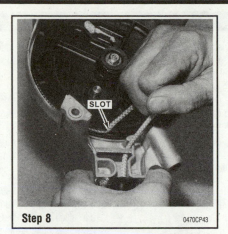

Step 8 — SLOT

0470CP43

Step 9 — PAWL POST, PAWL, PAWL SPRING

0470CP44

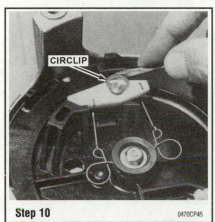

Step 10 — CIRCLIP

0470CP45

Step 11

0470CP46

Step 12

0470CP47

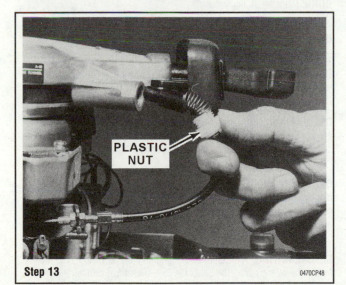

Step 13 — PLASTIC NUT

0470CP48

13. Slip the starter stop cable end through the spring and then into the recess of the plunger. Hold these parts together and slide them into the starter housing. Tighten the plastic nut snugly.

➡ If the cable adjustment at the other end was undisturbed, the no-start-in-gear protection system should perform satisfactorily. When the unit is not in neutral, the plunger should push out to lock the sheave and prevent it from rotating. This means an attempt to pull on the rope with the lower unit in any gear except neutral should fail.

ADJUSTMENT

If the no-start-in-gear protection system fails to function properly, first remove the rewind hand starter from the powerhead. Make an adjustment on the length of the cable at the two locknuts at either side of the bracket to bring the plunger flush with the inner surface of the starter housing. Install the starter on the powerhead and again check the no-start-in-gear system. If the system still fails to function correctly, replace the cable.

GLOSSARY

Understanding your mechanic is as important as understanding your marine engine. Most boaters know about their boats, but many boaters have difficulty understanding marine terminology. Talking the language of boats makes it easier to effectively communicate with professional mechanics. It isn't necessary (or recommended) that you diagnose the problem for him, but it will save him time, and you money, if you can accurately describe what is happening. It will also help you to know why your boat does what it is doing, and what repairs were made.

AFTER TOP DEAD CENTER (ATDC): The point after the piston reaches the top of its travel on the compression stroke.

AIR CLEANER: An assembly consisting of a housing, filter and any connecting ductwork. The filter element is made up of a porous paper or a wire mesh screening, and is designed to prevent airborne particles from entering the engine. Also see Intake Silencer.

AIR/FUEL RATIO: The ratio of air-to-fuel, by weight, drawn into the engine.

ALTERNATING CURRENT (AC): Electric current that flows first in one direction, then in the opposite direction, continually reversing flow.

ALTERNATOR: A device which produces AC (alternating current) which is converted to DC (direct current) to charge the battery.

AMMETER: An instrument, calibrated in amperes, used to measure the flow of an electrical current in a circuit. Ammeters are always connected in series with the circuit being tested.

AMP/HR. RATING (BATTERY): Measurement of the ability of a battery to deliver a stated amount of current for a stated period of time. The higher the amp/hr. rating, the better the battery.

AMPERE: The rate of flow of electrical current present when one volt of electrical pressure is applied against one ohm of electrical resistance.

ANTIFREEZE: A substance (ethylene or propylene glycol) added to the coolant to prevent freezing in cold weather.

ARMATURE: A laminated, soft iron core wrapped by a wire that converts electrical energy to mechanical energy as in a motor or relay. When rotated in a magnetic field, it changes mechanical energy into electrical energy as in a generator.

ATDC: After Top Dead Center.

ATMOSPHERIC PRESSURE: The pressure on the Earth's surface caused by the weight of the air in the atmosphere. At sea level, this pressure is 14.7 psi at 32°F (101 kPa at 0°C).

ATOMIZATION: The breaking down of a liquid into a fine mist that can be suspended in air.

AXIAL PLAY: Movement parallel to a shaft or bearing bore.

BACKFIRE: The sudden combustion of gases in the intake or exhaust system that results in a loud explosion.

BACKLASH: The clearance or play between two parts, such as meshed gears.

BALL BEARING: A bearing made up of hardened inner and outer races between which hardened steel balls roll.

BATTERY: A direct current electrical storage unit, consisting of the basic active materials of lead and sulphuric acid, which converts chemical energy into electrical energy. Used to provide current for the operation of the starter as well as other equipment, such as the radio, lighting, etc.

BEARING: A friction reducing, supportive device usually located between a stationary part and a moving part.

BEFORE TOP DEAD CENTER (BTDC): The point just before the piston reaches the top of its travel on the compression stroke.

BLOCK: See Engine Block.

BLOW-BY: Combustion gases, composed of water vapor and unburned fuel, that leak past the piston rings into the crankcase during normal engine operation. These gases are removed by the evacuation system to prevent the buildup of harmful acids in the crankcase.

BORE: Diameter of a cylinder.

BTDC: Before Top Dead Center.

BUSHING: A liner, usually removable, for a bearing; an anti-friction liner used in place of a bearing.

CAMSHAFT: A shaft in the engine on which are the lobes (cams) which operate the valves. The camshaft is driven by the crankshaft, via a belt, chain or gears, at one half the crankshaft speed.

CARBON MONOXIDE (CO): A colorless, odorless gas given off as a normal byproduct of combustion. It is poisonous and extremely dangerous in confined areas, building up slowly to toxic levels without warning if adequate ventilation is not available.

CETANE RATING: A measure of the ignition value of diesel fuel. The higher the cetane rating, the better the fuel. Diesel fuel cetane rating is roughly comparable to gasoline octane rating.

CHECK VALVE: Any one-way valve installed to permit the flow of air, fuel or vacuum in one direction only.

CIRCLIP: A split steel snapring that fits into a groove to hold various parts in place.

CIRCUIT BREAKER: A switch which protects an electrical circuit from overload by opening the circuit when the current flow exceeds a pre-determined level. Some circuit breakers must be reset manually, while most reset automatically.

CIRCUIT: Any unbroken path through which an electrical current can flow. Also used to describe fuel flow in some instances.

COMBUSTION CHAMBER: The part of the engine in the cylinder head where combustion takes place.

COMPRESSION CHECK: A test involving cranking the engine with a special high pressure gauge connected to an individual cylinder. Individual cylinder pressure as well as pressure variance across cylinders is used to determine general operating condition of the engine.

COMPRESSION RATIO: The ratio of the volume between the piston and cylinder head when the piston is at the bottom of its stroke (bottom dead center) and when the piston is at the top of its stroke (top dead center).

P>CONDUCTOR: Any material through which an electrical current can be transmitted easily.

CONNECTING ROD: The connecting link between the crankshaft and piston.

CONTINUITY: Continuous or complete circuit. Can be checked with an ohmmeter.

COOLANT: Mixture of water and anti-freeze circulated through the engine to carry off heat produced by the engine.

CRANKCASE: The lower part of an engine in which the crankshaft and related parts operate.

CRANKSHAFT: Engine component (connected to pistons by connecting rods) which converts the reciprocating (up and down) motion of pistons to rotary motion used to turn the driveshaft.

CYLINDER BLOCK: See engine block.

CYLINDER HEAD: The detachable portion of the engine, usually fastened to the top of the cylinder block and containing all or most of the combustion chambers. On overhead valve engines, it contains the valves and their operating parts. On overhead cam engines, it contains the camshaft as well.

CYLINDER: In an engine, the round hole in the engine block in which the piston(s) ride.

DETONATION: An unwanted explosion of the air/fuel mixture in the combustion chamber caused by excess heat and compression, advanced timing, or an overly lean mixture. Also referred to as "ping".

DIAPHRAGM: A thin, flexible wall separating two cavities, such as in a vacuum advance unit.

DIESELING: The engine continues to run after the it is shut off; caused by fuel continuing to be burned in the combustion chamber.

DIGITAL VOLT OHMMETER: An electronic diagnostic tool used to measure voltage, ohms and amps as well as several other functions, with the readings displayed on a digital screen in tenths, hundredths and thousandths.

DIODE: An electrical device that will allow current to flow in one direction only.

DIRECT CURRENT (DC): Electrical current that flows in one direction only.

DISPLACEMENT: The total volume of air that is displaced by all pistons as the engine turns through one complete revolution.

DOHC: Double overhead camshaft.

DOUBLE OVERHEAD CAMSHAFT: The engine utilizes two camshafts mounted in one cylinder head. One camshaft operates the exhaust valves, while the other operates the intake valves.

DVOM: Digital volt ohmmeter

ELECTROLYTE: A solution of water and sulfuric acid used to activate the battery. Electrolyte is extremely corrosive.

END-PLAY: The measured amount of axial movement in a shaft.

ENGINE: The primary motor or power apparatus of a vessel, which converts fuel into mechanical energy.

ENGINE BLOCK: The basic engine casting containing the cylinders, the crankshaft main bearings, as well as machined surfaces for the mounting of other components such as the cylinder head, oil pan, transmission, etc.

ETHYLENE GLYCOL: The base substance of antifreeze.

EXHAUST MANIFOLD: A set of cast passages or pipes which conduct exhaust gases from the engine.

FEELER GAUGE: A blade, usually metal, of precisely predetermined thickness, used to measure the clearance between two parts.

FIRING ORDER: The order in which combustion occurs in the cylinders of an engine.

FLAME FRONT: The term used to describe certain aspects of the fuel explosion in the cylinders. The flame front should move in a controlled pattern across the cylinder, rather than simply exploding immediately.

FLAT SPOT: A point during acceleration when the engine seems to lose power for an instant.

FLYWHEEL: A heavy disc of metal attached to the rear of the crankshaft. It smoothes the firing impulses of the engine and keeps the crankshaft turning during periods when no firing takes place. The starter also engages the flywheel to start the engine.

FOOT POUND (ft. lbs. or sometimes, ft. lb.): The amount of energy or work needed to raise an item weighing one pound, a distance of one foot.

FREEZE PLUG: A plug in the engine block which will be pushed out if the coolant freezes. Sometimes called expansion plugs, they protect the block from cracking should the coolant freeze.

FUEL FILTER: A component of the fuel system containing a porous paper element used to prevent any impurities from entering the engine through the fuel system. It usually takes the form of a canister-like housing, mounted in-line with the fuel hose, located anywhere on a vessel between the fuel tank and engine.

FUEL INJECTION: A system that sprays fuel into the cylinder through nozzles. The amount of fuel can be more precisely controlled with fuel injection.

FUSE: A protective device in a circuit which prevents circuit overload by breaking the circuit when a specific amperage is present. The device is constructed around a strip or wire of a lower amperage rating than the circuit it is designed to protect. When an amperage higher than that stamped on the fuse is present in the circuit, the strip or wire melts, opening the circuit.

FUSIBLE LINK: A piece of wire in a wiring harness that performs the same job as a fuse. If overloaded, the fusible link will melt and interrupt the circuit.

HORSEPOWER: A measurement of the amount of work; one horsepower is the amount of work necessary to lift 33,000 lbs. one foot in one minute. Brake horsepower (bhp) is the horsepower delivered by an engine on a dynamometer. Net horsepower is the power remaining (measured at the flywheel of the engine) that can be used to power the vessel after power is consumed through friction and running the engine accessories (water pump, alternator, fan etc.)

HYDROCARBON (HC): Any chemical compound made up of hydrogen and carbon. A major pollutant formed by the engine as a by-product of combustion.

HYDROMETER: An instrument used to measure the specific gravity of a solution.

INCH POUND (inch lbs.; sometimes in. lb. or in. lbs.): One twelfth of a foot pound.

INJECTOR: A device which receives metered fuel under relatively low pressure and is activated to inject the fuel into the engine under relatively high pressure at a predetermined time.

INTAKE MANIFOLD: A casting of passages or pipes used to conduct air or a fuel/air mixture to the cylinders.

INTAKE SILENCER: An assembly consisting of a housing, and sometimes a filter. The filter element is made up of a porous paper or a wire mesh screening, and is designed to prevent airborne particles from entering the engine. Also see Air Cleaner.

JOURNAL: The bearing surface within which a shaft operates.

JUMPER CABLES: Two heavy duty wires with large alligator clips used to provide power from a charged battery to a discharged battery.

JUMPSTART: Utilizing one sufficiently charged battery to start the engine of another vessel with a discharged battery by the use of jumper cables.

KNOCK: Noise which results from the spontaneous ignition of a portion of the air-fuel mixture in the engine cylinder.

LITHIUM-BASE GREASE: Bearing grease using lithium as a base. Not compatible with sodium-base grease.

LOCK RING: See Circlip or Snapring

MANIFOLD VACUUM: Low pressure in an engine intake manifold formed just below the throttle plates. Manifold vacuum is highest at idle and drops under acceleration.

MANIFOLD: A casting of passages or set of pipes which connect the cylinders to an inlet or outlet source.

MISFIRE: Condition occurring when the fuel mixture in a cylinder fails to ignite, causing the engine to run roughly.

MULTI-WEIGHT: Type of oil that provides adequate lubrication at both high and low temperatures.

needed to move one amp through a resistance of one ohm.

NEEDLE BEARING: A bearing which consists of a number (usually a large number) of long, thin rollers.

NITROGEN OXIDE (NOx): One of the three basic pollutants found in the exhaust emission of an internal combustion engine. The amount of NOx usually varies in an inverse proportion to the amount of HC and CO.

OEM: Original Equipment Manufactured. OEM equipment is that furnished standard by the manufacturer.

OHM: The unit used to measure the resistance of conductor-to-electrical flow. One ohm is the amount of resistance that limits current flow to one ampere in a circuit with one volt of pressure.

OHMMETER: An instrument used for measuring the resistance, in ohms, in an electrical circuit.

OVERHEAD CAMSHAFT (OHC): An engine configuration in which the camshaft is mounted on top of the cylinder head and operates the valve either directly or by means of rocker arms.

OVERHEAD VALVE (OHV): An engine configuration in which all of the valves are located in the cylinder head and the camshaft is located in the cylinder block. The camshaft operates the valves via lifters and pushrods.

OXIDES OF NITROGEN: See nitrogen oxide (NOx).

PING: A metallic rattling sound produced by the engine during acceleration. It is usually due to incorrect timing or a poor grade of fuel.

PISTON RING: An open-ended ring which fits into a groove on the outer diameter of the piston. Its chief function is to form a seal between the piston and cylinder wall. Most pistons have three rings: two for compression sealing; one for oil sealing.

POLARITY: Indication (positive or negative) of the two poles of a battery.

POWERTRAIN: See Drivetrain.

PPM: Parts per million; unit used to measure exhaust emissions.

PREIGNITION: Early ignition of fuel in the cylinder, sometimes due to glowing carbon deposits in the combustion chamber.

PRELOAD: A predetermined load placed on a bearing during assembly or by adjustment.

PRESS FIT: The mating of two parts under pressure, due to the inner diameter of one being smaller than the outer diameter of the other, or vice versa; an interference fit.

PSI: Pounds per square inch; a measurement of pressure.

PUSHROD: A steel rod between the hydraulic valve lifter and the valve rocker arm in overhead valve (OHV) engines.

RACE: The surface on the inner or outer ring of a bearing on which the balls, needles or rollers move.

RADIATOR: Part of the cooling system for some water-cooled engines. Through the radiator, excess combustion heat is dissipated into the atmosphere through forced convection using a water and glycol based mixture that circulates through, and cools, the engine.

REAR MAIN OIL SEAL: A synthetic or rope-type seal that prevents oil from leaking out of the engine past the rear main crankshaft bearing.

RECTIFIER: A device (used primarily in alternators) that permits electrical current to flow in one direction only.

REGULATOR: A device which maintains the amperage and/or voltage levels of a circuit at predetermined values.

RELAY: A switch which automatically opens and/or closes a circuit.

RESISTANCE: The opposition to the flow of current through a circuit or electrical device, and is measured in ohms. Resistance is equal to the voltage divided by the amperage.

RESISTOR: A device, usually made of wire, which offers a preset amount of resistance in an electrical circuit.

ROCKER ARM: A lever which rotates around a shaft pushing down (opening) the valve with an end when the other end is pushed up by the pushrod. Spring pressure will later close the valve.

ROLLER BEARING: A bearing made up of hardened inner and outer races between which hardened steel rollers move.

RPM: Revolutions per minute (usually indicates engine speed).

RUN-ON: Condition when the engine continues to run, even when the key is turned off. See dieseling.

SENDING UNIT: A mechanical, electrical, hydraulic or electromagnetic device which transmits information to a gauge.

SENSOR: Any device designed to measure engine operating conditions or ambient pressures and temperatures. Usually electronic in nature and designed to send a voltage signal to an on-board computer, some sensors may operate as a simple on/off switch or they may provide a variable voltage signal (like a potentiometer) as conditions or measured parameters change.

SHIM: Spacers of precise, predetermined thickness used between parts to establish a proper working relationship.

SHORT CIRCUIT: An electrical malfunction where current takes the path of least resistance to ground (usually through damaged insulation). Current flow is excessive from low resistance resulting in a blown fuse.

SINGLE OVERHEAD CAMSHAFT: See overhead camshaft.

SLUDGE: Thick, black deposits in engine formed from dirt, oil, water, etc. It is usually formed in engines when oil changes are neglected.

SNAP RING: A circular retaining clip used inside or outside a shaft or part to secure a shaft, such as a floating wrist pin.

SOHC: Single overhead camshaft.

SOLENOID: An electrically operated, magnetic switching device.

SPECIFIC GRAVITY (BATTERY): The relative weight of liquid (battery electrolyte) as compared to the weight of an equal volume of water.

SPLINES: Ridges machined or cast onto the outer diameter of a shaft or inner diameter of a bore to enable parts to mate without rotation.

STARTER: A high-torque electric motor used for the purpose of starting the engine, typically through a high ratio geared drive connected to the flywheel ring gear.

STROKE: The distance the piston travels from bottom dead center to top dead center.

TACHOMETER: A device used to measure the rotary speed of an engine, shaft, gear, etc., usually in rotations per minute.

TDC: Top dead center. The exact top of the piston's stroke.

THERMOSTAT: A valve, located in the cooling system of an engine, which is closed when cold and opens gradually in response to engine heating, controlling the temperature of the coolant and rate of coolant flow.

TOP DEAD CENTER (TDC): The point at which the piston reaches the top of its travel on the compression stroke.

TORQUE: Measurement of turning or twisting force, expressed as foot-pounds or inch-pounds.

TUNE-UP: A regular maintenance function, usually associated with the replacement and adjustment of parts and components in the electrical and fuel systems of a engine for the purpose of attaining optimum performance.

TURBOCHARGER: An exhaust driven pump which compresses intake air and forces it into the combustion chambers at higher than atmospheric pressures. The increased air pressure allows more fuel to be burned and results in increased horsepower being produced.

VACUUM GAUGE: An instrument used to measure the presence of vacuum in a chamber.

VALVE CLEARANCE: The measured gap between the end of the valve stem and the rocker arm, cam lobe or follower that activates the valve.

VALVE GUIDES: The guide through which the stem of the valve passes. The guide is designed to keep the valve in proper alignment.

VALVE LASH (clearance): The operating clearance in the valve train.

VALVE TRAIN: The system that operates intake and exhaust valves, consisting of camshaft, valves and springs, lifters, pushrods and rocker arms.

VALVE: A device which control the pressure, direction of flow or rate of flow of a liquid or gas.

VISCOSITY: The ability of a fluid to flow. The lower the viscosity rating, the easier the fluid will flow. 10 weight motor oil will flow much easier than 40 weight motor oil.

VOLT: Unit used to measure the force or pressure of electricity. It is defined as the pressure

VOLTAGE REGULATOR: A device that controls the current output of the alternator or generator.

VOLTMETER: An instrument used for measuring electrical force in units called volts. Voltmeters are always connected parallel with the circuit being tested.

WATER PUMP: A belt driven component of the cooling system that mounts on the engine, circulating the coolant under pressure.

ANCHORS   1-13
BATTERIES (ELECTRICAL)   9-2
    BATTERY AND CHARGING SAFETY PRECAUTIONS   9-5
    BATTERY CHARGERS   9-5
    BATTERY CONSTRUCTION   9-2
    BATTERY LOCATION   9-3
    BATTERY RATINGS   9-3
    BATTERY SERVICE   9-3
    BATTERY TERMINALS   9-5
    MARINE BATTERIES   9-2
    REPLACING BATTERY CABLES   9-5
    STORAGE   9-6
BATTERY (MAINTENANCE)   3-3
    BATTERY & CHARGING SAFETY PRECAUTIONS   3-5
    BATTERY CHARGERS   3-5
    BATTERY TERMINALS   3-5
    CHECKING SPECIFIC GRAVITY   3-4
    CLEANING   3-4
    REPLACING BATTERY CABLES   3-5
BATTERY (TUNING)   2-9
BATTERY STORAGE   3-16
BOATING ACCIDENT REPORTS   1-14
BREAK-IN PROCEDURES   8-66
BREAKER POINTS   6-8
BREAKER POINTS (MAGNETO) IGNITION SYSTEM   2-6
    ADJUSTMENT   2-8
    REPLACEMENT   2-7
    TESTING   2-7
BROKEN REED   2-6
C115 MODELS   7-17
    CARBURETOR LINKAGE   7-18
    IDLE SPEED   7-17
    IGNITION TIMING   7-17
    PICKUP TIMING   7-17
    TIMING PLATE POSITION   7-17
C25 MODEL   7-7
    CARBURETOR LINKAGE ADJUSTMENT   7-7
    IDLE SPEED   7-7
    IGNITION TIMING   7-7
    THROTTLE LINKAGE ADJUSTMENT   7-7
C40 (2-CYLINDER) MODEL   7-11
    CARBURETOR LINK   7-12
    DYNAMIC TIMING   7-11
    IDLE SPEED   7-13
    STATIC TIMING   7-12
    THROTTLE LINK   7-13
C55 MODELS   7-14
    CARBURETOR LINKAGE   7-15
    IDLE SPEED   7-15
    IGNITION TIMING   7-14
C75 HP AND C85 MODELS   7-16
    CARBURETOR LINKAGE   7-17
    IDLE SPEED   7-17
    IGNITION TIMING   7-16
    PICKUP TIMING   7-17
    TIMING PLATE POSITION   7-16
CAPACITOR DISCHARGE IGNITION (CDI) SYSTEM   6-3
CARBURETION   4-3
    BASIC FUNCTIONS   4-4
    CARBURETOR CIRCUITS   4-4
    DUAL-THROAT CARBURETORS   4-5
    GENERAL INFORMATION   4-3
    REMOVING FUEL FROM THE SYSTEM   4-5
CARBURETOR IDENTIFICATION   4-9
CARBURETOR SERVICE   4-9
CARBURETORS   2-9
    IDLE SPEED ADJUSTMENT   2-10
    TACHOMETER CONNECTIONS   2-9
CDI IGNITION SYSTEMS   2-9
CDI UNIT   6-12
CDI UNIT AND IGNITION COILS   6-33

MASTER

INDEX

INSTALLATION 6-35
REMOVAL 6-33
CDI UNIT TEST CHARTS 6-14
CHARGE COILS 6-10
CHARGING CIRCUIT 9-6
CHOKE SWITCH 12-2
TESTING 12-2
CLEANING AND INSPECTING 8-58
BLEED SYSTEM SERVICE 8-59
BLOCK & CYLINDER HEAD WARPAGE 8-64
CONNECTING ROD SERVICE 8-60
CRANKSHAFT SERVICE 8-59
CYLINDER BLOCK SERVICE 8-63
EXHAUST COVER 8-58
HONING CYLINDER WALLS 8-64
OVERSIZE PISTONS & RINGS 8-63
PISTON RING SIDE CLEARANCE 8-63
PISTON SERVICE 8-61
REED BLOCK SERVICE 8-58
RING END-GAP CLEARANCE 8-62
CLEANING, WAXING AND POLISHING 1-2
COMBUSTION 4-3
ABNORMAL COMBUSTION 4-3
FACTORS AFFECTING COMBUSTION 4-3
COMBUSTION RELATED PISTON FAILURES 4-9
COMPASS 1-12
COMPASS PRECAUTIONS 1-13
INSTALLATION 1-12
SELECTION 1-12
COMPRESSION 6-8
COMPRESSION CHECK 2-2
CHECKING COMPRESSION 2-2
LOW COMPRESSION 2-3
CONDENSER 6-8
CONTACT BREAKER POINTS IGNITION (MAGNETO IGNITION) 6-2
SERVICING 6-2
CONTROL BOX ASSEMBLY 12-3
ASSEMBLY 12-8
CLEANING & INSPECTION 12-7
DISASSEMBLY 12-4
REMOVAL 12-3
CONTROL UNIT 6-21
CONTROL UNIT FUNCTIONS 6-39
ENGINE START CONTROL 6-39
ENGINE WARM UP CONTROL 6-39
IDLE STABILIZING CONTROL 6-40
IGNITION TIMING CONTROL 6-40
KNOCK CONTROL 6-40
OPERATING VOLTAGE CONTROL 6-40
OVERHEATING CONTROL 6-40
OVERREV CONTROL 6-40
REVERSE DIRECTION CONTROL 6-40
CONTROLLED COMBUSTION SYSTEM 4-61
CONTROLLING CORROSION 1-2
USING ZINC ANODES 1-2
CRANKING CIRCUIT 9-11
CRANKING MOTOR 9-14
DESCRIPTION 9-14
CRANKING MOTOR CIRCUIT 9-11
TROUBLESHOOTING 9-11
CRANKING MOTOR RELAY 9-12
DESCRIPTION AND OPERATION 9-12
INSTALLATION 9-14
REMOVAL 9-13
TESTING 9-13
DESCRIPTION & OPERATION (HYDRO TILT LOCK SYSTEM) 11-2
LOWERING OUTBOARD UNIT 11-2
RAISING OUTBOARD UNIT 11-2

UNDERWATER STRIKE 11-2
DESCRIPTION & OPERATION (POWER TILT SYSTEM) 11-3
MANUAL OPERATION 11-4
SHOCK ABSORBER ACTION 11-4
TILT DOWN OPERATION 11-3
TILT UP OPERATION 11-3
DESCRIPTION & OPERATION (POWER TRIM/TILT SYSTEM) 11-7
SHOCK ABSORBER ACTION 11-8
TILT DOWN 11-8
TILT UP 11-8
TRIM DOWN 11-8
TRIM UP 11-7
DESCRIPTION AND OPERATION (CRANKING CIRCUIT) 9-11
FAULTY SYMPTOMS 9-11
MAINTENANCE 9-11
DESCRIPTION AND OPERATION (ELECTRICAL) 9-2
CHARGING CIRCUIT 9-2
CRANKING MOTOR CIRCUIT 9-2
IGNITION CIRCUIT 9-2
DESCRIPTION AND OPERATION (OIL INJECTION SYSTEM) 5-2
SYSTEM COMPONENTS 5-3
DESCRIPTION AND OPERATION (YAMAHA MICROCOMPUTER IGNITION SYSTEM) 6-37
CONTROL UNIT 6-37
CRANKSHAFT POSITION SENSOR 6-38
KNOCK SENSOR 6-39
SYSTEM TYPES 6-37
THERMO SENSOR 6-39
THROTTLE POSITION SENSOR 6-38
DIAGNOSIS CODE TABLES 6-41
EFI DIAGNOSTIC CODES 4-62
ELECTRICAL 9-2
ELECTRONIC FUEL INJECTION 4-59
EMERGENCY EQUIPMENT 1-10
FIRE EXTINGUISHERS 1-11
FIRST AID KITS 1-11
TYPES & QUANTITIES 1-10
VISUAL DISTRESS SIGNALS 1-10
EMERGENCY SERVICE 3-13
EMERGENCY TETHER 3-13
ENGINE REBUILDING SPECIFICATIONS 8-67
ENGINE TORQUE SPECIFICATIONS 8-69
ENGINE TUNE-UP SPECIFICATIONS 7-21
EXCEPT 1-2 CYLINDER POWERHEAD 10-33
ASSEMBLY 10-43
CLEANING AND INSPECTING 10-40
CLUTCH DOG 10-47
DISASSEMBLY 10-33
EXCEPT 1-2-CYLINDER FUEL PUMPS 4-54
ASSEMBLY & INSTALLATION 4-58
CLEANING & INSPECTION 4-57
DESCRIPTION & OPERATION 4-54
FUEL PUMP PRESSURE CHECK 4-55
REMOVAL & DISASSEMBLY 4-57
EXCEPT 2 HP POWERHEADS 13-6
ADJUSTMENT 13-9
ASSEMBLING & INSTALLATION 13-7
CLEANING & INSPECTION 13-7
REMOVAL & DISASSEMBLY 13-6
EXHAUST GASES 10-4
FIBERGLASS HULLS 3-2
BELOW WATERLINE 3-2
FLOAT HEIGHT 4-40
FLOTATION 1-8
LIFE PRESERVERS—PERSONAL FLOTATION DEVICES (PFDS) 1-8
FLYWHEEL AND STATOR PLATE 6-24
ASSEMBLY AND INSTALLATION 6-28

CLEANING AND INSPECTION 6-28
  REMOVAL 6-24
40 HP, 50 HP AND PRO 50 MODELS 7-14
  IDLE SPEED 7-14
  IGNITION TIMING 7-14
  OIL PUMP LINK 7-14
  THROTTLE CABLE 7-14
  THROTTLE LINKAGE 7-14
4 HP AND 5 HP MODELS (CARBURETOR SERVICE) 4-15
  ASSEMBLY & INSTALLATION 4-18
  CLEANING & INSPECTION 4-17
  DISASSEMBLY 4-17
  REMOVAL 4-16
4 HP AND 5 HP MODELS (TIMING AND
SYNCHRONIZATION) 7-4
  IDLE SPEED 7-4
  IGNITION TIMING 7-4
  THROTTLE LINKAGE ADJUSTMENT 7-4
FUEL 4-2
  ALCOHOL-BLENDED FUELS 4-2
  HIGH ALTITUDE OPERATION 4-2
  OCTANE RATING 4-2
  RECOMMENDATIONS 4-2
  THE BOTTOM LINE WITH FUELS 4-2
  VAPOR PRESSURE AND ADDITIVES 4-2
FUEL AND COMBUSTION 4-2
FUEL AND FUEL TANKS 3-5
FUEL INJECTION BASICS 4-59
FUEL INJECTION COMPONENTS 4-59
  AIR INDUCTION GROUP 4-61
  ELECTRONIC CONTROL SYSTEM 4-59
  FUEL DELIVERY SYSTEM 4-61
FUEL LINE 4-8
  COMMON PROBLEMS 4-9
FUEL PUMP (FUEL SYSTEM) 4-6
FUEL PUMP (TROUBLESHOOTING) 4-8
FUEL PUMP SERVICE 4-52
FUEL STABILIZER 3-15
FUEL SYSTEM 4-3
FUEL SYSTEM (GENERAL INFORMATION) 1-7
  FUEL TANK 1-7
  FUEL TANK GROUNDING 1-7
  STATIC ELECTRICITY 1-7
  TAKING ON FUEL 1-7
FUEL SYSTEM (TROUBLESHOOTING) 4-6
  COMMON PROBLEMS 4-7
  LOGICAL TROUBLESHOOTING 4-7
FUEL SYSTEM (TUNING) 2-11
  FUEL FILTER SERVICE 2-12
  FUEL INSPECTION 2-11
  FUEL PUMP INSPECTION 2-11
GEAR OIL CAPACITY 3-11
GENERAL ENGINE SPECIFICATIONS 2-16
GENERAL INFORMATION 1-2
GENERAL INFORMATION (LOWER UNIT) 10-2
GENERAL INFORMATION (LUBRICATION) 3-7
GENERAL INFORMATION (POWERHEAD MECHANICAL) 8-2
  CLEANLINESS 8-2
  INTRODUCTION 8-2
  POWERHEAD COMPONENTS 8-2
  REED VALVE SERVICE 8-2
  REPAIR PROCEDURES 8-2
  TORQUE VALUES 8-2
GENERAL INFORMATION (TROUBLESHOOTING) 5-7
  EXCESSIVE SMOKE AT IDLE 5-9
  MAIN (ENGINE) OIL TANK OVERFLOWING 5-7
  OIL WILL NOT TRANSFER 5-8
HAND REWIND STARTER 13-2

HORSEPOWER 1-8
HYDRO TILT LOCK SYSTEM 11-2
IGNITION COILS 6-11
IGNITION SYSTEM 6-2
IGNITION TESTING SPECIFICATIONS 6-23
INJECTION CONTROL LINK ROD 5-33
  ADJUSTMENT 5-33
INSIDE THE BOAT 3-9
INTERNAL WIRING HARNESS 2-9
INTRODUCTION (GENERAL INFORMATION) 1-2
INTRODUCTION (HAND REWIND STARTER) 13-2
INTRODUCTION (MAINTENANCE) 3-2
INTRODUCTION (TIMING AND SYNCHRONIZATION) 7-2
  PREPARATION 7-2
  SYNCHRONIZATION 7-2
  TIMING 7-2
INTRODUCTION (TRIM & TILT) 11-2
JET DRIVE (GENERAL INFORMATION) 1-6
  DESCRIPTION & OPERATION 1-6
  GRILLE BLOCKAGE 1-7
  IDENTIFICATION 1-6
  OPERATIONAL HINTS 1-6
  POWERHEAD STALL 1-6
JET DRIVE (LUBRICATION) 3-10
  FLUSHING 3-12
  LUBRICATION 3-10
JET DRIVE ADJUSTMENTS 10-61
  ADJUSTMENT 10-61
  TRIM ADJUSTMENT 10-62
JET DRIVE UNITS 2-14
  GATE POSITION & SHIFT LEVER 2-14
  IMPELLER 2-14
JUMP STARTING 3-14
  JUMP STARTING PRECAUTIONS 3-14
  JUMP STARTING PROCEDURE 3-14
  JUMPER CABLES 3-14
KILL SWITCH 12-3
  TESTING 12-3
LIGHTING COIL 6-11
LOADING 1-8
LOW OIL WARNING BUZZER 12-2
  TESTING 12-2
LOWER UNIT 10-2
LOWER UNIT (TUNING) 2-13
LOWER UNIT OVERHAUL 10-11
LOWER UNIT SERVICE 10-5
LOWER UNIT SERVICE JET DRIVE 10-54
  ASSEMBLING 10-57
  CLEANING AND INSPECTING 10-56
  DESCRIPTION AND OPERATION 10-54
  MODEL IDENTIFICATION AND SERIAL NUMBERS 10-54
  REMOVAL & DISASSEMBLY 10-55
LOWER UNIT—NO REVERSE GEAR 10-7
  INSTALLATION 10-8
  REMOVAL 10-7
LOWER UNIT—WITH REVERSE GEAR 10-9
  INSTALLATION 10-10
  REMOVAL 10-9
LUBRICANTS 3-9
LUBRICATION 3-7
MAIN OIL TANK 5-23
  INSTALLATION 5-23
  REMOVAL 5-23
  TESTING 5-24
MAINTENANCE 3-2
MAINTENANCE (POWER TILT SYSTEM) 11-4
  CHECKING HYDRAULIC FLUID LEVEL 11-4
  PURGING AIR FROM THE SYSTEM 11-4

MAINTENANCE (POWER TRIM/TILT SYSTEM) 11-8
    PURGING AIR FROM SYSTEM 11-8
MISCELLANEOUS EQUIPMENT 1-14
    BILGE PUMPS 1-14
NAVIGATION 1-15
    BUOYS 1-15
    WATERWAY RULES 1-15
NEUTRAL SAFETY SWITCH 12-2
    TESTING 12-2
9.9 HP AND 15 HP MODELS 7-5
    IDLE SPEED 7-7
    IGNITION TIMING 7-5
    THROTTLE LINKAGE ADJUSTMENT 7-6
NORMAL VS. FAIL SAFE CONTROL 4-62
    FAIL SAFE CONTROL (RETURN TO PORT) MODE 4-62
    NORMAL MODE 4-62
NORMAL VS. FAIL SAFE CONTROL MODES 4-62
OIL INJECTION SYSTEM 5-2
OIL INJECTION SYSTEM (SERVICING) 5-10
    ADJUSTMENT 5-17
    BLEEDING 5-15
    INSTALLATION 5-12
    REMOVAL 5-10
    TESTING 5-19
OIL INJECTION WARNING SYSTEM 5-33
    DESCRIPTION & OPERATION 5-33
    OPERATIONAL CHECK 5-36
    TROUBLESHOOTING 5-35
OIL PUMP (SERVICING) 5-21
    ASSEMBLY 5-22
    CLEANING & INSPECTING 5-21
    DISASSEMBLY 5-21
OIL PUMP (SERVICING) 5-27
    ASSEMBLY 5-29
    BLEEDING 5-32
    CLEANING & INSPECTING 5-28
    DISASSEMBLY 5-27
    INSTALLATION 5-31
    REMOVAL 5-27
OIL PUMP OUTPUT SPECIFICATIONS 5-9
OIL TRANSFER PUMP TROUBLESHOOTING CHART 5-8
1- AND 2-CYLINDER POWERHEAD CRANKING MOTOR 9-14
    INSTALLATION 9-15
    REMOVAL 9-14
1-2 CYLINDER POWERHEAD WITH REVERSE GEAR 10-16
    ASSEMBLY 10-23
    CLEANING AND INSPECTING 10-22
    DISASSEMBLY 10-16
1-2 CYLINDER POWERHEAD WITHOUT REVERSE GEAR 10-11
    ASSEMBLY 10-13
    CLEANING AND INSPECTING 10-12
    DISASSEMBLY 10-11
1-2-CYLINDER FUEL PUMPS 4-52
    DESCRIPTION & OPERATION 4-52
    FUEL PRESSURE CHECK 4-53
1-2-CYLINDER POWERHEADS 4-10
ONE-CYLINDER 2 HP AND 3 HP MODELS 8-4
    ASSEMBLY & INSTALLATION 8-6
    CLEANING & INSPECTION 8-6
    REMOVAL & DISASSEMBLY 8-4
ONE-CYLINDER 4 HP AND 5 HP MODELS 8-9
    ASSEMBLY & INSTALLATION 8-12
    CLEANING & INSPECTION 8-12
    REMOVAL & DISASSEMBLY 8-9
PERFORMANCE TESTING 2-15
PERIODIC LUBRICATION 3-9
PERIODIC MAINTENANCE 3-2

POLARITY CHECK 6-9
POWER TILT SYSTEM 11-3
POWER TRIM/TILT SWITCH 11-11
    TESTING 11-11
POWER TRIM/TILT SYSTEM 11-7
POWERHEAD MECHANICAL 8-2
POWERHEAD REFINISHING 8-58
PRE-SEASON CHECKLIST 3-6
PRO 60, 70 HP AND 90 HP MODELS 7-15
    CARBURETOR LINKAGE 7-16
    IDLE SPEED 7-16
    IGNITION TIMING 7-15
    OIL PUMP LINK 7-16
    PICKUP TIMING 7-15
    THROTTLE SENSOR CONTROL LINK 7-15
    TIMING PLATE POSITION 7-15
PROPELLER (LOWER UNIT SERVICE) 10-5
    INSTALLATION 10-6
    REMOVAL 10-5
PROPELLER (TUNING) 2-13
PROPELLER DRIVE 3-9
    DRAINING 3-9
    FILLING 3-10
    WATER IN THE LOWER UNIT 3-9
PROPELLER SERVICE 3-3
PROPELLERS (GENERAL INFORMATION) 1-3
    CAVITATION 1-4
    CUPPING 1-5
    DIAMETER & PITCH 1-3
    HIGH PERFORMANCE PROPELLERS 1-5
    PROGRESSIVE PITCH 1-5
    PROPELLER RAKE 1-4
    PROPELLER SELECTION 1-4
    ROTATION 1-5
    SHOCK ABSORBERS 1-4
    VIBRATION 1-4
PULSAR COILS 6-9
RECTIFIER 6-21
RECTIFIER TEST CHART 6-22
REMOTE CONTROL BOX 12-2
    DESCRIPTION & OPERATION 12-2
REMOTE CONTROLS 12-2
REMOTE OIL TANK 5-24
    CLEANING & INSPECTING 5-26
    INSTALLATION 5-26
    REMOVAL 5-25
    TESTING 5-24
RESISTANCE TESTING PRECAUTIONS 6-9
ROUTINE TUNE-UP 2-2
SAFETY 1-8
SELF DIAGNOSIS 6-40
SERIAL NUMBERS 1-3
SERVICING (IGNITION SYSTEM) 6-24
SERVICING (OIL INJECTION) 5-10
SERVICING (HYDRO TILT LOCK SYSTEM) 11-2
SERVICING (POWER TILT SYSTEM) 11-7
SERVICING (POWER TRIM/TILT SYSTEM) 11-12
    ASSEMBLY 11-15
    CLEANING & INSPECTION 11-14
    CLOSING TASKS 11-17
    DISASSEMBLY 11-12
    PRELIMINARY TASKS 11-12
SHIFTING PRINCIPLES 10-2
    COUNTERROTATING UNIT 10-3
    STANDARD ROTATING UNIT 10-2
SINGLE-PHASE CHARGING SYSTEM 9-8
    DESCRIPTION AND OPERATION 9-8

SERVICING   9-8
TROUBLESHOOTING   9-8
6 HP, 8 HP, 9.9 HP AND 15 HP MODELS   4-21
ASSEMBLY   4-25
CLEANING & INSPECTION   4-24
DISASSEMBLY   4-23
FLOAT ADJUSTMENT   4-25
INSTALLATION   4-27
REMOVAL   4-21
6 HP AND 8 HP MODELS   7-4
IDLE SPEED   7-5
IGNITION TIMING   7-4
THROTTLE LINKAGE ADJUSTMENT   7-5
SPARK PLUG WIRES   2-5
CHECKING & REPLACING   2-5
SPARK PLUGS (TROUBLESHOOTING)   6-7
SPARK PLUGS (TUNING)   2-3
GAPPING SPARK PLUGS   2-4
INSPECTION   2-4
INSTALLATION   2-4
READING SPARK PLUGS   2-4
REMOVAL   2-4
SPARK PLUG HEAT RANGE   2-3
SPARK PLUG SERVICE   2-4
SPECIFICATION CHARTS
CARBURETOR IDENTIFICATION   4-9
CDI UNIT TEST CHARTS   6-14
DIAGNOSIS CODE TABLES   6-41
ENGINE REBUILDING SPECIFICATIONS   8-67
ENGINE TORQUE SPECIFICATIONS   8-69
ENGINE TUNE-UP SPECIFICATIONS   7-21
FLOAT HEIGHT   4-40
GEAR OIL CAPACITY   3-11
GENERAL ENGINE SPECIFICATIONS   2-16
IGNITION TESTING SPECIFICATIONS   6-23
OIL PUMP OUTPUT SPECIFICATIONS   5-9
PERIODIC LUBRICATION   3-9
PERIODIC MAINTENANCE   3-2
RECTIFIER TEST CHART   6-22
YMIS SENSOR CHARACTERISTICS   6-43
YMIS SYSTEM APPLICATIONS   6-38
START BUTTON   12-3
TESTING   12-3
STARTER MOTOR   2-9
SUBMERGED ENGINE   3-13
SUBMERGED ENGINE—FRESH WATER   3-13
SUBMERGED ENGINE—SALT WATER   3-13
SUBMERGED ENGINE—WHILE RUNNING   3-13
TACHOMETERS   9-20
TACHOMETER CONNECTIONS   9-20
TESTING   6-43
CONTROL UNIT   6-43
CRANK POSITION SENSOR   6-44
KNOCK SENSOR   6-45
THERMOSENSOR   6-45
THERMOSWITCH TEST   6-45
THROTTLE POSITION SENSOR   6-46
YMIS POWER SUPPLY   6-44
30 HP (2-CYLINDER) MODEL   7-9
IDLE SPEED   7-9
IGNITION TIMING   7-9
THROTTLE CABLE   7-9
THROTTLE CONTROL LINK   7-9
30 HP (3-CYLINDER) MODEL   7-9
CARBURETOR LINKAGE   7-10
IDLE SPEED   7-10
IGNITION TIMING   7-9

OIL PUMP LINK ADJUSTMENT   7-11
PICKUP TIMING   7-10
THROTTLE CABLE ADJUSTMENT   7-11
3 HP MODEL   7-3
IDLE SPEED   7-3
IGNITION TIMING   7-3
3-CYLINDER POWERHEAD CRANKING MOTOR   9-16
INSTALLATION   9-17
REMOVAL   9-16
3-CYLINDER POWERHEADS (CARBURETOR SERVICE)   4-33
ASSEMBLY   4-39
CLEANING & INSPECTION   4-38
DISASSEMBLY   4-37
INSTALLATION   4-41
REMOVAL   4-34
TACHOMETER CONNECTIONS   4-44
3-CYLINDER POWERHEADS (SERVICING)   5-10
THREE-CYLINDER POWERHEADS   8-28
ASSEMBLY & INSTALLATION   8-32
CLEANING & INSPECTION   8-32
REMOVAL & DISASSEMBLY   8-28
THREE-PHASE CHARGING SYSTEM   9-8
DESCRIPTION AND OPERATION   9-8
SERVICING   9-9
TROUBLESHOOTING   9-9
TILT MOTOR   11-6
TESTING   11-6
TILT RELAY   11-5
TESTING   11-5
TILT SWITCH   11-6
TESTING   11-6
TIMING AND SYNCHRONIZATION   7-2
TRIM & TILT   11-2
TRIM SENSOR   11-12
ADJUSTMENT   11-12
TESTING   11-12
TRIM TABS AND LEAD WIRES   3-3
TRIM/TILT MOTOR   11-11
TESTING   11-11
TRIM/TILT RELAY   11-10
TESTING   11-10
TROUBLESHOOTING (FUEL SYSTEM)   4-6
TROUBLESHOOTING (IGNITION SYSTEM)   6-7
TROUBLESHOOTING (LOWER UNIT)   10-4
TROUBLESHOOTING (OIL INJECTION)   5-7
TROUBLESHOOTING (POWER TILT SYSTEM)   11-5
ELECTRICAL TESTING   11-5
HYDRAULIC TESTING   11-5
TROUBLESHOOTING (POWER TRIM/TILT SYSTEM)   11-9
HYDRAULIC TESTING   11-10
MANUAL OPERATION   11-9
PRELIMINARY INSPECTION   11-9
SYMPTOM DIAGNOSIS   11-9
TROUBLESHOOTING (YAMAHA MICROCOMPUTER IGNITION
SYSTEM)   6-42
1990-95 225 (2.6L) POWERHEAD   6-42
1990-95 250, 225X, 225U AND 1996-98 3.1L
POWERHEADS   6-43
1992-98 60, C60, C80 AND 90 POWERHEADS   6-42
1996-98 150-225L POWERHEADS   6-43
TROUBLESHOOTING CHARTS
EFI DIAGNOSTIC CODES   4-62
NORMAL VS. FAIL SAFE CONTROL MODES   4-62
OIL TRANSFER PUMP TROUBLESHOOTING CHART   5-8
TUNE-UP SEQUENCE   2-2
TUNING   2-2
25 HP AND 30 HP MODELS   4-28

ASSEMBLY 4-31
CLEANING & INSPECTION 4-31
DISASSEMBLY 4-29
INSTALLATION 4-33
REMOVAL 4-28
25 HP MODEL 7-7
IDLE SPEED 7-8
IGNITION TIMING 7-7
LINK ROD ADJUSTMENT 7-8
2 HP AND 3 HP MODEL 4-10
ASSEMBLLY & INSTALLATION 4-13
CLEANING & INSPECTION 4-13
REMOVAL & DISASSEMBLY 4-10
2 HP MODEL 7-2
IDLE SPEED 7-3
IGNITION TIMING 7-2
2 HP POWERHEADS 13-2
ASSEMBLY & INSTALLATION 13-3
CLEANING & INSPECTION 13-3
REMOVAL & DISASSEMBLY 13-2
TWO-CYLINDER 6 HP, 8 HP, 9.9 HP, 15 HP, 25 HP AND 30 HP
  MODELS 8-15
ASSEMBLY & INSTALLATION 8-20
CLEANING & INSPECTION 8-20
PREPARATION 8-15
REMOVAL & DISASSEMBLY 8-16
TWO-STROKE OPERATION 8-2
CONCLUSION 8-3
INTAKE/EXHAUST 8-2
LUBRICATION 8-2
PHYSICAL LAWS 8-2
POWER CYCLE 8-2
TIMING 8-3
TYPE II FUEL PUMP 4-54
ASSEMBLY & INSTALLATION 4-54
CLEANING & INSPECTION 4-54
REMOVAL & DISASSEMBLY 4-54
V4 & V6 POWERHEADS 4-44
ASSEMBLY 4-48
CHOKE SOLENOID ADJUSTMENT 4-51
CLEANING & INSPECTION 4-47

DISASSEMBLY 4-45
INSTALLATION 4-50
REMOVAL 4-44
V4 AND V6 EXCEPT YAMAHA MICROCOMPUTER IGNITION
  SYSTEM (YMIS) 7-18
CARBURETOR LINKAGE ADJUSTMENT 7-18
CARBURETOR PICKUP TIMING ADJUSTMENT 7-18
IDLE SPEED 7-19
IGNITION TIMING 7-18
OIL PUMP LINK 7-19
THROTTLE POSITION SENSOR (225 HP ONLY) 7-19
V4 AND V6 POWERHEAD CRANKING MOTORS 9-18
DESCRIPTION 9-18
INSTALLATION 9-19
REMOVAL 9-18
V4 AND V6 POWERHEAD SERVICE 8-40
ASSEMBLY & INSTALLATION 8-48
CLEANING & INSPECTION 8-48
REMOVAL & DISASSEMBLY 8-40
V4 AND V6 POWERHEADS 5-23
V4 AND V6 WITH YAMAHA MICROCOMPUTER IGNITION
  SYSTEM (YMIS) 7-19
CARBURETOR LINKAGE 7-19
CARBURETOR PICKUP TIMING 7-19
IDLE SPEED 7-20
THROTTLE POSITION SENSOR 7-20
V76 CHARGING SYSTEM 9-9
BATTERY CABLE DISCONNECT WARNING 9-9
SERVICING 9-11
TROUBLESHOOTING 9-9
WATER-COOLED RECTIFIER/REGULATOR 9-9
WATER PUMP CHECK 2-12
WINTER STORAGE 3-15
WIRE COLORS 5-7
WIRING DIAGRAMS (ELECTRICAL) 9-20
WIRING DIAGRAMS (OIL INJECTION) 5-38
**YAMAHA MICROCOMPUTER IGNITION
  SYSTEM (YMIS) 6-37**
YAMAHA TUNED PORT INJECTION 4-59
YMIS SENSOR CHARACTERISTICS 6-43
YMIS SYSTEM APPLICATIONS 6-38